OVERVIEW

FINANCIAL RISK MANAGEMENT PROCEDURES

FINANCIAL RISK MANAGEMENT

FINANCIAL RISK AND FINANCIAL RISK MANAGEMENT

RESEARCH IN INTERNATIONAL BUSINESS AND FINANCE

Series Editor: Thomas A. Fetherston

RESEARCH IN INTERNATIONAL BUSINESS AND FINANCE
VOLUME 16

FINANCIAL RISK AND FINANCIAL RISK MANAGEMENT

EDITED BY

JONATHAN A. BATTEN
Deakin University, Melbourne, Australia

THOMAS A. FETHERSTON
University of Alabama, Birmingham, USA

Emerald

United Kingdom – North America – Japan
India – Malaysia – China

Emerald Group Publishing Limited
Howard House, Wagon Lane, Bingley BD16 1WA, UK

Reprints and permission service
Contact: booksandseries@emeraldinsight.com

British Library Cataloguing in Publication Data
A catalogue record for this book is available from the British Library

ISBN: 978-0-76-230858-3
ISSN: 0275-5319 (Series)

CONTENTS

LIST OF CONTRIBUTORS

Carol Alexander	ISMA Centre, University of Reading, UK
David. E. Allen	Edith Cowan University, Perth, Australia
Tom Arnold	Louisiana State University, USA
Jonathan A. Batten	Deakin University, Australia
Theodore Bos	University of Alabama at Birmingham, USA
John Cadle	University of Birmingham, UK
Robert Faff	RMIT, Australia
Thomas A. Fetherston	University of Alabama, USA
Darren Filson	Claremont Graduate University, USA
Michel Gendron	Laval University, Canada
Ian Giblin	Pennoyer Capital Management, USA
Benton E. Gup	University of Alabama, USA
Pongsak Hoontrakul	Chulalongkorn University, Bangkok, Thailand
William C. Hunter	Federal Reserve Bank of Chicago, USA
Anna Kalemenova	Risk Lab Gmbh, Germany
Walter Kemmsies	UBS Warburg, London, UK
Heinz R. Kubli	Bank von Ernst & Cie AG, Switzerland
Van Son Lai	Laval University, Canada

François-Serge Lhabitant	Union Bancaire Privée/Thunderbird, Switzerland
Cornelis A. Los	Kent State University, USA
G. MacDonald	Curtin University, Perth, Australia
Andrew P. Marshall	University of Strathclyde, UK
Davide Meneguzzo	Università degli Studi di Padova, Italy
Lance Nail	University of Alabama at Birmingham, USA
Doowoo Nam	University of Southern Mississippi, USA
Terry D. Nixon	Miami University, USA
K. Ben Nowman	Durham University, UK
Ponladesh Poomimars	University of Birmingham, UK
Nidal Rashid Sabri	Birzeit University, Israel
Bernd Schmid	Risk Lab Gmbh, Germany
Issouf Soumaré	Laval University, Canada
Kessara Thanyalakpark	Chulalongkorn University, Bangkok, Thailand
Michael Theobald	University of Birmingham, UK
Walter Vecchiato	IntesaBci, Italy
Chris Viney	Deakin University, Australia
Niklas Wagner	Dresden University, Germany
David Walsh	Barclays Global, Sydney, Australia
Kathy Walsh	AGSM, UNSW, Sydney, Australia
Wayne Weddington III	Pennoyer Capital Management, USA
Elizabeth Wong	Deakin University, Australia

THE CURRENT FINANCIAL RISK SCENE

Jonathan A. Batten and Thomas A. Fetherston

Financial Risk Measurement and Management is an area of endeavor that has had its profile raised every time a significant monetary loss occurs as a result of the utilization (or abuse) of derivative instruments. However, the subject has transcended being only a subject of topical interest. An understanding of Financial Risk Measurement and Management has become essential to survival in all business activity. Financial Risk relates to the volatility of unexpected outcome or movements in financial variables. Financial risk variables arise generically in the form of interest rate risk, foreign exchange risk, equity risk and commodity risk. Some risk terminology (e.g. sigma, beta, duration, convexity, delta, gamma, theta etc.) has become a part of the everyday lexicon for those working with financial variables. Professional risk management has demonstrated its relevance in the corporate world by enhancing the bottom line. An organized professional society, *Risk and Insurance Management Society (RIMS)* in the U.S. and Canada has been instrumental in fostering the development of the risk management cause. The creation of a Chief Risk Officer position reporting directly to the board of directors is a direct outgrowth of the recognition and importance of the discipline. Further, the understanding and breadth of sophistication to handle unpleasant surprises and their likelihood has moved from the gut feeling stage to a new higher level. A well thought out Risk Management Strategy should be an integral core of every business and not just a fire brigade in time of emergency. A Company's management must identify and evaluate the financial risks it faces, and then they may select those that should be borne. A thorough process for identifying

Financial Risk and Financial Risk Management, Volume 16, pages 3–21.

ISBN: 0-7623-0858-3

and evaluating risks is the foundation of a risk management strategy. Risks must be prioritized akin to the matrix below:

Decision Matrix for Prioritizing Risk		
	High Impact Low likelihood	***High Impact High Likelihood***
Impact of Financial Risk	***Low Impact Low Likelihood***	***Low Impact High Likelihood***
	Likelihood of Financial Risk Occurring	

Source: FT Mastering Risks, Volume I.

Given the prioritization of the financial risks, management must decide in each case what their preferred method to deal with or avoid those risks will be. Strategies to be considered are accepting the risk; transferring it partially or totally to another risk bearer; eliminating it by get out of the business; controlling it as part of the ongoing operational process.

In the Finance arena there has been extensive research in the realm of "market risk" with the outcome of this research providing tremendous progress and understanding. Empirical efforts in this volume will add to the body of literature and understanding in the field. This volume is structured into three parts: an Overview section, a section with papers focusing Financial Risk Management Procedures and a third section devoted to papers on Financial Risk Measurement. There are twenty-one papers in the volume with forty authors, many of whom are prominent in the field, contributing their effort to this volume.

OVERVIEW

This section is comprised of three papers the first of which surveys the contributions of this volume, followed by a paper with a regulators view of financial crises and last by a chapter on the role and scope of regulatory capital and credit derivatives. The Hunter paper addresses the financial crises of the recent past and the lessons learned from them. The initial lessons to be taken from recent experiences are, first, that no one country should be consider itself immune to financial crisis and second, the cost of resolving a crisis once it has occurred is almost certain to be very high. In some East Asian countries the cost had been estimated to be as high as 20 to 60% of GDP. Countries suffering financial crises typically exhibit many of the same symptoms. In almost all of the crisis countries, significant financial sector problems e.g. government directed and connected lending, poor supervision of the financial system, an inadequate legal infrastructure, absence of a credit culture in which lenders and investors make judgments based on independent credit assessments and sound financial analysis, underdeveloped bond and long term capital markets, lack of adequate accounting disclosure and transparency, ineffective systems of corporate governance, excessive and imprudent risk-taking by financial institutions operating with explicit or implicit deposit insurance schemes or governmental guarantees, among others.

Hunter also pointed out unique elements that contributed and in many cases that set off their particular episodes e.g. weak fixed exchanges rate regimes (often pegged to the U.S. dollar), significant debt and asset priced deflation, and unstable short-term capital flows, among others. We learn that infrastructure matters. Countries with strong financial infrastructures including good systems of supervision and regulation, legal frameworks, and private property rights have tended to be more immune to financial shocks and have tended to enjoy more stable rates of growth. Such stability in the financial system breeds the necessary trust essential to a well functioning competitive financial system.

The Wong, Fetherston and Batten paper explores the application of regulatory capital models in risk management practices. The goal of their study is to determine the ability of regulatory capital models to meet prudential objectives in the realm of credit derivatives. It summarizes the pertinent literature and offers conclusions and direction for regulatory action. Combining conclusions drawn from the analysis of risk weighted, standard and internal regulatory capital models applied to credit derivatives, the need for regulatory capital to move closer to achieving the primary and specific prudential objectives is suggested. This paper identifies two specific goals for future regulatory capital guidelines for credit derivatives. One is to correct deficiencies of current regulatory capital models, which failed to recognize hedging benefits of credit derivatives. Second, is to increase consistency in national implementation of regulatory capital models for credit derivatives. It is important to understand that this paper has not argued for a complete reform of regulatory capital regulation. It is up to central banks and supervisory authorities to determine this macroeconomic question and to consider the impact of reformed capital rules on the overall safety and soundness of the banking system. Nonetheless, despite limitations this paper has emphasized the importance for regulatory capital models applied to credit derivatives to achieve prudential objectives, and thus has set the foundation for further conclusive research to ascertain the ability of regulatory capital modes applied to new risk management practices to achieve prudential objectives.

FINANCIAL RISK MANAGEMENT PROCEDURES

The state-of-the-art procedures introduced in this section offer guidelines for managers and modelers of Financial Risk. The Alexander, Giblin and Weddington paper demonstrates a classic hedge fund strategy: an investment vehicle whose key objective is to minimize investment risk in an attempt to deliver profits under all market circumstances. Such a strategy may be described as "non-directional" or "market-neutral": the hedge is designed to have minimal correlation with the market and, irrespective of market direction, the fund seeks to generate positive alpha. Market-neutral hedge strategies are presently in great demand, though the true condition of market-neutrality remains elusive to even the most well known hedge funds. Certain high profile market-neutral managers were very market-neutral. And in some cases, they were shown to be not-so-market-neutral in spectacular fashion. But, as a group, market neutral managers have done well in this era of high volatility: equity market-neutral funds in the U.S. returned 14.99% in 2000. The strategy that is described in this paper uses historical price patterns to project the future performance of a stock. A significant difference between this model and more traditional hedge fund strategies is that portfolio optimization is based upon the cointegration of prices rather than the correlation of returns. Cointegration refers not to co-movements in returns, but to co-movements in asset prices, exchange rates or yields. This widely used method in time series analysis springs from the seminal work of Engle and Granger (1987).

The Alexander, Giblin and Weddington strategy of cointegration between asset prices demonstrated in the paper, is based on the criterion that the hedge is mean-reverting to the benchmark; thus tracking errors are designed to be stationary. The strategy will accommodate investor's preferences for the alpha as well as flexible constraints on allocations. A sophisticated training and testing methodology is described for the selection of model parameters. Extensive back testing results are reported and those results demonstrate the ability of the model to capture market upswings whilst not compromising the downside protection.

The Nam and Gup effort attempts to improve on the widely implemented VaR model employed. The proliferation of VaR as a risk measurement and management tool can be attributed, for the most part, to three factors (Hull & White, 1998). First, the development of VaR has been greatly facilitated since 1994 when J. P. Morgan introduced RiskMetrics, a comprehensive VaR methodology for measuring market risk, and the database of daily volatilities and correlations for a variety of market risk factors freely available to the public who would intend to implement VaR systems based on RiskMetrics. Second, the decision of banking supervisory authorities to adopt VaR as a basis for estimating a bank's minimum regulatory capital served as a momentum for the banking industry to see the practical necessity of developing VaR frameworks. Finally, a series of embarrassing derivatives disasters (e.g. Metallgesellschaft, Orange County, Barings Bank, Sumitomo Corporation and LTCM) in recent years compelled all market participants to pay more keen attention than ever to accurate risk measurement as an essential prerequisite in order for any risk management system to be effective and sound.

Nam and Gup address the most imperative area requiring further VaR development and fineness by managing the issue of non-normality, namely, asymmetry and fat-tailedness in asset returns. Their new approach adopts the *g*-and-*h* distribution and, hence, it is named the *g*-and-*h* VaR method. The *g*-and-*h* distribution is defined in terms of quantiles, and its statistical properties can be found in Hoaglin (1983, 1985), Martinez and Iglewicz (1984), MacGillivray and Balanda (1988), and MacGillivray (1992). This methodology permits greater simplicity and flexibility in accommodating non-normality and combines the merits of the normal and the historical simulation methods. The empirical analysis is conducted using the interest and foreign exchange rate data. The back testing results show that the *g*-and-*h* VaR method significantly outperforms the normal method at the 99% or higher levels although the performance of both methods is equally satisfactory at the 95% confidence level.

The Kubli and Kemmsies effort attempts to model the risk/return profile of volatility trades, which lead to more profitable hedging activities for the options involved. The understanding of how the risks of such trading strategies are inter-twined is very important for risk managers. For the purpose of their analysis, the implied volatility of Deutsche Aktien Index (DAX) options and the implied volatility of Swiss Market Index (SMI) options are compared. However, this analysis is not restrictive to index options but can be applied also for options on single stocks, baskets and sectors, or any other highly correlated assets. The main feature of this paper is a simulation of the returns to trades that seek to profit from temporary divergences in equity volatilities. The risks for such positions include, but are not limited to (currency fluctuations, interest rate movements, funding cost risks, hedging risk, and Pin (assignment) risk). All of them have to be monitored in order to properly control and limit exposures. The simulation set-up for the option trading strategies follows the Hull/White (1990) model. The Kubli and Kemmsies analysis finds The largest risk for pair trades set up in order to capture the implied volatility gap of two closely related underlying assets, occurs when one of the underlying assets deviates from the strike price of the option, while the other does not. They find there is some profit potential if the underlying asset of the long call deviates from the strike price. On the contrary, there is a loss potential if the underlying asset of the short call deviates from the strike price, while the other assets remains at similar levels. The characteristics of time decay diverge and may shift expected profits down. Like most market neutral trading strategies, volatility mean-reverting trades also have to be carefully monitored and the results interpreted with caution. Special focus must be given to the short call option and its dynamic hedge.

The Faff and Marshall research effort focuses on international comparisons of the foreign exchange hedging practices of multinational companies in the USA, U.K. and Asia Pacific. The motivation for their survey paper is an attempt to add to the empirical studies that have tested the theoretical reasons for corporate risk management by considering not just a general definition of derivatives use versus non-use but instead consider the use or non-use of a large number of specific internal and external instruments. To get a broader view of hedging behavior than previous studies they gather information by surveying the largest MNCs in three regions (U.K., USA and Asia Pacific). They also use more specific definitions of currency risk, including transaction and translation exposure, to see if hedging activities vary with the type of risk being hedged. There are two main aims of their paper: (i) to see if internal and/or external instruments are considered to have special characteristics such that they are used to manage certain types of foreign exchange risk and if there are any relationships between instruments; and (ii) to consider the theoretical reasons for hedging by testing the use of explicit hedging instruments and the financial characteristics of the user.

In this study the approach is to consider only largest MNCs in each region as these companies are most likely be exposed to foreign exchange risk which follows the lead of Gezcy et al. (1997) and Graham and Rogers (2000) who also take this approach. Due to the large number of possible bivariate tests between the users of any one of the ten instruments and non-users for each region of the three regions and each type of currency risk and to allow for interactions between the explanatory variables, Faff and Marshall follow the approach of Nance et al. (1993) and others and estimate logistic regressions to distinguish among the potential explanations for hedging instruments use for their sample. They find that MNCs place most importance on transaction exposure in all regions but there is significant regional variation in the importance placed on translation exposure. Further, they find significant evidence that certain internal and external instruments are used primarily to manage translation or transaction exposure e.g. in the case of internal instruments netting is used primarily for transaction exposure while balance sheet hedging is used for translation exposure.

The Wagner contribution critically reviews a number of properties of the Hill estimator, Hill (1975) which are important to financial risk modeling. Prior discussions of the chances and pitfalls of applying extreme value statistics in finance can be found e.g. in Diebold et al. (1998) and Embrechts et al. (1997). Then, an application of the Hill estimator to modeling extreme changes in daily U.S.-Dollar/Deutsche M-Mark exchange rate is given. The study highlights issues relevant in financial risk assessment and proposes a tail index estimation based on the original data together with a simulation of the error distribution based on a suitable return model. A study in financial risk assessment is given for extremal exchange rate changes. The exchange rate returns are first modeled by a GARCH model. After demonstrating that this prominent model captures short-term dependencies quite well, the Hill estimator‘s small sample properties are simulated under the estimated model. Using information on potential estimation bias, tail thickness is then inferred from the original exchange rate observations. This procedure allows us to derive unconditional tail estimates without the potential disturbing effects of model and residual estimation, while, results on the distributional properties of the tail index estimates under GARCH-type dependence are derived from our simulations. The Wagner results indicate that an interpretation of tail index estimates heavily relies on a thorough preliminary analysis of the return series under examination. Simulating small sample bias under a GARCH model, he finds that bias is the dominant issue to cope with in a practical risk assessment situation. A reduction in estimation bias is suggested by varying the choice of a scaling parameter.

The Allen, MacDonald and Walsh research interest involves assessing whether a cointegrating relationship exists between futures prices and spot prices. The study of cointegration between spot and futures markets and its effect on estimation of mean variance hedge ratios (MVHRs) started with Ghosh (1993b), who showed that MVHRs are biased downwards due to misspecification if spot and futures are cointegrated and the error correction term is not included in the regression. Theoretical support is also provided by Lien (1996), who notes that "a hedger who omits the cointegration relationship will adopt a smaller than optimal futures position, which results in a relatively poor hedging performance" (p. 779). The analysis was performed on 10-Year Australian Government Treasury Bonds listed on the Sydney Futures Exchange. Daily closing prices of the Futures Contracts from 3/20/85 to

3/17/97 and the corresponding cash prices of the 10-year bonds were sourced from Datastream.

The paper addresses the question of the validity of using standard econometric techniques to estimate hedge ratios by stacking contracts into a time series. Such an approach makes the implicit assumption that the hedge ratio can be taken as a constant across the differing contracts. The findings are that, while the basic time series properties of the data show a high degree of homogeneity, this assumption is not valid, with the individual hedge ratio estimates differing significantly between contracts. They also find that the estimated parameters show considerably stronger evidence of stability when they look at the data on a contract-by-contract basis. For much of their analysis they are able to take advantage of the increased power of panel based testing procedures, such as tests for a unit root and cointegration.

The current Los research paper extends the limited empirical analysis of the previous paper Los (1998) in three ways. First, the portfolios of strategic investments are expanded from three to seven Asian countries – Hong Kong, Indonesia, Japan, Malaysia, the Philippines, Singapore and Thailand. In addition, a comparison is made between the return/risk profiles of such regional portfolios with more diversified portfolios, including investments in the United States and in Germany. Such portfolios are representative for investors in the ASEAN region. In contrast to Lee (1987), substantial interaction between the asset, cash and currency markets was found in Asia. Second, the original five-year period of analysis from June 1992 to June 1997 is extended by half a year to include the period of Asian currency turmoil in the second half of 1997. Third, using the developed framework, the notorious non-stationarity of investment risks in Asia is analyzed. It is found that the Asian countries went through three clearly discernible investment phases of each almost two years during this period: in the first phase most investment returns were obtained in the stock markets, followed by a phase in which capital was pulled out of the stock markets into cash investments, because of the two high risk levels in the stock markets. In the final phase, the global investors pulled out of Asia, because of the unpredictability of the systematic risks. Their departure and consequent reduction of credit availability (bank loans) led to the currency crisis. Since the Asian countries have experienced significant economic and financial upheavals, both the general level of portfolio risk as well as the structural changes in the Asian investment risk profile are analyzed using spectral decomposition of the data covariance matrices. This spectral analysis clearly shows that some Asian countries show more systematic risk than others. However, any portfolio manager investing in the Asian financial markets would have had a very difficult time.

The Poomimars, Cadle and Theobold work focuses on the risk arising for a portfolio where the risk is measured relative to a benchmark. Portfolio managers who optimize in terms of tracking errors relative to a benchmark are reflecting the choice that they face as between active management and passive management via tracking a benchmark. Many issues within the portfolio management area are now analyzed within a benchmark/tracking error framework (e.g. Grinold & Kahn, 2000; Ibbotson & Kaplan, 2000; Jacobs, Levy & Starer, 1998). The efficient frontier that is generated by optimizing in relative risk terms will not necessarily be efficient in absolute risk terms, particularly when the benchmark is not on the "absolute" efficient frontier. A third frontier – or more correctly space – is possible when optimizations are conducted jointly in terms of both relative and absolute risks. It would be anticipated that modeling the risk structure using differing techniques would impact upon the tracking error volatilities which they demonstrate both empirically and analytically in this paper. When risk does impact, however, they demonstrate empirically that using models that incorporate changes in the risk structure through time can improve the management of tracking error volatility. They demonstrate that for a two-asset class universes tracking error volatilities and the portfolio alteration vector for a return enhancement against the benchmark are independent of the risks (that is, the variance/covariance structure) of the asset classes. Since this result only holds for the two asset universe, the portfolio change vector will depend upon the benchmark in the sense that the asset change vector will differ as between benchmarks which have two or more than two asset classes included within their composition. They confirm these results empirically for a U.S. manager who invests across two asset universes – the U.S. market and developed international markets. When the manager allocates funds across three asset classes (the U.S., developed international and emerging markets) this result no longer holds and they demonstrate that tracking error volatility is dependent upon the risk estimators used and that more sophisticated models that incorporate the dynamics of the risk structure can lead to lower tracking error volatilities.

The Meneguzzo and Vecchiato work explores the VaR risk management procedure. Despite its conceptual simplicity, the measurement of VaR is a very challenging statistical problem. There are many models for calculating VaR which differ in the methodology they use, the assumptions they make and the way they are implemented. However, all the existing models follow a common genera structure, which can be summarized in three steps:

(1) the portfolio is marked to market daily;

(2) the distribution of portfolio returns is estimated;
(3) the VaR of the portfolio is computed.

The main difference among the existing models is related to the way they estimate the portfolio returns distribution. In this sense the VaR models can be classified into four categories:

(1) Parametric Models (Delta-Normal, Delta-Gamma Normal, RiskMetrics);
(2) Non-Parametric Models (Historical Simulation, Hybrid models);
(3) Semi parametric Models (Extreme Value Theory, QML GARCH);
(4) Simulative Models (Monte Carlo, Quasi-Monte Carlo).

Some of the methodologies listed before do not give accurate solutions and, often needless to say, the chosen methodology depends on the underlying assumptions for the returns distribution. Since VaR can be computed as the quantile of future portfolio returns, conditional on current information, and since the distribution of portfolio returns typically changes over time, Engle and Manganelli (1999) propose a new autoregressive model for the quantile called CAViaR (Conditional Autoregressive Value at Risk). The main purpose of this work is to summarize the results reached by Engle and Manganelli (1999) using the CAViaR model and to introduce the Extreme Value Theory (EVT) into the CAViaR framework. In this paper they also provide some applications of these new methodologies to the most important European Equity Indices and discuss other useful extensions to VaR measures.

FINANCIAL RISK MEASUREMENT

This section introduces some important recent empirical contributions to the body of Financial Risk Measurement literature. The Nowman effort delves into the empirical estimation of interest rate models in risk management that has only been a recent development in current financial market practice for practitioners. For risk management specialists the wide choice of models incorporating these features is extensive. The Nowman investigation employs the recently developed Gaussian estimation methods of Bergstrom (1983, 1984, 1985, 1986, 1990) for general linear continuous time models. These methods were first applied in finance to non-linear diffusions by Nowman (1997) who estimated the single factor Chan, Karolyi, Longstaff and Sanders (CKLS, 1992) model and its special cases. It was shown that the volatility of rates was not dependent on the level of rates in the U.K. in contrast to the CKLS results. This again will have implications for the risk management of portfolios in the U.K. and U.S. Nowman extends the approach of Nowman (1997, 2001) applying the Gaussian estimation methods. Earlier studies all indicated that the general

Gaussian estimation methodology worked well in practice and should provide an efficient way to discriminate between different models for risk management analysis. His aim in this paper is to review these Gaussian estimation methods for risk management specialists and to provide some new empirical results using the approach of Nowman (2001) for U.S. Treasury yields.

He finds that these models have important implications for the effective development of risk management tools in banks and are therefore important for practitioners in deciding which model to use. He has found that the relationship between the volatility of rates and the level of rates is much higher than assumed in previous work. He also finds that the general Gaussian estimation methods have much wider applications in general areas of financial modelling and further do have further research applications.

The Sabri study aims at examining factors that increase international linkages of global stock markets. First it presents the forms of linkages, which are considered as the main factors in creating interactions between stock markets and may lead to close market integration. Second it indicates to what extend the present interaction factors are increasing in the last decade. Third it examines the changes that occurred in the international stock market linkages using empirical investigation of the performance indices' movement during two different years (1994 to 1998). The forms of stock markets linkages include removing restrictions by stock exchanges imposed on foreign ownership fully or partially. Increasing of stock market liberalization dealing with foreign stocks. Introducing liberal regulatory rules in stock exchanges to attract foreign equities and investors. Increasing the flows of net private portfolio between developed and emerging markets. Increasing of the trading volume of firm's shares outside home exchanges. Increasing the number of cross-listed corporations in two or more stock exchanges. Increasing number of the cross listed corporations from emerging economies to be listed in other markets, and increasing the volume of foreign transactions of stocks' trading.

The analysis of published data related to the above factors as presented in stock exchange fact books, International Federation of stock Exchanges Database, IFC fact books and other related sources indicate that there has been a significant increase in the above factors that lead to more linkages among individual and regional stock markets. The study indicates that there were significant changes during the nineties arising from introducing liberal regulatory rules, in increasing foreign trading, increasing number of cross listed firms and transactions' activities and in equity portfolio flows. The increasing of stock market linkages is captured in the high correlation of stock price movements between the majorities of the world stock markets. The study finds that a significant correlation between 38 stock market pairs in 1994, and that increases to 117 stock market pairs in 1998.

The Thanyalakpark and Filson work analyzes region-wide (Asian) panic in 1997 that struck first in Thailand before spreading to Malaysia, the Philippines, Indonesia, Korea, and eventually to Taiwan and Hong Kong. Many analysts argue that the magnitude, severity and geographical reach of the crisis were amplified by contagion effects. However, it is not obvious that the crisis was caused by contagion effects rather than by shared economic weaknesses. The goal of this paper is to assess whether contagion took place. This is important for both investors and policy makers. If contagion occurs it undermines much of the benefits of international diversification. Understanding the source and transmission mechanisms of the crisis are important as policy makers contemplate financial market, institutional, and macro-political reforms to foster a recovery while preventing another crisis. Their analysis employs cross-market correlations to test for stock market contagion during the 1997 Asian crisis, but they propose a different approach to eliminate the bias in the conventional correlation coefficient. They compute the correlation matrix using time-varying estimates. This conditional correlation coefficient is measured at each point in time so it is automatically adjusted for the bias introduced by the change in market volatility. To compute the time-varying conditional variance they use an asymmetric Generalized Autoregressive Conditional Heteroscedasticity (GARCH) process where volatility responds more to negative shocks than to positive ones. The standard GARCH model allows for the variance to change over time as a function of past errors and the past conditional variance but assumes that volatility responds symmetrically to positive and negative shocks. This is crucial, because during the crisis, when most shocks are negative, the symmetry restriction in GARCH leads to a downward bias in the volatility processes – hence, they use an asymmetric GARCH. They find little evidence for contagion. The absence of significant increases in correlations between the different countries' stock markets suggests that co-movement across markets are simply due to their historically close relationships. We find evidence for contagion only from Thailand to Korea.

The purpose of the Gendron, Lai and Soumaré paper is to add to the literature on loan guarantees by considering a portfolio of loan guarantees held by a private guarantor, and accounting explicitly for the non-zero correlation among the borrowing firms themselves and between these firms and the guarantor. They use contingent claims analysis (CCA) to evaluate portfolios of private, hence vulnerable loan guarantees and investigate their risk diversification properties. They show how the value of the guarantee is affected by the covariance structure among the firms and between the firms and the guarantor. Positive correlations among the firms increase the risk of the guarantee portfolio, while negative correlations decrease it. Both positive and negative correlations between the borrowing firms and the guarantor increase the risk of the portfolio of guarantees. To analyze private loan guarantee portfolios, they first consider the value of single guarantees that they then aggregate into portfolios. Merton (1977) has established the isomorphism between a single default-free guarantee and a put option. Since they are dealing with private guarantees, this put becomes a complex option on both the value of the guaranteed firm and the guarantor. Under the standard Merton (1974) framework, they first describe the dynamics of the firm and the guarantor, then evaluate the loss per unit of face value, and finally calculate the value of the private loan guarantee.

Their results demonstrate that, depending on correlations, insuring the debts of five to fifteen firms produces a well-diversified portfolio of guarantees. These results parallel those in Evans and Archer (1968) for equity stocks as well as for bonds (McEnally & Boardman, 1979). They also demonstrate how the level of diversifiable credit risk (e.g. Babbel, 1989) can be reduced through an appropriate combination of volatilities and correlations of all parties involved. Their results suggest that, for very high leverage cases, guarantors can do better through size diversification, i.e. increasing the number of insured firms in the portfolio, than by seeking cross-sector diversification, i.e. reducing correlations among the insured firms.

Lhabitant proposes and tests a practical framework for the quantification of the market risk and the specific risk of hedge funds and hedge funds portfolios ("funds of hedge funds"). His model combines the style analysis approach of Sharpe (1988) with the factor push approach applied in stress testing and historical simulation. It is easy to implement, has a high explanatory power, and is not restricted by some of the assumptions that tie down traditional VaR approaches. He notes that trading rooms have adopted VaR more readily than asset management firms. While most asset managers are particularly proficient at measuring returns and constructing benchmarks to evaluate performance, they argue that this expertise does not extend to the measurement of risk. Indeed, asset managers view risk management in general, and VaR in particular, as being inherently at odds with their primary business mandate: taking risks. Nevertheless, this situation should change rapidly, particularly for asset managers whose portfolio holdings are not transparent to investors at all times. His particular focus is on hedge funds, commodities trading advisors (CTAs), and other eclectic investment pools, whose private partnership structure or offshore location frees them from local regulation and disclosure requirements that apply to mutual funds and banks. For all of these, VaR could be used to communicate risk figures in simple terms, answering both regulators and investors' concerns without imposing disclosure of portfolio holdings. His VaR model requires the estimation of extreme percentile returns of style indices (which is done once for all), and the calculation of the sensitivity coefficients of a hedge fund to style indices (which needs to be repeated for each fund). The resulting VaR can be split into a specific and a market (style) component. The sources of the latter are also known. Despite a relatively short observation period, he has tested his model on a large sample of hedge funds. The positive results provide additional comfort to investment managers by indicating that the realized risks would not be significantly different from the expected ones.

The Arnold, Nail and Nixon research focuses on American Depository Receipts (ADRs). To date, studies of American Depository Receipts have focused on two main topics: (1) pricing efficiency of ADRs relative to their underlying foreign security, and (2) potential international diversification benefits of ADRs in an individual's stock portfolio. They seek to make such a contribution to the existing international diversification benefits of ADR literature. The sample employed in this study consists of 85 ADRs traded continuously on the U.S. stock exchanges between 1990 and 1999. In particular, we measure the volatility of the ADRs in terms of their volatility in U.S. trading, volatility of trading in their home countries, and the volatility of exchange rates between the U.S. and the home country of the ADR. They then decompose the volatility of the ADR into terms attributable to either home country volatility or exchange rate volatility. Finally, we expand the ADR literature by conducting ex-post tests of the Capital Asset Pricing Model (CAPM) in both the U.S. and the home country of the ADR in order to determine the ability of CAPM to serve as an accurate predictor of returns for ADRs and/or their home country stocks.

Their results show that ADRs can add more diversification to a portfolio of U.S. stocks than the broad indices previously tested. We also find that ADR returns are significantly lower than their underlying stocks in emerging markets but that the opposite is true for developed countries. Their results also indicate that the volatility of ADRs as measured by the standard deviation of return is not significantly different from the volatility of their underlying home country stocks for either developed or emerging markets. However, the volatility in exchange rates causes the correlation between ADRs and the S&P 500 to be much lower than for the average U.S. stock relative to the same index. This result also leads to beta measures near zero for the ADRs in our study and indicates that ADRs can be used to reduce both systematic and unsystematic portfolio risk. We also cannot reject the validity of CAPM in generating expected returns for ADRs or home country stocks in developed countries. However, CAPM significantly overestimates expected returns in emerging markets.

The Viney paper focuses on banking institutions and their exposure and lack of standards to manage operational risk, incorporating business continuity risk. The elapsed time between when a disaster (such as 9/11/01) causes the loss of critical business functions, and when recovery of that function is essential to a bank's survival, is typically accepted as being less than twenty-four hours for a bank's computer center operations. However, some critical bank functions, such as foreign exchange trading, derivatives dealing and payments system settlements, are time sensitive within minutes. Banks are fundamentally reliant upon technology to support their information systems and deliver their products and services. Coupled with this absolute dependency on technology is an exposure to public confidence and market sentiment.

Banks are exposed to financial and operational risks. The failure of the majority of bank regulators and prudential supervisors to establish organizational disaster risk management standards, or guidelines, indicates that the potential consequences of this form of operational risk to banking institutions and financial systems remains an unresolved issue. It is evident from an analysis of the results of this paper, and further supported by a BIS survey, that there exists a resultant level of institutional and systemic risk within an undefined number of nation-state financial systems that should be of concern to bank regulators and prudential supervisors. Any contention that the majority of Australian banks have fully developed comprehensive organizational disaster risk management practices is not supported by the data. Furthermore, such a contention cannot be supported for foreign banks that operate within the Australian financial system. The results of this research clearly demonstrate that the majority of banks are in the formative stages of developing disaster recovery planning or disaster response processes throughout their organizations.

The Schmid and Kalemenova piece analyzes a defaultable term structure model, which is necessary for the valuation of defaultable bonds, defaultable interest rate options and credit derivatives. One important issue of using such a model in practice is the estimation of its parameter values. Their article presents a Kalman filtering method for estimating the parameter values of the Schmid and Zagst three factor defaultable term structure model Schmid and Zagst (2000). They apply this method to zero coupon bond data of German and Italian Government bonds between September 30, 1999 and October 23, 2000. For that time frame the exchange rates between the German and Italian currencies have already been fixed due to the membership of the two countries to the European Monetary Union. So they don't have to consider any exchange rate risk in their study. They analyze the development of the credit spreads between German and Italian bonds through time and examine for the ability of the Schmid and Zagst model to describe these dynamics realistically. The Schmid and Zagst model is a hybrid model and as such combines ideas of structural and reduced-form defaultable bond pricing models. The structural approach goes back to the initial proposal of Merton (1974), where he assumes that the dynamics of the value of the assets of a firm across time can be described by a diffusion-type stochastic process and the defaultable security can be regarded as a contingent claim on the value of the assets of the firm. for stochastic non-defaultable interest rates. Hybrid models like the Schmid and Zagst model combine the strengths of structural and reduced-form models. Their model is a direct credit spread model. One of the factors that determine the credit spread is the so-called uncertainty process, which can be understood as an aggregation of all information on the quality of the obligor currently available: The greater the value of the uncertainty process the lower the quality of the obligor. The model assumes the underlying short rate to follow either a mean-reverting Hull-White process or a mean-reverting square root process with time-dependent mean reversion level; the uncertainty process is assumed to follow a mean-reverting square root process; finally, in addition to the non-defaultable short rate and the uncertainty index, Schmid and Zagst directly model the short rate spread process.

The Bos and Hoontrakul work extends the Bos, Ding, and Fetherston (1998) attempt at improving the iterated cumulative sum of squares (ICSS) algorithm. That attempt used the critical boundaries of Tanazaki (1995) in the hope that those nonlinear boundaries would improve the estimates of the original ICCS which uses linear boundaries. Bos and Fetherston (1992) showed that the linear boundaries, first used by Brown, Durbin, and Evans (1975), lead to higher incidences of breaks in the middle of the data set.

In their empirical work, Bos, Ding, and Fetherston (1998) hypothesized that their estimated change points in the variance of Thai stock returns might be related to changes in the mean of those stock returns. This effort revisits that concern. Using Monte Carlo analysis they that changes in the mean of a process will indeed be picked up by the ICCS as changes in the variance. Thus the original ICCS procedure will pick up both changes in mean and variance. Further, they introduce a procedure that will estimate whether an estimated change point is either a change in mean, or variance, or both. This new procedure can be grafted to the original ICCS procedure. They demonstrate that the judicious use of partial mean and variance standardization of segments allows for the statistical identification of the type of change point. They assert correctly that a procedure that identifies when and what mean and variance changes occur in a time series is an interesting tool for financial research. Their analysis applied to daily returns of the index of the Stock Exchange of Thailand discovers that the nearly all, if not all, the estimated changes are attributed to changes in the mean. Some changes are estimated to be changes in both mean and variance.

REFERENCES

Alexander, C. (Ed.) (2001). *FT Mastering Risk, Volume II*. London: Prentice Hall.

Babbel, D. F. (1989). Insuring banks against systematic credit risk. *Journal of Futures, 9*, 487–505.

Bos, T., & Fetherston, T. A. (1992). Market Model Nonstationarity in the Korean Stock Market. In: G. Rhee & R. Chang (Eds), *Pacific-Basin Capital Markets Research* (Vol III). Amsterdam: North-Holland.

Bos, T., Ding, D., & Fetherston, T. A. (1998). Searching for Periods of Volatility: A Study of the Behavior of Volatility in Thai Stocks. *Pacific-Basin Finance Journal*.

Brown, R. L., Durbin, J., & Evans, J. M. (1975). Techniques for Testing the Constancy of Regression Relationships over Time. *JRSS(B), 37*(2), 149–163.

Chan, K. C., Karolyi, G. A., Longstaff, F. A., & Sanders, A. B. (1992). An empirical comparison of alternative models of the short-term interest rate. *Journal of Finance, 47*, 1209–1227.

Das, S. (1998). *Risk management and financial derivatives: a guide to the mathematics*. New York, McGraw Hill.

Diebold, F. X., Schuermann, T., & Stroughair, J. D. (1998). Pitfalls and Opportunities in the Use of Extreme Value Theory in Risk Management. In: A.-P. N. Refenes (Ed.).

Dunbar, N. (2000). *Inventing money: the story of Long-term Capital Management and the legends behind it*. Chichester: New York, Wiley.

Embrechts, P., Klüppelberg, C., & Mikosch, T. (1997). *Modelling Extremal Events for Insurance and Finance*. New York: Springer.

Engle, R. F., & Granger, C. W. J. (1987). Co-integration and error correction: representation, estimation, and testing. *Econometrica, 55*(2), 251–276.

Evans, J. L., & Archer, S. H. (1968). Diversification and the reduction of dispersion: An empirical analysis. *The Journal of Finance, 23*, 761–767.

Geczy, C., Minton, B. A., & Schrand, C. (1997). Why firms use currency derivatives. *Journal of Finance, 54*, 1323–1354.

Ghosh, A. (1993b). Hedging with Stock Index Futures: Estimation and Forecasting with Error Correction Model. *Journal of Futures Markets, 13*, 743–752.

Graham, J. R., & Rodgers, D. A. (2000). Does corporate hedging increase firm value? An empirical analysis. Northeastern University Working Paper.

Hill, B. M. (1975). A Simple General Approach to Inference about the Tail of a Distribution. *Annals of Statistics, 3*, 1163–1174.

Hoaglin, D. C. (1983). The *g*-and-*h*-Distributions, In: S. Kotz, N. L. Johnson & Campbell B. R. (Eds), *Encyclopedia of Statistical Sciences* (Vol. 3, pp. 298–301). New York: John Wiley & Sons.

Hoaglin, D. C. (1985). Summarizing Shape Numerically: The *g*-and-*h* Distributions. In: D. C. Hoaglin, F. Mosteller & J. W. Tukey (Eds), *Exploring Data Tables, Trends, and Shapes* (pp. 461–513). New York: John Wiley & Sons.
Hull, J. C., & White, A. (1990). Pricing Interest Rate Derivative Securities. *Review of Financial Studies, 3*(4), 573–592.
Hull, J. C., & White, A. (1998). Value at Risk When Daily Changes in Market Variables Are Not Normally Distributed. *Journal of Derivatives, 5* (Spring), 9–19.
Jorion, P. (1997). *Value at risk: the new benchmark for controlling market risk.* Chicago: Irwin Professional Pub.
Jorion, P., & Khoury, S. J. (1995). *Financial risk management: domestic and international dimensions.* Cambridge, Mass.: Blackwell Publishers.
Lee, A. F. (1987). International asset and currency allocation. *Journal of Portfolio Management, 14*, 68–73.
Lewis, M. (1990). *Liar's poker: rising through the wreckage on Wall Street.* New York, N.Y.: Penguin Books.
Lien, D. H. D. (1996). The Effect of the Cointegration Relationship on Futures Hedging: A Note. *Journal of Futures Markets, 16*, 773–780.
Los, C. A. (1998) Optimal multi-currency investment strategies with exact attribution in three Asian countries. *Journal of Multinational Financial Management, 8*, 169–198.
Lowenstein, R., & Long-term Capital Management (Firm). (2000). *When genius failed: the rise and fall of Long-Term Capital Management.* New York, Random House.
MacGillivray, H. L. (1992). Shape Properties of the *g*-and-*h* and Johnson Families. *Communications in Statistics – Theory and Methods, 21* (May), 1233–1250.
MacGillivray, H. L., & Balanda, K. P. (1988). The Relationships Between Skewness and Kurtosis. *Australian Journal of Statistics, 30* (December), 319–337.
Martinez, J., & Iglewicz, B. (1984). Some Properties of the Tukey, *g* and *h* Family of Distributions. *Communications in Statistics – Theory and Methods, 13* (September), 353–369.
Mayer, M. (1993). *Nightmare on Wall Street: Salomon Brothers and the corruption of the marketplace.* New York: Simon & Schuster.
McEnally, R. W., & Boardman, C. M. (1979). Aspects of corporate bonds portfolio diversification. *Journal of Financial Research, 2*, 27–36.
Merton, R. C. (1974). On the pricing of corporate debt: The risk structure of interest rates. *The Journal of Finance, 29*, 449–470.
Merton, R. C. (1977). An analytic derivation of the cost of deposit insurance and loan guarantees: An application of modern option pricing theory. *Journal of Banking and Finance, 1*, 3–11.
Nance, D. R., Smith, C. W., & Smithson, C. W. (1993). On the determinants of corporate hedging. *Journal of Finance, 48*, 267–284.
Nowman, K. B. (1997). Gaussian estimation of single-factor continuous time models of the term structure of interest rates. *Journal of Finance, 52*, 1695–1706.
Nowman, K. B. (2001). Gaussian estimation and forecasting of multi-factor term structure models with an application to Japan and the United Kingdom. *Asia Pacific Financial Markets*, in press.
Pickford, J. (Ed.) (2001). *FT Mastering Risk, Volume I.* London: Prentice Hall.
Schmid, B., & Zagst, R. (2000). A three-factor defaultable term structure model. *The Journal of Fixed Income, 10*(2), 63–79.
Sharpe, W. F. (1988). Determining a Fund's Effective Asset Mix. *Investment Management Review, 2*(6), 59–69.

Tanizaki, H. (1995). Asymptotically Exact Confidence Intervals of CUSUM and CUSUMSQ Tests: A Numerical Derivation Using Simulation Technique. Communications in Statistics. *Simulation and Computation*, *24*(4), 1019–1036.
Wolfe, T. (1987). *The bonfire of the vanities*. New York, Farrar Straus Giroux.

RECENT GLOBAL FINANCIAL CRISES: LESSONS LEARNED*

William C. Hunter

ABSTRACT

Since 1990, major banking and financial crises have occurred in many countries throughout the world – including Mexico and Latin America in 1994–1995, East Asia in 1997–1998, and Russia and Brazil in 1998 – with large costs both to the individual countries experiencing the crises and to other nations. As a result of these crises, considerable effort has been expended by economists and policymakers to identify the causes of these crises and to design programs with the aim of preventing similar crises from occurring in the future. This paper summarizes the key lessons that policymakers have learned from these recent crises.

INTRODUCTION

When Thailand was forced to devalue its currency in July of 1997, few, if any economists could have foreseen the turmoil that would follow. Over the succeeding two years, financial crises swept through the developing world with

* This paper draws on the discussions and materials presented at conferences devoted to financial crisis sponsored by the Federal Reserve Bank of Chicago. An earlier version of this paper is forthcoming in *Asymmetries in Financial Globalization* B. Batavia, N. Lash and A. Malliaris (Editors) Toronto: APF Press 2002. The views expressed are those of the author and not necessarily those of the Federal Reserve Bank of Chicago or the Board of Governors of the Federal Reserve System.

Financial Risk and Financial Risk Management, Volume 16, pages 23–31.

ISBN: 0-7623-0858-3

the force of several hurricanes. Indonesia, South Korea, Malaysia, the Philippines, Hong Kong, Russia, and Brazil were among the hardest hit, but few developing countries emerged unscathed. In the crises countries, currencies and equity prices plummeted, economic growth turned into recession, wealth evaporated, jobs were destroyed, and poverty and school drop out rates soared. Private capital flows to emerging economies nose-dived, while industrial countries saw their export markets shrink. In the fall of 1998, after Russia's debt default and devaluation and the near collapse of the hedge fund Long Term Capital Management, international financial markets seized-up for nearly all high-risk borrowers including those in the United States and other developed economies. At that time, the Federal Reserve's Federal Open Market Committee lower its intended or target federal funds rate three times (by a cumulative total of 75 basis points) in response to the systemic threat posed by these developments. Although systemic crisis was avoided, global growth slowed dramatically. In some quarters, doubts arose about the market and the market system as a reliable source or engine of prosperity. And confidence in the official institutions that manage financial crises was shaken, so much so, that there was serious talk of actually shutting the institutions down.

Despite this turmoil, it must be remembered that financial crises are nothing new. In the past 20 years alone, more than 125 countries, including the United States, have experienced at least one serious financial or banking crisis. In more than half of these episodes, a developing country's entire banking system became insolvent. In more than 40 cases the cost of resolving the crises averaged about 12.8% of GDP. In developing countries (over all) the percentage was even higher.

KEY LESSONS

The initial lessons to be taken from recent experiences are, first, that no one country should be consider itself immune to financial crisis and second, the cost of resolving a crisis once it has occurred is almost certain to be very high. In some East Asian countries the cost had been estimated to be as high as 20 to 60% of GDP. The specific details of these crises are well known and thus will not be repeated here. Suffice it to say that the countries suffering financial crises typically exhibited many of the same symptoms. In almost all of the crisis countries, significant financial sector problems included:

(1) government directed and connected lending;
(2) poor supervision of the financial system;
(3) an inadequate legal infrastructure;

(4) absence of a credit culture in which lenders and investors make judgements based on independent credit assessments and sound financial analysis;
(5) underdeveloped bond and long term capital markets;
(6) lack of adequate accounting disclosure and transparency;
(7) ineffective systems of corporate governance;
(8) excessive and imprudent risk-taking by financial institutions operating with explicit or implicit deposit insurance schemes or governmental guarantees, among others.

However, these same countries also has unique elements that contributed and in many cases, set off their particular episodes:

(1) weak fixed exchanges rate regimes (often pegged to the U.S. dollar);
(2) significant debt and asset priced deflation, and
(3) unstable short-term capital flows, among others.

Thus, the third lesson we have learned from recent global financial crises is that all crises are different and all crises are the same. The list of common problems suggests lessons in and of themselves.

Stated differently, the fourth (and perhaps most important) lesson we have learned is that infrastructure matters. Countries with strong financial infrastructures including good systems of supervision and regulation, legal frameworks, and private property rights have tended to be more immune to financial shocks and have tended to enjoy more stable rates of growth. Such stability in the financial system breeds the necessary trust that Federal Reserve System considers essential to a well functioning competitive financial system. Research presented at a 1999 Federal Reserve Bank of Chicago/Bank for International Settlements conference devoted to financial crises showed that weakness of legal institutions for corporate governance had an important effect on the extent of currency depreciations and stock market declines in the Asia crisis countries. By corporate governance we mean the effectiveness of legal mechanisms that prevent managers from stealing. Measures of legal protections, enforceability of contracts, corruption, and judiciary efficiency were all shown to be important in determining the depth of the crisis.

A corollary to the fourth lesson is something policymakers learned from the Russian financial crisis. To use a medical analogy, corruption and lawlessness are the quiet killers. They are equivalent to the hypertension of the financial system. The Russian crisis also taught policymakers about the complexities involving luck, economic policies, and institutions in generating a crisis and defining its depth. The interaction of these three factors tends to be critical. At the Chicago Fed/BIS financial crisis conference one expert on the Russian economy described a conversation he had with a Russian banker during the aftermath of the Russian default. In commenting on the Russian psyche, the banker said that: "the Russian soul is constituted such that when confronted with a choice between two evils, it chooses both!" According to some commentators, in Russia's case in 1998 it choose three evils all at once. It devalued its currency, it defaulted on domestic treasuries, and it imposed a private debt moratorium. Regarding luck, policies, and institutions, Russia had bad luck, bad policies, and bad institutions.

The fifth lesson policymakers have learned is one that was highlighted by former World Bank Chief Economist Joseph Stiglitz at this same crisis conference. Namely, a crisis is not over once financial markets stabilize. That is, we should never confuse financial variables with real economic variables or with the human dimension of a crisis. Exchange rates and interest rates are not ends in and of themselves but means to an end. We should be careful never to confuse ends with means, nor judge our success by anything other than an improvement in the ends themselves.

The sixth lesson learned involves the contributions academic scholars can make to good crisis management. The lesson is that modern finance (as a discipline) can be very useful in the design of economic institutions and policies just like modern macroeconomics can. Understanding such financial concepts such as market micro-structure and option value proved to be just as important in forecasting and mitigating crises as has been a sound understanding of modern macroeconomics. The Asian crisis is a good example of this given that most of the countries had good macroeconomic fundamentals but significant imbalances on the finance-side that escaped the scrutiny of economists and policy makers. In additional, such notions as agency costs, moral hazard, signaling, complete and incomplete markets, bankruptcy and strategic default, and other micro level incentive related concepts were critical in fully understanding the recent crises. In essence, finance is important and can prove to be very valuable for macroeconomic and monetary policy.

LOOKING TO THE FUTURE: MARKET DISCIPLINE AND INCENTIVE COMPATIBLE REGULATION

It seems clear that a country susceptible to financial crisis due to weak infrastructure is analogous to a human body with a weakened immune system. An immune system with strong fundamentals can shrug off minor infections without harm. However, the same low-grade concerns can wreck havoc on a weakened immune system leading to systemic crisis. In this case, as with financial crises, an ounce of prevention is worth a pound of cure. Since we can not fully protect against or eliminate every potential risk factor that might give rise to a crisis (financial or medical), devoting proper attention to preventive actions seems very appropriate. This includes coordinated actions to improve the global financial infrastructure or architecture (examples include efforts like the BIS capital standards and the core banking principles).

Although there seems to be a consensus regarding the value of a strong financial infrastructure, there is less of a consensus regarding the optimal design of this infrastructure, including among other things, the exact role to be played by the multilateral agencies in the grand design. Continuing with my medical analogy:

(1) What is the role of the doctor?
(2) What medicines should be prescribed?
(3) What is the correct dosage?
(4) How long should the patient continue on the medication?
(5) How will the patient be monitored? and
(6) When is the patient cured?

For some illnesses, the answers to these questions are well known. For other, more exotic diseases, more research is obviously required. Similarly, in the case of financial crises, more research is needed on issues related to the optimal design and implementation of a financial architecture. In this regard, another lesson we have learned is that direct measures of risk-taking can provide misleading assessments of overall exposure in an environment characterized by complex interconnections among policies, institutions, instruments, and markets. These interactions almost always produce non-normally distributed outcomes (the "so called fat tails" problem) or surprise correlations in situations where outcomes were thought to be ex ante independent. For example, direct lending exposure of global depository financial institutions to Thailand, Malaysia, and South Korea were limited at the time of the Asian crisis. However, proxy hedging of these risks in other more liquid and deep markets – including those in Hong Kong, Australia, Brazil, and Mexico proved costly when these markets were adversely impacted by the evolving events and their spillover effects.

This growing complexity of institutions and markets – highlighted by increased interconnectedness driven by advances in technology (both, information processing technology and financial technology or financial engineering) has been taken by some as grounds for supporting the case for a single global financial regulation. This growing desire for centralized regulation must be tempered with caution, given the inherent difficulties associated with the design and implementation of socially optimal regulation. As is well known, inappropriate implementation of even well designed regulation creates more problems than it solves. This is because regulation does not occur in a vacuum . . . firms and agents react to changes in regulation in ways to affect the effectiveness of the regulation. In essence, regulators must know exactly how economic agents will react in order to implement optimal regulatory rules. However, given that regulators are generally looking from the outside in, such understanding is difficult and elusive. This is why enhancing market discipline is so important to the overall process of international harmonization of regulation.

Market discipline compliments regulators' efforts allowing for more effective supervision. As I noted earlier, there is no way regulators can ensure a fail safe financial system. This is another key lesson we have learned from recent financial crises. We need help and market discipline provides a partial solution. Enhancing market discipline through dynamic incentive compatible approaches is the next challenge confronting the Federal Reserve System and regulators in general. From the perspective of the Federal Reserve, we must respond to the recently passed financial modernization legislation (the Gram Leach Bliley Act) which allows full affiliation of banking and securities and insurance activities creating large complex banking organizations which have to be effectively supervised and regulated. Clearly, that regulation must be adaptive. Similarly, in the case of emerging markets and transitioning economies, regulation must be dynamic and adaptive. This makes sense since these markets are emerging and in transition.

The Federal Reserve Bank of Chicago has long pushed for more market discipline through increased disclosure and transparency and through such schemes as mandatory issuance of subordinated debt by large complex banking organizations. In the Chicago Fed view, mandatory subordinated debt is incentive compatible in that it aligns the incentives and risk preferences of bondholders with those of bank supervisors. Being subordinated to other liabilities, the debt holders would be risk sensitive and would monitor and discipline bank behavior. They would demand higher rates from riskier banks (a direct effect) and have stronger incentives to quickly resolve problems and avoid forbearance and its associated costs. In addition, increases in interest rate spreads provide signals to supervisors that risk is increasing (an indirect effect). The Second Quarter 2000 issue of the Chicago Fed's journal – *Economic Perspectives* contains a comprehensive article on subordinated debt – "Subordinated debt as bank capital: A proposal for regulatory reform," by Douglas Evanoff (Chicago Fed) and Larry Wall (Atlanta Fed). This article discusses subordinated debt in banking and its advantages as a tool for regulators in supervising large complex banking organizations. It should noted that the U.S. Shadow Financial Regulatory Committee has endorsed the subordinated debt concept and it is likely to be endorsed by the shadow committees in Europe and Japan.

GROWTH, DERIVATIVES, AND MONETARY POLICY

Obviously, one could fill numerous pages describing other lessons that policymakers have learned from recent financial crises. In this section, let me offer a few observations regarding financial derivatives, economic growth, systemic risk, and the conduct of monetary policy.

Recent research (e.g. Ross Levine, "Stock Markets, Banks, and Economic Growth," (Word Bank mimeo, 1991); Ross Levine, "Stock Markets, Growth, and Tax Policy," *Journal of Finance*, (September 1991); and Ross Levine and Sara Zervos, "Capital Control Liberalization and Stock Market Development," (World Bank, mimeo, 1996)) has shown that financial market deepening (e.g. high stock market turnover) does have a positive impact on a country's rate of real economic growth. This is important given that only a years few many economists were of the opinion that finance and financial markets were just a side-show to economic growth which was thought to be determined solely by real factors (rate of capital accumulation, human capital, etc.). Luckily, this view has changed in light of recent research on the determinants of economic growth. Following up on some of this research, recent work at the Chicago Fed focuses on the impact of financial derivatives on economic growth (see for example, J. Hao & W. C. Hunter, "A Test of the Impact of Financial Innovation on Economic Growth," *Managerial Finance*, Vol. 23, No. 11 (1997), pp. 64–78). This work extends the existing literature by explicitly examining the impact of second stage financial deepening on real economic growth. Essentially, the study adds second stage financial innovation variables to standard growth regressions. In these regressions, variables such as education levels, population growth, investment share of gross domestic product (GDP), foreign direct investment and others are used to explain the real rate of growth in GDP for a broad cross section of developed and developing countries. The Chicago study considered the absence or presence of futures and options markets on underlying stock and debt markets along with various measures of financial market openness and the degree to which the banking system was liberalized. A total of 68 countries were examined and the results showed that second stage financial deepening of the type associated with well developed derivative markets was positively linked to real GDP growth.

Regarding financial derivatives and their role in contributing to financial crises and systemic risk, it turns out that all the talk about financial wizardry that allows unbundling and transferring of risks and the lightening speeds of transmission of these risks across markets was probably overblown. That is, recent crises remind us that by and large, the mistakes of the past few years were rather hum drum or ordinary and not so exotic – making bad loans (typically in real estate), failure to evaluate counterparty risk, or relying on the lofty reputations of firm principals (a la Long Term Capital Management). These are age-old problems (especially in the banking industry). The lesson here is that derivatives were not a major villain in recent crises. This suggests that maybe the first lesson we should learn is not to forget the old lessons!

With regards to matters monetary policy, there is much disagreement on the overall effectiveness of monetary policy in a world of sophisticated financial derivatives. It could be that derivatives, in addition to complicating monetary policy, might also reduce the impact monetary policy has on the real economy. That is, a given amount of monetary stimulus may have a smaller effect. For example, the existence of foreign exchange derivatives may reduce the ability of central banks to influence exchange rates. Since money should be neutral in a frictionless economy, the sources of monetary non-neutrality must lie in economic frictions such as informational imperfections and transactions costs. By increasing the liquidity, depth, flexibility and transactional efficiency of financial markets, derivatives increase the speed with which monetary policy actions are transmitted throughout the financial system. Lower transaction costs and reduced frictions resulting from derivatives activities increase the rate at which new information, including policy actions, is impounded into market prices. Since derivatives markets reduce these sorts of frictions, they provide a more efficient mechanism for price discovery, speed up information transmission, and reduce informational asymmetries. Thus, it follows that by reducing frictions, derivative markets may actually reduce the real effects of monetary policy actions.

Furthermore, derivative markets act as a mechanism for spreading shocks across the economy as a whole. To the extent that derivatives reduce the force of monetary policy, monetary policy may become a weaker tool for counter cyclical stabilization policy. However, if derivatives do provide the economy with the benefits cited by their proponents, that is, a more efficient, self-correcting and shock resistant economy, then there should be less of a need for counter cyclical monetary policy. Stated differently, derivatives activity might actually reduce the incidence and severity of business cycles themselves.

CONCLUSION

In conclusion, it is clear that policymakers have learned quite a lot from recent financial crises. However, it is also clear that policymakers can not become complacent regarding the potential for future financial crises to erupt. With this said, and despite the lessons learned in recent years, we must remember that the world is indeed complicated and that the challenge to policymakers is not to repeat the mistakes of the past.

THE ABILITY OF REGULATORY CAPITAL MODELS TO MEET PRUDENTIAL OBJECTIVES: A CREDIT DERIVATIVE PERSPECTIVE

Elizabeth Wong, Thomas A. Fetherston and Jonathan A. Batten

ABSTRACT

This survey study explores the application of regulatory capital models in risk management practices. The goal of this study is to determine the ability of regulatory capital models to meet prudential objectives in the realm of credit derivatives. It summarizes the pertinent literature and offers conclusions and direction for regulatory action.

INTRODUCTION

The focus of the paper is on the development of credit derivatives and their impact on capital regulation of banks. The increasing complexity of risk management practices has raised the need for regulators to manage and integrate credit, market, and operational risk under the one comprehensive capital regulation model (Smithson, 1999). Currently regulatory capital models are separated into credit (banking book) and market risk (trading book) models with operational risk models yet to be developed. The regulatory capital requirements imposed by banking and trading models fail to represent a

Financial Risk and Financial Risk Management, Volume 16, pages 33–61.

ISBN: 0-7623-0858-3

probability of insolvency, as regulatory measures of bank risk do not measure a bank's true economic risk. Regulatory capital requirements are required to reflect true economic risk, as Mizon (1998) highlights the shift from regulatory capital representing a regulatory review of a bank's risks, to a measure that is closely monitored by public rating agencies and stock analysts to represent a banks true stability and credit quality. Hence market participants require regulatory capital requirements to be accurate enough to reflect a bank's true soundness and safety. If regulators diverge from this prudential objective Wall and Peterson (1995) note that banks would be motivated to search for regulatory arbitrage opportunities, as regulatory capital would be deemed burdensome. From a regulatory perspective, bank participation in regulatory arbitrage is not desired as artificial adjustment of bank risk creates a realistic negative effect on the soundness and safety of the entire banking system. Therefore, it is imperative that regulatory capital models adhere to prudential objectives, in particular the primary objective of preserving the safety and soundness of the banking system, otherwise the market becomes extremely vulnerable to the chance of economic and financial crises. Accordingly, research attention on the ability for capital regulation when applied to new risk management practices to achieve prudential objectives is justified as the changing nature of risk management practices provide scope for capital regulations to stray from achieving prudential objectives.

Past empirical research such as Hovakimian and Kane (2000) conclude that U.S. capital regulations in general do fail to achieve the prudential objective of deterring financial crises. The Houpt (1999), study found the role of U.S. and U.K. banks to be expanding as there is a trend for increased cross border lending and derivative trading activities. Hall (1992) noted that U.S. and U.K. are also comparable, as there is little difference in their definition of capital and company law policies.[1] In addition, focus was given to U.S. and U.K., as both the Federal Reserve Board (FRB)[2] and the Financial Services Authority (FSA)[3] have implemented BIS risk weighted and standard regulatory capital models for credit derivatives. To date, FSA and FRB have not specifically implemented the internal regulatory capital approach to credit derivatives. As a result, the ability for the internal approach applied to credit derivatives to meet prudential objectives will be implied from internal model requirements set by BIS (1996).

The Capital Model impact of credit derivatives was chosen as a focus area as it has been quoted to " have the potential to revolutionise the way that credit risk is originated, distributed, measured and managed" (Mizon, 1997). Supporting the potential of credit derivatives, the British Bankers' Association most recent survey (BBA, 1999/2000) predicts that the global credit derivative market is set to reach $893 billion by the end of this year and $1581 billion by year 2002.[4] Clearly, this suggests that there is widespread agreement between market participants that credit derivatives will continue to grow. Banks in particular are drawn to use this new credit risk management, as credit risk comprises 85% of a bank's total risk (Federal Reserve Bank of Chicago, 1998). An examination of regulatory capital models applied to credit derivatives is important, as the expanding use of credit derivatives by banks will have an immense impact on bank capital regulation.

A reason for expected credit derivative growth identified by BBA (1999/2000) is the comparative advantages it offers over traditional credit risk management techniques. Primarily, it allows banks to trade the credit risk component of an asset in isolation whilst avoiding costs of selling or buying physical asset. Another distinct advantage of credit derivatives is the confidentiality and freedom to negotiate terms of credit derivative contracts, as reference to the client is not required. In sum, credit derivatives have altered traditional risk management practice to the extent that banks are able to hedge or offset unwanted exposure, whilst maintaining client relationships[5] (Davies, 1998). The question of whether such a change in risk management practice will affect the ability of regulatory capital proposed by BIS to achieve prudential objectives is investigated.

The 1988 Basle Accord formed by BIS established the first agreement amongst G-10 central banks to apply a common international risk weighted approach for bank capital treatment of credit risk held in the banking book.[6] Carmichael (2000) emphasised that it is not an easy task for financial regulators to develop one risk management framework that incorporates all potential risks a bank is to face. Consequently, the Basle Accord was amended in 1996 to address market risks arising from debt and equity securities held in the trading book. The amendment proposed a standard and internal approach to regulatory capital. At the heart of the Basle Accord Amendment (1996) is the division of a bank's activities into a banking and trading book, where items that do not fall within the trading book definition constitute the banking book.[7] The banking and trading account division is important, as it will determine the treatment of credit derivatives for regulatory capital purposes. To illustrate, under the banking book (risk weighted model) credit derivatives are treated in the same manner as interest rate swaps and other derivatives, where credit risk is calculated for regulatory capital purposes based on the reference asset. Under the trading book (standard approach) capital requirements for credit derivatives are based on price volatility and asset maturity, whilst internal Value at Risk (VaR) models are largely based on bank internal risk assessment methods.

The risk weighted, standard and internal (VaR) regulatory capital models, applied to credit derivatives are examined. In order to assess their ability to meet prudential objectives, this study adopts an analytical perspective similar to that used by Mingo (2000) and Berger, Herring and Szego (1995). Principally, Mingo (2000) analysed implications of credit risk based capital models for the banking industry as a whole, by examining the extent theoretical goals of regulatory capital are achieved. Similarly, Berger, Herring and Szego (1995) proposed a definition and measurement of regulatory capital based on achievement of regulatory capital objectives. The qualitative approach of assessing the impact of regulatory changes was preferred over empirical studies based on stock market data such as Cornett and Tehranian (1990) and Schwert (1981), as they are limited to the Modigliani and Miller proposition (M&M, 1958).

In support of the argument against adoption of the quantitative approach, Miller (1999) noted that the focus of finance research in the last 30 years has been on departures from the M&M proposition. The M&M proposition proposes that in a frictionless world of perfect information and markets, a firm's capital structure will have no effect on a firm's value. Consequently, if M&M propositions are supported then there would be no need for regulatory capital as in a frictionless world of perfect information and markets, the value of a firm is independent of capital structure. In practice this proposition is not supported, as Jones (1998) and Wagster (1996) are amongst many studies that indicate markets are not perfect as regulatory arbitrage opportunities can be identified.

Credit derivatives provide a distinct advantage as they allow a more flexible approach to management of credit concentration risk[8] than would be available through traditional credit risk management techniques. The management of concentration risk is vital, as large exposure to a particular issuer, industry, region with high default correlation will increase a bank's expected portfolio loss. It is desirable to manage credit risk by reducing/increasing exposure to a client to whom the bank is over/underexposed. Leah (1997) supports this strategy by demonstrating return on credit assets to be related to the size of exposure, pricing, and default correlation between credit assets.[9]

Types of Credit Derivatives

In terms of product range, the British Bankers' Association (BBA, 1996) is one of the first associations to identify four distinct categories of credit derivative contracts: *total return swaps, credit default swaps, credit spread contracts and credit linked notes.* A review of each product will not be undertaken, as an abundant amount of literature discussing the primary functions of each product already exists.[10] This section will limit the introduction of credit derivatives to the two most commonly used, as indicated by BBA (1999/2000) to be credit default swaps and total return swaps.

For credit default swaps, the protection seller receives a fixed stream of payment from the protection buyer in exchange for a payment conditional upon default. Hence, only the protection buyer is exposed to credit risk, as payment from sellers is conditional. Market risk is eliminated as default payment is based on the probability of defined default events,[11] and if positions are matched (in asset and maturity); specific risk is also eliminated. For a Total Return Swap, payments are unconditional as the buyer of protection makes a fixed set of payments in return for a payment from the seller, hence both sellers and buyers are exposed to credit risk. In addition, market risk is not eliminated as default payment is based on probability of default and change in market value, however specific risk may also be reduced if positions are matched.

Three advantages of credit derivatives that regulators should be aware of when setting regulatory capital for credit derivatives can be identified.

(1) Capital regulations need to adequately reflect the hedging benefits offered by credit derivatives, as credit derivatives have the ability to isolate and transfer credit exposures inherent in debt obligations. This allows sellers and buyers the ability to customise the size, term and structure of the commitment. Ultimately, it encourages optimal hedging benefits as specific needs of the institution are matched appropriately with risks and assets.

(2) If hedging benefits are not recognized by regulators, then the increase in bank efficiency in terms of liquidity and cost due to the temporary transfer and hedging of credit exposure to other firms better adapted to manage such risk will be lost. Liquidity of credit risk is enhanced significantly; as banks are able to trade credit derivatives at a faster rate than would be possible with bank loans. The cost of credit risk protection is reduced as on balance sheet management costs are avoided.

(3) Overall regulatory failure to recognize benefits offered by credit derivatives is dangerous; particularly as credit derivatives permit banks to take on additional exposure beyond limits dictated, and also occur without client knowledge that the credit risk has been sold to counterparty. Capital regulators need to ensure that both the benefits and limits of credit derivatives are adequately reflected in regulatory capital.

REGULATORY CAPITAL OF CREDIT DERIVATIVES

Regulatory capital models to be considered are those proposed by BIS (1988) and implemented by FRB SR 96-17 GEN (1996) and FSA (1998). Also the trading book models, proposed by BIS (1996) and implemented by FRB SR 97-18 GEN (1997) and FSA (1998) is covered.

Banking Book Model (See Fig. 1)

Regulators have been inclined to treat credit derivatives held under the banking account, as direct credit substitutes. The regulatory capital treatment of credit derivatives as direct substitutes for traditional credit instruments is supported by Smithson (1998), who notes that the basic concept behind credit derivatives is not entirely new as credit derivatives do share characteristics similar to that of traditional guarantees or letter of credit instruments. The banking book proposes a risk weighted regulatory capital model.

Under this model, regulatory capital is set for credit risk only, as market and specific risks are ignored. Regulatory capital for credit risk is calculated by a summation of capital, a maximum regulatory capital of 8% of the notional value applies for a credit derivative transaction marked at 100% risk weight. In addition, a 100% conversion risk weight is also applied to the nominal value in order to convert credit derivatives into on balance sheet credit items.[12]

Risk weightings depend on the category of the reference asset rather than credit quality and the maturity of credit derivative. Risk weights are determined by differentiating between Organisation for Economic Co-operation and Development (OECD) countries,[13] broadly 0% for sovereign OECD, 20% for OECD banks and 100% for non-sovereign and non-OECD banks.[14] Consequently, all loans are weighted with the same capital charge as risk weights fail to include features of a bank's true economic risk e.g. market risk, specific risk, diversification strategies. This unrepresentative risk weight will cause the risk weighted approach to be more onerous than required to maintain an adequate level of safety and soundness, and thus may influence users of credit derivatives towards trading book risk models in order to gain regulatory capital relief as diversification strategies are recognised.

To date, the U.S. FRB has released one paper regarding the regulatory capital treatment of credit derivatives held in the banking book: FRB SR 96-17 GEN. It extends the risk-weighted approach by allowing buyers the ability to reduce credit risk to that of the counterparty, provided the positions are perfectly matched. Failure to provide regulatory relief for unmatched hedges, as Francis et al. (1999) notes, poses a problem for credit default and total return swaps as most are generally of shorter maturities than the term of the underlying asset. Nonetheless, a joint release by FRB, FDIC, OCC and OTS (2000) has now considered recognition of unmatched positions by proposing an internal risk model for credit risk. In the U.K., FSA (1998) revised Bank of England's (1996) paper regarding credit derivatives, to produce a chapter of regulation that specifically deals with the "Regulatory Treatment of Credit Derivatives."

Trading Book Model (See Fig. 1)

Total return swap credit derivatives fit into the trading book/market risk framework, as Clark (1997) notes that total return swaps are possible to mark to the market as they are widely traded with market prices readily available. However, to mark credit default swaps to the market is complicated, as adverse price changes are not associated with the probability of default event. The trading book proposed two regulatory capital models: standard and internal.

Under the standard model, regulatory capital is the summation of credit, market and specific risk. This building block approach ignores dynamic trading strategies for risk control as it is based solely on a bank's current asset position.

FRB released SR 97-18 GEN to determine regulatory capital for credit derivatives, simply by dividing credit derivative transactions into open, matched or offsetting positions. The consideration of positions other than matched provides an advantage over the risk-weighted model, as it permits regulatory capital relief for diversification strategies adopted by banks. Contrasting, FSA (1998) is more comprehensive as it determines the measurement of regulatory capital for credit derivatives beyond the three positions defined under FRB SR 97-18 GEN.

The Basle Accord was amended in 1996 to allow credit, market and specific risk to be modelled by an internal (VaR) model. It was a regulatory attempt to account for bank trading strategies, volatile interest rates, and the rapid pace and complexity at which risk methods is developing.

VaR is derived from statistical estimates which details the loss or gain produced by a portfolio due to changes in underlying prices and confidence intervals over a given holding period.[15] To ensure that the objective of comparability is maintained the Basle Accord Amendment (1996) sets out quantitative and qualitative requirements for use of VaR models.

The quantitative standards are a 10-day holding period, a minimum observation period of 1 year and a standard confidence interval of 99%. Some qualitative requirements are that banks must operate an independent risk control unit and have senior management closely involved with risk control

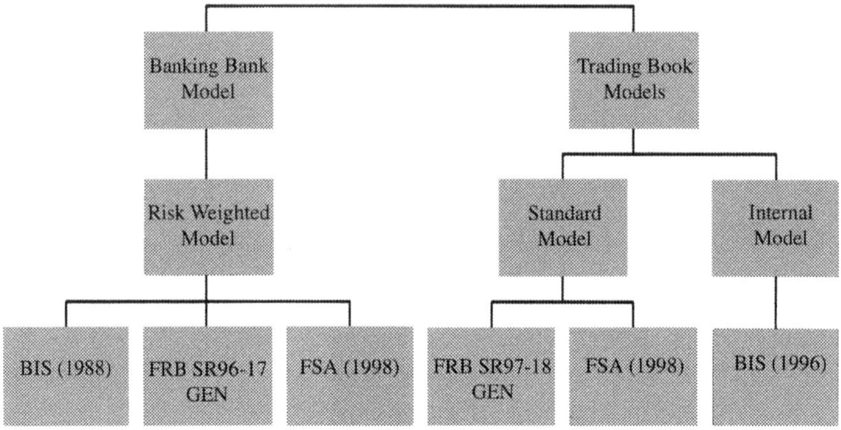

Fig. 1. Regulatory Capital Models for Credit Derivatives.

process. The internal model must also be closely integrated with both risk management and internal trading and exposures limits, be subject to routine and rigorous testing regime (e.g. back and stress testing) and regular independent reviews by an internal auditor.[16] Imposition of qualitative requirements in addition to stringent quantitative requirements are justified as the threat of market disturbances, which although have a low probability of occurrence however can have a high impact on bank capital if they occurred e.g. 1987 October stock market crash.

A Prudential objective will be developed from theoretical models of regulation proposed. Although there are several competing theories of regulation, only two of the leading theories will be discussed: Economic and Capture Theory.

Core Principles of Regulation

The Economic Theory of government regulation, attributable to Peltzman (1976) is an attempt to improve or generalize the Capture Theory first proposed by Stiger (1971), which proposed that the regulated and not the public are likely to influence the direction of government regulation. Comparatively, the Economic Theory extends on this basic proposition to consider the competitive nature of conflicting interest groups and implies that both the regulated and general public have an influential effect on regulators. To provide some clarity of which model is superior, Caudill, Im and Kaserman (1993) conducted a study to discriminate between theories of regulation and found the Economic Theory to be the superior model. Hence the following four core principles of regulation will be extracted from the Economic Theory.

(a) REDUCE SYSTEMIC RISK

Greenspan (1996) defines systemic risk as the chance that the failure of one financial institution in isolation may trigger a chain reaction in the economy. Hence, if a bank is in jeopardy it has potential to cause a domino effect on the entire financial and perhaps even non-financial system. To combat this, prudential regulation and government maintenance are needed to provide some form of insurance against systemic risk.

(b) PROTECT CONSUMERS

Consumers need protection as they are assumed to be unable to judge the safety and soundness of derivative transaction due to information asymmetry problems. In protecting consumers, financial products must be safe and reliable and potential hazards involved in credit derivatives trading must be adequately publicised. This is to ensure that the overall integrity of the markets is sustained.

(c) ENCOURAGE PRODUCT DEVELOPMENT

In addition to providing adequate levels of protection and control, it is also vital for a regulatory regime to encourage product development. For example, in order for regulatory capital to promote credit derivative development, the measurement of risk must adequately reflect the true benefits of credit derivatives offered. Ultimately, capital regulations need to be flexible enough to respond to market needs whilst balancing the need to encourage product development. Schachter (1997) notes that this is not an easy task as capital regulations that are too flexible will encourage regulatory capital arbitrage opportunities. Arbitrage opportunities are not desired, as artificial adjustment of bank risk will expose the market to a greater risk of economic and financial crises.

(d) ACHIEVEMENT OF SOCIAL OBJECTIVES

Goodhart et al. (1988) emphasised a social objective to be the protection of society from the dangers of monopolies. Regulations should control entry and behaviour of new and existing products to ensure fair and open competition, reduce competitive inequality, whilst also ensuring that participants have reasonable access to systems and information through appropriate disclosures.

Primary Objective of Regulatory Capital

In keeping with the core principles of regulation as inferred by the Economic Theory of regulation, a regulator should balance conflicting interests by simultaneously reducing systemic risk and protecting consumers. In addition, support product development without jeopardising achievement of social objectives. Hence underlying these core principles of regulation lies the primary objective of regulation: "to maintain safety and soundness of the banking system" in order to prevent crisis in the financial system. Mingo (2000), BIS (1997), Berger, Herring and Szego (1995), and Mussa (1986) support this assumption, amongst others.

Specific Objectives of Regulatory Capital

Regulatory capital models must also meet specific objectives outlined in BIS capital regulations. However as most of the specific objectives represent components of the primary prudential objective, this paper in most instances will discuss the ability for regulatory capital models to meet primary and specific prudential objectives concurrently.

(1) The Basle Accord (BIS, 1988, paragraph 3) states that the specific objectives are to ensure:
    (a) "That the new framework should serve to strengthen the soundness and safety of the international banking system."
    (b) "Secondly that the framework should be fair and have a high degree of consistency in its application to banks in different countries with a view to diminishing an existing source of competitive inequality amongst international banks."
(2) The Basle Accord Amendment Proposal (BIS, 1995, paragraph 3) states that the specific objective is to "balance the need to preserve the integrity and flexibility of banks internal models against the need to ensure the transparency and consistency of capital requirements across banks."
(3) U.S. and U.K. national credit derivative regulations do not set out any specific objectives. Hence as national regulations apply both Basle Accord (1988) and Basle Accord Amended (1996), it is assumed that national regulation will follow Basle prudential objectives.

How Effective are the Regulatory Capital Models?

The purpose of this section is to ascertain whether regulatory capital models for credit derivatives, in particular risk weighted, standard and internal models are capable of meeting primary and specific prudential objectives.

Under this account end users of credit derivatives must set regulatory capital for credit risk by adopting the risk-weighted approach proposed in the Basle Accord (1988). The ability of the risk weighted approach to meet the first objective of ensuring "that the new framework should serve to strengthen the soundness and safety of the international banking system" (BIS, 1988, paragraph 3). As this specific objective coincides with the primary objective, they will be discussed concurrently. The Basle Accord (1988) makes no direct comment on credit derivatives; hence the ability for risk-weighted approach applied to credit derivatives to achieve this objective will be inferred from the Basle Accord (1988).[17]

The second objective the risk weighted model will be assessed upon, is the ability to "be fair and have a high degree of consistency in its application to banks in different countries with a view to diminishing existing source of competitive inequality among international banks" (BIS, 1988, paragraph 3). The objective of reducing competitive inequality confirms Dale (1990) assertion that the effectiveness of Basle Accord (1988) will largely depend on the manner in which national supervisory authorities exercise the discretion available to them under the BIS agreement. Therefore, it is important to assay the national (U.S. and U.K.) implementation of the risk-weighted approach to credit derivatives in order to determine whether the risk-weighted model achieves the second prudential objective.

RISK WEIGHTED APPROACH: BASLE ACCORD (1988)

Following the lead of empirical studies into capital regulation of banks discussed below, the first objective towards strengthening the international banking system can be broken down into two components. The first component is whether the measure of risk is accurate in reflecting true economic risk. The second component is whether this model limits regulatory arbitrage opportunities. Only if both components are met will the risk-weighted approach achieve the first prudential objective.

Measure of Risk

Cordell, King and Kuester (1995) support that in order for the objective of strengthening safety and soundness of international banking system to be met, the measure of risk must be sufficiently distinguished among assets of differing risk classes so that true economic risk is represented. Wall (1996) disagreed on the need for risk measurement to be accurate enough to reflect true economic risk. He argued that the market is competent in only rewarding banks that meet capital requirements through profits from ordinary operations, as his study found banks that engaged in purely cosmetic accounting changes were disciplined by the market with a drop in stock price. However, as Wall's (1996) argument is based on the assumption of M&M (1956), the obvious existence of regulatory arbitrage opportunities cited in Jones (1998) and Wagster (1996) disproves his conclusion. Hence, the necessity for the evaluation of measure of risk in order for the first objective to be met remains valid.

Support for inaccuracy of the risk-weighted approach is provided by the 100% off balance sheet conversion risk weight applied to all credit derivatives. This unjustified conversion risk weight perversely penalizes relatively safe banks, as the conversion risk weight fails to include features of a bank's true economic risk e.g. term structure of credit risk, internal management systems and unmatched hedges. Avery and Berger (1991) also found evidence that supports the inaccuracy of current regulatory risk weights, as only a weak relationship between risk based regulatory capital requirements and market based capital requirements was found. Based on Dimson and Marsh (1994), a major implication of inaccurate risk measures is that banks may be discouraged from adopting risk reducing diversification strategies such as credit derivatives as they are inadequately rewarded.

A more direct implication of inaccurate risk weights is that for the purpose of offsetting regulatory capital, banks of the same risk weight will effectively seek to trade credit derivatives only with other banks in homogeneous risk classes. For example, consider that both Argentina and Mexico are potential buyers of credit derivatives. Argentina carries a 100% risk weight attracting an 8% regulatory capital, and has a BBB – sovereign rating.[18] Yet Mexico with 0% risk weight attracts 0% regulatory capital despite a lower BB + sovereign rating. From this example, it can be determined that a non-OECD bank is doomed to attract a higher regulatory capital than OECD banks. Hence OECD banks will be compelled to trade only with each other in order to offset the cost of transaction.

Clearly, this approach allows regulatory capital relief based solely on OECD status, as the sovereign rating of a particular country is disregarded. Although OECD favouritism can be tolerated if membership requirements reflected the status of a bank's safety and soundness, current OECD membership requirements however do not warrant preferential regulatory capital treatment.[19] In addition, equal risk weights apply to all corporate, non-retail and household exposures. Given this, regardless if non-OECD countries held high quality credit derivatives, there would still be no relief from regulatory capital set by Basle Accord. An implication of this bias towards OECD members is shown below.

100% Risk Weighted (Non OECD)		20% Risk Weighted (OECD)	
Asset Book Value	100.00%	Asset Book Value	100.00%
× Capital Risk Weight	100.00%	× Capital Risk Weight	20.00%
= % Risk Weighted Asset	100.00%	= % Risk Weighted Asset	20.00%
× Capital Requirement	8.00%	× Capital Requirement	8.00%
× Conversion Factor	100.00%	× Conversion Factor	100.00%
= % Risk Based Capital	8.00%	= % Risk Based Capital	1.60%
Notional Value	$1 Million	Notional Value	$1 Million
Net Income 50 bps	**$50,000**	**Net Income 50 bps**	**$50,000**
Regulatory Capital	$800,000	Regulatory Capital	$160,000
Return on Capital	**6.25%**	**Return on Capital**	**31.25%**

Adapted from Tavakoli (1998).

This illustration demonstrates that although risk and return are identical for both counterparties, the OECD bank with 20% risk weighting (31.25%) is able to optimise return on capital five times more than the non OECD bank with 100% risk weight (6.25%). Kwast and Passmore (1998) notes that in spite of little academic literature on bank motivation for wanting to appear well capitalised. An obvious benefit of lower regulatory capital (thus higher capital return) to the bank is the chance that market demand for the bank may increase, as consumers view capital return as a sufficient proxy for the stability of a bank. It is dangerous for consumers to assume that capital return is a sufficient proxy for bank's stability, as under this approach a high return on capital may not equally translate to a low probability of insolvency.

Regulatory Arbitrage

Koppenhaver and Stover (1991) concluded that as long as regulatory arbitrage opportunities exist, inaccurate risk based capital standards will increase motivation for banks to adopt credit derivative transactions in order to minimise the overall cost of complying with burdensome capital regulations. Although this conclusion meets a core principle of regulation (product encouragement), it is in conflict with the aforementioned conclusion by Dimson and Marsh (1994) that inaccurate risk weights will reduce the market potential for credit derivatives, as banks are not rewarded for adopting risk-reducing strategies.

To provide some resolution, Merton (1995) and Carlstrom and Samolyk (1995) concluded that Koppenhaver and Stover (1991) result is more likely. Their studies found banks reacted to higher regulatory capital requirements by taking on more and not less off balance sheet risk (e.g. credit derivatives) as it is exposure that is unobservable to regulators. Hence, burdensome regulatory capital requirements set by inaccurate risk weights will more likely encourage rather than impede credit derivative growth, as banks are motivated to use credit derivatives to artificially manipulate capital ratios.

Furthermore, risk weightings based on OECD status also facilitate international comparison of bank capital as OCED members rarely change their status.[20] However this benefit comprises the first objective of safety and soundness, as static risk weights do not reflect the constant changing state of a bank's soundness and safety. Although an amendment to add flexibility by revoking OECD status for a period of time if an OECD country "reschedules it's external sovereign debt" (BIS, 1994a, paragraph 35) was made, this amendment only had the subtle effect of making the risk weightings less static. Without enforcing market discipline into risk weights, this abstract measure of regulatory capital will continue to weaken the soundness and safety of banks, as credit derivative users will adopt regulatory arbitrage opportunities to reduce the burden of inaccurate regulatory capital.

Capital regulations that encourage arbitrage opportunities are not desired, as banks are focused on seizing regulatory arbitrage opportunities rather than achieving company goals. This will result in bank inefficiency, and at the same time will erode the overall safety and soundness of a bank. In support of regulatory capital arbitrage, Greenspan (1998) highlighted that arbitrage opportunities do offer the advantage of mitigating social effects of banks forced to exit low risk exposures in order to maximise return on capital by adopting high-risk exposures. Though this is a valid argument, the benefit received by society from a sound and stable banking system is far greater than the benefit identified by Greenspan (1998).

RISK WEIGHTED APPROACH: FRB SR 96-17 GEN (1996) and FSA (1998)

The second objective can also be broken down into two parts. First, whether the risk-weighted approach is fair and has a high degree of consistency in its application to banks in different countries. Second, whether the risk-weighted approach reduces competitive inequality amongst international banks.

Consistency

The national risk weighted models of FRB SR 96-17 GEN (1996) and FSA (1998), differ as FSA (1998) better reflects the risk reducing properties that credit derivatives contain by recognising the degree of protection a credit derivative transaction offers. For example, FSA (Section 9, 1998) allows recognition of credit derivative hedging benefits for buyers of the banking account and for sellers of the trading book subject to risk transfer requirements.[21] The specific requirements set by FSA offer an advantage, as to date FSA is the only regulator to clarify the degree of correlation a credit derivative transaction must have in order to be eligible for recognition of hedging benefits. Conversely, FRB SR 96-17 GEN can also offer an advantage as the degree of correlation needed for recognition of hedging benefits is subject to 'an examiner's satisfaction level'. This case-by-case approach represents an advantage as users of credit derivatives have some discretion to offset credit exposures within the portfolio, as there are no specific risk transfer requirements to meet.

Another inconsistency relates to the treatment of first to default credit derivatives. For FRB SR 96-17 GEN (1996) buyers of credit derivatives are allowed to choose one asset within the basket with the smallest dollar amount to base regulatory capital on, whilst the seller must assign the highest risk category appropriate to all the assets in the basket. In comparison, FSA (1998) requires the sellers to base regulatory capital on the aggregate exposure of all reference assets and allows buyers the freedom to select a reference asset to set their exposure against. From this, it can be implied that U.K. FSA regulators are more inclined than U.S. FRB regulators to recognize diversification benefits offered by first to default baskets for sellers, as FSA (1998) does not specifically impose the highest risk weight category.

In addition, FSA (1998) also differs as it allows the recognition of hedging benefits for maturity mismatched credit derivatives, at the cost of an additional forward exposure. Here buyers have the choice of assuming the risk weight of the underlying asset for the full term, or of the counterparty for the time credit protection is provided and the remainder of the term to be weighted at the original risk weight of the underlying asset.[22] This represents a distinct advantage for U.K. buyers of credit derivatives, as most credit derivative by nature are mismatched in maturity.

Comparatively, FRB SR 96-17 GEN does not specifically allow for recognition of hedging benefits for mismatched credit derivatives. However, a recent joint press release together with FDIC, OCC and OTS (1999) may offer wider recognition of hedging benefits than that proposed by the FSA (1998). This release proposes to measure credit risk capital requirements based on credit ratings of nationally recognized statistical rating agencies, for certain unrated direct credit substitutes now defined to explicitly include credit derivatives.[23]

This proposal is a move towards achieving a more flexible and market oriented measure of regulatory capital for credit risk, as the internal ratings approach for credit risk does provide more scope for recognition of hedging benefits than the traditional risk weighted approach. Yet, relatively small differences in risk may result to disproportionate large differences, as under this approach risk weights can only be classified between five broad categories. Consequently, this new approach merely presents another form of inaccurate regulatory risk measure, as narrow risk categories do not allow accurate reflection of true risk weights.

Competitive Inequality

The objective of competitive equality is justified by Cooke's (1991) survey. His international survey confirmed the notion that countries viewed national discretion of Basle Accord implementation as a means to alter capital regulations to their own advantage. For example, the inconsistencies discussed suggest that U.K. regulators use their discretion to allow U.K. credit derivative buyers recognition of benefits for both matched and mismatched hedges, and allow U.K. sellers of first to default basket credit derivatives the comparative advantage of not imposing the highest risk category. Hence, the risk weighted approach applied to credit derivatives fails to achieve the objective of reduced competitive inequality as U.K. FSA (1998) is not as equally restrictive as U.S. FRB SR 97-18 GEN (1996) in allowing users of credit derivatives to recognize hedging benefits.

This result coincides with U.S. studies such as Hall (1993), Haubrich and Wachtel (1993), Calem and Rob (1996) and Thakor (1996) which found U.S. banks when faced with restrictive regulatory capital tend to shift sharply from loans which attract high risk weight (corporate lending) to loans of low risk weights (government securities). Whilst Ediz, Michael and Perraudin (1998), a U.K. study found evidence that in times of restrictive regulatory capital requirements converse to the U.S., U.K. banks are not motivated to shift loans to lower risk weights suggesting perhaps less restrictive regulatory capital.

In addition to the failure of reducing competitive inequalities amongst the nations, U.S. and U.K. national implementation of the risk weighted approach also fail to reduce competitive inequality between sellers and buyers. As both FRB SR 96-17 GEN (1996) and FSA (1998) are consistent in allowing buyers to reduce category risk weight to that of the seller, provided a perfect match is recognised and that the seller has a lower capital charge. Otherwise, the buyer will hold capital against the full risk weight of the reference asset. Jones (1998), describes this advantage to represent a basic arbitrage where buyers are able to convert a bank's on balance sheet credit risk into an off balance sheet exposure to gain a lower risk weight.

While for sellers of credit derivatives, both regulators adopt a punitive approach as credit derivatives are treated as direct credit substitute. In the sense that regardless of a perfect hedge, sellers remain responsible for the full risk weight of the reference asset as the seller is assumed to be exposed to identical amounts of credit risk as the buyer. Consequently, failure to recognise hedging benefits for sellers of credit derivatives effectively imposes a double capital charge on the same exposure.

To this end, even though both buyers and sellers of credit derivatives are equally tempted to capture relief from burdensome capital regulations. The implementations of the risk weighted regulatory capital model by U.S. and U.K. poses a competitive advantage for buyers of credit derivatives only.

Trading Book

For credit derivatives booked under the trading account, dealers of credit derivatives have a choice to measure risk for regulatory capital purposes under a standard or internal (VaR) Model. In order for credit derivatives to qualify for treatment under the trading book, Basle Accord Amended (BIS, 1996, paragraph 2) sets out that credit derivatives must be held with trading intent and be marked to the market.

The objective of Basle Accord Amended (1996) is "to preserve the integrity and flexibility of banks internal models", we look at the internal approach proposed by the Basle Accord Amended (1996) and applied to credit derivatives. The primary objective of maintaining safety and soundness of the entire economy in order to prevent crisis in the financial system, is dependent on achievement of the specific objective of the Basle Accord Amended (BIS, paragraph 3 1995), accordingly both primary and specific objectives will be discussed concurrently.

STANDARD MODEL: FRB SR 97-18 GEN (1997) and FSA (1998)

Transparency and Consistency

Both FRB SR 97-18 GEN (1997) and FSA (1998) implement the standard model of risk measurement for credit, market and specific risk. However, regulations differ as FSA (1998) regulation better reflects the risk reducing properties of credit derivatives, as it is more comprehensive on three levels.

Firstly, it overruled the previous authority (Bank of England) decision to refuse credit default swap credit derivatives on the trading book. The Bank of England was justified in making this decision, as the probability of credit swap default is based on credit events that are difficult to mark to the market. However, FSA (1998) justified allowing credit swaps (illiquid assets) into the trading account, by imposing an additional reserve to be held specifically against the inability to mark to the market. Hence at the cost of an additional capital requirement, FSA (1998) specifically allows credit default swaps to be included into the trading account. This would work to strengthen soundness and safety of banks, as U.K. users of credit derivatives are no longer restricted to holding credit default swaps in the banking book.

Secondly, for specific risk FSA (1998) specifies regulatory capital treatment for basket and first to default basket of credit derivatives. This treatment reverses the FSA (1998) banking book treatment, as it imposes on buyers the aggregate exposure of all reference assets and allows sellers the freedom to select a reference asset to set their exposure against. The preferential treatment for sellers under the trading account is commended, as sellers consist mostly of dealers who often hold credit derivatives under the trading account.

Lastly, in addition to FSA (1998) risk weighted model setting out specific risk transfer requirements for matched credit derivative position. FSA (1998) standard model also considers credit derivatives that are mismatched in maturity, and permits specific risk to be offset against the longer reference asset maturity.

In comparison, the extent of FRB SR 97-18 GEN (1997) comprehensiveness is limited to the definition of credit derivative transactions into three positions and their associated credit, market and specific risk. The first position is matched where only credit risk is considered for regulatory capital as specific and market risks are eliminated due to identical structure, maturity, assets, default events and contract terms of positions. The second, offsetting positions exhibit different maturities or instruments, hence all three risks are considered, except market and specific risk are reduced as reference asset and seniority are matched under this category. Thirdly all other positions that fall outside the first and second categories are subject to all three risks and are considered under the Open position.

As noted earlier, FRB intentionally chose to refrain from providing highly specific written examination guidance for assessing capital adequacy, as a case-by-case approach was preferred. Although such an approach will allow the benefit of supervisory flexibility, Jones and Mingo (1999) note that this benefit is weighted against the inability for FRB to justify a bank to maintain regulatory capital above the minimum unless a bank is clearly in trouble. This implication works against achievement of the primary objectives, as in the event of crisis banks will hold insufficient regulatory capital to protect the economy, and will ultimately increase the general safety and soundness of the bank.

Despite that FSA (1998) is more transparent than FRB SR 97-18 GEN (1997), they both share the same measurement of specific and market risk under the standard model. Where specific risk capital charge for offsetting and matched positions is applied to the largest part of the transaction, and open position are treated the same as cash position instruments. Whilst market risk is calculated in the same manner as cash market debt instruments that is weighted against the reference asset. And credit risk is measured as the sum of the market value of credit derivative plus an add on factor to represent future exposure. There is scope for credit derivatives to add on factors used by both regulators to vary as BIS (1994b) fails to specify an add on factor for debt based securities. Hence, credit derivatives use interest rate, equity and commodity add on factors as proxies.

To illustrate the inconsistency of add on factors, FSA (1998) imposes on credit derivatives an interest rate add on factor for 'qualifying debts' and for all else applies an equity add on factor.[24] In contrast, FRB SR 97-18 GEN (1997) imposes on investment or unrated exposures with high quality collateral an equity factor, and for all other exposures the higher commodity add on factor.[25] Comparing them, U.S. FRB SR 97-18 GEN (1997) has a higher add on factor range between 6%–15%, whilst FSA (1998) has a lower add on factor range between 0–10%.

For the case of credit default swaps this comparative advantage is weighed against the added capital requirement that FSA (1998) sets for allowing credit default swaps into the trading account. Nevertheless, a significant competitive advantage for U.K. dealers of credit derivatives is identified, as banks with lower add on factors will evidently have lower capital ratios. Along with this implication, U.K. banks with lower capital ratios are able to earn a more competitive return on capital. This allows them to expand their market share at a greater pace and operate at a lower cost than a U.S. dealer. Ultimately, inconsistencies between U.S. and U.K. regulation of credit derivatives encourage competitive inequality and arbitrage opportunities that hinder achievement of prudential objectives.

Consequently, implementation of the standard approach under the Basle Accord Amendment (1996) by U.S. and U.K. fall to two extremes. U.S. regulators adopt a more comprehensive approach and offer a comparative advantage for credit derivative dealers. Whilst U.S. regulators intentionally adopt lose regulations to ensure flexibility of regulations to accommodate for future innovations. Despite the benefits of such flexibility, ambiguous regulations compromise the ability for regulatory capital regulations to ensure safety and soundness of a bank, as there is scope for regulatory capital arbitrage.

At this point it is appropriate to raise Kane's (1995) assertions that even the most comprehensive and consistent measurement system will not increase the ability for regulatory capital to achieve these prudential objectives, as the interests of regulated and the regulator are not aligned. In an effort to align interests, Kane (1995) suggested greater reliance be placed on 'private sector mechanisms for identifying, measuring and monitoring bank risk'. His suggestion is an introduction to the analysis of the internal approach proposed by the Basle Accord Amended (1996).

INTERNAL MODEL: AMENDMENT TO BASLE ACCORD (1996)

Integrity and Flexibility

An immediate assumption is that the use of internal model will meet the prudential objective of strengthening the soundness and safety of the economy. As in theory it restores a bank's internal model integrity as the model is based on day-to-day risk management practices of a bank and actual current default and recovery rates of bank positions. This point supports Scholes (2000) study that the use of an internal model allows banks to develop a comprehensive risk model that accounts for overall bank exposure, as internal models based on VaR (a product of portfolio theory) allows for recognition of diversification strategies particularly evident for credit derivatives. The only requirement that VaR sets in order to allow a firm to recognise hedging benefits for maturity and asset mismatches, is that a firm must be able to estimate the benefits of matching and offsetting.

The internal method is also more flexible as the discrimination between the trading and banking book is eliminated. The elimination of this distinction is especially important for innovations such as credit derivatives, as Jones and Mingo's (1999) study verifies that internal risk models represent the most useful model for setting regulatory capital requirements against instruments, which the Basle Accord is silent or ineffectual.

Recent academic literature also finds other advantages to this approach. Moskow (1997) conveys that this method of measuring regulatory capital limits the degree to which regulators intrude into a bank's trading business and appropriately focuses regulator attention on assessment of a bank's internal risk management practices. In addition, Hendricks and Hurtle (1997) proposed that if regulators were to make their assessment of bank internal models accessible to market participants, a new valuable source of information would be created. As over time, the information about the performance and accuracy of risk models will aid market participants to monitor the safety and soundness of banks. However the possible advantage identified in Hendricks and Hirtle's (1997) is based on the assumption that regulators will know as much as the bank management team who designed and built the models. Carey and Treacy (1998) point out that this advantage may be limited. As the task for regulators to develop and retain human and other resources, and also to approve, monitor and translate the diversity of models employed by firms into a common framework capable of adapting to developments and improvements is not a simple one.

Another limitation of identified benefits is highlighted by Figlewski (1994) to be risk ignorance. This limit is especially evident with credit derivatives or any other new product/process where the technical/environmental aspects are not fully understood, or where there exhibits constant change in the legal environment. He identified that in many cases risk ignorance increases the room of model errors.

Although the reduction of model errors is restricted to the lack of historical default data available for credit transactions, Christoffersen and Errunza (2000) made several broad suggestions to reduce model errors. The application of non-linear models is suggested, as many studies have concluded that most asset returns are not normally distributed but instead are fat tailed and skewed to the left (e.g. Fama, 1965; Duffie & Pan, 1997). As such the use of linear assumptions will severely underestimate the frequency of major loses. Kimball (2000) provides further support on the inappropriateness of the assumption of normality, as the probability of a crisis occurring has also been proven to be non-normal.

Also real time and high frequency data is preferred as the use of historical data restricts correlation to be stable across periods, when in reality Roll (1988), Longin and Solnik (1995) and Booth and Broussard (1998) have found actual correlation amongst asset return to be unstable. Similarly, Campbell, Lo and McKinlay (1997) find that returns arc positively serially correlated, hence the assumption that returns are serially independent will also add to the underestimation of a major loss.

Following on, the set of quantitative and qualitative requirements for banks wanting to use in-house models imposed by the Basle Accord Amendment (1996) also restrict the advantages of maintaining integrity and flexibility. Despite, support for qualitative and quantitative requirements seen in Jackson and Perraudin (1998), which argued that these requirements are necessary in order to ensure that only extremely unpredictable risky portfolios would fail to be covered by sufficient capital. And Jones and Mingo (1999) supporting the qualitative requirement of stress testing for the reason that hypothetical market disturbance scenarios provide useful checks on the reasonableness of regulatory capital generated by VaR models. A vast array of empirical papers have argued that the qualitative, more than the quantitative requirements set by Basle Accord Amended (1996), actually restrict the integrity and flexibility of a bank's internal model.

The main area of criticism concerns the conservative and unjustified nature of quantitative requirements. Firstly, Hendricks (1996) commented that the VaR minimum historical observation (one year long) can be considered a weakness, as shorter periods would more accurately model real economic risks that are generally volatile by nature. The argument for shorter periods is also supported by Kupiec and O'Brien (1995), founders of the VaR model who specifically noted a limitation of bank internal models to be the lack of ability to measure risk exposures over relatively lengthy time intervals. Secondly, Hendricks and Hirtle (1997) raises the point that the 10 day holding period is overly conservative, as under normal market conditions a bank's trading portfolio could be liquidated in less time. The Basle Accord Amended (1996) supports the long holding period, as a longer period will increase the chance of revealing smaller risk factor movements than that of a shorter period. However, in order for the integrity and flexibility of bank's internal models to be represented, both holding and observation periods should be more reflective of a market's true conditions.

Lastly, Schachter (1997) commented that the VaR figure is flawed, as there is no theoretical basis for the VaR figure to be multiplied by three. Although it is understood that VaR is multiplied by a number to allow for a margin of error due to by model errors identified above, there is however no justification that a factor of three is sufficient to cover margin of error. This area of criticism suggests that the conservative and unjustified of quantitative requirements for the internal model approach, is less than ideal for setting capital requirements against. A model that fails to be based on actual market conditions will not maintain the integrity and flexibility of a bank's true internal model.

Stringent qualitative requirements have also been argued to reduce bank internal model integrity and flexibility. An example of such is the back testing requirement, which requires banks to perform an ex-post comparison of the risk measure generated by the VaR model against actual daily changes in portfolio value over a substantial period of time. Diebold et al. (1997) highlighted such a long comparison period will reduce integrity and flexibility of a bank's internal model, as only extreme credit losses relative to model predictions will label the model insufficient. Thus, regulatory capital based on an internal model will not provide sufficient regulatory capital to protect consumers against crises, as only extremely inaccurate models will be rejected.

In sum, restrictive quantitative and qualitative standards of VaR eliminate much of the expected gain from basing regulatory capital for credit derivatives on an internal risk assessment model. In addition, Quigley (1997) pointed out that under this approach the integration of regulators and the regulated creates a false impression that the incentives of these two agents have been aligned. Their interests can only be aligned once internal models are deemed rigorous and consistent across banks in design and accuracy of risk measurement. Until interests are aligned and restrictive quantitative and qualitative standards are relaxed, the internal model will continue in failing to preserve the integrity and flexibility of a banks internal model.

CONCLUSION

Combining conclusions drawn from the analysis of risk weighted, standard and internal regulatory capital models applied to credit derivatives, the need for regulatory capital to move closer to achieving the primary and specific prudential objectives is suggested. This paper identified two specific goals for future regulatory capital guidelines for credit derivatives. One is to correct deficiencies of current regulatory capital models, which failed to recognise hedging benefits of credit derivatives. Second, is to increase consistency in national implementation of regulatory capital models for credit derivatives. It is important to understand that this paper has not argued for a complete reform of regulatory capital regulation. It is up to central banks and supervisory authorities to determine this macroeconomic question and to consider the impact of reformed capital rules on the overall safety and soundness of the banking system. Nonetheless, despite limitations this paper has emphasised the importance for regulatory capital models applied to credit derivatives to achieve prudential objectives, and thus has set the foundation for further research to ascertain the ability of regulatory capital modes applied to new risk management practices to achieve prudential objectives.

NOTES

1. See Hall (1992) for a full discussion.
2. FRB is the central regulator of U.S. state member banks and bank holing companies. FRB also works with Office of the Comptroller of the Currency (OCC – National Banks), OTS (Office of Thrift Supervision) and the Federal Deposit Insurance Corporation (FDIC – State, Co-operative, Industrial, Savings and Foreign Banks).
3. The FSA came into effect in the U.K. as of June 1, 1998. This mega regulator replaced the prudential and functional regulatory role of, amongst others, Banks (Bank of England), Insurance Companies (Department of Trade and Industry), Building Societies (Building Societies Commission) and the Securities and Futures Authorities. The idea behind FSA, was to create a single management structure to ensure consistent regulation whilst balancing the different nature of each business.
4. The BBA surveys' (BBA, 1996, 1997/1998 & 1999/2000) together represent one of the most comprehensive studies of the size, application, product type and constraints of the credit derivatives market. Their survey covers a large number of leading market practitioners as it is based on detailed questionnaires of 24 market leaders, as well as comments from a number of other market practitioners.
5. Banks have a strong desire to maintain client relationships as they hope to gain access to the clients non-credit business.
6. The 1988 Basle Capital Accord sets minimal capital requirements based on 8% of risk weights. The 1988 Basle Capital Accord applies to G-10 countries which consist of Belgium, Canada, France, Germany, Italy, Japan, Netherlands, Sweden, U.K. and U.S.
7. Banking book exposures arise from traditional lending activities. Trading book is defined by BIS (1993) to include: "a bank's proprietary positions in financial instruments which are taken on with the intention of benefiting in the short term from actual or expected difference between their buying and selling prices; of hedging other elements of the trading books; or which are held for resale; or in order to execute a trade with a customer."
8. Concentration of risk frequently arises as banks are forced to specialise, as the current state of credit markets lack assets with desired term, structure and industry characteristics appropriate for credit risk diversification.
9. Leah (1997) concludes that for credit risk to reach optimal diversity, approximately 350 names for debt portfolios compared to 30 names for equity portfolio is

required. This significant difference is attributed to credit risk exhibiting skewed and non linear properties, compared to equity positions with linear properties.

10. For detailed descriptions of credit derivative instruments refer to Neal (1996); Whittaker and Li (1997); Das (1998) and Francis et al. (1999).

11. For credit default swaps, payment only occurs when a pre-defined credit event occurs e.g. bankruptcy, insolvency receivership liquidation, material adverse restructuring of debt and rating downgrades. In some contracts a pre-determined materiality threshold may also trigger payment (OSFI, 1999).

12. The conversion weights for some off balance sheet instruments are as follows. Short term commitments incur 20% risk weight, contingent and long term commitments incur 50% risk weight, unfunded loans and direct credit substitutes incur 100% risk weight, and recourse commitments incur dollar for dollar risk weights (BIS, 1988: Annex 3).

13. Basle Accord's definition of OECD involves a group of countries, which have "special lending arrangements with the International Monetary Fund" (BIS, 1988, para 35).

14. For details of risk weights see BIS (1988) Annex 2.

15. The holding period refers to the time interval over which changes in the value of the portfolio are to be assessed, and the confidence interval is an estimate of the changes in portfolio value which are likely to occur some proportion of the time (Hendricks & Hirtle, 1997).

16. See BIS 1996, Part B.2 and B.4 for more detail.

17. At the time of proposal the Basle Accord (1988) was more concerned with capital standards for lending, and not the trading of credit risk.

18. Sovereign ratings obtained from rating agency Standard and Poors, as of September 22, 2000.

19. For OECD member requirements see www.oecd.org/about/general/member-countries.htm

20. Comparison is limited only to Tier 1 and not Tier 2 definition of capital, as the former is defined by common capital whilst the latter includes a combination of eligible capital elements.

21. See FSA (Section 9, 1998) Credit Derivative Guideline for risk transfer requirements.

22. Note FSA only allows mismatched hedges to be offset, provided the buyer is able to show the following: assets are obligations of the same legal entity and seniority, there exists a high correlation between the two instruments, and documentation exists to link the reference asset to the underlying asset.

23. Banks are permitted to use this rating system within limits e.g. ability to qualify for a risk weight of 100% or 200% but not for a risk weight less than 100%.

24. A qualifying debt is defined under s 5 of Interest Rate Position Risk, FSA (1998).

25. Equity add on factors for maturity less than one year is 6%, between 1–5 years is 8% and 5 or more years if 10%. Commodity factors are 12% for maturities of 0–5 years and any maturity over 5 years apply 15% add on factor. For add on factors of foreign exchange, precious metals and interest rate refer to Annex 3 of Basle Capital Accord (1994).

REFERENCES

Avery, R. B., & Berger, A. N. (1991). Risk Based Capital and Deposit Insurance Reform. *Journal of Banking and Finance*, *15*, 847–874.

Bank of England (1996). *Developing a Supervisory Approach to Credit Derivatives*. In: *Supervision and Surveillance Discussion Paper* (November 4). London.

Bank for International Settlements (BIS) (1997). *Core Principles for Effective Banking Supervision*. Basle, Switzerland.

Bank for International Settlements (BIS) (1996). *Amendment of the Capital Accord to Incorporate Market Risk*. January.

Bank for International Settlements (BIS) (1995). *Proposal to Issue A Supplement to the Basle Capital Accord to Cover Market Risk*. April.

Bank for International Settlements (BIS) (1994a). *Amendment to the Capital Accord of July 1988*. July.

Bank for International Settlements (BIS) (1994b). *Basle Capital Accord: The Treatment of the Credit Risk Associated with Certain Off Balance Sheet Items*. July.

Bank for International Settlements (BIS) (1988). *International Convergence of Capital Measurement and Capital Standard*. Commonly Referred To As "1988 Capital Accord." July.

Berger, A. N., Herring, R. J., & Szego, G. P. (1995). The Role of Capital in Financial Institutions. *Journal of Banking and Finance*, *19*, 393–430.

Booth, G. G., & Broussard, J. P. (1998). REIT Returns, Probability of Large Losses, and Asset Allocation. *Eli Broad Graduate School of Management*. Michigan State University. Processed.

British Bankers' Association (BBA) (1996). Global Credit Derivative Market: Survey. *BBA Publications*.

British Bankers' Association (BBA) (1997/1998). Global Credit Derivative Market: Survey. *BBA Publications*.

British Bankers' Association (BBA) (1999/2000). Global Credit Derivative Market: Survey. *BBA Publications*.

Calem, P. S., & Rob, R. (1996). The Impact of Capital Based Regulation on bank Risk Taking: A Dynamic Model. *Board of Governors of the Federal Reserve System, Finance and Economics Discussion Series*, 96–12.

Campbell, J. Y., Lo, A. W., & McKinlay, A. C. (1997). *The Econometrics of Financial Markets*. (Chap. 2). Princeton. NJ: Princeton University Press.

Carey, M., & Tracey, W. (1998). Internal Credit Risk Rating Systems at Large Banks. *Federal Reserve Bulletin*, *84*(1), 897–921.

Carmichael, J. (2000). Financial Regulation in the 21st Century. *PACAP – FMA Conference*. Melbourne. Australia. July 6th.

Carlstrom, C. T., & Samolyk, K. A. (1995). Loan Sales as A Response to Market Based Capital Requirements. *Journal of Banking and Finance*, *19*, 627–646.

Caudill, S. B., Im, B. G., & Kaserman, D. L. (1993). Modelling Regulatory Behaviour: The Economic Theory of Regulation versus Alternative Theories and Simple Rules of Thumb. *Journal of Regulatory Economics*, *3*(3), 251–262.

Chance, D. M. (1999). Research Trends in Derivatives and Risk Management Since Black-Scholes. *Journal of Portfolio Management*, 35–46.

Christoffersen, P., & Errunza, V. (2000). Towards a Global Financial Architecture: Capital Mobility and Risk Management Issues. *Emerging Markets Review*, *1*, 3–20.

Clark, A. (1997). Derivatives: A Regulator's Perspective. *Economic Notes*, *26*(2), 425–440.

Collins, B. M., & Fabozzi, F. J. (1999). Derivative and Risk Management. *Journal of Portfolio Management*, 16–27.

Cooke, P. (1991). *Bank Capital Adequacy and Capital Convergence*. Price Waterhouse. London. England.

Cordell, L., King, R., & Kuester, K. (1995). A Market Evaluation of the Risk Based Capital Standards for the U.S. Financial System. *Journal of Banking and Finance*, *19*(3–4), 531–562.

Cornett, M. M., & Tehranian, H. (1990). An Examination of the Impact of the Garn-St. Germain Depository Institutions Act of 1982 on Commercial Banks and Savings and Loans. *Journal of Finance*, *45*, 95–111.

Crouchy, M., Galai, D., & Mark, R. (2000). A Comparative Analysis of Current Credit Risk Models. *Journal of Banking and Finance*, *24*, 59–117.

Dale, R. (1990). Japan's Banking Regulation: Current Policy Issues, In: C. A. E. Goodhart & G. Sutija (Eds), *Japanese Financial Growth*. Macmillan.

Das, S. (1998). Credit Derivative Applications. In: S. Das (Ed.), *Credit Derivatives: Trading and Management of Credit and Default Risk* (1st ed.). John Wiley and Sons.

Davies, B. (1998). Using Credit Derivatives to Manage Credit Risk in Bank Loan Portfolios. *Barclays Bank*.

Diebold. F. X., Gunther, T. A., & Tay, A. S. (1997). Evaluating Density Forecasts. Technical Working Paper. No 215. *National Bureau of Economic Research*.

Dimson, E. & Marsh, P. (1994). The Debate on International Capital Requirements, The City Research Project, Subject Report VIII. *London Business School*. February.

Duffie, D., & Pan, J. (1997). An Overview of Value at Risk. *The Journal of Derivatives*, *493*, 7–49.

Ediz, T., Michael, I., & Perraudin, W. (1998). The Impact of Capital Requirements on U.K. Bank Behaviour. *Federal Reserve Bank of New York Economic Policy Review*. October.

Fama, E. F. (1965). The Behaviour of Stock Market Prices. *Journal of Business*, *3* (January), 34–105.

Federal Reserve Bank of Chicago (1998). *Chicago Fed Letter*, Number 130.

Federal Reserve Board (FRB) (1997). *SR 97–18 GEN: Application of Market Risk Capital Requirements to Credit Derivatives*. June 13th.

Federal Reserve Board (FRB) (1996). *SR 96–17 GEN: Supervisory Guidance for Credit Derivatives*. August 12th.

Federal Reserve Board (FRB), Federal Deposit Insurance Corporation (FDIC), Office of the Comptroller of the Currency Bank (OCC), & Office of Thrift Supervision (OTS) (2000). *Joint Press Release: Risk Based Capital Standards – Recourse and Direct Credit Substitutes*. February 17th.

Figlewski, S. (1994). How to Lose Money in Derivatives. *Journal of Derivatives*, *2*(2), 75–82.

Financial Services Authority (FSA) (1998). *Regulatory Treatment of Credit Derivatives*. July 2nd.

Francis, J., Frost, J., & Wittaker, J. (1999). *Handbook of Credit Derivatives*. NY: McGraw Hill.

Goodhart, C., Mortimer, J., & Duguid, A. (1988). Financial Regulation-or Over-Regulation? *Institute of Economic Affairs*.

Greenspan, A. (1998). The Role of Capital in Optimal Supervision and Regulation. Proceedings of a Conference on Capital in 21st Century. *Federal Reserve Bank of New York*. February.

Greenspan, A. (1996). *Remarks at the VIIIth Frankfurt International Banking Evening*. Frankfurt.

Hall, B. (1993). How Has the Basle Accord Affected Bank Portfolios? *Journal of Japanese and International Economies.*, *7*, 408–440.

Hall, M. (1992). Implementation of the BIS "Rules" on Capital Adequacy Assessment: A Comparative Study of the Approaches Adopted in the U.K., the U.S. and Japan. *BNL Quarterly Review*, *180*, 35–57.

Haubrich, J. G., & Wachtel, P. (1993). Capital Requirements and Shifts in Commercial Bank Portfolios. *Federal Reserve Bank of Cleveland Economic Review*, *29* (Quarter 3), 2–15.

Hendricks, D., & Hirtle, B. (1997). Bank Capital Requirement for Market Risk: The Internal Models Approach. *Federal Reserve Bank of New York Economic Pokily Review*, *3*(4), 1–12.

Hendricks, D., & Hirtle, B. (1996). Evaluation of Value at Risk Models Using Historical Data. *Federal Reserve Bank of New York Economic Policy Review*, *29*(1), 39–69.

Houpt, J. V. (1999). International Activities of U.S. Banks and in U.S. Banking Markets. *Federal Reserve Bulletin*, *85*(9), 599–615.

Hovakimian, A., & Kane, E. (2000). Effectiveness of Capital Regulation at U.S. Commercial Banks. 1985 to 1994. *Journal of Finance*, *LV*(1), 451–468.

Jackson, P., & Perraudin, W. (1998). Testing Value at Risk Approaches to Capital Adequacy. *Bank of England Quarterly Bulletin*, *38*(3), 256–266.

Jones, D. S., & Mingo, J. (1999). Credit Risk Modeling and Internal Capital Allocation Processes: Implications for a Models Based Regulatory Bank Capital Standard. *Journal of Economics and Business*, *51*, 79–108.

Jones, D. S., & Mingo, J. (1998). Emerging Problems with the Basle Capital Accord: Regulatory Capital Arbitrage and Related Issues. *Journal of Banking and Finance*, *24*, 35–58.

Kane, E. J. (1995). Three Paradigms for the Role of Capitalisation Requirements in Insured Financial Institutions. *Journal of Banking and Finance*, *14*, 431–459.

Kimball, R. C. (2000). Failures in Risk Management. *Federal Reserve Bank of Boston New England Economic Review*, (January–February), 3–12.

Koppenhaver, G. D., & Stover, R. D. (1991). Standby Letters of Credit and Large Bank Capital: An Empirical Analysis. *Journal of Banking and Finance*, (April), 315–327.

Kupiec, P., & O'Brien, J. (1997). The Pre-Commitment Approach: Using Incentives to Set Market Risk Capital Requirements. *Federal Reserve Board Finance and Economics Discussion Series*, *14* (March).

Kwast, M. L., & Passmore, S. W. (1998). The Subsidy Provided by the Federal Safety Net: Theory, Measurement and Containment. Proceedings of a Conference on Bank Structure and Competition. *Federal Reserve Bank of Chicago*, (May).

Leah, R. (1997). *Challenges of Managing Credit Portfolios*. JP Morgan Securities Inc.

Longin, F., & Solnik, B. (1995). Is the Correlation in International Equity Returns Constant? 1960–1990. *Journal of International Money and Finance*, *14*, 3–26.

Merton, R. C. (1995). Financial Innovation and the Management and Regulation of Financial Institutions. *Journal of Banking and Finance*, *19*, 461–481.

Miller, M. H. (1999). The Derivatives Revolution After Thirty Years. *Journal of Portfolio Management*, (May), 1–15.

Miller, M. H. (1995). Do the M & M Propositions Apply to Banks. *Journal of Banking and Finance*, *19*(3–4), 483–489.

Mingo, J. J. (2000). Policy Implications of Federal Reserve Study of Credit Risk Models at Major U.S. Banking Institutions. *Journal of Banking and Finance*, *24*, 15–33.

Mizon, G. (1998). *Credit Derivatives: A Primer*. JP Morgan.

Modigliani, F., & Miller, M. (1958). The Cost of Capital, Corporation Finance, and the Theory of Investment. *American Economic Review*, (June), 261–297.

Moskow, M. (1997). The Regulation of Derivatives. *Federal Reserve Bank of Chicago*, (March).

Mussa, M. (1986). Safety and Soundness as an Objective of Regulation of Depository Institutions. *Journal of Business*, *59*(11), 97–117.

Neal, R. S. (1996). Credit Derivatives: New Financial Instruments for Controlling Credit Risk, In: Federal Reserve Bank of Kansas City, *Economic Review*, (2nd Quarter), 15–27.

Office of the Superintendent of Financial Institutions (1999). *Credit Derivatives – Capital Treatment*. Interim Appendix to Guideline A: Parts I & II. November.

Peltzman, S. (1976). Toward a More General Theory of Regulation. *Journal of Economics and Law*, *19*(2), 211–240.

Quigley, N. (1997). Credit Risk in Banking. *Proceedings of a Conference at H. C. Cooms Center for Financial Studies*, (May 1–2).

Roll, R. R. (1988). The International Stock Market Crash of 1987. *Financial Analysts Journal*, *44*(5), 19–35.

Schachter, B. (1997). Derivatives, Regulation and Banking. New York: Elsevier Science B. V.

Scholes, M. (2000). Crisis and Risk Management. *The American Economic Review*, *90*(2), 17–21.

Schwert, G. W. (1981). Using Financial Data to Measure Effects of Regulation. *Journal of Law and Economics*, *24*, 121–158.

Smithson, C. W. (1999). Firm-Wide Risk: How Firms Are Integrating Risk Management. In: *Managing the Risk Management Process*. CIBC World Markets.

Smithson, C. W. (1998). *Managing Financial Risk* (p. 312). New York: McGraw-Hill.

Stigler, G. J. (1971). The Theory of Economic Regulation. *Journal of Economics*, *2*(1), 3–21.

Tavakoli, J. (1998). *Credit Derivatives: A Guide to Instruments and Applications*. John Wiley & Sons Inc.

Thakor, A. V. (1996). Capital Requirements, Monetary Policy and Aggregate Bank Lending: Theory and Empirical Evidence. *Journal of Finance*, *51*(1), 279–324.

Wagster, J. D. (1996). Impact of the 1988 Basle Accord on International Banks. *The Journal of Finance*, *LI*(4), 1321–1346.

Wall, L. D. (1996). Bank's Responses to Binding Regulatory Capital Requirements. Economic Review. *Federal Reserve Bank of Atlanta*, *81*(2), 1–17.

Wall, L. D., & Peterson, D. R. (1995). Bank Holding Company Targets in the Early 1990s: The Regulators versus the Markets. *Journal of Banking and Finance*, *19*, 563–574.

Whittaker, J., & Li, W. (1997). An Introduction to Credit Derivatives. *Risk: Credit Risk Supplement*, July.

COINTEGRATION AND ASSET ALLOCATION: A NEW ACTIVE HEDGE FUND STRATEGY

Carol Alexander, Ian Giblin and Wayne Weddington III

ABSTRACT

Models that are based on mean-variance analysis seek portfolio weights to minimise the variance of the portfolio for a given level of return. The portfolio variance is measured using a covariance matrix that represents the volatility and correlation of asset returns. However these matrices are notoriously difficult to estimate and ad hoc *methods often need to be applied to limit or smooth the mean-variance efficient allocations that are recommended by the model. Moreover the mean-variance criterion has nothing to ensure that tracking errors are stationary. Although the portfolios will be efficient, the tracking errors will in all probability be random walks. Therefore the replicating portfolio can drift very far from the benchmark unless it is frequently re-balanced.*

A significant difference between traditional hedge fund strategies and the model presented in this paper is that portfolio optimization is based upon the cointegration of asset prices rather than the correlation of asset returns. We show that it is possible to devise allocations that always have stationary tracking errors. Moreover, efficient market neutral long short hedge strategies may be achieved with relatively few stocks and with much lower turnover rates compared to traditional market neutral strategies.

Financial Risk and Financial Risk Management, Volume 16, pages 65–89.

ISBN: 0-7623-0858-3

1. INTRODUCTION

Investors recognize that traditional investment vehicles have become increasingly risky, and the managers of traditional long only investment styles are handicapped in that they can take advantage of only one side of the investment process. If they do not like an asset, then they simply do not buy it, whereas the hedge fund manager can actively sell those assets he does not like, presenting a "double alpha" opportunity. No matter how well the traditional manager selects his portfolio, he will still have significant market exposure. Beta-neutrality, dollar-neutrality, and sector-neutrality are all intended to make the hedged portfolio more predictable by eliminating systemic risk.

An unfortunate consequence of hedge funds' present popularity is that "hedge fund" can refer to many different investment styles. Traditionally, a hedge was meant to define a market opportunity in which the risk of the overall market was eliminated from the source of return. But it has become a term used to describe any fund that is not conventional, including long-only bonds, long-only equities (mutual funds), or long-only money markets. Some consider all absolute-return funds to fall within the hedge fund definition, even if these funds do not typically sell short.[1] Many funds are not hedged at all but use leverage to multiply their active market exposure. The returns can be high, but so can the losses, as leveraged directional investments (that are not hedged) tend to have a large impact on performance. It is noteworthy that most hedge fund databases still restrict their searches to absolute return.

The fundamental hedge fund proposition is that pure alpha depends upon dynamic asset selection rather than market direction. The hedge manager's expanded tool set provides greater opportunity to exercise relative value assessments: the manager can fully utilize a stock selection model and, most importantly, focus upon relative valuation rather than absolute valuation. The latter can be particularly profitable when 'all' stocks are over-valued, as the S&P100 stocks became in the quarter ending March 2000. Three types of hedge fund may be distinguished:

1. Directional

Directional hedge funds buy undervalued securities and sell short over valued securities for the purpose of making a profit. Profits are realised on long positions in undervalued assets by selling the asset at a price higher than their buying price; on short positions in overvalued assets profits are made by buying them back at a price lower than their sell price. If leverage is used the speculator is exposed to risk that is greater than the underlying security.

2. Arbitrage

Arbitrage funds operate by the simultaneous buying and selling of a security at two different prices in two different markets, resulting in profits without risk. Perfectly efficient markets present no arbitrage opportunities.

3. Classic Hedge

These funds aim to minimize the market risk by offsetting otherwise risky positions. They are non-directional and often maintain long and short positions for 'dollar' or 'market' neutrality.

Most hedge fund categories did well last year. The SP500-stock index was down 9.1%, the Nasdaq down 39%, while the average U.S. hedge fund was up 4.85% according to the CSFB/Tremont Hedge Fund Index. It is precisely these periods – when volatility is high or in bear markets – that hedge funds become 'hot.' It is amusing that hedge funds are relatively unpopular in strong equity markets, only to regain popularity when the market 'corrects.' Of course, hedge funds may not outperform the market during euphoric upswings. In their simplest market-neutral form, equity hedge funds only seek to provide a return greater than the short-term risk free rate that is, technically, their benchmark. When the markets are down, however, the performances of hedge funds are notable.

The truth is that hedge funds have consistently outperformed the U.S. mutual funds on a risk-adjusted basis (as opposed to absolute return). As investors become increasingly sophisticated regarding the value-at-risk of their investments, hedge funds cannot help but benefit. While the public's fascination with hedge funds has been on-again, off-again depending upon market conditions, each "on" cycle brings incrementally higher interest and higher capital allocations.

This paper presents a classic hedge fund strategy: an investment vehicle whose key objective is to minimize investment risk in an attempt to deliver profits under all market circumstances. Such a strategy may be described as "non-directional" or "market-neutral": the hedge is designed to have minimal correlation with the market and, irrespective of market direction, the fund seeks to generate positive alpha. Market-neutral hedge strategies are presently in great demand, though the true condition of market-neutrality remains elusive to even the most well known hedge funds. Certain high profile market-neutral managers were very market-neutral . . . until they weren't. And in some cases, they were shown to be not-so-market-neutral in spectacular fashion. But, as a group, market neutral managers have done well in this era of high volatility: equity market-neutral funds in the U.S. returned 14.99% in 2000.

The outline of the paper is as follows: Section 2 introduces the concept of cointegrated time series and explains the relationship between cointegrated prices and correlated returns with examples from different types of financial markets. Section 3 describes the methodology for tracking a benchmark using a basket of assets with a price that is cointegrated with the benchmark. Section 4 expands this methodology to a long-short hedge strategy that is based on cointegration. Section 5 reports the results of backtesting such a model for a long-short equity hedge of the S&P100 index, and Section 6 summarizes and concludes.

2. COINTEGRATION

The strategy that is described in this paper uses historical price patterns to project the future performance of a stock. A significant difference between this model and more traditional hedge fund strategies is that portfolio optimization is based upon the cointegration of prices rather than the correlation of returns. We shall see that this affects the character of portfolio performance: In particular turnover will be relatively low for a market-neutral strategy (approximately 2% per trading day) and each leg of the hedge will be independently convex to the market.[2]

Financial markets by their very nature are highly co-dependent. It is, however, unfortunate that many market practitioners still base their analysis of the relationships between assets on the very limited concept of correlation. Trying to model the complex inter-dependencies between financial assets with so restrictive a tool is like trying to surf the internet with an IBM AT. Therefore it is gratifying that more sophisticated dynamic models based on multivariate time series analysis are now being applied to analyze the complex relationships between financial assets.

Cointegration refers not to co-movements in returns, but to co-movements in asset prices, exchange rates or yields. If spreads are mean-reverting, asset prices are tied together in the long-term by a common stochastic trend, and we say that the prices are 'cointegrated'. Since the seminal work of Engle and Granger (1987) cointegration has become the prevalent tool of time series econometrics.[3] Cointegration has emerged as a powerful technique for investigating common trends in multivariate time series, and provides a sound methodology for modelling both long-run and short-run dynamics in a system.

Cointegration is a two step process: first any long-run equilibrium relationships between prices are established and then a dynamic correlation model of returns is estimated. This error correction model (ECM), so-called because short-term deviations from equilibrium are corrected, reveals the Granger causalities that must be present in a cointegrated system. Thus cointegration may be a sign of market inefficiency, but it can also be the result of market efficiency, as for example is the cointegration between spot and futures prices.

Although empirical models of cointegrated financial time series are common place in the academic literature, the practical implementation of these models into systems for investment analysis or portfolio risk is still in its early stages. This is because the traditional starting point for portfolio allocation and risk management is a correlation analysis of returns. In standard risk-return models the price data are differenced before the analysis is even begun, and differencing removes a-priori any long-term trends in the data. Of course these trends are implicit in the returns data, but any decision based on common trends in the price data is excluded in standard risk-return modelling. The aim of cointegration analysis, on the other hand, is to detect any common stochastic trends in the price data, and to use these common trends for a dynamic analysis of correlation in returns.

Correlation is based only on return data, which are stationary, denoted I(0). Cointegration is based on the raw price, rate or yield data as well as the return data. Price, rate or yield data are not normally stationary, in fact they are usually a random walk, or at least integrated of order 1, denoted I(1).[4] Since it is normally the case that log prices will be cointegrated when the actual prices are cointegrated it is standard, but not necessary, to perform the cointegration analysis on log prices. A set of I(1) series are termed 'cointegrated' if there is a linear combination of these series that is stationary. In the case of just two integrated series:

$$x \text{ and } y \text{ are cointegrated if } x, y \sim I(1) \text{ but there exists } \alpha$$
$$\text{such that } z = x - \alpha y \sim I(0).$$

The definition of cointegration given in Engle and Granger (1987) is far more general than this, but the basic definition presented here is sufficient for the purposes of this paper.

Cointegration and Correlation

Cointegration and correlation are related, but different concepts. High correlation does not imply high cointegration, and neither does high cointegration imply high correlation. In fact cointegrated series can have correlations that are quite low at times. For example a large and diversified portfolio of stocks in an equity index, where allocations are determined by their weights in the index, should be cointegrated with the index. Although the portfolio should move in line with the index in the long-term, there will be periods when stocks that are not in the portfolio have extreme price movements. Following this the empirical correlations between the portfolio and the index may be quite low for a time.

Conversely, high correlation of returns does not necessarily imply high cointegration in prices or rates either. An example is given in Fig. 1, with 8 years of daily data on U.S. dollar spot exchange rates of the German Mark (DEM) and the Dutch Guilder (NLG) from 1986 to 1992. Their returns are very highly correlated, in fact the unconditional correlation coefficient over the whole period is 0.9642. The rates themselves also appear to be moving together. The spread is very stable indeed and in fact they appear to be cointegrated, which is highly unusual for two exchange rates (Alexander & Johnston, 1992, 1994).

Now suppose that a very small incremental stochastic return is added to the spread, to create the NLG 'plus' series that is also shown in Fig. 1. The NLG 'plus' is clearly not cointegrated with DEM. They are not tied together by a stationary spread, in fact they are diverging. However the correlation between the returns to NLG 'plus' and the DEM is virtually unchanged, at 0.9620.

Thus high correlations may occur when there is cointegration, or when there is no cointegration. That is, correlation tells us nothing about the long-term

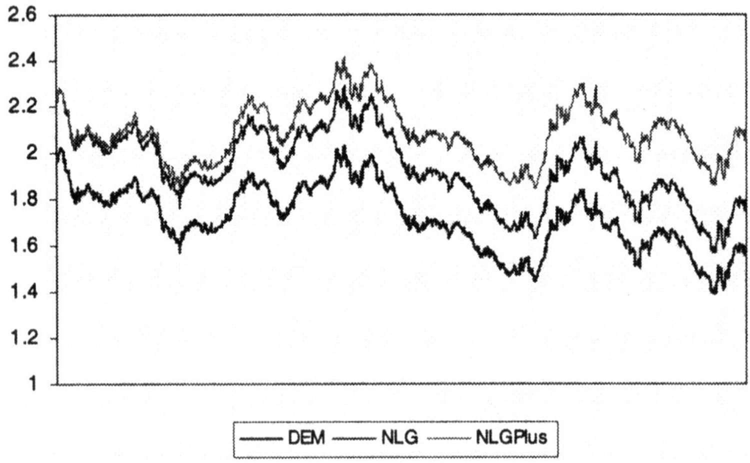

Fig. 1. DEM and NLG Daily FX Rates, Jan 1986–Dec 1992.

behaviour between two markets: they may or may not be moving together over long periods of time, and correlation is not an adequate tool for measuring this.

Correlation reflects co-movements in returns, which are liable to great instabilities over time. In fact, correlation is intrinsically a short-run measure because it is based on returns, which are short memory processes. Therefore classic hedge fund strategies that are based only correlations cannot guarantee long term performance. The model has no mechanism to ensure the reversion of the hedge to the underlying, there is nothing to prevent the tracking error from behaving in the unpredictable manner of a random walk and, consequently, correlation based hedge strategies will normally require frequent re-balancing. To avoid the erosion of profits by high transaction costs, sometimes there is limited re-balancing in direction only, or the optimal allocations are smoothed over time, or Bayesian methods are used to impose priors on the covariance matrix. Each of these strategies has the effect of increasing the fund volatility in a more or less *ad hoc* fashion.

Since high correlation is not sufficient to ensure the long-term performance of hedges, there is a need to augment standard risk-return modelling methodologies to take account of common long-term trends in prices. This is exactly what cointegration provides. Cointegration measures long-run co-movements in prices, which may occur even through periods when static correlations appear low. Therefore hedging methodologies based on cointegrated financial assets should be more effective in the long term. Moreover, the cointegration methodology loses none of the traditional methods. It merely augments the basic correlation model to include a preliminary stage in which the multivariate price data are analyzed and then extends the correlation model to include a dynamic analysis of the lead-lag behaviour between returns.

Common Trends and Long-Run Equilibria

When asset price time series are random walks, over a period of time they may have wandered virtually anywhere, because a random walk has infinite unconditional variance. There is little point in modelling them individually since the best forecast of any future value is the just value today plus the drift. However when two or more asset prices are cointegrated a multivariate model will be worthwhile because it reveals information about the long-run equilibrium in the system. For example, if a spread is found to be mean-reverting we know that, wherever one series is in several years time, the other series will be right there along with it.

Cointegrated log asset prices have a common stochastic trend (Stock & Watson, 1988). They are 'tied together' in the long-run even though they might drift apart in the short-run because the spread or some other linear combination is mean-reverting. A simple example[5] that illustrates why cointegrated series have a common stochastic trend is

$$\begin{aligned} x_t &= w_t + \varepsilon_{xt} \\ y_t &= w_t + \varepsilon_{yt} \\ w_t &= w_{t-1} + \varepsilon_t \end{aligned} \tag{1}$$

where all the errors are i.i.d. and independent of each other. In the example (1) the I(1) variables x and y are cointegrated because $x - y \sim I(0)$. They also have a common stochastic trend given by the random walk component w. Note that the correlation between Δx and Δy will be less than 1 and when the variances of ε_{xt} and/or ε_{yt} are large the correlation can be quite low.[6] Thus, as already mentioned above, cointegration does not imply high correlation.

The linear combination of I(1) variables that is stationary is denoted z. It is called the 'disequilibrium term' because it captures deviations from the long run equilibrium in the error correction model (for further details see chapter 12 of Alexander, 2001). The expectation of z gives the long-run equilibrium relationship between x and y and short-term periods of disequilibrium occur as the observed value of z varies around its expected value. The 'cointegrating vector' is the vector of weights in z. In the case of two I(1) variables x and y where $x - \alpha y \sim I(0)$ the cointegrating vector is $(1, -\alpha)$. When only two integrated series are considered for cointegration, there can be at most one cointegrating vector, because if there were two cointegrating vectors the original series would have to be stationary.

More generally cointegration exists between n integrated series if there exists at least one cointegrating vector, that is at least one linear combination of the I(1) series that is stationary. Each stationary linear combination acts like 'glue' in the system, and so the more cointegrating vectors found the more the coherence and co-movements in the prices. Cointegration can be thought of as a form of factor analysis similar to principal component analysis[7] so it is not surprising that cointegration analysis often works very well on the futures or interest rate term structures that are so successfully modelled by a principal component analysis. Most yield curves have very high cointegration. Often each of the $n - 1$ independent spreads is mean reverting, so there are $n - 1$ cointegrating vectors, the maximum possible number.

Cointegration in Financial Markets

Cointegration has been the subject of extensive research in many financial markets: within term structures, between spot and futures prices, and between international equity and bond market indices.[8] Research on cointegration of stock prices has been more limited, although findings of cointegration were recorded at least a decade ago (Cherchi & Havenner, 1988; Pindyck & Rothenberg, 1992).

This paper concerns the cointegration between a basket of stocks and the stock index. Since the index is, by definition, a linear combination of the constituents, there should be some basket of stocks that is cointegrated with the index. Assuming that the basket is sufficiently large and the index weights do not change too much over time, the tracking error will be stationary, that is, the basket will cointegrated with the index. What is, perhaps, surprising, is that a cointegrating basket can normally be found that contains relatively few stocks. Therefore transactions costs can be substantially reduced when this method is applied to track an index.

3. THE METHODOLOGY

When portfolios are constructed on the basis of mean-variance returns analysis, frequent re-balancing is usually necessary to keep the portfolio in line with the index. One of the reasons for this is that the portfolio variance will normally be measured using a covariance matrix, but these matrices are notoriously difficult to estimate. Unless they are based on very long term averages, which will not respond to current market conditions by definition, they often lack robustness. When the covariance matrix changes considerably from day to day, so will the efficient frontier and the corresponding recommendation for the optimal portfolio. Moreover the mean-variance criterion has nothing to ensure that tracking errors are stationary: indeed the tracking errors will in all probability be random walks. Therefore the replicating portfolio can drift arbitrarily far from the benchmark unless it is frequently re-balanced, and *ad hoc* adjustments are often employed to avoid onerous transactions costs.

The previous section has explained why the cointegration methodology can form the basis of a very powerful tool for investment analysis. When the allocations in a portfolio are designed so that the portfolio is cointegrated with the index, it will track the index over the long term. The portfolio and the index will deviate, but only in the short term, and over the longer term they will be tied together. This property, combined with the fact that cointegrating portfolios can often be formed using relatively few stocks, leads to the construction of optimal portfolios that have less risk, less turnover and lower transaction costs than the traditional mean-variance optimal portfolios.

Selection and Allocation

The criteria that are used in cointegration analysis are to maximise the stationarity and to minimise the variance of the tracking error. Thus, using cointegration it is possible to devise optimal portfolios that are tied to the benchmark and also have minimum risk tracking errors. A linear regression of log prices is employed: the dependent variable will be the log index price or some other benchmark, such as LIBOR, that is used to evaluate the performance of the portfolio;[9] the explanatory variables will be the log prices of the assets in the tracking portfolio; and the residuals are the tracking errors.[10]

There are two parts to the problem: first select the assets, and then optimise the portfolio weights. The asset selection process is perhaps the hardest but most important part, and can be approached in a number of ways. Selection methods range from a 'brute force' approach, such as when the number of assets is fixed and then linear models are fitted for all possible portfolios with this number of assets, to methods that are tailored to investors preferences over various types of stocks, or proprietory technical analysis.

The optimal allocation process uses least squares regression analysis: allocations are made according to a cointegrating regression, so that the fitted portfolio will be cointegrated with the benchmark and the tracking error will be stationary. Suppose a benchmark with log price index y is to be tracked with a number of assets with log prices $x_1, \ldots, x_n$. The Engle-Granger cointegration method is to regress y on a constant and $x_1, \ldots, x_n$, and then to test the residuals for stationarity.[11] The coefficients $\alpha_1, \ldots, \alpha_n$ in the Engle-Granger regression

$$y_1 = \alpha_0 + \alpha_1 x_{1,t} + \ldots + \alpha_n x_{n,t} + \varepsilon_t \tag{2}$$

are normalized to sum to one, thereby giving the portfolio weights. Thus the problem of finding the optimal replicating portfolio can be solved by finding the best assets with log prices $x_1, \ldots, x_n$ to use in the cointegrating regression, and then defining allocations to give the maximum stationarity in the tracking error ε. The more stationary the tracking error, the greater the cointegration between the benchmark and the candidate portfolio. In practice, a very high degree of cointegration can be found between the benchmark and the tracking portfolio, so the standard augmented Dickey-Fuller (ADF) unit root test will be sufficient to compare different portfolio specifications and choose those with the most stationary tracking errors.

When there are a large number of potential assets that could be used in a replicating portfolio it is not at all a trivial problem to test all possible portfolios to find the one that has the most stationary tracking error. If there are N assets in total one has to test N!/n!(N − n)! portfolios for every n less than or equal to N.

This strategy can be extended for global asset management models where the benchmark may be a global index such as the Morgan Stanley World Index. In this case there will be two-stages to the selection – allocation process. First select the country indices to track the global index and assign optimal country allocations, and then either buy/sell the country index futures (if available) or repeat the process for tracking the individual country indices with individual stocks. A single country model could also be approached in two stages: first select the industrial sectors and assign weights optimally, then select the stocks within each industry sector and optimize portfolios to track the industry indices.

Constrained Allocations

Examples of constrained allocations include:

- A fund manager may wish to go long-short in exactly twelve different countries, with the EAFE index as benchmark. The problem then becomes one of selecting the basket of twelve countries that are currently most highly cointegrated with the EAFE index.
- A small asset management company might seek a benchmark return of 5% per annum above the S&P 100 index, so in this case the benchmark index will be the S&P 100 'plus'.
- Assets may be selected according to quite specific preferences of investors. For example, 50% of the fund may have to be allocated to the U.K., or no more than 5% of capital can be allocated to any single asset.

Equality constraints on allocations, such as 40% in technology related stocks, are simple to implement. The dependent variable just becomes $y - \omega_j x_j$, where a fraction ω_j of the fund must be assigned to the jth asset; the other log asset prices are used as regressors with the constraint that the sum of the weights is $1 - \omega_j$. Similarly if more than one asset has a constrained allocation, the dependent variable becomes y – the weighted sum of the constrained log asset prices, and the remaining log asset prices are used as regressors.

Inequality constraints are more difficult to implement. How should one deal with the constraint of no short sales, $\omega_j > 0$ for all j? First perform an unconstrained estimation of the model by ordinary least squares (OLS) because if no constraint is violated there will be no problem. Suppose the constraints $\omega_j > 0$ for some j are violated. Then the model is restricted so that all these ω_j are set to zero, and re-estimated to ensure that no other coefficients that were originally positive have now become negative. If that is the case the resulting constrained OLS estimator is obtained, but it will of course be biased. That it is more efficient than the original estimator because it reflects the value of further information may be little compensation.

Problems arise when imposing the constraints causes more constraints to be violated, so that other coefficients that were positive in the unconstrained model become negative in the constrained model. The only feasible solution is to put those coefficients to zero, re-estimate a further constrained model, and to keep shooting coefficients to zero until a purely long portfolio of assets is obtained. Clearly this can cause severe bias in results: the more constraints that have to be imposed the further the model will be from a true underlying market equilibrium. Therefore the model developer needs to approach this exercise with caution, and to validate his or her judgment by thorough back testing.

Parameter Selection

The basic cointegration index tracking model can be defined in terms of certain parameters:

- Any 'alpha' return over and above the index;
- The time-span of daily data that is used in the cointegrating regression (2);
- The number of assets in the portfolio;[12]
- Any constraints on allocations that are defined by the preferences of the investor.

The optimal parameter values are chosen by recording a number of in-sample and post-sample performance measures for each set of parameters. The optimal parameter set is that which gives the 'best' performance measures and for the purposes of this paper the most important in-sample performance measures are:

- *Tracking error stationarity*: The standard ADF test is used to test the level of cointegration between the portfolio the benchmark on the historic data: the larger and more negative the ADF statistic, the greater the level of cointegration and the more stationary the tracking error;[13]
- *Standard error of the regression*: The in-sample tracking error will be stationary if the portfolio is cointegrated with the benchmark, so it cannot deviate from the benchmark for too long. However this does not imply that the short-term deviations between the portfolio and the benchmark are necessarily small. It is also important to choose a portfolio for which the in-sample tracking error has a low volatility, and this is measured by the standard error of the regression.
- *Turnover*: Only those portfolios showing realistic turnover projections as the model is rolled over the back test period should be considered. Typically

turnover projections from cointegration based strategies will be much lower than those based on mean-variance analysis.

Having specified the selections and the allocations on the in-sample 'training period', a fixed period of data immediately following the in-sample data is used to analyze the out-of-sample performance of the portfolio. These post-sample data are called the 'testing period'. If the strategy requires monthly re-balancing then it is normal to use a testing period of one month or two months for the post-sample diagnostics. Some typical post-sample diagnostics are:

- *Tracking error variance*: This is the variance of the daily tracking errors during the testing period. The tracking error variance is equivalent to the root mean square forecast error if it is measured as an equally weighted average;
- *Differential return:* The difference between the portfolio return and the benchmark return over the testing period;
- *Information ratio:* The ratio between the mean daily tracking error and the standard deviation of the daily tracking error over the testing period. In-sample information ratios are zero by design (because the residuals from ordinary least squares regression have zero mean) but a high positive post-sample information ratio is very important as a risk adjusted performance measure.

Consider a simple example of how to decide which parameters are optimal. The problem is to track the Morgan Stanley European, Asian and Far Eastern (EAFE) index with a one year buy-and-hold strategy. The alpha over the EAFE index is fixed at 3% per annum and there are no constraints on allocations. Thus there are only two model parameters to be chosen, the number of country indices in the portfolio (at the time of optimization the maximum was 23) and the training period for the model. Figure 2 shows the 12 month out-of-sample information ratios that are obtained as the number of assets selected varies from 5 to 15 and the length of training period varies from 10 to 130 months. From the figure it seems that the highest information ratio of 3.8 occurs when the training period is between 100 and 115 months and the number of assets is between 7 and 11.

Instead of fixing the alpha over an index – or indeed under an index – it may be preferable to fix the number of assets in the portfolio. In that case this type of two-dimensional 'heat map' can be used to determine the optimal choice of two other important parameters: the alpha over the index and the length of training period. Examples of such heat maps are given in the next section.

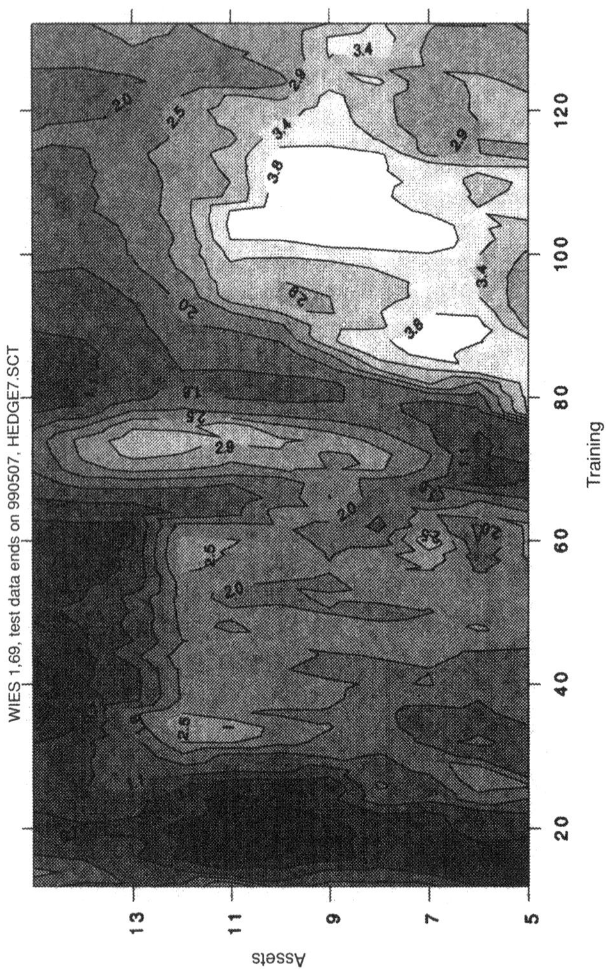

Fig. 2. Alpha 0.03 (outperformance) 12 month Information Ratio.

4. THE HEDGE FUND STRATEGY

The hedge strategy consists of two legs, a long and a short portfolio. Each leg of the long-short equity hedge consists of a portfolio of 75 stocks that will be used to track an S&P 100 index 'plus' benchmark. The model parameter specification stage begins with a heat map, similar to that shown in Fig. 2, that is generated by finding the 75 asset portfolio that is most highly cointegrated with the index plus alpha percent per annum. In this case the parameters to choose will be the alpha over the index (or under, if it is negative) and the length of training period.

Each time the alpha and the training period are changed the choice of assets and the allocations in the portfolio will change. These allocations are not recorded at this stage: all that will be stored are the in-sample and out-of-sample diagnostics that have been described above, for each parameter vector. Figure 3a shows the one month out-of-sample information ratios, and Fig. 3b shows the one month out-of-sample differential returns for a 75 stock portfolio in the S&P 100 index that is being optimised at the end of February 2000. Figures 3c and 3d are similar to Figs 3a and 3b but for the two month information ratio. The maps are colour coded to indicate the regions where better diagnostic test results are obtained.

These heat maps show a clear 'hot spot' when the alpha is negative but no more than about –7% per annum, and the training period is between 28 and 48 months. Another region that gives promising out-of-sample diagnostics is for a high, positive alpha and a very long training period. However the highest differential return and information ratio are in fact obtained within the 'hot spot' when the alpha is approximately –5% and the training period is about 3 years.

The heat maps in Fig. 3 also have a 'cold spot', that is a region where the parameter choices give rise to rather bad performance measures. In particular when the alpha is –12% and the training period is 72 months, the one-month and two-month out-of-sample information ratios are negative, as are the differential returns. For this parameter vector, the out-of-sample performance

Table 1. Long and Short Portfolio Parameter Choices, February 2000.

	Alpha	Training Months
Long	–5%	36
Short	–12%	72

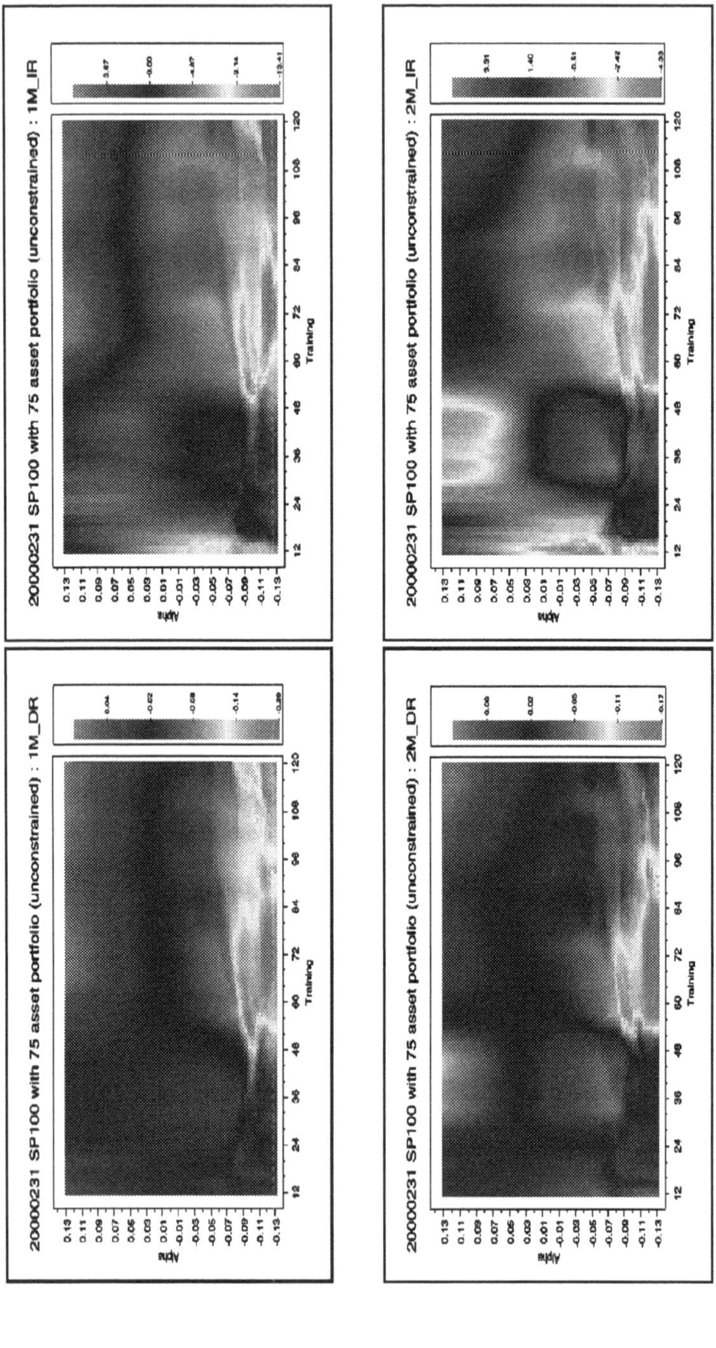

Fig. 3. Heat Maps for Model Parameter Optimization.

Table 2. Optimal Parameter Choices for S&P 100.

	Long		Short			Long		Short	
	Alpha	Training	Alpha	Training		Alpha	Training	Alpha	Training
Jan-95	–0.1	54	–0.06	24	Jan-98	0.04	24	–0.1	78
Feb-95	–0.12	30	0.09	30	Feb-98	0.12	90	–0.1	72
Mar-95	0.08	78	–0.05	72	Mar-98	0.12	90	–0.05	30
Apr-95	0	18	–0.05	66	Apr-98	0.12	102	–0.03	12
May-95	0.1	66	–0.05	18	May-98	0.12	84	–0.1	24
Jun-95	0.1	66	–0.1	102	Jun-98	0.12	84	–0.1	24
Jul-95	0.12	30	–0.12	102	Jul-98	0.12	12	–0.1	24
Aug-95	0.12	30	–0.12	96	Aug-98	0.12	84	–0.12	102
Sep-95	0.12	42	–0.12	36	Sep-98	0.12	30	–0.12	54
Oct-95	0.1	66	–0.07	12	Oct-98	–0.11	102	–0.1	12
Nov-95	0.12	60	–0.1	102	Nov-98	0.09	12	–0.1	12
Dec-95	0.12	54	–0.11	102	Dec-98	0.05	12	–0.04	18
Jan-96	–0.12	48	–0.12	102	Jan-99	0.12	78	–0.11	78
Feb-96	0.08	78	–0.12	102	Feb-99	0.12	102	–0.12	66
Mar-96	0.12	48	–0.05	90	Mar-99	0.03	48	–0.11	54
Apr-96	0.11	60	–0.08	96	Apr-99	0.06	102	0.04	36
May-96	0.02	72	–0.1	78	May-99	0.05	102	0.11	18
Jun-96	0.11	78	–0.09	78	Jun-99	–0.03	12	–0.08	30
Jul-96	0.12	78	–0.11	102	Jul-99	0.12	30	–0.09	30
Aug-96	0.12	78	–0.12	96	Aug-99	0.12	78	–0.12	96
Sep-96	0.01	42	0	96	Sep-99	0.12	78	–0.12	84
Oct-96	0.11	84	0	96	Oct-99	0.12	36	–0.11	102
Nov-96	0.12	78	–0.12	90	Nov-99	0.12	54	–0.1	36
Dec-96	–0.12	66	0.12	66	Dec-99	0.12	54	–0.11	96
Jan-97	0.01	24	0.11	66	Jan-00	0.12	16	–0.12	88
Feb-97	0.01	102	–0.12	54	Feb-00	0.12	6	–0.11	12
Mar-97	0.01	102	–0.12	102	Mar-00	0.12	64	–0.12	92
Apr-97	0.09	66	–0.12	30	Apr-00	0.12	64	–0.1	60
May-97	0.05	72	–0.12	12	May-00	0.12	16	–0.08	40
Jun-97	0.11	90	0	102	Jun-00	0.06	12	–0.08	28
Jul-97	0.11	96	–0.1	102	Jul-00	0.12	48	–0.1	88
Aug-97	0.11	96	–0.12	102	Aug-00	0.12	120	–0.13	20
Sep-97	–0.11	102	–0.12	36	Sep-00	0.12	120	–0.12	20
Oct-97	0.12	12	–0.11	12	Oct-00	0.11	108	–0.13	88
Nov-97	–0.08	12	0.12	12	Nov-00	–0.11	90	–0.12	24
Dec-97	0	18	0.12	96	Dec-00	–0.09	20	–0.09	26

of the portfolio is returning considerably less than the index. Therefore it would be possible to make money by going short this portfolio.

Note that this 'short' portfolio will itself contain long and short positions, unless the constraint of no short sales has been applied. Similarly the 'long' portfolio, the one that has the highest information ratio and differential return, will typically also consist of long and short positions. Then a hedged portfolio is obtained by matching the amount invested in the long portfolio with the same amount being shorted with the short portfolio.

When this type of long-short strategy is used with a 75 stock portfolio from the S&P 100, Fig. 3 indicates that the optimal parameter choices for February 2000 are shown in Tables 1 and 2.

Typically the optimal parameter choices will be different every month, and will depend on any allocation constraints. Table 2 shows the parameter choices that were actually used for the 75 asset long portfolio and a 75 asset short portfolio in the S&P 100 index. Note that in February 2000 the parameters are different from those shown in Table 1. This is because in Table 2 allocations were constrained so that the total (long + short) allocation to each asset will be no more than 5% of the fund.[14] Of course some of the same assets will be chosen in both portfolios, and the net position in these assets will be determined by the difference of their weight (positive or negative) in the long portfolio minus their weight (positive or negative) in the short portfolio.

5. THE RESULTS

This section describes two types of model back tests. The first type of back test is of a fixed parameter set that is optimal according to 'heat maps' of the type just described and the test is of its performance over an historic period. A simple snap-shot of portfolio performance at one instance in time as in Fig. 3, may not provide sufficient evidence that parameter choices are optimal. Dynamic performance measures can be obtained by running the model over time, for example month by month. Each month a new set of assets will be chosen and new allocations will be made, but the set of parameters remains fixed. Table 3 reports the in-sample ADF, the turnover percent, and the one-month, two-month and three-month out of sample information ratios for the long and the short portfolio parameters that were optimal in October 2000, given in Table 2. The rest of the table indicates how these parameter choices would have performed since January 1995. For example the first line of the table shows that the portfolio parameter choice of alpha 5% (long) and –8% (short) and training 30 months would not have been a good choice at all in

Table 3. Back Testing the October 2000 Parameter Choices.

	Long					Short				
	ADF	Turnover	1mth IR	2mth IR	3mth IR	ADF	Turnover	1mth IR	2mth IR	3mth IR
Jan-95	−10.57	0.78	−4.66	−2.47	−1.29	−10.59	0.77	9.09	2.54	2.14
Feb-95	−11.12	0.33	−4.32	−4.38	−2.80	−11.47	0.58	−0.22	4.16	1.69
Mar-95	−11.11	0.42	−0.63	−2.35	−3.31	−12.61	0.71	1.86	0.67	3.47
Apr-95	−10.93	0.47	0.13	−0.25	−1.47	−12.35	0.61	−3.22	−1.04	−0.76
May-95	−10.51	0.57	−0.32	−0.10	−0.27	−12.19	0.47	1.49	−0.85	−0.13
Jun-95	−10.74	0.36	3.79	1.39	0.93	−11.95	0.38	−4.91	−2.19	−2.50
Jul-95	−11.27	0.30	5.16	4.53	2.60	−12.16	0.64	−0.40	−2.80	−1.60
Aug-95	−10.88	0.38	3.97	4.61	4.37	−12.60	0.58	−4.74	−2.22	−3.26
Sep-95	−11.54	0.56	−2.13	0.42	1.86	−12.27	0.98	0.29	−2.29	−1.50
Oct-95	−11.57	0.39	3.50	0.75	1.57	−11.97	0.49	−6.04	−2.90	−3.54
Nov-95	−11.76	0.35	2.79	3.21	1.39	−12.33	0.99	2.26	−1.50	−0.96
Dec-95	−12.08	0.25	3.81	3.10	3.26	−12.06	0.70	1.75	2.05	−0.47
Jan-96	−11.52	0.26	3.36	3.54	3.43	−12.38	0.54	−3.32	−1.84	−0.25
Feb-96	−11.25	0.44	0.78	2.01	2.41	−12.26	0.82	−1.25	−2.46	−1.67
Mar-96	−11.94	0.42	3.77	2.06	2.52	−12.64	0.37	−0.68	−0.92	−1.81
Apr-96	−12.06	0.26	−0.35	1.56	1.27	−12.41	1.19	0.24	−0.26	−0.54
May-96	−12.65	0.38	2.68	1.15	1.96	−12.05	0.51	−2.08	−0.92	−0.84
Jun-96	−12.33	0.26	3.03	2.88	1.84	−11.57	0.87	3.85	0.83	0.64
Jul-96	−12.02	0.28	0.29	1.49	1.80	−11.62	0.60	−1.80	0.11	−0.44
Aug-96	−12.97	0.39	2.87	1.37	1.89	−12.99	1.08	−1.68	−1.74	−0.44
Sep-96	−12.28	0.53	−1.63	1.03	0.69	−12.68	0.82	−0.49	−1.18	−1.44
Oct-96	−12.19	0.26	−3.27	−2.57	−0.43	−13.18	1.03	1.38	0.60	−0.24
Nov-96	−12.26	0.23	−2.67	−3.00	−2.62	−12.40	1.19	2.79	2.04	1.32
Dec-96	−12.89	0.29	2.26	0.12	−0.89	−11.94	0.57	6.42	4.79	3.58
Jan-97	−12.00	0.31	−2.57	−0.40	−0.83	−12.07	0.76	−4.45	0.49	0.69
Feb-97	−12.48	0.17	5.54	0.10	0.80	−12.25	0.69	2.82	−0.33	1.33
Mar-97	−11.85	0.33	3.99	4.61	1.34	−12.19	0.46	−4.38	−0.54	−1.65
Apr-97	−12.79	0.26	3.06	3.50	3.93	−12.22	0.37	−2.78	−3.58	−1.30
May-97	−11.54	0.46	−0.98	1.54	2.35	−13.04	0.52	0.55	−1.23	−2.27
Jun-97	−12.32	0.26	3.40	1.38	2.09	−13.16	0.83	−0.08	0.20	−0.82
Jul-97	−11.97	0.16	1.00	2.03	1.21	−12.72	0.73	−3.94	−2.14	−1.39
Aug-97	−11.97	0.64	−3.27	−0.78	0.48	−12.26	1.01	2.46	−0.90	−0.65
Sep-97	−11.36	0.47	−2.58	−2.76	−1.52	−12.12	0.66	3.12	2.82	0.34
Oct-97	−10.67	0.64	−4.70	−3.58	−3.46	−12.62	1.50	0.96	1.87	2.06
Nov-97	−11.89	0.45	2.92	−1.13	−1.68	−12.76	1.13	−0.40	0.42	1.24
Dec-97	−11.37	0.37	2.26	2.55	0.19	−12.69	1.00	1.45	0.72	0.82

Table 3. Continued.

	Long					Short				
	ADF	Turnover	1mth IR	2mth IR	3mth IR	ADF	Turnover	1mth IR	2mth IR	3mth IR
Jan-98	−12.11	0.37	1.26	2.67	3.19	−13.27	0.41	−7.46	−1.17	−1.47
Feb-98	−12.55	0.34	3.03	2.01	2.75	−13.43	0.31	−2.87	−5.25	−1.59
Mar-98	−11.95	0.39	1.47	2.13	1.82	−12.95	1.08	−2.24	−2.45	−3.81
Apr-98	−11.99	0.43	8.43	4.79	4.33	−12.64	1.26	−2.26	−2.28	−2.39
May-98	−12.44	0.32	1.63	5.14	3.85	−12.48	1.12	−4.42	−3.24	−2.88
Jun-98	−11.98	0.56	2.47	2.11	4.19	−12.08	1.08	−5.76	−5.21	−4.23
Jul-98	−11.88	0.28	3.63	3.01	2.60	−11.83	1.72	−4.47	−5.11	−4.91
Aug-98	−10.76	0.65	−4.43	−1.59	−0.47	−11.43	1.61	5.82	1.82	0.08
Sep-98	−10.45	0.42	−2.89	−3.77	−2.00	−11.39	0.93	1.31	3.82	1.67
Oct-98	−11.85	0.28	6.13	2.00	−0.42	−12.27	1.10	−3.34	−1.24	1.35
Nov-98	−11.44	0.40	−2.66	3.14	1.07	−11.96	0.71	2.33	−1.22	−0.37
Dec-98	−11.75	0.25	3.81	1.16	3.34	−11.71	0.70	−4.85	−1.31	−2.19
Jan-99	−12.48	0.47	−3.93	−1.05	−1.88	−11.06	0.66	0.81	−2.63	−1.96
Feb-99	−12.37	0.32	2.10	−1.16	−0.07	−10.90	0.97	2.54	1.60	−1.02
Mar-99	−11.78	0.43	−3.73	−0.90	−2.00	−11.53	1.46	2.80	2.68	1.96
Apr-99	−11.78	0.41	1.82	−0.70	0.14	−11.51	1.26	1.71	1.99	2.14
May-99	−11.96	0.30	2.61	2.20	0.33	−11.48	0.51	−2.80	0.30	0.92
Jun-99	−12.27	0.49	3.28	2.98	2.55	−11.51	0.88	−5.27	−4.17	−1.14
Jul-99	−11.92	0.46	−0.64	1.36	1.80	−10.98	1.27	2.71	−2.03	−2.30
Aug-99	−12.59	0.27	3.16	1.35	2.00	−11.54	0.90	−2.05	−0.23	−2.05
Sep-99	−12.30	0.17	7.87	4.97	2.97	−11.44	0.72	−7.83	−4.16	−2.24
Oct-99	−11.48	0.43	−1.66	1.52	2.07	−12.27	1.20	−3.30	−4.86	−3.83
Nov-99	−12.01	0.45	−0.35	−1.08	0.91	−12.08	0.71	−0.10	−1.93	−3.37
Dec-99	−11.49	0.54	1.15	0.63	−0.02	−12.07	0.97	−9.05	−5.21	−4.60
Jan-00	−12.03	0.35	2.65	0.95	1.07	−11.82	1.04	4.99	−0.32	−0.83
Feb-00	−12.15	0.42	−5.15	−1.31	−1.15	−11.31	0.89	−2.00	1.88	−0.82
Mar-00	−13.12	0.50	−1.55	−3.04	−1.41	−11.48	0.95	1.40	0.13	1.69
Apr-00	−13.33	0.32	2.57	0.63	−0.79	−10.94	1.39	2.67	2.01	1.02
May-00	−12.65	0.27	1.77	2.18	0.88	−11.01	1.06	3.37	3.04	2.45
Jun-00	−12.07	0.44	−0.52	0.60	1.42	−11.68	1.45	−5.59	−0.97	0.25
Jul-00	−12.48	0.45	−1.18	−0.88	−0.08	−11.68	1.06	0.65	−2.79	−0.53
Aug-00	−12.01	0.36	−3.85	−1.94	−1.46	−10.97	1.23	−0.79	−0.12	−2.13
Sep-00	−11.80	0.25	4.05	1.64	0.73	−11.40	1.13	2.28	0.68	0.67
Oct-00	**−12.45**	**0.38**	**5.62**	**4.63**	**2.85**	**−11.40**	**1.36**	**−2.54**	**−0.40**	**−0.53**

January 1995. In fact with these choices the long portfolio under performed and the short portfolio out performed the index!

The object of this exercise is to check the robustness of the portfolio over time: this is fundamental to cointegration. Consistency between the 1 month, 2 month and 3 month information ratios is paramount: Table 3 indicates that if the 1 month information ratio is high so also, on the whole, are the 2 month and 3 month information ratios. Thus, if a portfolio starts well for the first month, it tends to perform well over several months. Similarly if the portfolio does not perform well during the first month, this tends to continue for subsequent months. Since the parameter choice for the current month is made on the basis of last month's performance, this autocorrelation in information ratios is a crucial performance indicator. Another robustness check for the portfolio is to ensure high ADFs and relatively low turnover projections when the portfolio is rebalanced using the same fixed parameters each month.[15]

It is evident from Table 2 that the same parameter selection is not usually optimal for two consecutive months. Therefore the most important back testing of the hedge fund strategy is to report the returns that are obtained when the alpha and training periods are re-optimized every month. Table 4 gives the consolidated returns from applying the long-short hedge strategy to the S&P 100 during three years that have been chosen as representative of difficult market conditions (1987, 1990 and 1993) and then continuously from 1995–2000.[16]

Note the large annual rates of return in 1998 and 1999: these were significantly strong years for the stock markets. Due to the inherent convexity

Table 4. Consolidated Returns from the Long-Short Strategy.

	1987	1990	1993	1995	1996	1997	1998	1999	2000
Compound Return									
SP100	8.9%	–4.4%	8.7%	37.2%	24.1%	29.8%	34.3%	33.7%	–13.4%
L-S HEDGE	14.3%	7.3%	15.8%	18.3%	13.6%	11.6%	46.4%	82.5%	34.9%
Fund Daily Returns:									
Maximum	4.6%	2.5%	2.9%	2.2%	2.0%	3.2%	3.8%	5.9%	4.3%
Minimum	–6.0%	–3.0%	–1.5%	–2.0%	–1.9%	–3.0%	–4.3%	–4.3%	–4.1%
Average	0.1%	0.0%	0.1%	0.1%	0.1%	0.0%	0.2%	0.2%	0.2%
Median	0.0%	0.0%	0.1%	0.1%	0.0%	0.0%	0.2%	0.1%	0.0%
Volatility (St Dev)	1.0%	0.7%	0.6%	0.7%	0.6%	0.9%	1.1%	1.5%	1.5%
Max 30-DayPeak-to-Trough	7.8%	10.2%	4.9%	7.3%	5.0%	12.6%	14.4%	10.1%	7.4%
Max 30-Day Trough-to-Peak	9.7%	9.8%	6.9%	8.7%	5.4%	13.9%	22.9%	24.0%	13.8%

Table 5. Monthly Consolidated Returns 1987, 1993 and 1998.

1987	SP100	L-S HEDGE	1993	SP100	L-S HEDGE	1998	SP100	L-S HEDGE
Jan-87	13.06%	1.72%	Jan-93	1.26%	–0.33%	Jan-98	2.04%	6.61%
Feb-87	3.89%	–0.37%	Feb-93	1.56%	4.54%	Feb-98	6.88%	–0.23%
Mar-87	3.31%	3.08%	Mar-93	1.69%	4.17%	Mar-98	5.30%	2.89%
Apr-87	0.68%	0.02%	Apr-93	–1.72%	–0.78%	Apr-98	1.49%	4.95%
May-87	0.68%	5.64%	May-93	2.59%	0.16%	May-98	–1.34%	3.33%
Jun-87	4.86%	0.30%	Jun-93	–0.17%	1.33%	Jun-98	4.83%	13.79%
Jul-87	4.26%	0.57%	Jul-93	–0.52%	1.84%	Jul-98	–0.54%	4.94%
Aug-87	4.50%	0.33%	Aug-93	3.31%	–0.89%	Aug-98	–15.16%	–8.83%
Sep-87	–3.09%	–1.91%	Sep-93	–1.53%	4.67%	Sep-98	5.10%	2.91%
Oct-87	–19.77%	2.27%	Oct-93	1.54%	–2.14%	Oct-98	8.78%	6.53%
Nov-87	–9.87%	–0.75%	Nov-93	–0.55%	0.42%	Nov-98	7.33%	–2.27%
Dec-87	6.00%	2.54%	Dec-93	0.88%	1.63%	Dec-98	4.73%	3.54%
Simple Return	8.51%	13.41%		8.34%	14.63%		29.46%	38.14%
Compound Return	8.88%	14.35%		8.70%	15.75%		34.26%	46.43%
Standard Deviation	8.10%	1.95%		1.52%	2.16%		6.08%	5.23%
Excess Return (Compound vs Index)		5.47%			7.05%			1.7%
Sharpe Ratio (Over Risk Free Rate 5%)		1.38			1.44			2.29

of the "long" side of the hedge (a long-biased combination of longs and shorts) the fund was able to capture market upswings. This did not compromise the downside protection of the "short" side of the hedge (a short-biased combination of shorts and longs) as shown in years in which the market retreated (1990, 2000). At all times the composite portfolio was dollar-neutral.

BARRA have performed a verification analysis of the 1999 returns.[17] They have shown that the strategy derives its excess returns primarily from risk assessment items such as earnings yield, earnings variation, momentum, size, and, as one would expect, some leverage. Both "Value" and "Growth" assessment are actually negative contributors to the return, which somewhat distinguishes the strategy from the status quo.

Monthly returns for some of the most difficult years for equity markets (1987, 1993 and 1998) are given in Table 5 above. The long-short strategy performs relatively well during the market crashes of October 1987 and August 1998. The returns are also much less volatile than the S&P 100 index returns, and during each of these years the fund outperformed the index considerably.

Over the entire back-test [1987, 1990, 1993, and 1995–2000]:

- the correlation between the hedge strategy and the S&P 100 was only –15.2%;
- the average annual Sharpe Ratio was 1.51;
- the average leverage was approximately 1.5 on both the long and the short legs of the hedge;
- the average annual returns were 27.2% and the average annual risk (annualized volatility from the monthly standard deviation of returns) was 11.4%.

6. SUMMARY AND CONCLUSIONS

This paper has described a long short hedge strategy that is based on cointegration between asset prices. Traditional strategies will not guarantee that the tracking error is stationary and will therefore require frequent rebalancing for the hedge to remain tied to the benchmark. The cointegration strategy, on the other hand, is based on the criterion that the hedge is mean-reverting to the benchmark; tracking errors are designed to be stationary and this may be achieved with relatively few stocks and with much lower turnover rates.

The strategy will accommodate investor's preferences for the alpha as well as flexible constraints on allocations. A sophisticated training and testing methodology has been described for the selection of model parameters. Extensive back testing results were reported and these have demonstrated the ability of the model to capture market upswings whilst not compromising the downside protection.

Hedge funds are clearly the future: not as a replacement to traditional investment techniques, but as an alternative investment tool. There is a growing consensus that the best hedge funds can deliver risk-adjusted returns that are superior to those from traditional "long only" strategies: they can augment a portfolio manager's risk adjusted returns because they are relatively uncorrelated with the returns from the traditional assets or funds in the portfolio. Transparency, liquidity and performance analytics offered by sophisticated on-line platforms will provide security for institutional investors to allocate in size. Indeed European pension funds, with less than 1% of their assets currently in hedge funds, are ready to more than quintuple their investment in alternative asset classes over the next three years. These developments will continue to fuel the growth in market neutral hedge fund strategies such as the one that has been described in this paper.

NOTES

1. TASS identifies 11 basic investment styles in hedge funds: Long/short Equity; Equity Market Neutral; Equity Trading; Event Driven; Convertible Arbitrage; Fixed Income Relative Value/Arbitrage; Global Macro; Short Sellers; Emerging Markets; Managed Futures; Funds of Funds.

2. Convex to the market means that if the market goes up by 10% the fund will increase by more than 10%; if the market goes down 10% the fund will decrease by less than 10%. In other words, the 'up market' beta is greater than the 'down market' beta; in fact the down market beta might even be negative. Convexity suggests market exposure, and indeed the empirical results described in this paper show that there is some degree of market exposure in certain years.

3. Every modern econometrics text covers the statistical theory necessary to master the practical application of cointegration, Hamilton (1994), Enders (1995) and Hendry (1996) being amongst the best sources.

4. A process is integrated of order 1 if it is not stationary, but becomes stationary after first differencing. Thus random walks are integrated of order 1, but not all I(1) series are random walk because there may be autocorrelation after first differencing.

5. Of course this example is very theoretical. It is unlikely cointegrated series will conform to this model in practice, but it useful for illustration.

6. This follows since $V(\Delta x) = \sigma^2 + 2\sigma_x^2$, $V(\Delta x) = \sigma^2 + 2\sigma_y^2$, and $COV(\Delta x, \Delta y) = \sigma^2$

7. The connection between these two methodologies is that a principal component analysis of cointegrated variables will yield the common stochastic trend as the first principal component. But the outputs of the two analyses differ: principal components gives two or three series which can be used to approximate a much larger set of series (such as the yield curve); cointegration gives all possible stationary linear combinations of a set of random walks. See Gouriereux et al. (1991).

8. Details of the extensive research in these areas are given, with many references, in Alexander (1999a, b and 2001).

9. In the case of tracking an index 'plus' alpha percent per annum, the dependent variable will be the log of the index 'plus' series (this is defined as the index price plus a small increment that amounts to alpha percent over the year).

10. Note the definition of 'tracking error' in this paper. Contrary to standard, but confusing, terminology, 'tracking error' here is *not* defined the variance or volatility of the difference between the portfolio and the benchmark.

11. Classical regression assumes the dependent and independent variables are stationary, so that the error term will be stationary by definition. However in a cointegrating regression the dependent and independent variables are integrated, therefore the error will only be stationary under special circumstances. Indeed, the error term will be stationary if and only if the dependent variable is cointegrated with the explanatory variables. Thus a statistical test for cointegration is to perform such a 'cointegrating regression' and then test the residuals for stationarity.

12. In fact the number of non-zero allocations need not be specified. Instead the number of assets chosen can depend on a bound that is set for the tracking error variance.

13. The 1% critical value of the ADF statistic is approximately –3.5, although much greater values than this are normally experienced in practice as for example in Table 3 and in Fig. 3d.

14. More information about the operation of this hedge fund strategy is available from www.pennoyercapital.com

15. The figures in Table 3 represent percentage turnover: that is, 1$ long in security X converted to 1$ short in the same security represents a 200% turnover.

16. The returns stated include transactions costs but no other fees. Daily closing prices on the S&P 100 stocks we taken from the University of Chicago Research in Securities Prices (CRISP) database. The prices were adjusted for splits, dividends and mergers.

17. While the data was correct with respect to stock splits and mergers, Pennoyer's analysis did not include dividend effects. BARRA's confirmation did, which most often resulted in slightly higher calculated returns from BARRA. Nonetheless, the difference was not significant.

REFERENCES

Alexander, C. O. (1999a). Optimal Hedging Using Cointegration. *Philosophical Transactions of the Royal Society, A357*, 2039–2058.

Alexander, C. O. (1999b). Cointegration and correlation in energy markets. In: *Managing Energy Price Risk* (2nd ed., Chap. 15, pp. 291–304). RISK Publications.

Alexander, C. O. (2001). *Market Models: A Guide to Financial Data Analysis*. John Wiley.

Alexander, C. O., & Johnson, A. (1992). Are foreign exchange markets really efficient? *Economics Letters, 40*, 449–453.

Alexander, C. O., & Johnson, A. (1994). Dynamic links. *RISK, 7*(2), 56–61.

Cerchi, M., & Havenner, A. (1988). Cointegration and stock prices. *Journal of Economic Dynamics and Control, 12*, 333–346.

Covey, T., & Bessler, D. A. (1992). Testing for Granger's full causality. *Review of Economics and Statistics*, 146–153.

Enders, W. (1995). *Applied Dynamic Econometrics*. John Wiley.

Engle, R. F., & Granger, C. W. J. (1987). Co-integration and error correction: representation, estimation, and testing. *Econometrica, 55*(2), 251–276.

Gourieroux, C., Monfort, A., & Renault, E. (1991). A general framework for factor models. *Institut National de la Statistique et des Etudes Economiques*, No. 9107.

Hamilton, J. D. (1994). *Time Series Analysis*. Princeton University Press.

Hendry, D. F. (1996). *Dynamic Econometrics*. Oxford University Press.

Pindyck, R. S., & Rothemberg, J. J. (1992). The comovement of stock prices. *Quarterly Journal of Economics*, 1073–1103.

Stock, J. H., & Watson, M. W. (1988). Testing for common trends. *Journal of the American Statistical Association, 83*(404), 1097–1107.

IMPROVING VALUE AT RISK FOR NON-NORMAL RETURN DISTRIBUTIONS

Doowoo Nam and Benton E. Gup

ABSTRACT

The non-normality of asset return distributions has been a stylized fact in the empirical finance literature. Fat-tailedness, in particular, can have significant impact on the accuracy in computing value at risk (VaR), which became popular from the mid-1990s as a primary measure of market risks arising from the trading activities of banks.

The primary purpose of this study is to develop a new VaR methodology to better handle skewness and fat-tailedness than the existing analytical VaR approaches, while at the same time being more flexible than the historical simulation approaches. The new approach adopts the g*-and-*h *distribution and, hence, it is named the* g*-and-*h *VaR method. The proposed methodology permits greater simplicity and flexibility in accommodating non-normality and combines the merits of the normal and the historical simulation methods.*

The empirical analysis is conducted using the interest and foreign exchange rate data. The backtesting results show that the g*-and-*h *VaR method significantly outperforms the normal method at the 99% or higher levels although the performance of both methods is equally satisfactory at the 95% confidence level.*

Financial Risk and Financial Risk Management, Volume 16, pages 91–116.

ISBN: 0-7623-0858-3

1. INTRODUCTION

There is no doubt that value at risk (VaR) has been one of the hottest research themes in finance since the mid-1990s. Its primary virtue of conceptual simplicity and practical attractiveness, which results from the capability of VaR to enable one to summarize various risks into a single number, thereby enhancing the communication of risk, has contributed to the surge in interest in VaR among banking institutions, non-bank financial institutions, supervisory authorities, and corporations alike. Hoppe (1999) described it as "VaR hysteria."

This proliferation of VaR as a risk measurement and management tool can be attributed, for the most part, to three factors (Hull & White, 1998). First, the development of VaR has been greatly facilitated since 1994 when J. P. Morgan introduced RiskMetrics,[1] a comprehensive VaR methodology for measuring market risk, and the database of daily volatilities and correlations for a variety of market risk factors freely available to the public who would intend to implement VaR systems based on RiskMetrics. Second, the decision of banking supervisory authorities to adopt VaR as a basis for estimating a bank's minimum regulatory capital served as a momentum for the banking industry to see the practical necessity of developing VaR frameworks. Prominent among the rules embodying those decisions are the European Union's Capital Adequacy Directive (CAD) agreed upon in 1993 (European Commission, 1993) and the 1996 Amendment to the Capital Accord of the Basle Committee on Banking Supervision (Basle Committee, 1996), both of which are intended to deal with market or price risks arising principally from banks' trading books. Subsequently, central banks throughout the world have implemented the Basle Amendment, including the Risk-Based Capital Standards set forth jointly by the U.S. federal bank regulatory agencies (Office of the Comptroller of the Currency, Board of Governors of the Federal Reserve System, and Federal Deposit Insurance Corporation, 1996).

Finally, a series of embarrassing derivatives disasters in recent years compelled all market participants to pay more keen attention than ever to accurate risk measurement as an essential prerequisite in order for any risk management system to be effective and sound. Such derivatives and other risk management disasters occurred in many organizations including a U.S. subsidiary of Metallgesellschaft due to the fall of oil prices in 1993, Orange County due to the hikes of interest rates in 1994, Barings Bank due to the precipitation of a Japanese stock index in 1995, Daiwa Bank in 1995 and Sumitomo Corporation in 1996 due to the accumulated losses for more than ten years by a rogue trader (Jorion, 1997; Dowd, 1998), and, more recently, Long-Term Capital Management,[2] to name but a few.

Indeed, the initiatives of both J. P. Morgan for developing its proprietary VaR methodology and the Basle Committee on Banking Supervision at the Bank for International Settlements (BIS) for requiring banks to establish minimum capital requirements based on VaR amounts calculated from their own internal models, which are subject to supervisory approval on the basis of some qualitative as well as quantitative criteria, can be regarded as the two most important factors contributing to the rapid development of various VaR methodologies (Lucas, 2000).

Despite much research effort having been devoted to VaR, there are still many issues to be resolved. From a methodological or theoretical standpoint, in particular, the most imperative area requiring further development and fineness is addressing an issue of non-normality, namely, asymmetry and fat-tailedness in asset returns. In the midst of his discussion at a symposium held in 1997, Alan Greenspan, Chairman of the Board of Governors of the Federal Reserve System, emphasized the importance of this issue in risk measurement and management by saying that "the biggest problem[s] we now have with the whole evaluation of risk is the fat-tail problem" (Federal Reserve Bank of Kansas City, 1997, p. 54). Danielsson and Morimoto (2000) also accentuated the need for incorporating non-normality into the risk measurement and management framework: "While normality may be a relatively innocuous assumption in many applications, in risk management it is disastrous, and the non-normality needs to be addressed" (p. 3).

The main problem of the normal VaR method is that it might seriously underestimate VaR in the presence of fatter tails than predicted by a normal distribution. Its main variant, the normal GARCH method, based on conditional volatility, achieved some degree of success, but the problem of fat-tailedness still remains, though it is mitigated, after modeling volatilities using GARCH. On the other hand, the historical simulation method has gained popularity in practice because it is free from the non-normality problem, but it has the limitation of requiring a large amount of data to ensure reliable VaR estimation.

The primary purpose of this study is to develop a new, alternative method of VaR estimation to better accommodate asymmetry and fat-tailedness, which are both stylized facts in the financial time series literature on asset returns, than the existing analytical VaR approaches, and at the same time to be more flexible than the historical simulation approaches. The new approach adopts the family of *g*-and-*h* distributions, which would permit greater simplicity and flexibility in embracing kurtosis as well as skewness than any other alternatives to a normal distribution. Indeed, the family of g-and-h distributions would provide the comprehensiveness in that it can model skewed distributions, fat-tailed distributions, or distributions exhibiting both characteristics. As will be seen later, the proposed approach combines the merits of both the normal VaR method and the historical simulation method.

The paper is organized as follows. Section 2 provides an overview of VaR and examines the merits and limitations of existing VaR methods. Section 3 proposes a new VaR approach, called the g-and-h VaR approach, while Section 4 performs the empirical analysis on our proposed VaR methodology. Section 5 concludes the paper.

2. OVERVIEW OF VaR

Financial decision making under uncertainty is necessarily beset with risk. Traditionally, the most popular measure of risk in modern finance is the standard deviation inherited from the study of Harry Markowitz on portfolio selection in the 1950s. However, one of the major limitations of standard deviation as a risk measure lies in its symmetry, which implies that favorable movements resulting in positive returns are viewed as having the same risk as unfavorable movements resulting in negative returns (Lucas, 2000). Therefore, the standard deviation of a portfolio does not provide a true risk exposure in that upside potentials and downside potentials are treated in the same manner.

To address the drawback of standard deviation as a risk measure, alternative measures have been suggested to consider only unfavorable movements or what is called downside risk. A downside risk measure receiving the most attention is VaR. VaR is defined as the maximum potential loss or adverse change in the value of a portfolio consisting of financial assets and/or commodities or of an individual asset in a specified time horizon (T) at a particular confidence level (CL) given that markets are in normal conditions:

$$\Pr[\Delta V \leq -VaR_{T,CL}] = 1 - CL. \tag{1}$$

Equation (1) provides the formal definition of VaR, and says that the probability of losses from adverse changes in value ($-\Delta V$) exceeding VaR is equal to 1 minus the confidence level specified. For example, a daily VaR estimate of \$1 million (i.e. $VaR_{1,0.99} = \$1$ million) for a portfolio at the 99% confidence level ($CL = 0.99$) implies that the daily losses of the portfolio will exceed \$1 million 1% of the time ($1 - CL = 0.01$; i.e. in only one day during

100 days). Equivalently, noting that the left-hand side of Eq. (1) is the definition of a cumulative distribution function, Eq. (1) can be expressed as:

$$F(-VaR_{T,CL}) = 1 - CL \tag{1$'$}$$

where $F(\cdot)$ is a cumulative distribution function of profits and losses.

Alternatively, using a quantile function or an inverse cumulative distribution function,[3] Eq. (1)′ can be written as:

$$VaR_{T,CL} = -F^{-1}(1 - CL) \tag{2}$$

where $F^{-1}(\cdot)$ is the inverse of a cumulative distribution function.

Many variants of VaR approaches have been proposed, but they are fundamentally classified into one of three classes:

(1) parametric, analytical, or variance-covariance methods;
(2) nonparametric, or historical simulation methods;
(3) Monte Carlo simulation methods.

In addition, as a fourth class, a new approach employing extreme value theory (EVT) to VaR estimation has recently received much interest. Increasing applications of the extreme value approach are mainly due to its notable advantage of reducing the statistical complexity by eliminating the need for estimating the whole distribution of asset returns and, hence, enabling us to better model the tail behavior of the distribution by focusing only on the tails, thereby leading to improvement in the precision of VaR estimation.

Overwhelming empirical evidence from studies evaluating various VaR models in terms of accuracy indicates that a single method does not dominate others on every aspect. The extent to which different models perform would depend critically on the choice of confidence levels (Hendricks, 1996). It should be noted that the influence of fat-tailedness on VaR would not be problematic at the 95% confidence level in general, but it can be serious at the 99% confidence level or higher (Minnich, 1998; De Raaji & Raunig, 1998).

Employing twelve variants of the variance-covariance and historical simulation VaR methods for the daily foreign exchange rate data, Hendricks (1996) concluded that all models seem appropriate at the 95% confidence level, but at the 99% confidence level only the historical simulation approach with a fairly long estimation period is accurate. The results suggest that tail fatness would pose a critical problem in estimating VaR at high confidence levels, say 99% or higher.

Applying three techniques, namely the variance-covariance, historical simulation, and extreme value methods, to the stock indices of the Netherlands and the U.S., Van den Goorbergh and Vlaar (1999) concluded that the VaR method based on a normal distribution performs quite satisfactorily at the 95% confidence level, and the property of fat-tailedness has to be reflected in modeling the return distributions for the 99% confidence level or higher. They also found that the historical simulation method is appropriate only with a substantially long estimation period and even in that case it underestimates VaR at the 95% confidence level. As regards the tail index technique based on extreme value theory, it fails at the 99% confidence level which is particularly important to banks for regulatory compliance and, in general, produces too conservative VaR estimates.[4]

Khindanova, Rachev, and Schwartz (1999) compared the performance of the stable Paretian distributions in VaR estimation with that of the normal method utilizing various foreign exchange rate and equity index data. The primary findings included that the normal method performs well at the 95% confidence level but underestimates VaR at the 99% confidence level due to the presence of fatter tails than expected by a normal distribution, while their stable method is more accurate at the 99% confidence level but at the 95% confidence level it underestimates VaR.

Empirical studies to date on various VaR models for different confidence levels seem to support De Raaji and Raunig's (1998) observation that "methods that do not incorporate excess kurtosis tend to underestimate VaR at the 99% confidence interval. On the other hand, the same methods tend to overestimate VaR at the 95% confidence interval" (p. 68). It is worth mentioning that the overestimation of VaR is undesirable as well in that it would result in more regulatory capital than necessary, implying the waste of shareholder wealth.

3. THE *g*-and-*h* VaR METHODOLOGY

3.1. Properties of the g-*and*-h *Distribution*

The *g*-and-*h* distribution can improve modeling the financial data that often exhibit non-normality by accounting for skewness and kurtosis. The *g*-and-*h* distribution is defined in terms of quantiles, and its statistical properties can be found in Hoaglin (1983, 1985), Martinez and Iglewicz (1984), MacGillivray and Balanda (1988), and MacGillivray (1992). The *g*-and-*h* distribution, which can be formed by two nonlinear transformations of the standard normal distribution, has two parameters to be estimated, namely, skewness and kurtosis (or elongation).

To define the *g*-and-*h* distribution, first let Y be a random variable, which is a function of a standard normal random variable (Z), that is, $Y = Y(Z)$ where

$Z \sim N(0,1)$. The random variable Y has the following distribution, named the g-and-h distribution:

$$Y_{g,h}(Z) = \left(\frac{\exp(gZ) - 1}{g}\right)\exp\left(\frac{hZ^2}{2}\right) \tag{3}$$

where the parameters g and h represent the degrees of skewness and kurtosis, respectively. In the right-hand side of Eq. (3), the first term, $\frac{\exp(gZ) - 1}{g}$, is called the g-distribution, denoted by $Y_g(Z)$, and accommodates skewness. The second term multiplied by Z, $Z\exp\left(\frac{hZ^2}{2}\right)$, is referred to as the h-distribution, $Y_h(Z)$, and accommodates kurtosis. Therefore, the g-distribution can be used to allow only for skewness, the h-distribution only for kurtosis, while the g-and-h distribution is used for both.

The distribution of Eq. (3) is location- and scale-free. To introduce the location and scale parameters, let X be a random variable created by a linear transformation of $Y_{g,h}(Z)$:

$$X = A + BY_{g,h}(Z) = A + B\left(\frac{\exp(gZ) - 1}{g}\right)\exp\left(\frac{hZ^2}{2}\right) \tag{4}$$

where A and B are the parameters for the location and scale, respectively. The result is that Eq. (4) has four parameters (location, scale, skewness, and kurtosis) that need to be estimated.

One of the major benefits of employing the g-and-h distribution when modeling empirical distributions lies in its greater flexibility in addressing a wider variety of properties of distributions (e.g. negative skewness, positive skewness, tail fatness, tail thinness, or a combination of any degrees of skewness and kurtosis) than other parametric distributions can provide. It nests or approximates a variety of theoretical distributions depending on the values of g and h (Martinez & Iglewicz, 1984). For example, it becomes the standard normal distribution when both g and h are zero (i.e. $Y_{0,0}(Z) = Z$), the lognormal distribution for $g = 1$ and $h = 0$ (i.e. $Y_{1,0}(Z) = \exp(Z) - 1$), and the Cauchy distribution for $g = 0$ and $h = 0.97$.[5] A positive (negative) value of h implies the fatter (thinner) tails of a distribution than the standard normal distribution (Badrinath & Chatterjee, 1991). The symmetric case with $h = 0$ (i.e. the standard normal distribution) defines neutral elongation, while the lognormal distribution is viewed as neutral elongation for the non-symmetric case with $h = 0$ (Hoaglin, 1985).

One convenient feature of the g-and-h distribution is obtaining the quantiles of the distribution from the quantiles of the standard normal distribution. Let z_p be the pth quantile of the standard normal distribution, and the pth quantile of the g-and-h distribution is given by:

$$Y_{g,h}(z_p) = y_p = \left(\frac{\exp(gz_p) - 1}{g} \right) \exp\left(\frac{hz_p^2}{2} \right). \tag{5}$$

For instance, when $g = 0$, the standard normal quantile ($h = 0$) at the 95% confidence level is 1.645, which changes to 0.836 and 3.236 for $h = -0.5$ and $h = 0.5$, respectively.

3.2. Procedures for Estimating Parameters

The estimation of parameters g and h can proceed in two ways. First, estimate the values of skewness and kurtosis. Then obtain the values of g and h by matching the estimates of skewness and kurtosis with the moments found from the moment generating function for the g-and-h distribution. Second, estimate the corresponding values of g by varying the quantiles (z_p). Then estimate h given the estimated value of g (Martinez & Iglewicz, 1984). All of these techniques can be used to fit empirical distributions as well as theoretical distributions.

Based on the second approach, the estimation procedure works with the entire order statistics for a small sample, and with the quantiles for a large sample (Hoaglin, 1983). For the latter case, the pth quantile of the random variable X is obtained using Eq. (4):

$$x_p = A + By_p \tag{6}$$

where $x_{0.5}$ is the median, which is an estimate of the location parameter A. The procedures of estimating other parameters, scale (B), skewness (g) and kurtosis (h), are discussed in Appendix.

3.3. VaR Based on the g-and-h Distribution

In this section, we develop a VaR estimation approach based on the g-and-h distribution, which is henceforth named the g-and-h VaR method. Given that all the four parameters are estimated, plugging the value of a standard normal quantile into Eq. (4) yields the quantile of the distribution. Therefore, a VaR estimate based on the *g*-and-*h* distribution is obtained, at a specified confidence level (*CL*), by

$$VaR_{CL} = -\left[A + B\left(\frac{\exp(gZ_{1-CL}) - 1}{g}\right)\exp\left(h\frac{Z_{1-CL}^2}{2}\right)\right] \tag{7}$$

where, in general, *CL* is set to 0.95 and 0.99 to calculate 95% and 99% VaRs, respectively.

In the *g*-and-*h* VaR method, a VaR estimate at a specified confidence level (*CL*) for one-day horizon can be obtained by Eq. (7). The estimation of VaR can be made for any confidence level, even for higher confidence levels than 99.9%, by varying *CL*. This flexibility is considered a clear advantage of the *g*-and-*h* method over the historical simulation method, which can address non-normality but has a limitation that VaR estimation for very high confidence levels will not be feasible unless the size of estimation window is very large.

For the non-normal financial data, it is expected that the VaR estimation method based on the *g*-and-*h* distribution would outperform the VaR methods based on the normal distribution, particularly, at higher confidence levels, owing to the capability of the *g*-and-*h* distribution to accommodate the non-normal behavior of financial asset returns. In addition, the method of fitting the quantiles of a distribution with letter values is always feasible, while other methods taking non-normality into account are not always feasible. For instance, the moment-matching methods that can address the non-normality utilizing the higher moments cannot be conducted in cases when those higher moments do not exist.

4. ESTIMATION OF VaR AND BACKTESTING

4.1. Data Description

The choice of the data sets used for our empirical analysis is primarily based on the level of significance in exposures to market risk factors arising from banks' trading activities, that is, in order of importance interest rate risk and foreign exchange rate risk. The data sets consist of the historical daily changes in the interest rates of the U.S. Treasury markets and the foreign exchange rates expressed in the price notation with the base currency of the U.S. dollar vis-à-vis currencies of some selective countries,[6] which, taken together, would, it is hoped, let us verify the veracity and the appropriateness of the *g*-and-*h* VaR methodology in different circumstances. The evaluation will be performed using in-sample as well as out-of-sample backtesting.

The historical data used in our VaR analysis are collected for the period of 1991–1998, which is divided into two sub-periods: the data for the period of 1991–1996 are used for VaR estimation; and the data for 1997 and 1998 are applied to backtesting. Therefore, the 1991–1996 period serves as the estimation or observation period for our empirical analysis, and the last two years (1997 and 1998) as the backtesting or evaluation period. The historical interest rate series, which are the secondary market yields on Treasury securities, are obtained from the H.15 Historical Data section of the Federal Reserve Statistical Release, and the historical foreign exchange rate series, which are expressed in the U.S. dollar against the foreign currencies, are collected from the database of the PACIFIC Exchange Rate Service.

The return distributions of Treasury securities can be obtained from the initial Treasury yield data in two steps: first, the Treasury price series are obtained by discounting cash flows with the corresponding yields; second, the returns are calculated by taking logarithm on Treasury price changes. The returns on foreign exchanges are also calculated by taking logarithm on exchange rate changes. In this way, the left tail of the return distributions consistently represents adverse changes in Treasury prices and foreign exchange rates.

The non-normality of the asset distributions can be seen in the summary statistics shown in Tables 1 and 2. Note that the odd moments (i.e. the mean and the skewness) of the Treasury return distributions in Table 1 have an opposite sign to the yield change distributions that are commonly used, but the even moments (i.e. the standard deviation and the kurtosis) are not affected. Treasury returns, or Treasury yields, exhibit significant excess kurtosis during the 1990s, which is common to all maturity ranges, with some skewness.

This significant non-normality of the Treasury markets seems due to the interest rate hikes in 1994. Year-by-year comparisons of excess kurtosis, however, reveal that the Treasury return series of 1992 and 1998 have very high degrees of excess kurtosis relative to other years. Only for 1-year Treasury bills does a high excess kurtosis value in 1994 affect the value of kurtosis of the entire sample upwardly. The European Rate Mechanism (ERM) crisis of 1992 and the Russian debacle and the collapse of Long-term Capital Management of 1998 are major factors in making the Treasury return distributions such highly leptokurtotic.

The descriptive statistics for the return distributions of currencies of nine G-10 countries in Table 2 also demonstrate the non-normality for all foreign exchange data examined though the extent of non-normality is varying from

Table 1. Summary Statistics for Treasury Return Distributions.

	Mean (%)	Standard Deviation (%)	Skewness	Kurtosis	AD Statistics	
3M T-Bill						
1991–1996	0.0002	0.0102	0.5005	7.6052	30.404	(0.00)
1991–1998	0.0003	0.0111	1.0337	12.9468	42.824	(0.00)
6M T-Bill						
1991–1996	0.0004	0.0211	0.4034	6.4719	27.841	(0.00)
1991–1998	0.0005	0.0211	0.7394	8.8406	37.931	(0.00)
1Y T-Bill						
1991–1996	0.0008	0.0499	− 0.1214	5.8686	19.661	(0.00)
1991–1998	0.0010	0.0481	0.1411	6.8651	30.021	(0.00)

Note: The *p*-values from the Anderson–Darling normality test are reported in parentheses. The numbers of observations included in the periods of 1991–1996 and 1997–1998 are 1,502 and 500, respectively.

currency to currency. As regards Table 2, several casual observations get our attention.

First, all exchange rates have the virtually zero mean returns, ranging from –0.0195% to 0.0104%, which seems to justify the convention of assuming the mean return of zero for daily data in calculating VaR. Another is that the mean returns are all negative except the Japanese yen.

Second, the Canadian dollar has significantly lower volatility than other currencies. That is, the standard deviation of the Canadian dollar is 0.2677% and 0.2872% for each period, while the standard deviations of all other currencies are in the range of 0.6052% to 0.7355%. It should be noted that the magnitude of the volatility is much larger than that of the mean for all currencies.

Third, the direction and degree of skewness differ from currency to currency: three currencies (Belgian franc, Japanese yen, and Dutch guilder) are positively skewed; four currencies (German mark, Italian lira, Swedish krona and British pound) are negatively skewed; two currencies (Canadian dollar and French franc) exhibit mixed signs.

Fourth, the currencies of all European G-10 countries except for the United Kingdom exhibit the lower degree of excess kurtosis in the whole period of 1991–1998 than in the estimation period of 1991–1996. This seems to be due to the impact of 1992 ERM crisis, and they have not experienced many extreme

Table 2. Summary Statistics for Foreign Exchange Return Distributions.

	Mean (%)	Deviation (%)	Skewness	Kurtosis	AD Statistics	
Belgium						
(Franc)						
1991–1996	− 0.0016	0.7052	0.0360	2.2367	9.503	(0.00)
1991–1998	− 0.0054	0.6798	0.0600	2.1504	10.690	(0.00)
Canada						
(Dollar)						
1991–1996	− 0.0108	0.2677	− 0.0554	2.7762	9.500	(0.00)
1991–1998	− 0.0136	0.2872	0.0238	3.2568	14.277	(0.00)
France						
(Franc)						
1991–1996	− 0.0011	0.6595	− 0.0325	1.9223	8.301	(0.00)
1991–1998	− 0.0045	0.6405	0.0265	1.7570	8.713	(0.00)
Germany						
(Mark)						
1991–1996	− 0.0018	0.7000	− 0.0915	2.0320	8.948	(0.00)
1991–1998	− 0.0053	0.6742	− 0.0325	1.9105	9.437	(0.00)
Italy						
(Lira)						
1991–1996	− 0.0195	0.7175	− 0.8459	6.0724	11.688	(0.00)
1991–1998	− 0.0188	0.7025	− 0.6235	5.0525	11.046	(0.00)
Japan						
(Yen)						
1991–1996	0.0104	0.6428	0.2621	3.4625	12.805	(0.00)
1991–1998	0.0090	0.7355	0.6792	5.3534	22.948	(0.00)
Netherlands						
(Guilder)						
1991–1996	− 0.0056	0.7085	0.0359	2.3245	9.067	(0.00)
1991–1998	− 0.0052	0.6805	0.0823	2.2296	10.141	(0.00)
Sweden						
(Krona)						
1991–1996	− 0.0125	0.7202	− 0.7460	7.2533	10.014	(0.00)
1991–1998	− 0.0180	0.7015	− 0.5327	6.3572	9.658	(0.00)
U.K.						
(Pound)						
1991–1996	− 0.0077	0.6369	–0.3508	2.9973	16.941	(0.00)
1991–1998	− 0.0073	0.6052	–0.3160	3.0325	19.322	(0.00)

Note: The p-values from the Anderson–Darling normality test are reported in parentheses.

movements in 1997 and 1998. Only the Japanese yen appears to be affected by the 1997 Asian crisis since its volatility and excess kurtosis values are significantly increased when the post-crisis data are included.

4.2. VaR Estimation Using the g-and-h Method

For the historical daily interest rate data of Treasury bill markets and the foreign exchange rate data for those nine countries mentioned previously, VaR estimates are calculated at the 95%, 99%, and 99.9% confidence levels, and then the estimates from the *g-and-h* method are compared with those from the analytical method based on a normal distribution. The evaluation will be made by means of counting the frequency of losses exceeding a VaR estimate (called exceptions or exceedances or failures), or equivalently computing the exception rate calculated as the ratio of the frequency of exceptions to the total number of observations in an evaluation sample, and then comparing it to the frequency or the exception rate expected from the data. For example, for an evaluation sample consisting of 500 data points the frequency exceeding a 99% VaR should be five or the exception rate should be 1%.

The backtesting is performed for the in-sample data of the estimation period (i.e. 1991–1996) as well as the out-of-sample data of the evaluation period (i.e. 1997–1998). The significance of backtesting results is examined using two-sided statistical tests, considering that both underestimation and overestimation are not desirable. To this end, we employ the likelihood ratio (LR) and the *Z*-score tests, which will be discussed later.

Table 3 presents the 95%, 99%, and 99.9% confidence level VaR estimates for the Treasury return data and the results from the in-sample backtesting. The data for the in-sample backtesting consist of the estimation sample which has 1,502 observations from 1991 through 1996. The number of exceptions, which is defined as losses exceeding VaRs, is counted and exception rates are calculated.

The accuracy of competing models from backtesting can be verified through statistical tests of significance. Given that either VaR overestimation or underestimation is equally undesirable from banks' perspectives, two-sided tests should be performed. For this purpose, the likelihood ratio (LR) test is widely used (Van den Goorbergh & Vlaar, 1999). In addition, we perform the *Z*-score test, which takes a positive statistic for underestimation and a negative statistic for overestimation. The LR and *Z*-score statistics are given as follows (Kupiec, 1995; Best, 1998):

Table 3. VaR Estimation and In-Sample Backtesting for Interest Rates.

Unit (bps)	*CL*	Normal VaR	No. of Exceptions	*g*-and-*h* VaR	No. of Exceptions
U.S. 3M T-Bill	95%	1.66	66 (4.4%)	1.59	66 (4.4%)
	99%	2.36	28 (1.9%)	2.93	15 (1.0%)
	99.9%	3.14	11 (0.7%)	4.55	1 (0.1%)
U.S. 6M T-Bill	95%	3.43	71 (4.7%)	3.28	71 (4.7%)
	99%	4.87	30 (2.0%)	6.02	15 (1.0%)
	99.9%	6.48	15 (1.0%)	9.49	2 (0.1%)
U.S. 1Y T-Bill	95%	8.12	64 (4.3%)	8.05	64 (4.3%)
	99%	11.52	29 (1.9%)	14.36	12 (0.8%)
	99.9%	15.33	10 (0.7%)	25.72	1 (0.1%)

Note: VaR figures are expressed in terms of basis points (bps). The estimation sample includes 1,502 observations from 1991 through 1996. The backtesting sample also consists of 1,502 observations, which means that the 5%, 1%, and 0.1% of the sample will be 75.1, 15, and 1.5, respectively. The percentages in parentheses are exception rates.

$$LR = 2\left[\ln\left(\frac{E}{N}\right)^{E}\left(1 - \frac{E}{N}\right)^{N-E} - \ln((1 - CL)^{E} CL^{N-E})\right] \tag{8}$$

$$Z\text{-score} = \frac{E - N(1 - CL)}{\sqrt{N(1 - CL)CL}} \tag{9}$$

where E represents the number of exceptions and N is the evaluation sample size. In general, the LR statistic has the chi-square distribution with degrees of freedom equal to the number of restrictions, which is 1 in our case,[7] and the Z-score statistic has the standard normal distribution.

Both tests are conducted for the in-sample Treasury return data, and the results are presented in Table 4.

As seen in the table, the normal VaR method is accepted only at the 95% confidence level, but is rejected for the higher confidence levels. The method is rejected more strongly as the confidence level specified in calculating gets higher. On the other hand, it can be seen that the g-and-h method produces very accurate VaR estimates for all confidence levels in which we are interested, in particular for the extreme tail region of below 1% (i.e. higher than the 99% confidence level). The method is accepted for all cases, and it should be noted

Table 4. Statistical Tests for In-Sample Backtesting Results.

	CL	Normal VaR		*g*-and-*h* VaR	
		LR Statistic	Z-Score	LR Statistic	Z-Score
U.S. 3M T-Bill	95%	1.208	− 1.077	1.208	− 1.077
	99%	9.032*	3.366*	0.000	− 0.005
	99.9%	24.868*	7.754*	0.191	− 0.410
U.S. 6M T-Bill	95%	0.240	− 0.485	0.240	− 0.485
	99%	11.700*	3.885*	0.000	− 0.005
	99.9%	42.163*	11.019*	0.150	0.407
U.S. 1Y T-Bill	95%	1.814	− 1.314	1.814	− 1.314
	99%	10.331*	3.625*	0.659	− 0.783
	99.9%	20.968*	6.937*	0.191	− 0.410

Note: The critical values for two-tailed testing are 3.842 for the likelihood ratio (LR) test and ± 1.96 for the *Z*-score test at the 95% level. * denotes the rejection of a method.

that the LR statistic and the absolute value of the *Z*-score statistic are very small for the high confidence levels of 99% and 99.9%. Hence, the results suggest that at the low confidence level of 95% both methods are equally appropriate, which implies that the normal method does not suffer from the problem of fat-tailedness, but for the high confidence levels of 99% and 99.9% we should take fat-tailedness into account and, therefore, the *g*-and-*h* method provides notable improvement in the accuracy in estimating VaR.

Table 5 presents results from the out-of-sample backtesting for the 1997 data,[8] and Table 6 shows results from testing the statistical significance of the backtesting results.

As seen in Table 5, both methods seem to perform equally well except for the normal method at the 99% confidence level for the 3-month Treasury.

Table 6 shows that the statistical significance tests on the out-of-sample backtesting give somewhat mixed results. The normal method is strongly rejected at the 99.9% confidence level for the 3-month Treasury, while both methods are marginally rejected at the 95% confidence level for both 6-month and 1-year Treasuries due to overestimation. Although too conservative estimation leads to the rejection of the methods, they will still be valid for the capital adequacy purpose since banking regulators are only concerned with underestimating VaR, which suggests that one-sided tests of significance should be used to discern models with underestimation. The term "n/c" in the

Table 5. VaRs and Out-of-Sample Backtesting for Treasury Returns.

Unit (bps)	*CL*	Normal VaR	No. of Exceptions	*g*-and-*h* VaR	No. of Exceptions
U.S. 3M T-Bill	95%	1.66	13 (5.2%)	1.59	13 (5.2%)
	99%	2.36	5 (2.0%)	2.93	2 (0.8%)
	99.9%	3.14	2 (0.8%)	4.55	0 (0.0%)
U.S. 6M T-Bill	95%	3.43	6 (2.4%)	3.28	6 (2.4%)
	99%	4.87	1 (0.4%)	6.02	0 (0.0%)
	99.9%	6.48	0 (0.0%)	9.49	0 (0.0%)
U.S. 1Y T-Bill	95%	8.12	4 (1.6%)	8.05	4 (1.6%)
	99%	11.52	0 (0.0%)	14.36	0 (0.0%)
	99.9%	15.33	0 (0.0%)	25.72	0 (0.0%)

Note: VaR figures are expressed in terms of basis points (bps). The estimation sample includes 1,502 observations from 1991 through 1996. The backtesting sample consists of 250 observations, which means that the 5%, 1%, and 0.1% of the sample will be 12.5, 2.5, and 0.3, respectively. The percentages in parentheses are exception rates.

Table 6. Statistical Tests for Out-of-Sample Backtesting Results.

	CL	Normal VaR		*g*-and-*h* VaR	
		LR Statistic	Z-Score	LR Statistic	Z-Score
U.S. 3M T-Bill	95%	0.017	0.130	0.017	0.130
	99%	1.937	1.580	0.113	− 0.324
	99.9%	4.816*	3.493*	n/c	− 0.501
U.S. 6M T-Bill	95%	4.423*	− 1.897	4.423*	− 1.897
	99%	1.189	− 0.958	n/c	− 1.592
	99.9%	n/c	− 0.501	n/c	− 0.501
U.S. 1Y T-Bill	95%	8.256*	− 2.476	8.256*	− 2.476
	99%	n/c	− 1.592	n/c	− 1.592
	99.9%	n/c	− 0.501	n/c	− 0.501

Note: The critical values for two-tailed testing are 3.842 for the likelihood ratio (LR) test and ± 1.96 for the *Z*-score test at the 95% level. * denotes the rejection of a method. The notation "n/c" stands for "not calculable," for there is zero exception, which results in the acceptance of a method.

table means not calculable, and indicates that the frequency of exceptions is zero, which suggests that a method be accepted.

Table 7 provides VaR estimates and in-sample backtesting results for the foreign exchange rate data. As with the Treasury return data, both methods appear to perform well at the 95% confidence level, but the *g*-and-*h* method clearly outperforms the normal method for the high confidence levels of 99% and 99.9%, which can be verified through the LR and *Z*-score tests. Specifically, the normal method produces the exception rate of 4.1%–5.1% at the 95% confidence level, but appears to significantly underestimate VaR with the exception rates of 1.6%–2.9% at the 99% level and of 0.5%–1.0% at the 99.9% level. In contrast, the exception rate of *g*-and-*h* method for each confidence level looks to be close to the percentage expected from the confidence level.

The significance of the backtesting results in Table 7 can be tested using the LR and *Z*-score tests. As can be seen in Table 8, the *g*-and-*h* method is accepted at all three confidence levels for all nine exchange rates, while the normal method is valid only at the 95% confidence level. It should be noted that the normal method is very strongly rejected for the 99% and 99.9% confidence levels. Therefore, we can again see that the fat-tailedness of financial asset return distributions is very problematic at extreme tails, and VaR methods based on a normal distribution would lead to the significant underestimation of VaR and thus will be inappropriate. As with the Treasury return data, the *g*-and-*h* method clearly outperforms the normal method for these extreme tail regions.

Next, we perform out-of-sample backtesting for the foreign exchange rate data of 1997 consisting of 251 daily observations, and statistical tests on the significance of the backtesting results. For the evaluation sample of 251 observations, we anticipate that the frequency of exceptions would be 12.5 (the exception rate of 5%), 2.5 (the exception rate of 1%), and 0.3 (the exception rate of 0.1%). The LR and *Z*-score tests are employed in statistical tests to determine whether a particular VaR method should be accepted or not. Models either with underestimation or with overestimation are rejected since both tests are basically two-tailed.

The results from the backtesting are provided in Table 9, which shows that at the 95% confidence level two cases have the number of exceedances greater than 12.5 for the normal method, and only one case for the *g*-and-*h* method, while for the higher confidence levels of 99% and 99.9%, three cases exceed the expected frequency for the normal method, and only one case at the 99% level and none at the 99.9% level for the *g*-and-*h* method.

Table 7. VaRs and In-Sample Backtesting for Foreign Exchanges.

Unit (%)	*CL*	Normal VaR	No. of Exceptions	*g*-and-*h* VaR	No. of Exceptions
Belgian Franc	95%	1.16	74 (4.8%)	1.15	77 (5.0%)
	99%	1.64	35 (2.3%)	1.97	15 (1.0%)
	99.9%	2.18	9 (0.6%)	2.69	3 (0.2%)
Canadian Dollar	95%	0.45	77 (5.0%)	0.46	70 (4.6%)
	99%	0.63	25 (1.6%)	0.80	14 (0.9%)
	99.9%	0.84	13 (0.8%)	1.23	1 (0.1%)
French Franc	95%	1.09	72 (4.7%)	1.08	72 (4.7%)
	99%	1.54	28 (2.8%)	1.85	17 (1.1%)
	99.9%	2.04	12 (0.8%)	2.56	3 (0.2%)
German Mark	95%	1.15	74 (4.8%)	1.16	74 (4.8%)
	99%	1.63	29 (1.9%)	2.00	16 (1.0%)
	99.9%	2.16	10 (0.7%)	2.91	2 (0.1%)
Italian Lira	95%	1.20	71 (4.6%)	1.16	72 (4.7%)
	99%	1.69	27 (1.8%)	2.04	18 (1.2%)
	99.9%	2.24	13 (0.8%)	4.02	3 (0.2%)
Japanese Yen	95%	1.05	63 (4.1%)	0.94	83 (5.4%)
	99%	1.49	24 (1.6%)	1.70	16 (1.0%)
	99.9%	1.98	9 (0.6%)	2.75	1 (0.1%)
Dutch Guilder (Netherlands)	95%	1.17	72 (4.7%)	1.13	77 (5.1%)
	99%	1.65	29 (2.9%)	1.98	17 (1.1%)
	99.9%	2.19	8 (0.5%)	2.96	1 (0.1%)
Swedish Krona	95%	1.20	73 (4.7%)	1.22	70 (4.6%)
	99%	1.69	27 (1.8%)	1.83	23 (1.5%)
	99.9%	2.24	8 (0.5%)	3.06	1 (0.1%)
U.K. Pound	95%	1.06	78 (5.1%)	1.09	73 (4.7%)
	99%	1.49	36 (2.3%)	1.97	15 (1.0%)
	99.9%	1.98	15 (1.0%)	2.89	1 (0.1%)

Note: VaR figures are expressed in terms of percent. The estimation sample includes 1,537 observations from 1991 through 1996. The backtesting sample consists of 1,537 observations, which means that the 5%, 1%, and 0.1% of the sample will be 76.9, 15.4, and 1.5, respectively. The percentages in parentheses are exception rates.

Table 10 reports the statistical significance of each method on the backtesting results. It shows that both normal and *g*-and-*h* methods perform equally satisfactorily for all confidence levels. Only two cases of failure occur:

the VaR estimate of the Japanese yen at the 99% confidence level for the normal method and the VaR estimate of the Swedish krona at the 95% level for the *g*-and-*h* method. The former involves underestimation, while the latter involves overestimation.

Table 8. Statistical Tests for In-Sample Backtesting Results.

	CL	Normal VaR		*g*-and-*h* VaR	
		LR Statistic	Z-Score	LR Statistic	Z-Score
Belgian Franc	95%	0.113	− 0.334	0.000	0.018
	99%	18.599*	5.032*	0.009	− 0.095
	99.9%	16.924*	6.023*	1.088	1.181
Canadian Dollar	95%	0.000	0.018	0.662	− 0.802
	99%	5.124*	2.469*	0.127	− 0.351
	99.9%	32.673*	9.251*	0.215	− 0.433
French Franc	95%	0.329	− 0.568	0.329	− 0.568
	99%	8.433*	3.238*	0.169	0.418
	99.9%	28.467*	8.444*	1.088	1.181
German Mark	95%	0.113	− 0.334	0.113	− 0.334
	99%	9.685*	3,494*	0.026	0.162
	99.9%	20.576*	6.830*	0.127	0.374
Italian Lira	95%	0.480	− 0.685	0.329	− 0.568
	99%	7.254*	2.981*	0.431	0.674
	99.9%	32.673*	9.251*	1.088	1.181
Japanese Yen	95%	2.792	− 1.621	0.505	0.720
	99%	4.180*	2.212*	0.026	0.162
	99.9%	16.923*	6.023*	0.215	− 0.433
Dutch Guilder (Netherlands)	95%	0.329	− 0.568	0.000	0.018
	99%	9.685*	3.494*	0.169	0.418
	99.9%	13.495*	5.216*	0.215	− 0.433
Swedish Krona	95%	0.206	− 0.451	0.662	− 0.802
	99%	7.254*	2.981*	3.320	1.956
	99.9%	13.495*	5.216*	0.215	− 0.433
U.K. Pound	95%	0.018	0.135	0.206	− 0.451
	99%	20.300*	5.289*	0.009	− 0.095
	99.9%	41.539*	10.865*	0.215	− 0.433

Note: The critical values for two-tailed testing are 3.842 for the likelihood ratio (LR) test and ± 1.96 for the *Z*-score test at the 95% level. * denotes the rejection of a method.

Table 9. VaRs and Out-of-Sample Backtesting for Foreign Exchanges.

Unit (%)	*CL*	Normal VaR	No. of Exceptions	*g*-and-*h* VaR	No. of Exceptions
Belgian Franc	95%	1.16	9 (3.6%)	1.15	9 (3.6%)
	99%	1.64	2 (0.8%)	1.97	1 (0.4%)
	99.9%	2.18	1 (0.4%)	2.69	0 (0.0%
Canadian Dollar	95%	0.45	13 (5.2%)	0.46	11 (4.4%)
	99%	0.63	1 (0.4%)	0.80	0 (0.0%)
	99.9%	0.84	0 (0.0%)	1.23	0 (0.0%)
French Franc	95%	1.09	7 (2.8%)	1.08	7 (2.8%)
	99%	1.54	3 (1.2%)	1.85	0 (0.0%)
	99.9%	2.04	0 (0.0%)	2.56	0 (0.0%)
German Mark	95%	1.15	9 (3.6%)	1.16	9 (3.6%)
	99%	1.63	2 (0.8%)	2.00	0 (0.0%)
	99.9%	2.16	0 (0.0%)	2.91	0 (0.0%)
Italian Lira	95%	1.20	11 (4.4%)	1.16	11 (4.4%)
	99%	1.69	1 (0.4%)	2.04	0 (0.0%)
	99.9%	2.24	0 (0.0%)	4.02	0 (0.0%)
Japanese Yen	95%	1.05	15 (6.0%)	0.94	18 (7.2%)
	99%	1.49	6 (2.4%)	1.70	4 (1.6%)
	99.9%	1.98	1 (0.4%)	2.75	0 (0.0%)
Dutch Guilder					
(Netherlands)	95%	1.17	7 (2.8%)	1.13	8 (3.2%)
	99%	1.65	0 (0.0%)	1.98	0 (0.0%)
	99.9%	2.19	0 (0.0%)	2.96	0 (0.0%)
Swedish Krona	95%	1.20	7 (2.8%)	1.22	5 (2.0%)
	99%	1.69	1 (0.4%)	1.83	0 (0.0%)
	99.9%	2.24	0 (0.0%)	3.06	0 (0.0%)
U.K. Pound	95%	1.06	7 (3.2%)	1.09	7 (2.8%)
	99%	1.49	3 (1.2%)	1.97	1 (0.4%)
	99.9%	1.98	1 (0.4%)	2.89	0 (0.0%)

Note: VaR figures are expressed in terms of percent. The estimation sample includes 1,537 observations from 1991 through 1996. The backtesting sample consists of 251 observations, which means that the 5%, 1%, and 0.1% of the sample will be 12.5, 2.5, and 0.3, respectively. The percentages in parentheses are exception rates.

Table 10. Statistical Tests for Out-of-Sample Backtesting Results.

	CL	Normal VaR		*g*-and-*h* VaR	
		LR Statistic	*Z*-Score	LR Statistic	*Z*-Score
Belgian Franc	95%	1.168	− 1.028	1.168	− 1.028
	99%	0.113	− 0.324	1.189	− 0.958
	99.9%	1.269	1.496	n/c	− 0.501
Canadian Dollar	95%	0.017	0.130	0.210	− 0.449
	99%	1.189	− 0.958	n/c	− 1.592
	99.9%	n/c	− 9.501	n/c	− 0.501
French Franc	95%	3.055	− 1.607	3.055	− 1.607
	99%	0.091	0.311	n/c	− 1.592
	99.9%	n/c	− 0.501	n/c	− 0.501
German Mark	95%	1.168	− 1.028	1.168	− 1.028
	99%	0.113	0.324	n/c	− 1.592
	99.9%	n/c	− 0.501	n/c	− 0.501
Italian Lira	95%	0.210	− 0.449	0.210	− 0.449
	99%	1.189	− 0.958	n/c	− 1.592
	99.9%	n/c	− 0.501	n/c	− 0.501
Japanese Yen	95%	0.475	0.710	2.209	1.578
	99%	3.527	2.214*	0.757	0.945
	99.9%	1.269	1.496	n/c	− 0.501
Dutch Guilder (Netherlands)	95%	3.055	− 1.607	1.982	− 1.318
	99%	n/c	− 1.592	n/c	− 1.592
	99.9%	n/c	− 0.501	n/c	− 0.501
Swedish Krona	95%	3.055	− 1.607	6.134*	− 2.187*
	99%	1.189	− 0.958	n/c	− 1.592
	99.9%	n/c	− 0.501	n/c	− 0.501
U.K. Pound	95%	3.055	− 1.607	3.055	− 1.607
	99%	0.091	0.311	1.189	− 0.958
	99.9%	1.269	1.496	n/c	− 0.501

Note: The critical values for two-tailed testing are 3.842 for the likelihood ratio (LR) test and ± 1.96 for the *Z*-score test at the 95% level. * denotes the rejection of a method. The notation "n/c" stands for "not calculable," for there is zero exception, which results in the acceptance of a method.

5. CONCLUSION

The non-normality of asset return distributions has been a stylized fact in the empirical finance literature. Fat-tailedness, in particular, can have significant impact on the accuracy in computing value at risk (VaR), which became popular from the mid-1990s as a primary measure of market risks arising from the trading activities of banks.

The normal VaR method might seriously underestimate VaR in the presence of fatter tails than predicted by a normal distribution. Its main variant, the normal GARCH method, based on conditional volatility, achieved some degree of success, but the problem of fat-tailedness still remains, though it is mitigated, after modeling volatilities using GARCH. On the other hand, the historical simulation method has gained popularity in practice because it is free from the non-normality problem, but it has the limitation of requiring a large amount of data to ensure reliable VaR estimation.

In this study, we develop a new VaR methodology to better handle skewness and fat-tailedness than the existing analytical VaR approaches, while at the same time being more flexible than the historical simulation approaches. The new approach adopts the *g*-and-*h* distribution and, hence, it is named the *g*-and-*h* VaR method. The proposed methodology permits greater simplicity and flexibility in accommodating non-normality and combines the merits of the normal and the historical simulation methods.

The empirical analysis is conducted using the interest and foreign exchange rate data. The results show that the *g*-and-*h* VaR method, in terms of the frequency of exceedances, significantly outperforms the normal method at the 99% or higher levels though the performance of both methods is equally satisfactory at the 95% confidence level.

NOTES

1. RiskMetrics, a registered trademark of J. P. Morgan & Co., rapidly became an industry standard. Its wide acceptance and the following success of a credit risk measurement methodology led RiskMetrics Group to emerge as an independent company through the spin-off from J. P. Morgan in September 1998.

2. The near-collapse of Long-Term Capital Management was due to several factors besides derivatives, and thus is not regarded as a derivatives disaster per se. It is, however, worth noting that the use of total-return swaps was a major contributing factor to the debacle.

3. A quantile function (QF) gives the value corresponding to a specified cumulative probability while a cumulative distribution function (CDF) provides the cumulative probability associated with a value of interest. The *p*th quantile (or percentile), denoted by q_p for $0 \leq p \leq 1$, is defined as a solution to $Q(p) = F^{-1}(p) = q_p$ where $Q(\cdot)$ and $F^{-1}(\cdot)$

are a QF and inverse CDF respectively, or, alternatively, as the smallest value q satisfying $F(q) \geq p$ where $F(\cdot)$ is a CDF (Mood, Graybill & Boes, 1974). For the simplest case, the 0.5th quantile, $q_{0.5}$, of a random variable or a distribution is its median.

4. Statistical significance of backtesting is verified via the use of a two-sided test developed by Kupiec (1995), instead of the one-sided test required by banking supervisory authorities. A two-sided test implies that models producing either too low or too high VaR estimates would be rejected.

5. In addition, for some pair of the values of g and h, the g-and-h distribution can approximate well such a variety of distributions as the uniform, the beta, the exponential, the Weibull, the Student-t, the logistic, and the double exponential distributions. See p. 363 of Martinez and Iglewicz (1984) for further details.

6. The foreign exchange rates chosen for our analysis include the currencies of the Group of Ten (G-10) countries, namely, the Belgian franc, the British pound, the Canadian dollar, the Dutch guilder, the French franc, the German mark, the Italian lira, the Japanese yen, the Swedish krona, and the U.S. dollar.

7. The only restriction is that the exception rate equals 1 minus the specified confidence level, that is, $\frac{E}{N} = (1 - CL)$, which is the null hypothesis for testing.

8. The use of the two-year out-of-sample data for 1997 and 1998 yielded similar results. Therefore, for the sake of avoiding redundancy, the results are not reported here. This also holds for the foreign exchange data.

REFERENCES

Badrinath, S. G., & Chatterjee, S. (1991). A Data-Analytic Look at Skewness and Elongation in Common-Stock-Return Distributions. *Journal of Business and Economic Statistics*, *9*(April), 223–233.

Basle Committee on Banking Supervision (1996). *Amendment to the Capital Accord to Incorporate Market Risks*. Bank for International Settlements, January.

Best, P. (1998). *Implementing Value at Risk*. Chichester, England: John Wiley & Sons.

Danielsson, J., & Morimoto, Y. (2000). Forecasting Extreme Financial Risk: A Critical Analysis of Practical Methods for the Japanese Market. Bank of Japan, IMES Discussion Paper Series, No. 2000-E-8, April.

De Raaji, G., & Raunig, B. (1998). A Comparison of Value at Risk Approaches and Their Implications for Regulators. *Focus on Austria*, *4* (Oesterreichische Nationalbank), 57–71.

Dowd, K. (1998). *Beyond Value at Risk*. Chichester, England: John Wiley & Sons.

European Commission (1993). *Directive on the Capital Adequacy of Investment Firms and Credit Institutions*. 93/6/EEC, European Union, March 15.

Federal Reserve Bank of Kansas City (1997). *1997 Symposium Proceedings: Maintaining Financial Stability in a Global Economy*.

Hendricks, D. (1996). Evaluation of Value-at-Risk Models Using Historical Data. *Economic Policy Review* (Federal Reserve Bank of New York), April, 39–69.

Hoaglin, D. C. (1983). g-and-h-Distributions. In: S. Kotz, N. L. Johnson & C. B. Read (Eds), *Encyclopedia of Statistical Sciences* (Vol. 3, pp. 298–301). New York: John Wiley & Sons.

Hoaglin, D. C. (1985). Summarizing Shape Numerically: The *g*-and-*h* Distributions. In: D. C. Hoaglin, F. Mosteller & J. W. Tukey (Eds), *Exploring Data Tables, Trends, and Shapes* (pp. 461–513). New York: John Wiley & Sons.

Hoppe, R. (1999). It's Time We Buried Value-at-Risk. *Risk Professional*, July/August, 14–17.

Hull, J. C., & White, A. (1998). Value at Risk When Daily Changes in Market Variables Are Not Normally Distributed. *Journal of Derivatives*, *5*(Spring), 9–19.

Jorion, P. (1997). *Value at Risk: The New Benchmark for Controlling Market Risk.* New York: McGraw-Hill.

Khindanova, I., Rachev, S., & Schwartz, E. (1999). Stable Modeling of Value at Risk. UCLA, Finance Working Paper, No. 7–99, May.

Kupiec, P. H. (1995). Techniques for Verifying the Accuracy of Risk Management Models. *Journal of Derivatives*, *2*(Winter), 73–84.

Lucas, A. (2000). A Note on Optimal Estimation From a Risk-Management Perspective Under Possibly Misspecified Tail Behavior. *Journal of Business & Economic Statistics*, *18*(January), 31–39.

MacGillivray, H. L. (1992). Shape Properties of the *g*-and-*h* and Johnson Families. *Communications in Statistics – Theory and Methods*, *21*(May), 1233–1250.

MacGillivray, H. L., & Balanda, K. P. (1988). The Relationships Between Skewness and Kurtosis. *Australian Journal of Statistics*, *30*(December), 319–337.

Martinez, J., & Iglewicz, B. (1984). Some Properties of the Tukey *g* and *h* Family of Distributions. *Communications in Statistics–Theory and Methods*, *13*(September), 353–369.

Minnich, M. (1998). A Primer on Value at Risk. In: F. J. Fabozzi (Ed.), *Perspectives on Interest Rate Risk Management for Money Managers and Traders* (pp. 39–50). New Hope, PA: Frank J. Fabozzi Associates.

Mood, A. M., Graybill, F. A., & Boes, D. C. (1974). *Introduction to the Theory of Statistics* (3rd ed.). New York: McGraw-Hill.

Office of the Comptroller of the Currency, Board of Governors of the Federal Reserve System, and Federal Deposit Insurance Corporation (1996). Risk-Based Capital Standards: Market Risk. *Federal Register*, *61*(September 6), 47357–47378.

Van den Goorbergh, R., & Vlaar, P. (1999). Value-at-Risk Analysis of Stock Returns: Historical Simulation, Variance Techniques or Tail Index Estimation? De Nederlandsche Bank, DNB Staff Report, No. 40.

APPENDIX

Procedure for Estimating the Parameters of the g-and-h Distribution

The skewness parameter g is estimated as the median of values of g_p, which can be calculated as:

$$g_p = -\frac{1}{z_p}\ln\left(\frac{x_{1-p} - x_{0.5}}{x_{0.5} - x_p}\right) \tag{A-1}$$

for $0 < p < 0.5$. For selecting the values of p or percentiles, the use of letter values is recommended, starting from M for the median, and halving the areas results in the fourths (F), and doing once more gives the eighths (E) (Hoaglin, 1985). In this manner, further halving the tail areas produces letter values of D, C, B, A, and so on.

Specifically, setting the median (the 0.5th percentile) of a distribution as a reference point, the letter values of F through W for the lower half and the upper half represent the corresponding percentiles as shown below:

Letter Values	Lower Half	Upper Half
F = 1/4	0.25	0.75
E = 1/8	0.125	0.875
D = 1/16	0.0625	0.9375
C = 1/32	0.0313	0.9687
B = 1/64	0.0156	0.9844
A = 1/128	0.0078	0.9922
Z = 1/256	0.0039	0.9961
Y = 1/512	0.00195	0.99805
X = 1/1024	0.00098	0.99902
W = 1/2048	0.0005	0.9995

A distance between the *p*th quantile and the median is referred to as the *p*th half-spread, which can be divided into two cases: for $p<0.5$, the distance between the median and the *p*th quantile (i.e. $x_{0.5}-x_p$) is called the *p*th lower half-spread (LHS), and the distance between the (1–*p*)th quantile and the median (i.e. $x_{1-p}-x_{0.5}$) is called the *p*th upper half-spread (UHS).

Given the estimate of the skewness parameter *g*, note that the *p*th letter spread $(x_{1-p}-x_p)$ of the *g*-and-*h* distribution is given by:

$$x_{1-p}-x_p=\frac{B}{g}[\exp(-gz_p)-1]\exp\left(\frac{hz_p^2}{2}\right). \qquad \text{(A-2)}$$

Multiplying Eq. (A-2) by $\dfrac{g}{\exp(-gz_p)-1}$ would abstract skewness from consideration:

$$\frac{g(x_{1-p}-x_p)}{\exp(-gz_p)-1}=B\exp\left(\frac{hz_p^2}{2}\right) \qquad \text{(A-2)}'$$

where the term on the left-hand side is called the corrected full spread (CFS).

Taking the logarithm of both sides, Eq. (A-2)′ becomes

$$\ln\left(\frac{g(x_{1-p}-x_p)}{\exp(-gz_p)-1}\right)=\ln B+h\,\frac{z_p^2}{2}. \tag{A-3}$$

It can be seen from Eq. (A-3) that an estimate of h is obtained as the slope coefficient in a regression of $\ln\left(\frac{g(x_{1-p}-x_p)}{\exp(-gz_p)-1}\right)$ against $\frac{z_p^2}{2}$, and the intercept gives the logarithm of an estimate of the scale parameter B.

EQUITY VOLATILITY TRADING STRATEGY IN TWO CLOSELY RELATED INDICES – A RISK MANAGEMENT PERSPECTIVE

Heinz R. Kubli and Walter Kemmsies

ABSTRACT

This paper investigates the potential and behaviour of profits of a trading strategy designed to gain from mean reversion in volatilities. The model allows for equity price and interest rate fluctuations, but excludes currency effects.

An important observation is that on average the profitability of such a trade is not revealed until 19% of the time horizon has been reached because of the possibility of lagged correlation effects. Risk managers need to be very cautious about busting positions before then.

INTRODUCTION

During the last decade investment management has changed dramatically in Europe. The introduction of the Euro reduced currency risk. Due to fewer currencies and regulatory efforts, country markets are more integrated than they were just a few years ago. Simultaneously, institutional investors have been switching from "top-down" country approaches in portfolio management, to "bottom-up" global sector-based approaches.

Financial Risk and Financial Risk Management, Volume 16, pages 117–135.

ISBN: 0-7623-0858-3

Corporate activity has also become more global. The number of multinational companies rose dramatically in the years leading up to the end of the 20th century. Cross border mergers and expanding investment have thus resulted in a situation where many companies' stock returns are better correlated within their industry on a global basis than with the equity index of the country where they are headquartered.

All these factors contribute to increasingly synchronised economic cycles across countries. In particular, convergence of:

(1) Companies earnings;
(2) Stock price returns; and
(3) Volatility.

In the last several years we have noticed that the volatility curves for the major equity market indexes are increasingly moving in tandem.

Also, the correlation between the return of European market indices has been increasing over the 20-year period starting in the late seventies.[1] Within this environment of convergence, the trading desks of investment banks and major institutional investors are taking on foreign exchange risk and correlation risk when they trade equities and equity options across borders.

In this paper we present an applied option trading strategy in closely related underlying assets where initial trades are based on implied volatility triggers. Our study attempts to model the risk/return profile of such volatility trades, which lead to more profitable hedging activities for the options involved. Understanding how the risks of such trading strategies are inter-twined is very important for risk managers.

ENVIRONMENT

For the purpose of this analysis, the implied volatility of Deutsche Aktien Index (DAX) options and the implied volatility of Swiss Market Index (SMI) options are compared. The set-up used, however, does not only apply to index options but also for options on single stocks, baskets and sectors, or any other highly correlated assets.

Exhibit 2 shows that DAX and SMI volatility mean reverts. Comparing a ratio of German volatility divided by Swiss volatilities over time illustrates that this ratio is mean-reverting, too.

This leaves the investor with a statistical arbitrage profit opportunity when trading the volatility spread. That means that in some market situations the volatilities of the closely related underlyings' returns diverge to an extent which is beyond or below an expected average volatility spread. These

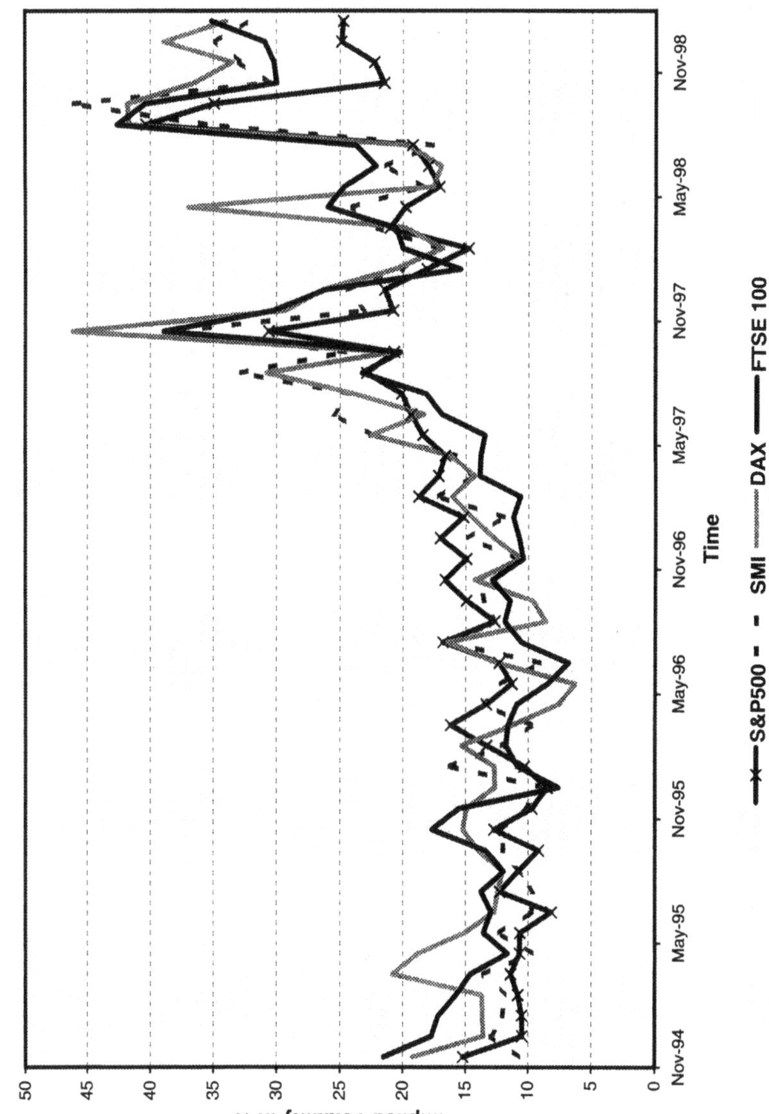

Exhibit 1. Volatility of Major Equity Indices.

Source: Author

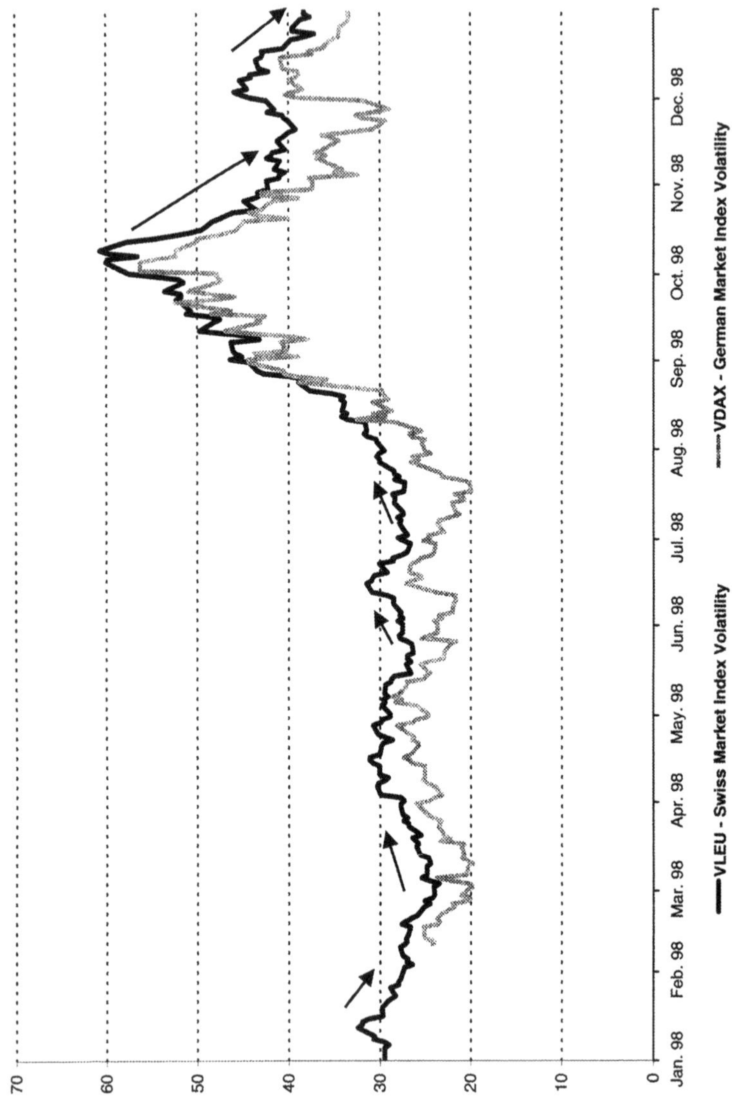

Source: Author

Exhibit 2. Mean Reversion of Volatility.

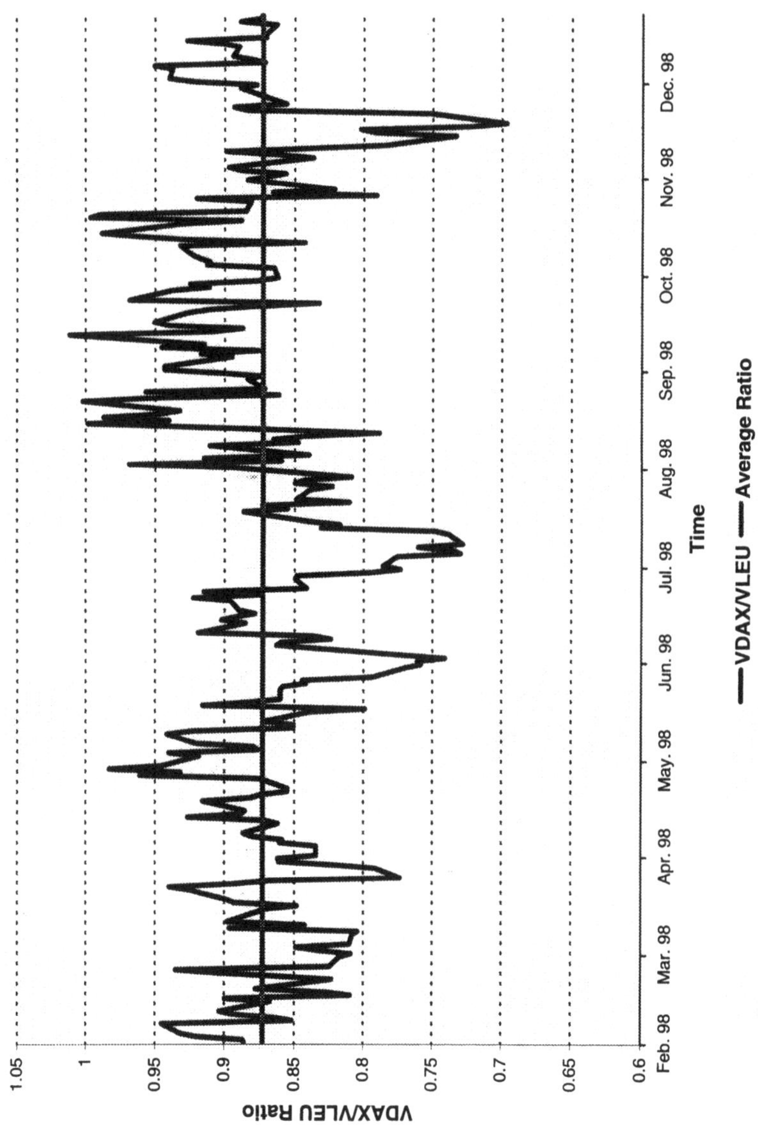

Exhibit 3. Mean Reversion of Volatility Ratio.

Source: Author

situations, present potential profit opportunities from selling and buying the volatility spread between the markets.

The main feature of this paper is a simulation of the returns to trades that seek to profit from temporary divergences in equity volatilities. The risks for such positions include, but are not limited to:

(1) currency fluctuations;
(2) interest rate movements;
(3) funding cost risks;
(4) hedging risk;
(5) pin risk.[2]

All of them have to be monitored in order to properly control and limit exposures.

Although currency risk is an issue in the simulated trading set-up involving German and Swiss equities, it would not be an issue for Euro zone member countries. Because we want to focus on improving the profits for a cross border/cross sector portfolio the presented model does not include foreign exchange changes. Inclusion of foreign exchange fluctuations makes it more difficult to derive insights from the already complex problems brought about by volatility and interest rate fluctuations.

Interest rate risk is modelled within the Hull/White (1990) framework. The model incorporates a time-dependent mean reversion level where the short rate is pulled to the mean level by a certain speed to mean reversion. Superimposed upon this "pull" is a normally distributed stochastic term. The volatility of the short rate is not dependent on the level of the interest rate.

The options are delta-hedged[3] with forwards in the simulation. The intention of delta hedging is to capture the volatility of both underlyings, while avoiding exposure to the underlyings' price movements. As forward trades do not have to be funded no funding costs for cash flows arise. However, they include credit risk, which is ignored here.

Pin risk is a situation where the underlying price is very close to the option strike price at expiry. This creates uncertainty for the option sellers about whether they will be assigned or not. For example, suppose we sold the 100 strike call and at expiry the market bid and ask prices are 99.50 and 99.75, respectively. Theoretically, the call is not an exercise. But if there is a broker fee greater than or equal to 0.25 and there is no broker fee on the purchase of shares via exercising the call, then even though the call technically is not in-the-money, it is still profitable to exercise the call if the owner of the call wishes to purchase shares. We have not modelled pin risks in this simulation.

SIMULATION SET-UP

The simulation set-up for the option trading strategies assumes:

(1) the Swiss Franc German Mark foreign exchange cross spot rate is fixed at CHF/DEM 0.81.
(2) Following the Hull/White (1990) model, interest rates for Germany and Switzerland are assumed to have a time dependent mean reversion level. A 2×2 Cholesky factorisation[4] is applied to determine the correlation between German and Swiss short-term interest rates.[5] Both volatilities of interest rate changes are constant. Interest rate changes are correlated with a correlation coefficient (rho) of 0.335. Interest rates are independent of other driving factors.
(3) For the Monte Carlo simulations the DAX, SMI, and the two volatility indices used for the calculation of option prices – the German volatility index (VDAX) and the Swiss volatility index (VLEU) – are linked in manner presented in exhibit 4. To implement the correlation in the random numbers of DAX, SMI, VDAX and VLEU, a 4×4 Cholesky matrix is applied.[6]

In the simulations, the correlation between the DAX and SMI was 0.65, between the DAX and VDAX 0.53, between the DAX and VLEU 0.17, between the SMI and VDAX 0.51, between the SMI and VLEU 0.19, and between the VDAX and VLEU 0.28.

The time series for the underlying indices, interest rates and volatilities have been simulated over 260 trading days. Whenever the trading rules were met over the course of this year, a pair trade was set up and is dynamically hedged until expiration. It is possible to set up more then one pair trade simultaneously, as long as they had different entry signals. The simulation of time series for the above factors was repeated for 547 trials.

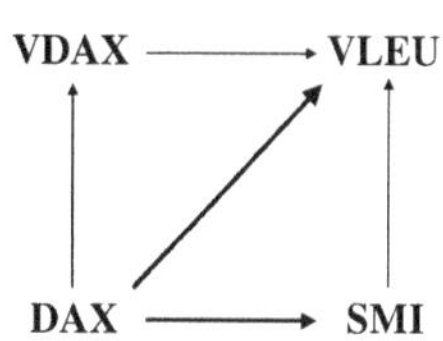

Source: Author

Exhibit 4. Interpendence in 4×4-Cholesky Matrix for Indices and Volatilities.

TRADING STRATEGY: THE FACTS

"Buy low/sell high" is an old adage. In the context of our analysis we mean buy one volatility low and sell the other high when the difference between them gets larger than approximately seven volatility percentage points or lower than approximately three volatility percentage points. When these volatilities have come apart or have come too close, it is assumed that within a reasonable time they will have to converge/revert to their previous relationship of an average difference of 4.5 volatility percentage points. The reason for doing the trade this way is that we hedge our exposure to rising volatilities. However, this is easier said than done – particular when it comes to managing the risks. Without further hedging effort the position quickly becomes exposed to equity market movements, foreign exchange movement, and interest rate movements.

There is another consideration for modelling the returns, which we have not considered here. Share prices and indices often move in response to country and industrial sector risk factors. Isolating these factors and their effect on returns is not a trivial matter, however, the rewards to doing so include more precise hedging. See Sefton and Kemmsies (2001) on how to disentangle these effects and use this to develop more accurate hedge ratios.

The DAX and SMI indices do not contain the same proportions of equivalent type stocks. Because the DAX contains more TMT (Technology, Media, and Telecommunication)[7] type companies than the SMI, and given the recent volatility of TMT company share prices, we would expect the DAX to be more volatile. But because of a higher number of companies included in the DAX compared to the SMI, the volatility index on the DAX tends to be lower due to diversification effect, which is why the ratio of VDAX to VLEU volatilities is usually less than one. Between February 10, 1998 and December 31, 1998 the VDAX/VLEU ratio traded in the range between 0.70 and 1.01.[8] The strategy analysed here involves buying and selling VLEU and VDAX volatility as they approach these extremes. The exact details are described in the following section.

TRADING STRATEGY: THE RULES

When a VDAX/VLEU ratio of 0.8 or lower occurs, we buy a 60-day[9] DAX option and sell a 60-day SMI option, each struck at the nearest at-the-money forward strike according to the EUREX strike price scheme. When a VDAX/VLEU ratio of 0.91 or larger occurs, we sell a 60-day DAX option and buy a 60-day SMI option, each struck at the nearest at-the-money forward strike.

If more then on of the same signals occur in a row, we only set up the trade at the moment of the first instance.

We re-hedge the options positions with the index forwards expiring on the same day as the index options.

MANAGING THE POSITION

We delta hedge the options with the index forwards on a daily basis. For the hedge, no cash flow is needed until unwind. For this hedging instrument there is no cash flow until the position is unwound or the expiry date.

EXAMPLE OF A TRADE AND HEDGES

Let's assume that the VDAX/VLEU ratio falls to 0.796, the DAX is at 3,592 and the SMI at 6,573. We buy a 60-day DAX call struck at 3,600 with a delta of 0.56 and we sell a 60-day SMI call struck at 6,600 with a delta of 0.52. For the DAX call we pay DEM133.8. For its hedge we sell 0.56 times the DAX forward price of DEM3613, which equals an amount of DEM2033.4. For the SMI call we receive CHF263.7 and buy an amount of 0.52 times the SMI forward price of CHF6583.7, which equals an amount of CHF3403.1, forward in 60 days. In the next step the DAX increases to 3637 and the SMI decreases to 6536.9. For the DAX call the delta increases to 0.62 and for the SMI call the delta decreases to 0.50. For the DAX call the new hedge trade multiples the delta difference between the initial trade and the next day of 0.06 times the new DAX forward price of DEM3657.8 resulting in an amount to sell forward of DEM206.7. For the SMI call an amount equal to the delta difference of 0.02 times the new SMI forward price of CHF6547, equal to CHF139.9, is sold forward.

If we were to bust the trade on the second day, with a DAX call price of DEM162.1 and an SMI call price of CHF245.5 at a constant exchange rate of CHF/DEM of 0.81, the total loss is DEM0.35 in forward terms.

SIMULATION INPUTS

In addition to the already mentioned input data the Swiss Franc (CHF) interest rate is 1%, the volatility of the interest rate changes is 6.2 basis points and the speed of mean reversion for the these rates used in the Hull/White model is 0.25.

The Deutsch Mark (DEM) interest rate is 3.5%, the volatility of the German interest rate changes is 0.98 basis points and the speed of mean reversion for these rates is 0.25.

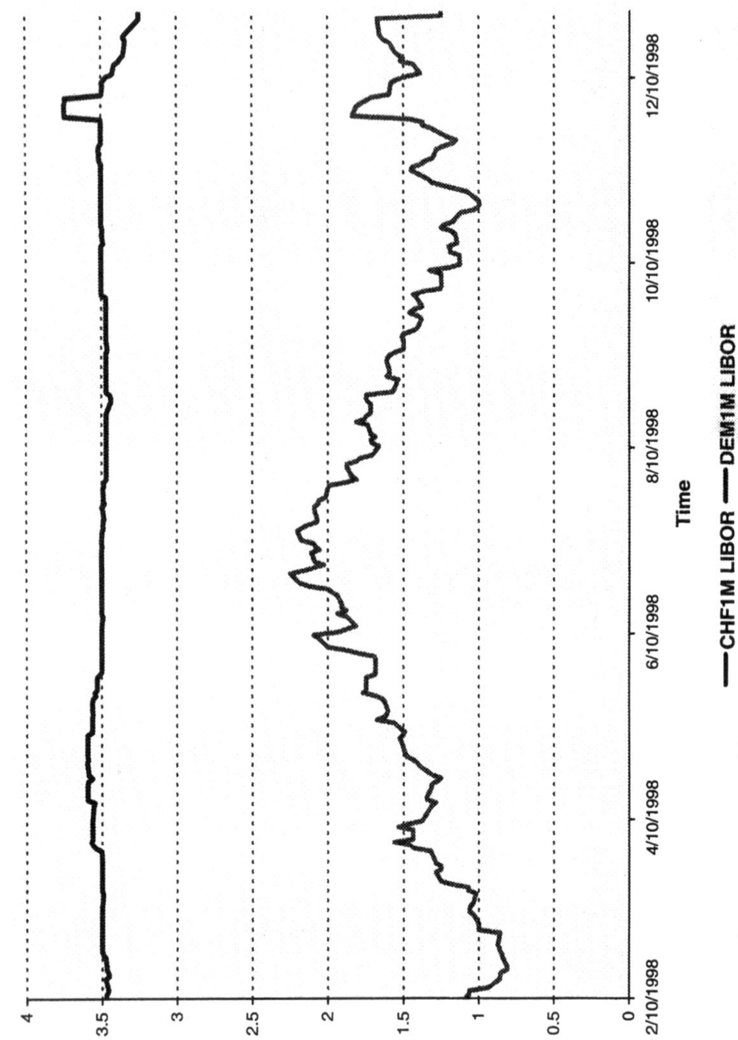

Exhibit 5. Interest Rates Over Time.

Source: Author

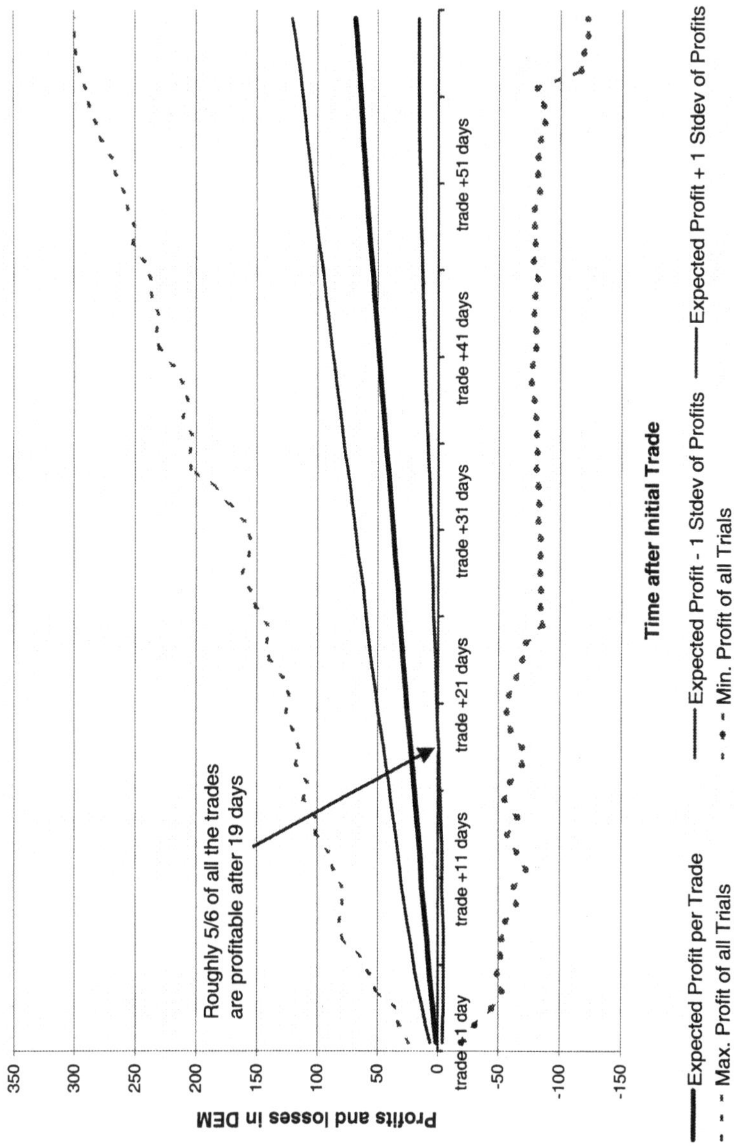

Source: Author

Exhibit 6. Profit and Loss.

PROFIT & LOSS

The results from the simulations in exhibit 6 show that profits from capturing the volatility gap between the two correlated assets increases over time and up to the expiration of the options after 60 days. Once the volatility ratio gets back to the targeted ratio level, the profit is not supposed to grow further. Of course, it could be that the volatility ratio further moves into a favourable direction towards the other extreme for the trades set up. But there is no statistical reason for holding the positions longer than to the day when the volatility ratio reaches the targeted level. This is because the VDAX/VLEU ratio is pulled towards the mean level when deviating from it, but there is no systematic "push away" from the mean level detected in practice nor modelled for the ratio.
Exhibit 7 shows typical patterns, if the underlying indices of both long and short calls are moving in tandem and are highly correlated with each other. But the high correlation is not persistent over time and high fluctuations in profit and losses of individual pair trades occur, as shown in exhibit 8.

For the correct set up of position management and risk control, the portfolio trader and risk manager have to know about the behaviour of these trades. There are certain effects observable in the simulated data series, which influence the outcome of risk management decisions. These effects may not be obvious.

EFFECTS OF MONEYNESS

One effect is the divergence of moneyness of the two calls, i.e. that the option characteristics of the long and the short call are not identical anymore after a certain time. Instead of both being at-the-money over the entire time period, the short call is getting either in-the-money or out-of-the-money, while the long call remains at-the-money. The time value wasted in the long at-the-money call cannot be made up with the lower absolute gains from the time value in the in-the-money call or an out-of-the-money call. The contrary is true, if the underlying of the long call is trending, while the short call's underlying remains at similar levels. Then, the time value profit in the short call would exceed the time value losses of the in-the-money or out-of-the-money long call.

EFFECTS OF DAILY HEDGING

Related to the trend in the short call's underlying position is the profit and loss from using daily rebalancing instead of continuous rebalancing in the hedging process. The trending index causes hedging errors[10] in the related options.

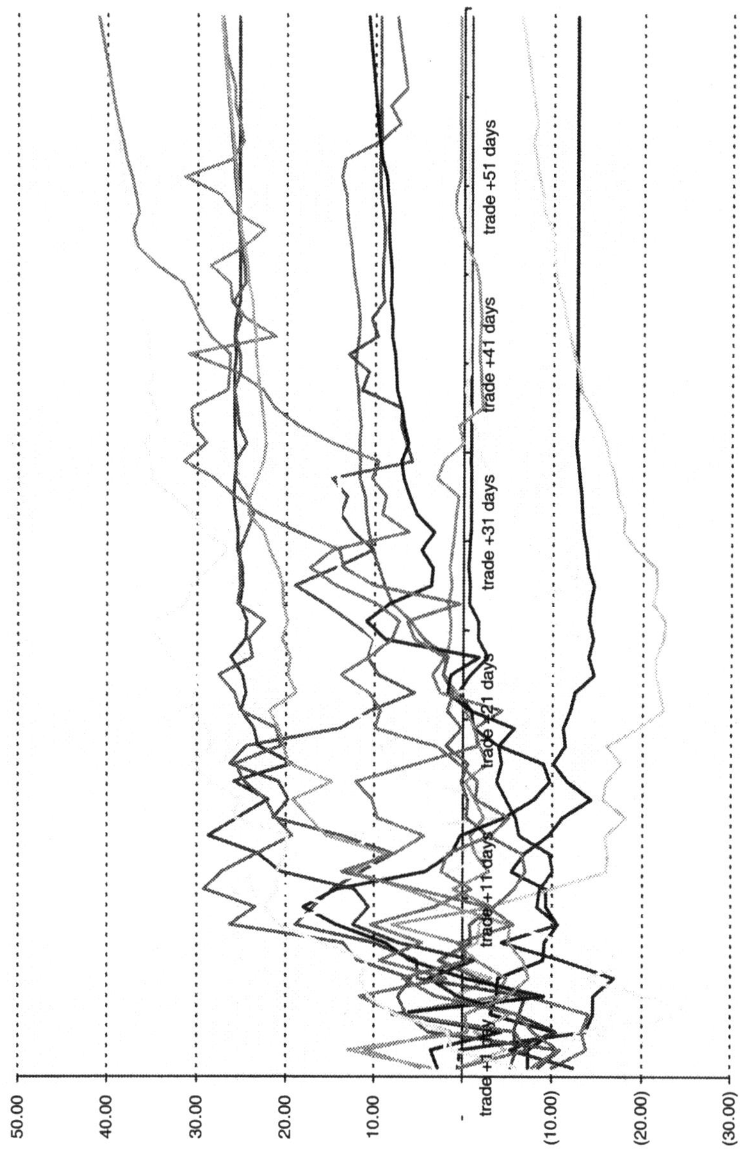

Source: Author

Exhibit 7. Typical Profit and Loss Petterns Over Time.

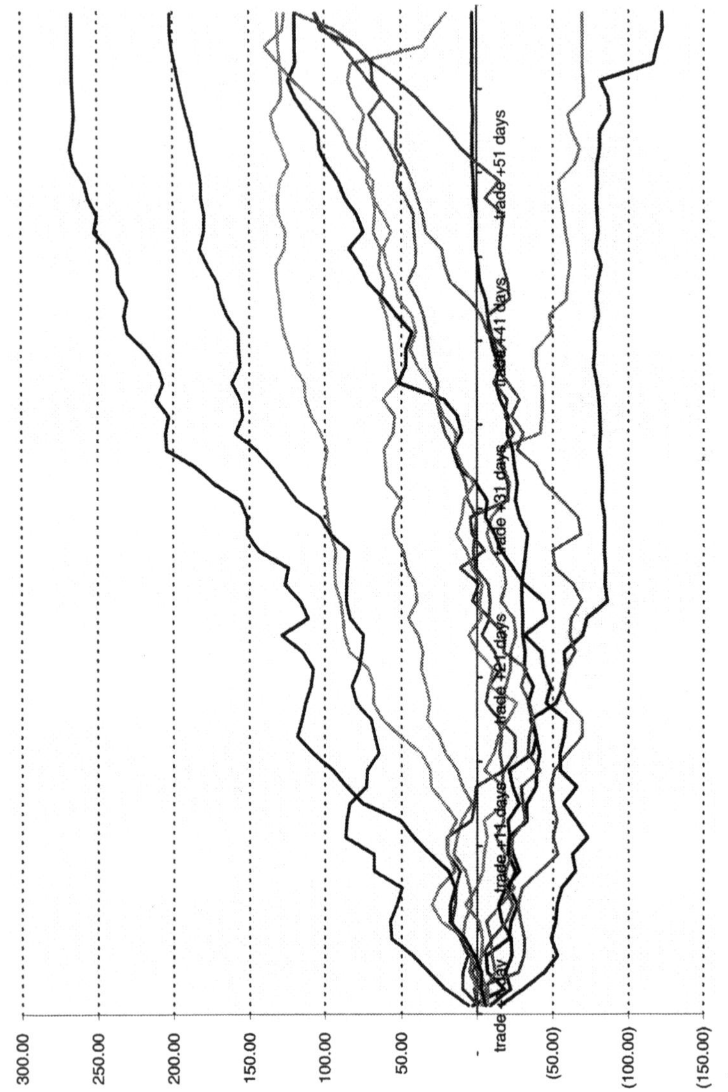

Source: Author

Exhibit 8. Typical Profit and Loss Patterns Over Time.

Assuming a large jump of an index, a short call position suffers from not being hedged sufficiently on the upside and being over-hedged on the downside. In order to rebalance the short call, the trader has to buy all forwards at a higher price compared to continuous hedging. This leads to losses.

If the underlying index of the short call is falling heavily, then the long position in forwards, is being readjusted at a lower price than it would be the case with continuous hedging. For the hedged long call option however, such large jumps increase profits.

On the upside the long call option increases faster than its hedge position. Forwards are therefore sold for a higher price than suggested in continuous hedging. On the downside the short position in forwards is adding value while the long call reduces its value to a lower extent.[11]

COMBINED EFFECTS

Trending markets for the long call option with the replication of the short call return profits from daily rehedging. It may also profit from time value effects in the options. A trending market for the short call option with a long call replication, however, leads to losses.

PREMATURE POSITION CLOSING

Over time, trends may not occur in both markets at the same time. Thus, with a large enough correlation of the underlyings, they should occur at similar times and decrease the risks of the presented trading strategy. Because some trend changes only occur with time lags, some trades may start off looking like losses, but then turn out to be profitable by expiry because of the time lag in the underlying trends. Pair trades that look profitable early on, may turn negative by expiration of the options. Thus, only at the expiration of the options can a clear picture on profits and losses be drawn. Unwinding pair trades during the life of the options may change the positive average outcome unfavourably.

If one trade is going seriously wrong during any partial period within the 60 days, it is not certain that the trade will end up losing money. A trade in the given set up may lose money when the underlying index of the short call is trending, while the underlying index of the long call remains at a constant level.

Notice that on average a trade indicates whether being profitable or not after 11.4 days, i.e. 19% of the time to maturity. Exhibit 6 shows that after 19 days roughly 5/6 of the distribution of the accumulated profits and losses is in the positive profit area.

This indicates that the downside risk on average is not as large as the upside potential.

Linearly increasing or decreasing the foreign exchange rate by 20% over the 60-day period of the pair trades as well as changing any other of the input variables does not significantly change the overall outcome of profits. The only requirement is that the trading strategy of buying low volatility and selling high volatility is followed strictly.

EXPECTED SHORTFALL

Exhibit 6 shows, that profits increase over time. Exhibit 9 indicates that the minimum expected shortfall is usually reached after approximately 53 days.

The expected shortfall calculates the number of losing trades on the ith day after the pair trade has been set up, divided by total number of trades on the ith day, on the basis of 547 trials. Losing trades are defined as trades with a negative net loss measured in Deutsch Marks.

The probability that a loss occurs decreases, as the trading strategy captures the volatility gap over time and the accumulated profits increase over time.

SUMMARY AND CONCLUSIONS

The largest risk for pair trades set up in order to capture the implied volatility gap of two closely related underlying assets, occurs when one of the underlying assets deviates from the strike price of the option, while the other does not. There is some profit potential if the underlying asset of the long call deviates from the strike price. On the contrary, there is a loss potential if the underlying asset of the short call deviates from the strike price, while the other asset's price remains at similar levels. The characteristics of time decay diverge and may shift expected profits down.

Large jumps in the underlying assets are preferable for the long call option being hedged with a dynamic short call replication. Jumps are critical in the underlying of the short call option, hedged with a dynamic long call replication.

Infinitesimal movements of the underlying assets, that remain on the same index levels as when the pair trades have been set up, do capture the volatility gap over time.

Like most market neutral trading strategies, volatility mean-reverting trades also have to be carefully monitored and the results interpreted with caution. Special focus must be given to the short call option and its dynamic hedge.

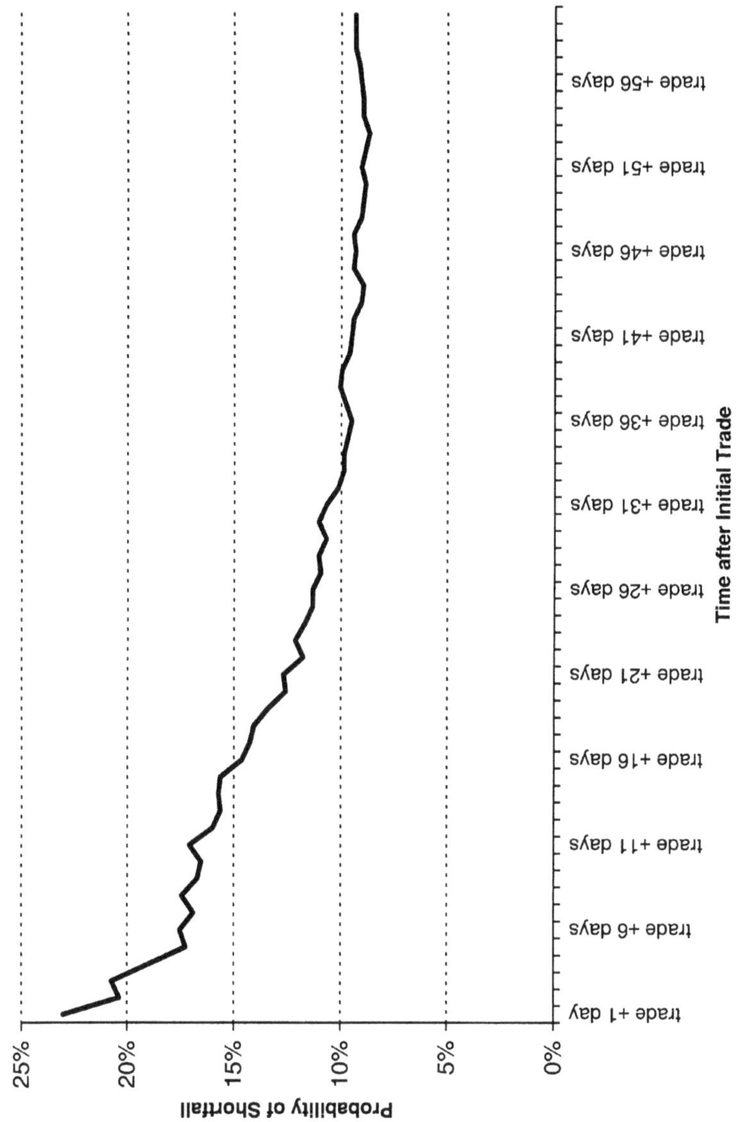

Source: Author

Exhibit 9. The Probability of Shortfall.

FURTHER ISSUES

One of the goals of this analysis is to improve hedging results in practice if specific country and sector hedges are applied[12] instead of hedging with the underlying asset. Further research is needed to determine whether it is possible to capture the volatility gap of two closely correlated underlying assets' prices by hedging one option position while dynamically replicating the second offsetting position.

The risk management process of the presented trades must focus on the short call option and its replication. Finding better trading rules for the management of the short call and its replication than described in this paper may lead to a substantial improvement of the results. From a practical point of view there may arise some implementation problems when using exchange-traded derivatives. These have to be studied before the implementation of such volatility trades. Also transaction costs may reduce the returns enough to make it unprofitable.

It has not been determined what happens when positions are rolled past the initial expiration date, i.e. if the volatility gap of the two underlying assets has not closed over the 60-day period during which the pair trades have been set up. An excellent generalization would be to allow the trades to be rolled forward if volatility reversion is too slow. Such assumptions are more realistic, but also could be deadly mistakes of a company, as illustrated by the analyses of well-known derivative disasters.

Pin risks should not change the picture very much, because the probability of getting pinned is relatively low and in the presented strategy we are dealing with repeated trades. But when getting pinned is imminent, it means that this one trade has to either be busted or rolled over immediately. Otherwise, the expected profit for the according pair trade may be given up.

Further research is needed to improve the accuracy of this and similar strategies' sensitivity to risk factors, in order to improve the process of risk-managing such trades.

NOTES

1. See Kubli (1998).
2. Pin risk is inherent in every model with options held to maturity. It is not modelled in the presented paper. Pin risk is the risk of an underlying being very close to the strike price near the expiry of the option, making it difficult to assess the likelihood of the option being exercised. This can be expensive if the trader has to buy the underlying for delivery, doesn't get assigned, and the price falls after the expiry date.
3. For an explanation of delta-hedging in length compare Kubli (2001), Chapter 6.

4. The Cholesky factorisation is briefly described in P. Wilmott (1998), pp. 682–683.
5. The Cholesky factorisation was suggested and explained to us by Dr. Xin Hai, UBS Warburg, Los Angeles.
6. By applying Cholesky factorisation a decomposition of the profit and loss of the trader to individual risk parameters is possible. We do not discuss the decomposition in this paper.
7. TMT refers to the Technology, Media, and Telecommunications sectors. During the time period studied in this analysis, the share prices of companies in these sectors were very volatile.
8. At the time when calculations have been proceeded for this paper, no longer time series have been available in both markets jointly.
9. Only trading days are counted.
10. For hedging errors compare Kubli (2001), chapters 6 to 9.
11. For the mathematical derivation of the explained hedge errors see Kubli (2001), pp. 49–50.
12. See Sefton and Kemmsies (2001).

REFERENCES

Kubli, H. R. (1998). Statistische Untersuchung zur Öffnung des schweizerischen Aktienmarktes. *Schweizerische Zeitschrift für Wirtschaftsrecht 5/1998*, 260–262.

Kubli, H. R. (2001). *Feedback effects from dynamic hedging on selected stocks – An empirical analysis in the Swiss stock market*. Bern: Paul Haupt Verlag.

Hull, J. C., & White, A. (1990). Pricing Interest Rate Derivative Securities. *Review of Financial Studies*, *3*(4), 573–592.

Sefton, J., & Kemmsies, W. (2001). Stripping out specific risk. *Risk*, (June), S12-3.

Wilmott, P. (1998). *Derivatives*. Chichester: John Wiley & Sons.

THE CHOICE OF FOREIGN EXCHANGE HEDGING TECHNIQUES: AN INTERNATIONAL STUDY

Robert Faff and Andrew P. Marshall

ABSTRACT

In this paper we consider an international comparison of the foreign exchange hedging practices of multinational companies in the USA, U.K. and Asia Pacific. Using the results of a survey we find that internal and external instruments are used primarily to manage specific types of risk and there were clear patterns in the use of hedging instruments. This was particularly the case in the use of complimentary internal instruments, especially in the USA. There were also clear regional differences in the emphasis on types of risk and the use of certain instruments to manage particular risks, indicating country specific factors could influence the use of hedging instruments. We then attempt to find financial characteristics that explain the emphasis on the main types of currency risk and use of distinct internal and external instruments. Using proxies of the theoretical relationships for hedging we found supporting evidence that the explanatory variables for liquidity, size and internationalisation exhibit discriminatory power for the emphasis on risk and the degree of utilisation of internal and external techniques. However, this evidence varied between the type of risk being managed, the particular instruments used and the different regions.

Financial Risk and Financial Risk Management, Volume 16, pages 137–172.

ISBN: 0-7623-0858-3

1. INTRODUCTION

Theoretical and empirical research on risk management and hedging has grown significantly since the 1980s. Nonetheless, many questions remain unanswered. One stream of this research has been the numerous empirical studies testing the theoretical explanations for risk management by examining the differences in financial characteristics between derivative users and non-users.[1] The findings of these studies have been mixed with conflicting results for the main theorised risk management hypotheses of effective corporate taxes (Smith & Stulz, 1985), financial distress (Smith & Stulz, 1985) and underinvestment (Froot et al., 1993). Extant research continues on this theme with use of new data sources[2] and refinements of the proxies of the theoretical relationships.[3] Rather than follow these approaches this study seeks to provide new insights into the hedging behaviour of multinational companies (MNCs) by trying to understand the choices made in the instruments used to hedge and the influences on the choice of individual hedging instruments rather than the overall hedging choice. We can do this by focusing explicitly on MNCs who actively hedge using internal and/or external hedging instruments.

Many of the previous empirical studies examining the reasons for hedging use a binary classification of companies as hedgers versus or non-hedgers based on derivative users versus non-users distinction. They have so far disregarded the possibility that companies may actively hedge their currency exposure by using one of the large number of internal hedging instruments. Companies therefore could be classified as non-hedgers as they do not use derivatives but actively hedge their currency risks by matching, netting, balance sheet hedging etc (see Beatty, 1999 for a discussion of this limitation).[4] There is considerable survey evidence that indicates firms use a wide range of internal techniques instead of or to complement an external hedging programme (see, Khoury & Chan, 1988; Marshall, 2000). The motivation for this paper is therefore an attempt to add to the empirical studies that have tested the theoretical reasons for corporate risk management by considering not just a general definition of derivatives use versus non-use but instead consider the use or non-use of a large number of specific internal and external instruments.

To get a broader view of hedging behaviour we gather our information by surveying the largest MNCs in three regions (U.K., USA and Asia Pacific). We also use more specific definitions of currency risk, including transaction and translation exposure, to see if hedging activities vary with the type of risk being hedged. There are two main aims of this paper: (i) to see if internal and/or external instruments are considered to have special characteristics such that they are used to manage certain types of foreign exchange risk and if there are any relationships between instruments; and (ii) to consider the theoretical reasons for hedging by testing the use of explicit hedging instruments and the financial characteristics of the user.

As yet only one empirical paper on the theories of hedging has considered the possibility that companies may not only hedge by using derivatives and considered a range of individual hedging instruments (Joseph, 2000). We add to Joseph (2000) in a number of ways including:

(i) a focus on companies that ex-ante have currency exposures. Previous research may have classified companies as non-hedgers despite the fact they have no currency exposure. In this study we consider only largest MNCs in each region as these companies are most likely be exposed to foreign exchange risk (Gezcy et al., 1997; Graham & Rogers, 2000 also take this approach).[5] In fact, all the MNCs in our sample hedge at least one form of foreign exchange exposure using internal and/or external instruments. The non-use of a hedging instrument in our sample can therefore be interpreted as a decision not to use the particular instrument rather than a lack of currency exposure.

(ii) an international comparison of foreign exchange hedging behaviour. Previous studies have considered the cross sectional results on one country (USA or U.K.), usually within an industry or across industries, but this is the first study to consider the decision to hedge across three regions using a simultaneous survey. There have been a number of comparative descriptive studies on the types of derivatives used and the corporate view of risk management and these have shown some similarities but also significant regional differences, see Marshall (2000).[6] Since we use the same questionnaire in three regions this study is not a mere comparison of the results but a comparable study. This is interesting, as it can potentially uncover alternative, country specific institutional factors that affect the hedging decision, not previously explored.

(iii) consideration of the emphasis on different types of currency risk. Previous studies on foreign exchange exposure have only considered total currency exposure. However, there are various types of currency exposure and companies place differing emphasis on these risks and use different techniques to manage them. For instance, Marshall (2000) has shown that firms place more emphasis on transaction exposure and therefore their use of hedging techniques may be related to the type of exposure they wish to hedge. Similar to Joseph (2000) we refine these studies by focusing on the individual types of foreign currency exposure and how these are hedged. However, from the questionnaire, for the first time we have a measure of the emphasis our sample place on the two main types of foreign exchange exposure that firms commonly face, transaction and translation, and relate this to their hedging behaviour. (Unlike Joseph, 2000 we do not consider economic exposure due to its long-term nature and the wide spread view that this exposure is difficult to hedge using the commonly available internal and external techniques, see Marshall, 2000 for a discussion of the views of MNCs on economic exposure and how they deal with it).

From an analysis of our responses we find that MNCs place most weight on transaction exposure in all regions but there was significant regional variation in the importance placed on translation exposure. We found significant evidence that certain internal and external instruments are used predominantly to manage translation or transaction exposure. However, there were also significant differences between the regions in the use of certain instruments with particular risks, for example there were significant regional variations in the use of internal methods to manage translation exposure. We also found distinct patterns in the use of some of the hedging instruments, especially external instruments to manage transaction exposure and internal instruments in managing translation exposure. Again, we found there were clear regional variations in this pattern of usage. In the second part of the study we attempted to explain the emphasis of the MNCs place on currency risk and degree of usage of internal and external instruments in terms of the financial characteristics predicted by theory. We discovered supporting evidence that some of the theoretical proxies had discriminatory power, however this varied between instruments and between regions. We found that MNCs with high levels of liquidity place least emphasis on translation and transaction exposure. Similarly, for the liquidity proxy there are significant negative relationships for some of the internal instruments used in managing transaction and translation exposure. Also, as predicted in theory, we found significant positive relationships between the use of a number of the internal and one external instrument for managing transaction exposure and the degree of internationalization. For the size proxy there were mixed results which is consistent with the ambiguous predictions from theory, for instance we found significant negative relationships with internal instruments and translation exposure, however there was a positive relationship with internal instruments and transaction exposure, highlighting the importance of consideration of different types of risk when considering the theories of hedging.

The paper is organised as follows, Section 2 provides information on the questionnaire and a detailed analysis of the relationships between the responses considering the importance on different types of currency risk and the use of various hedging methods. From this we attempt to gain an understanding of the overall hedging decision including the use of both internal and external instruments and the different types of currency risk. Section 3 describes the theoretical reasons for hedging, the proxies we employ in testing these theories in relation to our sample, descriptive characteristics of our sample and the methodology employed in the study. The results of this analysis are discussed in Section 4, where we link the emphasis on different types of currency risk, the use of internal and external hedging instruments to their financial characteristics. Conclusions are provided in Section 5.

2. QUESTIONNAIRE AND HEDGING RELATIONSHIPS FROM RESPONSES

2.1. Questionnaire

Despite some of the advances in the disclosure of risk management instruments in financial statements, these developments have not been at the same pace internationally. Also, these disclosures have focused almost exclusively on derivatives and not the internal methods of hedging. Consequently, to get a comparable view of risk management internationally, including information on internal hedging instruments it was decided that a survey approach was the optimal information source (a copy of the questionnaire is shown as Appendix 1). In July 1998 questionnaires were sent to the largest 200 U.K., USA and Asia Pacific MNCs (30 Australia, 30 Hong Kong, 100 Japanese and 40 Singapore). Responses arrived between July and September 1998 and the number of usable responses were 179, of which 79 were U.K., 47 USA, and 53 Asia Pacific (which consisted of 14 from Australia, 9 Hong Kong, 18 Japan and 12 Singapore, in general the responses of the Asia Pacific region were similar and we group the results together). The 30% overall response rate compares favourably with the previous studies in this area.[7] Tables 1 to 3 present the raw data from the questionnaires in terms of the emphasis on transaction and translation exposure and use of internal and external hedging techniques to manage these exposures. Regional differences on the extent of use of internal and external hedging instruments for the two types of risk and the emphasis on these risks are discussed in Marshall (2000) and we summarise the main findings here. Table 1 illustrates most MNCs in all regions placed most importance on transaction exposure, however there was a statistically significant regional difference on the degree of emphasis on translation exposure. Table 2 shows that almost all of the MNCs use external hedging instruments to manage transaction exposure and a very high proportion,

Table 1. Degree of Emphasis on Translation and Transaction Exposure by Region.

Exposure	Degree of emphasis		
	1–2 Number, (%)	3 Number, (%)	4–5 Number, (%)
Translation	Asia Pacific 9 (17%) U.K. 27 (34%) USA 29 (62%)	Asia Pacific 19 (36%) U.K. 21 (26%) USA 7 (15%)	Asia Pacific 25 (47%) U.K. 31 (40%) USA 11 (23%)
Transaction	Asia Pacific 3 (6%) U.K. 4 (5%) USA 4 (9%)	Asia Pacific 8 (15%) U.K. 10 (13%) USA 2 (4%)	Asia Pacific 42 (79%) U.K. 65 (82%) USA 41 (87%)

Responses taken from survey. Degree of emphasis measured on an ordinal scale from 1 (least important) to 5 (most important). USA (n = 47), U.K. (n = 79) and ASIA PACIFIC (n = 53).

Table 2. Internal and External Management of Transaction and Translation Exposure by Region.

	USA Number, (%)	U.K. Number, (%)	Asia Pacific Number, (%)
Internal methods used to manage transaction exposure			
YES	42 (89%)	65 (82%)	45 (86%)
NO	5 (11%)	14 (18%)	8 (14%)
External methods used to manage transaction exposure			
YES	46 (98%)	76 (96%)	51 (97%)
NO	1 (2%)	3 (4%)	2 (3%)
Internal methods used to manage translation exposure			
YES	27 (57%)	68 (86%)	49 (93%)
NO	20 (43%)	11 (14%)	4 (7%)
External methods used to manage translation exposure			
YES	21 (45%)	59 (75%)	20 (37%)
NO	26 (55%)	20 (25%)	33 (63%)

Responses taken from survey.

Table 3. Internal and External Instruments Used to Manage Translation and Transaction Exposure.

Internal Hedging Instrument	Region	Translation – Number (%)	Transaction – Number (%)
Netting	USA	11 (24%)	33 (70%)
	U.K.	21 (25%)	50 (62%)
	ASIA PACIFIC	13 (25%)	26 (49%)
Matching	USA	9 (19%)	22 (55%)
	U.K.	32 (39%)	42 (52%)
	ASIA PACIFIC	18 (34%)	26 (42%)
Leading and lagging	USA	3 (6%)	10 (21%)
	U.K.	2 (3%)	8 (10%)
	ASIA PACIFIC	2 (4%)	11 (21%)
Pricing policies	USA	9 (19%)	16 (34%)
	U.K.	1 (1%)	29 (35%)
	ASIA PACIFIC	6 (11%)	16 (30%)
Balance sheet hedging	U.S.	21 (45%)	10 (24%)
	U.K.	60 (72%)	9 (11%)
	ASIA PACIFIC	23 (43%)	12 (23%)
External Hedging Instruments			
Forward contracts	USA	13 (28%)	37 (79%)
	U.K.	34 (41%)	72 (89%)
	ASIA PACIFIC	19 (36%)	40 (75%)
Future contracts	USA	2 (4%)	3 (6%)
	U.K.	1 (1%)	2 (3%)
	ASIA PACIFIC	5 (9%)	10 (19%)
Options on currency future	USA	3 (6%)	2 (4%)
	U.K.	1 (1%)	4 (5%)
	ASIA PACIFIC	1 (2%)	5 (9%)
Currency options	USA	10 (21%)	28 (60%)
	U.K.	9 (11%)	40 (49%)
	ASIA PACIFIC	10 (19%)	17 (32%)
Currency swaps	USA	8 (17%)	22 (47%)
	U.K.	46 (56%)	28 (34%)
	ASIA PACIFIC	14 (26%)	25 (47%)

Responses taken from survey. Respondents can choose more than one method to reflect their overall hedging instrument use. USA (n = 47), U.K. (n = 79) and ASIA PACIFIC (n = 53).

averaging 85% between regions, use internal instruments. Clearly, many MNCs have hedging programs that encompass both methods to manage transaction exposure. There was less use of hedging instruments to manage translation exposure (although more than half use some hedging instrument). Reasons for this could include the difficulty in matching the maturity of the hedging instruments to the underlying translation exposure. Consequently, it is not surprising that the companies were more likely to use internal methods. Table 3 shows the range of instruments used for each exposure, showing the wide scale use of certain instruments to manage specific risks, for instance currency options for transaction exposure and balance sheet hedging for translation exposure. We formally investigate this more fully in Section 2.2. These results have similarities to Joseph (2000) in the emphasis on external instruments to manage transaction exposure but we find that our sample make a greater use of both internal and external instruments which is not surprising given our focus on MNCs with ex ante foreign exchange exposure and comparatively their larger size. In the next section we add to Marshall (2000) by considering for the first time the relationships between the emphasis of the two types of currency risk and the use of both internal and external hedging methods.

2.2. Hedging Relationships from Responses

We present some general results on the inter-relationships between the responses to our questionnaire considering three main questions:

(i) whether the emphasis the MNCs placed on transaction and translation exposure influenced their choice of instruments and the number of instruments used. For example, did MNCs that place most emphasis on these risks choose certain types of instruments or use more techniques. By investigating the number of instruments used we attempt to investigate whether there are economies of scale to running a hedging program. Previously, focusing exclusively on external instruments, Geczy et al. (1997) argue that the likelihood of using currency derivatives is positively affected by the use of other types of derivatives.

(ii) given the wide and extensive use of internal and external hedging instruments in our sample to manage transaction and translation exposure whether the MNCs perceive certain techniques to have distinct attributes such that they can only be used to hedge transaction or translation exposure. We therefore considered for each risk category the null hypothesis of no relationship within each type of instrument category and between the external and internal instruments. There is some evidence that the use of some hedging techniques are more appropriate to certain risks due to the short term nature of many external instruments in comparison to the long term nature of the risk and differences in the pay – off structures of the instruments and the underlying risks (see Joseph, 2000). In terms of the choice between external instruments the user must consider the costs involved with particular instruments including; liquidity costs, transaction costs of customisation and basis risk. Liquidity and transaction costs are greater for over the counter and long-term contracts but this reduces basis risk (Geczy et al., 1997).

(iii) the link between the utilisation rates of internal and external techniques in the management of transaction and translation exposure to determine whether there were any significant relationships between the sort of instruments used, for example are instruments complimentary such that the user of one specific internal or external instrument more likely to use another type of instrument or are they considered to be substitutes.

To test for statistical differences between the relationships from the above questions and between the different regions chi-square (χ^2) tests were used.[8]

2.2.1. Respondents' View of the Importance of Transaction and Translation Exposure and the Choice of Instrument

Tables 4 and 5 show the respondent's view of the importance of transaction and translation exposure and the choice of instrument for hedging this exposure. Table 4 shows that there were no significant relationships between the degree of emphasis on translation exposure and the use of internal and external instruments. However, the number of instruments used increased between the lowest degree of emphasis and the other two classifications, particularly for the USA MNCs and for external instruments, but there were no significant difference between these groupings.

From Table 5, there is an overall significant relationship between the degree of importance placed on transaction exposure and choice of external hedging instrument ($\chi^2(8) = 16.841$; ρ-value = 005), however the small numbers in the bottom two rankings mean that these results have to be treated with caution.[9] The widespread use of external hedging instruments in our sample is illustrated by the fact that even Asia Pacific and USA MNCs that ranked the transaction exposure as least important still frequently used forwards and currency swaps.

Table 4. Use of Hedging Instruments and Emphasis on Translation Exposure by Region.

Panel A – Internal Hedging Instruments – Translation Exposure, number (percentage)

Degree of Importance (rating 1 least to 5 most)	Netting	Matching	Leading and lagging	Pricing policies	Balance sheet hedging	Average number of instruments used
1 and 2						
Asia Pacific (n = 9)	3 (33)	1 (11)	0 (0)	3 (33)	3 (33)	1.1
U.K. (n = 27)	3 (11)	7 (26)	1 (4)	1 (4)	14 (27)	1.0
USA (n = 29)	5 (17)	5 (17)	1 (3)	4 (14)	9 (31)	0.8
3						
Asia Pacific (n = 19)	4 (21)	6 (31)	1 (5)	1 (5)	7 (37)	1.0
U.K. (n = 21)	6 (29)	10 (48)	0 (0)	0 (0)	18 (86)	1.6
USA (n = 7)	3 (43)	1 (14)	1 (14)	2 (29)	5 (72)	1.7
4 and 5						
Asia Pacific (n = 25)	6 (24)	11 (44)	1 (4)	2 (8)	13 (52)	1.3
U.K. (n = 31)	12 (39)	15 (48)	1 (3)	0 (0)	28 (90)	1.8
USA (n = 11)	3 (27)	3 (27)	1 (9)	3 (27)	7 (64)	1.6

Panel B – External Hedging Instruments – Translation Exposure, number (percentage)

Degree of importance (rating 1 least to 5 most)	Forward	Currency future	Options on currency future	Currency option	Currency swaps	Average number of instruments used
1 and 2						
Asia Pacific (n = 9)	1 (11)	1 (11)	0 (0)	0 (0)	0 (0)	0.2
U.K. (n = 27)	4 (15)	0 (0)	0 (0)	0 (0)	12 (44)	0.6
USA (n = 29)	5 (17)	1 (3)	1 (3)	3 (10)	3 (10)	0.4
3						
Asia Pacific (n = 9)	8 (89)	2 (22)	0 (0)	6 (67)	4 (44)	2.2
U.K. (n = 21)	13 (62)	1 (5)	1 (5)	2 (10)	16 (76)	1.6
USA (n = 7)	4 (57)	0 (0)	1 (14)	3 (42)	1 (14)	1.3
4 and 5						
Asia Pacific (n = 25)	10 (40)	2 (8)	1 (4)	4 (16)	10 (40)	1.1
U.K. (n = 31)	17 (55)	0 (0)	0 (0)	7 (23)	18 (58)	1.4
USA(n = 11)	4 (36)	1 (9)	1 (9)	4 (36)	4 (36)	1.3

Table 5. Use of Hedging Instruments and Emphasis on Transaction Exposure by Region.

Panel A – Internal Hedging Instruments – Transaction Exposure, number (percentage)

Degree of Importance (rating 1 least to 5 most)	Netting	Matching	Leading and lagging	Pricing policies	Balance sheet hedging	Average Number of Instruments Used
1 and 2						
Asia Pacific (n = 3)	1 (33)	1 (33)	0 (0)	1 (33)	0 (0)	1.0
U.K. (n = 4)	3 (75)	4 (100)	1 (25)	0 (0)	2 (50)	2.5
USA (n = 3)	1 (25)	2 (75)	0 (0)	1 (33)	2 (75)	2.0
3						
Asia Pacific (n = 8)	4 (50)	3 (38)	1 (13)	3 (38)	2 (25)	1.6
U.K. (n = 10)	6 (60)	5 (50)	0 (0)	2 (20)	1 (10)	1.4
USA (n = 2)	0 (0)	0 (0)	0 (0)	0 (0)	2 (100)	1.0
4 and 5						
Asia Pacific (n = 42)	21 (50)	22 (52)	10 (24)	12 (29)	10 (24)	1.8
U.K. (n = 65)	41 (63)	33 (51)	7 (11)	27 (42)	6 (9)	1.8
USA(n = 42)	32 (78)	20 (49)	10 (24)	15 (37)	8 (20)	2.0

Panel B – External Hedging Instruments – Transaction Exposure, number (percentage)

Degree of Importance (rating 1 least to 5 most)	Forward	Currency future	Options on currency future	Currency option	Currency swaps	Average Number of Instruments Used
1 and 2						
Asia Pacific (n = 3)	1 (33)	0 (0)	0 (0)	1 (33)	0 (0)	0.7
U.K. (n = 4)	2 (50)	0 (0)	0 (0)	1 (25)	1 (25)	1.0
USA (n = 3)	2 (67)	0 (0)	0 (0)	0 (0)	2 (67)	1.3
3						
Asia Pacific (n = 8)	6 (75)	5 (63)	2 (25)	2 (25)	3 (38)	2.3
U.K. (n = 10)	10 (100)	0 (0)	0 (0)	3 (30)	4 (40)	1.7
USA (n = 2)	1 (50)	1 (50)	0 (0)	0 (0)	0 (0)	1.0
4 and 5						
Asia Pacific (n = 42)	33 (79)	5 (12)	3 (7)	25 (60)	22 (53)	2.1
U.K. (n = 65)	60 (92)	2 (4)	4 (6)	36 (55)	23 (35)	1.9
USA (n = 42)	34 (83)	2 (5)	2 (5)	17 (40)	20 (48)	1.8

Responses taken from survey. Respondents can choose more than one method to reflect their overall hedging instrument use.

2.2.2. Hedging Exposures with Similar Methods

Internal instruments. The contingency Table 6 considers whether internal instruments are used primarily to manage specific types of risk. For example, do they have particular attributes that make them most appropriate for either transaction and translation exposure? The null hypothesis of no difference between the use of the instrument and the type of risk could be rejected in a number of cases. A number of the techniques such as netting and leading and lagging, are used primarily to manage the transaction risk. This is the case in all regions. However, there was significant regional variation in the use of pricing methods and the type of risk, as the null hypothesis could be rejected in U.K. and Asia, but not the USA. No U.K. MNCs used pricing policies for hedging translation exposure and few in Asia. However, almost half of USA respondents use pricing policies to manage translation exposure. This is evidence that country specific factors influence the hedging instrument choice as practice in the USA clearly favours using this method. We could reject the null hypothesis for matching for USA MNCs, who use it primarily for transaction exposure but there was no significant relationship for U.K. and Asia Pacific MNCs. There was no significant difference between the regions for matching.

In contrast to the other internal methods we found that balance sheet hedging is used primarily to hedge translation exposure in all regions. This was particularly true for the U.K. with 76% of MNCs using balance sheet hedging to hedge translation exposure with only 11% of these MNCs using this technique for hedging transaction exposure. This strong result for the U.K. causes a significant difference between the regions.

External instruments. Table 7 considers whether external techniques are perceived to have distinctive features such that they can only be used to hedge specific exposures. We found that forward contracts and currency options are used predominantly to hedge transaction exposure and the null hypothesis of no association can be rejected in all the regions (except the USA for currency options). There is no difference between the regions. The null hypothesis for currency swaps could be rejected in all regions, however unlike the other external instruments there is a significant difference between the regions in their use. U.K. MNCs stated that they primarily used currency swaps for hedging translation exposure (62%), which would seem to be consistent with matching the long-term nature of the risk with the maturities of the hedging instrument, while Asia Pacific (64%) and USA (73%) MNCs principally use currency swaps for hedging transaction exposure. The null hypothesis could

Table 6. Hedging Transaction and Translation Exposures with Internal Techniques.

Internal Instrument									
Netting	$\chi^2(1)$ C	Matching	$\chi^2(1)$ C	Leading and lagging	$\chi^2(1)$ C	Pricing policies	$\chi^2(1)$ C	Balance sheet hedging	$\chi^2(1)$ C
Asia Pacific (n = 30)	7.29***	Asia Pacific (n = 34)	2.69	Asia Pacific (n = 12)	7.20***	Asia Pacific (n = 19)	5.90**	Asia Pacific (n = 27)	5.44**
Translation only (4)	*0.39*	Translation (8)	*0.18*	Translation (1)	*0.39*	Translation (3)	*0.35*	Translation (15)	*0.33*
Transaction only (17)		Transaction (16)		Transaction (10)		Transaction (13)		Transaction (4)	
Both exposures (9)		Both exposures (10)		Both exposures (1)		Both exposures (3)		Both exposures (8)	
U.K. (n = 54)	21.51***	U.K. (n = 57)	2.54	U.K. (n = 9)	3.84*	U.K. (n = 29)	32.26***	U.K. (n = 63)	66.92***
Translation only (4)	*0.54*	Translation (15)	*0.24*	Translation (1)	*0.22*	Translation (0)	*0.64*	Translation (54)	*0.92*
Transaction only (33)		Transaction (25)		Transaction (7)		Transaction (28)		Transaction (3)	
Both exposures (17)		Both exposures (17)		Both exposures (1)		Both exposures (1)		Both exposures (6)	
USA (n = 37)	22.00***	USA (n = 25)	8.42***	USA (n = 11)	4.42**	USA (n = 21)	2.74	USA (n = 25)	6.02***
Translation only (4)	*0.71*	Translation (3)	*0.44*	Translation (1)	*0.32*	Translation (5)	*0.18*	Translation (15)	*0.37*
Transaction only (26)		Transaction (16)		Transaction (8)		Transaction (12)		Transaction (4)	
Both exposures (7)		Both exposures (6)		Both exposures (2)		Both exposures (4)		Both exposures (6)	
Difference between regions	2.64		3.31		0.59		12.01**		11.67**

We test for differences between the utilisation of internal hedging instruments in hedging translation and transaction exposure. The null hypothesis is no difference between degree of usage for each risk. The null hypothesis of no association is rejected for probability ρ-values less than or equal to 10%. The degrees of freedom for the χ^2 statistic is 1. We also test for difference between regions in use of the instruments for translation and transaction exposure. The null hypothesis of no association is rejected for probability ρ-values less than or equal to 10%. The degrees of freedom for the χ^2 statistic is 4. *** significant at 1% level, ** significant at 5% level and * significant at 10% level. The C value is the Crammer co-efficient which is a measure of the degree of association (see, Joseph, 2000).

Table 7. Hedging Transaction and Translation Exposures with External Techniques by Region.

External Instrument									
Forward	$\chi^2(1)$ C	Future	$\chi^2(1)$ C	Options on future	$\chi^2(1)$ C	Currency options	$\chi^2(1)$ C	Currency swaps	$\chi^2(1)$ C
Asia Pacific (n = 43)	19.39***	Asia Pacific (n = 12)	1.97	Asia Pacific (n = 5)	2.84*	Asia Pacific (n = 32)	14.11***	Asia Pacific (n = 30)	5.22**
Translation only (3)	*0.66*	Translation (2)		Translation (0)		Translation (4)		Translation (5)	
Transaction only (24)		Transaction (7)		Transaction (4)		Transaction (22)		Transaction (16)	
Both exposures (16)		Both exposures (3)		Both exposures (1)		Both exposures (6)		Both exposures (9)	
U.K. (n = 75)	41.39 ***	U.K. (n = 2)	0.34	U.K. (n = 4)	1.85	U.K. (n = 42)	28.43***	U.K. (n = 58)	8.23***
Translation only (3)	*0.72*	Translation (0)		Translation (0)		Translation (2)		Translation (30)	
Transaction only (41)		Transaction (1)		Transaction (3)		Transaction (33)		Transaction (12)	
Both exposures (31)		Both exposures (1)		Both exposures (1)		Both exposures (7)		Both exposures (16)	
USA (n = 40)	26.68 ***	USA (n = 5)	0.21	USA (n = 5)	0.21	USA (n = 23)	2.61	USA (n = 27)	9.91***
Translation only (3)	*0.78*	Translation (2)		Translation (3)		Translation (6)		Translation (5)	
Transaction only (27)		Transaction (3)		Transaction (2)		Transaction (13)		Transaction (19)	
Both exposures (10)		Both exposures (0)		Both exposures (0)		Both exposures (4)		Both exposures (3)	
Difference between regions	3.47		3.34		7.27		6.55		24.93***

We test for differences between the utilisation of external hedging instruments in hedging translation and transaction exposure. The null hypothesis is no difference between degree of usage for each risk. The null hypothesis of no association is rejected for probability ρ-values less than or equal to 10%. The degrees of freedom for the χ^2 statistic is 1. We also test for difference between regions in use of the instruments for translation and transaction exposure. The null hypothesis of no association is rejected for probability ρ-values less than or equal to 10%. The degrees of freedom for the χ^2 statistic is 4. *** significant at 1% level, ** significant at 5% level and * significant at 10% level. The C value is the Crammer co-efficient which is a measure of the degree of association (see, Joseph, 2000).

not be rejected for currency futures and the small numbers in this category limits the evidence on options on currency futures.

2.2.3. Hedging Currency Exposure with Different Techniques

Translation exposure. Given the mixed emphasis on translation exposure we were interested in any patterns in use of internal and external instruments. Table 3 shows that despite potential problems in matching the maturities of the external instrument to the underlying risk there was considerable use of external instruments. We found that Asia Pacific and U.K. MNCs who use currency futures are more likely to use options on currency futures (Asia $\chi^2(1) = 3.63$ ρ-value $= 0.08$ $C = 0.37$, U.K. $\chi^2(1) = 29.49$ ρr-value $= 0.00$). Expertise in using futures may develop into a use of other exchange-traded options. It should be noted that the numbers were small in this test. However, for the Asia Pacific sample, MNCs who use currency futures were unlikely to use currency swaps (Asia $\chi^2(1) = 4.91$ ρ-value $= 0.03$). This is unusual as these instruments could not be considered substitutes for each other given potential differences in their maturities and we are comparing a customised over the counter swap to an exchange-traded instrument.

In the analysis of the internal instruments the null hypothesis of no relationship between the uses of internal hedging instruments can be rejected for netting and leading and lagging for the U.K. and USA MNCs (U.K. $\chi^2(1) = 4.12$; ρ-value $= 0.04$ $C = 0.247$, U.K. $\chi^2(1) = 4.03$ ρ-value $= 0.04$; $C = 0.379$). For USA MNCs matching has also a significant relationship with leading and lagging (USA $\chi 2$ $(1) = 5.26$ ρ-value $= 0.03$; $C = 0.433$). This is consistent with our previous finding that these instruments are used primarily to manage translation exposure. It can also indicate the use of centralised cash management systems in the USA would develop expertise in the use of these internal methods. For USA MNCs there seems to be clear evidence of economies of scale in hedging activity.

In testing between internal and external instruments we found significant relationships in Asia Pacific MNCs for forwards and pricing policies ($\chi^2(1) = 3.84$ ρ-value $= 0.05$; $C = 0.345$), no user of forwards used pricing policies. These methods could be considered mutually exclusive as the certainty provided by either instrument would not require the use of the other (similar to Joseph, 2000 findings although we did not find any significant relationships for our U.K. sample). For USA MNCS there were significant relationships between the use of currency swaps and netting and leading and lagging, ($\chi^2(1) = 3.20$ ρ-value $= 0.08$; $C = 0.298$ and $\chi^2(1) = 3.42$ ρ-value $= 0.06$; $C = 256$, respectively). Users of swaps did not use leading and lagging and were also less likely to use netting. Although the time horizons of these techniques may differ given the differing views on the time horizon of translation risk these instruments may be considered substitutes for each other.

Transaction exposure. As we have demonstrated in Table 3 the MNCs in our sample hedge transaction exposure using primarily the external instruments of forwards, currency options and currency swaps but also a wide range of internal instruments, with netting and matching very popular. In testing relationships between external hedging instruments there is some evidence for both the U.K. and the USA sample that the MNCs that do not use forwards are more likely to use options on currency futures (U.K. $\chi^2(1) = 5.10$; ρ-value = 0.02; C = 0.26, USA $\chi^2(1) = 3.00$; ρ-value = 0.09; C = 0.27). Forwards are a comparatively low cost method for matching the payoffs of frequent transactions, however the pay-off profiles of the forward is different to the currency swaps. Therefore there is evidence that these instruments may be used in special circumstances, for example forwards provide certainty for transaction exposure but unlike the option does not allow for the MNCs to benefit from favourable movements. It was also interesting that their choice was for exchange-traded options as opposed to over the counter options, which may be due to differences in expertise or the premiums charged. There were no other significant relationships in the use of external instruments to manage transaction exposure.

For internal hedging instruments we found significant regional differences. The null hypothesis can be rejected for netting and leading and lagging for USA MNCs, where there is a significant relationship (USA $\chi^2(1) = 3.41$; ρ-value = 0.09). All the USA MNCs who use leading and lagging also use netting. Similarly, there was a significant relationship for USA MNCs between balance sheet hedging and leading and lagging, a sizeable percentage (60%) of users of balance sheet hedging use leading and lagging as opposed to 20% of non-users. Again, similar to the findings on internal instruments and translation exposure, this provides evidence that USA MNCs who manage transaction exposure tend to use complimentary hedging instruments to benefit from economies of scale, centralized cash management systems or expertise. There were no significant relationships the use of these internal instruments for U.K. and Asia Pacific MNCs and for all regions for the internal techniques of pricing and matching.

Joseph (2000) found significant relationships for U.K. companies between forwards and matching and two significant relationships for currency option, leading and lagging and pricing. We did not find any significant relationships in any region between internal and external instruments for transaction exposure. This may be due to the wider use of the various instruments in our sample due to the larger companies and the increased use of hedging instruments over time between the respective dates of the two surveys.

3. DETERMINANTS OF HEDGING INSTRUMENT USE

3.1. Introduction

In our second area of investigation of international hedging practices we focus on the relationships between hedging techniques and the characteristics of the respondent MNCs in attempt to isolate factors that influence the use of hedging instruments. Several theories of optimal hedging strategies offer us insight on the potential motives and benefits derived from hedging and a number of papers have considered these relationships. As mentioned previously most of these papers have dealt only with the external derivatives, focused on one country, the overall currency exposure and have produced varied results. Joseph (2000) is an exception and does consider internal hedging instruments. Unlike the other empirical papers he makes predictions for the use of both internal and external instruments for each of his risk types based on financial characteristics. His predictions are generalised as his questionnaire used the degree of usage of a specific instruments. He also argues that in general firms begin their hedging programme by using internal techniques and consequently the greater use of internal means less use of external. He also postulates a positive relationship with the financial proxies and internal hedging instruments but a negative relationship with external methods. It should also be noted that for his proxies Joseph (2000) uses variability measures of the financial variables based on the view that some hedging instruments are short term and may increase the variability of financial measures. We do not follow this approach as his predictions have problems for use in our sample as the previous sections indicate there is widespread use of both internal and external instruments. Some of the predictions are also inconsistent with previous theoretical arguments (see, Howton & Perfect, 1998) and the use of absolute rather than variability measures. We base our predictions on the majority of the empirical papers dealing with the general theories of hedging and not on specific internal or external instruments or type of risk as well as using absolute values.

Berkman and Bradbury (1996), Froot et al. (1993), Nance et al. (1993) and Howton and Perfect (1998) all provide comprehensive reviews of the theoretical determinants of hedging and the proxies for these detriments (good summaries are provided by Adam, 1999 and Graham & Rodgers, 2000). Since the theories are well established we provide only concise summaries. Due to the different regions financial data was obtained from a number of sources including Datastream and Global Access – Worldscope. We limited the number of proxies to the most widely used in the previous literature because of the difficulty of obtaining the required accounting information for MNCs in six countries. We focus on the main theories for explaining hedging in five groups: currency risk exposure, size, financial distress, liquidity and underinvestment. We do not consider the tax hypothesis of Smith and Stulz, (1985) due to the regional differences in tax treatment that mean that any proxy developed would have to be distinct to the region. In addition due to data restrictions we cannot include the managerial incentives theories as argued by DeMarzo and Duffie (1985). In the next section we define our financial variables implied by theory.

3.2. Corporate Hedging Theories

3.2.1. Currency Risk Exposure – Internationalisation Proxies

Mathur (1985) was one of the first to argue that there was a relationship between internationalisation and the extent of hedging, suggesting companies with higher levels of multinationality have greater risk and therefore receive superior benefits of hedging. Although our entire sample had some international business to measure the extent of internationalisation we use one binary proxy, which we have derived from the survey: (i) the percentage of overseas business of the MNCs (OVRBUS) and also a continuous variable; and (ii) five year average of foreign sales to total sales (FORSALES). These have similarities to the variables used by Howton and Perfect (1998) and Goldberg et al. (1998) and suggest a positive relationship between internationalisation and the use of hedging techniques.

3.2.2. Size

There are a number of explanations why size is associated with hedging, including; economies of scale, in the use of external hedging instruments and the ability to effectively use some of the internal hedging instruments is dependent on having a subsidiary companies trading throughout the world. Most of the previous research there has been a positive relationship between size and derivative use. For example, the log of sales was positively related to a firm's decision to hedge in Mian (1996) and Geczy et al. (1997). In contrast it has also been suggested a negative relationship is consistent with the extent of hedging increasing with information asymmetry and financial distress costs (Geczy et al., 1997). Consequently, we follow the previous research and make an ambiguous prediction for size proxy. To measure size, the following proxy is used: (i) log of five-year average of sales (LOGSALES).

3.2.3. Financial Distress

One of the commonly used theories of hedging is that it can reduce the potential for financial distress by reducing the variability of certain measures and improve debt terms or capacity. By tapering the distribution of company values, hedging can reduce the expected costs of financial distress. We follow Berkman and Bradbury (1996) and Howton and Perfect (1998) and use a leverage measure to capture the expected costs of financial distress and argue higher leverage ratios are associated with greater use of hedging instruments. To measure the degree of financial distress we use: (i) five year average of long-term borrowing to ordinary shareholders' equity and reserves (LTBOR).

3.2.4. Hedging Substitutes – Liquidity

Companies can reduce the probability of default by carrying more liquid assets. It has been suggested that there would be less use of hedging instruments if companies have substitutes for derivatives (Tufano, 1996; Geczy et al., 1997), such that more liquid companies have greater flexibility in meeting cash flow needs and thus they have less need to use these instruments. To measure the degree of liquidity we use two proxies: (i) five year average quick asset ratio: total current assets less stock and work in progress to total current liabilities (QAR); and (ii) five year average working capital ratio: total current assets/total current liabilities (WCR). Theory predicts a negative relationship between these proxies and the use of hedging instruments.

3.2.5. Underinvestment Problem

It has been argued that hedging reduces the probability that shareholders will find it beneficial to forgo valuable projects, commonly known as the underinvestment problem (Froot et al., 1993). Theory implies that the underinvestment problem is most severe for companies with valuable investment opportunities. The underinvestment problem is an increasing function of the growth options in the companies' investment opportunity set. We follow Nance et al. (1993), Gauy (1999) and Graham and Rodgers (2000) and postulate a negative relationship between our proxy for the level of growth options: (i) the five-year average ratio of the book value of the assets to the market value (BOOKMV) and the use of hedging instruments. This would indicate the importance of the underinvestment problem in the decision to use hedging instruments.

More details of the proxies are given in Appendix 2.

3.3. Data Description

One of the problems in using the different regions is that the largest MNCs in each region could still differ regionally in terms of our proxies of the theoretical hedging relationships. Table 8 shows the descriptive statistics for each financial proxy for each region and the numbers for the independent dummy variable. There was a significant difference in the size of the responding MNCs with

Table 8. Descriptive Statistics of Theoretical Proxies for the Regions.

Theoretical proxy – financial characteristics	USA **Mean** *Standard deviation*	U.K. **Mean** *Standard deviation*	Asia Pacific **Mean** *Standard deviation*
Internationalisation			
FORSALES	34.3	46.7	34.5
	17.9	*26.9*	*23.5*
Size			
TOTSALES	10,871,447	3,528,798	1,419,576
	3,234,581	*1,879,954*	*1,321,189*
Financial distress			
LTBOR	0.66	0.52	0.83
	1.29	*0.37*	*1.03*
Liquidity			
QAR	0.90	1.00	0.94
	0.38	*0.36*	*0.44*
WCR	1.25	1.39	1.27
	0.44	*0.46*	*0.49*
Underinvestment			
BOOKMV	4.68	6.26	2.23
	7.39	*27.94*	*1.51*
Theoretical proxy – dummy variable	USA **Number, %** 0 for 1–50%, 1 for 51–100%	U.K. **Number, %** 0 for 1–50%, 1 for 51–100%	Asia Pacific **Number, %** 0 for 1–50%, 1 for 51–100%
Internationalisation			
OVRBUS	0–40 (85%)	0–37 (48%)	0–37 (70%)
	1–7 (15%)	1–42 (52%)	1–16 (30%)

Information for the financial proxies obtained from Datastream and Worldscope. Information for the dummy variable obtained from the questionnaire.

unsurprisingly the USA MNCs being the largest. This is inevitable given the aim of the survey was to survey the 200 largest in each region. The U.K. MNCs are on average larger than the Asia Pacific MNCs, however there is a high standard deviation for the Asia Pacific MNCs, which is primarily due to some large Japanese MNCs in this sample. There is also a significant difference in the responding region and percentage of overseas business ($\chi^2(6) = 24.98$ ρ-value = 0.001). Despite the growing presence of USA MNCs in the world market, their revenues from their overseas business remain low compared with the revenues from home markets. Given their large single currency home markets, this was not surprising. The Asia Pacific MNCs have approximately the same levels of overseas business, as USA MNCs. U.K. MNCs appear to be the most reliant on overseas trade. The Asia Pacific MNCs had higher levels of leverage than the other regions and as widely reported U.K. MNCs have comparatively low leverage ratios. There was some variation in the proxy for growth opportunities as the book to market value ratios for U.K. MNCs were high but with the large standard deviation for these U.K. MNCs the differences between the regions was not statistically different. The five-year average for the liquidity ratios for all three regions were very similar.

3.4. Methodology

Due to the large number of possible bivariate tests between the users of any one of the ten instruments and non-users for each region of the three regions and each type of currency risk and to allow for interactions between the explanatory variables, we follow the approach of Nance et al. (1993) and others and estimate logistic regressions to distinguish among the potential explanations for hedging instruments use for our sample. The dependent variable indicating use of a particular internal or external instrument under each of the exposure type for the full sample and for each region is coded 0 if the instrument is not used and 1 if used. The independent variables are drawn from the theoretical papers on the decision to hedge as shown in the previous section. Despite using a number of information sources we had missing explanatory variables for 30 MNCs, producing a final sample for the logistic regression of 68 U.K., 42 Asia Pacific and 39 USA MNCs. Following the approach of Joseph (2000) we only carry out regressions for the models where at least 20% of the MNCs can be allocated to either group 0 or 1 of the dependent variable. We consider the results of the regression in three categories:

(i) the importance on translation and transaction exposure and the financial characteristics;

(ii) translation exposure hedging instruments and financial characteristics; and
(iii) transaction exposure hedging instruments and financial characteristics.

Due to the large number of regressions necessary for this analysis we present the results only where we have significant relationships.

4. EMPIRICAL RESULTS

4.1. Emphasis on Currency Risk and Financial Characteristics

Although our financial characteristic proxies are based on the theories of hedging we also decided to consider if they explain the weight the MNCs place on the different types of currency risk. Table 9 shows that for translation exposure there was significant negative relationship for one of the liquidity ratios for the whole and Asia Pacific samples. The strong results for the Asia Pacific sample are interesting given the strong weight MNCs in this region place on translation exposure. MNCs in Asia Pacific and for the full sample with high levels of liquidity place least importance on translation exposure. For the U.K. sample there was a significant relationship with the proxy for growth options but the sign was opposite to that predicted. The only significant relationship for the emphasis on transaction exposure was for the liquidity proxy for the full and U.K. samples. Again the higher the liquidity the less weight was placed on transaction exposure. Consequently, we have evidence to suggest that more liquid MNCs have greater flexibility in meeting cash flow needs and thus they place less importance on currency exposure.

4.2. Translation Exposure Hedging Instruments and Financial Characteristics

Unlike Joseph (2000), who finds no significant relationships for internal instruments and translation exposure, Table 10 panel A indicates that the independent proxies display some discriminatory power for the use of internal instruments and the financial characteristics. There are significant negative relationships for the size proxy and netting for U.K. and USA MNCs and balance sheet hedging for the full sample indicating less use of these instruments the larger the size of the MNCs. This would contradict the general findings of the previous evidence of a positive relationship between the size proxy and external derivative use. However, this is consistent with arguments that the smaller MNCs should hedge more because of the inverse relationship with size and bankruptcy costs and greater information asymmetries. Consistent with our findings on the emphasis on currency risk the table also shows that there was significant negative relationship for the liquidity ratios for matching and balance sheet hedging for the Asia Pacific and USA samples respectively. We have some significant results for our internationalization measures and the growth proxy, however the signs on the coefficients were

Table 9. Logistic Reegression for the Emphasis on Transaction and Translation Exposure and the Characteristics of the Firms.

Emphasis on *Translation* Exposure – **Full Sample**		Coefficient	Standard errors	p value
Independent variable	QUICK	−1.5627	0.9168	0.088*
	Constant	2.04	1.442	0.157
$N_0 = 97$, $N_1 = 52$				
Emphasis on *Translation* Exposure – **Asia Pacific Sample**				
Independent variable	QUICK	−0.5125	0.2668	0.055*
	Constant	0.145	2.359	0.952
$N_0 = 20$, $N_1 = 22$				
Emphasis on *Translation* Exposure – **U.K. Sample**				
Independent variable	BOOKMV	0.2467	0.1438	0.086*
	Constant	2.21	1.53	0.667
$N_0 = 45$, $N_1 = 23$				
Emphasis on *Transaction* Exposure – **Full Sample**				
Independent variable	QUICK	−0.2521	0.1231	0.023**
	Constant	1.382	1.931	0.474
$N_0 = 28$, $N_1 = 121$				
Emphasis on *Transaction* Exposure – **U.K. Sample**				
Independent variable	QUICK	−0.3953	0.2187	0.071*
	Constant	1.274	0.609	0.834
$N_0 = 13$, $N_1 = 55$				

A logistic regression was carried out between the dependent variable which was taken from responses from survey with the degree of emphasis measured on an ordinal scale from 1 (least important) to 5 (most important) and independent variable based on financial characteristics. The dummy variable was 0 for MNCs that rated their emphasis as 1 to 3 and 1 for a rating of 4 or 5. N_0 indicates the number who rated their emphasis as 1 to 3 and N_1 indicates the number who rated their emphasis 4 or 5. The independent variables are shown in Appendix 2. *** significant at 1% level, ** significant at 5% level and * significant at 10% level. No evidence was found that dubious large regression residuals had an adverse effect on the estimated coefficients.

Table 10. Logistic Regression for the Use of Internal and External Hedging Techniques for Translation Exposure and the Characteristics of the Firms.

Panel A – Internal instruments – translation exposure

Internal instruments *Netting* – **U.K. Sample**		Coefficient	Standard errors	p value
Independent variable	LOGSALES	–1.463	0.8577	0.088*
	Constant	0.5674	0.553	0.117
$N_0 = 53$, $N_1 = 15$				
Internal instruments				
Netting – **USA Sample**				
Independent variable	LOGSALES	–0.5245	0.2733	0.055*
	FORSALES	–0.069	0.04	0.084*
	Constant	0.3313	0.1817	0.068*
$N_0 = 29$, $N_1 = 10$				
Internal instruments				
Matching – **Full Sample**				
Independent variable	BOOKMV	–0.2219	0.0931	0.017**
	Constant	0.913	1.563	0.559
$N_0 = 104$, $N_1 = 45$				
Internal instruments				
Matching – **U.K. Sample**				
Independent variable	BOOKMV	0.2634	0.1359	0.053*
	Constant	–0.4291	0.5317	0.403
$N_0 = 45$, $N_1 = 23$				
Internal instruments				
Matching – **Asia Pacific Sample**				
Independent variable	WCR	–0.1108	0.5462	0.042**
	LTBOR	–0.1114	0.5301	0.036**
	BOOKMV	–1.155	0.5788	0.046**
	OVRBUS	–0.434	0.2025	0.032**
	Constant	0.6903	0.3758	0.066*
$N_0 = 27$, $N_1 = 15$				
Internal instruments				
Balance sheet hedging – **Full Sample**				
Independent variable	LOGSALES	–0.343	0.2028	0.093*
	Constant	1.307	1.461	0.371
$N_0 = 84$, $N_1 = 65$				
Internal instruments				
Balance sheet hedging – **USA Sample**				
Independent variable	QUICK	–0.5226	0.2617	0.046**
	Constant	1.95	0.115	0.865
$N_0 = 17$, $N_1 = 22$				
Internal instruments				
Balance sheet hedging – **Asia Pacific Sample**				
Independent variable	FORSALES	0.042	0.0194	0.03**
	Constant	0.361	2.298	0.875
$N_0 = 21$, $N_1 = 21$				

Table 10. Continued.

Panel B – External instruments – translation exposure

External instruments *Forward* – **Full Sample**		Coefficient	Standard errors	p value
Independent variable	LTBOR	–0.3173	0.1865	0.089*
	Constant	–0.042	1.585	0.979
$N_0 = 53$, $N_1 = 95$				
External instruments				
Forward – **U.K. Sample**				
Independent variable	BOOKMV	–0.265	0.1523	0.082*
	Constant	–0.009	2.893	0.590
$N_0 = 26$, $N_1 = 42$				
External instruments				
Forward – **USA sample**				
Independent variable	WCR	0.4947	0.2638	0.061*
	BOOKMV	0.332	0.2008	0.098*
	Constant	0.1392	0.1325	0.293
$N_0 = 11$, $N_1 = 28$				
External instruments				
Forward – **Asia Pacific sample**				
Independent variable	WCR	–0.1019	0.4451	0.022**
	Constant	0.3467	0.3046	0.255
$N_0 = 16$, $N_1 = 25$				

Panel C – Internal instruments – transaction exposure

Internal instruments *Netting* – **Full Sample**		Coefficient	Standard errors	p value
Independent variable	OVRBUS	0.1154	0.447	0.01***
	Constant	–0.2248	1.513	0.106
$N_0 = 60$, $N_1 = 89$				
Internal instruments				
Netting – **U.K. Sample**				
Independent variable	FORSALES	0.1753	0.0715	0.014**
	Constant	0.276	0.4907	0.899
$N_0 = 39$, $N_1 = 29$				
Internal instruments				
Matching – **Full Sample**				
Independent variable	LOGSALES	0.338	0.1991	0.089*
	Constant	–0.278	1.466	0.058
$N_0 = 73$, $N_1 = 76$				
Internal instruments				
Matching – **U.K. Sample**				
Independent variable	OVRBUS	0.1168	0.0669	0.081*
	Constant	–0.0659	0.8795	0.453
$N_0 = 35$, $N_1 = 33$				

Table 10. Continued.

Panel C – Continued				
Internal instruments *Matching* – **Asia Pacific Sample**		Coefficient	Standard errors	p value
Independent variable	LOGSALES	0.0763	0.0425	0.073*
	BOOKMV	–0.133	0.0614	0.031**
	Constant	–0.301	0.2947	0.307
$N_0 = 18$, $N_1 = 24$				
Internal instruments				
Matching – **USA Sample**				
Independent variable	BOOKMV	0.0156	0.0919	0.089*
	Constant	–0.16	0.1054	0.128
$N_0 = 20$, $N_1 = 19$				
Internal instruments				
Pricing – **Full Sample**				
Independent variable	QUICK	–0.2122	0.978	0.024**
	Constant	–1.6613	1.5	0.267
$N_0 = 97$, $N_1 = 52$				
Internal instruments				
Pricing – **U.K. Sample**				
	QUICK	–0.388	0.168	0.02**
	Constant	–0.7509	0.5739	0.191
$N_0 = 43$, $N_1 = 25$				
Internal instruments				
Pricing – **Asia Pacific Sample**				
	LTBOR	–0.3313	0.1645	0.045**
	Constant	–1.143	0.262	0.663
$N_0 = 29$, $N_1 = 13$				
Internal instruments				
Pricing – **USA sample**				
	BOOKMV	0.6371	0.325	0.05**
	Constant	–0.8527	0.9284	0.358
$N_0 = 25$, $N_1 = 14$				

Panel D – External instruments – transaction exposure				
External instruments *Forward* – **U.K. Sample**		Coefficient	Standard errors	p value
Independent variable	OVRBUS	0.2102	0.1027	0.041**
	Constant	0.3157	0.7148	0.659
$N_0 = 10$, $N_1 = 58$				
External instruments				
Forward – **USA Sample**				
Independent variable	FORSALES	0.0818	0.0495	0.099*
	Constant	0.616	0.117	0.599
$N_0 = 7$, $N_1 = 32$				

Table 10. Continued.

Panel D – Continued		Coefficient	Standard errors	*p* value
External instruments				
Currency Option – **USA Sample**				
Independent variable	LTBOR	–0.2652	0.1337	0.047**
	Constant	–0.1362	1.088	0.211
External instruments		Coefficient	Standard errors	p value
Forward – **U.K. Sample**				
$N_0 = 24$, $N_1 = 15$				
External instruments				
Currency Option – **Asia Pacific Sample**				
Independent variable	LTBOR	–0.8492	0.3093	0.093*
	Constant	–0.505	0.5056	0.103
$N_0 = 24$, $N_1 = 18$				
External instruments				
Currency Swap – **U.K. Sample**				
Independent variable	LOGSALES	–0.1414	0.855	0.098*
	Constant	0.6098	0.548	0.267
$N_0 = 48$, $N_1 = 20$				
External instruments				
Currency Swap – **USA Sample**				
Independent variable	LTBOR	–0.1223	0.6565	0.062*
	Constant	–0.3776	0.9808	0.70
$N_0 = 23$, $N_1 = 16$				

A logistic regression was estimated between the dependent variable coded 1 for a user of the hedging instrument, 0 otherwise and the financial characteristics. The independent variables are shown in Appendix 2. N_0 indicates the number who did not use the hedging instrument and N_1 indicates the number who use the instrument. *** significant at 1% level, ** significant at 5% level and * significant at 10% level. No evidence was found that dubious large regression residuals had an adverse effect on the estimated coefficients.

mixed between instruments and regions and some were different from that predicted by theory. The significant findings for some regions but not for others could indicate that there should be consideration of the general applicability of the theories of hedging.

There were less significant relationships for external instruments and translation exposure, Table 10 panel C. We did find for forwards that there were significant coefficients carrying the correct sign for liquidity for the Asia Pacific sample, providing further support for this theory. We also found a significant relationship for growth options for the U.K. sample. The significant coefficients for the use of forwards and leverage for the full sample and for forwards and liquidity for the USA sample were mixed with some coefficients in the wrong direction.

4.3. Transaction Exposure Hedging Instruments and Financial Characteristics

Table 10, panel C provides evidence that there are significant positive coefficients between the use of a number of the internal instruments for transaction exposure and the degree of internationalization, particularly for the U.K. MNCs. For example, netting for the full and U.K. samples and matching for the U.K. sample (which is similar to Joseph's (2000) finding for his U.K. sample). Also, consistent with the findings for translation exposure, there was evidence of a negative relationship between liquidity and the use of pricing for the full and U.K. samples. However, in comparison to our findings for translation exposure, there was a positive relationship with the size proxy and the use of matching for the full and Asia Pacific samples. This is important, as the difference in predictions for the size proxy may be due to consideration of the different types of currency risk and future theoretical predictions may have to take this into account. The significant results for leverage and the use of pricing are in the opposite direction to expected and the results for growth proxies the results are mixed.

There was further evidence of the degree of internationalisation and the use of hedging instruments as Table 10, panel D indicates a positive relationship with the use of forwards and internationalistaion proxies for the U.K. and USA samples. There was also a negative relationship with size and the use of currency swaps for the U.K. sample. However, despite the fact there are significant relationships with leverage and currency options and currency swaps for USA and U.K. samples the sign of the coefficients are in the opposite direction to expected.

5. CONCLUSION

In this paper we consider the currency hedging practices of companies in the U.K., USA and Asia Pacific by surveying the largest multinational companies (MNCs) in each region. We specifically considered companies that actively hedge by focusing on MNCs with an ex-ante a foreign currency exposure and were using at least one internal and/or external instrument(s). We add to the empirical studies that have tested the theoretical reasons for hedging by considering not just a general definition of derivatives but the use of specific internal and external instruments. It was also considered important to split the analysis of the instruments into the types of risk hedged. A regional analysis was important to determine if there were any country specific institutional factors that influence the hedging decision. Specifically, we provide empirical evidence in two main areas: (i) an analysis of the emphasis on currency risk, the use of and inter-relationships between internal and external instruments to manage transaction and translation exposures; and (ii) an examination of the financial characteristics of MNCs that might explain the emphasis on the types of risk and the degree of usage of both internal and external instruments to manage transaction and translation exposure.

From an analysis of our responses we find that MNCs place most importance on transaction exposure in all regions but there was significant regional variation in the importance placed on translation exposure. However, we did not find for any region strong evidence to suggest that the MNCs that placed most significance on both types of exposure were more likely to use hedging instruments (except for the USA sample) and their choice of hedging instrument was not statistically different from the low emphasis group. We found significant evidence that certain internal and external instruments are used primarily to manage translation or transaction exposure. For instance, in the case of internal instruments. netting is used primarily for transaction exposure while balance sheet hedging is used for translation exposure. We did find evidence that there maybe country specific factors that influence the use of hedging instruments. For internal instruments, pricing policies are used to manage translation exposure in the USA, in contrast to the other two regions and for external instruments; currency swaps are used in the U.K. to manage translation exposure, while USA and Asia Pacific primarily use them for management of transaction exposure. Finally, we were interested in whether hedging instruments are used to compliment or as substitutes for one another. Here, we also found distinct regional patterns in the use of some of the hedging instruments indicating country specific factors may influence hedging programme. For instance, USA MNCs tended to use other internal instruments to compliment their use of leading and lagging in managing transaction and translation exposure to benefit from economies of scale, centralized cash management systems or expertise. There was also some indication that some hedging instruments were considered as substitutes for one another and again this tended to depend on the region. In terms of translation exposure for example, in the Asia Pacific sample no user of forwards used pricing policies.

In the second part of the paper we try to isolate factors that influence the importance on transaction and translation exposure and the usage of individual internal or external instruments. To empirically test the hedging theories against our responses from the questionnaire we generate a number of proxies based on their financial characteristics. We found supporting evidence that the explanatory variables for liquidity, size and internationalisation exhibit some discriminatory power for the emphasis on risk and the degree of utilisation of internal and external techniques. However, some of these relationships were particular to some regions, indicating regional factors could play a significant factor in the choice of hedging instruments and therefore the general applicability of the theories. The strongest evidence was for our liquidity proxy. Consistent with theory for a number of instruments for both translation and transaction exposures, MNCs with high levels of liquidity tended to use less of the instruments. Also, there was supporting evidence that MNCs with higher levels of international business use more hedging instruments to manage transaction exposure. Interestingly, for our size proxy we found conflicting results for the different types of risks being hedged. The theories related to hedging and size provide ambiguous predictions; consequently consideration of the type of risk being hedged may help resolve this contradiction. We did not find evidence supporting the theories connecting financial distress to hedging and for the proxy used for underinvestment theory. This is not entirely unexpected as the use of leverage as a measure of financial distress is not without controversy due to disagreements about the causality and the proxy used to capture growth options to test the underinvestment could also surrogate for a number of other factors.

Our findings indicate that future empirical papers testing the theoretical explanations for hedging should take into account the differing emphasis companies have on different types of currency risk and the wide spread use of internal instruments Regional factors should also be important in future empirical test of hedging theories as we found regional variations in the emphasis on risk, the use of certain instruments to manage specific risks and in the significant financial characteristics that influenced the degree of usage. The general applicability of the theories of hedging to the different types of currency risk and to both internal and external hedging instruments requires further theoretical analysis and this paper has attempted to begin this process.

NOTES

1. See, Nance et al. (1993), Dolde (1993), Mian (1996), Geczy et al. (1997) and Howton and Perfect (1998). Graham and Rodgers (2000) provide a useful survey.

2. Empirical examination of hedging theories has been affected by the general unavailability of data on hedging activities. Early USA studies were reliant on survey data (e.g. Nance et al., 1993) and used a binary classification of derivative versus non-derivative use (e.g. Geczy et al., 1997) but increased accounting disclosure notes in the USA have meant that that more information is available on the derivative type,

the notional amounts and whether the position is long or short. Recent studies are therefore able to include derivative notional amounts as a continuous variable, see Goldberg et al. (1998) and Howton and Perfect (1998) and are now refining the dependent variables for long and short payoff positions, see Graham and Rodgers (2000).

3. Due to the earlier weak empirical results a number of recent papers have not investigated all of the theoretical risk management hypotheses but rather focus on improving the proxies for one particular theory, see Graham and Smith (2000) on tax incentives, Crain et al. (2000) on capital structure and Rodgers (2000) on managerial incentives.

4. Alternatively, a company could be classified as a non-hedger because they have taken a view on foreign exchange rates to enable them to benefit from an unhedged position. Alternatively, they may simply lack confidence in using derivative instruments and prefer internal techniques.

5. Joseph (2000) considered the use of internal and external hedging instruments but only for 74 U.K. companies of the top 300 U.K. companies in 1994. From a review of the previous studies on derivative use and foreign exchange exposure this suggested we concentrate only the largest MNCs. Analogous to previous research we define companies with ex ante currency exposure if they disclose foreign sales or have at least one overseas subsidiary over which it has financial and management control.

6. Marshall (2000) found that although U.K. and USA MNCs have similar policies there were significant differences between these regions and the Asia Pacific region. A few surveys of non-USA and U.K. companies have recently appeared, including Belguim, Germany, Finland, and New Zealand. These papers do not simultaneously survey the different regions but simply compare their survey to previous U.K. or USA work, see Berkman et al. (1997), Hakkarainen et al. (1998), Prevost et al. (2000), Fatemi and Glaum (2000), and De Ceuster et al. (2000). Only one paper has empirically tried to explain the relationship between the theoretical determinants and the actual derivative use, Berkman and Bradbury (1996) for New Zealand firms.

7. A comparison of this response rate with the other major studies is discussed Marshall (2000). Although we were only targeting the largest 200 MNCs in each region the Kruskal Wallis test was applied to test for non-response bias between the respondents and non-respondents in each region. No evidence was found of significant differences between the samples, except for two variables, total assets and sales, in a few regions. The mean for the respondents in some years was larger than the non-respondents. However, since we were interested in the largest MNCs in each region this bias is in the desired direction. We also considered the industry sector of the response sample in comparison to the non-response sample for each region and found no significant differences in any of the regions. Nonetheless, the normal caveats apply when dealing with questionnaire survey data.

8. We do not set out formal hypothesis; the null hypothesis is no association. Throughout the paper the null hypothesis of no association is rejected for probability ρ-values less than or equal to 10%. The degrees of freedom following the χ^2 statistic are in parenthesis.

9. There was significant differences for Asia Pacific and USA MNCs instrument, $\chi^2(8) = 13.56$; ρ-value $= 0.10$ and $\chi^2(8) = 117.72$; ρ-value $= 0.025$ respectively.

ACKNOWLEDGMENTS

The authors would like to thank Fah Mei Lee, You Koong Szto and Joan Tang who undertook the initial survey as part of their MBA project, Martin Kemmit for further research assistance and all the companies who took part in the project. All errors remain our own.

REFERENCES

Adam, T. R. (1999). Do firms use derivatives to reduce their dependence on external capital markets. Hong Kong University of Science and Technology Working Paper.

Beatty, A. (1999). Assessing the use of derivatives as part of a risk management strategy. *Journal of Accounting and Economics*, *26*, 353–357.

Berkman, H., & Bradbury, M. E. (1996). Empirical evidence on the corporate use of derivatives. *Financial Management*, *25*(2), 5–9.

Berkman, H., Bradbury, M. E., & Magan, S. (1997). An international comparison of derivative use. *Financial Management*, *26*(4), 69–73.

Crain, S. J., So, J. C., & Bharati, R. (2000). Hedging and the optimal capital structure of firms. Southern Illinois University Edwardsville Working Paper.

De Ceuster, M. J. K., Durinck, E., Laveren, E., & Lodewyckx, J. (1999). A survey into the use of derivatives by large non-financial firms operating in Belgium. *European Financial Management*, *6*(3), 301–318.

DeMarzo, P. M., & Duffie, D. (1995). Corporate incentives for hedging and hedge accounting. *The Review of Financial Studies*, *8*(3), 743–771.

Dolde, W. (1993). The trajectory of corporate financial risk management. *Journal of Applied Corporate Finance*, *6*(3), 33–41.

Fatemi, A., & Glaum, M. (2000). Risk management practices of German firms. *Managerial Finance*, *26*(3), 1–17.

Froot, K. A., Scharfstein, D., & Stein, J. C. (1993). Risk management: coordinating corporate investment and financing policies. *Journal of Finance*, *48*, 1629–1658.

Froot, K. A., Scharfstein, D., & Stein, J. C. (1994). A framework for risk management. *Harvard Business Review*, *72*(6), 91–103.

Geczy, C., Minton, B. A., & Schrand, C. (1997). Why firms use currency derivatives. *Journal of Finance*, *54*, 1323–1354.

Guay, W. R. (1999). The impact of derivatives on firm risk: an empirical examination of new derivative users. *Journal of Accounting and Economics*, *26*, 319–351.

Goldberg, S. R, Godwin, J. H., Kim, M. N., & Tritschler, C. A. (1998). On the determinants of corporate usage of financial derivatives. *Journal of International Financial Management and Accounting*, *9*(2), 132–166.

Graham, J. R., & Rodgers, D. A. (2000). Does corporate hedging increase firm value? An empirical analysis. Northeastern University Working Paper.

Graham, J. R., & Smith, C. W. (2000). Tax incentives to hedge. Forthcoming *Journal of Finance*.

Grant, K., & Marshall, A. P. (1997). Large U.K. companies and derivatives. *European Financial Management*, *3*(2), 191–208.

Hakkarainen, A., Nathan, J., Eero, K., & Puttonnen, V. (1998). The foreign exchange exposure management practices of Finnish industrial firms. *Journal of International Financial Management and Accounting*, *9*(1), 34–57.

Howton, S. D., & Perfect, S. B. (1998). Currency and interest rate derivatives use in U.S. firms. *Financial Management*, *27*(4), 111–121.

Joseph, N. L. (2000). The choice of hedging techniques and the characteristics of U.K. industrial firms. *Journal of Multinational Financial Management*, *10*, 161–184.

Khoury, S., & Chan, K. (1988). Hedging foreign exchange risk: selecting the optimal tool. *Midland Corporate Finance Journal*, (Winter), 40–52.

Marshall, A. P. (2000). Foreign exchange risk management in U.K., USA and Asia Pacific multinational companies. *Journal of Multinational Financial Management*, *10*, 185–211.

Main, S. L. (1996). Evidence on corporate hedging policy. *Journal of Financial and Quantitative Analysis*, (September), 419–439.

Mathur, I. (1985). Managing foreign exchange risk: strategy considerations. *Managerial Finance*, *11*, 7–11.

Nance, D. R., Smith, C. W., & Smithson, C. W. (1993). On the determinants of corporate hedging. *Journal of Finance*, *48*, 267–284.

Prevost, A. K., Rose, L. C., & Miller, G. (2000). Derivatives usage and financial risk management in large and small economies: a comparative analysis. *Journal of Business Finance and Accounting*, *27*(5&6), 733–759.

Rogers, D. A. (2000). Does executive portfolio structure affect risk management? CEO risk-taking incentives and corporate derivative usage. Northeastern University Working Paper.

Smith, C. W., & Stulz, R. M. (1985). The determinants of firms' hedging policies. *Journal of Financial and Quantitative Analysis*, *20*, 391–405.

Tufano, P. (1996). Who manages risk? An empirical examination of risk-management practices in the gold mining industry. *Journal of Finance*, *51*, 1097–1137.

APPENDIX 1

Questionnaire

SURVEY OF FOREIGN EXCHANGE RISK MANAGEMENT IN THE U.K., THE USA AND ASIA PACIFIC

Indicate the contribution of overseas business (i.e. other than home country) to total revenues.

1% to 25% 26% to 50% 51% to 75% 76% to 100%

Indicate the degree of emphasis your company places on the following risk: (1 for least important and 5 for most important – please tick one box for each type of risk)

	1	2	3	4	5
Translation risk (uncertain domestic value of a net accounting position denominated in a foreign currency)					
Transaction risk (uncertain domestic currency of an open position denominated in a foreign currency with respect to a known transaction)					

Which of the following non-derivative method(s) does your company in managing the following foreign exchange risks use? (You may tick more than one box)

	Translation Risk	Transaction Risk
Netting		
Matching		
Leading and lagging		
Pricing policies		
Balance sheet hedging		

Which of the following derivative(s) does your company in managing the following foreign exchange risks use? (You may tick more than one box)

	Translation Risk	Transaction Risk
Currency forward contracts		
Currency future contracts		
Currency future options		
Currency options		
Currency swaps		

APPENDIX 2

Proxies for the Theoretical Relationships, Predicted Sign, Variable Description and Data Source

Variable Name	Predicted Sign	Variable Description	Data Source
Internationalisation			
OVRBUS	+	the percentage of overseas business to total business	Survey Dummy Variable Measured 0 for 1–50%, 1 for 51–100%.
FORSALES	+	the percentage of group's turnover generated overseas: foreign sales to total sales.	Datastream/ Worldscope Measured as 3 year average 1996 to 1998
Size			
LOGSALES	+/-	log of sales	Datastream/ Worldscope Measured as 5 year average 1995 to 1998
Financial Distress			
LTBOR	+	long-term borrowing to ordinary shareholders' equity and reserves	Datasteam/ Worldscope Measured as 5 year average 1995 to 1998
Liquidity			
QAR	-	quick asset ratio: total current assets less stock and work in progress to total current liabilities	Datastream/ Worldscope Measured as 5 year average 1995 to 1998

Appendix 2 – Continued

Variable Name	Predicted Sign	Variable Description	Data Source
Liquidity – Continued			
WCR	-	working capital ratio: total current assets/ total current liabilities	Datasteam/ Worldscope Measured as 5 year average 1995 to 1998
Underinvestment			
BOOKMV	-	book value of company assets to market value	Datasteam/ Worldscope Measured as 5 year average 1995 to 1998

The logistic regression analysis is performed using these independent variables against the dependent variable of the degree of emphasis on the types of currency risk and the use or non-use of the hedging instrument. The financial variables are obtained from Datastream and Worldscope and the independent dummy is obtained from the survey. The predicted signs are based on the previous theoretical literature.

THE HILL ESTIMATOR IN FINANCIAL RISK ASSESSMENT AND AN APPLICATION TO EXTREMAL EXCHANGE RATE RISK

Niklas Wagner

ABSTRACT

Extremal price changes are of vital interest in financial risk management. The present empirical investigation studies the tail index α of U.S.-Dollar/Deutschmark exchange rate changes and highlights issues in the application of the prominent Hill estimator: Adaptive selection of an appropriate subsample, small sample bias and non-linear time-series dependence. Conducting a preliminary analysis of the exchange rate series and simulating small sample bias under a fitted GARCH model, we find that bias is a dominant issue to cope with in financial risk assessment. Reducing estimation bias is suggested by variation of a scaling parameter in the Drees et al. (2000) estimation approach: Compared to a traditional approach, our α-estimate is reduced by roughly one quarter and thereby indicates a substantially higher risk in the tails of the exchange rate distribution.

1. INTRODUCTION

Extreme value theory as outlined for example in Beirlant et al. (1996), Coles (1999) and Embrechts et al. (1997) characterizes the asymptotic tail behavior

Financial Risk and Financial Risk Management, Volume 16, pages 173–187.

ISBN: 0-7623-0858-3

of some stationary distribution function $F(r)$. It turns out that the distribution tails can be characterized by a single parameter, the so-called "tail index" frequently denoted as α. One approach to its estimation is based on a proposal by Hill (1975). The Hill estimator is suitable for financial applications: The semi-parametric estimation approach is based on the assumption that the underlying distribution is in the maximum domain of attraction of the Fréchet extreme value distribution (cp. Embrechts et al., 1997). This generally holds for fat-tailed distributions as analyzed in finance. Unlike other competing estimation approaches, the estimator does not require that exact asymptotic limits are met. Applications in the empirical finance literature include an early study on exchange rates by Koedijk et al. (1990). Further examples are Dacarogna et al. (1995), Danielsson and de Vries (1997), Krämer and Runde (1996) and Jondeau and Rockinger (1999). Putting a critical light on previous studies, Annaert et al. (2001) use Hill estimation results in distinguishing between stable and non-stable fat-tailed distributional alternatives.

This contribution first critically reviews a number of properties of the Hill estimator which are important to financial risk modeling. Prior discussions of the chances and pitfalls of applying extreme value statistics in finance can be found e.g. in Diebold et al. (1998) and Embrechts et al. (1997). Then, an application of the Hill estimator to modeling extremal changes in daily U.S.-Dollar/Deutschmark exchange rate is given. The study highlights issues relevant in financial risk assessment and proposes tail index estimation based on the original data together with a simulation of the error distribution based on a suitable return model.

2. METHODOLOGY

2.1. The Hill Estimator

By construction, the estimator

$$\hat{\alpha} = \frac{1}{k} \sum_{i=1}^{k} \ln R_{i,T} - \ln R_{k,T} \tag{2.1}$$

is optimal in a maximum likelihood sense under k independent draws $R_{i,T}$ from an exact Pareto distribution with distribution function, $G(r) = 1 - cr^{-\alpha}$, $c > 0$, $\alpha > 0$. In extreme value statistics, the Hill estimator (2.1) is based on k upper order statistics $R_{i,T}$, $i = 1, \ldots, k$, with $R_{i,T} > R_{i+1,T}$ from T sample observations of some stationary distribution function $F(r)$ in the maximum domain of attraction of the Fréchet extreme value distribution. It is therefore constructed as a maximum likelihood estimator (MLE) *conditional* on some *known* threshold level $R_{k,T}$ (cp. e.g. Embrechts et al., 1997). Given that k approaches infinity with T, but k remains a small portion of the overall sample, one can then show that the conditional maximum likelihood estimator is asymptotically normally distributed:

$$\sqrt{k}(\hat{\alpha} - \alpha) \xrightarrow{d} N(0,\alpha^2). \qquad (2.2)$$

Note that the normal limit in (2.2) does not contain an asymptotic bias term when the threshold is assumed to be known.

2.2. Applications in Financial Risk Assessment

In applications, the threshold is unknown and financial return observations are typically dependent. Therefore, the estimator looses its optimality properties in financial risk assessment. Particularly, the following four issues have to be taken into account:

- The *threshold has to be estimated*, i.e. a certain number of sample observations from the tail under investigation has to be selected. This is essential to the Hill estimator's bias/variance trade-off: Selecting too many potential tail observations reduces variance but introduces bias and vice versa. As the estimator is biased, overall estimation performance is typically measured by mean squared estimation error. Apart from graphical methods based on the so-called Hill plot (cp. Embrechts et al., 1997), various adaptive, data-driven, criteria have been proposed. One approach widely applied in the finance literature is the subsample bootstrap by Hall (1990), Dacarogna et al. (1995) and Danielsson and de Vries (1997). The maximum occupation time estimator by Drees et al. (2000) is an algorithmic version of graphical Hill plot approaches.
- Small sample bias is crucial in an appropriate risk assessment: Small sample results indicate that not only sampling variance as given in (2.2) but also *bias relates to the magnitude of the tail index*. As a consequence, the extremal risk of high risk (i.e. low α) assets may potentially be underestimated and vice versa (cp. Huisman et al., 2001; Wagner & Marsh, 2000).
- The estimator has to be robust with respect to *small sample deviations from the exact, asymptotic Pareto model*. As the statistical results only hold asymptotically, finite sample observations do not exactly come from a Pareto tail. This makes small sample tail approximations necessary, which converge to the Pareto tail as the sample size increases. Furthermore, although the theoretical results suggest that the Hill estimator is a general approach to measuring tail thickness for distributions in the class of the Fréchet

maximum domain of attraction, it turns out that the estimator is severely biased under stable distributions within this maximum domain of attraction. This was noted in the Hill estimation proposal by DuMouchel (1983) and critically pointed out by several authors thereafter (cp. e.g. Dewachter & Gielens, 1994; McCulloch, 1997; Mittnik et al., 1998; Wagner & Marsh, 2000; Annaert et al., 2001). The Hill estimator should therefore rather be employed under non-stable alternatives, the latter typically including the student-t distribution.

- In financial applications, returns typically display *nonlinear dependence*, with autoregressive conditional heteroskedasticity (ARCH) being most prominent model approach. It is therefore desirable that the tail index estimator is also robust with respect to the independence assumption of the classical extreme value theory. Although there are theoretical results indicating consistency of the Hill estimator under different types of time-series dependence including ARCH (cp. Resnick & Starica, 1998), the estimator's small sample properties may exhibit substantial estimation error under ARCH-type dependence; see Kearns and Pagan (1997) for integrated GARCH processes and Wagner and Marsh (2000) for a general class of finite-variance stationary GARCH processes with student-t innovations. One approach suggested e.g. by Embrechts et al. (1997), Frey and McNeil (2000), and Lauridsen (2001) is to measure tail thickness of ARCH model residuals. In this contribution we propose an alternative approach which estimates tail thickness based on the original data and simulates the error distribution based on a suitable model.

3. MODELING EXTREMAL CHANGES IN DAILY EXCHANGE RATES

In this section, a study in financial risk assessment is given for extremal exchange rate changes. The exchange rate returns are first modeled by a GARCH model. After demonstrating that this prominent model captures short-term dependencies quite well, the Hill estimator‘s small sample properties are simulated under the estimated model. Using information on potential estimation bias, tail thickness is then inferred from the original exchange rate observations. This procedure allows us to derive unconditional tail estimates without the potential disturbing effects of model and residual estimation, while, results on the distributional properties of the tail index estimates under GARCH-type dependence are derived from our simulations.

3.1. The Exchange Rate Dataset

The empirical investigation is based on logarithmic changes R_t, $t = 1, \ldots, T$, in daily USD/DEM exchange rates during the period 1988 to 1994.

The time series and a histogram of exchange rate changes are plotted in Fig. 1. The sample period was chosen as an approximately stationary period of exchange rates without severe exogenous policy impact or structural breaks. Removing holidays from the Datastream database yields a sample of $T = 1716$ daily observations. The plots illustrate the typical fat-tailed characteristics of the data, which are further examined in the following.

3.2. Modeling Exchange Rate Changes

3.2.1. Assumptions and the GARCH Model

In the following assume that the logarithmic changes or returns, R_t, $t = 1, \ldots, T$, are generated by a GARCH(1,1)-t(v) model

$$R_t = \sigma_t Z_t,$$

$$\sigma_t^2 = \beta_0 + \beta_1 R_{t-1}^2 + \beta_2 \sigma_{t-1}^2, \ \beta_0 > 0, \ \beta_1, \beta_2 \geq 0, \tag{3.1}$$

where the Z_ts are iid draws from a student-t distribution function with density $f(z)$ and v degrees of freedom. Note that under the student distribution the innovations' asymptotic tail behavior is given by a Pareto tail, i.e.: $1 - F(z) \sim dz^{-v}$, $d > 0$, $v > 0$ as $z \to \infty$.

For model (3.1) a stationary marginal distribution $F(r)$ for the returns exists under the following necessary and sufficient condition:

$$\int_{-\infty}^{\infty} \ln |\beta_1 z^2 + \beta_2| f(z) dz < 0. \tag{3.2}$$

The stationary marginal distribution will then exhibit fat-tailed behavior according to the Pareto law with some tail index exponent α, i.e.: $1 - F(r) \sim cr^{-\alpha}$, $c > 0$, $\alpha > 0$ as $r \to \infty$.[1]

3.2.2. GARCH Estimation Results

Estimation of the GARCH model with student-t innovations (3.1) is carried out by maximum likelihood as outlined in Hamilton (1994). The parameter estimation results are given in Table 1. As typically observed for GARCH estimation in finance, all estimates differ from zero at high confidence levels and the sum of the estimates of β_1 and β_2 is close to, but smaller than, one. The maximum likelihood estimate of v turns out to be close to six, which we assume as the number of degrees of freedom for the model innovations.

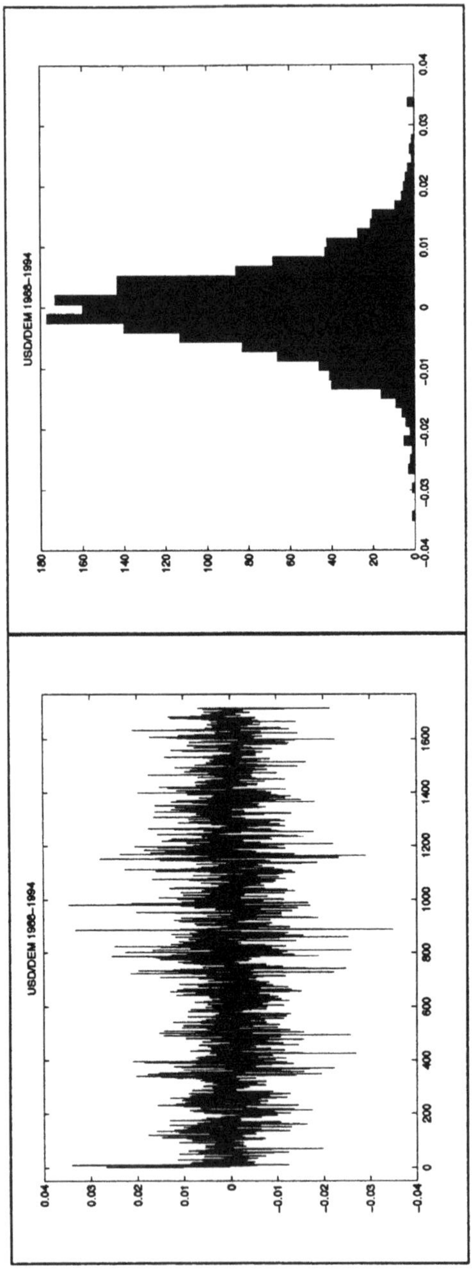

Fig. 1. Plot of the USD/DEM Exchange Rate Changes 1988 to 1994 (Left) and the Corresponding Histogram (Right).

Table 1. MLE Results for the GARCH(1,1)-t(v) Model for USD/DEM Exchange Rate Returns in the Period 1988 to 1994 with $T=1716$. MLE Start Values are Obtained from Fitting the GARCH Model with Normal Innovations. Standard Errors in Parenthesis.

Model-Parameter:	β_0	β_1	β_2	v
MLE	$1.28\ 10^{-6}$ ($6.17\ 10^{-7}$)	0.0410 (0.0108)	0.937 (0.0184)	6.01 (0.890)

For the given point estimates and $v=6$, the stationarity condition (3.2) can be verified numerically and a theoretical tail index $\alpha=2.41$ or $\xi=1/\alpha=0.41$ results. Note that this theoretical tail index derived from GARCH estimation gives a rough idea of the magnitude of the tail index for the data.[2] It further allows for a simulation of the sample properties of the Hill estimator under such model, which is performed in the following section.

GARCH model estimation diagnostics are given in Fig. 2 and Table 2. Exchange rate changes' and the model residuals' empirical quantiles are each plotted against quantiles of the student-t(6) distribution quantiles in Fig. 2. The results indicate an approximate fit of the student distribution, where fitting the GARCH model improves the fit in the center of the distribution but also points out that the very extremal observations should rather be captured by a specific modeling approach.

Table 2 provides estimates of the autocorrelation, partial autocorrelations and Ljung-Box Q-statistics for the model residuals and squared model residuals up to a lag of 15 trading days. There is no indication of linear dependence in both cases: none of the estimated correlation coefficients is significant at the 10% level, the same holds for the corresponding Q-statistics.[3]

3.3. Inferring Tail Thickness of the Distribution of Exchange Rate Changes

In this section we use the Hill estimator to infer tail thickness for our sample of exchange rate changes where three different approaches to adaptive estimator selection are chosen.

A naive Hill estimator ('H-INI') is based on $k=[2T^{1/2}]$ (where $[n]$ denotes the largest integer smaller or equal to n). As an automated subset selection criterion the bootstrap estimator by Hall (1990) and modified by Dacarogna et al. (1995) and Danielsson and de Vries (1997) is used. Following results in the literature, the second order parameter is set equal to one, which gives the estimator 'H-

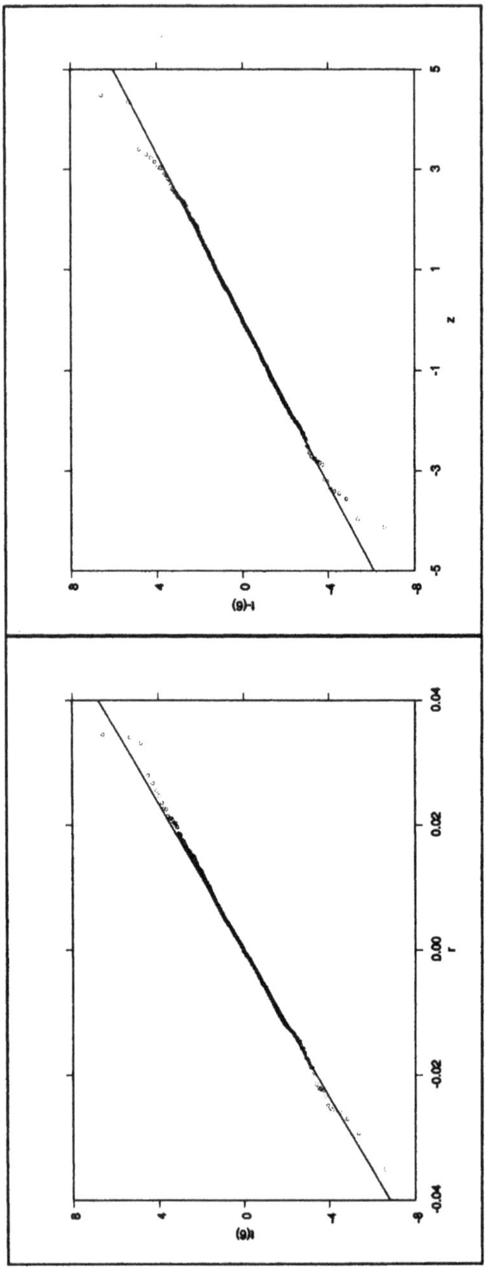

Fig. 2. Quantile Plots of Exchange Rate Changes (Left) and Standardized GARCH Residuals (Right) Each Against Quantiles of the Student-t Distribution with Six Degrees of Freedom.

Table 2. Sample Autocorrelations SACF, Partial Autocorrelations SPACF and Ljung-Box Q-statistics for the Standardized GARCH Residuals (Columns 2 to 5) and Squared Standardized GARCH Residuals (Columns 6 to 9).

Lag l	z_t SACF	SPACF	$Q(l)$	Prob.	z_t^2 SACF	SPACF	$Q(l)$	Prob.
1	0.031	0.031	1.6295	0.202	− 0.025	− 0.025	1.0521	0.305
2	− 0.032	− 0.033	3.4006	0.183	− 0.002	− 0.002	1.0560	0.590
3	− 0.003	− 0.001	3.4147	0.332	− 0.011	− 0.011	1.2720	0.736
4	0.020	0.019	4.0826	0.395	− 0.008	− 0.008	1.3715	0.849
5	0.027	0.026	5.3704	0.372	0.025	0.024	2.4400	0.785
6	− 0.026	− 0.027	6.5723	0.362	− 0.002	− 0.001	2.4496	0.874
7	− 0.008	− 0.005	6.6868	0.462	− 0.033	− 0.033	4.2890	0.746
8	0.008	0.007	6.8082	0.557	0.021	0.020	5.0756	0.749
9	0.039	0.037	9.4274	0.399	0.012	0.013	5.3131	0.806
10	0.038	0.037	11.965	0.287	− 0.001	− 0.002	5.3145	0.869
11	− 0.025	− 0.023	13.040	0.291	0.022	0.022	6.1677	0.862
12	0.003	0.006	13.055	0.365	− 0.007	− 0.004	6.2495	0.903
13	− 0.016	− 0.020	13.496	0.410	0.034	0.033	8.2832	0.825
14	0.006	0.005	13.564	0.483	0.008	0.009	8.3926	0.868
15	0.007	0.007	13.658	0.552	− 0.024	− 0.022	9.3928	0.856

BSC'. Considering graphical approaches based on a smoothed version of the Hill plot, the so-called maximum occupation time estimator by Drees et al. (2000) is used as an alternative automated estimation criterion. In the latter approach, occupation in a neighborhood of some α is defined by an interval, which is constructed form the standard deviation of the Hill estimator times a scaling constant m. Here, the scaling parameter is set equal to three different values yielding 'H-MOT' with $m=1, m=5$ and $m=10$. For details on the implemented procedures compare also Wagner and Marsh (2000).

3.3.1. Simulated Hill Estimator Sample Properties under the GARCH Model
Before turning to an application of the Hill estimator to our sample, we now study the error distributions under GARCH-type dependence. Recall that the results from Table 1 imply a stationary marginal distribution for the returns and a theoretical tail index $\alpha=2.41$ or $\xi=1/\alpha=0.41$. Assuming the estimated model was the true return generating process and a sample size of $T=1716$, we can then simulate the error distributions of different Hill estimation procedures under 500 independent Monte Carlo runs.

The simulation results are given in Table 3, which reports the mean estimate (M), the mean error (ME), the standard deviation of the errors (STD) and the square root of the mean squared errors (RMSE). As a graphical illustration, smoothed kernel density plots of the simulated error distributions with scaling parameter $m=5$ for the maximum occupation time estimator are plotted in Fig. 3.

Under our GARCH model the simulation results reveal a negative bias for all estimation approaches. Under a scaling parameter m of the maximum

Table 3. Simulated Small Sample Properties of Hill Estimator for $\xi=1/\alpha=0.41$ and $T=1716$ Under 500 Monte Carlo Runs from the Estimated GARCH Model. The Hill Estimators Include the Initial Hill Estimator (H-INI) with Asymptotic Standard Error $k^{-1/2}\xi=[2T^{1/2}]^{-1/2}\xi=0.050$, the Bootstrap Estimator Under 100 Bootstrap Runs (H-BSC) and the Maximum Occupation Time Estimator (H-MOT) with Different Scaling Parameters m.

Estimator:	H-INI	H-BSC	H-MOT $m=1$	H-MOT $m=5$	H-MOT $m=10$
M	0.31	0.26	0.24	0.38	0.36
ME	− 0.10	− 0.15	− 0.17	− 0.035	− 0.059
STD	0.052	0.073	0.061	0.043	0.043
RMSE	0.12	0.17	0.18	0.055	0.076

occupation estimator MOT equal to one, the naive Hill estimator H-INI dominates the two adaptive approaches. The performance of the MOT can be improved by increasing m, which reveals reduced bias and improved RMSE.

3.3.2. Hill Estimation Results

A classical Hill plot $\{(k, \hat{\alpha}_{k,T}): k = 1, \ldots, 600\}$ for our series of exchange rate data is given in Fig. 4. As it is well-known that time series dependence strongly influences the properties of the Hill plot, one may point out that the plot obviously does not only not converge against some limit as k becomes larger (the problem of selecting an appropriate subset of tail observations) but may also be shifted up- or downwardly (i.e. exhibit bias) due to the non-linear dependence in the data. Apart from these difficulties, visual inspection of the plot reveals a nearly flat area of Hill estimates with moderate variability in an

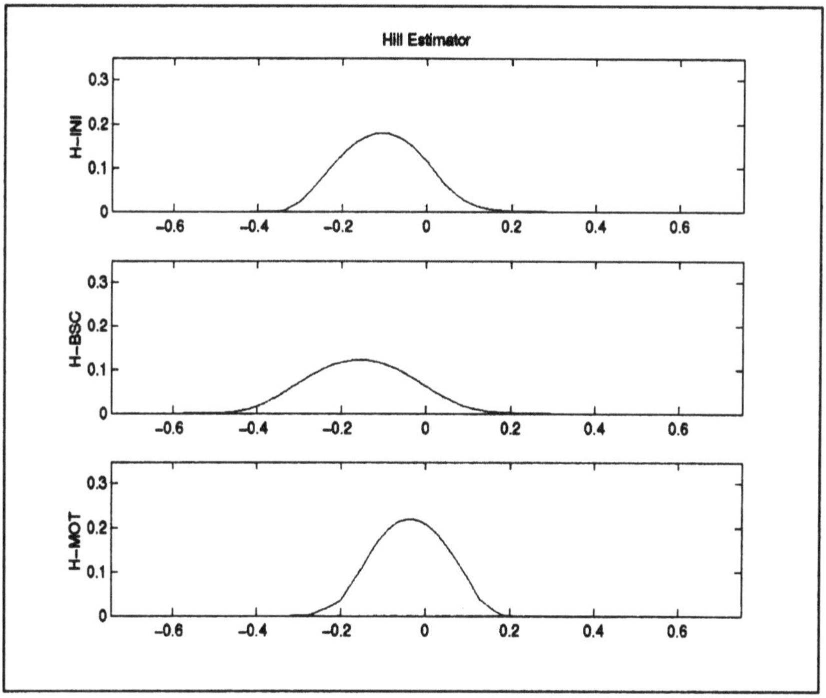

Fig. 3. kernel Density Plots of the Simulated Error Distributions for the Tail Index Estimates $\xi = 1/\alpha$ Under the Assumed GARCH Model with $T = 1716$ Observations; H-MOT Given for $m = 5$.

interval roughly between $k=60$ and $k=90$. A classical approach would be to choose an estimator from that range which would imply a tail index estimate of about 3.7 to 4.

Table 4 summarizes our tail index estimation results. The naive and the bootstrap estimator give results similar to our visual inspection above. Interestingly, this is not true for the maximum occupation time estimator, which is designed to find a flat region in a *smoothed* version of the Hill plot. The estimators' behavior corresponds surprisingly well to our previous simulation results: H-MOT with $m=5$ yields a lower estimate of α than H-MOT with $m=1$. Of course, by selection under the theoretical model, H-MOT with $m=5$ is also expected to give an estimate which comes closest to the theoretical tail index of $\alpha=2.41$.

Once we rely on the GARCH model as a suitable representation of the dependence in our data and in its impact on the Hill estimator's small sample properties, we may therefore conclude that the tail index α for the exchange rate changes is in some interval around 2.90 and potentially below 3. One may

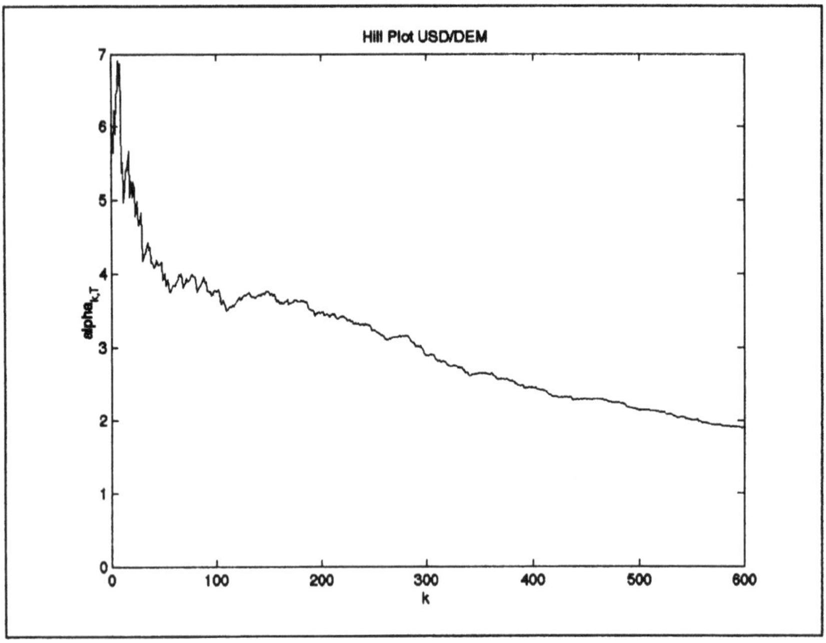

Fig. 4. Hill Plot for the Exchange Rate Changes, $k=1, \ldots, 600$, $T=1716$.

Table 4. Hill Estimation Results from the Naive Estimator H-INI, the Bootstrap Estimator H-BSC with 100 Bootstrap Runs and the Maximum Occupation Time Estimator H-MOT with Different Scaling Parameters *m*. Available Standard Errors in Parenthesis.

Estimator:	H-INI	H-BSC	H-MOT $m=1$	H-MOT $m=5$	H-MOT $m=10$
k	82	84	–	–	–
α	3.99	3.96	5.56	2.90	3.24
	(0.44)	(0.43)			
ξ	0.25	0.25	0.18	0.35	0.31
	(0.028)	(0.028)			

therefore rather doubt the existence of the third moment of the underlying distribution, although an interpretation of traditional results (e.g. from the bootstrap estimation approach H-BSC)[4] would not necessarily come to such a conclusion.

4. CONCLUSION

The following conclusions can be drawn from the present study:

- Although the true return generating process is (and will always be) unknown, we can consider the small sample properties of our estimator under GARCH-type dependence, assuming that our sample is drawn from a generating process with some stationary marginal distribution.
- Time series dependence complicates tail index estimation, but small sample bias, which is also present under independence, is the dominant issue to cope with in a practical risk assessment situation.
- Adaptive selection criteria do unfortunately not prevent from potentially substantial small sample estimation bias.
- The bootstrap approach improves estimation quality under an increased number of bootstrap runs, which, however, sooner or later reaches computational and time restrictions. For the maximum occupation time estimator the scaling parameter turns out to be critical.
- Contrary to the findings in most other studies on bias of the Hill estimator in finance, evidence suggests in our setting that the estimation bias in the tail index is positive. This implies e.g. that the number of existing moments of the underlying distribution is potentially overestimated or, correspondingly,

that risk assessment yields too low measures of risk in the form of quantiles of a loss distribution. The finding is in accordance with the observation by Wagner and Marsh (2000) that tail index estimation methods may come to results where high-risk assets' risk is potentially under- and low-risk assets' risk is potentially over-estimated.

- The simulation results for the maximum occupation time estimator indicate that there might be an optimal parameter choice for the scaling parameter depending on the magnitude of the tail index. Approaches reducing estimation bias by an adaptive choice of the parameter may hence offer a perspective for future research.

NOTES

1. Cp. e.g. Wagner and Marsh (2000) and the literature therein for a review on model stationarity conditions, tail behavior of the marginal distribution function and the numerical approximation of the theoretical tail index α.

2. Previous research as cited in Coles (1999) indicates that using this theoretical tail index estimate is a crude estimate of the true tail index, which results from its dependence on the model specification.

3. Note that for conclusions drawn from the results on the squared residuals, the assumption of the existence of the forth moment (i.e. $\alpha > 4$) of the distribution of the noise terms $F(z)$ is crucial. As our empirical results indicate a student-t distribution with six degrees of freedom for the residuals, this assumption does not appear to be violated in the given application.

4. The asymptotic 95% confidence band for H-BSC does not contain the tail index value 3. Note that unreported calculations showed that increasing the number of bootstrap runs increases the stability of the estimator of the optimal k. Performing 5000 instead of 100 bootstrap runs gave an optimal k equal to 79 which is still nearby the naive selection criterion and does not have substantial impact on the tail index estimate. Although performing additional bootstrap runs obviously reduces mean squared estimation error, this finding does not indicate a substantial reduction in estimation bias under the assumed GARCH model.

REFERENCES

Annaert, J., De Ceuster, M., & Hodgson, A. (2001). Moment Condition Failure – Australian Evidence. Working Paper, University of Antwerp.

Beirlant, J., Vynckier, P., & Teugels, J. L. (1996). *Practical Analysis of Extreme Values*. Leuven University Press.

Coles, S. G. (1999). Extreme Value Theory and Applications. Manuscript, University of Bristol.

Dacorogna, M. M., Müller, U. A., Pictet, O. V., & de Vries, C. G. (1995). *The Distribution of Extremal Foreign Exchange Rate Returns in Extremely Large Data Sets*. Zürich: O&A Preprint.

Danielsson, J., & de Vries, C. G. (1997). Tail Index and Quantile Estimation with Very High Frequency Data. *Journal of Empirical Finance*, *4*, 241–257.

Diebold, F. X., Schuermann, T., & Stroughair, J. D. (1998). Pitfalls and Opportunities in the Use of Extreme Value Theory in Risk Management. In: A.-P. N. Refenes, A. N. Burgess & J. E. Moody (Eds), *Decision Technologies for Computational Finance* (pp. 3–12). Dordrecht: Kluwer.

Drees, H., de Haan, L., & Resnick, S. (2000). How to Make a Hill Plot. *Annals of Statistics*, *28*, 254–274.

DuMouchel, W. H. (1983). Estimating the Stable Index α in Order to Measure Tail Thickness: A Critique. *Annals of Statistics*, *11*, 1019–1031.

Embrechts, P., Klüppelberg, C., & Mikosch, T. (1997). *Modelling Extremal Events for Insurance and Finance*. New York: Springer.

Frey, R., & McNeil, A. J. (2000). Estimation of Tail-Related Measures for Heteroscedastic Financial Time Series: An Extreme Value Approach. *Journal of Empirical Finance*, *7*, 271–300.

Hall, P. (1990). Using the Bootstrap to Estimate Mean Squared Error and Select Smoothing Parameters in Nonparametric Problems. *Journal of Multivariate Analysis*, *32*, 177–203.

Hamilton, J. D. (1994). *Time Series Analysis*. Princeton: Princeton University Press.

Hill, B. M. (1975). A Simple General Approach to Inference about the Tail of a Distribution. *Annals of Statistics*, *3*, 1163–1174.

Huisman, R., Koedijk, K. G., Kool, C. J. M., & Palm, F. (2001). Tail-Index Estimates in Small Samples. *Journal of Business and Economic Statistics*, *19*, 208–216.

Jondeau, E., & Rockinger, M. (1999). The Tail Behavior of Stock Returns: Emerging versus Mature Markets, Working Paper, HEC-School of Management.

Kearns, P., & Pagan, A. (1997). Estimating the Density Tail Index for Financial Time Series. *Review of Economics and Statistics*, *79*, 171–175.

Koedijk, K. G., Schafgans, M. M., & de Vries, C. G. (1990). The Tail Index of Exchange Rate Returns. *Journal of International Economics*, *29*, 93–108.

Krämer, W., & Runde, R. (1996). Stochastic Properties of German Stock Returns. *Empirical Economics*, *21*, 281–306.

Lauridsen, S. (2001). Estimation of Value at Risk by Extreme Value Methods. *Extremes*, *3*, 107–144.

McCulloch, J. H. (1997). Measuring Tail Thickness to Estimate the Stable Index α: A Critique. *Journal of Business and Economic Statistics*, *15*, 74–81.

Mittnik, S., Paolella, M. S., & Rachev, S. T. (1998). A Tail Estimator for the Index of the Stable Paretian Distribution. *Communication in Statistics – Theory and Methods*, *27*, 1239–1262.

Resnick, S., & Starica, C. (1998). Tail Index Estimation for Dependent Data. *Annals of Applied Probability*, *8*, 1156–1183.

Wagner, N., & Marsh, T. A. (2000). On Adaptive Tail Index Estimation for Financial Return Models, Working Paper No. RPF-295, U.C. Berkeley.

USING REGRESSION TECHNIQUES TO ESTIMATE FUTURES HEDGE RATIOS, SOME RESULTS FROM ALTERNATIVE APPROACHES APPLIED TO AUSTRALIAN 10 YEAR TREASURY BOND FUTURES

D. E. Allen, G. MacDonald, D. Walsh and K. Walsh

ABSTRACT

Using data from the Sydney futures market this paper critically assesses some of the potential problems involved in the use of cointegration techniques in the calculation of minimum variance hedge ratios. Following the work of Ghosh (1993a, b) there have been a number of papers which have made use of these techniques. The simple point made by Ghosh, and demonstrated clearly in Lien (1996), is that if spot and futures prices are cointegrated then the non-inclusion of an error correction term in the VAR model used to estimate the hedge ratio will lead to mis-specification problems and the under-estimation of the true optimal hedge ratio. Using data from the Sydney Futures Exchange we examine the use of such regression techniques in the calculation of hedge ratios.

Financial Risk and Financial Risk Management, Volume 16, pages 189–214.

ISBN: 0-7623-0858-3

In particular we consider the extent to which the stacking of the data into a time series, which effectively constrains the estimated hedge ratio to a single value over the span of the data, influences the results of such techniques. If the hedge ratio differs by contract, the movement from one contract to the next is likely to lead to instability in the estimated regression coefficients. Tests for parameter instability in the estimated regression suggest that this is indeed the case and our conclusion is that it is preferable to consider the estimation of the hedge ratio in a panel setting with each individual contract considered as an observational unit. One problem in the past with such a move has been the lack of tests for cointegration and unit roots in such a setting, fortunately these are now available and we take advantage of them in this paper. In such a panel setting we find that the result that the spot and futures prices are cointegrated still holds but that the estimated hedge ratios are not constant between contracts, throwing doubt on the applicability of regression methods which make such an assumption.

BACKGROUND AND MOTIVATION

Estimation of optimal hedge ratios arises from work as far back as Working (1953), Johnson (1960) and Stein (1961). Ederington (1979) formalises these ideas. He shows that a minimum variance hedge ratio (MVHR) is simply defined as the ratio of the covariance of futures price and spot price to the variance of futures price.[1] Ederington then shows that the MVHR is just the slope coefficient from a properly specified OLS regression, where futures price is the explanatory variable and spot price is the dependent variable.

It is also possible to measure the ex post effectiveness of the hedge as the ratio of the difference in variances of the hedged and unhedged positions to the variance of the unhedged positions (i.e. the percentage risk reduced by the hedge). This can easily be shown to be the R^2 from the OLS regression above (see, for example, Malliaris & Urrutia, 1991).

This approach to the estimation of MVHRs is clearly constrained to those that are constant and can be applied to hedges that exactly match the sampling interval of the regression data. However, even given this, they have been widely estimated and studied.[2] In a sense, they are timeless in that they implicitly assume that the covariability between spot and futures prices are constant, not time dependent. Ferguson and Leistikow (1998) argue that this is the case and suggest that "the commonly held view that in direct, near-to-maturity hedges the HR (hedge ratio) is approximately 1 for most assets is broadly supported by the data". However, the general thrust of recent work has been in a very different direction.

More recent directions have been to extend the OLS regression specification. For example, Myers and Thompson (1989) derive a MVHR that allows for conditioning information like seasonal effects. Howard and d'Antonio (1991) develop a multiperiod hedging strategy (generalised by Lien and Luo (1993) to allow for markets that are cointegrated and again by Lien and Luo (1994) to allow for conditional volatility). "Dynamic" hedging approaches have been suggested by Lence, Kimle and Hayenga (1993) and Myers and Hanson (1996).

A recent and very popular direction has been to relax the constant MVHR assumption, and use a more sophisticated technique that allows for time variation.[3] This involves estimating the time-varying hedge ratio using conditional volatility estimates from a bivariate GARCH model. While this topic is not the focus of this paper, it does help to throw light on restrictions and assumptions placed by other techniques.[4]

These other directions will not be discussed here.[5] Our interest involves assessing whether a cointegrating relationship exists between futures prices and spot prices. The study of cointegration between spot and futures markets and its effect on estimation of MVHRs probably started with Ghosh (1993b), who showed that MVHRs are biased downwards due to misspecification if spot and futures are cointegrated and the error correction term is not included in the regression. Theoretical support is provided by Lien (1996), who notes that "a hedger who omits the cointegration relationship will adopt a smaller than optimal futures position, which results in a relatively poor hedging performance" (p. 779).

However, Lien (1996) assumes that the equilbrium position is when spot and futures prices converge. This only holds at the end of the futures contract on the point of delivery. Prior to maturity we have the linkage between spot and futures prices constrained by the cost of carry relationship. We believe that we can get a fresh insight on hedging by viewing it from another angle, namely the option pricing view which provides a means of estimating an instantaneous hedge ratio.

Fisher (1978) and Margrabe (1978) provide a valuation for exchange options. This is the case when the exercise price is unknown. The valuation depends on the standard deviation of the two assets and the correlation between them.

$$C(S_t, F_t, T) = S_t\, N(d_1) - F_t\, N(d_2) \tag{1}$$

Where S_t is the spot at time t, F_t futures at time t, and the time to maturity is T.

$$\text{Also } d_1 = \frac{\ln(S_t/F_t) + \sigma^2 T}{\sigma\sqrt{T}}$$

$$d_2 = d_1 - \sigma\sqrt{T}$$

$$\text{and } \sigma^2 = \sigma^2_{St} - 2\rho_{StTt}\sigma_{St}\sigma_{Tt} + \sigma^2_{Ft}$$

The hedge ratio in the option context of spot on futures is N d_1. Prior to maturity the hedge ratio will depend on the variances of the two price series, their respective levels, standard deviations and correlations. In a sense this is what we are either running the OLS or ECM to calculate. At delivery the two prices are the same, the correlation is one and their variances are the same. At delivery of the futures contract the spot price and the futures prices are one and the same thing and have the same instantaneous variance of their rate of return, assumed constant in Black/Scholes. This means that $\sigma^2 = 0$, $T = 0$ and the hedge ratio $N(d_1) = 1$. This is the equilibrium assumed by Lien.

Prior to maturity we must have the cost of carry relationship holding between spot and futures. If we ignore dividends for the moment and marking to market we have:

$$_tF_T = E(S_{t=T})$$

$$_tF_T = S_t e^{trT} \tag{2}$$

If we substitute this value back in expression (1) we are assuming a known constant risk-free rate we get the following:

$$C(S_t, F_t, T) = S_t N(d_1) - S_t e^{trT} N(d_2) \tag{3}$$

where

$$d_1 = \frac{\ln(S_t/St\ e^{trT}) + \sigma^2 T}{\sigma\sqrt{T}}$$

Other things being equal, the ratio of the two prices suggests that the hedge ratio will be less than one prior to expiry, but this assumes the same diffusion process, constant interest rates etc., Lien incorrectly states that the ECM reduces the problem of underhedging.

Heaney (1998) has tested the cost of carry relationship using the London Metal Exchange lead contract. He points out that the variables underlying the cost of carry relationship may be non-stationary. This may particularly be the case with interest rates. He concludes that his data set suggests the existence of one cointegrating vector which consists of futures price, spot price, interest rate to maturity, stock level and a constant term. This implies that estimating a single cointegrating vector between spot and futures prices but omitting cost of carry terms may lead to mispecification of the vars.

Until now in this paper, we have motivated the study of cointegration between futures and spot through the estimation of MVHRs. However, there is a second motivation for this study. The issue of price discovery on futures and spot markets has long been a topic of interest to students of market microstructure and market efficiency. The idea is as follows: new price-sensitive information arriving at a market will be rapidly incorporated in price, in the process known as price discovery. However, when there are two markets that react to the same price-sensitive information (for example, futures and spot), which market reacts first? Whether the information is privately held or is a public announcement, the issues are very similar; design of markets, design of information release strategies and regulation of insider trading are among many motivations for study.

An early study that examined this relationship was Garbade and Silber (1982), which found the futures market leading the spot. However, this was not a strict causality test in the sense of Granger (1969) or Sims (1972), so more sophisticated vector autoregression (VAR) tests of causality were introduced, probably first by Stoll and Whaley (1990). Evidence from these and other papers suggests that futures markets usually lead spot markets by between 15 and 45 minutes.

However, if cointegration is present the nature of the VAR (and hence the causality test) is affected. Principally, causality tests then need to rely on a vector error correction (VEC) approach because a VEC model is required for causality tests in the presence of cointegration. This point is made strongly in Wahab and Lashgari (1993) and to a lesser extent in Ghosh (1993a). Both of these papers demonstrate how the VEC approach to estimation improves the ability to test for causality, in that models that do not allow for the presence of cointegration can draw incorrect inference regarding causality. However, using this approach, the direction of causality does not change, the lead of the futures market is largely unchanged and the size of the effect on the lag coefficients is not great, as seen in Tse (1995). Nevertheless, in the search for a correct specification, it is clear that the error correction term is statistically significant.[6]

Having said that both MVHRs and tests for causality are indeed affected by cointegration, a question that remains is whether or not futures and spot markets are indeed cointegrated. It seems that there is substantial (if somewhat superficial)[7] evidence that supports this, for financial and non-financial assets. Examples include Fortenbery and Zapata (1994) and Crowder and Hamed (1994).

One last point that needs to be made before discussing our method and the layout in the paper is that at least two papers have considered the use of tests of cointegration in the presence of conditional volatility (i.e. GARCH) effects. Kim and Schmidt (1993) show that the accuracy of the Dickey-Fuller test decreases as we approach integration of the conditional volatility equation (that is, as we approach IGARCH) with a non-zero constant term in the volatility equation. (Both of these are quite likely in practice.) The effect of this is that the DF test rejects the null of a unit root too often; the incidence of Type I errors increases. Lee and Tse (1996) find a similar effect using the Johansen test. However, both of these papers conclude that the effect is not great.

Leading from all of this, our study has two main emphases. Firstly, we question the significance of the cointegration between spot and futures, both from statistical and economic viewpoints. Secondly, we criticise the application of the standard cointegration approaches to data which are stacked (inducing systematic patterns and outliers in the data) and in which frequent mean and trend changes have occurred. It is clear from previous studies that not enough attention has been paid to these important issues. Questions like why the data are stacked, what impact convergence has, what impact trend changes and outliers have, and so on have not been addressed.

COINTEGRATION AND THE CALCULATION OF MVHR'S

Following on from the work of Ghosh (1993a, b), Lien (1996) demonstrates that in the context of the calculation of the optimal hedge ratio the existence of cointegration between spot and futures prices will typically lead to a downwardly biased hedge ratio if the error correction term is not allowed for in the calculation. Using a simple theoretical model Lien notes that the costs of omission of the cointegrating relationship from the calculation rise with the importance of the long run relationship for the dynamics of spot and futures prices. Thus it would seem sensible as a starting point to see how much the omission of the cointegrating relationship, if it exists, affects the calculated hedge ratio. Denoting s_t as the (log) spot price and f_t as the (log) futures price, then if s_t and f_t are not cointegrated the optimal hedge ratio can be calculated from a standard VAR model, using first differences of the variables, of the form:

$$\Delta S_t = \sum_{i=1}^{k} \beta_i \Delta S_{t-i} + \sum_{j=1}^{k} \delta_j \Delta f_{t-j} + \varepsilon_{1t}$$

$$\Delta f_t = \sum_{i=1}^{k} \gamma \Delta S_{t-i} + \sum_{j=1}^{k} \lambda \Delta f_{t-j} + \varepsilon_{2t} \tag{4}$$

and the hedge ratio is calculated as $\rho(\sigma_1/\sigma_2)$ where ρ is the correlation coefficient between ε_{1t} and ε_{2t} and σ_i is the variance of ε_{it} $i = 1,2$. However, the finding that s_t and f_t are cointegrated implies that the above VAR is mis-specified and that the cointegrating vectors must be included in the VAR, yielding a Vector Error Correction Model (VECM). In this case, since we only have two variables, there can be only one cointegrating vector, if we denote the error correction term derived from this vector as z then the VECM can be written as:

$$\Delta S_t = \sum_{i=1}^{i=n} \beta \Delta S_{t-i} + \sum_{j=1}^{j=k} \delta \Delta f_{t-j} - \alpha_s z_{t-1} + \varepsilon_{1t}$$

$$\Delta f_t = \sum_{i=1}^{i=n} \gamma \Delta S_{t-i} + \sum_{j=1}^{j=k} \lambda \Delta f_{t-j} + \alpha_f z_{t-1} + \varepsilon_{2t} \tag{5}$$

The hedge ratio can now be calculated using the same formula as above. The co-efficients, α_s and α_f can be interpreted as speed of adjustment factors. They measure how quickly each market responds to deviations from the long run equilibriating relationship. Thus if the cointegrating vector between s_t and f_t were denoted $(1, -\beta)$ then the error correcting term z_{t-1} is equivalent to $(s_t - \beta f_t)$. So, in the Δs_t equation if the disequilibrium is positive ie the spot rate is "too high" relative to the futures rate then this implies that the error correction term should be pushing it down, back to the equilibrium, hence we would expect the coefficient on α_s to be negative. In the Δf_t equation the same disequilibrium should cause f_t to rise, again this is reflected in the different signs given to the error correcting term. Of course it is possible for one of the error correcting terms to have a zero coefficient. This would imply that whilst the two markets move in an equilibrium relationship one of the markets does *all* of the re-adjustment. Thus if, above $\alpha_s = 0$ then if a positive disequilibrium arises then it is the futures market which does all of the adjusting back to equilibrium. On the other hand, it is not possible for $\alpha_s = \alpha_f = 0$ since then we would have a normal VAR in differences and the two variables would not be cointegrated.

THE TIME SERIES DATA

Our analysis was performed on 10-Year Government Treasury Bonds[9] listed on the Sydney Futures Exchange. We collected daily closing prices of the Futures Contracts from 20/3/85 to 17/3/97.[10] The corresponding cash prices of the 10-year bonds were sourced from Datastream.

In order to achieve a 'time series' of data the contracts were stacked in the following manner. The first data point at 20/3/85 was the price of a June 85 futures contract (60 days from expiration). We collected the June prices until the contract expired on 17/06/85. From the 18/06/85 we then collected the prices of the September Futures contract until expiration. This resulted in a time series of matched pairs of future and cash prices of 'nearest time to maturity' contracts.

To sort the data into panel format we needed to match the time to maturity cross-sectionally. We therefore selected the matched pairs from 60 days to maturity until expiration for each contract. This resulted in 49 columns of matched pairs with 60 data points in each column.

Firstly standard ADF tests were carried out on the time series data. We initially estimated an ADF with lag order of 8 and then sequentially reduced lag order, stopping when the last included lag was significant. For both spot and futures this occurred at lag 5 and the ADF statistics were –2.13 and –2.21 respectively, there was no evidence of serial correlation in the residuals and thus the tests could not reject the null of a unit root. On first differencing the two series the test statistics, using the same procedure were highly significant, − 23.22 for the spot rate and − 23.35 for the futures. Thus we conclude that the series are I(1) and it is possible to test for cointegration.

The first step in the Johansen estimation is the choice of the lag length in the VAR. We tested down from an, arbitrarily, chosen lag length of 10 and selected a lag length of 6 on the basis of F tests on the model reduction process[11] and calculation of the likelihood ratio test for the VAR reduction suggested by Sims,[12] see Table 1. Since the test is distributed as $\chi^2(4)$ the critical value is approximately 7.8 for 10% and 9.5 for 5% so the restriction from 6 to 5 is rejected.

The Johansen test and its associated critical values are based on the assumption of serially uncorrelated and normally distributed innovations.

Table 1. Var Reduction Test Statistics.

lag	10 to 9	9 to 8	8 to 7	7 to 6	6 to 5	5 to 4
Test Statistic	4.62	0	2.31	2.9	10.7	14.8

Whilst our estimated VAR passes the test of non correlated residuals it fails the test for normality. Fortunately monte carlo tests carried out by Cheung and Lai (1993) suggests that Johansens test, and in particular the trace test, is reasonably robust to the presence of non normality and that any bias is of a relatively low order.

Bearing all of the above in mind, Table 2 reports the standard maximum Eigenvalue and trace test statistics for testing for cointegration using Johansens method. As can be seen the test statistics suggest the presence of a single cointegrating vector.[13]

Based on the assumption that the rank of the long run matrix $\alpha\beta' = \Pi$ is unity we can carry out a number of simple tests based on restrictions on the α and β' matrices (under the assumption of a single cointegrating vector these matrices will in fact be a 1 by 2 row vector and a 2 by 1 column vector). Firstly by restricting the β' matrix so that $\beta_{11} = 0$ and $\beta_{12} = 1$ we can re test the unit root hypothesis. If the future series is I(1) it should reject this restriction. We can also test the unit root in the spot rate by a similar restriction, $\beta_{11} = 1$ and $\beta_{12} = 0$. These multivariate unit root tests are reported in the table below and confirm the non stationary status of the two series. A similar test can be used to test whether the cointegrating vector is (1, –1), and this restriction cannot be rejected by the data at the 5% level.

We can also test if either of the variables are weakly exogenous by restricting the weighting coefficients in the α matrix. Thus the spot rate is weakly exogenous if the relevant α coefficient cannot reject a zero restriction, implying that the cointegrating vector does not enter the spot equation of the system. Again these results are below (Table 3) and interestingly we find that the spot equation is weakly exogenous and does not therefore adjust for any of the long run disequilibrium in the system in the manner suggested above.

Using the error correction term calculated as $s_t - f_t$ we then estimated a VECM as in (2) above with $k = n = 5$. Whilst the error correction term was correctly signed in both equations and significant for the system as a whole, it was not significantly different from zero in the Δs_t equation but was significant in the Δf_t equation, thus supporting the above results that, in the long run, it is the futures rate which makes any adjustment back to the long run equilibrium

Table 2. Cointegration Analysis.

Eigenvalue	Null Hypothesis	Max. Eigenvalue test (unadjusted)	Max. Eigenvalue test (adjusted)	95% critical value	Trace test (unadjusted)	Trace test (adjusted)	95% critical value
0.016055	r = 0	47.47	47.28	14.1	48.01	47.81	15.4
0.000183	r = 0	0.5368	0.5347	3.8	0.5368	0.5347	3.8

Standardised β′ eigenvectors

Variable	Lspot	Lfuture
	$\beta_{11} = 1.0000$	$\beta_{12} = -1.0082$
	$\beta_{21} = -2.0983$	$\beta_{22} = 1.0000$

Standardised α coefficients

Lspot	0.000159	0.000470
Lfuture	0.059085	0.000469

Table 3. Restricted Estimation.

Multivariate unit root tests

Variable	Test statistic ($\chi^2(1)$)	p-value
Lspot	46.89	<0.01
Lfuture	46.75	<0.01

Test on cointegrating vector being (1,–1)

Test statistic ($\chi^2(1)$)	p-value
2.7143	0.0995

Weak exogeneity tests

Variable	Test statistic ($\chi^2(1)$)	p-value
Lspot	0.00001	0.99
Lfuture	6.59	0.01

relationship. Secondly whilst the coefficient on the error correction term in the futures equation is quite small in size, suggesting it takes approximately 20 periods to correct, this is well within the contract period which is 60 days. The VECM was then used to calculate the optimal hedge ratio as 0.86137. Now, supposing that the hedger was ignorant of the cointegration between spot and futures, s/he would estimate a simple VAR of the form given in (1) above, ignoring the error correction term. Doing so led to the calculation of the hedge ratio as 0.85963. Thus the analysis suggested by Lien is justified by the data in that the hedge ratio is smaller, however, given the small size of the coefficient on the error correcting term and the fact that it is insignificant in the spot equation, the error is as would have been expected small in absolute magnitude. Thus, the results of standard testing procedures suggest that the spot and futures price are I(1) processes which cointegrate. However the bias induced by ignoring the error correction term in the calculation of the hedge ratio appears to be small for this data set.

As noted in the introduction the primary focus of the paper is the validity of the assumption that we can calculate a single hedge ratio over this period using data stacked into a panel. In practice it is possible that the hedge ratio is not a constant but, for example varies over the contracts. Whilst we use more direct tests of this assumption below, when we organise the data into a set of panels, with each contract representing an observational unit, we can gain some insight into the validity of this assumption by testing for parameter stability in the cointegrating regression. In order to do this we apply a test to the cointegrating regression directly using a sequence of tests suggested by Hansen (1992). Hansen uses the Fully Modified OLS estimation procedure (FMOLS) suggested by Phillips and Hansen (1990) as a framework for testing parameter stability in regressions with I(1) variables. FMOLS is an alternative method of estimating cointegrating vectors which avoids the problem of finite sample bias in a static regression involving I(1) variables.[14] Johansen estimation attempts to solve the problem using a full system maximum likelihood estimator. FM-OLS is asymptotically equivalent and is based on non parametric correction for simultaneity bias and residual autocorrelation and depends on estimation of the long run variance covariance matrix using a kernel estimator. FM-OLS has the further advantage of being the estimator suggested by Hansen (1992) in his work on testing for parameter instability in regressions involving I(1) processes. In his paper Hansen (1992) suggests three tests for parameter instability, all of which posit a structural change in the regression equation parameters at an unknown date,[15] these are the supF, mean F and Lc test.[16] These tests provide a solution to the problem that standard Chow tests are based on *a priori* knowledge of the break date. Selection of such a break date leads to the same sort of problems as have become well-known in the literature on testing for a unit root in the presence of structural breaks in the underlying trend function (Perron, 1989; Banerjee, Lumsdaine & Stock, 1992; Zivot & Andrews, 1992). Hansen's solution is the same as the one adopted there, to calculate the test statistics allowing the assumed break point to move, sequentially through the sample. Clearly under such circumstance the critical values of the test statistic would be non standard, and Hansen (1992) provides such critical values. Hansen (1992) also shows that one of the test statistics, the Lc test can be considered as a test of the null hypothesis of cointegration against the alternative of non cointegration. In applying the tests we allowed a constant to enter the coinrtegrating regression and assumed possible drift in the I(1) processes.[17] What we find (see Table 4) is that the FMOLS estimate of the cointegrating parameter is close to that obtained from the Johansen estimation, being 1.0066, with a standard error of 0.002 (the Johansen estimation yielded a parameter estimate of 1.0082). However all three of the tests suggest a strong rejection of the null of parameter stability, this is reflected in the plot of the recursively estimated F tests, see Fig. 1.

Table 4. Results of FM-OLS and Hansen.

Sample size 2940.0000

Variable	Coefficient	Std. error
Log of Future	1.0066248	0.00218
Constant	–0.57584314	0.19480

Tests for Parameter Stability

	Test Statistic	P-value ('0.20′ means ′>=0.20′)
LC	1.24	0.01
MeanF	14.85	0.01
SupF	31.8	0.01

Whilst the above test is suggestive of instability it would be preferable to have a more formal test of the constancy of the hedge ratio across the contracts. In order to provide this we now move to estimation based on the re-ordering into a set of 49 contracts which could be considered as a panel.

Moving to an examination of the hedge ratio on a contract by contract basis leads to the potential criticism of loss of power due to the small sample size (60 observations). However by considering the data as a panel we can considerably improve the power properties of our test. Indeed in the context of unit root and cointegration tests the use of panels has been seen as an advantage in the literature recently.

The first step is to test the data, stacked by contract, for a unit root. The test we apply here is that of Im, Pesaran and Shin (IPS henceforth). This test is based on a simple average of the individual series ADF tests and has a standard normal distribution once adjusted in the manner suggested by IPS using their monte carlo based estimates of its mean and variance. The test has the advantage of allowing for different parameter estimates and autocorrelation structures amongst the various series across the panel. The test has been shown by IPS using monte carlo studies to have better finite sample performance than the other commonly used panel unit root test suggested by Levin and Lin (1993). There are, however, a number of questionable aspects of these tests. Firstly, despite the increase in power gained from the use of a panel the test is still based on the null that the series in question are unit root processes.

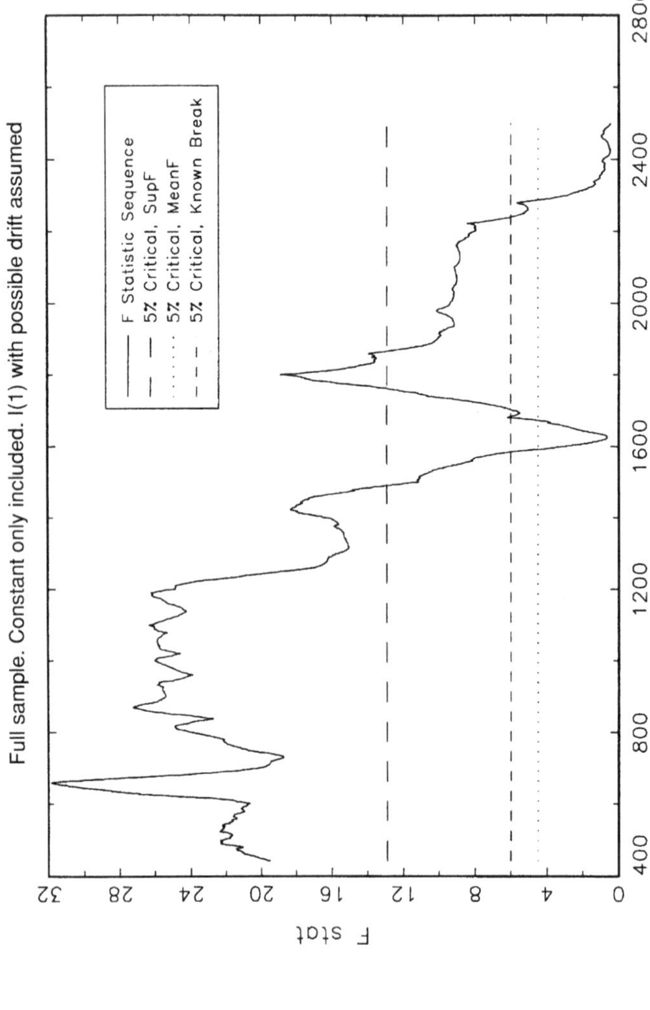
Full sample. Constant only included. I(1) with possible drift assumed
F stat
32
28
24
20
16
12
8
4
0
400
800
1200
1600
2000
2400
2800
F Statistic Sequence
5% Critical, SupF
5% Critical, MeanF
5% Critical, Known Break

Fig. 1.

Secondly the null hypothesis is that all of the series in the panel contain a unit root against the alternative that none do. This assumption has been criticised recently by Hansen and King (1998) who argue that it is thus possible that outliers (in the sense of a relatively high or low ADF for a particular series) have the potential to bias the results and that the all or nothing approach is unattractive. On the other hand, and as noted by McCoskey and Selden (1998) if it were the case that series were of different orders of integration this would put into question their aggregation across panels. Clearly these are important issues which need resolving before the confident application of such tests. However, in the current context, where we expect a high degree of homogeneity across the panel's, in the sense that whilst parameter variation is quite possible (and allowed for in the test) we would expect the basic time series properties of the series to be the same and hence the test would seem to be appropriate.

In terms of application the test is simple. We ran ADF tests (including a constant and time trend) on both the spot and future data for each of the 49 contracts. The lag order for each series and each panel was chosen by testing down from a maximum lag of 8 in the ADF, stopping if and when the last included lag was significant. The test statistic is then calculated as:

$$\Psi_{\bar{t}} = \frac{\sqrt{N}\left\{\bar{t}_{NT} - \frac{1}{N}\sum_{i=1}^{N} E[t_{iT}(p_i,0)]\right\}}{\sqrt{\frac{1}{N}\sum_{i=1}^{N} Var[t_{iT}(p_i,0)]}} \tag{6}$$

where N is the number of panels, $\bar{t}_{NT}$ and values for $E[t_{iT}(p_i,0)]$ and $Var[t_{iT}(p_i,0)]$ are obtained from the results of the monte carlo simulation carried out by IPS.[18] The resultant test statistic has a standard normal distribution.

When the above test was carried out the value of the test statistic for the spot data was -0.43162 and that for the futures data was -0.42687, neither of which, therefore can reject the unit root null. Once we took the first difference of the data the results were -35.85 (spot) and -36.79 (future). Thus the results confirm our earlier finding in that the panel tests cannot reject the null of a unit root in the levels but can on first differencing. Thus we conclude that the spot and futures rates are both I(1) in each individual contract. Thus it is valid to test for cointegration in a panel setting.

The panel cointegration tests used were based on those suggested by Pedroni (1997, 1998) and discussed in McCoskey and Kao (1997) in their comparison of panel cointegration tests. The actual test applied is the equivalent to the panel unit root test discussed above in that it is a group mean estimator which is converted to standard Normal using means and variances estimated via monte carlo simulations (we used those reported in McCoskey & Kao, 1997). Once again the test has the attractive feature of leading to an increase in power but at the same time allowing the cointegrating vector to vary so that each contract can have an individual cointegrating vector.

The test statistic is constructed using the following result (McCoskey & Kao, 1997):

$$\sqrt{N}(\bar{t}_{ADF} - \mu_{ADF}) \Rightarrow N(0, \sigma^2_{ADF}) \tag{7}$$

where μ_{ADF} and σ^2_{ADF} are given by the monte carlo simulations and $\bar{t}_{ADF}$ is the average of the individual ADF tests carried out on the residuals from the cointegrating regression for each of the individual contracts. Thus in practice the test involves estimating the ols cointegrating regression for each contract (thus allowing different slope estimates for each), retrieving the residuals and constructing the appropriate ADF (again each contract is allowed to have differing lag lengths in the ADF test to allow for differing autocorrelation structures). Again a potential criticism of the test procedure is that the null is no cointegration for the panel as a whole. The null will be rejected only when a sufficiently large number of the individual elements of the panel (the contracts) generate test statistics that are sufficiently far away from the mean value predicted by the theory under the assumption of the null. Thus a number of the individual elements could reject no cointegration but the constructed test might still fail to reject the null hypothesis that none can reject the null of no cointegration. In our case using the values for the mean and standard deviation obtained by McKoskey and Kao, of 2.0261 and 0.82, the value of $\bar{t}_{ADF}$ was calculated as -2.36941 and the test statistic thus evaluates to -2.93, thus rejecting the null of no cointegration. Overall therefore we are willing to proceed on the basis that there is evidence that spots and futures cointegrate. To find out how robust this evidence was to the length of contract period considered we re-estimated the above test statistics lifting each contract at an arbitrary point, we chose 50% of the way through. Using such a technique reflects the idea that the hedger may well not hold the contract to maturity but lift at some point through the sample and move to the next nearest futures contract. Doing this restricts us to only 30 observations in each contract, if we were unable to take advantage of the panel properties of the data this would be too few observations on which to base any sensible inference. Using panel tests we found continued support for the notion that the spot and the futures price cointegrate with the test statistic for the null of non unit root in the residuals from the cointegrating regression being -2.26 (once converted to standard normal) thus rejecting the unit root and suggesting that once again we have cointegration between spot and futures.

Once again we apply Hansens tests for parameter stability to the data on a panel by panel basis. Table 5 shows the results. We chose to categorise the results as showing evidence of instability whenever there was agreement between the three tests at the 5% level. Where at least one test was significant at 5% but at least one of the other three was not we categorised the test as "inconclusive." Only where none of the three tests was significant at 5% did we conclude that there was no evidence of instability. As can be seen from Table 5 the tests reject stability on 3 occasions and are inconclusive on 12 occasions. Thus there is evidence of stability in 34 out of the 49 individual contracts, some 79% of the sample, and only clear evidence of instability in 6% of the cases.

Our results suggest that it is appropriate, on a contract by contract basis, to assume that in each contract the spot and futures rates are I(1) and that they cointegrate. We wish now to formally test the assumption that the hedge ratios are equal across the contracts. To do so we consider a variation of the Hildreth/Houck/Swamy random coefficients model. The random coefficients model (rcm) allows the estimated coefficients in each of the contracts to vary stochastically. If we consider an example where we have n contracts, each with m observations then the model can be expressed as follows:

$$\mathbf{y}_{\mathrm{i}} = \mathbf{X}_{\mathrm{i}}\boldsymbol{\beta}_{i} + \boldsymbol{\varepsilon}_{\mathrm{i}}$$

where (8)

$$\boldsymbol{\beta}_{\mathrm{i}} = \boldsymbol{\beta} + \boldsymbol{v}_{i} \quad \text{with } E[\boldsymbol{v}_{i}] = 0 \text{ and } E[\boldsymbol{v}_{i}, \boldsymbol{v}_{i}] = \boldsymbol{\Gamma}$$

then the β_{i} for any of the individual contracts is the outcome of a random process with mean vector β and covariance matrix Γ.

Combining equations the model is:

$$\mathbf{y}_{\mathrm{i}} = \mathbf{X}_{\mathrm{i}}\boldsymbol{\beta}_{i} + (\boldsymbol{\varepsilon}_{\mathrm{i}} + \mathbf{X}_{\mathrm{i}}\mathbf{v}_{\mathrm{i}})$$

$$= \mathbf{X}_{\mathrm{i}}\boldsymbol{\beta}_{i} + \mathbf{w}_{\mathrm{i}}$$

where (9)

$$E[\mathbf{w}i] = \mathbf{0} \text{ and } E[w_i w_i' = \sigma_i^2 \mathbf{I} + \mathbf{X}_i \boldsymbol{\Gamma} \mathbf{X}_i' = \boldsymbol{\Pi}_i$$

Table 5. Tests for Cointegration and Parameter Stability in the Individual Contracts.

Instability	Cointegrates	Contract	Lc	Mean F	Sup F	beta	se beta	t beta
No	Yes	1	0.20 (0.20)	1.97 (0.20)	5.21 (0.20)	0.79	0.044	18
Inconclusive	Yes	2	0.45 (0.10)	4.59 (0.05)	9.32 (0.16)	1.15	0.027	43
No	Yes	3	0.16 (0.20)	2.69 (0.20)	4.76 (0.20)	0.95	0.014	68
No	Yes	4	0.30 (0.20)	2.01 (0.20)	3.62 (0.20)	1.15	0.065	18
No	Yes	5	0.28 (0.20)	2.03 (0.20)	5.0 (0.20)	0.83	0.035	24
No	Yes	6	0.34 (0.19)	2.85 (0.20)	6.65 (0.20)	0.97	0.019	51
No	Yes	7	0.33 (0.20)	1.81 (0.20)	4.10 (0.20)	0.54	0.102	5
Inconclusive	Yes	8	0.53 (0.06)	4.44 (0.06)	14.41 (0.02)	0.87	0.03	29
No	Yes	9	0.46 (0.09)	3.63 (0.11)	7.62 (0.20)	1.02	0.045	23
No	Yes	10	0.16 (0.20)	1.33 (0.20)	4.04 (0.20)	0.92	0.04	23
Inconclusive	Yes	11	0.34 (0.19)	7.44 (0.01)	12.53 (0.05)	0.95	0.03	32
No	Yes	12	0.51 (0.07)	4.31 (0.06)	5.63 (0.20)	0.85	0.036	24
No	Yes	13	0.20 (0.20)	1.29 (0.20)	1.81 (0.20)	1.13	0.28	4
Inconclusive	No	14	0.67 (0.03)	4.77 (0.04)	8.10 (0.20)	0.73	0.16	5
No	Yes	15	0.26 (0.20)	1.92 (0.20)	9.27 (0.17)	1.17	0.23	5
No	Yes	16	0.43 (0.11)	3.03 (0.17)	6.32 (0.20)	0.94	0.016	59
Yes	No	17	0.81 (0.01)	6.43 (0.01)	15.04 (0.02)	0.81	0.042	19
No	Yes	18	0.24 (0.20)	2.50 (0.20)	5.89 (0.20)	1.23	0.074	17
Yes	No	19	0.58 (0.05)	6.20 (0.01)	16.81 (0.01)	1.16	0.025	46
No	Yes	20	0.19 (0.20)	2.58 (0.20)	7.70 (0.20)	0.77	0.066	12
No	Yes	21	0.18 (0.20)	1.51 (0.20)	4.28 (0.20)	0.65	0.12	5
Inconclusive	Yes	22	0.47 (0.08)	4.74 (0.05)	9.42 (0.16)	0.96	0.031	31
No	Yes	23	0.14 (0.20)	1.72 (0.20)	3.90 (.020)	1.04	0.011	95
No	Yes	24	0.10 (0.20)	1.29 (0.20)	7.39 (0.20)	0.96	0.044	22
No	Yes	25	0.04 (0.20)	0.053 (0.20)	2.04 (0.20)	0.94	0.065	14
Inconclusive	Yes	26	0.52 (0.07)	4.50 (0.05)	13.83 (0.03)	0.92	0.009	102
No	Yes	27	0.41 (0.13)	2.71 (0.20)	5.72 (0.20)	0.72	0.02	36

Table 5. Continued.

Instability	Cointegrates	Contract	Lc	Mean F	Sup F	beta	se beta	t beta
Inconclusive	Yes	28	0.35 (0.18)	8.12 (0.01)	18.25 (0.01)	0.85	0.029	29
No	Yes	29	0.19 (0.20)	2.14 (0.20)	5.41 (0.20)	0.86	0.02	43
Inconclusive	Yes	30	0.14 (0.20)	2.30 (0.20)	16.97 (0.01)	0.89	0.019	47
Inconclusive	No	31	0.63 (0.04)	3.60 (0.11)	6.96 (0.20)	0.56	0.28	2
Inconclusive	Yes	32	0.39 (0.14)	14.90 (0.01)	191.32 (0.01)	0.92	0.014	66
No	Yes	33	0.24 (0.20)	1.66 (0.20)	3.88 (0.20)	0.69	0.094	7
No	Yes	34	0.11 (0.20)	1.78 (0.20)	8.93 (0.19)	0.92	0.009	102
No	Yes	35	0.10 (0.20)	0.71 (0.20)	2.73 (0.20)	0.95	0.112	8
Inconclusive	Yes	36	0.23 (0.20)	7.09 (0.01)	26.04 (0.10)	1.03	0.037	28
No	Yes	37	0.24 (0.20)	1.59 (0.20)	3.72 (0.20)	1.06	0.024	44
No	Yes	38	0.45 (0.10)	2.04 (0.20)	5.33 (0.20)	0.98	0.085	12
No	Yes	39	0.21 (0.20)	2.61 (0.20)	7.68 (0.20)	0.73	0.179	4
No	Yes	40	0.27 (0.20)	1.99 (0.20)	4.20 (0.20)	0.87	0.066	13
Inconclusive	Yes	41	0.29 (0.20)	3.26 (0.14)	15.99 (0.01)	0.93	0.014	66
No	Yes	42	0.25 (0.20)	1.99 (0.20)	5.23 (0.20)	0.96	0.007	137
Yes	No	43	1.16 (0.01)	25.64 (0.01)	64.09 (0.01)	0.74	0.036	21
No	Yes	44	0.48 (0.08)	2.78 (0.20)	7.92 (0.20)	1	0.011	91
No	Yes	45	0.19 (0.20)	1.40 (0.20)	3.54 (0.20)	0.79	0.074	11
No	Yes	46	0.39 (0.14)	3.41 (0.13)	5.22 (0.20)	0.92	0.008	115
No	Yes	47	0.30 (0.20)	2.39 (0.20)	3.97 (0.20)	1.02	0.009	113
No	Yes	48	0.17 (0.20)	1.98 (0.20)	7.29 (0.20)	1.18	0.129	9
No	Yes	49	0.27 (0.20)	2.68 (0.20)	4.51 (0.20)	0.88	0.0173	51

p values in parenthesis after test statistic.

The GLS estimator turns out[20] to be a weighted average of the OLS estimates of the individual coefficients with the weights given by:

$$\mathbf{W}_i = \left\{ \sum_{i=1}^{n} [\boldsymbol{\Gamma} + \mathbf{V}_i]^{-1} \right\}^{-1} [\boldsymbol{\Gamma} + \mathbf{V}_i]^{-1}$$

where (10)

$$\mathbf{V}_i = \boldsymbol{\sigma}_i^2 [\mathbf{X}_i' \mathbf{X}_i]^{-1}$$

Swamy (1971) suggests a two step approach which allows estimation of $\mathbf{V}_i$ and Γ and uses initial OLS estimates of the coefficients, $\mathbf{b}_i$ to provide an estimator of β

$$\hat{\boldsymbol{\beta}} = \sum_i \mathbf{W}_i \mathbf{b}_i$$

and

$$\hat{\boldsymbol{\Gamma}} = \frac{1}{n-1}\left(\sum_i \mathbf{b}_i \mathbf{b}_i' - n\bar{\mathbf{b}}\bar{\mathbf{b}}' \right) - \frac{1}{n} \sum_i \mathbf{V}_i$$

where

$$\bar{\mathbf{b}} = \frac{1}{n} \sum_i \mathbf{b}_i$$

Swamy (1971) provides a test of the random coefficients model which can be viewed as a test for the constancy of the regression parameters in a classical regression model. Swamy's test is asymptotically distributed as χ^2 with K(n − 1) degress of freedom and is constructed as:

$$\chi^2 = \sum_i [\mathbf{b}_i - \tilde{\bar{\mathbf{b}}}]' \hat{\mathbf{V}}_i^{-1} [\mathbf{b}_i - \tilde{\bar{\mathbf{b}}}],$$

where

$$\tilde{\bar{\mathbf{b}}} = \left[\sum_i \hat{\mathbf{V}}_i^{-1} \right]^{-1} \sum_i \hat{\mathbf{V}}_i^{-1} \mathbf{b}_i \quad (11)$$

This tests the null that all of the parameters in the model are equal. In our case we wish to test the null that a subset of the parameters (the ones relevant to the calculation of the hedge ratio) are equal. In order to implement this test we stacked the system in the following way

$$\begin{bmatrix} y_1 \\ y_2 \\ \cdot \\ \cdot \\ y_n \end{bmatrix} = \begin{bmatrix} \mathbf{X}_1 & \mathbf{0} & \dots & \mathbf{0} & \mathbf{0} \\ \mathbf{0} & \mathbf{X}_2 & \dots & \dots & \mathbf{0} \\ \cdot & \cdot & \cdot & \dots & \cdot \\ \mathbf{0} & \cdot & \dots & \mathbf{X}_{n-1} & \cdot \\ \mathbf{0} & \mathbf{0} & \dots & \dots & \mathbf{X}_n \end{bmatrix} \begin{bmatrix} \beta_1 \\ \beta_2 \\ \cdot \\ \cdot \\ \beta_n \end{bmatrix} + \begin{bmatrix} \varepsilon_1 \\ \varepsilon_2 \\ \cdot \\ \cdot \\ \varepsilon_n \end{bmatrix}$$

estimated the system by OLS, and calculated the test statistic as:

$$g = (\mathbf{R}\hat{\boldsymbol{\beta}} - \mathbf{r})'(\mathbf{RCR}')^{-1}(\mathbf{R}\hat{\boldsymbol{\beta}} - \mathbf{r}) \sim \chi^2_{(J)}$$

where (12)

$$\mathbf{C} = [\mathbf{X}'(\boldsymbol{\Sigma}^{-1} \otimes \mathbf{I}_m)\mathbf{X}]^{-1}$$

and

$$\Sigma = \begin{bmatrix} \sigma_1^2 & 0 & 0 & 0 \\ 0 & \sigma_2^2 & 0 & 0 \\ 0 & 0 & \cdot & 0 \\ 0 & 0 & 0 & \sigma_n^2 \end{bmatrix}$$

J is the number of restrictions imposed and we use $\frac{\varepsilon_i \varepsilon_i'}{m-k}$ as our estimator of σ_i^2. The first step was to estimate the cointegrating regression on each contract and test whether the cointegrating vector was the same. This involved running the following regression, by OLS for each contract:

$$Y_{it} = \alpha_i + \beta_i X_{it} + \upsilon_{it} \tag{13}$$

And using the above procedure to test whether we could reject the null that all of the β_i were equal across the panels. The calculated test statistic was $\chi^2(48) = 2075$ strongly rejecting the null, implying that the cointegrating vectors are not the same across the contracts.

We now estimated the VECM model using the estimation techniques described above. Since the above test rejected the null that the cointegrating vectors were constant we used the estimated parameters from the FM-OLS estimation, on a contract by contract basis, in order to construct the error correction terms. Thus for contract 1 the error correction term was calculated as:

$$\Psi = s_t - 0.79(f_t)$$

We then estimated the following regression equation using the random coefficients model:

$$\Delta Lspot_{it} = \beta_i \Delta Lfuture_{it} + \sum_{j=1}^{k} \delta_i \Delta Lfuture_{i,t-j} + \sum_{j=1}^{k} \lambda_i \Delta Lspot_{i,t-j} + \alpha_i \Psi_{i,t-1} + \xi_{i,t} \quad (14)$$

where the coefficient β will give us a direct estimate of the hedge ratio. Prior to estimation two issues required resolving. A further issue here was the lag order in the VECM, because of the use of panel based estimation the lag orders had to be the same across the contracts. We estimated the equation on a contract by contract basis in order to get some idea of the required lag order and found that a lag order of 2 was adequate in most cases. Whilst we accept that the sample size is small we found that the results and the diagnostics on the models were remarkably good, and that most of the diagnostic problems faced using the stacked time series data were eliminated.

Once again we used the test statistic described above to test the null that the coefficient β, the estimate of the hedge ratio, was constant across contracts and once again we found strong evidence against the null hypothesis, with the test statistic being $\chi^2(48) = 298.8$ which strongly rejects the null at normal significance levels. We carried out the above estimation using the full sample of data (60 observations per contract) and so once again it seemed worthwhile to see if the results were robust to a lifting of the contract halfway through the 60 days. Once again the test statistic ($\chi^2(48) = 175.1$) rejected the null that the hedge ratios were constant across the contracts.

CONCLUSIONS

This paper has addressed the question of the validity of using standard econometric techniques to estimate hedge ratios by stacking contracts into a time series. Such an approach makes the implicit assumption that the hedge ratio can be taken as a constant across the differing contracts. Our findings are that, whilst the basic time series properties of the data show a high degree of homogeneity, this assumption is not valid, with the individual hedge ratio estimates differing significantly between contracts. We also find that the estimated parameters show considerably stronger evidence of stability when we look at the data on a contract by contract basis. For much of our analysis we are able to take advantage of the increased power of panel based testing procedures, such as tests for a unit root and cointegration, and it seems likely that further developments in the econometrics of panel based testing will lead to fruitful applications in this area.

NOTES

1. We could also use price change or return for futures and spot, and the definition remains the same. Most studies (including us) use the price change version.
2. See, for example, Figlewski (1984, 1985), and Hill and Schneeweis (1984).
3. But note that McNew and Fackler (1994) develop a test of a constant hedge ratio and cannot reject the null hypothesis that the hedge ratio is indeed constant.
4. The interested reader is directed to Baillie and Myers (1991), Chan, Chan and Karolyi (1991), Myers and Hanson (1993), Park and Switzer (1995) and Choudhry (1997). For a general overview of the GARCH literature, see Bollerslev, Chou and Kroner (1992).
5. In particular, evaluation of the applicability of bivariate GARCH estimation is the subject of further research by us at present.
6. Note that this is extended in work by Chatrath and Song (1997) and Choudhry (1997) allow for both bivariate GARCH and VEC in what is sometimes known as a GARCH-X model. They find that most parameters are significant but that the causal structure does not change. Neither paper examines the impact on MVHRs.
7. It is exactly this point that we address.
8. As well as Ghosh (1993a) and Wahab and Lashgari (1993).
9. $100,000 face value, 12% pa coupon rate, Mar, Jun, Sep, Dec up to 2 quarter months ahead. The contracts expire at 12:00pm on the 15th day of the contract month (or next business day).
10. This information is publicly available from the Sydney Future Exchange at http://www.sfe.com.au
11. Most of the estimation in this paper was carried out using PC-GIVE and PC-FIML professional version 9 (Doornik & Hendry, 1997), full results are available from the corresponding author on request.
12. However we should note that one positive aspect of the tests was that the cointegration results were remarkably robust to a variety of lag lengths in the VAR an issue considered by Hall (1991).
13. The column headed "using T-nm uses a degrees of freedom correction suggested by Reimers (1992) (where T is sample size, m the lag order and n the number of variables in the cointegrating vector. The test statistic can then be compared to asymptotic critical values from the appropriate source. Cheung and Lai (1993) suggest that this scaling factor is biased (in favour of over rejection of the null) and they present response surface estimates which allow for the scaling of the asymptotic critical values. In this case both methods suggest a single cointegrating vector.
14. The validity of the procedure depends on the assumption that the right hand side variables in the cointegrating regression are I(1) and not cointegrated amongst themselves, in our case with only one explanatory variable this assumption clearly holds.

15. The break date is constrained so as not to lie close to the beginning or end of the sample and for practical purposes we do not consider breaks in the first or last 15% of the sample.

16. Estimation was carried out using GAU.S.S and we are grateful to Prof. Hansen who made the program for estimation of the supF, meanF and Lc tests available via his web page.

17. The results were however robust to alternative specifications of the trends in the model.

18. P refers to the lag order in the ADF, IPS report values for the mean and variance for values of p ranging from 0 to 8 for regression models with a constant only and with a constant and trend in the ADF.

19. All of the test results on the panels are available from the corresponding author on request.

20. See Greene (1993) pp. 459–460.

REFERENCES

Banerjee, A., Lumsdaine, R. L., & Stock, J. H. (1992). Recursive and sequential tests of the unit root and trend break hypothesis: Theory and international evidence. *Journal of Business and Economic Statistics*, *10*, 271–287.

Baillie, R., & Myers, R. (1991). Bivariate GARCH Estimation of the Optimal Commodity Futures Hedge. *Journal of Applied Econometrics*, *6*, 109–124.

Bollerslev, T., Chou, R. Y., & Kroner, K. F. (1992). Arch Modelling in Finance: a Review of the Theory and Empirical Evidence. *Journal of Econometrics*, *52*, 5–59.

Chan, K., Chan, K. C., & Karolyi, G. A. (1991). Intraday Volatility in the Stock Index and Stock Index Futures Markets. *Review of Financial Studies*, *4*(4), 657–684.

Cheung, Y-W., & Lai, K. S. (1993). Finite sample sizes of Johansen's likelihood ratio test for cointegration. *Oxford Bulletin of Economics and Statistics*, *55*(3), 313–328.

Choudhry, T. (1997). Short-Run Deviations and Volatility in Spot and Futures Markets: Evidence from Australia, Hong Kong and Japan. *Journal of Futures Markets*, *17*(6), 689–705.

Crowder, W. J., & Hamed, A. (1993). A Cointegration Test of Oil Futures Market Efficiency. *Journal of Futures Markets*, *13*, 933–941.

Doornik, J. A., & Hendry, D. F. (1997). *PC-GIVE and PC-FIML 9.0 for windows.ITP publishing*. London.

Ederington, L. (1979). The Hedging Performance of the New Futures Markets. *Journal of Finance*, *34*, 157–170.

Ferguson, R., & Leistikow, D. (1998). Are regression approach futures hedge ratios stationary? *Journal of Futures Markets*, *18*, 851–866.

Fisher, S. (1978). Call option pricing when the exercise price is uncertain and the valuation of index bonds. *Journal of Finance*, 169–176.

Figlewski, S. (1984). Hedging Performance and Basis Risk in Stock Index Futures. *Journal of Finance*, *39*, 657–669.

Figlewski, S. (1985). Hedging with Stock Index Futures: Theory and Application in a New Market. *Journal of Futures Markets*, *5*, 183–199.

Fortenbery, T. R., & Zapata, H. O. (1993). An Examination of Cointegration Relations between Futures and Local Grain Markets. *Journal of Futures Markets*, *13*, 921–932.

Garbade, K. D., & Silber, W. L. (1982). Best Exceution in Securities Markets: An Application of Signalling and Agency Theory. *Journal of Finance*, *37*, 493–504.

Ghosh, A. (1993a). Cointegration and Error Correction Models: Intertemporal Causality between Index and Futures Prices. *Journal of Futures Markets*, *13*, 193–198.

Ghosh, A. (1993b). Hedging with Stock Index Futures: Estimation and Forecasting with Error Correction Model. *Journal of Futures Markets*, *13*, 743–752.

Granger, C. W. (1969). Investigating Causal Relations by Econometric Models and Cross-Spectral Methods. *Econometrica*, *37*, pp. 424–438.

Greene, W. H. (1993). *Econometric Analysis*, (2nd ed.). New York: Macmillan Publishing.

Hall, S. G. (1991). The effects of varying length VAR models on the maximum likelihood estimates of cointegrating vectors. *Scottish Journal of Political Economy*, *38*(4), 317–323.

Hansen, B. E. (1992). Tests for parameter instability in regressions with I(1) processes. *Journal of Business and Economic Statistics*, *10*(3), 321–335.

Hansen, P., & King, A. (1998). Heath care expenditure and GDP: panel data unit root test results – comment. *Journal of Health Economics*, *17*, 377–381.

Heaney, R. H. (1998). A Test of the cost-of-carry relationship using the London Metal Exchange Lead contract. *Journal of Futures Markets*, *18*, 177–200.

Hildreth, C., & Houck, C. (1968). Some estimators for a linear model with random coefficients. *Journal of the American Statistical Association*, *63*, 584–595.

Hill, J., & Schneeweis, T. (1984). Reducing Volatility with Financial Futures. *Financial Analysts Journal*, *30*, 34–40.

Hsiao, C. (1975). Some estimation methods for a random coefficient model. *Econometrica*, *43*, 305–325.

Howard, C. T., & d'Antonio, L. J. (1991). Multiperiod Hedging Using Futures: A Risk Minimisation Approach in the Presence of Autocorrelation. *Journal of Futures Markets*, *11*, 697–710.

Im, K. S., Pesaran, M. H., & Shim, Y. (1996). Testing for unit roots in panel data. Dept. of Applied Economics, University of Cambridge, Working Paper, July 1996 revision.

Johnson, L. (1960). The Theory of Hedging and Speculation in Commodity Markets. *Review of Economic Studies*, *27*, 139–151.

Kim, K., & Schmidt, P. (1993). Unit-Root Tests with Conditional Heteroscedasticity. *Journal of Econometrics*, *59*(3), 287–300.

Lee, T. H., & Tse, Y. (1996). Cointegration Tests with Conditional Heteroscedasticity. *Journal of Econometrics*, *73*(2), 401–410.

Lence, S., Kimle, K. L., & Hayenga, M. L. (1993). A Dynamic Minimum Variance Hedge. *American Journal of Agricultural Economics*, *75*, 1063–1071.

Levin, A., & Lin, C. (1993). Unit root tests in panel data: asymptotic and finite sample properties. University of California, San Diego, Discussion paper.

Lien, D. H. D. (1996). The Effect of the Cointegration Relationship on Futures Hedging: A Note. *Journal of Futures Markets*, *16*, 773–780.

Lien, D. H. D., & Luo, X. (1993). Estimating Multiperiod Hedge Ratios in Cointegrated Markets. *Journal of Futures Markets*, *13*(8), 909–920.

Lien, D. H. D., & Luo, X. (1994). Multiperiod Hedging in the Presence of Conditional Heteroscedasticity. *Journal of Futures Markets*, *14*(8), 927–955.

Malliaris, A. G., & Urrutia, J. L. (1991). The Impact of the Lengths of Estimation Periods and Hedging Horizons on the Effectiveness of a Hedge: Evidence from Foreign Currency Futures. *Journal of Futures Markets*, *11*(3), 271–289.

Margrabe, W. (1978). The value of an option to exchange one asset for another. *Journal of Finance*, 177–186.

McCoskey, S., & Kao, C. (1998). A residual based test of the null of cointegration in panel data. *Econometric Reviews*, *17*(1), 57–84.

McCoskey, S., & Selden, T. M. (1998). Health care expenditures and GDP: panel data unit root test results. *Journal of Health Economics*, *17*, 369–376.

McNew, K. P., & Fackler, P. L. (1994). Nonconstant Optimal Hedge Ratio: Estimation and Nested Hypotheses Tests. *Journal of Futures Markets*, *14*(5), 619–635.

Myers, R., & Hanson, S. D. (1993). Pricing Commodity Options when the Underlying Futures Price Exhibits Time-Varying Volatility. *American Journal of Agricultural Economics*, *75*, 121–130.

Myers, R., & Hanson, S. D. (1996). Optimal Dynamic Hedging in Unbiased Futures Markets. *American Journal of Agricultural Economics*, *78*, 13–20.

Myers, R., & Thompson, S. R. (1989). Generalised Optimal Hedge Ratio Estimation. *American Journal of Agricultural Economics*, *71*, 858–868.

Park, T. H., & Switzer, L. N. (1995). Bivariate GARCH Estimation of the Optimal Hedge Ratios for Stock Index Futures: A Note. *Journal of Futures Markets*, *15*(1), 61–67.

Perron, P. (1989). The great crash, the oil price shock and the unit root hypothesis. *Econometrica*, *57*, 1361–1401.

Phillips, P. C. B., & Hansen, B. E. (1990). Statistical inference in instrumental variables regression with I(1) processes. *Review of Economic Studies*, *57*, 99–125.

Reimers, H.-E. (1992). Comparisons of tests for multivariate cointegration. *Statistical Papers*, *33*, 335–359.

Sims, C. A. (1972). Money, Income and Causality. *American Economic Review*, *62*, 540–552.

Stein, J. (1961). The Simultaneous Determination of Spot and Futures Prices. *American Economic Review*, *51*, 1012–1025.

Stoll. H. R., & Whaley, R. E. (1990). The Dynamics of Stock Index and Stock Index Futures Returns. *Journal of Financial and Quantitative Analysis*, *25*, 441–468.

Swamy, P. (1971). *Statistical inference in a random coefficient regression model*. New York: Springer-Verlag.

Tse, Y. K. (1995). Lead-Lag Relationship between Spot Index and Futures Price of the Nikkei Stock Average. *Journal of Forecasting*, *14*, 553–563.

Wahab, M., & Lashgari, M. (1993). Price Dynamics and Error Correction in Stock Index and Stock Index Futures Markets: A Cointegration Approach. *Journal of Futures Markets*, *13*, 711–742.

Working, H. (1953). Futures Trading and Hedging. *American Economic Review*, *43*, 314–343.

Zivot, E., & Andrews, D. W. K. (1992). Further evidence on the great crash, oil price shock and the unit root hypothesis. *Journal of Business and Economic Statistics*, *10*, 251–270.

OPTIMAL ASIAN MULTI-CURRENCY STRATEGY PORTFOLIOS WITH EXACT RISK ATTRIBUTION

Cornelis A. Los

ABSTRACT

In an earlier paper (Los, 1998), the exact and complete return attribution framework of Singer and Karnosky (1995) was extended to include market risk measurements for n *countries. Using simple tensor algebra and cash accounting identities, the degenerate portfolio choice problem is solved as a lower dimensional, non-degenerate problem of fundamental investment choices between stock market premiums and currency swap returns. The original* n^2 *multi-currency strategic investment allocations are uniquely retrieved from the resulting* 2n *optimal fundamental choice allocations. This new optimal, return-risk attribution, accounting framework is applied to monthly return data of Hong Kong, Indonesia, Japan, Malaysia, the Philippines, Singapore, Thailand, the USA and Germany from June 1992 through December 1997. This period includes the illustrative period of the Asian currency crisis of July–December 1997. The USA and Germany are included as alternative low risk strategic investment allocations in the Asian portfolio for further diversification. Throughout this five and a half year period, Asian risk levels, as measured by the GMV standard deviations of return, were about five times the corresponding average returns. The evidence shows that most of the strategic investment risk in Asian countries is attributable to the risk amplitudes of the stock markets,*

Financial Risk and Financial Risk Management, Volume 16, pages 215–260.

ISBN: 0-7623-0858-3

followed by those of the currency markets and, last, of the cash markets. The Thai stock market was the most volatile market to invest in throughout the period. The currency swaps facilitated the spreading contagion. For a U.S. dollar based Asian investor, GMV portfolio risk could have been reduced by half and his return could have been doubled, when the USA would have been included in his portfolio. In contrast, diversification to Germany (Europe) would only marginally have contributed to portfolio risk reduction. Risk management in Asia was hazardous. Spectral analysis of the covariance risks shows that during the investigated period the Asian portfolio efficiency frontier was highly non-stationary. Both the overall Asian diversification risk and the systematic risk in a few specific Asian countries changed considerably during this period.

1. INTRODUCTION

The Asian currency crisis, which erupted in July 1997 and developed into a full-blown financial crisis, has considerably increased interest in optimal multi-currency investment management in Southeast Asia, i.e. financial management that seeks not only to maximize returns on multi-currency investments, but takes explicit account of quantifiable investment risks (Gardner & Wuiloloud, 1995).[1]

As was demonstrated in Los (1998), such an investment approach requires an exact, unified accounting framework combined with the optimization of the performance of complex portfolios, involving various market assets, currencies and cross-currency hedging swaps or currency overlays. The resulting exact portfolio optimization cum cash accounting framework is an extension of the continuously compounding cash accounting framework of Karnosky and Singer (1994; Singer & Karnosky 1995; Singer, 1996). Los (1998) allow for a breakdown of the asset allocations and currency overlays by countries.

Earlier, Lee (1987) discussed asset and currency allocation in the context of international fixed income markets based on a review of the historical returns and risks in the period 1971–1985. Lee found local asset returns to be relatively independent of currency movements and suggested to analyze them independently from each other. He recommended active currency management to enhance portfolio return. Allen (1991) further developed on Lee's framework, suggested seven specific factors in evaluating portfolio returns, and measured the marginal impact of both policy and active management decisions on the portfolio returns. However, his framework focused on the total portfolio hedged return and didn't allow for country by country attribution analysis, in contrast to the current paper.

By using simple Kronecker product algebra, Los (1998) combines Singer and Karnosky's exact accounting framework with Markowitz' mean-variance optimization of global multi-currency investment portfolios (Markowitz, 1952, 1987, 1991). In the process, an interesting rank problem is solved, which has stymied many international portfolio managers, e.g. JP Morgan.

The current paper extends the limited empirical analysis of the previous paper in three ways. First, the portfolios of strategic investments are expanded from three to seven Asian countries – Hong Kong, Indonesia, Japan, Malaysia, the Philippines, Singapore and Thailand. In addition, a comparison is made between the return/risk profiles of such regional portfolios with more diversified portfolios, including investments in the United States and in Germany.[2] Such portfolios are representative for investors in the ASEAN region. In contrast to Lee (1987), substantial interaction between the asset, cash and currency markets was found in Asia.

Second, the original five year period of analysis from June 1992 to June 1997 is extended by half a year to include the period of Asian currency turmoil in the second half of 1997.

Third, using the developed framework, the notorious non-stationarity of investment risks in Asia is analyzed, although the dynamization of the current framework with one-period ahead predictions, by using Kalman-information filters as in Los (1984), must await another paper.

It is found that the Asian countries went through three clearly discernible investment phases of each almost two years during this period: in the first phase most investment returns were obtained in the stock markets, followed by a phase in which capital was pulled out of the stock markets into cash investments, because of the two high risk levels in the stock markets. In the final phase, the global investors pulled out of Asia, because of the unpredictability of the systematic risks. Their departure and consequent reduction of credit availability (bank loans) led to the currency crisis. Since the Asian countries have experienced significant economic and financial upheavals, both the general level of portfolio risk as well as the structural changes in the Asian investment risk profile are analyzed using spectral decomposition of the data covariance matrices. This spectral analysis clearly shows that some Asian countries show more systematic risk than others. However, any portfolio manager investing in the Asian financial markets would have had a very difficult time to keep his or her portfolio on track, because of the fundamental nonstationarity of the Asian financial returns and risks.

Section 2 develops the accounting framework of exact attribution, which is combined with Markowitz mean-variance analysis in Section 3, where the problem of the singularity of the risk matrix, implied by exact accounting, is elucidated. Section 4 analyzes the nonstationarity of the portfolio returns and risks by spectral analysis and indicates which Asian countries showed more or less changes in multidimensional systematic risk with respect to the stock market risk premia and the cash swap returns.

All data series were obtained from Datastream, Dow Jones Telerate. Their definitions are given in Appendix A. It is emphasized that this paper contains an ex-post historical analysis. It observed the severe nonstationarity of the Asian returns and risks and the consequent difficulty for formulating consistent and optimal portfolio strategies. But it makes no predictions about the future Asian financial markets and its returns and risks.

2. EXACT ATTRIBUTION

2.1. Exact Investment Strategy Return Attribution

At time t an investor has three possible investment instruments:

(1) investment in an asset in country i, e.g. a stock or a bond, with rate of return $r_i(t)$;
(2) a cash swap with rate of return $c_j(t) - c_i(t)$, with $c_j(t)$ the cash rate in country j into which the nominal is swapped, and $c_i(t)$ the cash rate in country i out of which the nominal is swapped; and
(3) the foreign currency (foreign currency) appreciation rate $\varepsilon_j(t)$ of country j.

Thus one particular bilateral investment strategy at time t is represented by the strategic rate of return

$$s_{ij}(t) = r_i(t) + [c_j(t) - c_i(t)] + \varepsilon_j(t) \tag{1}$$

Such a strategy return is equivalent to the sum of a risk premium and a cash return, i.e. the local market i risk premium $[r_i(t) - c_i(t)]$ and the cash return on currency j, $[c_j(t) + \varepsilon_j(t)]$:

$$s_{ij}(t) = [r_i(t) - c_i(t)] + [c_j(t) + \varepsilon_j(t)] \tag{2}$$

This is also equivalent to the sum of a local market i return, the return on a currency forward cross hedge and the foreign currency j appreciation rate, since

$$\begin{aligned} s_{ij}(t) &= r_i(t) + [\{c_1(t) - c_i(t)\} - \{c_1(t) - c_j(t)\}] + \varepsilon_j(t) \\ &= r_i(t) + [f_i(t) - f_j(t)] + \varepsilon_j(t) \\ &= r_i(t) + f_{ij}(t) + \varepsilon_j(t) \end{aligned} \tag{3}$$

The return on a currency forward is $f_i(t) = c_1(t) - c_i(t)$, with $c_1(t)$ the cash return of the base currency. The return on a currency forward cross hedge $f_{ij}(t)$ consists of the difference between the return on the long domestic forward $f_i(t)$ and the return on the short foreign forward $f_j(t)$. An $n \times n$ non-symmetric strategy matrix at time t is a matrix containing all n^2 bilateral investment strategies

$$\mathbf{S}(t) = \{s_{ij}(t);\ i, j = 1, \ldots, n\} \tag{4}$$

For example, for $i, j = 1, 2, 3$ we have the 3×3 non-symmetric strategy matrix at time t

$$\mathbf{S}(t) = \begin{bmatrix} s_{11}(t) & s_{12}(t) & s_{13}(t) \\ s_{21}(t) & s_{22}(t) & s_{23}(t) \\ s_{31}(t) & s_{32}(t) & s_{33}(t) \end{bmatrix}$$

$$= \left[\begin{bmatrix} r_1(t) \\ r_2(t) \\ r_3(t) \end{bmatrix} - \begin{bmatrix} c_1(t) \\ c_2(t) \\ c_3(t) \end{bmatrix} \right] [1 \quad 1 \quad 1]$$

$$+ \left\{ \left[\begin{bmatrix} c_1(t) \\ c_2(t) \\ c_3(t) \end{bmatrix} + \begin{bmatrix} \varepsilon_1(t) \\ \varepsilon_2(t) \\ \varepsilon_3(t) \end{bmatrix} \right] [1 \quad 1 \quad 1] \right\}'$$

$$= \begin{bmatrix} r_1(t) + \varepsilon_1(t) & r_1(t) - c_1(t) + c_2(t) + \varepsilon_2(t) & r_1(t) - c_1(t) + c_3(t) + \varepsilon_3(t) \\ r_2(t) - c_2(t) + c_1(t) + \varepsilon_1(t) & r_2(t) + \varepsilon_2(t) & r_2(t) - c_2(t) + c_3(t) + \varepsilon_3(t) \\ r_3(t) - c_3(t) + c_1(t) + \varepsilon_1(t) & r_3(t) - c_3(t) + c_2(t) + \varepsilon_2(t) & r_3(t) + \varepsilon_3(t) \end{bmatrix} \tag{5}$$

Table 1 provides for June 1997 the annualized monthly rates of return on the respective stock markets indices of Hong Kong, Indonesia, Japan, Malaysia, the Philippines, Singapore and Thailand as the seven Asian countries of interest, plus those of the United States and Germany for comparison, the respective 30-day bank lending rates, and the respective rates of return on the currencies. From those rates the risk premia $[r_i(t) - c_i(t)]$, $i = 1, 2, \ldots, 9$ and the cash returns $[c_j(t) + \varepsilon_j(t)]$, $j = 1, 2, \ldots, 9$ are also calculated. While the annualized risk premia in June 1997 were positive for Hong Kong, Indonesia,

Table 1. Annualized Rates of Return (%) in June 1997.

	Stock (1)	Cash (2)	FX (3)	Risk Premium (1) − (2)	Cash Returns (2) + (3)
Hong Kong	35.2	6.0	0.2	29.1	6.3
Indonesia	48.2	14.5	0.2	33.7	14.7
Japan	31.6	0.6	16.9	31.0	17.6
Malaysia	− 30.3	7.4	− 5.6	− 37.6	1.7
Philippines	− 0.1	11.0	0.0	− 11.1	11.0
Singapore	− 45.9	3.6	− 0.9	− 49.5	2.6
Thailand	− 74.8	16.8	4.4	− 91.5	21.1
Germany	75.5	3.1	− 24.0	72.4	− 21.0
USA	51.0	5.7	0.0	45.4	5.7

Japan, Germany and the USA, they were negative for Malaysia, the Philippines, Singapore and, in particular, Thailand. All the June 1997 cash returns were positive, with the exception of Germany.

Table 2 presents the corresponding matrix of strategic multi-currency investment returns $\mathbf{S}(t)$ for June 1997. Notice that on the diagonal of this investment strategy matrix we find all results for the simple buy-and-hold strategy of investing in country i, where the return is the combination of what is earned in the stock market and what is earned on the currency. Thus, in June 1997 Hong Kong earned 35.4%/yr at an annualized monthly rate on domestic investments, namely 35.2%/yr in the stock market and 0.2%/yr on cash, while Singapore lost 46.8%/yr on domestic investments, resulting from a 45.9%/yr loss in the stock market, combined with a 0.9%/yr loss on the Singapore dollar.[3]

In contrast, the off-diagonal elements contain the strategies of buying stock in country i and swapping into the cash of country j. What is earned in such a strategy is a combination of stock market, swap earnings and exchange rate earnings, i.e. the sum of risk premium and foreign cash earnings. Thus in June 1997 an investor could earn an annualized 75.5%/yr in the German stock market, but by swapping from the Deutschemark into Thailand's baht, he could earn an extra 16.8% − 3.1% = 13.7%/yr on the rate differential in cash lending and 4.4%/yr on the baht. Consequently, the rate of return on his stock investment-cum-multi-currency-swap strategy would have been a whopping 93.5%/yr at an annualized rate, i.e. 18.1 percentage points more, on an annualized basis, than what was earned by staying fully invested in Germany. Of course, such an investment strategy would ignore the risks involved in international currency swaps, but since Thailand's baht had been stable for a

Table 2. Strategic Investment Returns (%) in June 1997.

	CURRENCIES								
MARKETS	Hong Kong	Indonesia	Japan	Malaysia	Philippines	Singapore	Thailand	Germany	USA
Hong Kong	35.4	43.9	46.7	30.9	40.1	31.8	50.2	8.2	34.8
Indonesia	40.0	48.5	51.3	35.4	44.7	36.4	54.8	12.8	39.4
Japan	37.3	45.8	48.6	32.7	42.0	33.6	52.1	10.1	36.7
Malaysia	− 31.4	− 22.9	− 20.1	− 35.9	− 26.7	− 35.0	− 16.5	− 58.6	− 31.9
Philippines	− 4.8	3.7	6.5	− 9.3	− 0.1	− 8.4	10.0	− 32.0	− 5.4
Singapore	− 43.2	− 34.7	− 31.9	− 47.7	− 38.5	− 46.8	− 28.4	− 70.4	− 43.8
Thailand	− 85.3	− 76.8	− 74.0	− 89.9	− 80.6	− 88.9	− 70.4	− 112.5	− 85.8
Germany	78.6	87.1	89.9	74.1	83.3	75.0	93.5	51.4	78.1
USA	51.6	60.1	62.9	47.1	56.3	48.0	66.5	24.4	51.0

fairly long time that was exactly what transpired. Two days into July 1997 this preferred cash management strategy of swapping into Thai baht started to rapidly disintegrate.

It is easy to translate this rate of return story into investment dollars, since, by first order approximation[4], an initial investment $P(0)$, e.g. of \$100*mln*, invested in a strategy earning $s_{ij}(t)$, grows in one period t as follows

$$P_{ij}(t) = P(0)(1 + s_{ij}(t)) = P(0)e^{s_{ij}(t)} \tag{6}$$

the value of a strategy investment portfolio at time t can be represented by the weighted average

$$\begin{aligned} P(t) &= \sum_{i,j} w_{ij} P_{ij}(t) \\ &= P(0)\left[1 + \sum_{i,j}^{n} w_{ij} s_{ij}(t)\right] \\ &= P(0)e^{\Sigma_{i,j}^{n} w_{ij} s_{ij}(t)} \\ &= P(0)e^{s_p(t)} \end{aligned} \tag{7}$$

where w_{ij} is the share of the investment capital allocated to strategy $s_{ij}(t)$ with $\Sigma_{i,j}^{n} w_{ij} = 1$ and $s_p(t) = \Sigma_{i,j}^{n} w_{ij} s_{ij}(t)$ the average portfolio rate of return in period t. Thus the terminal value of such portfolio of multi-currency investment strategies is

$$P(T) = \sum_{i,j} w_{ij} P_{ij}(T) = P(0) \prod_{t}^{T} e^{s_p(t)} \tag{8}$$

Returning to the rates of return, the strategy matrix $S(t)$ at time t can now be generalized, by using matrix algebra, as follows

$$\begin{aligned} \mathbf{S}(t) &= [\mathbf{r}(t) - \mathbf{c}(t)]\boldsymbol{\iota}_n' + \{[\mathbf{c}(t) + \boldsymbol{\varepsilon}(t)]\boldsymbol{\iota}_n'\}' \\ &= [\mathbf{r}(t) - \mathbf{c}(t)]\boldsymbol{\iota}_n' + \boldsymbol{\iota}_n[\mathbf{c}(t) + \boldsymbol{\varepsilon}(t)]', \end{aligned} \tag{9}$$

where $\mathbf{r}(t)$, $\mathbf{c}(t)$ and $\boldsymbol{\varepsilon}(t)$ are $n \times 1$ data vectors of asset rates, cash rates and foreign currency appreciation rates at time t, respectively, as in Table 1, and $\boldsymbol{\iota}_n'$ is a $1 \times n$ unit vector, i.e. a vector consisting of n units, $\boldsymbol{\iota}_n' = [1, 1, \ldots, 1]$.

Next, the 3-dimensional $n \times n \times T$ historical investment strategy *array* $\mathbf{S}$ is the *sequence* of such strategy matrices $\mathbf{S} = \{S(t); t = 1, \ldots, T\}$. However, covariance risk analysis with three-dimensional arrays is very difficult and it is easier when these arrays are translated into simpler two-dimensional arrays by vectorization. The proper vectorization. of this strategy array is[5]

$$\begin{aligned}\mathbf{VEC(S)} &= [vec(\mathbf{S}(1)), vec(\mathbf{S}(2)), \ldots, vec(\mathbf{S}(T))] \\ &= [\boldsymbol{\iota}_n \otimes \mathbf{I}_n][\mathbf{r} - \mathbf{c}] + [\mathbf{I}_n \otimes \boldsymbol{\iota}_n][\mathbf{c} + \boldsymbol{\varepsilon}] \\ &= \mathbf{H}\begin{bmatrix} [\mathbf{r} - \mathbf{c}] \\ [\mathbf{c} + \boldsymbol{\varepsilon}] \end{bmatrix}\end{aligned} \tag{10}$$

where $\mathbf{r}$ is the $n \times T$ matrix of T observations on the rates of return of n country assets, $\mathbf{c}$ is the $n \times T$ matrix of observations on the n cash rates, and $\boldsymbol{\varepsilon}$ is the $n \times T$ matrix of T observations on the n currency appreciation rates, all with $T > 2n$. Consequently, $[\mathbf{r} - \mathbf{c}]$ is the $n \times T$ matrix of T observations on the n country risk premia and $[\mathbf{c} + \boldsymbol{\varepsilon}]$ is the $n \times T$ matrix of observations on the n country cash earning rates. $\mathbf{H} = [[\boldsymbol{\iota}_n \otimes \mathbf{I}_n] \quad [\mathbf{I}_n \otimes \boldsymbol{\iota}_n]]$ is the crucial $n^2 \times 2n$ selector matrix, which embodies the exact cash accounting identities, i.e. the exact cash accounting framework of Singer and Karnosky (1995).

2.2. *Exact Investment Strategy Risk Attribution*

In this section vectorization is implemented to prepare for the mean-variance analysis. The holding horizon averages of each of the n strategies are given by the $n^2 \times 1$ vector

$$\overline{\mathbf{VEC(S)}} = \frac{\mathbf{VEC(S)} \,.\, \boldsymbol{\iota}_T}{T} \tag{11}$$

where $\boldsymbol{\iota}_T$ is the $T \times 1$ unit vector. Thus

$$\overline{\mathbf{VEC(S)}} = \mathbf{H}\begin{bmatrix} [\bar{\mathbf{r}} - \bar{\mathbf{c}}] \\ [\bar{\mathbf{c}} + \bar{\boldsymbol{\varepsilon}}] \end{bmatrix} \tag{12}$$

In the case of the seven-plus Asian countries the $5\frac{1}{2}$-year ($T = 66$) averages for the annualized stock market premia are given in Table 3. Thus, in the period July 1992 through December 1997, on average, the stock market gained most in the USA and Germany – 15.7%/yr and 14.2%/yr, respectively – and not in

Table 3. Average Annualized Rates of Return (%), July 1997–December 1997.

	Stock (1)	Cash (2)	FX (3)	Risk Premium (1) − (2)	Cash Returns (2) + (3)
Hong Kong	10.2	5.1	0.0	5.1	5.1
Indonesia	4.5	14.0	− 14.0	− 9.5	0.1
Japan	− 0.8	1.8	− 0.7	− 2.6	1.1
Malaysia	0.1	6.7	− 8.0	− 6.7	− 1.3
Philippines	3.3	12.7	− 8.6	− 9.4	4.1
Singapore	0.6	2.9	− 0.7	− 2.4	2.3
Thailand	− 9.3	11.1	− 11.7	− 20.3	− 0.6
Germany	14.2	5.2	− 3.0	9.0	2.2
USA	15.7	4.8	0.0	10.9	4.8

Asia. The best average result was obtained in Hong Kong: 10.2%/yr. Notice that these average figures are much more subdued than the monthly figures of June 1997. That is already a first indication that the monthly returns must be very volatile.

Similarly we have the averages for the domestic cash lending earnings, also in Table 3. *A substantial part of the global multi-currency strategy returns was earned in the Asian cash overlay markets.* On average, the international investor could earn on cash 14.0%/yr in Indonesia, 12.7% in the Philippines and 11.1%/yr in Thailand. The advanced countries, Germany, the USA, Japan, and also Singapore, provided much lower average cash returns, mostly reflecting lower domestic inflation rates and more liquid cash markets. Thus, disregarding exchange rate risk, a natural incentive was created for cash to flow from those countries into Asia. But a closer look at Table 3 shows that most of the Asian cash rates were just compensating for the average exchange rate losses. For example, in Indonesia the domestic cash lending rate was 14%/yr, and this exactly compensated for the 14%/yr average annual loss on the rupiah, while in Thailand the 11.1%/yr cash rate did not even fully compensate the 11.7%/yr average currency depreciation. Only the Philippines' cash rate of 12.7%/yr appears to have added real value, since the peso only depreciated an average 8.6%/yr. Of course, the Hong Kong dollar stayed pegged to the U.S. dollar and its appreciation was 0%.

In Table 4 these average return strategy vectors are reconstituted into the better recognizable matrix of average strategy returns $\bar{\mathbf{S}}$. In the period July 1992 through December 1997, Singer and Karnosky's *maximizing average return*

Table 4. Average Strategic Investment Returns (%) July 1992–December 1997.

	CURRENCIES								
MARKETS	Hong Kong	Indonesia	Japan	Malaysia	Philippines	Singapore	Thailand	Germany	USA
Hong Kong	10.2	5.2	6.2	3.8	9.2	7.4	4.4	7.3	9.9
Indonesia	− 4.4	− 9.5	− 8.4	− 10.8	− 5.4	− 7.2	− 10.2	− 7.3	− 4.7
Japan	2.5	− 2.5	− 1.5	− 3.9	1.5	− 0.3	− 3.2	− 0.4	2.2
Malaysia	− 1.6	− 6.6	− 5.5	− 7.9	− 2.6	− 4.4	− 7.3	− 4.4	− 1.8
Philippines	− 4.3	− 9.3	− 8.3	− 10.7	− 5.3	− 7.1	− 10.1	− 7.2	− 4.6
Singapore	2.7	− 2.3	− 1.2	− 3.6	1.7	− 0.1	− 3.0	− 0.1	2.5
Thailand	− 15.2	− 20.3	− 19.2	− 21.6	− 16.2	− 18.0	− 21.0	− 18.1	− 15.5
Germany	14.1	9.1	10.1	7.7	13.1	11.3	8.3	11.2	13.8
USA	16.0	11.0	12.0	9.6	15.0	13.2	10.3	13.1	15.7

strategy would have been to invest in the USA to earn a 15.7%/yr and then, perhaps, to swap into the Hong Kong dollar to pick up an extra $5.1\% - 4.8\% = 0.3\%$, or 30 basis points per year. After the hand-over of Hong Kong to the People's Republic of China, such a "sure" swap has now lost its attraction too.

Interestingly, Table 4 also shows that investing in Thailand's stock market would have been unprofitable on average (but await the final verdict until Section 4, where we analyze the three sub-periods), because Thailand's row in Table 4 presents all negative returns, no matter what currency swaps are implemented. Similar results hold true for the stock markets of Indonesia, Malaysia and the Philippines. These countries were attractive for the global investors from the USA and Germany (and, because of the currency peg, from Hong Kong), not for their stock markets, but for their currency returns.

We can now compute the $n^2 \times n^2 = 81 \times 81$ strategy risk matrix Σ of the $n^2 = 81$ investment strategies and exactly decompose it into its various stock market and cash return risks

$$\begin{aligned}
\boldsymbol{\Sigma} &= \frac{\mathbf{DEV(S)}\,.\,\mathbf{DEV(S)}'}{T} \\
&= \frac{\left\{\mathbf{H}\begin{bmatrix}[\mathbf{r}-\mathbf{c}]\\ [\mathbf{c}+\boldsymbol{\varepsilon}]\end{bmatrix}\left[\mathbf{I}_T - \frac{\boldsymbol{\iota}_T\boldsymbol{\iota}_T'}{T}\right]\right\}\left\{\mathbf{H}\begin{bmatrix}[\mathbf{r}-\mathbf{c}]\\ [\mathbf{c}+\boldsymbol{\varepsilon}]\end{bmatrix}\left[\mathbf{I}_T - \frac{\boldsymbol{\iota}_T\boldsymbol{\iota}_T'}{T}\right]\right\}'}{T} \\
&= \mathbf{H}\boldsymbol{\Phi}\mathbf{H}' \\
&= \boldsymbol{\iota}_n\boldsymbol{\iota}_n' \otimes [\boldsymbol{\Sigma}_{rr} + \boldsymbol{\Sigma}_{cc} - \boldsymbol{\Sigma}_{rc} - \boldsymbol{\Sigma}_{rc}'] + [\boldsymbol{\Sigma}_{cc} + \boldsymbol{\Sigma}_{\varepsilon\varepsilon} + \boldsymbol{\Sigma}_{c\varepsilon} + \boldsymbol{\Sigma}_{c\varepsilon}'] \otimes \boldsymbol{\iota}_n\boldsymbol{\iota}_n' \\
&\quad + \boldsymbol{\iota}_n \otimes [\boldsymbol{\Sigma}_{rc} + \boldsymbol{\Sigma}_{r\varepsilon} - \boldsymbol{\Sigma}_{cc} - \boldsymbol{\Sigma}_{c\varepsilon}] \otimes \boldsymbol{\iota}_n' + \boldsymbol{\iota}_n' \otimes [\boldsymbol{\Sigma}_{rc} + \boldsymbol{\Sigma}_{r\varepsilon} - \boldsymbol{\Sigma}_{cc} - \boldsymbol{\Sigma}_{c\varepsilon}]' \otimes \boldsymbol{\iota}_n \qquad (13)
\end{aligned}$$

where $\boldsymbol{\Phi}$ is the $2n \times 2n = 18 \times 18$ risk premium – cash return covariance matrix. All the sub-matrices of the strategy risk matrix $\boldsymbol{\Sigma}$ are given in Table 5, with the $\boldsymbol{\Sigma}_{rr}$, $\boldsymbol{\Sigma}_{cc}$ and $\boldsymbol{\Sigma}_{ee}$ covariance submatrices along the diagonal of the $(3n \times 3n) = 27 \times 27$ data covariance matrix $\boldsymbol{\Omega}$. Notice that the stock market returns exhibit the highest level of covariance risk, followed by the currencies, while the cash returns show the lowest level of covariance risk. While the Hong Kong dollar is pegged, it clearly is not convertible into the U.S. dollar at a fixed rate. Otherwise the Hong Kong covariances would be also zero, like the ones of the U.S. dollar base currency.

The, for mean-variance analysis relevant, covariance matrix $\boldsymbol{\Phi}$ is given in Table 6 for the period July 1992–December 1997. The Asian risk premia

Table 5. Numerical Data Covariance Matrix Ω (27×27). Data Series: July 1992–December 1997.

	Stock market rates of return: r									Cash rates of return: c									FX rates of appreciation: ε								
	10590.5	6678.6	1710.8	6808.6	7184.7	4969.6	8599.5	3628.7	1963.7	(72.5)	(71.1)	2.4	1.4	(35.2)	(29.1)	(34.6)	6 1	(15.0)	20.4	899.6	(123.7)	158.0	(499.1)	263.4	799.9	(661.7)	0.0
	6678.6	9969.0	1232.1	6370.4	6842.0	3478.5	8233.8	2907.8	1717.9	(64.4)	(62.4)	9.6	(6.0)	(77.8)	(42.5)	(87.4)	18.1	(21.6)	18.8	966.0	58.6	937.0	(88.0)	252.5	817.3	(667.8)	0.0
	1710.8	1232.1	5588.4	740.4	1253.0	1673.4	1169.6	881.6	759.8	(32.9)	(23.6)	6.6	(2.9)	(32.6)	(10.7)	(41.7)	19.4	(12.0)	2.3	780.4	(78.2)	453.2	258.2	325.1	831.1	(142.3)	0.0
	68086	6370.4	740.4	9030.3	7389.4	4171.5	7570.5	2361.5	777.5	(79.4)	(93.1)	24.3	(9.8)	(28.9)	(35.3)	(79.7)	36.8	(28.5)	5.5	772.5	427.6	469.2	(357.2)	230.8	962.0	(251.1)	0.0
r	7184.7	6842.0	1253.0	7389.4	10950.3	4269.5	8890.9	3385.0	917.4	(64.7)	(74.3)	14.1	(5.9)	(15.0)	(27.2)	(70.7)	23.6	(29.6)	4.6	884.8	(73.0)	579.5	(348.5)	253.6	947.7	(405.1)	0.0
	4969.6	3478.5	1673.4	4171.5	4269.5	4337.1	4900.0	1957.6	985.2	(50.4)	(47.5)	16.1	(3.5)	(19.1)	(21.3)	(42.8)	27.4	(18.5)	12.0	749.3	(65.5)	155.6	(80.1)	283.2	942.5	(323.1)	0.0
	8599.5	8733.8	1169.6	7570.5	8890.9	4900.0	16967.0	4256.7	1633.0	(91.4)	(106.9)	42.6	(17.4)	(9.8)	(54.3)	(118.9)	66.9	(42.6)	25.6	879.9	(797.5)	437.5	(966.7)	128.4	(575.1)	(1196.8)	0.0
	3628.7	2907.8	881.6	2361.5	3385.0	1957.6	4256.7	3953.9	1136.7	(11.1)	(2.4)	(13.5)	12.9	(27.8)	1.6	10.3	(21.8)	3.8	(3.2)	(26.8)	(672.2)	(143.8)	(804.2)	(199.1)	(641.9)	(1093.0)	0.0
	1963.7	1717.9	759.8	777.5	917.4	935.2	1633.0	1136.7	1256.4	2.7	25.7	(8.1)	5.9	(14.3)	(3.0)	22.7	(12.6)	8.7	3.1	47.3	(152.3)	(0.1)	(379.1)	27.8	(154.2)	(289.6)	0.0
	(72.5)	(64.4)	(32.9)	(79.4)	(64.7)	(50.4)	(91.4)	(11.1)	2.7	2.8	3.9	(1.4)	0.3	0.4	1.0	3.3	(2.3)	1.4	(0.0)	(34.5)	(14.9)	(23.6)	(15.6)	(12.1)	(37.8)	1.7	0.0
	(71.1)	(62.4)	(23.6)	(93.1)	(74.3)	(47.5)	(106.9)	(2.4)	25.7	3.9	11.9	(1.4)	2.2	1.4	1.4	7.5	(1.8)	1.8	0.0	(66.6)	(26.7)	(50.2)	(47.6)	(24.6)	(58.0)	(3.1)	0.0
	2.4	9.6	6.6	24.3	14.1	16.1	42.6	(13.5)	(8.1)	(1.4)	(1.4)	1.5	(0.1)	0.5	(0.5)	(1.4)	2.4	(1.1)	(0.0)	11.6	15.0	7.9	6.4	4.6	13.6	3.4	0.0
	1.4	(6.0)	(2.9)	(9.8)	(5.9)	(3.5)	(17.4)	12.9	5.9	0.3	2.2	(0.1)	1.3	0.8	0.2	1.5	0.2	(0.2)	(0.0)	(16.0)	(5.8)	(14.7)	(17.2)	(8.7)	(21.0)	(11.0)	0.0
c	(35.2)	(77.8)	(32.6)	(28.9)	(15.0)	(19.1)	(9.8)	(27.8)	(14.3)	0.4	1.4	0.5	0.8	5.5	0.4	2.2	1.1	(0.7)	(0.1)	(40.5)	6.9	(34.3)	(14.6)	(11.0)	(38.6)	7.4	0.0
	(29.1)	(42.5)	(10.7)	(35.3)	(27.2)	(21.3)	(54.3)	1.6	(3.0)	1.0	1.4	(0.5)	0.2	0.4	1.1	1.7	(1.0)	0.4	(0.2)	(25.5)	(6.9)	(18.8)	(13.9)	(6.9)	(25.4)	2.8	0.0
	(34.6)	(87.4)	(41.7)	(79.7)	(70.7)	(42.8)	(118.9)	10.3	22.7	3.3	75	(1.4)	1.5	2.2	1.7	8.7	(2.1)	1.5	(0.3)	(78.2)	(1.8)	(55.8)	(62.6)	(21.9)	(69.0)	2.6	0.0
	6.1	18.1	19.4	36.8	23.6	27.4	66.9	(21.8)	(12.6)	(2.3)	(1.8)	2.4	0.2	1.1	(1.0)	(21)	4.1	(1.9)	0.0	19.5	19.3	11.5	11.4	5 8	21.8	2.3	0.0
	(15.0)	(21.6)	(12.0)	(28.5)	(29.6)	(18.5)	(42.6)	3.8	8.7	1.4	1.8	(1.1)	(0.2)	(0.7)	0.4	1.5	(1.9)	1.2	(0.1)	(9.3)	(9.6)	(4.7)	(4.6)	(2.9)	(9.9)	0.	0.0
	20.4	18.8	2.3	5.5	4.6	12.0	25.6	(3.2)	3.1	(0.0)	0.0	(0.0)	(0.0)	(0.1)	(0.2)	(0.3)	0.0	(0.1)	1.0	4.7	3.1	1.8	(0.1)	3.6	1.9	13.5	0.0
	899.6	966.0	780.4	772.5	884.8	749.3	879.9	(26.8)	47.3	(34.5)	(666)	11.6	(16.0)	(40.5)	(25.5)	(78.2)	19.5	(9.3)	4.7	1433.8	180.4	982.9	1057.5	399.5	1423.5	(33.5)	0.0
	(123.7)	58.6	(78.2)	427.6	(73.0)	(65.5)	(797.5)	(672.2)	(152.3)	(14.9)	(26.7)	15.0	(5.8)	6.9	(6.9)	(1.8)	19.3	(9.6)	3.1	180.4	1513.5	263.8	54.6	264.6	534.6	662.0	0.0
	158.0	937.0	453.2	469.2	579.5	155.6	437.5	(143.8)	(0.1)	(23.6)	(50.2)	7.9	(14.7)	(34.3)	(1a.8)	(55.8)	11.5	(4.7)	1.8	982.9	263.8	968.5	678.3	316.1	921.4	68.7	0.0
ε	(499.1)	(88.0)	258.2	(357.2)	(348.5)	(80.1)	(966.7)	(804.2)	(379.1)	(15.6)	(47.6)	6.4	(17.2)	(14.6)	(13.9)	(62.6)	11.4	(4.6)	(0.1)	1057.5	54.6	678.3	1743.3	278.0	1290.7	96.3	0.0
	263.4	252.5	325.1	230.8	253.6	283.2	128.4	(199.1)	27.8	(12.1)	(24.6)	4.6	(8.7)	(11.0)	(6.9)	(21.9)	5.8	(2.9)	3.6	399.5	2&4.6	316.1	278.0	208.2	507.1	2.42	0.0
	799.9	817.3	831.1	962.0	947.7	942.5	(575.1)	(641.9)	(154.2)	(37.8)	(58.0)	13.6	(21.0)	(38.6)	(25.4)	(69.0)	21.8	(9.9)	1.9	1423.5	534.6	921.4	1289.7	507.1	2424.0	326.2	0.0
	(661.7)	(667.8)	(142.3)	(251.1)	(405.1)	(323.1)	(1196.8)	(1093.0)	(289.6)	1.7	(3.1)	3.4	(11.0)	7.4	2.8	2.6	2.3	0.7	13.5	(33.5)	652.0	68.7	96.3	204.2	326.2	1206.4	0.0
	0.0	0.0	0.0	0.0	0.0	0.0	0.0	0.0	0.0	0.0	0.0	0.0	0.0	0.0	0.0	0.0	0.0	0.0	0.0	0.0	0.0	0.0	0.0	0.0	0.0	0.0	0.0

Data Series: July 1992–December 1997.

Table 6. Risk Premium – Cash Return Covariance Matrix Φ (18 × 18) July 1992–December 1997.

	r − c									c + ε								
	10738.2	6818.0	1740.0	6886.8	7285.1	5050.1	8728.8	3631.4	1977.5	(54.8)	859.1	(105.1)	182.8	(519.1)	245.4	799.7	(655.0)	(16.5)
	6818.0	10105.7	1244.8	6471.7	6995.5	3669.9	3435.6	2890.4	1715.7	(49.5)	958.3	96.3	970.0	(119.6)	233.2	780.4	(644.8)	(23.5)
	1740.0	1244.8	5576.7	718.9	1272.1	1667.5	1167.3	878.0	778.8	(29.3)	746.5	(88.1)	442.5	218.7	310.4	777.1	(128.7)	(10.9)
	6886.8	6471.7	718.9	9051.2	7425.1	4210.5	7669.1	2311.9	800.0	(74.2)	693.1	457.9	472.8	(369.8)	240.0	901.7	(203.4)	(28.3)
r − c	7286.1	6995.5	1272.1	7425.1	10985.8	4316.2	8973.6	3390.3	960.6	(60.4)	849.6	(66.4)	607.1	(354.4)	237.0	913.4	(390.0)	(28.9)
	5050.1	3569.9	1667.5	4210.5	4316.2	4380.7	4998.8	1927.6	1007.1	(39.3)	725.9	(42.1)	170.7	(85.7)	267.7	923.4	(297.5)	(18.9)
	8728.8	8435.6	1167.3	7669.1	1973.6	4998.8	17213.6	4177.3	1651.4	(68.8)	843.7	(751.7)	474.4	(916.1)	94.2	(633.8)	(1130.2)	(44.1)
	3631.4	2890.4	878.0	2311.9	3390.3	1927.6	4177.3	4001.5	1143.7	(12.1)	(46.9)	(707.4)	(142.5)	(844.4)	(202.4)	(651.3)	(1121.1)	5.7
	1977.5	1715.7	778.8	800.0	960.6	1007.1	1654.4	1143.7	1240.3	4.5	80.4	(149.8)	10.7	(388.2)	27.3	(123.1)	(301.1)	7.4
	(54.8)	(49.5)	(29.3)	(74.2)	(60.4)	(39.3)	(68.8)	(12.1)	4.5	3.7	(25.9)	(13.2)	(21.5)	(15.4)	(7.7)	(32.8)	12.9	1.3
	859.1	958.3	746.5	693.1	849.6	725.9	843.7	(46.9)	80.4	(25.9)	1312.5	164.0	918.9	970.8	350.5	1294.9	(18.9)	(7.5)
	(105.1)	96.3	(88.1)	457.9	(66.4)	(42.1)	(751.7)	(707.4)	(149.8)	(13.2)	164.0	1544.9	265.8	68.4	261.8	545.1	677.1	(10.7)
	182.8	979.0	442.5	472.8	607.1	170.7	474.4	(142.5)	10.7	(21.5)	918.9	265.8	940.3	627.7	288.8	846.1	69.4	(4.9)
c + ε	(519.1)	(119.6)	218.7	(369.8)	(354.4)	(85.7)	(916.1)	(844.4)	(388.2)	(15.4)	970.8	68.4	627.7	1719.6	253.5	1190.7	116.2	(5.2)
	245.4	233.2	310.4	204.0	237.0	267.7	94.2	(202.4)	27.3	(7.7)	350.8	261.8	288.8	253.5	195.4	461.5	211.8	(2.5)
	799.7	780.4	777.1	901.7	913.4	923.4	(633.8)	(651.3)	(123.1)	(32.8)	1294.9	545.1	846.1	1190.7	461.5	2294.8	348.4	(8.4)
	(655.0)	(644.8)	(128.7)	(203.4)	(390.0)	(297.5)	(1130.2)	(1121.1)	(301.1)	12.9	(18.9)	677.1	69.4	116.2	211.8	348.4	1215.0	(1.1)
	(16.5)	(23.5)	(10.9)	(28.3)	(28.9)	(18.9)	(44.1)	5.7	7.4	1.3	(7.5)	(10.7)	(4.9)	(5.2)	(2.5)	(8.4)	(1.1)	1.2

Determinant = 44E + 49
Product of Variances = 18E + 56
18D Noise/Data Ratio = 24E − 07
18D Signal/Noise Ratio = 42E + 06
For 18-dimensional Noise/Data and Signal/Noise Ratios, see Los (2001).

showed five to twenty times more risk than the cash returns, but most of the cash returns still showed very high levels of volatility risk. Cash in Asia has definitely not been risk free. As Table 6 shows, one of the reasons for the cash return risks is the correlation between the risk premia earned in the Asian stock markets and the cash returns earned in the cash lending and foreign exchange markets.

The $n \times n = 9 \times 9$ covariance matrix of the risk premia $[\mathbf{\Sigma}_{rr} + \mathbf{\Sigma}_{cc} - \mathbf{\Sigma}_{rc} - \mathbf{\Sigma}'_{rc}]$ consists of the covariance matrices of the stock markets $\mathbf{\Sigma}_{rr}$, of the cash markets $\mathbf{\Sigma}_{cc}$ and of the interaction between the stock and cash markets $\mathbf{\Sigma}_{rc}$. The matrix $\mathbf{\Sigma}_{rr}$ measures all covariances between the $n = 9$ stock markets. The matrix $\mathbf{\Sigma}_{cc}$ measures all covariances between the $n = 9$ cash markets. Considering that covariance matrices are positive definite, this expression shows that the interaction between the stock and cash markets, as measured by $\mathbf{\Sigma}_{rc}$, reduces the overall market risk $\mathbf{\Sigma}_{rr} + \mathbf{\Sigma}_{cc}$ emanating from both types of markets.

Notice from both Tables 5 and 6 that: (1) *most of the risk resides in the Asian stock markets* and that the German and, in particular, U.S. stock markets show much less risk, and (2) the stock and cash interaction risk matrix, Σ_{rc}, is asymmetric! The most volatile stock markets were Thailand, the Philippines and Indonesia.

The $n \times n = 9 \times 9$ covariance matrix of the cash earnings $[\mathbf{\Sigma}_{cc} + \mathbf{\Sigma}_{\varepsilon\varepsilon} + \mathbf{\Sigma}_{c\varepsilon} + \mathbf{\Sigma}'_{c\varepsilon}]$ contains the covariance matrices of the cash markets $\mathbf{\Sigma}_{cc}$, of the foreign currency markets $\mathbf{\Sigma}_{\varepsilon\varepsilon}$ and of the interaction between the cash and foreign currency markets. This expression shows that the interaction between the cash and foreign currency markets as measured by $\mathbf{\Sigma}_{c\varepsilon}$ increases the overall market risk $\mathbf{\Sigma}_{cc} + \mathbf{\Sigma}_{\varepsilon\varepsilon}$ emanating from both types of markets.

According to the numbers in Table 5 *the currency markets exhibited more risk than the local cash markets*. In the period July 1992 through December 1997, the Thai baht was the most volatile currency, followed by the Philippine peso, the Japanese Yen and the Indonesian rupiah. The volatility of the Japanese Yen is, perhaps, the most surprising observation, coming from a mature industrialized country. But the period July 1992–December 1997 covers Japan's painful and too long structural adjustment period, which has led, at least in global investors' circles, to a lot of disillusionment with Japan.

Third, the two cross terms involving the risk premia and the cash earnings contain $[\mathbf{\Sigma}_{rc} + \mathbf{\Sigma}_{r\varepsilon} - \mathbf{\Sigma}_{cc} - \mathbf{\Sigma}_{c\varepsilon}]$. In both cases the cross risk, emanating from the interaction between the stock and the cash and the stock and foreign currency markets, $\mathbf{\Sigma}_{rc} + \mathbf{\Sigma}_{r\varepsilon}$, is reduced by the interaction between the cash markets, $\mathbf{\Sigma}_{cc}$. and between the cash and the foreign currency markets, $\mathbf{\Sigma}_{c\varepsilon}$.

Clearly, the risk of the investment strategies, as measured by the strategy risk matrix $\mathbf{\Sigma}$, is a convoluted expression of the risks of the stock, cash and foreign currency markets and their inter-correlations. It makes sense to compute this risk matrix $\mathbf{\Sigma}$ and analyze it for a fixed number of observations T only when each of its six constituent market risk matrices – $\mathbf{\Sigma}_{rr}$, $\mathbf{\Sigma}_{rc}$, $\mathbf{\Sigma}_{cc}$, $\mathbf{\Sigma}_{c\varepsilon}$, $\mathbf{\Sigma}_{\varepsilon\varepsilon}$, $\mathbf{\Sigma}_{r\varepsilon}$ – is constant, i.e. when the financial market pricing processes are stationary. When such stationarity prevails, mean-variance portfolio optimization, as in the next Section, could be valuable. However if such direct stationarity does not prevail in the financial markets, a complete projective search should be conducted to determine what systematic forces change these financial market pricing processes (Los, 2001, Ch. 5). More discussion of this issue of the (lack of) return and risk stationarity in Asia, and therefore of the difficulty of the risk assessment in Asia, follows in Section 4.

3. MEAN-VARIANCE OPTIMIZATION

For strategic global portfolio management the fundamental question is: are there combinations of investment strategies that either lead to lowering overall risk for a comparable level of average return, or, *vice versa*, to a higher return for a comparable level of risk? (Black & Litterman, 1992). Markowitz' original mean-variance optimization of portfolios, which answers this question, requires that the central risk matrix is positive definite, i.e. nonsingular (Markowitz, 1952, 1991). Markowitz reformulated his problem in the 1980s to incorporate the possibility of a positive semi-definite risk matrix $\mathbf{\Sigma}$ (cf., in particular, Markowitz, 1987, p. 43).[6] But since the strategy risk matrix $\mathbf{\Sigma}$ based on exact accounting must be singular and we want to adopt Markowitz' optimization, not by fudging or avoiding, but by exploiting the exact accounting identities, the following simple exposition was developed using tensor algebra and the Kuhn-Tucker Theorem.

3.1. Singularity of Strategy Risk Matrix

It is easy to proof that the strategy risk matrix is singular, but this fact has stymied a lot of portfolio managers. It must singular, since

$$rank(\mathbf{\Sigma}) = 2n - 1 < n^2, \text{ for integer } n > 1$$

This is proved by determining the rank of the strategy deviations **DEV(S)**, which is the same as the rank of the strategy risk matrix $\mathbf{\Sigma}$. (cf. Proposition 7 of Dhrymes, 1978, p. 437).

$$rank\{\mathbf{DEV(S)}\} = rank\left\{\mathbf{H}\begin{bmatrix}[\mathbf{r}-\mathbf{c}]\\ [\mathbf{c}+\boldsymbol{\varepsilon}]\end{bmatrix}\left[\mathbf{I}_T - \frac{\boldsymbol{\iota}_T\boldsymbol{\iota}_T'}{T}\right]\right\}$$

$$\leq Min\left\{rank(\mathbf{H}),\ rank\begin{bmatrix}[\mathbf{r}-\mathbf{c}]\\ [\mathbf{c}+\boldsymbol{\varepsilon}]\end{bmatrix},\ rank\left[\mathbf{I}_T - \frac{\boldsymbol{\iota}_T\boldsymbol{\iota}_T'}{T}\right]\right\}$$

$$= Min\{2n-1, 2n, T-1\} = 2n-1 < n^2 \qquad (15)$$

since $\mathbf{H}$ is the $n^2 \times 2n$ selector matrix of rank $2n-1$,

$$\begin{bmatrix}[\mathbf{r}-\mathbf{c}]\\ [\mathbf{c}+\boldsymbol{\varepsilon}]\end{bmatrix}$$

is a risk-premium and cash return $2n \times T$ matrix of rank $2n$, and

$$\left[\mathbf{I}_T - \frac{\boldsymbol{\iota}_T\boldsymbol{\iota}_T'}{T}\right]$$

is the deviations producing $T \times T$ matrix of rank $T-1$, where it is required that $T > 2n$. This result can be illustrated by computing the rank of the selector matrix $\mathbf{H}$ for our nine countries. Since $\mathbf{H}$ consists of zeros and ones only, this is easily done. For our empirical example

$$rank(\mathbf{H}) = 2n - 1 = 17 < 81 = n^2$$

Remark. It should be emphasized that when one would numerically compute the rank of the strategy risk matrix in Table 5, the numerically computed result would deceptively show a *full* $rank(\boldsymbol{\Sigma}) = 81$, because of the imprecision of the numerical computation caused by the finite memory registers of a computer. Thus the strategy risk matrix appears to be of full rank.[7] However, the exact algebraic $rank\ (\boldsymbol{\Sigma}) = 17 < 81$ and thus the strategy risk matrix must logically be singular. The imprecision of the computed result is expressed by the determinant of $\boldsymbol{\Sigma}$ as the product of the resulting eigenvalues $|\boldsymbol{\Sigma}| = \Pi_{i=1}^{n^2}\lambda_i$. Although in our example $81 - 17 = 64$ eigenvalues are exactly zero, and consequently the determinant $|\boldsymbol{\Sigma}| = 0$, the (finite) computer shows these 64 eigenvalues to be numerically very close, but unequal, to zero at any available level of numerical computing precision of the data covariance matrix $\boldsymbol{\Omega}$.

3.2. Extended Markowitz Procedure

How we can exploit the accounting identities to get around the problem of the singular strategy risk matrix? The mean portfolio rate of return $\bar{s}_p$ for the holding period T is the allocated linear combination of the average strategy rates of return of the strategies, $\overline{\mathbf{VEC(S)}}$, contained in the portfolio

$$\bar{s}_p = \mathbf{w}'\overline{\mathbf{VEC(S)}} = \mathbf{w}'\mathbf{H}\begin{bmatrix} [\bar{\mathbf{r}} - \bar{\mathbf{c}}] \\ [\bar{\mathbf{c}} + \bar{\boldsymbol{\varepsilon}}] \end{bmatrix} = \mathbf{v}'\begin{bmatrix} [\bar{\mathbf{r}} - \bar{\mathbf{c}}] \\ [\bar{\mathbf{c}} + \bar{\boldsymbol{\varepsilon}}] \end{bmatrix} \tag{17}$$

w is a $n^2 \times 1 = 81 \times 1$ vector of portfolio allocations, such that the sum of the allocations equals unity, $\mathbf{w}'\boldsymbol{\iota}_{n^2} = 1$, where $\boldsymbol{\iota}_{n^2}$ is the $n^2 \times 1 = 81 \times 1$ unit vector; $\mathbf{v}$ is the $2n \times 1 = 18 \times 1$ vector of the combined portfolio allocations $\mathbf{v} = \mathbf{H}'\mathbf{w}$, such that $\mathbf{v}'\boldsymbol{\iota}_{2n} = 2$, where $\boldsymbol{\iota}_{2n}$ is the $2n \times 1 = 18 \times 1$ unit vector. The overall investment strategy portfolio risk, σ_{pp}, is the variance of the portfolio rates of return,

$$\sigma_{pp} = \mathbf{w}'\boldsymbol{\Sigma}\mathbf{w} = \mathbf{w}'\mathbf{H}\boldsymbol{\Phi}\mathbf{H}'\mathbf{w} = \mathbf{v}'\boldsymbol{\Phi}\mathbf{v} \tag{18}$$

Notice that the first $n = 9$ combined allocations $v_{i.}$, $i = 1, 2, \ldots, 9$, refer to the strategy choice of how much of the capital to invest in which stock market to earn a risk premium, while the second $n = 9$ allocations $v_{.j}$, $j = 1, 2, \ldots, 9$, refer to the strategy choice of how much of the capital to invest in which currency to earn a cash return. The allocations $\mathbf{v}$ exhaust the capital allocation based on these two fundamental choices of investments in stock markets and in currencies, because of the accounting identities,

$$\mathbf{v}' = \mathbf{v}'\left[\begin{bmatrix} \boldsymbol{\iota}_n \\ \mathbf{0} \end{bmatrix} + \begin{bmatrix} \mathbf{0} \\ \boldsymbol{\iota}_n \end{bmatrix}\right]$$

with

$$\mathbf{v}'\begin{bmatrix} \boldsymbol{\iota}_n \\ \mathbf{0} \end{bmatrix} = \mathbf{w}'\mathbf{H}\begin{bmatrix} \boldsymbol{\iota}_n \\ \mathbf{0} \end{bmatrix} = \mathbf{w}'\boldsymbol{\iota}_{n^2} = 1$$

and

$$\mathbf{v}'\begin{bmatrix} \mathbf{0} \\ \boldsymbol{\iota}_n \end{bmatrix} = \mathbf{w}'\mathbf{H}\begin{bmatrix} \mathbf{0} \\ \boldsymbol{\iota}_n \end{bmatrix} = \mathbf{w}'\boldsymbol{\iota}_{n^2} = 1. \tag{19}$$

Now the procedure has once again become similar to Markowitz' original nonsingular case, which we solve using the familiar Kuhn-Tucker Theorem for constraint optimization (Kuhn & Tucker, 1951). First, form the Lagrangian with the three accounting constraints:

$$L(\mathbf{v}, \lambda_1, \lambda_2, \lambda_3) = \mathbf{v}'\mathbf{\Phi}\mathbf{v} + \lambda_1\left[1 - \mathbf{v}'\begin{bmatrix}\boldsymbol{\iota}_n \\ \mathbf{0}\end{bmatrix}\right] + \lambda_2\left[1 - \mathbf{v}'\begin{bmatrix}\mathbf{0} \\ \boldsymbol{\iota}_n\end{bmatrix}\right]$$

$$+ \lambda_3\left[\bar{s}_p - \mathbf{v}'\begin{bmatrix}[\bar{\mathbf{r}} - \bar{\mathbf{c}}] \\ [\bar{\mathbf{c}} + \bar{\boldsymbol{\varepsilon}}]\end{bmatrix}\right] \tag{20}$$

Next, to find the optimum of this Lagrangian, set the $2n+3$ partial first derivatives equal to zero, i.e. the derivatives with respect to the $2n$ elements of the allocation vector $\mathbf{v}$ and to the three Lagrangian multipliers λ_1, λ_2 and λ_3.

The optimal Lagrangian multipliers λ_1^{opt}, λ_2^{opt} and λ_3^{opt} are given by

$$\begin{bmatrix}\lambda_1^{opt} \\ \lambda_2^{opt} \\ \lambda_3^{opt}\end{bmatrix} = 2.\mathbf{\Delta}^{-1}.\begin{bmatrix}1 \\ 1 \\ \bar{s}_p\end{bmatrix} \tag{21}$$

where the 3×3 symmetric and positive definite matrix $\mathbf{\Delta}$ is such that

$$\mathbf{\Delta} = \begin{bmatrix} [\boldsymbol{\iota}_n' \quad \mathbf{0}]\mathbf{\Phi}^{-1}\begin{bmatrix}\boldsymbol{\iota}_n \\ \mathbf{0}\end{bmatrix} & [\mathbf{0} \quad \boldsymbol{\iota}_n']\mathbf{\Phi}^{-1}\begin{bmatrix}\boldsymbol{\iota}_n \\ \mathbf{0}\end{bmatrix} & [[\bar{\mathbf{r}} - \bar{\mathbf{c}}]' \quad [\bar{\mathbf{c}} + \bar{\varepsilon}]']\mathbf{\Phi}^{-1}\begin{bmatrix}\boldsymbol{\iota}_n \\ \mathbf{0}\end{bmatrix} \\ [\boldsymbol{\iota}_n' \quad \mathbf{0}]\mathbf{\Phi}^{-1}\begin{bmatrix}\mathbf{0} \\ \boldsymbol{\iota}_n\end{bmatrix} & [\mathbf{0} \quad \boldsymbol{\iota}_n']\mathbf{\Phi}^{-1}\begin{bmatrix}\mathbf{0} \\ \boldsymbol{\iota}_n\end{bmatrix} & [[\bar{\mathbf{r}} - \bar{\mathbf{c}}]' \quad [\bar{\mathbf{c}} + \bar{\varepsilon}]']\mathbf{\Phi}^{-1}\begin{bmatrix}\mathbf{0} \\ \boldsymbol{\iota}_n\end{bmatrix} \\ [\boldsymbol{\iota}_n' \quad \mathbf{0}]\mathbf{\Phi}^{-1}\begin{bmatrix}[\bar{\mathbf{r}} - \bar{\mathbf{c}}] \\ [\bar{\mathbf{c}} + \bar{\varepsilon}]\end{bmatrix} & [\mathbf{0} \quad \boldsymbol{\iota}_n']\mathbf{\Phi}^{-1}\begin{bmatrix}[\bar{\mathbf{r}} - \bar{\mathbf{c}}] \\ [\bar{\mathbf{c}} + \bar{\varepsilon}]\end{bmatrix} & [[\bar{\mathbf{r}} - \bar{\mathbf{c}}]' \quad [\bar{\mathbf{c}} + \bar{\varepsilon}]']\mathbf{\Phi}^{-1}\begin{bmatrix}[\bar{\mathbf{r}} - \bar{\mathbf{c}}] \\ [\bar{\mathbf{c}} + \bar{\varepsilon}]\end{bmatrix} \end{bmatrix} \tag{22}$$

So that by substitution, the optimal fundamental choice allocations are determined to be

$$\mathbf{v}^{opt} = \frac{\mathbf{\Phi}^{-1}\left[\lambda_1^{opt}\begin{bmatrix}\boldsymbol{\iota}_n \\ \mathbf{0}\end{bmatrix} + \lambda_2^{opt}\begin{bmatrix}\mathbf{0} \\ \boldsymbol{\iota}_n\end{bmatrix} + \lambda_3^{opt}\begin{bmatrix}[\bar{\mathbf{r}} - \bar{\mathbf{c}}] \\ [\bar{\mathbf{c}} + \bar{\varepsilon}]\end{bmatrix}\right]}{2} \tag{23}$$

Remark. The $(2n+3)\times(2n+3)$ matrix of partial second derivatives is positive definite, since the full rank $2n\times 2n$ covariance matrix $\boldsymbol{\Phi}>0$, so that the optimum is, indeed, a – constrained – *minimum*.

We have now the two equations of Markowitz' Efficient Portfolio Frontier for $2n$ strategy investment choices, which can be plotted in a two-dimensional graph. For every portfolio strategy return $\bar{s}_p^{opt}$ there is a corresponding portfolio strategy risk σ_p^{opt}:

$$\bar{s}_p^{opt} = \mathbf{v}^{opt\prime}\begin{bmatrix}[\bar{\mathbf{r}}-\bar{\mathbf{c}}]\\ [\bar{\mathbf{c}}+\bar{\varepsilon}]\end{bmatrix} \tag{24}$$

$$\sigma_p^{opt} = \sqrt{(\mathbf{v}^{opt})\boldsymbol{\Phi}'\mathbf{v}^{opt}} \tag{25}$$

Figure 1 provides the efficiency frontier of the strategic multi-currency investment portfolios with exact risk attribution for the period July 1992–December 1997 for all $n=9$ countries, given by the bottom parabola. We compare this with the parabolic minimum variance frontiers of the 7 Asian countries by themselves, given by the top parabola, and with the parabolic minimum variance frontiers, when either Germany or the U.S. alone is included in the Asian portfolio. The optimal portfolio risk σ_p^{opt} is measured on the vertical axis, while the average portfolio return is measured on the horizontal axis.

3.3. Retrieval of the Optimal Strategy Allocations

The original portfolio investment strategy portfolio allocations $\boldsymbol{w}$ can be uniquely retrieved from the fundamental market choice portfolio allocations $\boldsymbol{v}$, via the two accounting identities imposed by the geometry of the original strategy matrix $\mathbf{S}(t)$, for example, when $n=3$,

$$[\mathbf{I}_n \quad \mathbf{0}]\mathbf{v}\mathbf{v}'\begin{bmatrix}\mathbf{0}\\ \mathbf{I}_n\end{bmatrix} = \begin{bmatrix} v_1v_4 & v_1v_5 & v_1v_6\\ v_2v_4 & v_2v_5 & v_2v_6\\ v_3v_4 & v_3v_5 & v_3v_6\end{bmatrix} = [\mathbf{I}_n \quad \mathbf{0}]\mathbf{H}'\mathbf{w}\mathbf{w}'\mathbf{H}\begin{bmatrix}\mathbf{0}\\ \mathbf{I}_n\end{bmatrix}$$

$$= \mathbf{W} = \begin{bmatrix} w_{11} & w_{12} & w_{13}\\ w_{21} & w_{22} & w_{23}\\ w_{31} & w_{32} & w_{33}\end{bmatrix} \tag{26}$$

Thus the investment strategy portfolio allocations $\mathbf{w}_{ij}$ are simply the *products* of the fundamental market choice portfolio allocations. Table 7 provides the

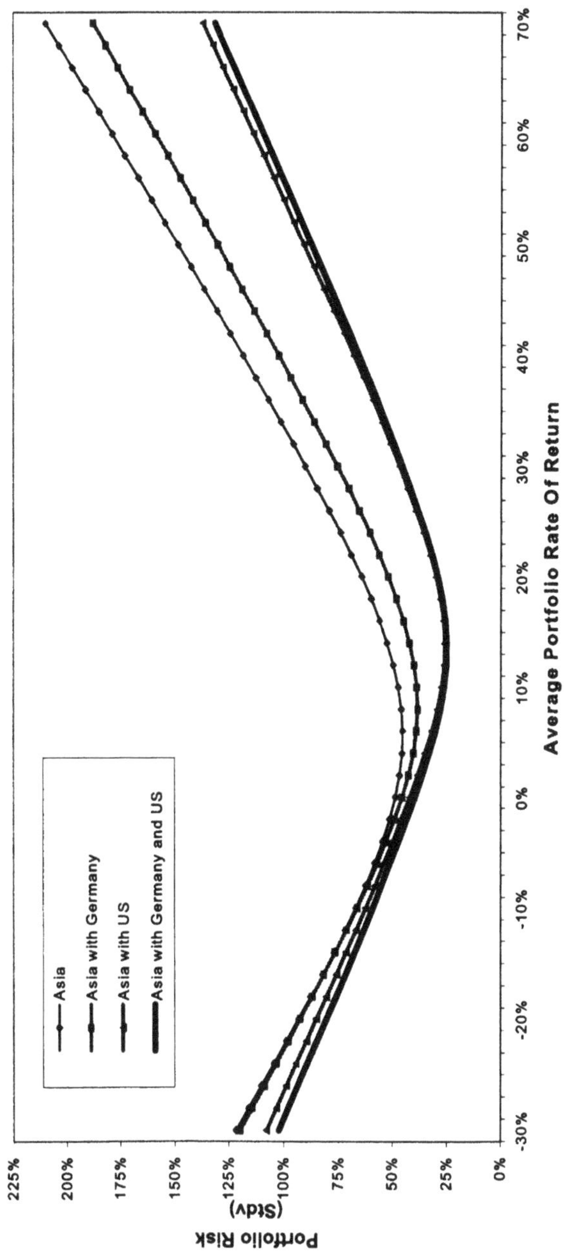

Fig. 1. Efficient Portfolio Frontiers of Strategic Multi-Currency Investments in Asia, July 1992–December 1997.

Table 7. Optimal GMV Strategic Allocations for Asian Countries, Together with USA and Germany, July 1992–December 1997.

			Hong Kong	Indonesia	Japan	Malaysia	Philippines	Singapore	Thailand	Germany	USA	
	cash returns weights		$v_{1.}$	$v_{.2}$	$v_{.3}$	$v_{.4}$	$v_{.5}$	$v_{.6}$	$v_{.7}$	$v_{.8}$	$v_{.9}$	
	risk premium weights		110.5%	− 48.7%	11.4%	41.4%	41.6%	− 99.2%	11.8%	25.4%	5.9%	100.0%
Hong Kong	$v_{1.}$	− 13.7%	− 15.2%	6.7%	− 1.6%	− 5.7%	− 5.7%	− 13.6%	− 1.6%	− 3.5%	− 0.8%	− 13.7%
Indonesia	$v_{2.}$	− 14.1%	− 15.6%	6.9%	− 1.6%	− 5.8%	− 5.9%	14.0%	− 1.7%	− 3.6%	− 0.8%	− 14.1%
Japan	$v_{3.}$	6.2%	6.9%	− 3.0%	0.7%	2.6%	2.6%	− 6.2%	0.7%	1.6%	0.4%	6.2%
Malaysia	$v_{4.}$	11.4%	12.6%	− 5.5%	1.3%	4.7%	4.7%	− 11.3%	1.3%	2.9%	0.7%	11.4%
Philippines	$v_{5.}$	2.7%	3.0%	− 1.3%	0.3%	1.1%	1.1%	− 2.7%	0.3%	0.7%	0.2%	2.7%
Singapore	$v_{6.}$	11.6%	12.8%	− 5.6%	1.3%	4.8%	4.8%	− 11.5%	1.4%	2.9%	0.7%	11.6%
Thailand	$v_{7.}$	3.7%	4.1%	− 1.8%	0.4%	1.5%	1.5%	− 3.7%	0.4%	0.9%	0.2%	3.7%
Germany	$v_{8.}$	11.9%	13.2%	− 5.8%	1.4%	4.9%	5.0%	− 11.8%	1.4%	3.0%	0.7%	11.9%
USA	$v_{9.}$	80.3%	88.7%	− 39.1%	9.1%	33.2%	33.4%	− 79.7%	9.4%	20.4%	4.7%	80.3%
		100.0%	110.5%	− 48.7%	11.4%	41.4%	41.6%	− 99.2%	11.8%	25.4%	5.9%	200.0%

Average portfolio return = 13.7%.
Average portfolio risk (stdv) – 25.3%.

optimal portfolio allocations for all nine countries combined based on the total investment of a five and a half year investment horizon (July 1992–December 1997) for the General Minimum-Variance (GMV) allocation, i.e. for the absolute minimum risk point of the lowest parabolic efficiency frontier in Fig. 1, where the average optimal portfolio return is $\bar{s}_p^{opt} = 13.7\%$/yr and the average portfolio risk $\sigma_p^{opt}(GMV) = 25.3\%$ within one year.

At the left side we find the column of risk premium weights $v_{i.}$, $i = 1, 2, \ldots, 9$ and in the top row the cash return weights $v_{.j}$, $j = 1,2, \ldots, 9$. In the surrounded rectangular we find the matrix **W** of investment strategy weights, which corresponds with the $n \times n = 9 \times 9$ investment strategy matrix **S**(t). The **W** matrix contains the "recipe" for optimal portfolio allocations for strategic multi-currency investments and can be computed for each point along the portfolio minimum variance frontier.

Notice that in Table 7 the exact accounting identities are maintained. Positive numbers for elements of **v** indicate buying or taking long positions; negative numbers indicate short selling or unwinding of long positions.[8] Table 7 shows that to achieve the GMV return and risk combination in the period, 80.3% of the initial capital $P(0)$ should have been invested in the U.S. stock market, with 11.9% in Germany, 11.6% in Singapore, 11.4% in Malaysia, and a smattering in Japan, Thailand, and the Philippines, with extensive short positions in the stock markets of 14.1% in Indonesia and 13.7% in Hong Kong. Such positions could have been achieved by buying and selling futures on the stock markets (if and when they had existed!).

The next step would have been to arrange cash swaps so that 110.5% of the capital value would have been swapped into the Hong Kong dollar and 41.4% and 41.6% would have been swapped into the Yen and the Ringgit, respectively, and 25.4% into the Deutschemark. The short currency positions would be 99.2% of the capital value against the Singapore dollar, 48.7% against the Rupiah, while only 5.9% would remain in the U.S. dollar. This would, of course, be the accumulated swap positions *resulting* from the 81 strategic investment allocations![9]

The rationale for such complex allocations is found in the covariance risk matrices of Tables 5 and 6. Such complex investment strategy allocations reduce the overall portfolio risk. Notice though, that, in each individual market, sometimes considerable gross leveraging occurs for some strategies, with allocations > 1 in absolute value, while on a net basis such leveraging cancels out.

On average, the portfolio approach to strategy investment does reduce portfolio risk. But the Asian risk levels remain high. The GMV risk is two times larger than the average return! Los (1998) found for the three country portfolio of Indonesia, Singapore and Malaysia that the risk level was six times higher than the return. Thus diversification considerably reduces the overall GMV risk, by including more international stock markets and currencies. The fundamental reason is that all three Asian stock markets exhibited very high levels of risk in the five and a half year period. Because the stock and currency markets are interrelated via the incessant capital flows, this stock market risk spills over into the currency markets.

From Fig. 1 it is also clear that any investor restricting his investment strategies only to Asia would not have been able to avoid the overall high level of GMV risk of close to 50% and a return of only 2.5%. By diversifying to the stable and regularly high earning U.S. stock market the GMV risk could have been halved and the return increased by five-fold. Only by more extensive globalization of the strategic Asian investment portfolios could the overall portfolio risk level of Asian investors have been reduced to more acceptable levels. This can be achieved by moving more capital to the more mature and stable markets of North America and Europe, which exhibited lower overall risk levels over the same time period.

4. NONSTATIONARITY OF ASIAN INVESTMENT RETURNS

Conventionally, Markowitz' mean-variance analysis assumes that the return data series are stationary in their first and second moments, i.e. that the average return rates and the covariance matrices don't change significantly over time. Since recently the Asian countries underwent significant economic and financial upheavals, it is a relevant research question to analyze if this assumption holds true.

In this section we analyze the changes in the average rates of return, changes in the general level of portfolio risk, as well as possible structural changes in the Asian investment risk profile in the period July 1992–December 1997. We do this by, rather crudely, windowing the empirical data set. Because of the minimal mathematical requirements for our mean-variance cum exact attribution analysis, $T > 2n = 18$, the complete data set of 66 monthly observations was, somewhat arbitrarily, divided into three equally sized windows, or data subsets, of each 22 observations. These three subsets cover the periods July 1992–April 1994, May 1994–February 1996 and March 1996–December 1997.

4.1. Level of Average Asian Strategic Investment Returns Over Time

It appears that the average levels of the Asian strategic investment returns went through three major changes over time and were far from stationary.

4.1.1. July 1992–April 1994

Chart 1 shows that in this period all of the cash returns and risk premia were positive. They ranged from substantial to large in Asia, but were very small in Germany and the USA. This period was dominated by very large risk premia of 20–25%/yr in the stock markets in Thailand, Malaysia, the Philippines and Singapore, closely followed by 17.5% in Hong Kong. The cash returns in Indonesia and Japan were slightly less than half that size and in Germany and the USA five to ten times smaller. It is clear that in this period fortunes were made in the stock markets of Asia, while Germany (Europe) and the USA were much less attractive places for equity investments.

Japan exhibited a very substantial average cash return of 14.9%/yr, followed by Thailand with 9.6%/yr and the Philippines with 8.6%/yr. Thus, under the assumption of unchanging FX regimes, a strategic multi-currency investor could reap a whopping 39.9%/yr by investing in the stock market in Thailand, earning a 25% risk premium, and swapping into Japanese Yen for an extra 14.9% cash return, as is shown in Table 8.

An equally profitable maximizing return strategy would have been to invest in the Malaysian stock market for the 24.4%/yr average risk premium, and then to swap into Yen, for a total average return of 39.3%/yr. The USA and Germany could never reach these return levels, even not with the currency overlays. Investing in the German stock market and swapping into Yen would have earned 18.9%/yr, a respectable return, but less than half of what was achievable in Asia. Since capital was attracted to Asia by its stock markets, cash returns could overall stay relatively low in Asia

4.1.2. May 1994–February 1996

Less than two years later the situation had already drastically changed. Chart 2 shows that all the stock markets in Asia delivered negative, or close to zero, risk premia, with the exception of Hong Kong. The stock market in the Philippines was losing on average 10.9%/yr. In contrast, the stock market in the USA was already showing a very healthy rebound en produced average risk premia of 13.5%/yr.

Since capital was now induced to return to the USA, the Asian countries had to raise their cash lending rates considerably. This made it attractive for money managers to swap into Asian bonds and to lend directly to governments and the

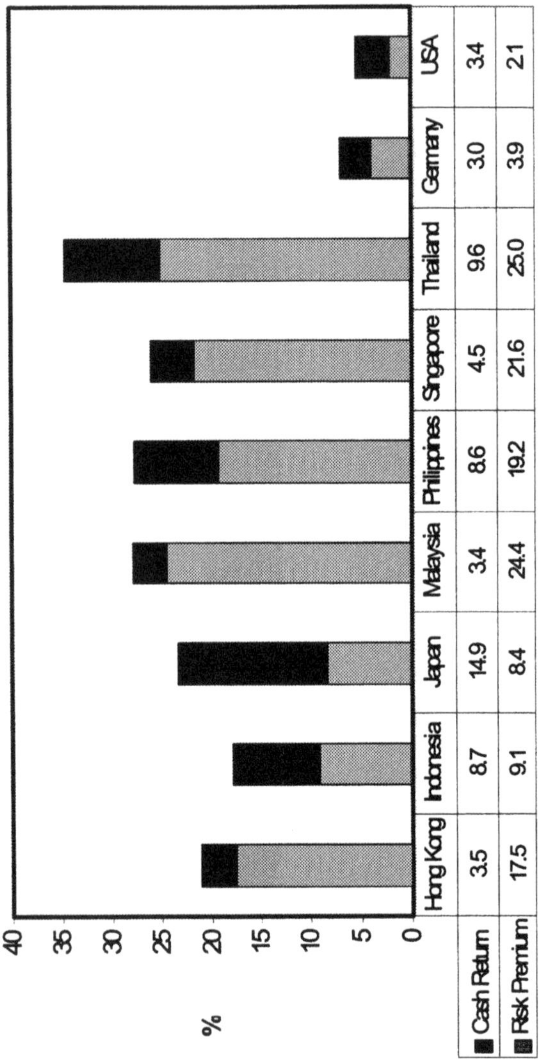

Chart 1. Risk Premia and Cash Returns, July 1992 – April 1994.

Table 8. Average Strategic Investment Returns (%), July 1992–April 1994.

	CURRENCIES								
MARKETS	Hong Kong	Indonesia	Japan	Malaysia	Philippines	Singapore	Thailand	Germany	USA
Hong Kong	21.0	26.2	32.4	20.9	26.1	22.0	27.1	20.5	20.8
Indonesia	12.6	17.8	24.0	12.5	17.7	13.6	18.7	12.1	12.5
Japan	11.9	17.1	23.3	11.8	17.0	12.9	18.0	11.3	11.7
Malaysia	27.9	33.1	39.3	27.8	33.0	28.9	34.0	27.4	27.8
Philippines	22.7	27.8	34.1	22.5	27.8	23.7	28.8	22.1	22.5
Singapore	25.1	30.2	36.5	24.9	30.2	26.1	31.2	24.5	24.9
Thailand	28.5	33.7	39.9	28.4	33.6	29.5	34.6	28.0	28.4
Germany	7.5	12.6	18.9	7.3	12.5	8.4	13.5	6.9	7.3
USA	5.6	10.7	17.0	5.5	10.7	6.6	11.7	5.0	5.4

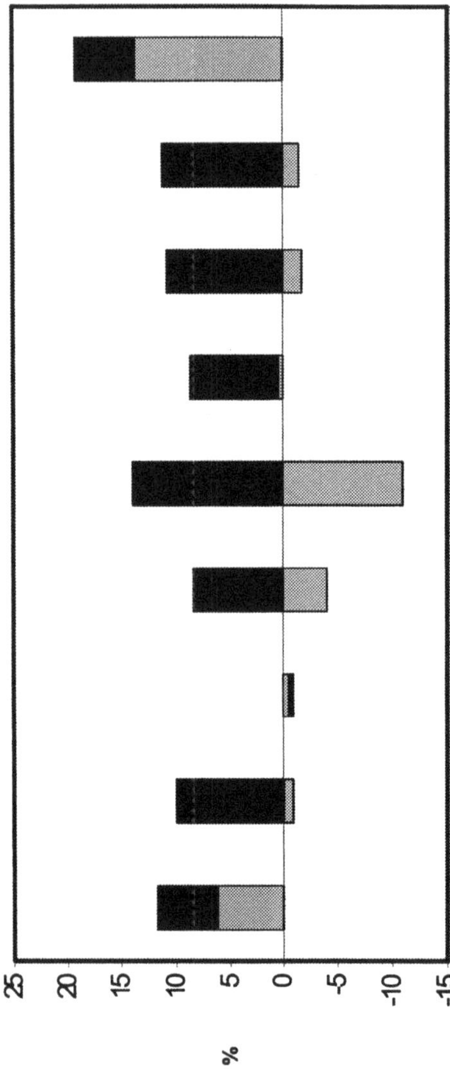

	Hong Kong	Indonesia	Japan	Malaysia	Philippines	Singapore	Thailand	Germany	USA
Cash Return	5.5	10.0	-0.4	8.3	13.8	8.1	10.8	11.2	5.6
Risk Premium	6.2	-0.9	-0.5	-4.0	-10.9	0.5	-1.7	-1.4	13.5

Chart 2. Risk Premia and Cash Returns, May 1994 – February 1996.

private sector alike. The highest cash returns in Asia could be earned in the Philippines, Thailand and Indonesia, 13.8%, 10.8% and 10.0% per year, respectively. At that time Germany was stepping on the inflationary brakes under the requirement of the Maastricht Treaty to prepare Europe for the Monetary Union. The German cash returns were 11.2%/yr, comparable to the Asian cash returns.

Because of the rebound in the stock market in the USA, the overall investment strategy, which clearly disregarded covariance risk, was to invest in the stock market in the USA to earn a 13.5%/yr risk premium and then to swap into an Asian currency or into Deutschemark. Table 9 shows that the total returns thus earned, were all above 20%/yr, with the highest strategic investment return of 27.4%/yr coming from investing in the USA and swapping into the Philippines' peso. Direct investments into the Philippines had become decidedly unattractive.

4.1.3. March 1996–December 1997

Chart 3 shows that in this third window of time the situation in Asia turned for the worse. Only six months of the 22 months in this window cover the currency turmoil and contagion, but, as a very detailed data analysis proves, the problems started actually in the Asian stock markets, spilled over into the cash lending markets and from there into the FX markets. Many of the direct investments and the financed government and private lending projects didn't deliver the returns expected. Most often, because hype combined with greed and lack of proper due diligence, many capitalized projects in Asia exhibited less than the marginally required returns. The risk premia in all Asian countries, including Japan, turned negative in this period, and so, with the exception of Hong Kong (because of the peg), did all the Asian cash returns.

In Thailand the risk premium was an average negative 84.2%/yr and the cash return, because of the collapse of the Thai baht, a negative 22.3%, so that capital was destroyed in Thailand at an average rate of 106.6%/yr, i.e. a complete annihilation of capital! Looking at the row for Thailand in Table 10, it is clear that no currency swap could have overcome the capital destruction in Thailand's stock market, since all the rates are about a negative 80–100%. Other hard hit countries were Malaysia, Indonesia and the Philippines, with domestic total returns of − 55.9%/yr, − 55.3%/yr and − 46.6%/yr, respectively.

As Table 10 shows, in this period of overall capital destruction, the best total returns could be earned by investing in the German stock market to earn a very healthy risk premium of 24.4%/yr, in advance of the European Union, and by swapping into the U.S.' or Hong Kong dollars to earn an extra 5.6%/yr,

Table 9. Average Strategic Investment Returns (%), May 1994–February 1996.

	CURRENCIES								
MARKETS	Hong Kong	Indonesia	Japan	Malaysia	Philippines	Singapore	Thailand	Germany	USA
Hong Kong	11.7	16.2	5.8	14.5	20.0	14.3	17.0	17.4	11.8
Indonesia	4.7	9.1	− 1.3	7.4	13.0	7.3	9.9	10.3	4.7
Japan	5.1	9.5	− 0.9	7.8	13.4	7.6	10.3	10.7	5.1
Malaysia	1.5	5.9	− 4.5	4.2	9.8	4.1	6.8	7.2	1.6
Philippines	− 5.4	− 0.9	− 11.3	− 2.6	2.9	− 2.8	− 0.1	0.3	− 5.3
Singapore	6.0	10.4	0.0	8.7	14.3	8.6	11.3	11.7	6.1
Thailand	3.8	8.2	− 2.2	6.5	12.1	6.4	9.1	9.5	3.8
Germany	4.1	8.6	− 1.8	6.9	12.4	6.7	9.4	9.8	4.2
USA	19.1	23.5	13.1	21.8	27.4	21.7	24.3	24.8	19.1

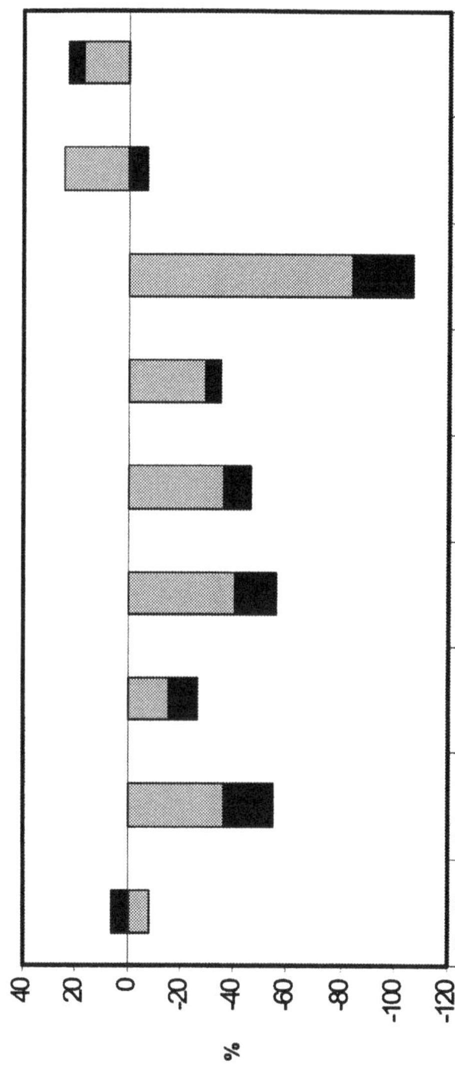

	Hong Kong	Indonesia	Japan	Malaysia	Philippines	Singapore	Thailand	Germany	USA
Cash Return	6.3	-18.4	-11.1	-15.5	-10.1	-5.8	-22.3	-7.5	5.6
Risk Premium	-8.4	-36.8	-15.7	-40.4	-36.5	-29.1	-84.2	24.4	17.1

Chart 3. Risk Premia and Cash Returns, March 1996 – December 1997.

Table 10. Average Strategic Investment Returns (%), March 1996–December 1997.

	CURRENCIES								
MARKETS	Hong Kong	Indonesia	Japan	Malaysia	Philippines	Singapore	Thailand	Germany	USA
Hong Kong	− 2.1	− 26.8	− 19.5	− 23.9	− 18.5	− 14.2	− 30.7	− 15.9	− 2.8
Indonesia	− 30.6	− 55.3	− 48.0	− 52.3	− 47.0	− 42.6	− 59.2	− 44.3	− 31.3
Japan	− 9.4	− 34.1	− 26.8	− 31.2	− 25.8	− 21.5	− 38.0	− 23.2	− 10.1
Malaysia	− 34.1	− 58.8	− 51.5	− 55.9	− 50.5	− 46.2	− 62.7	− 47.9	− 34.8
Philippines	− 30.2	− 54.9	− 47.6	− 52.0	− 46.6	− 42.3	− 58.8	− 44.0	− 30.9
Singapore	− 22.8	− 47.5	− 40.2	− 44.6	− 39.2	− 34.9	− 51.4	− 36.6	− 23.5
Thailand	− 78.0	− 102.7	− 95.4	− 99.8	− 94.4	− 90.1	− 106.6	− 91.8	− 78.7
Germany	30.7	6.0	13.3	8.9	14.3	18.6	2.1	16.9	30.0
USA	23.4	− 1.3	6.0	1.6	7.0	11.3	− 5.2	9.6	22.7

respectively 6.3%/yr cash return. As long as the Hong Kong peg holds, the swap in the Hong Kong dollar appears to be as attractive as the swap into the U.S. dollar. But the swap into the U.S. dollar eliminates all FX risk for the U.S. dollar based investor and is therefore probably more attractive.

4.2. Level of Asian Investment Risk Over Time

In the preceding subsection we discussed the average levels of total returns in three consecutive windows and found that they changed drastically over time. In this section we look closely at the level of covariance risk in the various markets in Asia. The general level of portfolio risk can be measured by the GMV risk of the portfolio minimum variance frontiers in the respective data windows. The first window ($h = 1$) ranges from July 1992 through April 1994, the second window ($h = 2$) from May 1994 through February 1996 and the third window ($h = 3$) from March 1996 through December 1997. For each window set the average returns were computed as in Charts 1, 2 and 3, and the corresponding $2n \times 2n$ risk-premium and cash return covariance matrix $\mathbf{\Phi}_h$, $h = 1, 2, 3$ (available in Appendix B) From these windowed data sets three respective minimum variance frontiers traced in the risk return space in Fig. 2, using the preceding procedures.

In the first window period, the highest risk premium volatility resided already in Thailand, followed by the Philippines and Hong Kong, while the highest cash return risk was in the Philippines. In the second window period, the order of the risk premium volatility remained unchanged, but Japan showed the highest cash return risk, resulting from high Yen volatility. In the third window period, the highest risk premium volatility remained in Thailand, followed by Indonesia, while the highest cash return volatility shifted now to Thailand, when the Thai baht collapsed.

Figure 2 shows that the GMV portfolio risk level declined from the first window period to the second and then sharply increased again moving from the second to the third period. At the same time the overall average strategic investment returns shifted down from the early to the middle and late 1990s. This conclusion is confirmed by the GMV return risk profiles in Table 11, which also provides the commensurate GMV portfolio fundamental choice allocations.

Most of that rate decline, from 10.0% to 3.0%, occurred from the first to the second window, when the risk level declined by 270 basis points from 10.8% to 8.1%, due to the fact that investors switched from investments in Asian stock markets to investments in Asian cash. But the transition from the second to the third window was clearly different; the GMV portfolio risk level increased by

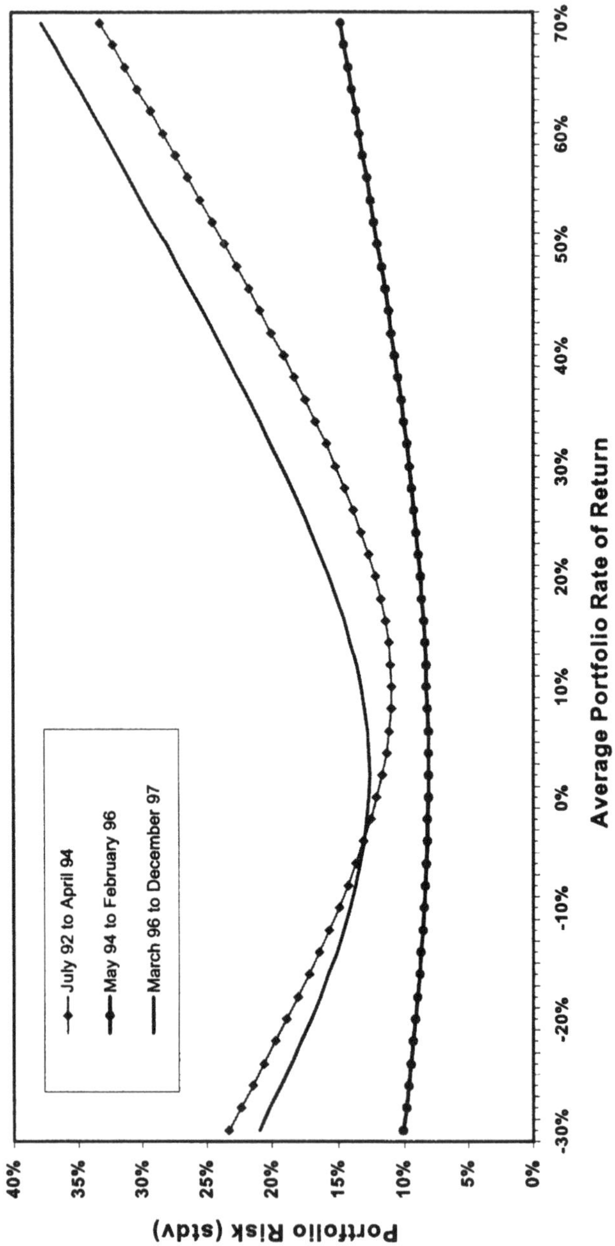

Fig. 2. Efficient Frontiers Over Time for Globally Diversified Asian Portfolio (3 windows of each 22 months).

Table 11.

		GMV	PORTFOLIO	PROFILES
		Jul 92–Apr 94	May 94–Feb 96	Mar 96–Dec 97
Average Return	$\bar{s}_p$	10.0%	3.0%	2.0%
Average Risk (stdv)	$\frac{3}{4}_p$	10.8%	8.1%	12.5%
Asset allocations	$v_{1.}$	− 0.29	− 0.02	0.11
	$v_{2.}$	0.02	− 0.19	0.15
	$v_{3.}$	0.21	− 0.09	0.08
	$v_{4.}$	− 0.04	0.17	− 0.09
	$v_{5.}$	0.30	− 0.48	− 0.12
	$v_{6.}$	0.00	0.84	0.52
	$v_{7.}$	0.05	0.02	0.01
	$v_{8.}$	− 0.11	0.19	0.07
	$v_{9.}$	0.85	0.60	0.28
Currency allocations	$v_{.1}$	15.70	− 4.02	− 4.40
	$v_{.2}$	− 0.57	− 1.61	− 0.56
	$v_{.3}$	0.09	0.05	− 0.01
	$v_{.4}$	1.23	1.93	0.58
	$v_{.5}$	0.49	0.50	1.40
	$v_{.6}$	0.08	− 0.72	− 3.20
	$v_{.7}$	− 0.21	3.57	− 0.36
	$v_{.8}$	− 0.72	0.50	1.31
	$v_{.9}$	− 14.09	7.95	6.25

440 basis points from 8.1% to 12.5%, without a commensurate increase in GMV portfolio return. Instead, the GMV portfolio average return declined further from 3.0% to 2.0%. In contradiction to static finance theory, there was a pure, uncompensated, increase in risk: sharp unpredictable declines in stock markets gradually, combined in the second half of 1997 with sharp unpredictable currency depreciations.

Table 11 also reveals other remarkable differences between the periods. Notice, for example, that the GMV portfolios required a positive allocation of 30% of capital to the stock market in the Philippines, but pulled such a capital allocation out in the second and third periods. The heavy and leveraged Hong Kong dollar based GMV strategy (+ 15.7) combined with the heavy shorting of the U.S. dollar (− 14.09) of the first period, was totally reversed in the second and third periods, when we had strategy combinations (− 4.02, + 7.95) and (− 4.40, + 6.25) respectively. Most likely, this was related to the global portfolio cautiousness in advance of the Hong Kong hand-over.

4.3. Structural Changes in Asian Investment Risk

In Fig. 2 it is obvious that between July 1992 and December 1997 not only the level of portfolio risk changed in Asia, but also its "shape": the three windowed portfolio frontiers have different shapes. In particular, the parabolic shape of the portfolio frontier in the second window for the period May 1994 to February 1997 shows much less curvature than the parabolic frontiers of the first window period from July 1992 to April 1994 and of the third window period from March 1996 to December 1997. The efficiency frontiers of the first and second window have remarkably similar curvatures.

A possible reason is that, in both the first and second window periods, the risky Asian stock market premia were dominant; in the first window period they were positive and in the third window period they were negative. But in the second period, from May 1994 to February 1996, low risk cash returns were dominant. One can discern the considerable difference between the risk premium $(\mathbf{r}-\mathbf{c})$ blocks of the $2n \times 2n$ covariance matrices $\mathbf{\Phi}_h$ and the cash return $(\mathbf{c}+\boldsymbol{\varepsilon})$ blocks of the same $\mathbf{\Phi}_h$ matrices. First, the cash return blocks are bordered by the very low and mostly negative covariances of the Hong Kong and U.S.' cash returns. Second, we can discern the flip-flopping changes from positive to negative covariances and vice versa, going from one window to the next, again suggesting the instability of the covariance risks.

But a more formal analysis is possible. The $2n = 18$-dimensional covariance risk ellipsoids, which are implied by the covariance matrices $\mathbf{\Phi}_h$, $h = 1, 2, 3$, since $\mathbf{w}_h'\mathbf{\Phi}_h\mathbf{w}_h = c$ (= arbitrary constant), can be analyzed to see if there were significant structural changes in the Asian investment portfolio (= diversification) risk profile. For this analysis each covariance matrix is spectrally decomposed as follows

$$\mathbf{\Phi}_h = \mathbf{V}_h \Lambda_h \mathbf{V}_h', \tag{27}$$

where Λ_h is the diagonal matrix with the 18 eigenvalues λ_{hi}, $h = 1, 2, 3$; $i = 1, 2, \ldots, 18$, on the diagonal and $\mathbf{V}_h$ the corresponding matrix of eigenvectors, providing the rotational information with respect to the data frame of reference. The squared (all positive) eigenvalues λ_{hi} provide the amplitudes for the 18-dimensional scatter plots of the data vectors $[(\mathbf{r}-\mathbf{c}), (\mathbf{c}+\boldsymbol{\varepsilon})]$ from which the shape of each 18-dimensional covariance ellipsoid is derived. Since the matrix of eigenvectors is orthonormal, we can, by plotting simultaneously the three scree plots of eigenvalues, observe if significant structural changes have taken place in the shape of each covariance ellipsoid, and thus in the unsystematic covariance risk.

In Fig. 3 these amplitudes are standardized, i.e. the maximum amplitude along the main axis of the covariance risk ellipsoid in each window is set equal to 100% and is not plotted in Fig. 3. Only the second, third, etc. up to the 18th amplitude are plotted, since all but the first (maximum) amplitude represent the diversification risk (=volume of the risk ellipsoid). Notice that the second amplitude is only 31.2% of the maximum amplitude in the first window, (July 1992–April 1994), indicating that there is a strong, unifying global market movement in the risk premia and cash returns. However, the second amplitude drops sharply to 20.2% in the second window (May 1994–February 1996) and returns to 24.5% in the third window (March 1996–December 1997). This represents, respectively, the lower curvature of the minimum variance frontier in the second window compared with the one in the first window, and the partial return to a higher curvature in the third window. The diversification risk in Asia was clearly not stable. The Asian diversification risk was very extensive in the mid-1990s and this probably caused considerable allocation problems for strategic portfolio managers investing in Asia.

What about the changes in systematic risk? Since the mapping from one covariance risk ellipsoid into the next can be described as follows: $\mathbf{\Phi}_h \rightarrow \mathbf{\Phi}_k$ is equivalent to $\mathbf{V}_h\mathbf{\Lambda}_h\mathbf{V}_h' \rightarrow \mathbf{V}_k\mathbf{\Lambda}_k\mathbf{V}_k'$, there occurred also simultaneous rotation in the direction of the systematic covariance risk, as represented by the change in the matrices of eigenvectors $\mathbf{V}_h$, $h=1, 2, 3$ to $\mathbf{V}_k$, $k=1, 2, 3$, respectively. While the matrices of eigenvectors are orthonormal, per definition – within each data window $\mathbf{V}_h\mathbf{V}_h' = \mathbf{I} = \mathbf{V}_h'\mathbf{V}_h$, they are usually not orthonormal between windows: $\mathbf{V}_h\mathbf{V}_k' \neq \mathbf{I} \neq \mathbf{V}_h'\mathbf{V}_k$ for $h \neq k$.[10] Because of the orthonormality within each window, it is sufficient to focus on the 18-dimensional direction of the maximum axis of the covariance risk ellipsoid, since the other seventeen axes are orthogonal to the maximum axis. A change in the direction of the maximum axis represents a change in the systematic risk and implies similar direction changes in the other seventeen axes.

In Fig. 4 a radar diagram shows the $2n = 18$ direction coefficients of the eigenvector of the maximum axis of the Asian covariance risk ellipsoid for the three consecutive windows periods. Each direction coefficient is measured from the center (which is at -60% of the unit length of the eigenvector). The first nine axes (1–9) correspond with the data axes of the risk premia, i.e. the stock markets. The second nine (10–18) correspond with the data axes of the cash returns, i.e. the currency swap markets.[11]

First, there is an initial impression of general similarity of each of the coefficients between the windows and thus of overall stability of systematic risk. Second, the systematic risk is mostly related to the risk premia, i.e. the stock markets, since the first nine coefficients in each of the three consecutive

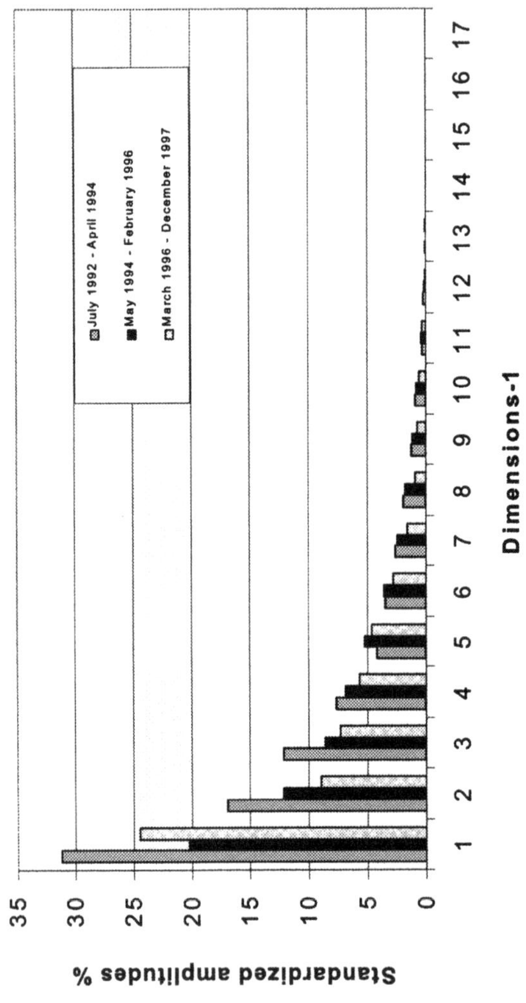

Fig. 3. Standardized Amplitudes of 18D Covariance Risk Ellipsoid.

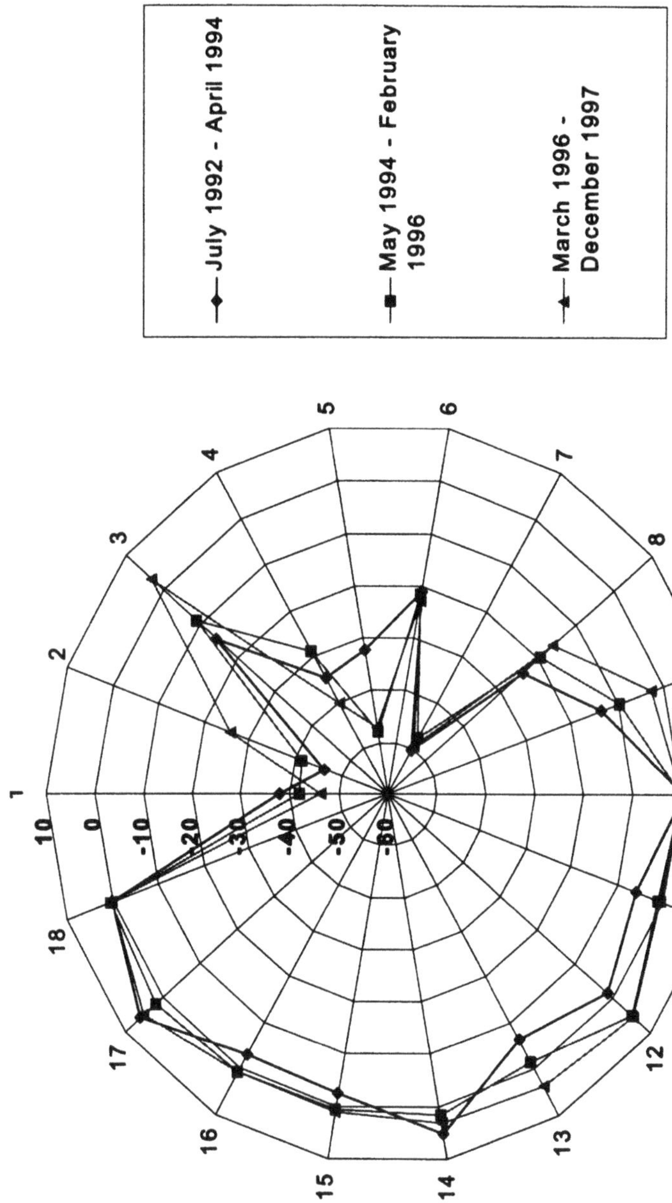

Fig. 4. 18D Analysis of Changes in Systematic Risk.

periods are closest to the center of the diagram. Hong Kong, the Philippines, Thailand and Malaysia show most stock market related systematic risk: their coefficients are closest to the center. There is much less systematic risk related to the currency swap markets: the currency return coefficients are close to zero and they shift for five of the seven Asian countries from negative to positive.

Third, there are specific country related changes discernible in the systematic risk. The largest decrease in systematic risk occurred in the stock market of Indonesia between the second window (May 1994–February 1996) and the third window (March 1996–December 1997). During the same transition there occurred also an decrease in the systematic stock market risk of Japan. Interestingly, for both Indonesia and Japan the systematic currency swap risk switched signs between the early and the later 1990s. A substantial increase in systematic risk of the stock market in the Philippines also occurred between the first and second window period. In the period July 1992–December 1997, Germany and the USA saw a gradual decrease in systematic stock market risk.

From the point of view of our Asian + portfolio, Singapore and Thailand surprisingly exhibited most stability in systematic risk in its stock market dimension, while Hong Kong and the USA, as expected, exhibited most stability in systematic risk in their respective currency return dimensions. Neither the USA nor Hong Kong showed systematic currency swap risk in any of the three periods: their systematic cash return coefficients remained zero.

5. CONCLUSIONS

Singer and Karnosky's (1994, 1995) complete and exact cash growth accounting framework produces a singular strategy risk matrix based on simple growth strategy investment allocations, which prevents mean-variance portfolio optimization. With the help of simple tensor algebra, and by exploiting the accounting identities, the exact accounting framework of Singer and Karnosky is reformulated, so that the fundamental choice covariance matrix is nonsingular. and Markowitz mean-variance portfolio optimization can be implemented with complete and exact attribution. This implies that finally commercial procedures, such as RiskMetrics^{TM} and CreditMetrics^{TM} can properly implement portfolio optimization combined with exact, cash flow based, return attribution. Thus far, their optimization procedures have been based on singular risk matrices, which only appear nonsingular, because of errors introduced by finite computer memory registers.

This new optimal return-risk attribution accounting framework is implemented to the stock market, cash market and FX return data for seven Asian countries, plus the USA and Germany, in the period July 1992 through December 1997. In this five and a half year investment horizon, out of 81 possible bilateral investment strategies, the optimal investment strategy would have been to invest 80.3% of the investable capital in the U.S. stock market, with smaller allocations of 11.5% into Malaysia, Singapore and Germany and with some short selling of around 14% in Hong Kong and Indonesia. This stock market allocation should have been combined with currency swaps, with 110% in the Hong Kong dollar, around 41.5% in Malaysian Ringgit and Philippines' peso and 25.4% in German Deutschemark, with almost 100% short selling of the Singapore dollar. The result? An annual average portfolio return of 13.7% with average portfolio risk (measured by one standard deviation of 25.3%. Was the total GMV portfolio return enough to compensate for the GMV portfolio risk? The historical facts tell us no! Even diversification into the stable and liquid markets of the USA and Germany would have been insufficient for an investor bent on investing in Asia.

There is ample evidence that many global investors disregarded normal portfolio risk considerations and that they based their strategic investment allocations strictly on policies of maximizing returns, but not on minimizing risks. Perhaps, because Asian diversification risk was non-stationary and thus essentially unpredictable, overall risk was foolishly ignored as a serious strategic investment consideration. Stock market volatility made Asia a high investment risk area[12] Thailand showed the highest risk premium volatility throughout the period, and the highest cash return volatility in the early period of July 1992 to April 1994 and again in the period March 1996 to December 1997. This stock market volatility was caused by non-existent, unreliable, or non-transparent fundamental stock valuations. Consequently, the Asian stock markets operated more as speculative casinos than as mechanisms for reliable equity valuation and arbitrage.

In addition, there was latent currency risk, because of mercantilistic trade policies. The cash returns in Japan were the most volatile in the second window period, because of Yen volatility. Their mercantilistic trade policies forced most Asian countries to artificially "peg" their currencies to the U.S. dollar. The enormous surpluses of accumulated foreign reserves in several of the Asian countries clearly indicate that these currencies should have appreciated, but were prevented from doing so by continued U.S. dollar buying by their central banks. This caused enormous pressures on the Asian FX rates. These pressured broke into the open, when in 1997 the Asian stock market risks spilled over into and were then amplified by the Asian currency crisis.[13]

By a detailed analysis of the nonstationarity of the portfolio return-risk profiles, we discern three distinct, although somewhat arbitrarily timed, window periods within this five and a half year period. In the first period, July 1992–April 1994, the Asian stock markets delivered high risk premia, combined with moderate cash returns. Simultaneously the risk premia and cash returns in the USA and Germany were low. This situation induced a capital flow to Asia.

In the second period, May 1994–February 1996, the Asian stock markets produced zero risk premia on average, but liquidity crunches combined with the continuing capital inflows raised the cash returns to very high levels. However, the USA stock market started to produce substantial risk premia and many portfolio managers invested in the USA stock market, but swapped their cash into Asian currencies, for public and private lending.

In the third period, the Asian stock markets collapsed and sharply produced negative risk premia. This was combined with negative cash returns, when the promised cash returns on bank lending projects failed to materialize. Foreign capital started then to pull out of the region and Asian currencies began to depreciate at fast rates. The multi-lateral currency swaps transmitted the volatility fast throughout the ASEAN countries and thus the Asian financial crises resembled the progression of viral contagion.

While from the first to the second period the GMV return decline was accompanied by a decline in risk, when capital was shifted from the stock markets into cash, in the second transition this was no longer true. In the second transition from the second to the third period, GMV portfolio risk increased sharply together with a decline in total GMV return, when all capital was pulled out of Asia.

Spectral analysis of the fundamental covariance risks between the (mostly Asian) risk premia and the cash returns, demonstrates that the diversification risks within the Asian portfolio were sharply changing between the three window periods. The Asian financial markets suffered from severe non-stationarity of the second moments of their return distributions (and probably, also of the third and higher moments).The Asian portfolio diversification risks were largest in the mid-1990s. Such non-stationarity changes the shape of the portfolio minimum variance frontier over time. Hong Kong, Thailand, the Philippines and Malaysia exhibited the largest systematic risks.

But these systematic risks were changing too. The Philippines' systematic risk increased in the early 1990s, between the first and second window periods. The systematic risks of Indonesia and Japan both were dramatically reduced between the second and third window periods in the mid-1990s. Meanwhile the systematic risk in Thailand and Singapore remained unchanged throughout. Only intensive dynamic monitoring by Kalman-information filtering (= using moving windows) may, perhaps, make it possible for a portfolio manager to project, perhaps, one or two months ahead for dynamic portfolio allocation, when the monthly data would be timely and accurate. However, because the portfolio would have to be adjusted continuously, the transaction costs may become prohibitive for such an exercise.

NOTES

1. Montes (1998) timely examined the economic basis for the Asian currency crisis and characterizes the nature of the policy weaknesses that led to the crisis. A short, sober and critical ex-post commentary can be found in Bomhoff (1999).

2. Since January 1, 1999, this can be investments in the European Union and in the Euro.

3. Rounding errors prevent exactness of some summations in the digit behind the decimal point.

4. The approximation is more accurate when the periods $t = 1, 2, \ldots, T$ and thus the periodic rates $s_{ij}(t)$ are smaller. For example, daily valuations are more accurate than weekly valuations, which are more accurate than monthly, which are more accurate than quarterly valuations, etc. An increasing number of global financial institutions is able to compute daily valuations of their portfolios, thanks to electronic accounting systems, and as strongly recommended by the Association for Investment Management and Research, 1997, p. 66.

5. When A is an $m \times n$ matrix and B a $p \times q$ matrix, then the *Kronecker product* of these two matrices is defined by $A \otimes B = [a_{ij}B]$ and $vec(AB) = (B' \otimes I)vec(A) = (I \otimes A)$ $vec(B)$. For proof cf. Dhrymes, 1978, p. 519. For a compilation of useful Kronecker product results, cf. Los, 1984, pp. 543–548.

6. Since Markowitz (1987) is currently out of print, Professor Markowitz drew my attention to the generality of his 1980s presentation in reaction to Los (1998), by courteously sending me a copy of his book. Of course, one may question the relevance of symmetric mean-variance optimization, since there are observable asymmetries in the regional risk distributions. An optimization based on the empirical asymmetrical and leptokurtic return distributions would require the computation of third and fourth moments. But then the procedure of this would quickly become quickly very complex, without elucidating the issues of combining portfolio optimization with complete and exact attribution and the resulting singularity of the risk matrix.

7. As, indeed, is the case in RiskMetrics^{TM}, confirmed by Professor Mark Garman, when he revealed the instability and unreliability of RiskMetrics^{TM}'s information matrix $\mathbf{\Sigma}^{-1}$ in a research seminar on March 7, 1996 at the Nanyang Technological University. It was again confirmed by e-mail on April 23, 1998 by Peter Zangari of J. P. Morgan.

8. Until recently, Malaysia, like many Asian countries, didn't allow shorting of stocks, thereby introducing an unnecessary market inefficiency. This inefficiency was removed in October 1997.

9. Anybody who thinks that the computation of 81 strategic investment allocations for one portfolio is excessive has not recently been on the trading floor of a modern advanced investment firm, where much higher dimensional strategy matrices can be observed on the screens of the traders.

10. Although, interestingly, it is true that $(\mathbf{V}_h\mathbf{V}_k')(\mathbf{V}_h\mathbf{V}_k')' = \mathbf{I}$, clearly demonstrating the rotational nature of these orthonormalized matrices of eigenvectors.

11. **Risk premia of stock markets**: 1 = Hong Kong, 2 = Indonesia, 3 = Japan, 4 = Malaysia, 5 = Philippines, 6 = Singapore, 7 = Thailand, 8 = Germany, 9 = USA.
Cash returns of swaps: 10 = Hong Kong, 11 = Indonesia, 12 = Japan, 13 = Malaysia, 14 = Philippines, 15 = Singapore, 16 = Thailand, 17 = Germany, 18 = USA.

12. Elsewhere, Los (1997) shows that for Singapore, Malaysia and to a somewhat lesser extent Indonesia, the volatility of the stock markets is closely related to the instability of the local economies and not to the risks of the local cash markets. In fact, the local cash markets operate almost independently from the local stock markets and the local economies.

13. The Asian currency crisis resembles very much the breakdown of the artificial European Monetary System in 1992–1993, when the Pound Sterling, the Italian Lire, the Swedish Krone, the French Franc, etc. came under attack of currency arbitragers. In Asia in 1997, the mercantilistic "monetary system" of artificially pegged exchange rates broke down for a similar reason. The artificially created currency disequilibria, expressed by the enormous foreign exchange surpluses, formed an inviting opportunity for major currency arbitragers to force an Asian FX equilibrium (cf. Bomhoff, 1999).

ACKNOWLEDGMENTS

I thank my former students Ho Su-Ping, Lim Cheer Hwi and Jeyanthi Karuppiah at the Nanyang Business School of the Nanyang Technological University in Singapore, who collected the data and performed the computations, Professor Markowitz for his kind correction, and Dr. Li Zhi-Feng for discussing the representation of changes in the multi-dimensional systematic investment risk. This paper has been presented at the Sixth Conference on Pacific Basin Business, Economics and Finance in Hong Kong, 28–29 May, 1998 and received an Outstanding Paper Award from the Asia-Pacific Risk and Insurance Association at its Second Annual Conference in Singapore, 19–22 July 1998.

REFERENCES

AIMR (1997). *Performance Presentation Standards Handbook* (2nd ed.). Association for Investment Managers and Research, Charlottesville, NC.

Allen, G. C. (1991). Performance attribution for global equity portfolios. *Journal of Portfolio Management, 17*, 59–65.

Black, F., & Litterman, R. (1992). Global portfolio optimization. *Financial Analysts Journal, 48*, 28–43.

Bomhoff, E. J. (1999). Lessons from the Asian financial crisis. *Accounting and Business Review, 6*, 1–16.

Dhrymes, P. (1978). *Introductory Econometrics*. New York, NY: Springer-Verlag.

Gardner, G. W., & Wuiloloud, T. (1995). Currency risk in international portfolios: how satisfying is optimal hedging? *Journal of Portfolio Management, 21*, 59–67.

Karnosky, D. S., & Singer, B. D. (1994). *Global Asset Management and Performance Attribution*. The Research Foundation of the Institute of Chartered Financial Analysts, Charlottesville, VA.
Kuhn, H. W., & Tucker, A. W. (1951). Nonlinear programming. In: J. Neyman (Ed.), *Proceedings of the Second Berkeley Symposium on Mathematical Statistics and Probability*. Berkeley, CA: University of California Press.
Lee, A. F. (1987). International asset and currency allocation. *Journal of Portfolio Management*, *14*, 68–73.
Los, C. A. (1984). Econometrics of Models with Evolutionary Parameter Structures. PhD thesis, New York, NY: Columbia University.
Los, C. A. (1997). Valuation of six Asian stock markets: financial system identification in noisy environments. In: *Proceedings of the Econometric Society Australasian Meeting* (Vol. 4, pp. 589–621.
Los, C. A. (1998). Optimal multi-currency investment strategies with exact attribution in three Asian countries. *Journal of Multinational Financial Management*, *8*, 169–198.
Los, C. A. (2001). *Computational Finance: A Scientific Perspective*. Singapore: World Scientific Publishing Co.
Markowitz, H. M. (1952). Portfolio selection. *Journal of Finance*, *7*, 77–91.
Markowitz, H. M. (1987). *Mean-Variance Analysis in Portfolio Choice and Capital Markets*. Cambridge, MA: Basil Blackwell.
Markowitz, H. M. (1991) (Original 1959). *Portfolio Selection: Efficient Diversification of Investments*. Cambridge, MA: Basil Blackwell.
Montes, M. F. (1998). *The Currency Crisis in Southeast Asia* (updated ed.). Institute of Southeast Asian Studies, Singapore.
Singer, B. D. (1996). Evaluation of portfolio performance: attribution analysis. *The Journal of Performance Measurement*, *1*, 45–55.
Singer, B. D., & Karnosky, D. S. (1995). The general framework for global investment management and performance attribution. *The Journal of Portfolio Management*, *21*, 84–92.

APPENDIX A: LIST OF DATA SERIES

All series were obtained from Datastream, Dow Jones Telerate, for the period July 1992–December 1997.

Stock Market Indices

Hong Kong: Hang Seng – Price Index
Indonesia: Jakarta SE – Price Index
Japan: Nikkei 225 Stock Average – Price Index
Malaysia: Kuala Lumpur Composite – Price Index
Philippines: Philippines SE Composite – Price Index
Singapore: Straits Times Industrial Index

Thailand: Thailand DS Market – Price Index
Germany: DAX 'KURS' – Price Index
United States: S&P 500 Composite – Price Index

Interest Rates

Hong Kong: HK Inter-bank 1 Month (Middle Rate)
Indonesia: Indonesia Deposit 1 Month (Middle Rate)
Japan: Japan Inter-bank 1 Month (Middle Rate)
Malaysia: Malaysia Inter-bank 1 Month (Middle Rate)
Philippines: Philippines T-Bill 91 Days (Middle Rate)
Singapore: Singapore Inter-bank 1 Month (Middle Rate)
Thailand: Average of 3 banks Offered Rates

(1) Thailand Inter-bank 1 Month (BB) – Offered Rate
(2) Thailand Inter-bank 1 Month (SC) – Offered Rate
(3) Thailand Inter-bank 1 Month (TF) – Offered Rate

Germany: Germany Inter-bank 1 Month (LDN:BBA – Offered Rate)
United States: U.S. Inter-bank 1 Month (LDN:BBA – Offered Rate)

Exchange Rates

Hong Kong: Hong Kong$ to U.S.$ – Exchange Rate
Indonesia: Indonesian Rupiah to U.S.$ – Exchange Rate
Japan: Japanese Yen to U.S.$ – Exchange Rate
Malaysia: Malaysian Ringitt to U.S.$ – Exchange Rate
Philippines: Philippine Peso to U.S.$ – Exchange Rate
Singapore: Singapore$ to U.S.$ – Exchange Rate
Thailand: Thai Bhat to U.S.$ – Exchange Rate
Germany: German Mark DM to U.S.$ – Exchange Rate

TRACKING ERRORS, CHANGING RISKS AND THE ASSET UNIVERSE

Ponladesh Poomimars, John Cadle and
Michael Theobald

ABSTRACT

The management of tracking errors is demonstrated to be independent of the risk structure and risk estimation procedures when the asset universe is restricted to two asset classes (i.e. stocks vs. bonds, domestic vs. international stocks). When there are more than two asset classes, however, tracking errors will be dependent upon risk. Using a relatively straightforward risk estimation procedure that incorporates changes in variances and covariances through time leads to the generation of portfolios with lower tracking errors.

INTRODUCTION

The risk of a portfolio may be managed either in total (or absolute) risk terms, that is the standard deviation of returns, or in relative risk terms, where the risk is measured relative to a benchmark (see, for example, Chow, 1995; Franks, 1992; Roll, 1992). Portfolio managers who optimise in terms of tracking errors relative to a benchmark (Wang, 1999 analyses the issue of multiple benchmarks) are reflecting the choice that they face as between active management and passive management via tracking a benchmark (or employing an index fund). Many issues within the portfolio management area are now

Financial Risk and Financial Risk Management, Volume 16, pages 261–273.

ISBN: 0-7623-0858-3

analysed within a benchmark/tracking error framework (see, for example, Grinold & Kahn, 2000; Ibbotson & Kaplan, 2000; Jacobs, Levy & Starer, 1998). The efficient frontier that is generated by optimising in relative risk terms will not necessarily be efficient in absolute risk terms, particularly when the benchmark is not on the "absolute" efficient frontier. A third frontier – or more correctly space – is possible when optimisations are conducted jointly in terms of both relative and absolute risks (Chow, 1995).

Roll (1992) generated a number of useful and interesting insights into the properties and characteristics of optimisations that minimise tracking error variance for a given level of tracking error. For example, he demonstrates that optimising in tracking error terms will not normally generate Markowitz efficient frontiers and that the same trades will be conducted by portfolio managers irrespective of the benchmark against which they are assessed, provided they face the same asset universe and have homogeneous expectations. It would be anticipated that modelling the risk structure using differing techniques would impact upon the tracking error volatilities. For example, modelling the covariance structure by incorporating changes in this structure through time would be expected to improve the management of tracking errors. However, this will not be the case for certain types of asset universe and estimation procedures as we demonstrate both empirically and analytically in this paper. When risk does impact, however, we demonstrate empirically that using models that incorporate changes in the risk structure through time can improve the management of tracking error volatility.

As part of a top down approach, portfolio managers may often conduct analyses across two broad asset classes such as stocks and bonds, domestic and international assets or developed and emerging markets. (Elton & Gruber, 1995, chapters 5 and 6 provide simple examples of this type of asset allocation decision). We demonstrate that for such two asset class universes tracking error volatilities and the portfolio alteration vector for a return enhancement against the benchmark are independent of the risks (that is, the variance/covariance structure) of the asset classes. Since this result only holds for the two asset universe, the portfolio change vector will depend upon the benchmark in the sense that the asset change vector will differ as between benchmarks which have two or more than two asset classes included within their composition. We confirm these results empirically for a U.S. manager who invests across two asset universes – the U.S. market and developed international markets. When the manager allocates funds across three asset classes (the U.S., developed international and emerging markets) this result no longer holds and we demonstrate that tracking error volatility is dependent upon the risk estimators used and that more sophisticated models that incorporate the dynamics of the risk structure can lead to lower tracking error volatilities.

TRACKING ERRORS AND THE ASSET UNIVERSE

An important variable in this analysis is the portfolio alteration vector which represents the modifications introduced by the manager, stock by stock, relative to the benchmark in forming the managed portfolio. The actual portfolio will then equal the benchmark plus the portfolio alteration vector. Roll (1992) demonstrates that the self-financing portfolio alteration vector, **X**, is given by

$$\mathbf{X} = D\,(\mathbf{q}_1 - \mathbf{q}_0) \tag{1}$$

where $D = (R_p - R_B)/(R_1 - R_0)$ with R_p, the expected return on the manager's portfolio (equalling $\mathbf{q}_p'\mathbf{R}$, where $\mathbf{R}$ is the $N \times 1$ vector of expected asset returns, $\mathbf{q}_p$ the investment proportions vector) and R_B, the expected benchmark return, given by $\mathbf{q}_p'\mathbf{R}$ where $\mathbf{q}_B$ is the benchmark investment proportions vector (the prime "′", denotes a vector transpose). R_0 and R_1 represent the returns on the global minimum variance portfolio and the returns on the Markowitz efficient portfolio at the point where a ray through the origin and the global minimum variance portfolio intersects the frontier ($\mathbf{q}_0$ and $\mathbf{q}_1$ are the corresponding investment proportion vectors for these portfolios). D is, effectively, a relative performance target; the larger this target, the larger the **X** vector elements since the tilt away from benchmark will need to be greater.

While Eq. (1) has a particularly simple form and it can provide the basis for a number of important insights as developed by Roll (1992), it is expressed in terms of two arbitrary portfolios. The expression can be rearranged in terms of the returns and the variances/covariances of all the assets available to the investor, making the result somewhat more general in form (and, potentially, more amenable to computing/programming applications). The risk dependence/independence issue is more amenable to interpretation when this more general formulation is employed.

In the appendix to this paper we demonstrate that[1]

$$\mathbf{X} = G^* \frac{(\mathbf{V}^{-1}\mathbf{Z}\mathbf{V}^{-1})\,\mathbf{i}}{\mathbf{R}'\,(\mathbf{V}^{-1}\mathbf{Z}\mathbf{V}^{-1})\,\mathbf{i}} \tag{2}$$

(see Eq. (A6)) where $\mathbf{V}^{-1}$ is the inverse of the variance/covariance matrix, **i** is the unit vector, **Z** is an $N \times N$ matrix with zero diagonal elements and off-diagonal elements $Z(i, j)$ given by $R_i - R_j$ (note that the numerator is a $N \times 1$ vector and the denominator a scalar) and $G = R_p - R_B$, i.e. the gain relative to the benchmark. When the asset universe available in both the portfolio, P, and benchmark, B, is restricted to two the portfolio change vector, **X**, is given by

$$\mathbf{X} = \frac{G}{\Delta R}\begin{bmatrix} 1 \\ -1 \end{bmatrix} \tag{3}$$

see the appendix (Eq. A(11)), with ΔR the difference in the returns of the two available assets or asset classes. Thus, in this two asset universe case the portfolio change vector will be independent of the risk structure, i.e. the variance/covariance matrix. By extension, tracking error volatilities will be similarly independent of the risk structure. Note that in this case both the two-asset benchmark and the manager's portfolio will lie on the Markowitz efficient frontier. Effectively, this result derives in general from the analyses in Merton (1972) and Roll (1977) wherein it is demonstrated that the Markowitz efficient frontier can be generated by any two assets or portfolios lying on the efficient frontier. The intuition underlying this result is most easily developed by noting that in a two asset (class) universe all feasible combinations of the assets will lie on the Markowitz efficient frontier. Shifts away from benchmark to achieve a particular return "pick up" will be determined only by the return differential since the resultant portfolio, being on the efficient frontier, will have minimum risk (both absolute and relative) for that particular level of return. When, however, the asset universe comprises more than two assets (asset classes) the portfolio change vector will not be independent of the variance/covariance matrix (see appendix, Eq. A(12)).

The results that were derived, above, assumed that the benchmark portfolio was similarly restricted to two assets or asset classes. Clearly, when the benchmark comprises only one asset class the previous results will again apply. That is, the single asset class will figure on the efficient frontier and exactly similar intuitive arguments apply as before (in analytic terms this situation corresponds to the situation where one of the two elements in $\mathbf{q}_B$ is zero and the other is one). When the number of assets included in the benchmark is greater than two, however, the portfolio change vector will depend upon the variance/covariance matrix as demonstrated in the appendix. Effectively, then, the nature of the portfolio change vector will depend upon the benchmark selected.

TRACKING ERRORS AND CHANGING RISKS

One particular asset allocation decision that a portfolio manager has to address in a top down strategy is the allocation between domestic and international equities. A two asset class universe in this context would comprise U.S. and developed international equities; while a three asset class universe would add emerging equity markets to these two asset classes. The tracking error volatilities are estimated for a two asset class universe (using the S&P 500 and MSCI EAFE indices) and a three asset class universe (comprising the S&P 500, MSCI EAFE and Emerging Markets (Free) indices) using a dataset comprising 558 weekly return observations on these three indices for the period from 3rd January, 1990 to 6th September, 2000. The impact of differing risks upon tracking error volatilities was analysed by using differing estimators of the variances and covariances. The variance/covariance matrix was estimated using the static historic sample moments and by using two dynamic estimators – the constant correlation model, where the conditional covariances are proportional to the product of the conditional GARCH standard deviations (Bollerslev, 1990) and the asymmetric dynamic covariance model, a generalised dynamic covariance model incorporating asymmetric effects (see Kroner & Ng, 1998).

The static model assumes that the variances and covariances of the asset classes remain constant over the whole of the period. The constant correlation model assumes that the correlation between markets remains constant over the sample frame, but that the covariances change with GARCH volatilities. The asymmetric dynamic covariance model relaxes the assumption of a constant correlation through time and introduces asymmetric effects – that is, an unexpected decline in price will lead to a higher volatility in a subsequent period than an unexpected price increase.

The estimates of the variances and covariances of each of the three indices using each of the three estimators are contained in Table 1. The variance/

Table 1. Variance/Covariance Estimates.

	Var {S&P}	Var {EAFE}	Var {EM}	Cov {S&P, EAFE}	Cov {S&P, EM}	Cov {EAFE, EM}
Static Historic	6.967	7.011	10.749	4.635	6.667	6.032
Constant Correlation	4.259	3.902	5.907	2.063	2.495	2.563
Asymmetric Dynamic	3.765	4.311	5.360	2.575	2.252	2.179

Key:
Var = variance operator
Cov = covariance operator
S&P = S&P 500 index
EAFE = MSCI EAFE index
EM = MSCI emerging markets index

covariance estimates differ across the estimators, with the averages of the two dynamic estimators having more similar estimates than with the static historic estimator.

Various characteristics of the efficient frontier and optimal portfolios are contained in Table 2. Table 2, Panel A contains various results for a two asset universe where the manager is determining the asset allocation to domestic (U.S.) equity investment and to international equity investment in developed markets using the S&P 500 and EAFE indices to proxy these equity investment opportunities respectively; the results were generated for a 1% p.a. return pick-up against benchmark (assuming a two asset class benchmark). As can be seen, the investment proportions vectors for the global minimum variance portfolio ($\mathbf{q_0}$) and the efficient portfolio at the intersection of the ray through the origin and global minimum variance portfolio ($\mathbf{q_1}$) differ across the variance/covariance estimators. However, the self-financing portfolio alteration vector is constant across each estimator (i.e. is independent of the risk structure) as indicated by the analytics in this section for this two asset case scenario.

Table 2. Optimal Portfolio Characteristics.

Panel A – Two Asset Case {S&P 500; EAFE}

	q_0		q_1		X	
Model	S&P	EAFE	S&P	EAFE	S&P	EAFE
Static Historic	0.505	0.495	1.572	−0.572	0.092	−0.092
Constant Correlation	0.456	0.544	1.141	−0.141	0.092	−0.092
Asymmetric Dynamic	0.593	0.407	1.494	−0.494	0.092	−0.092

Panel B – Three Asset Case {S&P 500; EAFE; EM}

	q_0			q_1			X		
Model	S&P	EAFE	EM	S&P	EAFE	EM	S&P	EAFE	EM
Static Historic	0.597	0.547	−0.144	3.176	0.793	−2.969	0.026	0.003	−0.029
Constant Correlation	0.396	0.468	0.136	2.650	1.054	−2.704	0.024	0.006	−0.027
Asymmetric Dynamic	0.437	0.310	0.252	4.977	−0.143	−3.833	0.030	−0.003	−0.027

Key:
q_0 = Investment proportions for global minimum variance portfolio
q_1 = Investment proportions for efficient portfolio at the intersection of a ray through the origin and global minimum variance portfolio
X = Investment proportions for the self financing alteration portfolio

Essentially, risk has no impact in this case. In Table 2, Panel B we report the corresponding results for a three asset universe where the manager allocates funds across three asset classes – domestic, developed international and the emerging markets. The investment proportions vectors, $\mathbf{q}_0$ and $\mathbf{q}_1$ again differ across the estimators but, in this case, in moving to a three asset universe the self-financing portfolio alteration vector, **X**, differs across the risk estimators (i.e. it is dependent upon the risk structure of the asset universe).

When the tracking errors for a 1% return pick up in Table 3, Panel A, are analysed it becomes apparent that there are no differences in tracking errors with changes in risk estimation for the two asset case. However, for the three asset class case (Table 3, Panel B) the tracking error volatilities do differ with the estimation technique, corresponding to the analytics presented in the previous section.

In Table 3, Panel B, we report the tracking error volatilities both in sample and out of sample (the tracking error volatilities are plotted in Fig. 1) for the three asset universe. As can be seen, the results are quite similar across the three estimators, both numerically and visually, although the asymmetric dynamic covariance model is generally the most volatile; it is a general characteristic of this model that it is more sensitive to shocks in return series. The out-of-sample results are the most pertinent from a practical perspective and Table 3, Panel B indicates that both for the one year forward and whole

Table 3. Tracking Error Volatilities (TEV).

Panel A – Two Asset Case {S&P 500; EAFE}

Model	IN-SAMPLE TEV 8 year period	IN-SAMPLE TEV 1 year period	OUT-OF-SAMPLE TEV 1 year forward
Static Historic	1.823	2.073	1.758
Constant Correlation	1.823	2.073	1.758
Asymmetric Dynamic	1.823	2.073	1.758

Panel B – Three Asset Case {S&P 500; EAFE; EM}

Model	IN-SAMPLE TEV 8 year period	IN-SAMPLE TEV 1 year period	OUT-OF-SAMPLE TEV 1 year forward	OUT-OF-SAMPLE TEV whole sample average
Static Historic	0.232	0.173	0.311	0.631
Constant Correlation	0.235	0.176	0.292	0.615
Asymmetric Dynamic	0.235	0.181	0.343	0.645

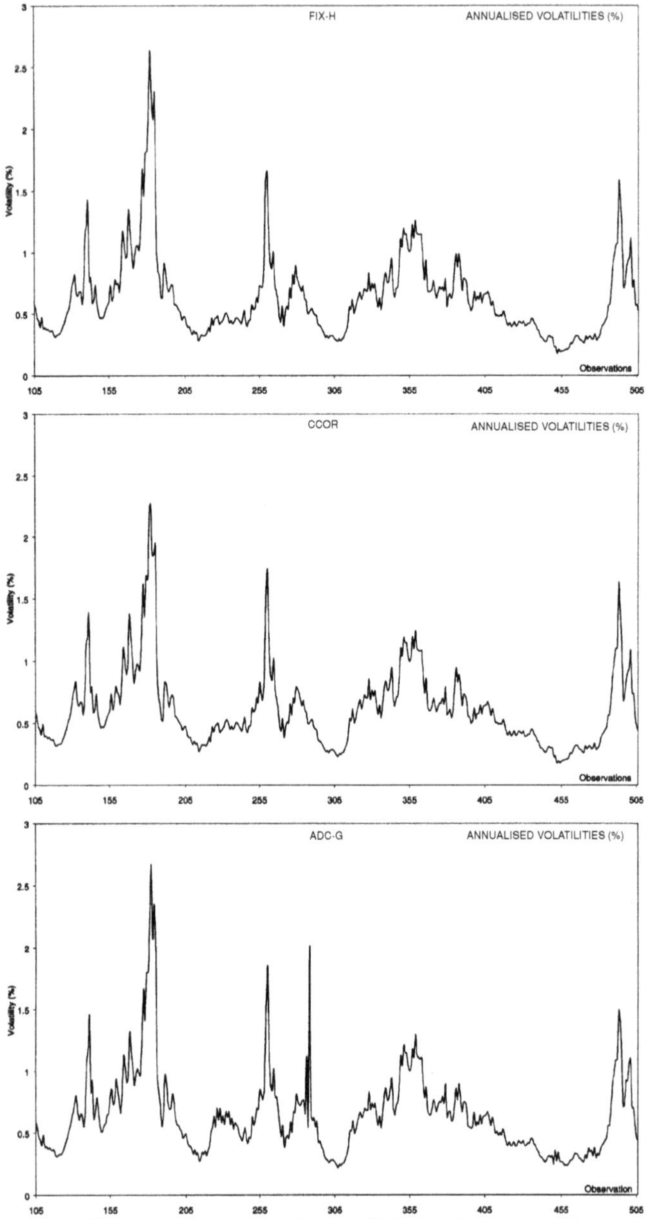

Fig. 1. Tracking Error Volatilities.

sample average cases the constant correlation estimator provides tracking errors with the lowest volatility. By contrast, the other dynamic model, the asymmetric dynamic model provides out-of-sample tracking errors with the highest volatilities. On average, tracking error volatilities generated by the constant correlation model are statistically significantly lower at the 1% level (using bootstrapped Z-statistics) than those for the static historic model, while the asymmetric dynamic model has statistically significantly higher tracking error volatilities. Thus, reflecting changes in risks through time will lead to improvements in tracking error volatilities, but only when a relatively simple dynamic specification (i.e. the constant correlation model) is employed.[2] The asymmetric dynamic model generates poorer performance, a result that derives from its greater sensitivity to shocks than either of the other two models (see, for example, the additional spike in this estimator's tracking error series at observation number 288). This greater shock sensitivity leads to poorer benchmark tracking. Effectively, then, when the risk structure is relevant (i.e. where there are more than two asset classes) using a relatively simple dynamic covariance estimator does improve the management of tracking error.

CONCLUSIONS

The portfolio alteration vector developed in Roll (1992) may be expressed as a direct function of the returns and risks of the available set of assets. When a portfolio manager is optimising within a relative risk/tracking error framework with only two asset classes (such as stocks and bonds) the shift in investment proportions desired will be a function of returns only, i.e. asset class risk characteristics are irrelevant. In such simple top down scenarios the asset allocation changes for particular performances relative to benchmark are easily computed. The analytical results were empirically confirmed by using three differing estimators of the variance/covariance matrix using two and three asset class universes. When risk is relevant, that is, when optimising across more than two asset classes, modelling the dynamics of the risk structure does improve the management of tracking error volatility.

NOTES

1. The alteration vector, **X**, for a benchmark return pick-up of "y" percent will be scaled upwards or downwards by this amount relative to the 1% return pick-up used in the previous section as a result of the form of Eq. (2). The tracking error volatilities, which will be given by $\mathbf{x}'\mathbf{V}\mathbf{x}$ will be similarly proportionately scaled upwards or downwards; hence the rank order preservation referred to in footnote 1.

2. The rank order of the results is preserved for other return pick-ups (see next section, footnote 2), i.e. the tracking error volatilities for a 0.5% benchmark return pick-up will be half those of the 1% pick-up for all estimators (in standard deviation terms).

REFERENCES

Bollerslev, T. (1990). Modelling the Coherence in Short-Run Nominal Exchange Rates: A Multivariate Generalized ARCH Approach. *Review of Economics and Statistics*, *72*, 498–505.

Chow, G. (1995). Portfolio Selection Based on Return, Risk and Relative Performance. *Financial Analysts Journal*, (March–April), 54–60.

Elton, E., & Gruber, M. (1995). *Modern Portfolio Theory and Investment Analysis* (5th ed.). John Wiley and Sons Inc.

Franks, E. (1992). Targeting Excess-of-Benchmark Returns. *Journal of Portfolio Management*, (Summer), 6–12.

Grinold, R., & Kahn, R. (2000). The Efficiency Gains of Long-Short Investing. *Financial Analysts Journal*, (November–December), 40–52.

Ibbotson, R., & Kaplan, P. (2000). Does Asset Allocation Policy Explain 40, 90 or 100 Percent of Performance? *Financial Analysts Journal*, (January–February), 26–33.

Jacobs, B., Levy, K., & Starer, D. (1998). On the Optimality of Long-Short Strategies. *Financial Analysts Journal*, (March–April), 40–51.

Kroner, K., & Ng, V. (1998). Modelling Asymmetric Comovements of Asset Returns. *Review of Financial Studies*, *11*, 817–844.

Merton, R. (1972). An Analytic Derivation of the Efficient Portfolio Frontier. *Journal of Financial and Quantitative Analysis*, *7*, 1851–1872.

Roll, R. (1977). A Critique of the Asset Pricing Theory's Tests: Part I. *Journal of Financial Economics*, *4*, 129–176.

Roll, R. (1992). A Mean/Variance Analysis of Tracking Error. *Journal of Portfolio Management*, *Summer*, 13–22.

Wang, M. (1999). Multiple-Benchmark and Multiple-Portfolio Optimization. *Financial Analysts Journal*, (January–February), 63–72.

APPENDIX

Equation (1) was derived by Roll (1992) as,

$$\mathbf{X} = \frac{G}{R_1 - R_0}(\mathbf{q}_1 - \mathbf{q}_0) \tag{1A}$$

where $R_1 = a/b$, $R_0 = b/c$, $\mathbf{q}_1 = \mathbf{V}^{-1}\mathbf{R}/b$ and $\mathbf{q}_0 = \mathbf{V}^{-1}i/c$ with the efficient set information matrix, $\mathbf{A}$, given by

$$\mathbf{A} = \begin{bmatrix} \mathbf{R}'\mathbf{V}^{-1}\mathbf{R} & \mathbf{R}'\mathbf{V}^{-1}\mathbf{i} \\ \mathbf{R}'\mathbf{V}^{-1}\mathbf{i} & \mathbf{i}'\mathbf{V}^{-1}\mathbf{i} \end{bmatrix} \equiv \begin{bmatrix} a & b \\ b & c \end{bmatrix}$$

(A1) may be expressed, by substitution, as

$$\mathbf{X} = \frac{G}{ac - b^2} (\mathbf{V}^{-1}\mathbf{R}c - \mathbf{V}^{-1}\mathbf{i}b) \tag{A2}$$

Now, $ac - b^2$

$$= \mathbf{R}'\mathbf{V}^{-1}\mathbf{R}\mathbf{i}^1\mathbf{V}^{-1}\mathbf{i} - \mathbf{R}'\mathbf{V}^{-1}\mathbf{i}\mathbf{R}'\mathbf{V}^{-1}\mathbf{i}$$

$$= \mathbf{R}'\mathbf{V}^{-1}(\mathbf{R}\mathbf{i}' - \mathbf{i}\mathbf{R}')\mathbf{V}^{-1}\mathbf{i} \tag{A3}$$

and similarly

$$\mathbf{V}^{-1}\mathbf{R}c - \mathbf{V}^{-1}\mathbf{i}b$$

$$= \mathbf{V}^{-1}\mathbf{R}\mathbf{i}'\mathbf{V}^{-1}\mathbf{i} - \mathbf{V}^{-1}\mathbf{i}\mathbf{R}'\mathbf{V}^{-1}\mathbf{i}$$

$$= \mathbf{V}^{-1}(\mathbf{R}\mathbf{i}' - \mathbf{i}\mathbf{R}')\mathbf{V}^{-1}\mathbf{i} \tag{A4}$$

It is easily demonstrated that

$$\mathbf{R}\mathbf{i}' - \mathbf{i}\mathbf{R}' = \begin{Bmatrix} 0 \; R_a - R_b \; R_a - R_c \dots R_a - R_n \\ R_b - R_a \; 0 \; R_b - R_c \dots R_b - R_n \\ \vdots \quad \cdot \quad \cdot \quad \vdots \\ R_n - R_a \; R_n - R_b \dots\dots\dots 0 \end{Bmatrix} \equiv Z \tag{A5}$$

Substituting (A3), (A4) and (A5) in (A2) yields

$$\mathbf{X} = \frac{G(\mathbf{V}^{-1}\mathbf{Z}\mathbf{V}^{-1})\mathbf{i}}{\mathbf{R}'(\mathbf{V}^{-1}\mathbf{Z}\mathbf{V}^{-1})\mathbf{i}} \tag{A6}$$

That is, the portfolio alteration vector, **X**, is expressed as a direct function of the asset universe return and risk structure rather than in terms of two arbitrary portfolios.

Since the unit vector is effectively a summation vector, (A6) may be expressed as

$$\mathbf{X} = \frac{G\begin{bmatrix} \Sigma \text{ row 1 of matrix B} \\ \Sigma \text{ row 2 of matrix B} \\ \vdots \\ \Sigma \text{ row n of matrix B} \end{bmatrix}}{R_a(\Sigma \text{ row 1 of matrix B}) + \dots R_n(\Sigma \text{ row n of matrix B})} \tag{A7}$$

where $\mathbf{B} = \mathbf{V}^{-1}\mathbf{Z}\mathbf{V}^{-1}$.

When the number of assets is two, the **B** matrix will have the general form

$$\begin{bmatrix} o & m \\ -m & o \end{bmatrix} \tag{A8}$$

That is, in this case, V^{-1} may be represented as, in general terms,

$$\begin{bmatrix} w & x \\ x & y \end{bmatrix} \tag{A9}$$

and

$$V^{-1}ZV^{-1} = \begin{bmatrix} w & x \\ x & y \end{bmatrix} \begin{bmatrix} 0 & R_a - R_b \\ -(R_a - R_b) & 0 \end{bmatrix} \begin{bmatrix} w & x \\ x & y \end{bmatrix}$$

$$= (R_a - R_b)\begin{bmatrix} 0 & wy - x^2 \\ -(wy - x^2) & 0 \end{bmatrix} \tag{A10}$$

where R_a and R_b are the returns on the two asset classes.
For $N = 2$, we have, then,

$$\mathbf{X} = \frac{G\begin{bmatrix} m \\ -m \end{bmatrix}}{R_a m - R_b m}$$

$$= \frac{G}{R_a - R_b}\begin{bmatrix} 1 \\ -1 \end{bmatrix} \tag{A11}$$

i.e. the alteration vector is independent of the variance/covariance matrix, **V**. This result will, however, not hold for the general case where $N > 2$. For example, with $N = 3$, the **B** matrix will have the form

$$\begin{bmatrix} 0 & m & n \\ -m & 0 & s \\ -n & -s & 0 \end{bmatrix} \tag{A12}$$

and the row sums will necessarily be more complicated than in the two asset case and the simple cancellations above not available. Note also that if the asset universe is restricted to two assets, but the benchmark has more than two assets, the variance/covariance independence result no longer holds. That is, the **X** vector may be partitioned as

$$\mathbf{X} = \begin{bmatrix} \mathbf{q}_p^I - \mathbf{q}_B^I \\ \hline - \mathbf{q}_B^N \end{bmatrix} \tag{A13}$$

where $\mathbf{q}_p^I - \mathbf{q}_B^I$ is a 2×1 vector relating to the assets included in the portfolio and $\mathbf{q}_B^N$ is a $N \times 1$ vector comprising the N assets in the benchmark not contained in the portfolio. Shifts in the $\mathbf{q}_p^I - \mathbf{q}_B^I$ will depend upon **V** since, again, the simple cancellations at (A11) are no longer available.

IMPROVEMENTS ON VALUE AT RISK MEASURES BY COMBINING CONDITIONAL AUTOREGRESSIVE AND EXTREME VALUE APPROACHES

Davide Meneguzzo and Walter Vecchiato

ABSTRACT

This paper describes a new methodology called Conditional Autoregressive Value at Risk (CAViaR) proposed by Engle and Manganelli (1999) for computing Value at Risk (VaR) measures. Following Manganelli (2000) we introduce the Extreme Value Theory (EVT) into the CAViaR framework trying to improve VaR estimation for very low probability levels, and we propose some useful statistical tests to compare different approaches for calculating VaR. Finally we present an empirical application to the most common European equity indexes where we find a distinctive out-performance of this new approach.

1. INTRODUCTION

Over the last decades many financial institutions have significantly increased their trading activities. Jorion (1997) identifies increased volatility, technologically enhanced physical equipment, advances in financial theory and political developments, such as more market-oriented policies and deregulation of financial markets, as the driving force behind this process. In addition, many

Financial Risk and Financial Risk Management, Volume 16, pages 275–324.

ISBN: 0-7623-0858-3

new financial products have been developed, some in response to regulation. Although such products may offer certain advantages in hedging financial risks or provide speculative opportunities, under certain circumstances they may also generate huge losses. The last decade has, indeed, seen spectacular financial disasters. Most of those could probably have been avoided, if properly functioning internal controls and adequate risk management systems had been in place.

Financial institutions and regulatory authorities have clearly recognized that, in order to ensure financial stability, it is imperative to accurately measure financial risk perceived as the uncertainty about unknown future movements of net returns. In particular, Banks are now required to hold a certain amount of capital to absorb adverse markets movements. According to the Capital Adequacy Directive by the Bank for International Settlement (BIS) in Basle, the risk capital of a bank must be sufficient to cover losses on the bank's trading portfolio over ten-day holding periods in 99% of occurrences. This value is referred to as *Value at Risk* (VaR). VaR is now the standard measure used by financial analysts to quantify financial risks. VaR is simply defined as the maximum potential loss in a portfolio value to be expected with a given probability over a certain horizon. Of course, holding period and confidence interval may vary according to application. Despite its conceptual simplicity, the measurement of VaR is a very challenging statistical problem. There are a lot of models for calculating VaR which differ in the methodology they use, the assumptions they make and the way they are implemented. However, all the existing models follow a common general structure, which can be summarized in three steps:

(1) the portfolio is marked to market daily;
(2) the distribution of portfolio returns is estimated;
(3) the VaR of the portfolio is computed.

The main difference among the existing models is related to the way they estimate the portfolio returns distribution. In this sense the VaR models can be classified into four categories:

(1) Parametric Models (Delta-Normal, Delta-Gamma Normal, RiskMetrics);
(2) Non-Parametric Models (Historical Simulation, Hybrid models);
(3) Semiparametric Models (Extreme Value Theory, QML GARCH);
(4) Simulative Models (Monte Carlo, Quasi-Monte Carlo).

Some of the methodologies listed before do not give accurate solutions and, often needless to say, the chosen methodology depends on the underlying assumptions for the returns distribution. Since VaR can be computed as the quantile of future portfolio returns, conditional on current information, and since the distribution of portfolio returns typically changes over time, Engle and Manganelli (1999) propose a new autoregressive model for the quantile called CAViaR (Conditional Autoregressive Value at Risk).

The main purpose of the next pages is to summarize the results reached by Engle and Manganelli (1999) using the CAViaR model and to introduce the Extreme Value Theory (EVT) into the CAViaR framework. In this paper we also provide some applications of these new methodologies to the most important European Equity Indexes and we discuss other useful extensions to VaR measures.

The contents are organized as follows. Section two briefly introduces the reader to the CAViaR specification models, the way the parameters can be estimated and their asymptotic distribution. Section three provides an overview of the role of EVT in the risk management environment, and in particular it concentrates on the peaks-over-threshold model. Section four deals with a new approach which combines extreme value theory and CAViaR model. Section five shows some empirical results for CAViaR model, and proposes a possible way to plug EVT into the CAViaR model. Besides that, there are some comparisons obtained by applying different VaR approaches that we are going to discuss. Section six concludes the paper.

2. CAViaR MODEL

The aim of the CAViaR is to model directly the quantile of the conditional returns distribution skipping the estimation of the distribution issue. The basic idea stems from the empirical evidence that volatility of stock market returns tends to cluster over time. In general this behavior is described by conditional heteroskedasticity models as the GARCH-type models. Consequently, since the VaR is linked to the standard deviation of the returns distribution, it is natural to think that it should exhibit a similar behavior and for that reason it could be useful to adopt an autoregressive model.

A general specification for the CAViaR might be the following[1]:

$$VaR_t = \alpha_0 + \sum_{i=1}^{p} \alpha_i VaR_{t-i} + \ell(\alpha_{p+1}, \ldots, \alpha_{p+q}; \Omega_{t-1}) \tag{1}$$

where Ω_{t-1} is the information set available at time t and $\ell(\cdot)$ is a function that has the role to link the level of VaR_t to the value of other known exogenous variables.

In most empirical cases the formulation (1) can be reduced to a first order model:

$$VaR_t = \alpha_0 + \alpha_1 VaR_{t-1} + l(\alpha_2, y_{t-1}, VaR_{t-1}) \tag{2}$$

With this formulation the value of the *VaR* changes smoothly over time by the autoregressive term $\alpha_1 VaR_{t-1}$ and at the same time is linked with the level of the return y_{t-1} by the function $\ell(\cdot)$. What we would expect is that the value of VaR_t increases as y_{t-1} becomes very negative.

Different models can be estimated by choosing different specifications for the function $\ell(\cdot)$. Some of these models, proposed by Engle and Manganelli (1999) are:

(1) Adaptive:

$$VaR_t = VaR_{t-1} + \alpha[I(y_{t-1} \leq -VaR_{t-1}) - \theta] \tag{3}$$

where θ is the coverage probability for which the VaR is measured and $I(y_{t-1} \leq -VaR_{t-1})$ is an indicator function that assumes value 1 if the VaR is exceeded. With this model whenever the VaR is exceeded it is immediately increased, but when it is not exceeded, it is decreased very slightly.

(2) Proportional Symmetric Adaptive:

$$VaR_t = VaR_{t-1} + \alpha_1(|y_{t-1}| - VaR_{t-1})^+ - \alpha_2(|y_{t-1}| - VaR_{t-1})^- \tag{4}$$

where

$$(|y_{t-1}| - VaR_{t-1})^+ = \max((|y_{t-1}| - VaR_{t-1}), 0)$$

and

$$(|y_{t-1}| - VaR_{t-1})^- = \min((|y_{t-1}| - VaR_{t-1}), 0).$$

(3) Symmetric Absolute Value:

$$VaR_t = \alpha_0 + \alpha_1 VaR_{t-1} + \alpha_2 |y_{t-1}| \tag{5}$$

with this model positive and negative values of the returns are considered in the same manner.

(4) Asymmetric Absolute Value:

$$VaR_t = \alpha_0 + \alpha_1 VaR_{t-1} + \alpha_2 |y_{t-1} - \alpha_3| \tag{6}$$

where, with the introduction of α_3, negative and positive values of the returns are asymmetrically considered; negative shocks are amplified, positive shocks are reduced.

(5) Asymmetric Slope:

$$VaR_t = \alpha_0 + \alpha_1 VaR_{t-1} + \alpha_2(y_{t-1})^+ - \alpha_3(y_{t-1})^- \tag{7}$$

where $(y_{t-1})^+$ is $\max(y_{t-1}, 0)$ and $(y_{t-1})^-$ is $\min(y_{t-1}, 0)$. With this specification the model gives different parameters to positive and negative returns, so that their influence to the estimation of VaR is asymmetric.

(6) Indirect GARCH(1,1):

$$VaR_t = (\alpha_1 + \alpha_2 VaR^2_{t-1} + \alpha_3 y^2_{t-1})^{1/2} \tag{8}$$

this model is correctly specified if the underlying data were truly a GARCH(1,1) with i.i.d. error distribution. For this reason this model is useful for simulation.

The unknown parameters of the CAViaR specifications are estimated using the regression quantile techniques. The quantile regression model, first introduced by Koenker and Basset (1978), can be viewed as a location model.

Specifically, let (y_i, x_i), $i = 1, \ldots, n$, be a sample from some population, where x_i is a $K \times 1$ vector of regressors. It is assumed that:

$$F_{y_i}(\tau \mid x_i) = \Pr(y_i \leq \tau \mid x_i) = F_{u_\theta}(\tau - x_i'\beta_\theta \mid x_i), \qquad i = 1, \ldots, n. \tag{9}$$

This relation, in a different and perhaps more familiar formulation, can be written as:

$$y_i = x_i'\beta_\theta + u_{\theta_i}, \qquad Quant_\theta(y_i \mid x_i) = x_i'\beta_\theta \tag{10}$$

where $Quant_\theta(y_i \mid x_i)$ denotes the θ-quantile of y_i conditional on the regressor vector x_i. If $F_{u_\theta}(\cdot)$ were known then various techniques could be used to estimate β_θ. However, here the distribution of the error term $u_{\theta i}$ is left unspecified. As is implied by (10), it is only assumed that $u_{\theta i}$ satisfies the quantile restriction $Quant_\theta(u_{\theta i} \mid x_i) = 0$, that simply means that the θ-quantile of the error term is 0.

In general, the θth sample quantile $(0 < \theta < 1)$ of y, solves:

$$\min_{\beta \in R} \left[\sum_{t: y_t \geq \beta} \theta \mid y_t - \beta \mid + \sum_{t: y_t < \beta} (1 - \theta) \mid y_t - x_t'\beta \mid \right] \tag{11}$$

The analogue for the linear model for the θth quantile is defined in a similar manner. That is, $\hat{\beta}_\theta$, the estimator solution for β_θ in (10), termed the θth quantile regression, solves:

$$\min_{\beta \in R} \left[\sum_{t: y_t \geq x'_t\beta} \theta \mid y_t - x_t'\beta \mid + \sum_{t: y_t < x'_t\beta} (1 - \theta) \mid y_t - x_t'\beta \mid \right] \tag{12}$$

We stress that with the CAViaR specifications we are in the context of nonlinear models. The most important results for nonlinear models are those reached by White (1994) who has shown that the minimization of the regression quantile objective function (12) is able to deliver consistent estimates, under suitable assumptions. Engle and Manganelli (1999) have also shown how to derive the asymptotic distribution of the estimator obtained by (12) in order to perform hypothesis tests as the Wald and LM statistics.

In the appendix we briefly present these results assuming that the conditions necessary for the consistency and the asymptotically normal convergence for $\hat{\beta}_\theta$ are essentially those sufficient to prove the consistency and asymptotic normality of an estimator obtained from the minimization of a nonlinear criterion function.

In this section we also explain how to test if a CAViaR model is correctly specified. For this purpose we present the DQ test introduced by Engle and Manganelli (1999). Let the *Hit* as:

$$Hit(y_t, x_t, \theta) \equiv Hit_{\theta t} \equiv I(y_t < -VaR_t) - \theta \tag{13}$$

the *Hit* function assumes value $(1-\theta)$ every time y_t is less than VaR_t (in this case a *Hit* is realized) and $(-\theta)$ otherwise.

From the definition of the quantile function, a good model must present a sequence of Hit_t uncorrelated with any available information at time $t-1$. It is possible to verify that by regressing Hit_t on any variables that are function of the past information[2] and by testing if the coefficients estimated are jointly zeros. This regression may be written so:

$$Hit_t = \mathbf{X}\underline{\boldsymbol{\alpha}} + u_t \qquad u_t = \begin{cases} -\theta & \textit{with} \Pr(1-\theta) \\ (1-\theta) & \textit{with} \Pr\theta \end{cases} \tag{14}$$

After having estimated the s $\underline{\alpha}$-parameters by OLS, the Dynamic Quantile statistic test for the null hypothesis $H_0\!:\!\underline{\boldsymbol{\alpha}} = 0$ is defined as:

$$\frac{\hat{\underline{\boldsymbol{\alpha}}}'_{OLS}\mathbf{X}'\mathbf{X}\hat{\underline{\boldsymbol{\alpha}}}_{OLS}}{\theta(1-\theta)} \overset{a}{\sim} \chi^2_S \tag{15}$$

If the null hypothesis is accepted it is clear that there is not only the correct marginal fraction of exceedances but also the correct conditional coverage without any type of clustering for the *Hits*.

3. EVT

A major problem facing VaR practitioners is that the VaR is an extreme quantile on a return distribution, and yet we have relatively few extreme observations with which to estimate it. Our VaR estimates are not therefore precise, and become even more so as we move further out into the tail of the distribution. A response to this problem could be provided by the Extreme Value Theory (EVT).[3] There are two kinds of models for extreme values, the former is the so called block maxima models and the latter is the peaks-over-threshold models.

In the context of block maxima models the main result is due to the theorem by Fisher and Tippett (1928), which characterizes the limiting behavior of appropriately normalized sample maxima. Suppose we have a sequence of infinite i.i.d. random variables $X_1, X_2, \ldots$ from an unknown distribution F. We denote the maximum of the first n observations by $M_n = \max(X_1, \ldots, X_n)$. Suppose further that we can find a sequence of real numbers $a_n > 0$ and b_n such that $(M_n - b_n)/a_n$, the sequence of normalized maxima, converges in distribution:

$$\lim_{n \to \infty} \Pr\{(M_n - b_n)/a_n \leq x\} = \lim_{n \to \infty} F^n(a_n x + b_n) = H(x) \tag{16}$$

for some non-degenerate distribution function $H(x)$. If condition (16) holds Fisher and Tippet (1928) showed that $H(x)$ is of the type:

$$H_\xi(x) = \begin{cases} \exp(-(1+\xi x)^{-\frac{1}{\xi}}) & \xi \neq 0 \\ \exp(-e^{-x}) & \xi = 0 \end{cases} \tag{17}$$

where x is such that $1 + \xi x > 0$ and ξ is the shape parameter. $H_\xi(x)$ is called Generalized Extreme Distribution (GEV). Broadly speaking, the Fisher-Tippett theorem suggests the fitting of the GEV to data on sample maxima, when such data can be collected. We don't deal with the block maxima models since recent researches have developed more tractable models (peaks-over-threshold models). For a thorough analysis on the block maxima models see Embrechts et al. (1997), Gumbel (1958) and McNeil (1998).

The rest of the section is concentrated on the Peaks-Over-Threshold models (POT). The POT models are generally considered to be more useful for practical applications, due to their more efficient use of data. Within the POT class it is possible to distinguish two types of analysis: (1) the semiparametric model based on the Hill estimator and its relatives; (2) the parametric model based on the Generalized Pareto Distribution (GPD). Even if both approaches are correct and theoretically justified we prefer the GPD approach for the following reasons: (a) the GPD-based quantile estimator is more stable (in terms of mean squared error) with respect to the choice of the threshold k than the Hill estimator; (b) for high quantiles with $\theta \geq 0.99$ the GPD method is at least as efficient as the Hill method (c) the GPD method is applicable to light-tailed data ($\xi = 0$) or even short tailed ($\xi < 0$), whereas the Hill estimator is designed only for heavy-tailed distributions ($\xi > 0$).[4]

The most important result for peaks-over-threshold models is due to Pickands (1975). Let $x_H = \sup\{x \in R: F(x) < 1\}$ be the finite or infinite right endpoint of the distribution of returns F. Define the distribution function of the exceedances over the threshold u as:

$$F_u(x) = \Pr\{X - u \leq x \mid X > u\} = \frac{F(x+u) - F(u)}{1 - F(u)} \tag{18}$$

for $0 \leq x < x_H - u$. The Pickands theorem shows that under condition (16) the Generalized Pareto Distribution = ≠ wline

$$G_{\xi,\beta}(x) = \begin{cases} 1 - \left(1 + \frac{\xi x}{\beta}\right)^{-\frac{1}{\xi}} & \xi \neq 0 \\ 1 - \exp\left(-\frac{x}{\beta}\right) & \xi = 0 \end{cases} \tag{19}$$

(where $\beta > 0$, and the support is $x \geq 0$ when $\xi \geq 0$ and $0 \leq x \leq -\frac{\beta}{\xi}$ when $\xi < 0$) is the limiting distribution for the distribution of exceedances (18), as the threshold tends to x_H. Pickands (1975) shows that for a positive measurable function $\beta(u)$

$$F \in MDA(H_\xi) \Leftrightarrow \lim_{u \to x_H} \sup_{0 \leq y < x_H - u} |F_u(x) - G_{\xi,\beta(u)}(x)| = 0 \tag{20}$$

The theorem states that if F belongs to the Maximum Domain of Attraction of a GEV, as the threshold u approaches the endpoint of F, the GPD becomes an accurate estimator of the excess distribution F_u. It practically suggests that, for a sufficiently high threshold u, the excess distribution may be taken as a GPD for some ξ and β:

$$F_u(x) \approx G_{\xi,\beta}(x) \tag{21}$$

Supposing that there are N_u observations exceeding the chosen threshold u, the parameters ξ and β of the GPD are estimated by maximum likelihood:

$$\max_{\xi,\beta} \left\{ -N \ln \ \beta - \left(1 + \frac{1}{\xi}\right) \sum_{i=1}^{N} \ln\left(1 + \frac{\xi}{\beta}(X_{k_i} - u)\right) \right\}$$

$$\sum_{i=1}^{N} \ln \left\{ \left[I(\xi > 0) I(X_{k_i} - u > 0) + I(\xi < 0) I\left(0 \leq X_{k_i} - u \leq -\frac{\beta}{\xi}\right) \right] I(\beta > 0) \right\} \tag{22}$$

where $X_{k_1}, X_{k_2}, \ldots, X_{k_N}$ are the upper order statistics exceeding the threshold.

By setting $y = x + u$ and combining expressions (18) and (21) it is now possible to write:

$$F(y) = (1 - F(u))G_{\xi,\beta}(y - u) + F(u) \tag{23}$$

for $y > u$. This formula may be used to construct an estimator for the tail of the distribution. The only additional element it requires is an estimate of $F(u)$ that is obtained by the empirical estimator $(n - N_u)/n$. Putting $\hat{F}(u)$ and the maximum likelihood estimates of the parameters of the GPD together we arrive at the tail estimator:

$$\hat{F}(y) = 1 - \frac{N_u}{n}\left(1 + \hat{\xi}\frac{y - u}{\hat{\beta}}\right)^{-\frac{1}{\hat{\xi}}} \tag{24}$$

for $y > u$.

For a given probability $q > F(u)$ it is now possible to calculate the VaR by inverting the tail estimation formula (24) to get:

$$\widehat{VaR}_q = u + \frac{\hat{\beta}}{\hat{\xi}}\left(\left(\frac{n}{N_u}(1 - q)\right)^{-\hat{\xi}} - 1\right) \tag{25}$$

Due to their importance in the selection of the threshold u in the empirical applications it is also necessary to specify in this section the mean excess function and the mean excess function plot.[5] For a fixed $u < x_H$ the mean excess function[6] and the mean excess function plot are defined respectively as:

$$e(u) = E(X - u \mid X > u) \tag{26}$$

and

$$\{(u, e_n(u)), X_{1:n} < u < X_{n:n}\} \tag{27}$$

where $X_{1:n}$ and $X_{n:n}$ are the first nth order statistics and $e_n(u)$ is the sample mean excess function given by:

$$e_n(u) = \frac{\sum_{i=1}^{n} (X_i - u)^+}{\sum_{i=1}^{n} I(X_i > u)} \tag{28}$$

where $(X_i - u)^+$ is $\max((X_i - u), 0)$ and $I(X_i > u)$ is an indicator function that assumes value 1 if $X_i > u$ and 0 otherwise.

4. CAViaR AND EXTREME VALUE THEORY

Recently some empirical analysis have shown that the CAViaR approach works well for the 5% and 1% probability levels (see Manganelli & Engle, 1999), however for more extreme quantiles there might be some problems due to the finite size of the sample that we are analyzing. An evidence of this behavior for low confidence levels for the CAViaR could be found in a Monte Carlo study made by Engle and Manganelli (1999) where it is shown that the mean of the estimated parameters of the GARCH model, obtained indirectly by the Indirect GARCH CAViaR specification, differs significantly from their true values with a high variance. For such low quantiles a better alternative might be obtained by combining the extreme value theory in the CAViaR approach.

Following Manganelli (2000) we adopt a pre-whitening strategy.

As first step we fit the CAViaR model to our data to have an estimate of the θth quantile ($\hat{q}_{t,\theta}$) with θ that assumes values in the range between 5% and 10%. A high value of θ is necessary to have more precise estimates of the parameters. It is now possible to construct the series of the "standardized" quantile residuals:

$$\frac{\hat{\varepsilon}_{t,\theta}}{\hat{q}_{t,\theta}} = \left(\frac{y_t}{\hat{q}_{t,\theta}}\right) - 1 \tag{29}$$

and to define $f_t(\cdot)$ as the conditional density function of the standardized quantile residuals.

Before proceeding with the second step it is necessary to assume that:

$$f_t\left(\frac{\hat{\varepsilon}_{t,\theta}}{\hat{q}_{t,\theta}}\right) = f\left(\frac{\hat{\varepsilon}_{t,\theta}}{\hat{q}_{t,\theta}}\right) \text{ for all } \frac{\hat{\varepsilon}_{t,\theta}}{\hat{q}_{t,\theta}} > 0, \text{ for all } t, \text{ provided that } \hat{q}_{t,\theta} \neq 0 \text{ for all } t \tag{30}$$

That is, the distribution of the standardized quantile residuals is not time varying beyond the $(1-\theta)$ quantile[7]. This assumption (30) requires only that the standardized quantile residuals are i.i.d. in the right tail, allowing any type of behavior in the rest of the distribution.

Now it is possible to implement the second step of the strategy by applying the EVT to the standardized residuals to have an estimate of the right tail. Writing the relation:

$$\Pr(y_t < q_{t,p}) = \Pr(y_t < -q_{t,\theta} + (q_{t,\theta} - q_{t,p})) = \Pr\left(\frac{y_t}{q_{t,\theta}} - 1 > z\right) = p \qquad \text{for } p < \theta \tag{31}$$

where $z = \frac{q_{t,p}}{q_{t,\theta}} - 1$ is the $(1 - p) - quantile$ of the standardized quantile residuals, if z_p is the EVT estimate of the $(1 - p) - quantile$, the corresponding $p - quantile$ of portfolio returns is defined by

$$\hat{q}_{t,p} = \hat{q}_{t,\theta}(1 + \hat{z}_p) \tag{32}$$

5. EMPIRICAL APPLICATION

5.1. Data and Sample

The data used in this study cover a period of nearly 7 years from January 1993 to May 2000. Data are daily observations from closed levels of the most important European equity indexes (Mib30, Cac40, Dax, Ibex, Ftse, Aex, Omx and Smi).

So our data set is composed by eight time series. For each time series we proceed via standard statistical preliminary analysis: skewness, kurtosis, normality tests, autocorrelation tests and so on. Table 1 reports these results.

Each univariate time series of daily returns presents fat tails and it is more peaked than the normal distribution, it has volatility clusters and all other well known facts reported by the financial literature.[8] In our analysis we choose the first 1605 data in sample and the last 250 observations for out of sample analysis.

Table 1. Summary Statistics, Jarque-Bera Test for Normality and Autocorrelation for the Log-returns from Analyzed Indices.

	MIB30	CAC40	DAX	IBEX	FTSE	AEX	OMX	SMI
T	1855	1855	1855	1855	1855	1855	1855	1855
Mean	0,0008	0,0007	0,0008	0,0008	0,0004	0,0009	0,0011	0,0007
Median	0,0005	0,0008	0,0015	0,0011	0,0006	0,0013	0,0014	0,0011
Maximum	0,0697	0,0610	0,0611	0,0632	0,0435	0,0573	0,1102	0,0746
Minimum	-0,0643	-0,0563	-0,0838	-0,0734	-0,0389	-0,0612	-0,0688	-0,0523
Std.Dev.	0,0153	0,0124	0,0128	0,0128	0,0095	0,1158	0,0133	0,0110
Skewness	-0,0708	-0,1469	-0,5042	-0,3645	-0,1374	-0,3771	0,0986	-0,2596
Kurtosis	4,3791	4,5561	6,3383	6,6209	4,5575	6,4770	6,9499	6,5005
Jarque-Bera	148,7854	193,8181	945,0258	1057,2860	194,8996	989,9775	1212,7900	973,6747
Probability	0,0000	0,0000	0,0000	0,0000	0,0000	0,0000	0,0000	0,0000
Q-Stat$_{15}(y)$	30,2350	46,3710	51,5730	66,9160	50,6750	43,7320	58,5550	26,3280
Probability	0,0110	0,0000	0,0000	0,0000	0,0000	0,0000	0,0000	0,0350
Q-Stat$_{15}(y^2)$	625,7400	514,0600	789,5100	1102,7000	943,2000	1419,3000	586,2000	1527,0000
Probability	0,0000	0,0000	0,0000	0,0000	0,0000	0,0000	0,0000	0,0000

5.2. Results

5.2.1. Selection of the Best CAViaR Model

VaR measures are estimated at three different levels: 5%, 1% and 0.1%. We estimated all proposed CAViaR models and we adopt the following strategy to select the best model. Our strategy may be explained in two steps:

(1) Discard all the models for which the Dynamic Quantile Test doesn't accept the null hypothesis, both in and out of sample. To identify the causes of the rejection we use 4 different sets of regressors in the regression (14): (1) the constant and the first five lagged hits, (2) the VaR estimate, (3) the constant, the first lagged hit and the VaR estimate, (4) the constant, the first five lagged hits and the VaR estimate.
(2) Select among the remaining models, the one for which the value of the regression quantile objective function at the optimum is minimum for the data outside the sample.

At the end of this paper, in tables from 4 to 9 for each CAViaR specification we report the value of the estimated parameters,[9] the corresponding standard errors[10] and one-sided p-value, the value of the objective function defined in (12) calculated at the optimum, the sample mean of the excesses for VaR, and the p-values of the DQ test for the regressions described.

According to the strategy proposed we have tried to select at each level of probability the best model for the 8 series analyzed. We have to stress that for the 0.1% quantile it is necessary to take with extreme caution the estimates obtained even if the performance in terms of number of hits is acceptable. For this level it is not possible to select the best model using the strategy proposed due to the low power of the DQ test that consists in just 1 observation in sample.

At the 1% and 5% the best models for the series analyzed are presented in Table 2.

It is interesting what we notice with Dax series. It is the only series for which we are not able to choose the best CAViaR model at the 1% confidence level. The problem is due to the DQ test for the observations out of sample. To solve this problem we have tried to introduce the volume as new economic variable in the CAViaR specifications. The choice of this variable has been suggested from the results obtained by Clark (1973). The new CAViaR models estimated are:

$$VaR_t = (\gamma_1 + \gamma_2 VaR_{t-1}^2 + \gamma_3 y_{t-1}^2 + \gamma_4 \ln(\ln(vol_{t-1})))^{\frac{1}{2}} \tag{33}$$

$$VaR_t = \gamma_0 + \gamma_1 VaR_{t-1} + \gamma_2 (y_{t-1})^+ - \gamma_3 (y_{t-1})^- + \gamma_4 \ln(\ln(\mathrm{vol}_{t-1})) \tag{34}$$

Table 2. Selected CAViaR Models at 1% and 5% Level of Confidence.

	VaR at 1%	VaR at 5%
Mib30	Asymmetric Slope	Indirect GARCH(1,1)
Cac40	Indirect GARCH(1,1)	Indirect GARCH(1,1)
Dax	***	Indirect GARCH(1,1)
Ibex	Asymmetric Slope	Asymmetric Slope
Ftse	Indirect GARCH(1,1)	Proportional Symmetric Adaptive
Aex	Indirect GARCH(1,1)	Asymmetric Slope
Omx	Indirect GARCH(1,1)	Symmetic Absolute Value
Smi	Symmetic Absolute Value	Symmetic Absolute Value

We have chosen these two models since the Indirect GARCH(1,1) and the Asymmetric Slope seem to be the best models among those estimated with the six CAViaR specifications. The results obtained, reported in Table 11, show that the new variable is not significant and that the DQ test still rejects the null hypothesis.

We have also tried to estimate the following models:

$$VaR_t = (\gamma_1 + \gamma_2 VaR_{t-1}^2 + \gamma_3 y_{t-1}^2 + \gamma_4 VaR_{t-2}^2)^{\frac{1}{2}} \tag{35}$$

$$VaR_t = (\gamma_1 + \gamma_2 VaR_{t-1}^2 + \gamma_3 y_{t-1}^2 + \gamma_4 y_{t-2}^2)^{\frac{1}{2}} \tag{36}$$

to understand if the introduction of a second order specification for the CAViaR could be able to establish a model with a correct specification. The results obtained, reported in Table 11, show that the new variable is not significant and that the DQ test refuses the null hypothesis.

Not being able to solve the problem exposed above with the introduction of new variables, we verify if the problem depends on the *instability* of the model. We estimate recursively the parameters of the Indirect GARCH(1,1)[11] starting with 1100 observations and we add for each iteration a new observation. For the 1213*th* observation (28 October 1997)[12] there is a consistent variation on the value of the estimated parameters. The average value of γ_2 and γ_3 in the specification (8) changes respectively from 0.94 to 0.64 and from 0.13 to 2. To test if there is a structural change in the model we apply the Wald test in Theorem 4 (51). First we break up the series in two subsets, using different break points centered in the observation 1213, than we estimate the regression:

$$\begin{bmatrix} VaR_{t,1} \\ VaR_{t,2} \end{bmatrix} = \begin{bmatrix} 1 & VaR_{t-1,1} & y_{t-1,1} & 0 & 0 \\ 1 & 0 & 0 & VaR_{t-1,2} & y_{t-1,2} \end{bmatrix} \begin{bmatrix} \gamma_1 \\ \gamma_2 \\ \gamma_3 \\ \gamma_4 \\ \gamma_5 \end{bmatrix} \tag{37}$$

After having estimated the parameters of this model we apply the Wald test for verifying the null hypothesis $H_o{:}R\underline{\gamma} = \underline{r}$ where:

$$r' = [0,0] \tag{38}$$

and

$$R = \begin{bmatrix} 0 & -1 & 0 & 1 & 0 \\ 0 & 0 & -1 & 0 & 1 \end{bmatrix} \tag{39}$$

if we want to test the hypothesis of coefficients jointly equal, or:

$$R = [0 \quad -1 \quad 0 \quad 1 \quad 0] \tag{40}$$

if we test the null hypothesis that the coefficients of VaR_{t-1} are equal, or:

$$R = [0 \quad 0 \quad -1 \quad 0 \quad 1] \tag{41}$$

if we test if the coefficients of y_{t-1} are the same.

The results reported in Table 10 show that the Wald test rejects the null hypothesis of jointly null coefficients for the break point corresponding to the observations 1212 and 1213. Therefore we can say that the data might be divided in two subsets for which we have to estimate a different model. A possible solution could be the introduction of a dummy variable with zeros until the 1213*th* observation and ones from the 1214*th* observation. More interesting, we are going to see that by using the CAViaR & EVT approach we will be able to solve the problem.

5.2.2. *Comparison With the Current Approaches to VaR Estimation*

In this subsection we estimate the VaR by applying six well known methodologies. Also in this case, we choose 1605 data in sample and the last 250 observations out of sample. The implemented methodologies are the following:

(1) **Historical Simulation.** For this technique we have chosen a window size of 300 observation referring to the results obtained by Van de Goorbergh and Vlaar (1999). Remember that depending on the choice for the window

size, the VaR prediction may be steady or volatile: large windows keep data points for a long time which can lead sustained periods of constant\VaR prediction, while small windows reject data points relatively fast resulting in swift changes in the VaR predictions.

(2) **Extreme value theory.** Between the different methodologies for the implementation of the extreme value theory we have decided to model the exceedances over the threshold u by the Generalized Pareto Distribution (GPD). For the choice of u we have plotted the mean excess function and the estimates of the shape parameter by decreasing number of exceedances (or equivalently by increasing threshold). In particular, if the empirical plot of the mean excess function (27) seems to follow a reasonably straight line with positive gradient above a certain value u, this is the threshold that we should choose. Otherwise, referring to the plot of the shape parameter ξ of the GPD the best threshold is that for which ξ is sufficiently stable. In Figs 7 and 8 we also report the QQ-plot against the exponential distribution,[13] the distribution function of excesses $F_u(x)$ as defined in (18), the function $1 - F(x)$ and the plot of the 0.95, 0.99, 0.999 quantile estimates for increasing threshold.

(3) **GARCH with Normal innovations.** We adopt the standard GARCH(1,1) model proposed by Bollerslev (1996) with normal innovations.[14] For some series we also estimate a GARCH-in mean process trying to capture more instability in the data.

(4) **J. P. Morgan RiskMetrics.** Referring to the 'JP Morgan RiskMetrics Technical Document [4° Edition]', the returns are supposed to follow a normal distribution with a time varying variance determined as:

$$\sigma^2_{i,t/t-1} = \lambda^t \sigma^2_{i,0} + (1 - \lambda) \sum_{k=1}^{t-1} \lambda^k r^2_{i,t-k} \tag{42}$$

where $\lambda = 0.94$ and $\sigma^2_{i,0}$ fixed equal to the sample variance.

(5) **QML GARCH.** It consists in a Normal GARCH model estimation and then in computing VaR measures by the application of the historical simulation or the EVT approach for residuals. Therefore, the conditional VaR is defined as:

$$VaR_t = \mu + \alpha r_{t-1} - e * \sigma_{t-1} \tag{43}$$

where e is the selected quantile of the residuals distribution.

5.2.3. *Tests*

We wish to compare the different approaches applied to calculate VaR by using the tests proposed by Christoffersen (1998). The author interprets the VaR as a forecast that the portfolio return will lie in $(-\infty, v)$ with probability p and emphasizes the necessity to test not only the marginal coverage but also the conditional coverage of the interval forecasts. The importance of testing "conditional" coverage arises from the observation of volatility clustering in many financial series. Christoffersen's test is a three steps procedure: a test for correct unconditional coverage (Kupiec (1995) test), a test for independence, and a test for correct conditional coverage. In the test for correct conditional coverage, the null hypothesis of the failure probability being equal to p is tested against the alternative hypothesis of the failure probability being different from p under the assumption of an independent failure process. In the test for independence, the hypothesis of an independent distributed failure process is tested against the alternative hypothesis of the failure process being a first order Markov process. The test for correct conditional coverage is done by testing the hypothesis of correct failure probability under independence of the failure process against the hypothesis of a first order Markov failure process with a transition probability matrix different from that of an independent process.

All tests are carried out using the likelihood ratio (LR) methodology. The likelihood ratio statistic for each test are:

(1) *LR statistic for the test of unconditional coverage (Kupiec's test):*

$$LR_{uc} = -2\log\left[\frac{p^{n_1}(1-p)^{n_0}}{\tilde{\pi}^{n_1}(1-\tilde{\pi})^{n_0}}\right] \overset{a}{\sim} \chi^2_{(1)} \tag{44}$$

where

p = tolerance level at which VaR is estimated
n_1 = number of $(1-\theta)$'s in the indicator series (13)
n_0 = number of θ's in the indicator series (13)
$\tilde{\pi} = \dfrac{n_1}{n_0 + n_1}$

(2) *LR statistic for the test of independence hypothesis:*

$$LR_{ind} = -2\log\left[\frac{(1-\tilde{\pi}_2)^{(n_{00}+n_{10})}\tilde{\pi}_2^{(n_{01}+n_{11})}}{(1-\tilde{\pi}_{01})^{n_{00}}\tilde{\pi}_{01}^{n_{01}}(1-\tilde{\pi}_{11})^{n_{01}}\tilde{\pi}_{11}^{n_{11}}}\right] \overset{a}{\sim} \chi^2_{(1)} \tag{45}$$

where:

$n_{i,j}$ = number of i values followed by a j value in the series (13), $(i, j = 1, 0)$
$\pi_{ij} = \Pr\{I_t = i \mid I_{t-1} = j\}$, $(i, j = 0, 1)$

$$\tilde{\pi}_{01} = \frac{n_{01}}{n_{00} + n_{01}}$$

$$\tilde{\pi}_{11} = \frac{n_{11}}{n_{10} + n_{11}}$$

$$\tilde{\pi}_{2} = \frac{n_{01} + n_{11}}{n_{00} + n_{01} + n_{10} + n_{11}}$$

(3) *LR statistic for the test of correct conditional coverage:*

$$LR_{cc} = -2\log\left[\frac{(1-p)^{n_0}p^{n_1}}{(1-\tilde{\pi}_{01})^{n_{00}}\tilde{\pi}_{01}^{n_{01}}(1-\tilde{\pi}_{11})^{n_{10}}\tilde{\pi}_{11}^{n_{11}}}\right] \overset{a}{\sim} \chi^2_{(2)} \tag{46}$$

By the testing procedure, a model may be rejected if it fails to produce the correct unconditional coverage, if the failure are not independent or both. A model which fails to produce correct unconditional coverage will produce coverage probabilities p which are statistically different from the theoretical coverage probability. Failure to display the independence property also leads to the rejection of a model because it fails to capture the volatility dynamics of the return process. A model which captures the volatility dynamic of the returns will produce high VaR measures during periods of high volatility and low VaR during periods of low volatility, so that the exceedances are spread over the entire sample, and do not come in clusters.

5.2.4. Summary of Results and Tables

A first look at the value of the various LR statistics reveals that models which display correct unconditional coverage might not show a correct conditional coverage.

By analyzing the results obtained for the 5% VaR we notice that the Historical Simulation and the EVT approach display correct conditional coverage but not independence. This behavior shows that the assumption of i.i.d. returns, that is innate in this two methodologies, contradicts the volatility clustering that is observed in our data. On the contrary, the methodologies based on the GARCH model[15] show in general their attitude to model dynamically the quantile. However analyzing specifically the series of Cac40, Ibex, Omx and Aex, we note that the GARCH model with percentile calculated by the EVT presents a wrong unconditional coverage. This behavior might be determined by an estimated quantile lower than that of the normal distribution. At this level of confidence for the VaR we can think, referring to the in sample analysis, that the hypothesis of normality for the residuals of the GARCH model could be a good approximation for describing the left tail of the returns distribution. An exception to what we have said may be the results obtained for the RiskMetrics approach applied to the Mib30 and to the Ibex. For these two indexes the p-value of the LR test for unconditional coverage is zero. This result could be determined from the fact that the RiskMetrics approach imposes fixed values for the parameters of the autoregressive process for the variance and does not estimate them by the data. Analyzing now the results of the tests for the CAViaR model[16] we note that this approach not only shows a correct number of exceedances but also a correct conditional coverage. The behavior of the analyzed models in and out of sample is reported in Tables 14–15. We also notice in this case the problems previously mentioned for the Historical Simulation and the EVT approach. Moreover we observe that some methodologies correct in sample should be refused for the data out of sample in the back-test. We now summarize the best approach for each index for the 5% VaR referring to the LR statistics in sample and out of sample:

- Mib30: GARCH with normal innovations, QML GARCH with historical simulation, CAViaR;
- Cac40: all the methodologies but the QML GARCH with EVT;
- Dax: Historical Simulation, GARCH with normal innovations, RiskMetrics, CAViaR;
- Ibex: GARCH with normal innovations, CAViaR;
- Ftse: GARCH with normal innovations, RiskMetrics, QML GARCH with historical simulation, QML GARCH with EVT, CAViaR;
- Aex: GARCH with normal innovations, RiskMetrics, QML GARCH with historical simulation, CAViaR;
- Omx: GARCH with normal innovations, RiskMetrics, QML GARCH with historical simulation, CAViaR;
- Smi: RiskMetrics, QML GARCH with historical simulation, CAViaR.

The reader may refer to figures from 1 to 6 and from 9 to 16 for some depictive results.

At the 1% level of confidence, in general we notice that the Historical Simulation doesn't present the dependence of the exceedances and the wrong conditional coverage that we have observed for the 5% VaR but a number of exceedances greater than that expected. The EVT approach shows the same problem of dependence of the exceedances already observed unless for the series of Mib30, Ftse and Aex. It is also important to observe that the number of exceedances for the GARCH with normal innovations and the RiskMetrics approach is greater, referring to the expected value, than that obtained by the implementation of the QML GARCH with EVT. Hence, we can say that the introduction of the extreme value theory in the GARCH might be a good strategy at such a low level of confidence. While at the 5% level the quantile could be well determined by the Normal distribution, now a better approximation may be obtained by fitting to the data the generalized Pareto distribution (refer to Table 12). Analyzing now the CAViaR model we note that the number of the exceedances is very close to that expected. Also the p-values of the LR_{uc}, LR_{ind} and LR_{cc} statistics are always statistically significant (refer to Tables from 16 to 19).

Finally the selected models for each index are:

- Mib30:QML GARCH with EVT;
- Cac40: CAViaR;
- Dax: CAViaR;
- Ibex: QML GARCH with historical simulation, QML GARCH with EVT;
- Ftse: QML GARCH with EVT, CAViaR;
- Aex: CAViaR;
- Omx: QML GARCH with EVT, CAViaR;
- Smi: QML GARCH with historical simulation.

At the 0.1% level of confidence we noted that the historical simulation presents a high number of exceedances with respect to the expected ones. The null hypothesis for LR_{uc} test is rejected for all indices but Mib30 index. As for the application based on the EVT we observe that the number of exceedances is correct due to the significance of the p-value for the LR_{uc} test. We stressed that due to the low value for the chosen confidence level the use of GARCH-type methodology, where the desired quantile from standardized residuals is computed by EVT, leads to a better estimation for VaR than those ones based on standard normality assumption. As for Dax index we noted a number of exceedances with RiskMetrics methodology is 12 times higher than one obtained via a GARCH model with the desired quantile computed from GPD. In the application of CAViaR models we noted the performance referred to the number of exceedances is reliable (see Tables 13 and 20).

5.2.5. CAViaR & EVT

In this subsection we apply the new methodology presented in section 4 to our eight time series. The first step of the approach is implemented by estimating the CAViaR specifications for a sufficiently high level of probability θ fixed equals to 0.075 and by selecting the best CAViaR model following the strategy exposed in the previous subsection. The best CAViaR specification for each time series is reported in Table 3.

We can now construct the series of the standardized quantile residuals defined in (29) and fit them by the GPD for determining the *pth* quantile. The

Table 3. Best CAViaR Specifications at 7.5% Confidence Level.

7.5% quantile	Selected model
MIB30	Asymmetric Absolute Value
CAC40	Proportional Symmetric Adaptive
DAX	Indirect Garch
IBEX	Asymmetric Slope
FTSE	Asymmetric Slope
AEX	Asymmetric Slope
OMX	Proportional Symmetric Adaptive
SMI	Indirect Garch

exceedances used to estimate the GPD are always fixed equal to 100 following the results obtained by the Monte Carlo simulation in McNeil (1999) and Manganelli (2000).

After that the series of the $p\%$ VaR is obtained by relation (32).

We applied this methodology to all financial time series in hand. We choose to report the results obtained for Dax index because it is the only series that presents some specification problems on selecting CAViaR model at 1% confidence level.[17] For Dax index the residuals of the CAViaR model presents a positive value of the shape parameter of the GPD that indicates the presence of fat tails. At 1% level of confidence it is important to observe that while by using the CAViaR is not possible to select a suitable model due to the DQ test, now, by applying the CAViaR & EVT it is. At this level of confidence by applying the CAViaR & EVT we do not have only a correct marginal coverage as shown by the number of Hits reported in Table 20, but also a correct conditional coverage as shown by the DQ test that always accepts the null hypothesis of joint zeros coefficients. From comparing the results pictured on figures 15 and 16 we note a distinctive outperformance for CAViaR & EVT on computing VaR measure, hence it represents a more efficient allocation for financial institution's capital.

CONCLUSION

In this paper we found empirical evidence that it is possible to reach a significant improvement for calculating VaR measures by using a conditional autoregressive approach combined with extreme value theory.

We also provide some statistical tests to evaluate the chosen specification, the performance of the models and the reliability of the estimates.

A possible extension and also a work in progress for us will be to investigate the applications of this methodology on selecting the optimum portfolio for asset allocation problems.

NOTES

1. We omit the θ (confidence level) subscript for notational convenience.
2. For example Hit_{t-1}, Hit_{t-2}, . . . , VaR_t, . . . , σ_t^2 (calculated by the GARCH model) and so on.
3. Many applications of EVT can be found in a large variety of fields, finance included.
4. For a more detailed explaination of these concepts the reader may refer to Embrechts et al. (1997).
5. The interpretation of the mean excess plot is explained in Beirlant, Teugels and Vyckier (1996), Embrecht et al. (1997) and Hogg and Klugman (1984).
6. The mean excess function is commonly known as Shortfall function.
7. Here we assume that $q_{t,\theta}$ is a negative number.
8. See for example Mandelbrot (1963) and Fama (1965).
9. The estimated parameters are obtained by the implementation of the genetic algorithm. In particular we have first generated 5000 random vectors in the interval [0,2] and then select the fittest one to develop the new generations. For a more detailed explaination see Price and Storn (1997).
10. The standard errors are obtained by the kernel function defined in Theorem 3 with a banwidth of 0.1.
11. We have chosen this model for computational convenience.
12. Dax index fell as much as 13% as Asia's stock market slump spread to Europe.
13. A concave departure from the ideal shape indicates an heavier tailed distribution whereas convexity indicates a shorter tailed distribution.
14. Also we used t-student innovations to capture the fatness of the empirical distribution but we did not find any improvement.
15. Remember that also the RiskMetrics approach can be obtained from a GARCH model with Normal innovations with proper constrains for the parameters.
16. We have calculated the tests only for the CAViaR specification selected before.
17. Upon request we can provide the other results for all other indexes used in this analysis. For the rest of time series we find similar results as those obtained in CAViaR specifications.
18. The proofs of the cited theorems may be found in White (1994) and Engle and Manganelli (1999).

ACKNOWLEDGMENT

We greatly appreciated useful comments that have improved the contents of our paper from Nunzio Cappuccio, Simone Manganelli, Vladimiro Ceci and Marco Bee. Clearly all errors remain ours.

DISCLAIMER

The contents of this paper do not constitute a commitment by IntesaBci S.p.A. and any other its conglomerates and subsidiaries.

REFERENCES

Basle Committee on Banking Supervision (1995). An Internal Model-Based Approch to Market Risk Capital Requirements. Basle: Basle Commitee on Banking Supervision.

Basle Committee on Banking Supervision (1996). Supplement to the Capital Accord to Incorporate Market Risk. Basle: Basle Commitee on Banking Supervision.

Beder, T. S. (1995). VaR: Seductive but Dangerous. *Financial Analyst Journal*, (Sep.–Oct.), 12–24.

Beirlant, J., Teugels, J., & Vynckier, P. (1996), *Practical Analysis of Extreme Values*. Leuven: Leuven University Press.

Bollerslev, T. (1986). Generalized Autoregressive Conditional Heteroskedasticity. *Journal of Econometrics*, *31*, 307–327.

Bollerslev, T. (1987). A Conditionally Heteroskedastic Time Series Model For Speculative Prices and Rates of Return. *The Review of Economics and Statistics*, *8*, 542–547.

Bollerslev, T., & Woolridge, J. M. (1992). Quasi-Maximum-Likelihood Estimation and Inference in Dynamic Models with Time Varying Covariances, *Econometric Reviews*, *11*, 143–172.

Boudoukh, J., Richardson, M., & Whitelaw, R. (1998). The best of both Worlds. *Risk*, *11*, 64–67.

Boyle, P., Broadie, M., & Glasserman, P. (1997). Monte Carlo methods for security pricing. *Journal of Economic Dynamics an Control*, *21*, 1267–1321.

Brealey, R. A., Myers, S. C., & Sandri, S. (1999). *Principi di Finanza Aziendale* (3rd ed.). Milano: McGraw-Hill.

Brooks, C., & Persand, G. (2000). The pitfalls of VaR estimates. *Risk*, *5*, 63–65.

Brotherton-Ratcliffe, R. (1994). Monte Carlo monitoring. *Risk*, *7*, 53–57.

Buchinsky, M. (1997). *Recent Advances in Quantile Regression Models: A Practical Guideline for Empirical Research*. Brown University.

Chernozhukov, V., & Umantsev, L. (2000). *Conditional Value At Risk: Aspects of Modelling and Estimation*. Stanford: Stanford University.

Christoffersen, P. F. (1998). Evaluating Interval Forecast. *International Economic Review*, *39*, 841–862.

Christoffersen, P. F., Hahn, J., & Inoue, A. (1999). *Testing Comparing, and Combining Value-at-Risk Measures*. Montreal: McGill University.

Clark, P. K. (1973). A Subordinated Stocastic Process Model with Finite Variance for Speculative Prices. *Econometrica*, *41*, 135–155.

Clewlow, L., & Carverhill, A. (1994). Quicker on the curves. *Risk*, *7*, 63–65.

Cowles, A., & Jones, H. (1937). Some a posteriori probabilities in stock market action. *Econometrica*, *5*, 280–294.

Crnkovic, C., & Dranchman, J. (1996). Quality Control, *Risk*, *9*, 138–143.

Danielsson J., & de Vries, C. G. (1997). *Value-at-Risk and Extreme Returns*. London: London School of Economics.

Danielsson, J., & de Vries, C. G. (1998). *Beyond the sample: extreme quantile and probability estimation*. London: London School of Economics.

Dongcheol K., & Kon Stanley, J. (1994). Alternative Models for the Conditional Heteroscedasticity of Stock Returns. *Journal of Business*, *67*, 563–598.

Dowd, K. (1998). *Beyond Value at Risk*. London: John Wiley & Sons.

Duffie, D., & Pan, J. (1997). An Overview of Value at Risk. *Journal of Derivatives*, *8*, 7–49.

Embrechts, P., Kluppelberg, C., & Mikosch, T. (1997). *Modelling Extremal Events for Insurance and Finance* (1st ed.). Berlin: Springer.

Engle, R. F. (1982). Autoregressive Conditional Heteroskdastiticity with Estimates of the Variance of UK Inflation. *Econometrica*, *50*, 987–1008.

Engle, R. F., & Gonzalez-Rivera (1991), Semiparametric ARCH Models. *Journal of Business and Economic Statistics*, *9*, 345–359.

Engle, R. F., & Manganelli, S. (1999). *CAViaR: Conditional Value at Risk by Quantile Regression*. San Diego: University of California.

Engle, R. F., & Ng, V. (1993). Mesuring and Testing the Impact of News On Volatility. *Journal of Finance*, *48*, 1749–1778.

Fabozzi, F. J., & Modigliani, F. (1992). *Mercati Finanziari: Strumenti e Istituzioni*. Bologna: il Mulino.

Falk, M., Husler, J., & Reiss, R. (1994). *Laws of Small numbers: extremes and rare events,*. Basel: Birkhauser.

Fama, E. F. (1965). The Behavior of stock prices. *Journal of Business*, *38*, 34–105.

Fisher, R., & Tippet, L. (1928). Limiting forms of the frequency distribution of the largest or smallest member of a sample. *Proceedings of the Cambridge Philosophical Society*, *24*, 180–190.

Foresi, S., & Peracchi, F. (1995). The conditional distribution of excess returns: an empirical analysis. *Journal of American Statistical Association*, *90*, 451–466.

Goldberg, D. E. (1989). *Genetic algorithms in search, optimisation, and machine learning*. Reading: Addison-Wesley Publishing Corporation Inc.

Van den Goorbergh, R. W. J., & Vlaar, P. J. G. (1999). *Value-at-Risk Analysis of Stock Returns: Historical Simulation, Variance Techniques or Tail Index Estimation?* De Nederlandsche Bank.

Gourieroux, C., & Jasak, J. (1998). Truncated Maximum Likelihood, Goodness of Fit Tests and Tail Analysis. Unpublished Manuscript.

Greene, W. H. (1997). *Econometric Analysis*. New York: MacMillan.

Hamilton, D. J. (1995). *Time Series Analysis*. Princeton: Princeton University Press.

Hendricks, D. (1996). Evaluation of value-at-risk models using historical data. *Economic Police Review*, *2*, 39–70. Federal Reserve Bank of New York.

Johnson, N. L. (1949). Systems of frequency curves generated by methods of traslation. *Biometrica*, 149–175.

Johnston, J. (1993). *Econometrica*. Milano: F.Angeli.

Jorion, P. (1995). Predicting volatility in the foreing exchange market. *Journal of Finance*, *50*, 507–528.

Jorion, P. (1997). *Value at Risk: The New Benchmark for Controlling Market Risk*. Chicago: Irwin Professional Publishing.

Joy, C., Boyle, P. P., & Tan, K. S. (1995). Quasi Monte Carlo methods in numerical finance.*Mimeo*. Waterloo: Univerisity of Waterloo.

J. P. Morgan/Reuters (1996). *RiskMetrics – Technical Document* (4th ed.). New York.

Koenker, R., & Basset, G. (1978). Regression quantiles. *Econometrica*, *46*, 33–50.

Kupiec, P. (1995). Tecniques for Verifying the Accurancy of Risk Mesurement Models. *Journal of Derivatives*, *2*, 73–84.

Linsmeier, T., & Pearson, N. (1996). *Risk Measurement: An Introduction to Value at Risk.* University of Illinois.
Ljung, G., & Box, G. (1979). On a measure of lack of fit in time series models. *Biometrica, 66,* 265–270.
Lopez, J. A. (1998). Methods for Evaluating Value-at-Risk Estimates, Technical Report 9802. Federal Reserve Bank of New York, New York. Research Paper.
Mandelbrot, B. (1963). The variation of certain speculative prices. *Journal of Business, 36,* 394–419.
Manganelli S. (2000). *Value-At-Risk Models in Finance.* San Diego: University of California.
McNeil A. (1996). *Estimating the Tails of Loss Severity Distributions using Extreme Value Theory.* ETH Zentrum.
McNeil A. (1998). *Calculating Quantile Risk Measures for Financial Return Series using Extreme Value Theory.* ETH Zentrum.
McNeil A. (1999). *Extreme Value Theory for Risk Managers.* ETH Zentrum.
McNeil A., & Frey, R. (1999). *Estimation of Tail-Related Risk Measures for Heteroscedastic Financial Time Series: an Extreme Value Approch.* ETH Zentrum.
Mood, A. (1940). The distribution theory of runs. *Annals of Mathematical Statistics, 11,* 367–392.
Neiderreiter, H., & Xing, C. (1995). Low-discrepancy sequences and global function fields with many rational places, *Mimeo.* Wien: Austrian Academy of Sciences.
Newey W., & Powell, J. (1990). Efficient estimation of linear and type I censored regression models under conditional quantile restriction. *Econometric Theory, 6,* 295–317.
Owen, A. B., & Tavella, A. (1996). Scrambled nets for value at risk calculations. *Mimeo.* Stanford: Stanford University.
Paskov, S., & Traub, J. (1995). Faster valuation of financial derivatives. *Journal of Portafolio Management, 22,* 113–120.
Pickands, J. (1975). Statistical inference using extreme order statistics. *The Annals of Statistics, 3,* 119–131.
Powell, J. (1984). Least absolute deviations estimation for censored regression model. *Journal of Econometrics, 25,* 303–325.
Powell, J. (1986). Censored regression quantiles. *Journal of Econometrics, 32,* 143–155.
Price, K., & Storn, R. (1997). Differential Evolution. *Dr. Dobb's Journal,* (April), 18–24.
Reiss, R., & Thomas, M. (1996). Statistical Analysis of Extreme Values. Documentation for XTREMES software package.
Sarma, M., Thomas, S., & Shah, A. (2000). *Performance Evaluation of Alternative VaR Models.* Indira Ghandi Institute of Development Research.
Silverman, B. W. (1986). *Density Estimation for Statistics and Data Analysis.* London: Chapman and Hall.
Sironi, A., & Marsella M. (1997). *La misurazione e la gestione dei rischi di mercato.* Bologna: il Mulino.
Weiss, H. (1991). Estimating non linear dynamic models using least absolute error estimation. *Econometric Theory, 7,* 46–68.
White, H. (1994). *Estimation, Inference and specification Analysis.* Cambridge University Press.
White, H., & Domowitz, I. (1984). Nonlinear regression with dependent observations. *Econometrica, 52,* 143–161.

APPENDIX

Here we state some theorems useful for convergence and asymptotic properties of the estimators defined in the previous sections (refer to Engle & Manganelli, 1999, for a deeper discussion).

Considering the model:

$$y_t = f(x_t, \beta_\theta) + \varepsilon_{t\theta} \qquad Quant_\theta(\varepsilon_t \mid \Omega_{t-1}) = 0 \qquad t = 1, \ldots, n \tag{47}$$

we have[18]:

Theorem 1 (Consistency). *In model (47)* $\hat{\beta}_\theta \xrightarrow{p} \beta_\theta$ *as* $n \to \infty$ *where* $\hat{\beta}_\theta$ *is the solution of (12).*

Theorem 2 (Asymptotic Normality). *In the model (47) if the estimator is consistent, then:*

$$\sqrt{\frac{n}{\theta(1-\theta)}}\, A_n^{-\frac{1}{2}} D_n(\hat{\beta}_\theta - \beta_\theta) \xrightarrow{d} N(0, I) \tag{48}$$

where

$$A_n = n^{-1} \Sigma\, E\left[\frac{\partial f(x_t, \beta_\theta)}{\partial \beta_\theta} \frac{\partial f(x_t, \beta_\theta)}{\partial \beta'_\theta}\right],\ D_n = n^{-1} \Sigma\, E\left[h_t(0) \frac{\partial f(x_t, \beta_\theta)}{\partial \beta'_\theta} \frac{\partial f(x_t, \beta_\theta)}{\partial \beta'_\theta}\right]$$

with $h_t(0)$ *the density function of the error term* $h_t(\varepsilon_{t\theta})$ *calculated in zero, and* $\hat{\beta}_\theta$ *estimated by the (12).*

Theorem 3 (Estimation of the Asymptotic Variance-Covariance Matrix). *Under the following assumptions:*

(1) $g_t\left(\frac{\hat{\varepsilon}_{t\theta}}{f(x_t, \hat{\beta}_\theta)}\right)\Big|_0 = g\left(\frac{\hat{\varepsilon}_{t\theta}}{f(x_t, \hat{\beta}_\theta)}\right)\Big|_0$ for all t is not time varying, provided that $f(x_t, \hat{\beta}_\theta) \neq 0$ for all t. Where $g_t(\cdot)$ is the density function of the standardized quantile residuals.

(2) $\hat{c}_n / c_n \to 1$, where the nonstochastic sequence c_n satisfies $c_n = o(1)$ and $c_n^{-1} = o(n^{\frac{1}{2}})$.

(3) the elements of $\frac{\partial f(x_t, \beta_\theta)}{\partial \beta_\theta}$ are uniformly 4-dominated.

Defining the estimated variance-covariance matrix D_n as:

$$\hat{D}_n = (\hat{c}_n n)^{-1} \Sigma\, k\left(\frac{\hat{\varepsilon}_{t,n}}{f(x_t, \hat{\beta}_\theta)} \Big/ \hat{c}_n \right) \Sigma\, n^{-1} \left(\left(\frac{\partial f(x_t, \beta_\theta)}{\partial \beta_\theta} \frac{\partial f(x_t, \beta_\theta)}{\partial \beta'_\theta} \right) |_{\hat{\beta}_\theta} / f(x_t, \hat{\beta}_\theta) \right)$$

$$= \hat{g}(0)\hat{C}_n$$

where

$$k(u) = I(|u| \leq 1)/2$$

is the kernel for $g(\cdot)$,

$$\hat{g}(0) = (\hat{c}_n n)^{-1} \Sigma\, k\left(\frac{\hat{\varepsilon}_{t,n}}{f(x_t, \hat{\beta}_\theta)} \Big/ \hat{c}_n \right)$$

and

$$\hat{C}_n \equiv n^{-1} \Sigma \left(\left(\frac{\partial f(x_t, \hat{\beta}_\theta)}{\partial \beta_\theta} \frac{\partial f(x_t, \hat{\beta}_\theta)}{\partial \beta'_\theta} \right) \Big/ f(x_t, \hat{\beta}_\theta) \right)$$

we have that:

$$\hat{D}_{n} - D_n \xrightarrow{p} 0 \tag{50}$$

Theorem 4 (Wald and LM Test). *If the same conditions as Theorem 3 hold, under* $H_0: R\beta_\theta = r$:

$$W_n \equiv \frac{n}{\theta(1-\theta)} [\hat{g}(0)]^2 (R\hat{\beta}_\theta - r)' [R\hat{C}_n^{-1} \hat{A}_n \hat{C}_n^{-1} R']^{-1} (R\hat{\beta}_\theta - r) \overset{a}{\sim} \chi^2_q \tag{51}$$

$$LM_n \equiv d_n(\tilde{\beta}_\theta)' \tilde{C}_n^{-1} R' [R\tilde{C}_n^{-1} \tilde{A}_n \tilde{C}_n^{-1} R']^{-1} R\tilde{C}_n^{-1} d_n(\tilde{\beta}_\theta) \overset{a}{\sim} \chi^2_q \tag{52}$$

where:

$$\hat{A}_n = n^{-1} \Sigma\, \nabla f_t(\hat{\beta}_\theta) \nabla' f_t(\hat{\beta}_\theta)$$

$$\hat{C}_n = n^{-1} \Sigma\, [f(x_t, \hat{\beta}_\theta)]^{-1} \nabla f_t(\hat{\beta}_\theta) \nabla' f_t(\hat{\beta}_\theta)$$

$$d_n(\tilde{\beta}_\theta) = n^{-1/2} \Sigma\, \nabla f_t(\tilde{\beta}_\theta) Hit_t(\tilde{\beta}_\theta)$$

$$Hit_t(\beta_\theta) = I(y_t < -x'_t \beta_\theta) - \theta$$

$\hat{g}(0)$ *is computed as Theorem 3 and* ~ *denotes that the variables are evaluated at the restricted estimates.*

TABLES 4–20 (inclusive)

Table 4. Parameter Estimates and Relevant Statistics for the Adaptive Model.

0.1% quantile	MIB30	CAC40	DAX	IBEX	FTSE	AEX	OMX	SMI
Gamma1	0,00000002	0,02145866	0,02082639	0,02329344	0,01812307	0,03351668	0,03852692	0,02859961
Standard Errors	-	-	-	-	-	-	-	-
P-values	-	-	-	-	-	-	-	-
RQ in sample	0,10367516	0,07270237	0,11894698	0,11226627	0,05301965	0,08365087	0,07661523	0,08036945
RQ out of sample	0,01604065	0,01464536	0,01787059	0,01992817	0,01179840	0,01631332	0,01807553	0,01501472
Hit in sample (%)	0,12	0,12	0,12	0,12	0,12	0,12	0,12	0,12
Hit out of sample(%)	0,00	0,00	0,00	0,00	0,40	0,00	0,00	0,00
DQ in sample (p-values)								
1)[c,hit(-1 to -5)]	-	-	-	-	-	-	-	-
2)[VaR]	-	-	-	-	-	-	-	-
3)[c,hit(-1),VaR]	-	-	-	-	-	-	-	-
4)[c,hit(-1 to -5),VaR]	-	-	-	-	-	-	-	-
DQ out of sample (p-values)								
1)[c,hit(-1 to -5)]	-	-	-	-	-	-	-	-
2)[VaR]	-	-	-	-	-	-	-	-
3)[c,hit(-1),VaR]	-	-	-	-	-	-	-	-
4)[c,hit(-1 to -5),VaR]	-	-	-	-	-	-	-	-

1% quantile	MIB30	CAC40	DAX	IBEX	FTSE	AEX	OMX	SMI
Gamma1	0,00604256	0,01356179	0,01664703	0,01280263	0,00432169	0,01060507	0,00515669	0,01295017
Standard Errors	0,00078514	0,00112204	0,00182279	0,00098651	0,00036199	0,00065840	0,00078113	0,00124362
P-values	0,00000000	0,00000000	0,00000000	0,00000000	0,00000000	0,00000000	0,00000000	0,00000000
RQ in sample	0,74958662	0,54763409	0,72560026	0,68044958	0,41278389	0,58423870	0,61254645	0,55481895
RQ out of sample	0,12228345	0,10178530	0,10148898	0,13804613	0,08792982	0,12895532	0,12010828	0,09380856
Hit in sample (%)	1,12	1,00	1,00	1,18	1,12	1,12	1,18	1,00
Hit out of sample(%)	0,40	1,20	0,80	0,80	0,80	0,40	0,80	0,80
DQ in sample (p-values)								
1)[c,hit(-1 to -5)]	0,21612926	0,99064747	0,12504536	0,56809278	0,00281464	0,96135414	0,10806582	0,99064747
2)[VaR]	0,79381379	0,40612043	0,38331731	0,81247980	0,81490440	0,97342046	0,56805177	0,39745695
3)[c,hit(-1),VaR]	0,17456663	0,05727918	0,09228353	0,64762353	0,75757974	0,60425347	0,78769180	0,06214199
4)[c,hit(-1 to -5),VaR]	0,22096483	0,35729372	0,01457612	0,58028846	0,00394145	0,91903499	0,14373620	0,37368010
DQ out of sample (p-values)								
1)[c,hit(-1 to -5)]	0,98989733	0,99910405	0,99992863	0,30041407	0,99992863	0,98989733	0,99995440	0,99992863
2)[VaR]	0,31705745	0,99541501	0,58750014	0,12064818	0,68737494	0,30041407	0,69954727	0,57347822
3)[c,hit(-1),VaR]	0,53261455	0,46742429	0,25626432	0,22699791	0,25640897	0,54750296	0,22699791	0,29943352
4)[c,hit(-1 to -5),VaR]	0,94800776	0,92344927	0,74801669	0,80954283	0,77356417	0,95278781	0,73910619	0,80954283

5% quantile	MIB30	CAC40	DAX	IBEX	FTSE	AEX	OMX	SMI
Gamma1	0,00858164	0,00461756	0,00441414	0,00613962	0,00309962	0,00722534	0,00508778	0,00616854
Standard Errors	0,00075641	0,00060261	0,00034075	0,00048889	0,00026855	0,00065737	0,00053417	0,00071092
P-values	0,00000000	0,00000000	0,00000000	0,00000000	0,00000000	0,00000000	0,00000000	0,00000000
RQ in sample	2,66029076	2,13309737	2,26760112	2,22284243	1,48438361	2,00694100	2,10502371	1,98863957
RQ out of sample	0,36489769	0,40136452	0,40748201	0,34550981	0,34572364	0,34372426	0,42197092	0,31120259
Hit in sample (%)	4,98	5,05	5,11	4,98	5,17	5,05	4,98	5,05
Hit out of sample(%)	5,20	6,00	5,20	6,00	5,60	5,20	6,80	4,80
DQ in sample (p-values)								
1)[c,hit(-1 to -5)]	0,60277530	0,68219217	0,75335644	0,27412493	0,94202520	0,67380771	0,41546889	0,01340171
2)[VaR]	0,15910956	0,34332525	0,49920055	0,21601920	0,59542429	0,16935199	0,30260146	0,21341005
3)[c,hit(-1),VaR]	0,00178789	0,03666916	0,13205155	0,00753355	0,11515259	0,03163216	0,01075433	0,02341887
4)[c,hit(-1 to -5),VaR]	0,00362744	0,08626085	0,37221318	0,02610360	0,52008851	0,10108254	0,06355329	0,00093951
DQ out of sample (p-values)								
1)[c,hit(-1 to -5)]	0,91753926	0,92347163	0,89826854	0,50796802	0,21100465	0,82539233	0,26941504	0,87219946
2)[VaR]	0,65211761	0,55836474	0,94028063	0,69934986	0,99789702	0,69383104	0,26161493	0,38115047
3)[c,hit(-1),VaR]	0,19607550	0,80255957	0,42330816	0,14792940	0,48134350	0,15737400	0,51220449	0,01768859
4)[c,hit(-1 to -5),VaR]	0,51560204	0,94811609	0,70682090	0,40126737	0,09249468	0,45838091	0,33991972	0,11719734

Table 5. Parameter Estimates and Relevant Statistics for the Prop. Sym. Adaptive Model.

0.1% quantile	MIB30	CAC40	DAX	IBEX	FTSE	AEX	OMX	SMI
Gamma1	0,00000855	8,34526846	12,79869478	3,70632973	1,57144503	11,58215624	1,33564724	0,00005861
Standard Errors	-	-	-	-	-	-	-	-
P-values	-	-	-	-	-	-	-	-
Gamma2	0,00000002	0,00306566	0,00098865	0,00044906	0,00054924	0,00194547	0,00020854	0,00000000
Standard Errors	-	-	-	-	-	-	-	-
P-values	-	-	-	-	-	-	-	-
RQ in sample	0,10386338	0,06717868	0,08893282	0,10147019	0,04833006	0,06774215	0,10247667	0,08506075
RQ out of sample	0,01585216	0,01753563	0,01404880	0,01630832	0,01061917	0,03324411	0,02963310	0,01295572
Hit in sample (%)	0,12	0,31	0,12	0,00	0,06	0,12	0,00	0,12
Hit out of sample(%)	0,00	0,40	0,00	0,00	0,00	0,40	0,00	0,00
DQ in sample (p-values)								
1)[c,hit(-1 to -5)]	-	-	-	-	-	-	-	-
2)[VaR]	-	-	-	-	-	-	-	-
3)[c,hit(-1),VaR]	-	-	-	-	-	-	-	-
4)[c,hit(-1 to -5),VaR]	-	-	-	-	-	-	-	-
DQ out of sample (p-values)								
1)[c,hit(-1 to -5)]	-	-	-	-	-	-	-	-
2)[VaR]	-	-	-	-	-	-	-	-
3)[c,hit(-1),VaR]	-	-	-	-	-	-	-	-
4)[c,hit(-1 to -5),VaR]	-	-	-	-	-	-	-	-

1% quantile	MIB30	CAC40	DAX	IBEX	FTSE	AEX	OMX	SMI
Gamma1	1,00001805	1,02373468	0,54099273	1,70393463	1,14941751	1,68357224	2,06958712	0,74051181
Standard Errors	0,23289804	0,26861600	0,27173642	0,25695526	0,28706855	0,61012275	0,21957414	0,17855171
P-values	0,00000878	0,00006916	0,02324742	0,00000000	0,00003114	0,00289539	0,00000000	0,00001682
Gamma2	0,01000876	0,00723657	0,00186603	0,01616649	0,00437198	0,00285521	0,02248608	0,00553330
Standard Errors	0,00234039	0,00150670	0,00112789	0,00213608	0,00103448	0,00094837	0,00169105	0,00134633
P-values	0,00000949	0,00000078	0,04901826	0,00000000	0,00001188	0,00130346	0,00000000	0,00001979
RQ in sample	0,76446355	0,58516273	0,73810823	0,68982489	0,39605667	0,57418794	0,63108114	0,59157854
RQ out of sample	0,09987553	0,11047842	0,11067153	0,10209656	0,09480022	0,13214477	0,11566983	0,09461301
Hit in sample (%)	1,60	1,40	1,00	1,60	1,00	0,80	1,80	1,61
Hit out of sample(%)	2,00	1,60	0,00	2,00	0,80	0,40	2,00	0,80
DQ in sample (p-values)								
1)[c,hit(-1 to -5)]	0,00000000	0,00132150	0,00009061	0,05424832	0,98210785	0,98484388	0,01107153	0,00000000
2)[VaR]	0,07201834	0,36630311	0,98145167	0,11248655	0,88410831	0,43950277	0,03254390	0,00003026
3)[c,hit(-1),VaR]	0,00035331	0,00026507	0,98177047	0,00180096	0,95286759	0,87462080	0,00070221	0,02731511
4)[c,hit(-1 to -5),VaR]	0,00000000	0,00062347	0,00020788	0,01712520	0,99249038	0,99411026	0,00428236	0,00000000
DQ out of sample (p-values)								
1)[c,hit(-1 to -5)]	0,69667538	0,95422512	-	0,69667538	0,99992863	0,98989733	0,00285988	0,99992863
2)[VaR]	0,20074968	0,42958685	-	0,49344385	0,58224592	0,27587255	0,58094202	0,54815858
3)[c,hit(-1),VaR]	0,19894317	0,53844698	-	0,00569580	0,54195594	0,66385339	0,00002275	0,27804382
4)[c,hit(-1 to -5),VaR]	0,62261459	0,93838318	-	0,07508339	0,95103118	0,97881434	0,00068707	0,79322200

5% quantile	MIB30	CAC40	DAX	IBEX	FTSE	AEX	OMX	SMI
Gamma1	0,45969398	0,25752441	0,34274771	0,73241975	0,27299099	0,93436185	0,52715993	0,30378267
Standard Errors	0,08311747	0,08666943	0,09544338	0,14537874	0,08827606	0,23294676	0,14875931	0,11838702
P-values	0,00000002	0,00148251	0,00016464	0,00000024	0,00099249	0,00003022	0,00019727	0,00514375
Gamma2	0,03091623	0,01247384	0,02269550	0,05637001	0,01285129	0,05872172	0,04487253	0,01975497
Standard Errors	0,00483325	0,00384767	0,00571877	0,00995447	0,00407091	0,01261793	0,01082286	0,00671350
P-values	0,00000000	0,00059363	0,00003615	0,00000001	0,00079739	0,00000163	0,00001691	0,00162748
RQ in sample	2,62013173	2,12276221	2,21015624	2,19723397	1,47637125	1,97600444	2,11525148	1,96338885
RQ out of sample	0,37249959	0,37744255	0,39302856	0,34987692	0,32333588	0,36001265	0,41406275	0,30824897
Hit in sample (%)	5,42	5,48	5,61	5,92	5,05	5,86	5,86	5,36
Hit out of sample(%)	6,80	5,60	6,40	7,20	6,00	5,60	5,60	5,20
DQ in sample (p-values)								
1)[c,hit(-1 to -5)]	0,00164030	0,15887696	0,05954304	0,01144235	0,29570493	0,40568086	0,01334489	0,04100225
2)[VaR]	0,81547683	0,68414238	0,65328276	0,32347647	0,93379434	0,74769119	0,48724925	0,72317516
3)[c,hit(-1),VaR]	0,29557965	0,33125576	0,14807274	0,20200608	0,95113255	0,06093649	0,04151144	0,55740038
4)[c,hit(-1 to -5),VaR]	0,00051899	0,13311833	0,04672056	0,00546796	0,39399446	0,10555930	0,00508978	0,05905291
DQ out of sample (p-values)								
1)[c,hit(-1 to -5)]	0,35486618	0,88143394	0,24231414	0,15131878	0,67957089	0,81920226	0,51456847	0,76930128
2)[VaR]	0,28154070	0,56070842	0,34044757	0,21981346	0,79969230	0,79906318	0,60249153	0,52768007
3)[c,hit(-1),VaR]	0,37414462	0,92738236	0,65538423	0,15541704	0,97502281	0,47022558	0,32734505	0,16910122
4)[c,hit(-1 to -5),VaR]	0,32196249	0,90788923	0,29409706	0,10799180	0,78112296	0,75784752	0,63048444	0,46425801

Table 6. Parameter Estimates and Relevant Statistics for the Sym. Absolute Value Model.

0.1% quantile	MIB30	CAC40	DAX	IBEX	FTSE	AEX	OMX	SMI
Gamma1	0,01017748	0,00187643	0,02878388	0,00467862	0,00515509	0,00000000	0,00149659	0,00602056
Standard Errors	-	-	-	-	-	-	-	-
P-values	-	-	-	-	-	-	-	-
Gamma2	0,52154706	0,89086777	0,19953157	0,79058091	0,67945344	0,98447349	0,79824859	0,69867483
Standard Errors	-	-	-	-	-	-	-	-
P-values	-	-	-	-	-	-	-	-
Gamma3	1,12039096	0,24954487	1,17162096	0,57468943	0,55912002	0,08029806	0,65869526	0.48298098
Standard Errors	-	-	-	-	-	-	-	-
P-values	-	-	-	-	-	-	-	-
RQ in sample	0,07962237	0,06416528	0,08033973	0,09767676	0,04523004	0,06868378	0,06719402	0,05404500
RQ out of sample	0,01197601	0,01529948	0,01343813	0,01249577	0,01788191	0,02015520	0,01240048	0,01773909
Hit in sample (%)	0,19	0,06	0,12	0,12	0,06	0,12	0,06	0,06
Hit out of sample(%)	0,00	0,40	0,00	0,00	0,40	0,40	0,00	0,40
DQ in sample (p-values)								
1)[c,hit(-1 to -5)]	-	-	-	-	-	-	-	-
2)[VaR]	-	-	-	-	-	-	-	-
3)[c,hit(-1),VaR]	-	-	-	-	-	-	-	-
4)[c,hit(-1 to -5),VaR]	-	-	-	-	-	-	-	-
DQ out of sample (p-values)								
1)[c,hit(-1 to -5)]	-	-	-	-	-	-	-	-
2)[VaR]	-	-	-	-	-	-	-	-
3)[c,hit(-1),VaR]	-	-	-	-	-	-	-	-
4)[c,hit(-1 to -5),VaR]	-	-	-	-	-	-	-	-

1% quantile	MIB30	CAC40	DAX	IBEX	FTSE	AEX	OMX	SMI
Gamma1	0,00225710	0,00020892	0,00435431	0,00000011	0,00016802	0,00027648	0,00179128	0.00177629
Standard Errors	0,00099902	0,00035525	0,00224579	0,00054900	0,00021604	0,00024708	0,00094674	0.00072777
P-values	0,01193188	0,27823570	0,02625798	0,49991834	0,21836099	0,13156580	0,02924182	0,00732899
Gamma2	0,74654191	0,93797314	0,61089275	0,86829726	0,95133850	0,88747615	0,70679396	0.79042682
Standard Errors	0,04692279	0,02738123	0,11485227	0,04520578	0,02862632	0,02686583	0,05687032	0,05220716
P-values	0,00000000	0,00000000	0,00000005	0,00000000	0,00000000	0,00000000	0,00000000	0,00000000
Gamma3	0,57146484	0,17687085	0,91335026	0,40748570	0,13114216	0,34720059	0,70036165	0,45524519
Standard Errors	0,09693732	0,07500776	0,26505078	0,13485992	0,07511716	0,08329692	0,12799140	0,10858581
P-values	0,00000000	0,00918600	0,00028453	0,00125743	0,04041982	0,00001535	0,00000002	0,00001380
RQ in sample	0,66407404	0,55356048	0,62120125	0,62174464	0,40106882	0,51004803	0,54497068	0,47428422
RQ out of sample	0,09195961	0,10399911	0,13812428	0,10240888	0,09239388	0,11175049	0,11168526	0,08054556
Hit in sample (%)	1,06	1,00	1,00	1,00	1,00	1,06	1,00	1.00
Hit out of sample(%)	1,60	0,80	2,00	2,00	0,80	0,80	1,60	1,20
DQ in sample (p-values)								
1)[c,hit(-1 to -5)]	0,00091633	0,04112139	0,53528390	0,99064747	0,51952942	0,55607587	0,99064747	0,99064747
2)[VaR]	0,77485039	0,99411288	0,99700206	0,96239988	0,98312507	0,77254459	0,90014964	0,97521798
3)[c,hit(-1),VaR]	0,95910705	0,20967813	0,98311661	0,97976734	0,98294231	0,96187397	0,95867735	0,98277810
4)[c,hit(-1 to -5),VaR]	0,00167342	0,06644494	0,65118809	0,99545423	0,63611831	0,66889276	0,98951936	0,99682300
DQ out of sample (p-values)								
1)[c,hit(-1 to -5)]	0,95422512	0,99992863	0,00285938	0,00285938	0,99992863	0,99992863	0,00059624	0,99910405
2)[VaR]	0,74846220	0,59171423	0,72683169	0,53644273	0,61042724	0,61166912	0,46766664	0,95137511
3)[c,hit(-1),VaR]	0,11725682	0,68104017	0,00000036	0,00000034	0,44696633	0,76396530	0,00002459	0,25687646
4)[c,hit(-1 to -5),VaR]	0,53273335	0,97974433	0,00000563	0,00002078	0,90766128	0,99176285	0,00106531	0.77204398

5% quantile	MIB30	CAC40	DAX	IBEX	FTSE	AEX	OMX	SMI
Gamma1	0,00094907	0,00000002	0,00009389	0,00000860	0,00000007	0,00040769	0,00022304	0,00029713
Standard Errors	0,00052787	0,00017249	0,00013724	0,00021208	0,00007254	0,00026810	0,00037929	0,00038034
P-values	0,03609542	0,49995139	0,24694686	0,48382557	0,49961777	0,05417054	0,27824914	0,21733282
Gamma2	0,87249576	0,95800723	0,93383142	0,89444398	0,94324053	0,86755327	0,89567854	0,87636518
Standard Errors	0,03773378	0,02182978	0,02214849	0,02733710	0,01677281	0,04219003	0,04255965	0,05370243
P-values	0,00000000	0,00000000	0,00000000	0,00000000	0,00000000	0,00000000	0,00000000	0,00000000
Gamma3	0,18182374	0,08954878	0,12508081	0,21465463	0,11548358	0,22910003	0,18414004	0,22359475
Standard Errors	0,04852606	0,04503965	0,04114782	0,05380378	0,03323356	0,07304363	0,07133795	0,09483878
P-values	0,00008951	0,02339362	0,00118371	0,00003309	0,00025551	0,00085494	0,00492237	0,00919601
RQ in sample	2,58439882	2,11958332	2,18334057	2,15073110	1,46682981	1,93733283	2,06775870	1,88054859
RQ out of sample	0,37668757	0,37954818	0,40550320	0,34617186	0,34039886	0,35540170	0,39155765	0,29310720
Hit in sample (%)	4,98	4,98	5,05	4,98	4,92	4.98	5,05	5,05
Hit out of sample(%)	6,00	4,40	6,80	6,00	7,20	5,60	6,00	6,80
DQ in sample (p-values)								
1)[c,hit(-1 to -5)]	0,00429868	0,74219436	0,26666532	0,49858240	0,38148769	0,25866562	0,17934539	0,30486070
2)[VaR]	0,99049237	0,99016333	0,88337189	0,95878683	0,90212161	0,99662921	0,88616618	0,93433506
3)[c,hit(-1),VaR]	0,79140165	0,93477065	0,95202314	0,77512387	0,79489190	0,99999973	0,73402593	0,44520256
4)[c,hit(-1 to -5),VaR]	0,00735022	0,82928901	0,36535468	0,60742827	0,49219750	0,34772028	0,25500574	0,40997736
DQ out of sample (p-values)								
1)[c,hit(-1 to -5)]	0,87709339	0,86988611	0,35486618	0,08827111	0,43226303	0,86944779	0,17402324	0,75600172
2)[VaR]	0,68900069	0,80493892	0,26484830	0,80619042	0,35961606	0,90834801	0,39692378	0,75833095
3)[c,hit(-1),VaR]	0,30297488	0,84409837	0,35482561	0,13574481	0,53309181	0,27538993	0,36953969	0,07841526
4)[c,hit(-1 to -5),VaR]	0,56217711	0,91418531	0,32305577	0,02400732	0,41355159	0,58329370	0,25320319	0,28709452

Table 7. Parameter Estimates and Relevant Statistics for the Asym. Absolute Value Model.

0.1% quantile	MIB30	CAC40	DAX	IBEX	FTSE	AEX	OMX	SMI
Gamma1	0,00651225	0,00267596	0,00375283	0,03502143	0,00383982	0,00161121	0,00145947	0,00592265
Standard Errors	-	-	-	-	-	-	-	-
P-values	-	-	-	-	-	-	-	-
Gamma2	0,64478016	0,85392196	0,80254584	0,01630866	0,70798037	0,73330381	0,79954297	0,69637619
Standard Errors	-	-	-	-	-	-	-	-
P-values	-	-	-	-	-	-	-	-
Gamma3	0,65534766	0,32273725	0,57438866	0,96986739	0,56445601	0,85524577	0,65550006	0,48464401
Standard Errors	-	-	-	-	-	-	-	-
P-values	-	-	-	-	-	-	-	-
Gamma4	0,01052868	0,00170263	0,00124102	0,01475489	0,00390983	0,00429563	0,00000003	0,00110120
Standard Errors	-	-	-	-	-	-	-	-
P-values	-	-	-	-	-	-	-	-
RQ in sample	0,07372998	0,06331964	0,07413844	0,08734146	0,04440462	0,07201753	0,06728103	0,05309826
RQ out of sample	0,01993126	0,01525034	0,01292489	0,01271655	0,02527336	0,03888488	0,01232389	0,01942904
Hit in sample (%)	0,06	0,12	0,19	0,12	0,12	0,06	0,12	0,12
Hit out of sample(%)	0,81	0,40	0,00	0,00	0,40	0,40	0,00	0,40
DQ in sample (p-values)								
1)[c,hit(-1 to -5)]	-	-	-	-	-	-	-	-
2)[VaR]	-	-	-	-	-	-	-	-
3)[c,hit(-1),VaR]	-	-	-	-	-	-	-	-
4)[c,hit(-1 to -5),VaR]	-	-	-	-	-	-	-	-
DQ out of sample (p-values)								
1)[c,hit(-1 to -5)]	-	-	-	-	-	-	-	-
2)[VaR]	-	-	-	-	-	-	-	-
3)[c,hit(-1),VaR]	-	-	-	-	-	-	-	-
4)[c,hit(-1 to -5),VaR]	-	-	-	-	-	-	-	-

1% quantile	MIB30	CAC40	DAX	IBEX	FTSE	AEX	OMX	SMI
Gamma1	0,00222812	0,00007786	0,00337941	0,00025829	0,00005021	0,00027090	0,00158263	0,00177268
Standard Errors	0,00130094	0,00044164	0,00149708	0,00060397	0,00076381	0,00038727	0,00081569	0,00119880
P-values	0,04338376	0,43002876	0,01199357	0,33444975	0,47379348	0,24211722	0,02617556	0,06960969
Gamma2	0,74488891	0,95215277	0,64220508	0,80883855	0,81552989	0,87488378	0,73646027	0,74716777
Standard Errors	0,05725996	0,02590735	0,08219808	0,03723497	0,05794960	0,03614701	0,05209298	0,08067598
P-values	0,00000000	0,00000000	0,00000000	0,00000000	0,00000000	0,00000000	0,00000000	0,00000000
Gamma3	0,51319545	0,13178406	0,86600325	0,49231376	0,47010677	0,38059117	0,62044547	0,49264930
Standard Errors	0,10239912	0,06558664	0,19419557	0,08849704	0,13101473	0,10795069	0,11684173	0,14679564
P-values	0,00000027	0,02225199	0,00000411	0,00000001	0,00016649	0,00021126	0,00000005	0,00039536
Gamma4	0,00675435	0,00578359	0,00255601	0,00699514	0,00583231	0,00287016	0,00142351	0,00588279
Standard Errors	0,00140941	0,00361232	0,00094873	0,00093986	0,00120449	0,00111821	0,00076533	0,00143602
P-values	0,00000082	0,05468000	0,00352841	0,00000000	0,00000064	0,00513286	0,03144336	0,00002096
RQ in sample	0,63302556	0,54421539	0,61112817	0,61032973	0,39152347	0,50248674	0,53614938	0,46887915
RQ out of sample	0,12567239	0,10359310	0,13395137	0,10260176	0,09830665	0,11329561	0,11379364	0,09474038
Hit in sample (%)	1,06	0,93	1,00	1,06	1,00	1,06	0,93	1,06
Hit out of sample(%)	1,20	2,00	2,00	1,20	1,20	0,80	1,60	1,20
DQ in sample (p-values)								
1)[c,hit(-1 to -5)]	0,55607587	0,08712381	0,49886433	0,98210785	0,99064747	0,55607587	0,99306111	0,55607587
2)[VaR]	0,85307730	0,76762261	0,96574507	0,57059791	0,93590835	0,84250812	0,99435932	0,80064960
3)[c,hit(-1),VaR]	0,96435522	0,97141886	0,98426701	0,78177359	0,97720724	0,98743877	0,89199197	0,96621223
4)[c,hit(-1 to -5),VaR]	0,66381834	0,13149746	0,60170251	0,91577104	0,99688229	0,67101947	0,97990255	0,67156824
DQ out of sample (p-values)								
1)[c,hit(-1 to -5)]	0,99910405	0,00179594	0,00285938	0,99910405	0,99921875	0,99992863	0,00059624	0,99910405
2)[VaR]	0,99873638	0,16502088	0,66655316	0,58532450	0,98542542	0,58958526	0,47500547	0,84908580
3)[c,hit(-1),VaR]	0,60453767	0,24325744	0,00000034	0,01534700	0,65779939	0,73326160	0,00002221	0,12105770
4)[c,hit(-1 to -5),VaR]	0,96666624	0,00291496	0,00002621	0,15695142	0,97654095	0,98872301	0,00006481	0,56042390

5% quantile	MIB30	CAC40	DAX	IBEX	FTSE	AEX	OMX	SMI
Gamma1	0,00034503	0,00000001	0,00010769	0,00000000	0,00000001	0,00004205	0,00017696	0,00000003
Standard Errors	0,00053638	0,00039342	0,00027736	0,00029309	0,00016088	0,00031725	0,00039109	0,00050920
P-values	0,26002815	0,49998331	0,34891110	0,49999758	0,49997174	0,44727832	0,32544284	0,49997601
Gamma2	0,84146328	0,91944968	0,89729658	0,86995972	0,92483781	0,83533311	0,82690874	0,77298089
Standard Errors	0,03688698	0,03352141	0,03009467	0,03401993	0,02496020	0,03886508	0,03735763	0,05219172
P-values	0,00000000	0,00000000	0,00000000	0,00000000	0,00000000	0,00000000	0,00000000	0,00000000
Gamma3	0,28242893	0,14483658	0,18125837	0,26808188	0,14232965	0,30762899	0,28616587	0,43157475
Standard Errors	0,05843005	0,05422069	0,04907698	0,06753304	0,04402454	0,05997476	0,05726985	0,09196082
P-values	0,00000067	0,00377856	0,00011066	0,00003599	0,00061257	0,00000551	0,00000029	0,00000135
Gamma4	0,00570594	0,00718762	0,00488180	0,00316815	0,00392724	0,00535203	0,00728228	0,00615406
Standard Errors	0,00148346	0,00248360	0,00137419	0,00121819	0,00126805	0,00095491	0,00118431	0,00097119
P-values	0,00005994	0,00195097	0,00019079	0,00465171	0,00097725	0,00000001	0,00000000	0,00000000
RQ in sample	2,52864356	2,09332818	2,16527553	2,12745402	1,45155973	1,89360620	1,99541083	1,81994067
RQ out of sample	0,37843529	0,39059255	0,42109656	0,34138137	0,33846874	0,35985899	0,44820388	0,33496718
Hit in sample (%)	5,05	4,86	4,92	4,80	4,86	4,92	4,98	4,92
Hit out of sample(%)	6,80	6,40	8,80	6,00	7,60	4,40	9,20	7,60
DQ in sample (p-values)								
1)[c,hit(-1 to -5)]	0,10047733	0,52811950	0,94071928	0,93329340	0,19183840	0,99586873	0,13549259	0,72132700
2)[VaR]	0,88464026	0,86860325	0,88836893	0,92401725	0,93095411	0,91898718	0,97836671	0,91670898
3)[c,hit(-1),VaR]	0,73571162	0,83601571	0,80468143	0,90106585	0,58700566	0,99927695	0,45941078	0,46889556
4)[c,hit(-1 to -5),VaR]	0,15552983	0,62506133	0,97202881	0,96214145	0,23445613	0,99880560	0,18610526	0,81084739
DQ out of sample (p-values)								
1)[c,hit(-1 to -5)]	0,21243046	0,16798959	0,10746994	0,51230744	0,40285230	0,81532339	0,04617256	0,20897449
2)[VaR]	0,39196364	0,24207813	0,04329530	0,80400731	0,23837443	0,40009916	0,00491782	0,81885506
3)[c,hit(-1),VaR]	0,16352875	0,35428068	0,01604813	0,18471393	0,42138391	0,30770901	0,01623784	0,00000452
4)[c,hit(-1 to -5),VaR]	0,10104938	0,23073816	0,06187828	0,21284165	0,41466504	0,50901287	0,06599732	0,00008467

Table 8. Parameter Estimates and Relevant Statistics for the Asym. Slope Model.

0.1% quantile	MIB30	CAC40	DAX	IBEX	FTSE	AEX	OMX	SMI
Gamma1	0.01007765	0,00258095	0,00671476	0,04819600	0,00491918	0.00318665	0,00242638	0.00544883
Standard Errors	-	-	-	-	-	-	-	-
P-values	-	-	-	-	-	-	-	-
Gamma2	0,59694362	0,86159655	0,66146665	0,02649685	0,69602140	0,76348800	0,73422801	0,73140669
Standard Errors	-	-	-	-	-	-	-	-
P-values	-	-	-	-	-	-	-	-
Gamma3	0.44933285	0,24816669	0,60933995	0,00002721	0.45874168	0.30683296	0,95832363	0.35092002
Standard Errors	-	-	-	-	-	-	-	-
P-values	-	-	-	-	-	-	-	-
Gamma4	0,95867857	0,36437483	1,24366280	0,99685916	0,57949628	0,85376604	0.74618293	0,46536049
Standard Errors	-	-	-	-	-	-	-	-
P-values	-	-	-	-	-	-	-	-
RQ in sample	0.07361618	0,06333747	0,07196071	0,09187641	0,04484599	0,07168957	0,06588283	0,05320901
RQ out of sample	0,01131711	0,01647238	0,01263459	0,01369970	0,01956268	0,03647876	0,01295003	0,01931674
Hit in sample (%)	0,08	0,06	0.12	0,06	0.12	0,06	0,06	0,19
Hit out of sample(%)	0.40	0,40	0,00	0.00	0,40	0,80	0,00	0.40
DQ in sample (p-values)								
1)[c,hit(-1 to -5)]	-	-	-	-	-	-	-	-
2)[VaR]	-	-						
3)[c,hit(-1),VaR]	-	-	-	-	-	-	-	-
4)[c,hit(-1 to -5),VaR]			-	-	-	-	-	-
DQ out of sample (p-values)								
1)[c,hit(-1 to -5)]	-	-						
2)[VaR]	-	-	-	-	-	-	-	-
3)[c,hit(-1),VaR]			-	-	-	-	-	-
4)[c,hit(-1 to -5),VaR]	-	-	-	-	-	-	-	-

1% quantile	MIB30	CAC40	DAX	IBEX	FTSE	AEX	OMX	SMI
Gamma1	0,00274571	0,00028571	0,00252997	0,00173696	0,00196076	0,00052807	0,00133627	0,00308710
Standard Errors	0,00116096	0,00024864	0,00132510	0,00073055	0,00097656	0,00028519	0,00047479	0,00099373
P-values	0,00901395	0,12525439	0,02811333	0,00871278	0,02233129	0,03203613	0,00244312	0,00094632
Gamma2	0.80144924	0,95010682	0,76250096	0,79461817	0,75692360	0,87248657	0,91800145	0.74393510
Standard Errors	0,05287381	0,01758361	0,08175392	0,04771263	0,07618309	0,02916311	0,03350462	0,06466932
P-values	0,00000000	0,00000000	0,00000000	0,00000000	0,00000000	0,00000000	0,00000000	0,00000000
Gamma3	0,19001680	0,05833705	0,35941651	0,23005344	0,26469698	0.26418184	0,22583220	0.23788785
Standard Errors	0.08295779	0,05074017	0,19681370	0,09839115	0,14999148	0,08625270	0,06883433	0,11069775
P-values	0,01099548	0,12512935	0,03391185	0,00968969	0,03880317	0,00109608	0.00051755	0,01581778
Gamma4	0,51999470	0,21858151	0,78909616	0,68960410	0,78734702	0,45704378	0,52461789	0,64251665
Standard Errors	0.12487773	0,06472637	0,25500139	0,15277027	0,22767616	0.10168572	0,09086633	0.15081009
P-values	0,00001563	0.00036639	0,00098580	0,00000318	0,00027191	0,00000348	0,00000000	0,00001020
RQ in sample	0,64783438	0,54777619	0,61097274	0,61728281	0,40468855	0,50087117	0,53145945	0,46092204
RQ out of sample	0,10288632	0,10646337	0,11630069	0,09508177	0,09853712	0,11432073	0,12319306	0,09320685
Hit in sample (%)	1,00	1,00	1.00	1,00	1.00	1,00	1,06	1,12
Hit out of sample(%)	0,80	1,20	2.00	0,80	1,60	1,60	2,40	1,60
DQ in sample (p-values)								
1)[c,hit(-1 to -5)]	0,51952942	0,12570855	0,53528390	0,99064747	0,99064747	0,99064747	0,55607587	0,96135414
2)[VaR]	0.95220358	0,99673091	0,95965744	0,99623609	0,98619415	0,93075827	0,89611454	0.56300270
3)[c,hit(-1),VaR]	0,97205821	0,98326160	0,97798679	0,98307979	0,98327701	0,97928343	0,95653914	0,89303535
4)[c,hit(-1 to -5),VaR]	0,63437158	0,18721247	0,65120170	0,99548960	0,99609920	0,99686683	0.65707789	0,96539330
DQ out of sample (p-values)								
1)[c,hit(-1 to -5)]	0.99992863	0,00000175	0,69667538	0,99992863	0,95422512	0.95422512	0,00000175	0.95422512
2)[VaR]	0,71503427	0,93115084	0,43882140	0,47124991	0,73332496	0,64992814	0.05011910	0,66723835
3)[c,hit(-1),VaR]	0,97690112	0,29146923	0,01303622	0,46604150	0,11276842	0,14076428	0,00005767	0,06665835
4)[c,hit(-1 to -5),VaR]	0.99996496	0,00000121	0,14689625	0,92127201	0,54048033	0.60005704	0,00000153	0.40509256

5% quantile	MIB30	CAC40	DAX	IBEX	FTSE	AEX	OMX	SMI
Gamma1	0.00125324	0,00002509	0,00057612	0,00018487	0,00011653	0,00093708	0,00082231	0,00143056
Standard Errors	0,00071773	0,00014468	0,00032234	0,00023778	0,00010724	0,00036828	0,00038234	0,00049054
P-values	0.04039629	0,43116989	0,03694557	0,21843982	0,13858823	0,00547196	0,01574987	0.00177105
Gamma2	0,83521689	0,95707898	0.88504432	0,89312760	0,94105886	0.82262114	0,85497610	0.76765438
Standard Errors	0.04879889	0,01645519	0,04099494	0,02760132	0,02266837	0,04672156	0,03720383	0,05157669
P-values	0,00000000	0,00000000	0,00000000	0,00000000	0,00000000	0,00000000	0,00000000	0,00000000
Gamma3	0,11735834	0.03900505	0,08184844	0,09275516	0,06775656	0,12805921	0,07679764	0,09695122
Standard Errors	0,06140570	0,03540911	0,06380620	0,04803210	0,04535518	0.06656319	0,05503566	0.07157060
P-values	0.02798968	0.13532784	0,09978698	0,02673487	0,06759959	0,02718518	0,08144482	0,08776875
Gamma4	0.36321569	0,14103196	0,27106946	0.30274286	0,14907100	0,41192514	0,33684333	0,58885158
Standard Errors	0,09708589	0,04617475	0,08482238	0.07319042	0,05042497	0.10265008	0,07899142	0.12400703
P-values	0,00009158	0,00112790	0.00069739	0,00001764	0,00155681	0.00002999	0,00001003	0.00000103
RQ in sample	2,54396526	2,09956890	2,15853049	2,11442608	1,45746330	1,89514595	1,98644896	1,81697045
RQ out of sample	0,38444406	0,38403630	0,41965080	0,33817263	0,33707825	0,33598512	0,45251029	0,32176644
Hit in sample (%)	4.86	4,98	4,98	4,98	4,92	5,05	4,86	4,98
Hit out of sample(%)	6,00	5,60	8,00	6.40	7,60	4,80	9,60	6,80
DQ in sample (p-values)								
1)[c,hit(-1 to -5)]	0.19035689	0.26852600	0,84793199	0,86579087	0,06860823	0,99999975	0,18481075	0,89176518
2)[VaR]	0,84865618	0,91810124	0,98770336	0,97797818	0,85752806	0,95080346	0,70905873	0,88617259
3)[c,hit(-1),VaR]	0.49712682	0,99954912	0,78315299	0,76476463	0,79110472	0.99916000	0,24254864	0.79424655
4)[c,hit(-1 to -5),VaR]	0,27388198	0,35887395	0,90828782	0,92394530	0,10538829	0,99999998	0,25384039	0,92818434
DQ out of sample (p-values)								
1)[c,hit(-1 to -5)]	0.70574180	0,88143394	0,02361866	0,45776257	0,40285230	0,84047108	0,00279093	0,60146876
2)[VaR]	0.84099249	0,62417872	0,06057472	0,51996073	0,24477164	0.57420416	0,00191405	0.98001602
3)[c,hit(-1),VaR]	0,14782943	0,95415180	0,03329767	0,34531013	0,34699590	0,32773084	0,00108329	0,00240061
4)[c,hit(-1 to -5),VaR]	0,23666487	0,93336657	0,01890478	0,35484512	0,36375842	0,55881172	0,00538125	0,03053200

Table 9. Parameter Estimates and Relevant Statistics for the Indirect GARCH(1,1) Model.

0.1% quantile	MIB30	CAC40	DAX	IBEX	FTSE	AEX	OMX	SMI
Gamma1	0,00064609	0,00008622	0,00014797	0,00042717	0,00014529	0,00000705	0,00000005	0,00015345
Standard Errors	-	-	-	-	-	-	-	-
P-values	-	-	-	-	-	-	-	-
Gamma2	0,41635293	0,90221208	0,83828451	0,79133566	0,64276638	0,86463513	0,78729128	0,72854358
Standard Errors	-	-	-	-	-	-	-	-
P-values	-	-	-	-	-	-	-	-
Gamma3	3,23637327	0,44844568	1,51071071	1,26644188	1,83159785	1,37377147	2,50365037	1,23994221
Standard Errors	-	-	-	-	-	-	-	-
P-values	-	-	-	-	-	-	-	-
RQ in sample	0,07754602	0,06458125	0,07663348	0,09425287	0,04553213	0,07417376	0,06898635	0,05384694
RQ out of sample	0,01172993	0,01423142	0,01349307	0,01366393	0,01840896	0,03255371	0,01334092	0,01970088
Hit in sample (%)	0,12	0,06	0,12	0,06	0,06	0,06	0,12	0,06
Hit out of sample(%)	0,00	0,40	0,00	0,00	0,40	0,40	0,00	0,40
DQ in sample (p-values)								
1)[c,hit(-1 to -5)]	-	-	-	-	-	-	-	-
2)[VaR]	-	-	-	-	-	-	-	-
3)[c,hit(-1),VaR]	-	-	-	-	-	-	-	-
4)[c,hit(-1 to -5),VaR]	-	-	-	-	-	-	-	-
DQ out of sample (p-values)								
1)[c,hit(-1 to -5)]	-	-	-	-	-	-	-	-
2)[VaR]	-	-	-	-	-	-	-	-
3)[c,hit(-1),VaR]	-	-	-	-	-	-	-	-
4)[c,hit(-1 to -5),VaR]	-	-	-	-	-	-	-	-

1% quantile	MIB30	CAC40	DAX	IBEX	FTSE	AEX	OMX	SMI
Gamma1	0,00008011	0,00000657	0,00011998	0,00001677	0,00000083	0,00000831	0,00003899	0,00003934
Standard Errors	0,00003065	0,00000723	0,00007004	0,00001962	0,00000224	0,00000784	0,00001990	0,00001573
P-values	0,00447801	0,18189934	0,04334944	0,19635691	0,35472493	0,14449525	0,02505878	0,00618294
Gamma2	0,77589768	0,94139174	0,65637915	0,81016566	0,97618325	0,87311607	0,76899912	0,74229156
Standard Errors	0,04564368	0,02141225	0,12853325	0,06764858	0,01477432	0,03910702	0,05287923	0,05030063
P-values	0,00000000	0,00000000	0,00000016	0,00000000	0,00000000	0,00000000	0,00000000	0,00000000
Gamma3	0,91901688	0,33464810	2,05647851	1,05927162	0,14135056	0,82101179	1,08220814	1,46308580
Standard Errors	0,19613455	0,12743925	0,88877015	0,41508361	0,08478331	0,28067594	0,26543589	0,31733494
P-values	0,00000140	0,00432047	0,01033805	0,00535613	0,04773752	0,00172160	0,00002280	0,00000201
RQ in sample	0,65238196	0,54523106	0,63133102	0,62624323	0,40360202	0,50993885	0,54775189	0,48017072
RQ out of sample	0,08979436	0,09102608	0,11963475	0,10133091	0,08790270	0,10011108	0,10548820	0,09300954
Hit in sample (%)	1,00	1,00	1,00	0,93	0,93	1,00	1,00	1,06
Hit out of sample(%)	0,80	0,80	2,00	1,20	0,80	1,20	1,20	1,20
DQ in sample (p-values)								
1)[c,hit(-1 to -5)]	0,00043677	0,14293681	0,99064747	0,99306111	0,46068356	0,99064747	0,17904018	0,56878521
2)[VaR]	0,95207305	0,97524116	0,85489872	0,88616554	0,75220235	0,85427740	0,94310736	0,85275240
3)[c,hit(-1),VaR]	0,97974241	0,20497133	0,94766910	0,96634841	0,96852679	0,95804262	0,98032190	0,96673886
4)[c,hit(-1 to -5),VaR]	0,00064845	0,20459187	0,99651948	0,99444825	0,57075743	0,99590541	0,23464263	0,68232861
DQ out of sample (p-values)								
1)[c,hit(-1 to -5)]	0,99992863	0,99992863	0,95422512	0,99910405	0,99992863	0,99910405	0,99910405	0,99910405
2)[VaR]	0,91185431	0,80282176	0,84750478	0,79141337	0,64222690	0,96390085	0,87092839	0,91177967
3)[c,hit(-1),VaR]	0,86515814	0,67452662	0,02194630	0,11299339	0,22797040	0,62180750	0,91607400	0,31405494
4)[c,hit(-1 to -5),VaR]	0,99322473	0,97980596	0,20353025	0,54234495	0,72582937	0,97076290	0,99877250	0,82286184

5% quantile	MIB30	CAC40	DAX	IBEX	FTSE	AEX	OMX	SMI
Gamma1	0,00001852	0,00000049	0,00000223	0,00000414	0,00000048	0,00000668	0,00000868	0,00000797
Standard Errors	0,00001250	0,00000237	0,00000271	0,00000493	0,00000111	0,00000529	0,00000727	0,00000809
P-values	0,06926199	0,41809325	0,20545774	0,20068190	0,33249815	0,10348084	0,11642562	0,16233992
Gamma2	0,86768331	0,96064865	0,92598300	0,84640322	0,93690806	0,84301360	0,87063646	0,83918200
Standard Errors	0,04206798	0,01794557	0,02734498	0,04135796	0,02196843	0,05905718	0,04510508	0,06628811
P-values	0,00000000	0,00000000	0,00000000	0,00000000	0,00000000	0,00000000	0,00000000	0,00000000
Gamma3	0,26549929	0,10702089	0,17664509	0,38828402	0,15959611	0,38543898	0,27754588	0,43197872
Standard Errors	0,08581875	0,05054131	0,06925872	0,11348535	0,05614958	0,16122010	0,10287388	0,19306075
P-values	0,00098831	0,01710901	0,00537826	0,00031145	0,00223919	0,00840671	0,00348867	0,01262595
RQ in sample	2,58271652	2,11254276	2,18929044	2,16207416	1,46694912	1,93912154	2,07802345	1,90288664
RQ out of sample	0,35704102	0,35785789	0,39400503	0,34645312	0,33624511	0,35974794	0,41711738	0,31531460
Hit in sample (%)	4,92	4,98	4,98	4,98	4,98	4,98	4,98	5,05
Hit out of sample(%)	5,60	5,20	6,80	7,20	6,80	6,00	6,00	6,00
DQ in sample (p-values)								
1)[c,hit(-1 to -5)]	0,06176044	0,61717495	0,67950541	0,52025393	0,31326260	0,24603004	0,29384203	0,12038389
2)[VaR]	0,94386283	0,96888415	0,99253260	0,93158991	0,99144110	0,88778828	0,96224249	0,89738989
3)[c,hit(-1),VaR]	0,96519409	0,94736080	0,96850783	0,77412718	0,77233484	0,99124284	0,75510594	0,41261077
4)[c,hit(-1 to -5),VaR]	0,09506856	0,72713531	0,77761786	0,61467604	0,41906192	0,34170772	0,39329733	0,18271572
DQ out of sample (p-values)								
1)[c,hit(-1 to -5)]	0,95474673	0,80637690	0,23750781	0,00624322	0,74373530	0,87886651	0,33573878	0,69614055
2)[VaR]	0,92970879	0,65125201	0,39177357	0,24894098	0,48242439	0,94805704	0,43583701	0,96273899
3)[c,hit(-1),VaR]	0,24360933	0,67305855	0,50099983	0,07970197	0,79606890	0,26111375	0,36976739	0,05315058
4)[c,hit(-1 to -5),VaR]	0,62130844	0,61251670	0,23009717	0,00267431	0,77632853	0,61275286	0,44425374	0,24258182

Table 10. Estimated Parameters and Standard Errors for the Model (37) with Break Point Fixed Equal to the Observations 1212, 1213, 1214, 1215. This Table Also Shows the Value of the p-Value of the Wald Test with Restrictions (39), (40), (41).

	1212	1213	1214	1215
GAMMA 1	0,00006095	0,00006289	0,00006189	0,00006466
Standard Errors	0,00002936	0,00003234	0,00003380	0,00003583
GAMMA 2	0,63001203	0,58053647	0,70818086	0,70640935
Standard Errors	0,07456628	0,07936215	0,08428493	0,09048549
GAMMA 3	2,73149609	3,32059610	1,94499825	1,94790786
Standard Errors	0,66517856	0,78838696	0,64311749	0,69613665
GAMMA 4	0,85203332	0,84735334	0,85060953	0,84445421
Standard Errors	0,05940175	0,06549995	0,06834656	0,06404104
GAMMA 5	0,73389671	0,76385068	0,74006671	0,76977594
Standard Errors	0,41131245	0,45543336	0,47370601	0,45707948
Wald test p-value 1	0,02131234	0,00921231	0,27422324	0,30573242
Wald test p-value 2	0,00612142	0,00241259	0,11352352	0,14322434
Wald test p-value 3	0,00951242	0,00462345	0,12217980	0,14850707

Table 11. Estimated Parameters and Relevant Statistics for the Models "Indirect GARCH with Volume" (33), "Asymmetric Slope with Volume" (34), "IGARCH(1,2)" (36) and "IGARCH(2,1)" (35) for the Dax Index.

1% quantile	IGARCH with VOLUME	ASYM.SLOPE with VOLUME	IGARCH(1,2)	IGARCH(2,1)
Gamma1	0,00000004	2,62709E-07	0,00025821	0,00012001
Standard Errors	0,00134447	0,015693538	0,00007830	0,00007472
P-values	0,49998762	0,499993322	0,00048765	0,05411711
Gamma2	0,65560878	0,744331937	0,19882197	0,65616029
Standard Errors	0,13100397	0,081949296	0,12950079	0.123480941
P-values	0,00000028	5,28914E-20	0,06235565	0,00000005
Gamma3	2,05714611	0,416173098	2,28676550	0,00015235
Standard Errors	0,90386003	0,198361888	0,68684552	0,40278774
P-values	0,01142431	0,017950378	0,00043521	0,49984910
Gamma4	0,00004289	0,79356514	2,57836827	2,05674008
Standard Errors	0,00049209	0,242734307	0,96454460	1,02918441
P-values	0,46527083	0,000539118	0,00375718	0,02283571
Gamma5	-	0,00107224	-	-
Standard Errors	-	0,005794561	-	-
P-values	-	0,426597856	-	-
RQ in sample	0,63178156	0,609969023	0,62698934	0,63237254
RQ out of sample	0,11834749	0,15482084	0,15024798	0,11859389
Hit in sample (%)	1,12	1,00	1,00	1,00
Hit out of sample(%)	1,60	2,00	3,60	1,60
DQ in sample (p-values)				
1)[c,hit(-1 to -5)]	0,58469337	0,990741988	0,99074199	0,99074199
2)[VaR]	0,44000469	0,915831192	0,96686860	0,84854658
3)[c,hit(-1),VaR]	0,72119902	0,976611212	0,98309195	0,94712943
4)[c,hit(-1 to -5),VaR]	0,58658941	0,996915015	0,99593683	0,99653876
DQ out of sample (p-values)				
1)[c,hit(-1 to -5)]	0,94938862	0,464045385	0,00008244	0,94938862
2)[VaR]	0,83166208	0,371358567	0,04696342	0,83457372
3)[c,hit(-1),VaR]	0,02002093	0,000172864	0,00000000	0,01979282
4)[c,hit(-1 to -5),VaR]	0,19138357	0,005488179	0,00000000	0,18996783

Table 12. Estimated Parameters and Standard Errors for the GPD Distribution for a Fixed Number of Exceedances.

	MIB30	CAC40	DAX	IBEX	FTSE	AEX	OMX	SMI
Xi	0,0252125	0,0076498	0,1351397	0,2262775	0,0139824	0,1782819	0,0743450	0,0796783
Standard Errors	0,0692058	0,0784601	0,0920454	0,0955796	0,0885735	0,0860874	0,0822369	0,0737386
Beta	0,0092848	0,0080886	0,0086272	0,0070084	0,0059017	0,0074860	0,0077205	0,0077984
Standard Errors	0,0011661	0,0008939	0,0011188	0,0009446	0,0007371	0,0009085	0,0008947	0,0008103
Number of exceedences	130	165	135	135	130	160	160	200
0.1% quantile	-0,06300378	-0,05130085	-0,06725726	-0,06870650	-0,03794718	-0,06517363	-0,05586907	-0,05576212
1% quantile	-0,03979995	-0,03217323	-0,03618382	-0,03441773	-0,02372697	-0,03305987	-0,03286478	-0,03166536
5% quantile	-0,02436271	-0,01782551	-0,01954381	-0,01911082	-0,01405583	-0,01727847	-0,01897033	-0,01726345

Table 13. Estimated 0.1%, 1% and 5% Quantile of the Standardized Residuals of the GARCH(1,1) Model by Using the Historical Simulation and the EVT.

	MIB30	CAC40	DAX	IBEX	FTSE	AEX	OMX	SMI
0.1% quantile								
Empirical quantile	-3,1398138	-3,3430734	-4,3505951	-4,0773907	-3,6525172	-3,3256099	-3,5306533	-3,5911020
EVT quantile	-3,1858217	-3,2754747	-4,6109965	-4,1063843	-3,6125115	-3,7821132	-3,3299590	-3,4165100
1% quantile								
Empirical quantile	-2,3584120	-2,5197349	-2,8159265	-2,5709877	-2,5551355	-2,6327012	-2,3766764	-2,6431396
EVT quantile	-2,3822553	-2,4851578	-2,6264625	-2,5544407	-2,4314618	-2,6176399	-2,3970685	-2,5985848
5% quantile								
Empirical quantile	-1,6157244	-1,6187977	-1,5829160	-1,5951814	-1,6005809	-1,6475738	-1,6000128	-2,6431396
EVT quantile	-1,5988528	-1,5371934	-1,5930416	-1,5407728	-1,5939294	-1,6071782	-1,5465780	-2,5985848

Table 14. Number of Exceedances and Percentage of Coverage for All the Model Estimated. The Results Reported are Referring to the In Sample Data.[19]

0.1% quantile Sample = 1305 obs. Expected exceeses = 1/2	MIB30	CAC40	DAX	IBEX	FTSE	AEX	OMX	SMI
Historical Simulation	0,0031	0,0069	0,0038	0,0077	0,0046	0,0069	0,0046	0,0069
	4	9	5	10	6	9	6	9
Evt	0,0008	0,0015	0,0008	0,0046	0,0000	0,0000	0,0015	0,0000
	1	2	1	3	0	0	2	0
GARCH	0,0031	0,0031	0,0084	0,0023	0,0046	0,0031	0,0023	0,0031
with normal innovations	4	4	11	6	6	4	3	4
J.P Morgan's	0,0031	0,0031	0,0092	0,0054	0,0054	0,0061	0,0023	0,0061
RiskMetrics	4	4	12	7	7	8	3	8
QML GARCH	0,0008	0,0015	0,0023	0,0008	0,0008	0,0015	0,0015	0,0008
with empirical quantile	1	2	3	1	1	2	2	1
QML GARCH	0,0008	0,0015	0,0008	0,0008	0,0008	0,0008	0,0023	0,0008
with Evt quantile	1	2	1	1	1	1	3	1
CAViaR	0,0008	0,0015	0,0015	0,0015	0,0015	0,0015	0,0015	0,0015
Adaptive	1	2	2	2	2	2	2	2
	0,0008	0,0015	0,0015	0,0015	0,0015	0,0015	0,0015	0,0015
Prop. Sym. Adaptive	1	2	2	2	2	2	2	2
	0,0023	0,0008	0,0015	0,0015	0,0008	0,0015	0,0008	0,0008
Sym. Absolute Value	3	1	2	2	1	2	1	1
	0,0008	0,0008	0,0015	0,0015	0,0008	0,0015	0,0008	0,0008
Asym. Absolute Value	1	1	2	2	1	2	1	1
	0,0008	0,0008	0,0015	0,0008	0,0015	0,0008	0,0000	0,0023
Asymmetric Slope	1	1	2	1	2	1	0	3
	0,0015	0,0008	0,0015	0,0008	0,0008	0,0008	0,0015	0,0015
Indirect Garch	2	1	2	1	1	1	2	2
1% quantile Sample = 1305 obs. Expected exceeses = 13	MIB30	CAC40	DAX	IBEX	FTSE	AEX	OMX	SMI
Historical Simulation	0,0130	0,0145	0,0115	0,0168	0,0138	0,0145	0,0123	0,0130
	17	19	15	22	18	19	16	17
Evt	0,0123	0,0130	0,0130	0,0107	0,0138	0,0153	0,0115	0,0138
	16	17	17	14	18	20	15	18
GARCH	0,0138	0,0207	0,0191	0,0138	0,0145	0,0176	0,0123	0,0214
with normal innovations	18	27	25	18	19	23	16	28
J.P Morgan's	0,0145	0,0199	0,0176	0,0168	0,0161	0,0207	0,0130	0,0191
RiskMetrics	19	26	23	22	21	27	17	25
QML GARCH	0,0123	0,0123	0,0123	0,0092	0,0107	0,0115	0,0123	0,0107
with empirical quantile	16	16	16	12	14	15	16	14
QML GARCH	0,0100	0,0138	0,0130	0,0092	0,0123	0,0123	0,0107	0,0115
with Evt quantile	13	18	17	12	16	16	14	15
CAViaR								
Adaptive	-	-	0,0100	-	-	-	-	-
	-	-	13	-	-	-	-	-
Prop. Sym. Adaptive	-	-	0,0115	-	-	-	-	-
	-	-	15	-	-	-	-	-
Sym. Absolute Value	-	-	0,0115		-	-	-	0,0115
	-	-	15	-	-	-	-	15
Asym. Absolute Value	-	-	0,0115	-	-	-	-	-
	-	-	15	-	-	-	-	-
Asymmetric Slope	0,0092	-	0,0115	0,0115	-	-	-	-
	12	-	15	15	-	-	-	-
Indirect Garch	-	0,0100	0,0115	-	0,0107	0,0100	0,0092	-
	-	13	15	-	14	13	12	-
5% quantile Sample = 1305 obs. Expected exceeses = 65	MIB30	CAC40	DAX	IBEX	FTSE	AEX	OMX	SMI
Historical Simulation	0,0567	0,0574	0,0582	0,0574	202143951/100	0,0597	0,0574	0,0574
	74	75	76	75	87	78	75	75
Evt	0,0528	0,0590	0,0536	0,0582	0,0551	0,0528	0,0536	0,0544
	69	77	70	76	72	69	70	71
GARCH	0,0490	0,0567	0,0521	0,0513	0,0544	0,0574	0,0521	0,0582
with normal innovations	64	74	68	67	71	75	68	76
J.P Morgan's	0,0429	0,0582	0,0498	0,0467	0,0505	0,0544	0,0490	0,0567
RiskMetrics	56	76	65	61	66	71	64	74
QML GARCH	0,0505	0,0574	0,0574	0,0574	0,0590	0,0574	0,0613	0,0551
with empirical quantile	66	75	75	75	77	75	80	72
QML GARCH	0,0521	0,0666	0,0574	0,0597	0,0590	0,0620	0,0658	0,0582
with Evt quantile	68	87	75	78	77	81	86	76
CAViaR								
Adaptive	-	-	-	-	-	-	-	-
	-	-	-	-	-	-	-	-
Prop. Sym. Adaptive	-	-	-	-	0,0521	-	-	-
	-	-	-	-	68	-	-	-
Sym. Absolute Value	-	-	-	-	-	-	0,0536	0,0505
	-	-	-	-	-	-	70	66
Asym. Absolute Value	-	-	-	-	-	-	-	-
	-	-	-	-	-	-	-	-
Asymmetric Slope	-	-	-	0,0490	-	0,0521	-	-
	-	-	-	64	-	68	-	-
Indirect Garch	0,0482	0,0521	0,0521	-	-	-	-	-
	63	68	68	-	-	-	-	-

Table 15. Number of Exceedances and Percentage of Coverage for All the Model Estimated. The Results Reported are Referring to the Out of Sample Data.[20]

0.1% quantile Sample = 250 obs. Expected exceeses = 0/1	MIB30	CAC40	DAX	IBEX	FTSE	AEX	OMX	SMI
Historical Simulation	0,000	0,004	0,000	0	0,004	0	0,000	0,000
	0	1	0	0	1	0	0	0
Evt	0,000	0	0,000	0,000	0,004	0,000	0,000	0,000
	0	0	0	0	1	0	0	0
GARCH	0,000	0,004	0,004	0,004	0,004	0,004	0,000	0,004
with normal innovations	0	1	1	1	1	1	0	1
J.P Morgan's	0,000	0,004	0,004	0,8	0,004	0,004	0,000	0,004
RiskMetrics	0	1	1	2	1	1	0	1
QML GARCH	0,000	0,004	0,000	0,000	0,004	0,004	0,000	0,004
with empirical quantile	0	1	0	0	1	1	0	1
QML GARCH	0,000	0,004	0,000	0,000	0,004	0,004	0,000	0,004
with Evt quantile	0	1	0	0	1	1	0	1
CAViaR								
Adaptive	0,000	0,000	0,000	0,000	0,004	0,000	0,000	0,000
	0	0	0	0	1	0	0	0
Prop. Sym. Adaptive	0,000	0,000	0,000	0,000	0,004	0,000	0,000	0,000
	0	0	0	0	1	0	0	0
Sym. Absolute Value	0,000	0,004	0,000	0,000	0,004	0,004	0,000	0,004
	0	1	0	0	1	1	0	1
Asym. Absolute Value	0,008	0,004	0,000	0,000	0,004	0,004	0,000	0,004
	2	1	0	0	1	1	0	1
Asymmetric Slope	0,004	0,004	0,000	0,000	0,004	0,008	0,000	0,004
	1	1	0	0	1	2	0	1
Indirect Garch	0,000	0,004	0,000	0,000	0,004	0,004	0,000	0,004
	0	1	0	0	1	1	0	1

1% quantile Sample = 250 obs. Expected exceeses = 2/3	MIB30	CAC40	DAX	IBEX	FTSE	AEX	OMX	SMI
Historical Simulation	0,008	0,020	0,004	0,008	0,008	0,004	0,020	0,004
	2	5	1	2	2	1	5	1
Evt	0,004	0,016	0,000	0,004	0,036	0,004	0,020	0,004
	1	4	0	1	9	1	5	1
GARCH	0,008	0,016	0,020	0,016	0,016	0,016	0,020	0,016
with normal innovations	2	4	5	4	4	4	5	4
J.P Morgan's	0,024	0,012	0,012	0,024	0,008	0,016	0,008	0,008
RiskMetrics	6	3	3	6	2	4	2	2
QML GARCH	0,008	0,012	0,012	0,012	0,008	0,016	0,016	0,008
with empirical quantile	2	3	3	3	2	4	4	2
QML GARCH	0,008	0,012	0,012	0,012	0,008	0,016	0,012	0,008
with Evt quantile	2	3	3	3	2	4	3	2
CAViaR								
Adaptive	-	-	0,008	-	-	-	-	-
	-	-	2	-	-	-	-	-
Prop. Sym. Adaptive	-	-	0,000	-	-	-	-	-
	-	-	0	-	-	-	-	-
Sym. Absolute Value	-	-	0,020	-	-	-	-	0,012
	-	-	5	-	-	-	-	3
Asym. Absolute Value	-	-	0,020	-	-	-	-	-
	-	-	5	-	-	-	-	-
Asymmetric Slope	0,008	-	0,020	0,008		-	-	-
	2	-	5	2		-	-	-
Indirect Garch	-	0,008	0,016	-	0,008	0,012	0,012	-
	-	2	4	-	2	3	3	-

5% quantile Sample = 250 obs. Expected exceeses = 12/13	MIB30	CAC40	DAX	IBEX	FTSE	AEX	OMX	SMI
Historical Simulation	0,048	0,052	0,044	0,052	0,044	0,040	0,084	0,012
	12	13	11	13	11	10	21	3
Evt	0,048	0,076	0,104	0,080	0,120	0,068	0,112	0,052
	12	19	26	20	30	17	28	13
GARCH	0,072	0,056	0,072	0,076	0,068	0,064	0,064	0,088
with normal innovations	18	14	18	19	17	16	16	22
J.P Morgan's	0,064	0,056	0,064	0,064	0,064	0,052	0,044	0,052
RiskMetrics	16	14	16	16	16	13	11	13
QML GARCH	0,076	0,060	0,076	0,076	0,072	0,064	0,064	0,072
with empirical quantile	19	15	19	19	18	16	16	18
QML GARCH	0,076	0,068	0,076	0,084	0,072	0,068	0,080	0,076
with Evt quantile	19	17	19	21	18	17	20	19
CAViaR								
Adaptive	-	-	-	-	-	-	-	-
	-	-	-	-	-	-	-	-
Prop. Sym. Adaptive	-	-	-	-	0,060	-	-	-
	-	-	-	-	15	-	-	-
Sym. Absolute Value	-	-	-	-	-	-	0,060	0,048
	-	-	-	-	-	-	15	12
Asym. Absolute Value	-	-	-	-	-	-	-	-
	-	-	-	-	-	-	-	-
Asymmetric Slope	-	-	-	6,400	-	0,048	-	-
	-	-	-	16	-	12	-	-
Indirect Garch	0,056	0,052	0,068	-	-	-	-	-
	14	13	17	-	-	-	-	-

Table 16. This Table Shows the Components of Christoffersen's Test Applied to Our Family of Models for the In Sample Data (at 5% Level of Significance). The First Column Gives the Name of the Model, the Next Columns Give for Each Index the Value of the Estimated LR Statistics and the p-Value.

	MIB30			CAC40			DAX			IBEX			FTSE			AEX			OMX			SMI		
	LRuc	LRind	LRcc	LRuc	LRind	LRcc	LRuc	LRind	LRcc	LRuc	LRind	LRcc	LRuc	LRind	LRcc	LRuc	LRind	LRcc	LRuc	LRind	LRcc	LRuc	LRind	LRcc
Historical Simulation	1,172	6,783	8,071	1,450	0,119	1,688	1,757	2,697	4,574	1,450	13,618	15,186	6,905	4,385	11,428	2,454	5,408	7,985	1,450	4,526	6,097	1,450	6,421	7,990
p-value	0,279	0,009	0,018	0,228	0,730	0,430	0,185	0,101	0,102	0,228	0,000	0,001	0,009	0,036	0,003	0,117	0,020	0,018	0,228	0,033	0,047	0,228	0,011	0,018
Evt	0,217	27,728	28,053	2,092	1,312	3,525	0,348	6,298	6,757	1,757	8,184	10,041	0,701	12,507	13,321	0,348	10,847	11,306	0,348	10,847	11,306	0,510	13,044	13,666
p-value	0,641	0,000	0,000	0,148	0,252	0,172	0,555	0,012	0,034	0,185	0,004	0,007	0,402	0,000	0,001	0,555	0,001	0,004	0,555	0,001	0,004	0,475	0,000	0,001
GARCH with normal innovations	0,027	2,333	2,461	1,172	0,164	1,453	0,116	0,648	0,871	0,046	1,770	1,922	0,510	0,346	0,968	1,757	0,081	1,958	0,116	0,648	0,871	1,757	0,048	1,925
p-value	0,868	0,127	0,292	0,279	0,685	0,484	0,733	0,421	0,647	0,830	0,183	0,383	0,475	0,556	0,616	0,185	0,776	0,376	0,733	0,421	0,647	0,185	0,827	0,382
J.P Morgan's RiskMetrics	1,462	6,604	8,154	1,757	0,081	1,958	0,001	2,234	2,337	0,304	4,897	5,298	0,008	1,948	2,060	0,027	0,007	0,135	0,027	0,007	0,135	1,172	0,780	2,069
p-value	0,227	0,010	0,017	0,185	0,776	0,376	0,970	0,135	0,311	0,581	0,027	0,071	0,929	0,163	0,357	0,868	0,934	0,935	0,868	0,934	0,935	0,279	0,377	0,355
QML GARCH with empirical quantile	0,008	1,948	2,060	1,450	0,673	2,242	1,450	0,726	2,295	1,450	6,421	7,990	2,092	0,050	2,264	3,260	0,262	3,648	3,260	0,262	3,648	0,701	0,289	1,104
p-value	0,929	0,163	0,357	0,228	0,412	0,326	0,228	0,394	0,317	0,228	0,011	0,018	0,148	0,822	0,322	0,071	0,609	0,161	0,071	0,609	0,161	0,402	0,591	0,576
QML GARCH with EVT quantile	0,116	1,602	1,825	6,805	0,270	7,313	1,450	0,726	2,295	2,454	9,581	12,159	2,092	0,050	2,264	6,308	0,022	6,467	6,308	0,022	6,467	1,757	0,048	1,925
p-value	0,733	0,206	0,402	0,009	0,604	0,026	0,228	0,394	0,317	0,117	0,002	0,002	0,148	0,822	0,322	0,012	0,882	0,039	0,012	0,882	0,039	0,185	0,827	0,382
CAViaR *Adaptive*	-	-	-	-	-	-	-	-	-	-	-	-	-	-	-	-	-	-	-	-	-	0,007	0,352	0,463
p-value	-	-	-	-	-	-	-	-	-	-	-	-	-	-	-	-	-	-	-	-	-	0,932	0,553	0,793
Prop. Sym. Adaptive	-	-	-	-	-	-	-	-	-	-	-	-	0,006	0,212	0,322	-	-	-	-	-	-	-	-	-
p-value	-	-	-	-	-	-	-	-	-	-	-	-	0,936	0,645	0,851	-	-	-	-	-	-	-	-	-
Sym. Absolute Value	-	-	-	-	-	-	-	-	-	-	-	-	-	-	-	-	-	-	0,007	0,211	0,322	0,007	0,211	0,322
p-value	-	-	-	-	-	-	-	-	-	-	-	-	-	-	-	-	-	-	0,932	0,646	0,851	0,932	0,646	0,851
Asym. Absolute Value	-	-	-	-	-	-	-	-	-	-	-	-	-	-	-	-	-	-	-	-	-	-	-	-
p-value	-	-	-	-	-	-	-	-	-	-	-	-	-	-	-	-	-	-	-	-	-	-	-	-
Asymmetric Slope	-	-	-	-	-	-	-	-	-	0,119	0,828	1,053	-	-	-	0,007	0,002	0,113	-	-	-	-	-	-
p-value	-	-	-	-	-	-	-	-	-	0,731	0,363	0,591	-	-	-	0,932	0,962	0,945	-	-	-	-	-	-
Indirect Garch	0,021	3,784	3,906	0,001	1,139	1,243	0,202	0,178	0,488	-	-	-	-	-	-	-	-	-	-	-	-	-	-	-
p-value	0,886	0,052	0,142	0,979	0,266	0,537	0,653	0,673	0,784	-	-	-	-	-	-	-	-	-	-	-	-	-	-	-

Table 17. This Table Shows the Components of Christoffersen's Test Applied to our Family of Models for the In Sample Data (at 1% Level of Significance). The First Column Gives the Name of the Model, the Next Columns Give for Each Index the Value of the Estimated LR Statistics and the p-Value.

	MIB30			CAC40			DAX			IBEX			FTSE			AEX			OMX			SMI		
	LRuc	LRind	LRcc	LRuc	LRind	LRcc	LRuc	LRind	LRcc	LRuc	LRind	LRcc	LRuc	LRind	LRcc	LRuc	LRind	LRcc	LRuc	LRind	LRcc	LRuc	LRind	LRcc
Historical Simulation	1,096	11,062	12,184	2,393	0,561	2,984	0,278	1,955	2,256	5,127	0,763	5,924	1,688	0,504	2,220	2,393	0,561	2,984	0,624	1,734	2,382	1,096	0,449	1,571
p-value	0,295	0,001	0,002	0,122	0,454	0,225	0,598	0,162	0,324	0,024	0,382	0,052	0,194	0,478	0,330	0,122	0,454	0,225	0,430	0,188	0,304	0,295	0,503	0,456
Evt	0,624	1,734	2,382	1,096	1,532	2,654	1,096	5,639	6,762	0,067	13,536	13,624	1,688	1,348	3,064	3,204	1,028	4,263	0,278	6,622	6,923	1,688	10,354	12,071
p-value	0,430	0,188	0,304	0,295	0,216	0,265	0,295	0,018	0,034	0,796	0,000	0,001	0,194	0,246	0,216	0,073	0,311	0,119	0,598	0,010	0,031	0,194	0,001	0,002
GARCH with normal innovations	1,688	0,504	2,220	11,490	1,141	12,673	8,697	0,937	9,673	1,688	0,504	2,220	2,393	0,561	2,984	6,230	0,825	7,091	0,624	0,504	2,220	13,002	0,232	13,278
p-value	0,194	0,478	0,330	0,001	0,285	0,002	0,003	0,333	0,008	0,194	0,478	0,330	0,122	0,454	0,225	0,013	0,364	0,029	0,430	0,478	0,330	0,000	0,630	0,001
J.P Morgan's RiskMetrics	2,393	1,180	3,603	10,054	1,057	11,152	6,230	0,649	6,914	5,127	0,763	5,924	4,118	0,687	4,837	11,490	0,297	11,829	1,096	1,532	2,654	8,897	0,453	9,188
p-value	0,122	0,277	0,165	0,002	0,304	0,004	0,013	0,421	0,032	0,024	0,382	0,052	0,042	0,407	0,089	0,001	0,586	0,003	0,295	0,216	0,265	0,003	0,501	0,010
QML GARCH with empirical quantile	0,624	0,397	1,046	0,624	0,397	1,046	0,624	0,397	1,046	0,089	0,223	0,331	0,067	0,304	0,392	0,278	0,349	0,650	0,624	0,397	1,046	0,067	0,304	0,392
p-value	0,430	0,529	0,593	0,430	0,529	0,593	0,430	0,529	0,593	0,765	0,637	0,848	0,796	0,582	0,822	0,598	0,555	0,723	0,430	0,529	0,593	0,796	0,582	0,822
QML GARCH with EVT quantile	0,000	0,262	0,282	1,688	0,504	2,220	1,096	0,449	1,571	0,089	0,223	0,331	0,624	0,397	1,046	0,624	0,397	1,046	0,067	0,304	0,392	0,278	0,349	0,650
p-value	0,987	0,609	0,869	0,194	0,478	0,330	0,295	0,503	0,456	0,765	0,637	0,848	0,430	0,529	0,593	0,430	0,529	0,593	0,796	0,582	0,822	0,598	0,555	0,723
CAViaR *Adaptive*	-	-	-	-	-	-	0,000	2,081	2,101	-	-	-	-	-	-	-	-	-	-	-	-	-	-	-
p-value	-	-	-	-	-	-	0,990	0,149	0,350	-	-	-	-	-	-	-	-	-	-	-	-	-	-	-
Prop. Sym. Adaptive	-	-	-	-	-	-	0,000	6,880	6,900	-	-	-	-	-	-	-	-	-	-	-	-	-	-	-
p-value	-	-	-	-	-	-	0,990	0,009	0,032	-	-	-	-	-	-	-	-	-	-	-	-	-	-	-
Sym. Absolute Value	-	-	-	-	-	-	0,000	0,322	0,343	-	-	-	-	-	-	-	-	-	-	-	-	0,000	0,322	0,343
p-value	-	-	-	-	-	-	0,990	0,570	0,843	-	-	-	-	-	-	-	-	-	-	-	-	0,990	0,570	0,843
Asym. Absolute Value	-	-	-	-	-	-	0,000	0,302	0,322	-	-	-	-	-	-	-	-	-	-	-	-	-	-	-
p-value	-	-	-	-	-	-	0,990	0,583	0,851	-	-	-	-	-	-	-	-	-	-	-	-	-	-	-
Asymmetric Slope	0,000	0,322	0,343	-	-	-	0,000	0,322	0,343	0,000	0,322	0,343	-	-	-	-	-	-	-	-	-	-	-	-
p-value	0,990	0,570	0,843	-	-	-	0,990	0,570	0,843	0,990	0,570	0,843	-	-	-	-	-	-	-	-	-	-	-	-
Indirect Garch	-	-	-	0,000	0,322	0,343	0,000	0,322	0,343	-	-	-	0,071	0,283	0,373	0,000	0,322	0,343	0,000	0,322	0,343	-	-	-
p-value				0,990	0,570	0,843	0,990	0,570	0,843	-	-	-	0,790	0,595	0,830	0,990	0,570	0,843	0,990	0,570	0,843	-	-	-

Table 18. This Table Shows the Components of Christoffersen's Test Applied to Our Family of Models for the Out of Sample Data (at 5% Level of Significance). The First Column Gives the Name of the Model, the Next Columns Give for Each Index the Value of the Estimated LR Statistics and the p-Value.

	MIB30			CAC40			DAX			IBEX			FTSE			AEX			OMX			SMI		
	LRuc	LRind	LRcc	LRuc	LRind	LRcc	LRuc	LRind	LRcc	LRuc	LRind	LRcc	LRuc	LRind	LRcc	LRuc	LRind	LRcc	LRuc	LRind	LRcc	LRuc	LRind	LRcc
Historical Simulation	0,021	2,498	2,618	0,021	0,150	0,278	0,197	0,467	0,755	0,021	0,150	0,278	0,197	0,467	0,755	0,563	0,837	1,482	5,097	0,872	6,145	10,812	0,073	10,910
p-value	0,884	0,114	0,270	0,885	0,699	0,870	0,657	0,494	0,686	0,885	0,699	0,870	0,657	0,494	0,686	0,453	0,360	0,477	0,024	0,350	0,046	0,001	0,787	0,004
Evt	0,021	2,498	2,618	3,091	0,181	3,430	11,865	1,536	13,622	4,040	3,190	7,397	18,850	0,093	19,200	1,540	2,494	4,175	15,197	2,757	18,192	0,021	1,433	1,561
p-value	0,884	0,114	0,270	0,079	0,671	0,180	0,001	0,215	0,001	0,044	0,074	0,025	0,000	0,760	0,000	0,215	0,114	0,124	0,000	0,097	0,000	0,885	0,231	0,458
GARCH with normal innovations	2,256	0,087	2,492	0,183	0,060	0,358	2,256	2,808	5,213	3,091	0,181	3,430	1,540	0,592	2,273	0,951	2,199	3,283	0,951	0,851	1,935	6,259	4,271	10,715
p-value	0,133	0,768	0,288	0,669	0,806	0,836	0,133	0,094	0,074	0,079	0,671	0,180	0,215	0,442	0,321	0,329	0,138	0,194	0,329	0,356	0,380	0,012	0,039	0,005
J.P. Morgan's RiskMetrics	0,951	0,001	1,085	0,183	0,060	0,358	0,951	2,199	3,283	0,951	0,001	1,085	0,951	0,851	1,935	0,021	1,433	1,561	0,197	0,467	0,755	0,021	1,433	1,561
p-value	0,329	0,976	0,581	0,669	0,806	0,836	0,329	0,138	0,194	0,329	0,976	0,581	0,329	0,356	0,380	0,885	0,231	0,458	0,657	0,494	0,686	0,885	0,231	0,458
QML GARCH with empirical quantile	3,091	0,181	3,430	0,496	0,011	0,631	3,091	3,143	6,392	3,091	0,181	3,430	2,256	0,383	2,789	0,951	2,199	3,283	0,951	0,851	1,935	2,256	2,808	5,213
p-value	0,079	0,671	0,180	0,481	0,915	0,729	0,079	0,076	0,041	0,079	0,671	0,180	0,133	0,536	0,248	0,329	0,138	0,194	0,329	0,356	0,380	0,133	0,094	0,074
QML GARCH with EVT quantile	3,091	0,181	3,430	1,540	0,027	1,708	3,091	3,143	6,392	5,097	0,463	5,736	2,256	0,383	2,789	1,540	0,027	1,708	4,040	1,186	5,393	3,091	3,143	6,392
p-value	0,079	0,671	0,180	0,215	0,870	0,426	0,079	0,076	0,041	0,024	0,496	0,057	0,133	0,536	0,248	0,215	0,870	0,426	0,044	0,276	0,067	0,079	0,076	0,041
CAViaR *Adaptive*	-	-	-	-	-	-	-	-	-	-	-	-	-	-	-	-	-	-	-	-	-	0,021	1,216	1,336
p-value	-	-	-	-	-	-	-	-	-	-	-	-	-	-	-	-	-	-	-	-	-	0,884	0,270	0,513
Prop. Sym. Adaptive	-	-	-	-	-	-	-	-	-	-	-	-	0,496	1,166	1,786	-	-	-	-	-	-	-	-	-
p-value	-	-	-	-	-	-	-	-	-	-	-	-	0,481	0,280	0,409	-	-	-	-	-	-	-	-	-
Sym. Absolute Value	-	-	-	-	-	-	-	-	-	-	-	-	-	-	-	-	-	-	0,496	1,166	1,786	0,021	1,216	1,336
p-value	-	-	-	-	-	-	-	-	-	-	-	-	-	-	-	-	-	-	0,481	0,280	0,409	0,884	0,270	0,513
Asym. Absolute Value	-	-	-	-	-	-	-	-	-	-	-	-	-	-	-	-	-	-	-	-	-	-	-	-
p-value	-	-	-	-	-	-	-	-	-	-	-	-	-	-	-	-	-	-	-	-	-	-	-	-
Asymmetric Slope	-	-	-	-	-	-	-	-	-	0,951	0,001	1,085	-	-	-	0,021	1,216	1,336	-	-	-	-	-	-
p-value	-	-	-	-	-	-	-	-	-	0,329	0,976	0,581	-	-	-	0,884	0,270	0,513	-	-	-	-	-	-
Indirect Garch	0,183	0,060	0,358	0,021	0,150	0,278	1,540	2,494	4,175	-	-	-	-	-	-	-	-	-	0,496	1,166	1,786	-	-	-
p-value	0,669	0,806	0,836	0,885	0,699	0,870	0,215	0,114	0,124	-	-	-	-	-	-	-	-	-	0,481	0,280	0,409	-	-	-

Table 19. This Table Shows the Components of Christoffersen's Test Applied to Our Family of Models for the Out of Sample Data (at 1% Level of Significance). The First Column Gives the Name of the Model, the Next Columns Give for Each Index the Value of the Estimated LR Statistics and the p-Value.

	MIB30			CAC40			DAX			IBEX			FTSE			AEX			OMX			SMI		
	LRuc	LRind	LRcc	LRuc	LRind	LRcc	LRuc	LRind	LRcc	LRuc	LRind	LRcc	LRuc	LRind	LRcc	LRuc	LRind	LRcc	LRuc	LRind	LRcc	LRuc	LRind	LRcc
Historical Simulation	0,108	0,032	0,157	1,957	0,205	2,202	1,176	-	-	1,176	0,008	1,193	0,108	0,032	0,157	1,176	-	-	1,957	3,154	5,151	1,176	-	-
p-value	0,742	0,857	0,925	0,162	0,651	0,333	0,278	-	-	0,278	0,928	0,551	0,742	0,857	0,925	0,278	-	-	0,162	0,076	0,076	0,278	-	-
Evt	1,176	-	-	0,769	4,107	4,908	5,025	-	-	1,176	-	-	10,229	1,006	11,309	1,176	-	-	1,957	3,154	5,151	1,176	-	-
p-value	0,278	-	-	0,380	0,043	0,086	0,025	-	-	0,278	-	-	0,001	0,316	0,004	0,278	-	-	0,162	0,076	0,076	0,278	-	-
GARCH with normal innovations	0,108	0,032	0,157	0,769	4,107	4,908	1,957	0,205	2,202	0,769	0,131	0,932	0,769	0,131	0,932	0,769	0,131	0,932	1,957	0,205	2,202	0,769	0,131	0,932
p-value	0,742	0,857	0,925	0,380	0,043	0,086	0,162	0,651	0,333	0,380	0,718	0,627	0,380	0,718	0,627	0,380	0,718	0,627	0,162	0,651	0,333	0,380	0,718	0,627
J.P. Morgan's RiskMetrics	3,555	2,423	6,027	0,095	0,073	0,192	0,095	0,073	0,192	3,555	2,423	6,027	0,108	0,032	0,157	0,769	0,131	0,932	0,108	0,032	0,157	0,108	0,032	0,157
p-value	0,059	0,120	0,049	0,758	0,787	0,908	0,758	0,787	0,908	0,059	0,120	0,049	0,742	0,857	0,925	0,380	0,718	0,627	0,742	0,857	0,925	0,742	0,857	0,925
QML GARCH with empirical quantile	0,108	0,032	0,157	0,095	0,073	0,192	0,095	0,073	0,192	0,095	0,073	0,192	0,108	0,032	0,157	0,769	0,131	0,932	0,769	0,131	0,932	0,108	0,032	0,157
p-value	0,742	0,857	0,925	0,758	0,787	0,908	0,758	0,787	0,908	0,758	0,787	0,908	0,742	0,857	0,925	0,380	0,718	0,627	0,380	0,718	0,627	0,742	0,857	0,925
QML GARCH with EVT quantile	0,108	0,032	0,157	0,095	0,073	0,192	0,095	0,073	0,192	0,095	0,073	0,192	0,108	0,032	0,157	0,769	0,131	0,932	0,095	0,073	0,192	0,108	0,032	0,157
p-value	0,742	0,857	0,925	0,758	0,787	0,908	0,758	0,787	0,908	0,758	0,787	0,908	0,742	0,857	0,925	0,380	0,718	0,627	0,758	0,787	0,908	0,742	0,857	0,925
CAViaR *Adaptive*	-	-	-	-	-	-	0,108	0,032	0,157	-	-	-	-	-	-	-	-	-	-	-	-	-	-	-
p-value	-	-	-	-	-	-	0,742	0,857	0,925	-	-	-	-	-	-	-	-	-	-	-	-	-	-	-
Prop. Sym. Adaptive	-	-	-	-	-	-	-	-	-	-	-	-	-	-	-	-	-	-	-	-	-	-	-	-
p-value	-	-	-	-	-	-	-	-	-	-	-	-	-	-	-	-	-	-	-	-	-	-	-	-
Sym. Absolute Value	-	-	-	-	-	-	1,957	0,205	2,202	-	-	-	-	-	-	-	-	-	-	-	-	0,095	0,073	0,192
p-value	-	-	-	-	-	-	0,162	0,651	0,333	-	-	-	-	-	-	-	-	-	-	-	-	0,758	0,787	0,908
Asym. Absolute Value	-	-	-	-	-	-	1,957	0,205	2,202	-	-	-	-	-	-	-	-	-	-	-	-	-	-	-
p-value	-	-	-	-	-	-	0,162	0,651	0,333	-	-	-	-	-	-	-	-	-	-	-	-	-	-	-
Asymmetric Slope	0,108	0,032	0,157	-	-	-	1,957	0,205	2,202	0,108	0,032	0,157	-	-	-	-	-	-	-	-	-	-	-	-
p-value	0,742	0,857	0,925	-	-	-	0,162	0,651	0,333	0,742	0,857	0,925	-	-	-	-	-	-	-	-	-	-	-	-
Indirect Garch	-	-	-	0,108	0,032	0,157	0,769	0,131	0,932	-	-	-	0,108	0,032	0,157	0,095	0,073	0,192	0,095	0,073	0,192	-	-	-
p-value	-	-	-	0,742	0,857	0,925	0,380	0,718	0,627	-	-	-	0,742	0,857	0,925	0,758	0,787	0,908	0,758	0,787	0,908	-	-	-

Table 20. The Table Reports: (1) The Parameter Estimates and the Relevant Statistics for the 7.5% CAViaR Specifications; (2) The Estimated Parameter of the GPD Fitted to the Standardized Quantile Residuals of the 7.5% CAViaR Model; (3) the DQ Test and the Number of Hit for CAViaR & EVT.

Percentile 7.5%	Adaptive	Prop.Sym.	Sym.Abs.	Asym.Abs	Asym.Slope	IGARCH
Gamma1	0,00152011	0,32595068	0,00015076	0,00000001	0,00026448	0,00000264
Standard Errors	-	0,03009037	0,00001761	0,00017086	0,00004271	0,00000333
P-values	-	0,00000000	0,00000000	0,49998784	0,00000000	0,09133729
Gamma2	-	0,04258856	0,90370936	0,90663055	0,91050090	0,89581288
Standard Errors	-	0,00355589	0,00316837	0,02211825	0,00706042	0,02787111
P-values	-	0,00000000	0,00000000	0,00000000	0,00000000	0,00000000
Gamma3	-	-	0,15202921	0,15944406	0,06889494	0,18323654
Standard Errors	-	-	0,00491398	0,03517938	0,01078514	0,04028949
P-values	-	-	0,00000000	0,00000292	0,00000000	0,01902688
Gamma4	-	-	-	0,00425182	0,19425153	-
Standard Errors	-	-	-	0,00114213	0,01356474	-
P-values	-	-	-	0,00009854	0,00000000	-
RQ in sample	2,97542847	2,91690081	2,90338619	2,87391367	2,87236976	2,90801377
RQ out of sample	0,55337940	0,54550721	0,55533630	0,56414260	0,55775695	0,54886433
Hit in sample (%)	7,77	7,90	7,46	7,41	7,46	7,52
Hit out of sample (%)	7,69	9,72	9,31	10,40	10,12	8,50
DQ in sample (p-values)						
1)[c,hit(-1 to -5)]	0,29543379	0,71156864	0,64322958	0,87377205	0,61833846	0,57432062
2)[VaR]	0,97794069	0,86496854	0,97237777	0,99244659	0,98919600	0,96549937
3)[c,hit(-1),VaR]	0,64275612	0,71075859	0,99276726	0,76668602	0,57108416	0,99976000
4)[c,hit(-1 to -5),VaR]	0,26963463	0,66607768	0,74368316	0,90759139	0,72114971	0,68030125
DQ out of sample (p-values)						
1)[c,hit(-1 to -5)]	0,04137183	0,47124106	0,87606510	0,74006500	0,70460601	0,69539524
2)[VaR]	0,94286326	0,22064225	0,35872166	0,26471824	0,17705092	0,73521924
3)[c,hit(-1),VaR]	0,39400500	0,17419545	0,49546052	0,13441664	0,25335698	0,79615135
4)[c,hit(-1 to -5),VaR]	0,02197122	0,50320050	0,81812538	0,50641672	0,71167774	0,70099546

	0.1%	1%	5%
Hit in sample (%)	0,19	0,93	5,05
Hit out of sample(%)	0,00	1,20	6,80
DQ in sample (p-values)			
1)[c,hit(-1 to -5)]	-	0,47627139	0,68575649
2)[VaR]	-	0,59432401	0,95872689
3)[c,hit(-1),VaR]	-	0,86497979	0,73870004
4)[c,hit(-1 to -5),VaR]	-	0,51021037	0,76991768
DQ out of sample (p-values)			
1)[c,hit(-1 to -5)]	-	0,99910405	0,23750781
2)[VaR]	-	0,93572453	0,43596834
3)[c,hit(-1),VaR]	-	0,27188427	0,39280354
4)[c,hit(-1 to -5),VaR]	-	0,77171614	0,18361333

N. of exceedances	100
Threshold	0,0593
Xi	0,0665
Standard Errors	0,1241
Beta	0,4737
Standard Errors	0,0692
0.1% quantile	2,3107
1% quantile	0,9794
5% quantile	0,1628

FIGURES 1–16 (inclusive)

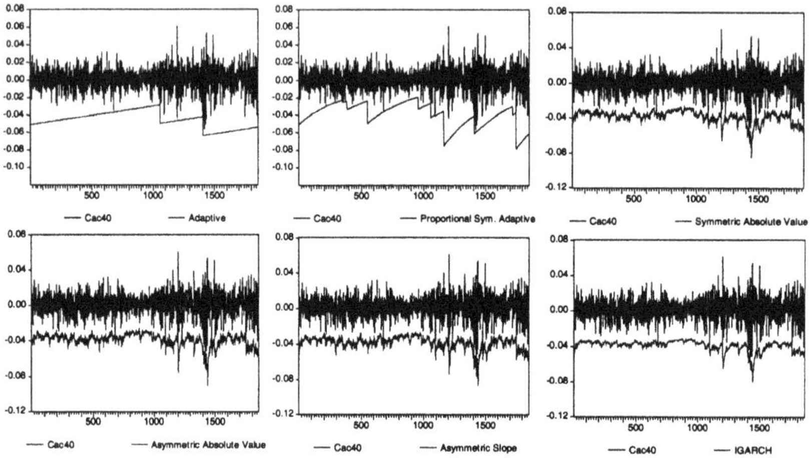

Fig. 1. 0.1% CAViaR Plots for Cac40.

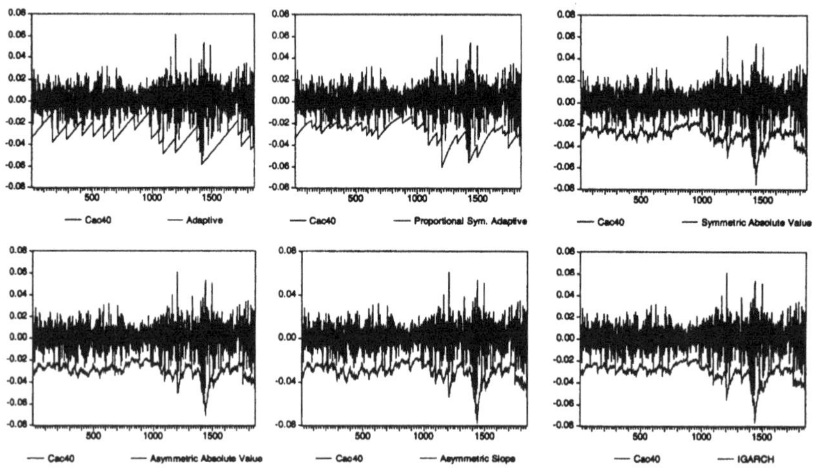

Fig. 2. 1% CAViaR Plots for Cac40.

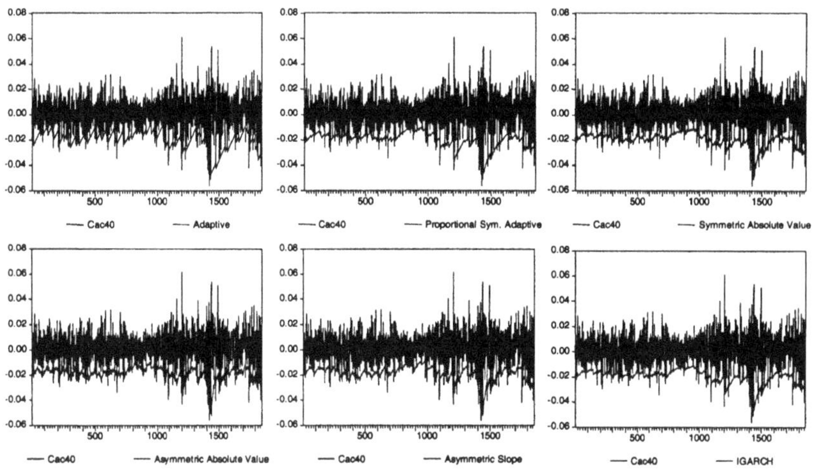

Fig. 3. 5% CAViaR Plots for Cac40.

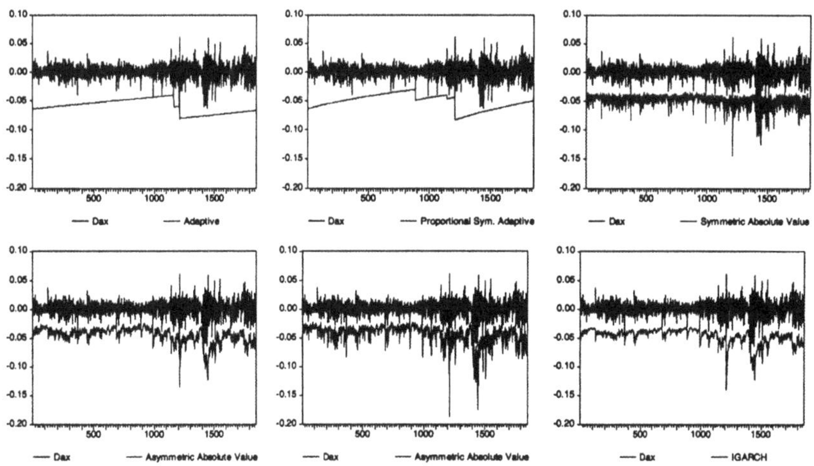

Fig. 4. 0.1% CAViaR Plots for Dax.

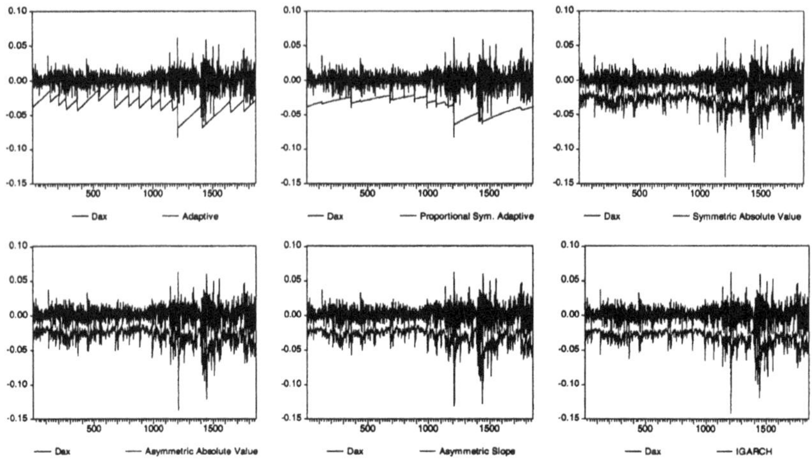

Fig. 5. 1% CAViaR Plots for Dax.

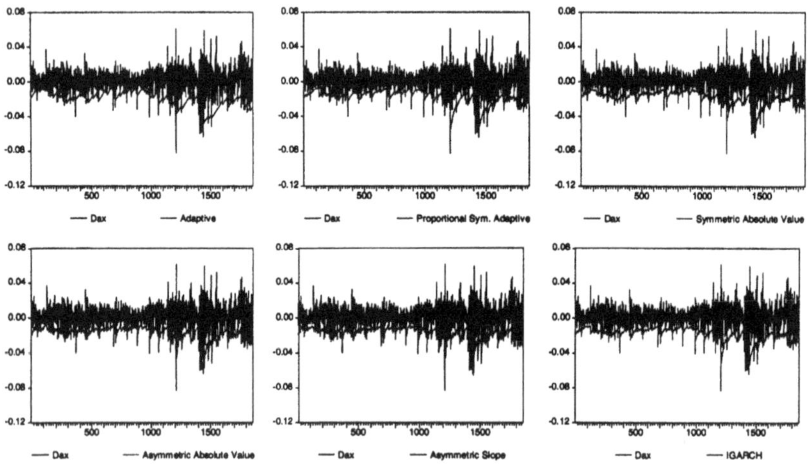

Fig. 6. 5% CAViaR Plots for Dax.

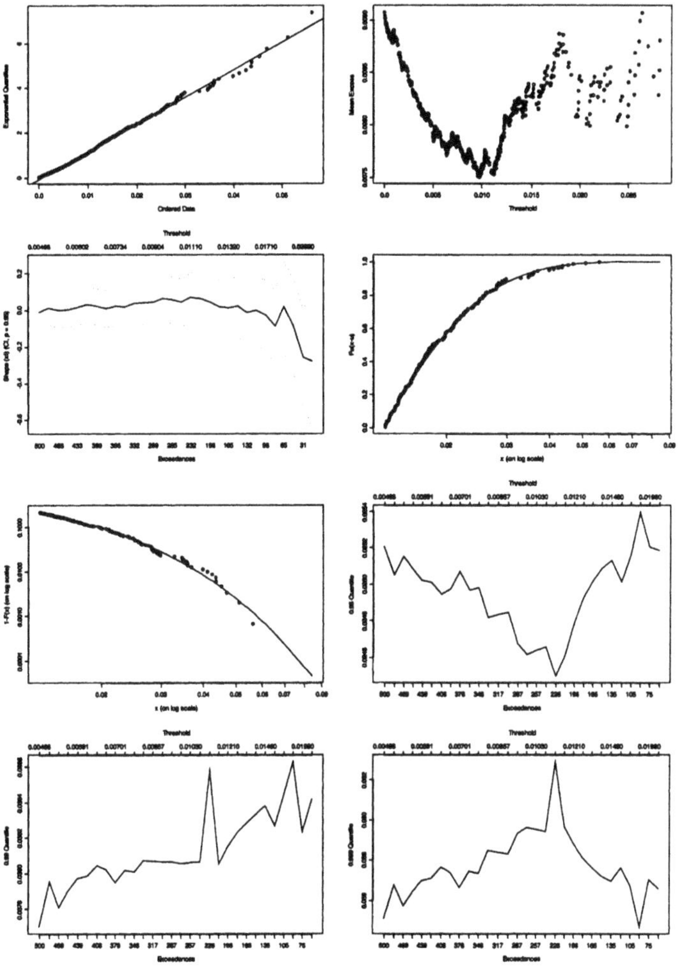

Fig. 7. Analysis of the Index Cac40. Starting from the Left Top we have the QQ-Plot Against the Exponential Distribution, the Mean Excess Function Plot, the Plot of the Shape Parameter by Decreasing Threshold and Decreasing Number of Exceedances, the Excess Function Calculated for the Estimated Parameters ($\xi = 0.2262$, $\beta = 0.0070$), the Estimate of the Tail of the GPD by using the Estimated Parameters, and then the 0.1%, 1%, 5% Quantile Estimates for Increasing Threshold and Decreasing Number of Exceedances.

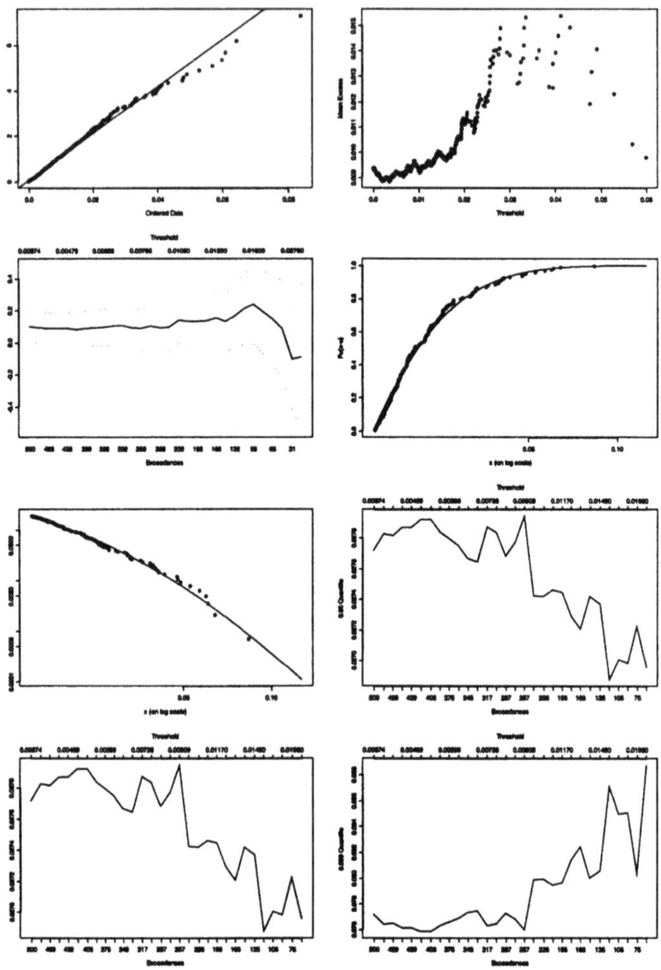

Fig. 8. Analysis of the Index Cac40. Starting from the Left Top we have the QQ-Plot Against the Exponential Distribution, the Mean Excess Function Plot, the Plot of the Shape Parameter by Increasing Threshold and Decreasing Number of Exceedances, the Excess Function Calculated for the Estimated Parameters ($\xi = 0.1351$, $\beta = 0.0086$), the Estimate of the Tail of the GPD by using the Estimated Parameters, and then the 0.1%, 1%, 5% Quantile Estimates for Increasing Threshold and Decreasing Number of Exceedances.

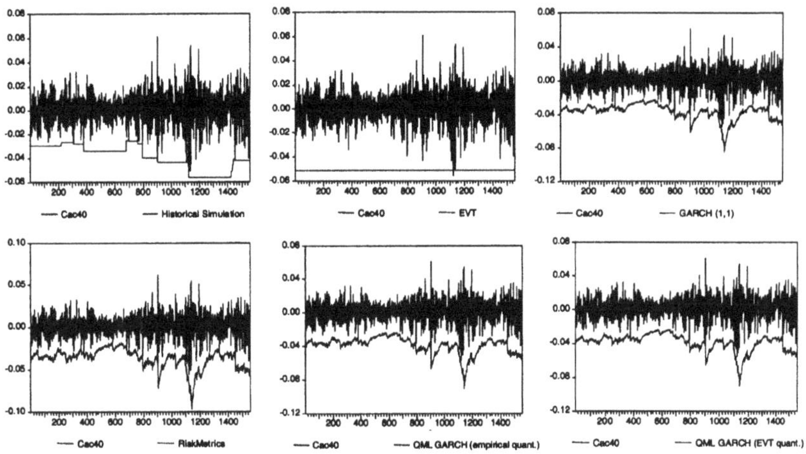

Fig. 9. 0.1% VaR for the Models Applied to Cac40.

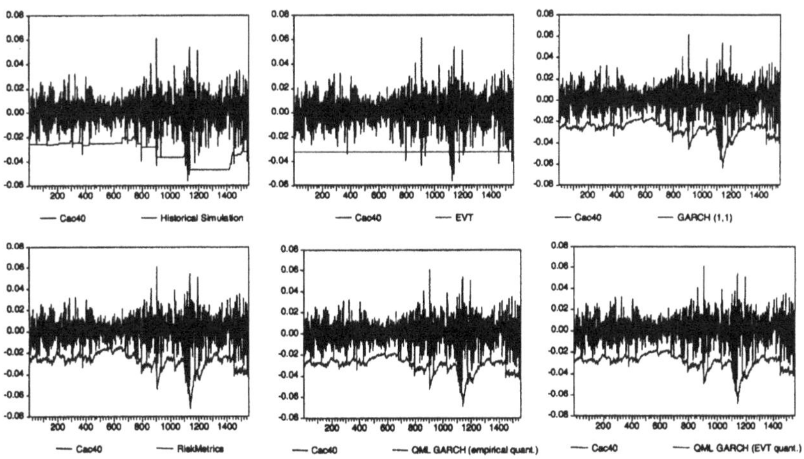

Fig. 10. 1% VaR for the Models Applied to Cac40.

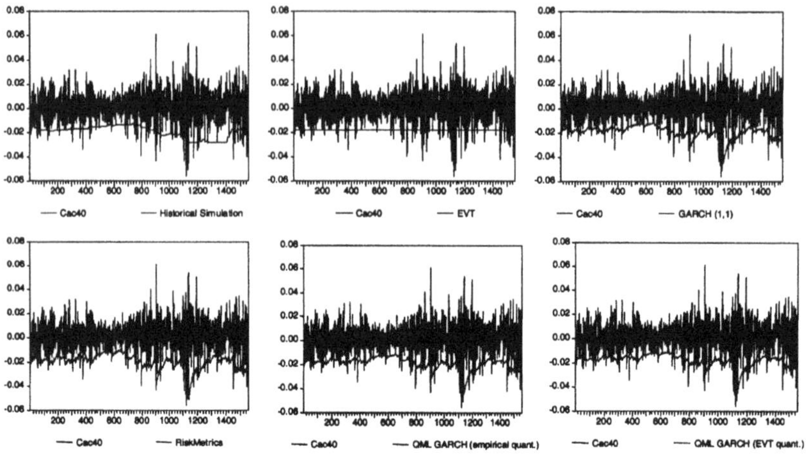

Fig. 11. 5% VaR for the Models Applied to Cac40.

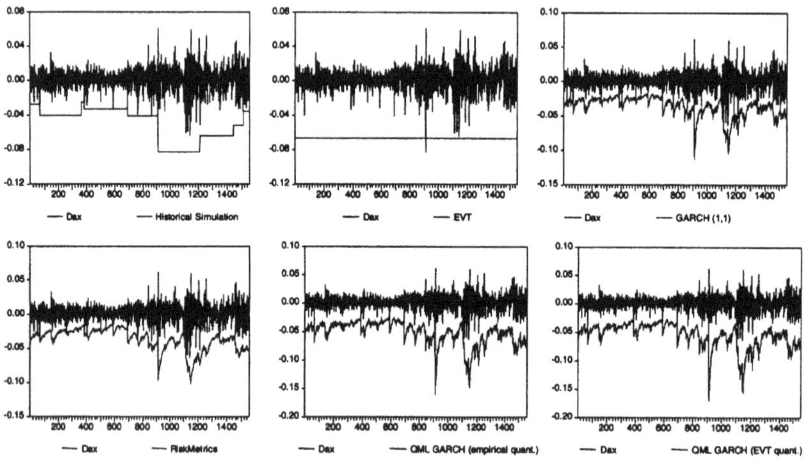

Fig. 12. 0.1% VaR for the Models Applied to Dax.

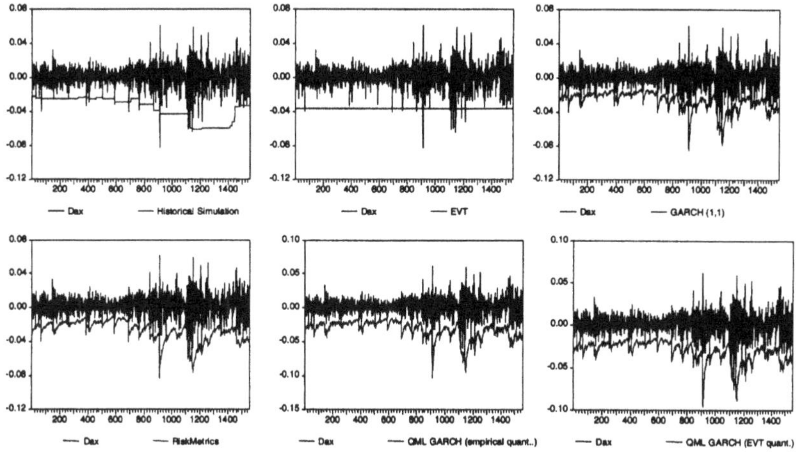

Fig. 13. 1% VaR for the Models Applied to Dax.

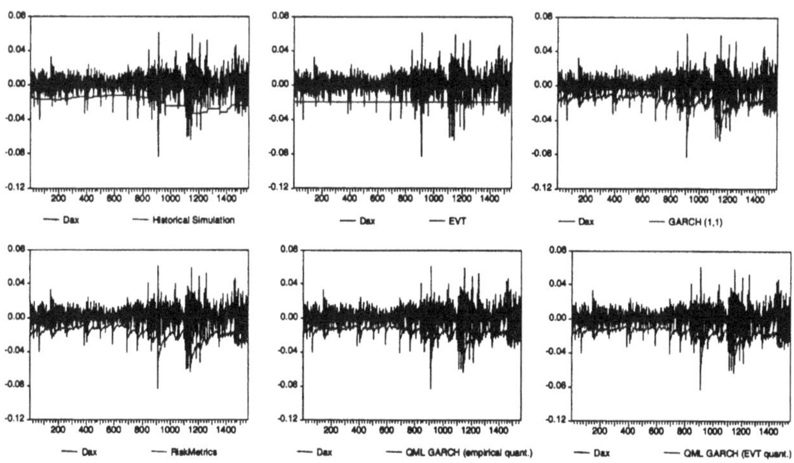

Fig. 14. 5% VaR for the Models Applied to Dax.

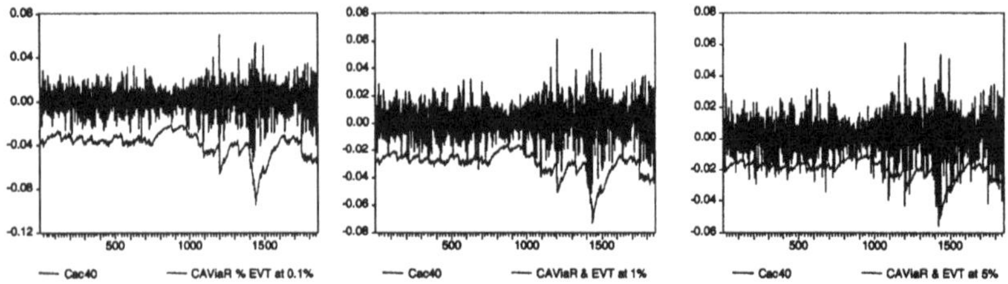

Fig. 15. 0.1%, 1% and 5% CAViaR&EVT plots Cac40.

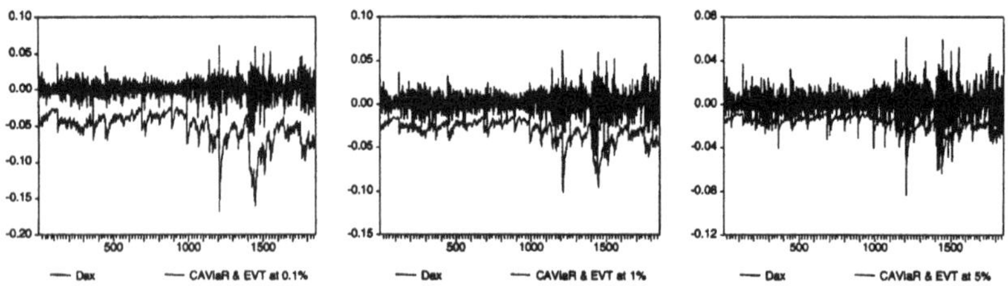

Fig. 16. 0.1%, 1% and 5% CAViaR&EVT plots Dax.

INTEREST RATE MODELS IN RISK MANAGEMENT: RESULTS FOR U.S. TREASURY YIELDS

K. Ben Nowman

ABSTRACT

This paper reviews recent developments in the empirical analysis of one and two-factor interest rate models used in risk management analysis. These models differ in their assumption between the volatility of rates and the level of rates. We discuss the empirical estimation of these models using monthly U.S. Treasury times series data and the recent approach of Gaussian estimation by Nowman (1997, 2001). We also compare optimal dynamic forecasts over a six-month period with those from a VAR model. The results indicate a strong volatility-level effect across maturities.

INTRODUCTION

The role of short-term interest rate models in the development of effective risk management procedures in banks is an important area of research in finance for academics and practitioners. The empirical estimation of these interest rate models in risk management has only been a recent development in current financial market practice for practitioners. Historically, it has been observed that when interest rates become very high they tend to revert to normal levels and vice versa. This is refereed to as mean reversion. In addition, interest rate models tend to incorporate either some relationship between the volatility of

Financial Risk and Financial Risk Management, Volume 16, pages 325–345.

ISBN: 0-7623-0858-3

rates and the level of rates or to assume no relationship. For risk management specialists the wide choice of models incorporating these features is extensive. The seminal paper by Chan, Karolyi, Longstaff and Sanders (1992, CKLS thereafter) developed a general single factor interest rate model which incorporated these general features and had the advantage of nesting a number of well known models developed previously. These included the models by Merton (1973), Vasicek (1977), Cox, Ingersoll, and Ross (1985, CIR thereafter), Dothan (1978), Brennan and Schwartz (1980), Cox, Ingersoll and Ross (1980) and the Constant Elasticity of Variance (CEV) and Geometric Brownian Motion (GBM) models. In CKLS they applied the estimation method of Generalized Method of Moments to one-month U.S. T-bill data and found that term structure models incorporating a relationship between the volatility of rates and the level of rates had a better fit to the data and indeed that this relationship was more dependent than the assumed relationship in those models. They also found weak evidence of mean reversion in interest rates. These empirical results have important implications for the choice of models for risk management. Since then a number of studies have followed the CKLS study for other international currencies, for example, Tse (1995), Dahlquist (1996), Hiraki and Takezawa (1997), Adkins and Krehbiel (1999).

An alternative approach to estimating these models is to use recently developed Gaussian estimation methods of Bergstrom (1983, 1984, 1985, 1986, 1990) for general linear continuous time models. These methods were first applied in finance to non-linear diffusions by Nowman (1997) who estimated the single factor CKLS model and its special cases. It was shown that the volatility of rates was not dependent on the level of rates in the U.K. in contrast to the CKLS results. This again will have implications for the risk management of portfolios in the U.K. and U.S. Further studies using this approach to other international markets are given in Nowman (1998), Byers and Nowman (1998), Nowman and Sorwar (1999) and Episcopos (2000).

One of the important questions in modelling the term structure is whether to use a multi-factor model which could allow a better representation of the dynamics of the term structure. Many models have been developed, for example, Brennan and Schwartz (1979), Langetieg (1980), Longstaff and Schwartz (1992) and Babbs and Nowman (1999).

In Nowman (2001) the Guassian estimation methods were extended using the approach of Nowman (1997) to estimate two-factor versions of the CKLS, Vasicek and CIR models. An application to one-month Euro-currency data for Japan and the U.K. indicated that the estimation method worked well in practice and provided realistic estimates. Nowman (2001) also used the optimal forecasting method developed by Bergstrom (1989) based on the discrete model used for estimation and compared the forecasting performance across the models (see also Byers & Nowman, 1998, 2001). In Bergstrom and Nowman (1999) the Gaussian estimation methods were extended to handle unobserved state variables and the likelihood function derived to estimate the multi-factor term structure model of Babbs and Nowman (1999). More recently, Saltoglu (2000) also applied the Gaussian estimation methods to the multi-factor model of Brennan and Schwartz (1979) with Canadian data. These studies all indicated that the general Gaussian estimation methodology worked well in practice and should provide an efficient way to discriminate between different models for risk management analysis. Our aims in this paper are to review these Gaussian estimation methods for risk management specialists and to provide some new empirical results using the approach of Nowman (2001) for U.S. Treasury yields.

The structure of the paper is as follows. In the second section we describe the different single and two-factor models. In the third section we discuss the econometric estimation of these models using the Gaussian estimation methods of Nowman (1997, 2001). In the fourth section we describe the data used in our empirical application. In the fifth section we discuss the empirical results and the forecasting performance of the models. The final section offers some conclusions.

ONE AND TWO FACTOR INTEREST RATE MODELS

In this section we discuss the single and two-factor interest rate models starting with the CKLS and its special cases. The CKLS model of the short-term interest rate is represented by equation (1) below. The equation allows the conditional mean and variance to depend on the level r

$$dr(t) = \{\alpha + \beta r(t)\}dt + \sigma r^{\gamma}(t)d\zeta(t) \qquad (t \geq 0) \tag{1}$$

where $\{r(t), t > 0\}$ is the short-term interest rate, α and β are the unknown drift and mean reversion structural parameters; σ is the volatility of the short-term rate and γ is the proportional volatility exponent. The error term is usually assumed to be a Wiener process. We use a weaker assumption using the theory of random measures applied to the error term by Bergstrom (1983, Theorem 1, 1984).

Assumption 1 Nowman (1997): ζ is a random measure defined on all subsets of the half line $0 < t < \infty$ with finite Lebesgue measure, such that: $E[\zeta(dt)] = 0$ and $E[\zeta(dt)^2] = dt$ and $E[\zeta(\Delta_1)\zeta(\Delta_2)] = 0$ for any disjoint sets Δ_1 and Δ_2 on the half line $0 < t < \infty$.

Table 1. Single Factor Interest Rate Models.

Model	α	β	σ^2	γ
CKLS $dr(t) = \{\alpha + \beta r(t)\}dt + \sigma r^{\gamma}(t)\zeta(dt)$				
Merton $dr(t) = \alpha dt + \sigma\zeta(dt)$		0		0
Vasicek $dr(t) = \{\alpha + \beta r(t)\}dt + \sigma\zeta(dt)$				0
CIR $dr(t) = \{\alpha + \beta r(t)\}dt + \sigma r^{1/2}(t)\zeta(dt)$				$1/2$
Dothan $dr(t) = \sigma r(t)\zeta(dt)$	0	0		1
GBM $dr(t) = \beta r(t)dt + \sigma r(t)\zeta(dt)$	0			1
Brennan-Schwartz $dr(t) = \{\alpha + \beta r(t)\}dt + \sigma r(t)\zeta(dt)$				1
CIR VR $dr(t) = \sigma r^{3/2}(t)\zeta(dt)$	0	0		$3/2$
CEV $dr(t) = \beta r(t)dt + \sigma r^{\gamma}(t)\zeta(dt)$	0			

Following CKLS we can obtain the various term structure models nested in CKLS as special cases by imposing the necessary restrictions on the structural parameters α, β, γ. The resulting term structure specifications are summarised in Table 1.

See CKLS for a discussion of these models in the literature. Nowman (1997) assumed that as an approximation to the true underlying model given by Eq. (1) that over the interval [0,T], $r(t)$ satisfied the stochastic differential equation

$$dr(t) = \{\alpha + \beta r(t)\}dt + \sigma\{r(t' - 1)\}^{\gamma} \quad \zeta(dt) \tag{2}$$

where $t' - 1$ is the largest integer less than t. Nowman (1997) assumed in Eq. (2) that the volatility of the interest rate changes at the beginning of the unit observation period and then remained constant. This assumption was made in order to use the Bergstrom (1983, 1990) formulation of the continuous time models (see Nowman, 1997, for further details). In Nowman (1997) Eq. (2) is interpreted as meaning that $r(t)$ satisfies the stochastic integral equation

$$r(t) - r(t' - 1) = \int_{t'-1}^{t} [\alpha + \beta r(s)]ds + \sigma\{r(t' - 1)\}^{\gamma} \int_{t'-1}^{t} d\zeta(s) \tag{3}$$

for all t in $[t' - 1, t']$

where

$$t' - 1 < t \leq t'$$

and

$$\int_{t'-1}^{t} d\zeta(s) = \zeta[t' - 1, t].$$

Table 2. Volatility – Level Assumptions for Two Factor Models.

Model	γ_1	γ_2
CKLS		
Vasicek	0	0
CIR	$^1/_2$	$^1/_2$

Two-Factor CKLS, Vasicek and CIR Models: Nowman (2001) considered the following two-factor CKLS version with correlated factors given by Eqs (4) and (5):

$$dr_1(t) = \{\alpha_1 + \beta_1 r_1(t)\}dt + \zeta_1(dt) \qquad (t \geq 0) \tag{4}$$

$$dr_2(t) = \{\alpha_2 + \beta_2 r_2(t)\}dt + \zeta_2(dt) \qquad (t \geq 0) \tag{5}$$

where $r_1(t)$ and $r_2(t)$ represented the short and long term interest rates and α_1, α_2, β_1 and β_2 are the drift and mean reversion parameters. Nowman (2001) assumed the error terms satisfied Assumption 2 below:

Assumption 2 Nowman (2001): ζ_1 and ζ_2 are random measures defined on all subsets of the half line $0 < t < \infty$ with finite Lebesgue measure, such that: $E[\zeta_1(dt)] = 0$, $E[\zeta_2(dt)] = 0$ and $E[\zeta_1(dt)\zeta_2(dt)] = (dt)\Sigma(r,t)$ where $\Sigma(r,t)$ was a positive definite matrix assumed in Nowman (2001, Eq. 4) to be:

$$\sum(r,t) = \begin{bmatrix} \sigma_1^2 r_1^{2\gamma_1}(t) & \rho_{12}\sigma_1\sigma_2 r_1^{\gamma_1}(t) r_2^{\gamma_2}(t) \\ \rho_{21}\sigma_2\sigma_1 r_2^{\gamma_2}(t) r_1^{\gamma_1}(t) & \sigma_2^2 r_2^{2\gamma_2}(t) \end{bmatrix}. \tag{6}$$

The assumption used in CKLS for the single-factor is represented by the first element. Nowman (2001) used the same assumption for the second factor but allowed them to be correlated. Nowman (2001) then used the assumption of constant volatility over the unit observation period applied to (6) as used in the single factor model case in Nowman (1997). The volatility-level assumptions for the two-factor models are given in Table 2.

GAUSSIAN ESTIMATION OF INTEREST RATE MODELS

The problem faced with testing which model one should use in developing effective risk management tools is that the available interest rate data is only available at discrete time periods, for example daily. We do not have a continuous time record of observations. Indeed, most macroeconomic data will be available only on a monthly or quarterly basis. Therefore, we must find a way of mapping the available discrete time data so that we can estimate the parameters of our continuous time model. Early work on estimating the parameters of continuous time models using discrete data was done by Bergstrom (1966) (see Bergstrom, 1988, 1996, for recent surveys). This work was based on using a discrete approximation to the continuous time model which had the disadvantage that the estimates were biased (see Bergstrom, 1984). It was shown in a important Monte Carlo study by Phillips (1972) that more efficient estimates of a continuous time model could be obtained by using an exact discrete model derived from the solution of the continuous time model rather than use the discrete approximation. The exact discrete model was suggested by Bergstrom (1966) but its practical implementation was not feasible given the computer resources of the day. Hence the discrete approximation become the standard approach to estimating continuous time models in the 1970s and 1980s (see Gandolfo, 1993, and the papers contained therein).

More recently new Gaussian estimation methods were developed in a seminal paper by Bergstrom (1983) based on the exact discrete model and in further related work for example, by Bergstrom (1984, 1985, 1986, 1990), Agbeyegbe (1984, 1987, 1988), Chambers (1991, 1996, 1998, 1999, 2000), Chambers and McGarry (2001), McGarry (2000), and Nowman (1991, 1993). The exact discrete model approach has the advantage that asymptotically efficient estimates of the continuous time model can be obtained (see Bergstrom, 1990, for full details).

For the single factor models Nowman (1997, Eqs 4–6) used the discrete model based on Bergstrom (1966, 1984, Theorem 2) modified for heteroscedasticity corresponding to Eq. (2) for estimation given below:

$$r(t) = e^{\beta} r(t-1) + \frac{\alpha}{\beta}(e^{\beta} - 1) + \eta_t \qquad (t = 1, 2, \ldots, T) \tag{7}$$

where η_t $(t = 1, 2, \ldots, T)$ satisfied the conditions

$$E(\eta_s \eta_t) = 0 \quad (s \neq t) \tag{8}$$

$$E(\eta_t^2) = \int_{t-1}^{t} e^{2(t-\tau)\beta} \sigma^2 \{r(t-1)\}^{2\gamma} d\tau = \frac{\sigma^2}{2\beta}(e^{2\beta} - 1)\{r(t-1)\}^{2\gamma} = m_{tt}^2. \tag{9}$$

Let the complete vector of parameters be defined as $\theta = [\alpha, \beta, \gamma, \sigma^2]$. Nowman (1997, Eq. 7) then defined $L(\theta)$ as minus twice the logarithm of the Gaussian likelihood function given below:

$$L(\theta) = \sum_{t=1}^{T} \left[2\, log\, m_{tt} + \frac{\{r(t) - e^{\beta} r(t-1) - \frac{\alpha}{\beta}(e^{\beta} - 1)\}^2}{m_{tt}^2} \right] \tag{10}$$

Nowman (1997) then used the Gaussian likelihood function in the same formulation used by Bergstrom (1983, 1990) given below:

$$L(\theta) = \sum_{t=1}^{T} [2 \log m_{tt} + \varepsilon_t^2] \tag{11}$$

where $\varepsilon_1, \ldots, \varepsilon_T$ can be computed from $m_{tt}\ \varepsilon_t = \eta_t$. As a more formal check on the dynamic specification of each continuous time model a Box-Pierce type portmanteau test statistic proposed by Bergstrom (1990) can be used. This uses the vector of transformed residuals which, if the model is correct, are independent and have variance 1. The statistic is given by

$$S = \frac{1}{n(T-l)} \sum_{i=1}^{l} \left(\sum_{t=l+1}^{T} \hat{\varepsilon}_t' \hat{\varepsilon}_{t-i} \right)^2$$

and is asymptotically distributed as chi-squared with l degrees of freedom $n = 1$ (see Bergstrom, 1990) for further details).

Turning to the estimation of the two-factor versions of the CKLS, Vasicek and CIR models. Nowman (2001, Eq. 6) used Bergstrom's (1984, Theorem 3) discrete model corresponding to Eqs (4–5) modified using the constant volatility assumption of Nowman (1997) given by Eq. (12) below. This exact discrete model was used first in empirical finance by Brennan and Schwartz (1979) to estimate their two-factor model (see Brennan & Schwartz, 1979) for the precise specification of their model and the implied exact discrete model coefficients).

$$r_t = e^{\beta} r_{t-1} + (e^{\beta} - I)\beta^{-1}\alpha + \varepsilon_t \qquad (t = 1, 2, \ldots, T) \tag{12}$$

where

$$e^{\beta} = I + \sum_{i=1}^{\infty} \frac{1}{i!}\beta^{i}$$

$$E(\varepsilon_t \varepsilon_t') = \int_0^1 e^{r\beta} \sum {}^{*}(r,t) e^{r\beta'} dr = \Omega(r,t)$$

$$\alpha = \begin{bmatrix} \alpha_1 \\ \alpha_2 \end{bmatrix}, \ \beta = \begin{bmatrix} \beta_1 & 0 \\ 0 & \beta_2 \end{bmatrix}$$

and Σ^* has the same general form as Eq. (6) above but subject to the constant volatility assumption over the unit observation period (see Nowman, 2001). Nowman (2001, Eq. 7) obtained the Gaussian estimates from numerical optimization of the Gaussian likelihood function below:

$$L(\theta) = \sum_{t=1}^{T} \log(|\Omega(r,t)|) + \sum_{t=1}^{T} \varepsilon_t' \Omega^{-1}(r,t) \varepsilon_t \qquad (13)$$

INTEREST RATE DATA

The interest rates used in this study are monthly U.S. Treasury constant maturities obtained from the Federal Reserve Statistical Release, H.15. The short end is represented by the three-month rate (r_1) and the long end is taken to be the one, two, three, five, seven and ten year rates (r_2) in each estimation case. The period covered in the empirical work is January 1982 to June 2000 giving a total of 221 observations. The last six-months are used for forecasting comparisons. Table 3 reports the summary statistics. The mean and standard deviations of the different series are as follows: three-month rate has a mean and standard deviation of 6.3743 and 2.2339%; one-year rate has a mean and standard deviation of 6.8827 and 2.3948%; two-year rate has a mean and standard deviation of 7.3601 and 2.4229%; three-year rate has a mean and standard deviation of 7.5606 and 2.4015%; five-year rate has a mean

Table 3. Monthly U.S. Treasury Yields.

$r(t)$	Mean	Standard Deviation
3-Month	0.0637	0.0223
1-Year	0.0688	0.0239
2-Year	0.0736	0.0242
3-Year	0.0756	0.0240
5-Year	0.0783	0.0235
7-Year	0.0804	0.0232
10-Year	0.0813	0.0230

and standard deviation of 7.8385 and 2.3598%; seven-year rate has a mean and standard deviation of 8.0482 and 2.3275%; ten-year rate has a mean and standard deviation of 8.1382 and 2.3002%.

EMPIRICAL RESULTS

In this section we present the Gaussian estimates (standard errors in brackets) of the two-factor term structure models. First estimating the one-factor CKLS model using Nowman (1997) on the three-month rate gave an estimate of $\gamma = 1.5780$. Following Nowman (1997, 2001) the explanatory power of each model is compared to the unrestricted model using the maximised Gaussian log likelihood function value. The first factor is always taken as the three-month rate.

One-Year:
We first estimated the model using the long rate as the one-year rate. Based on the maximized Gaussian log likelihood values compared to the unrestricted two-factor CKLS model the two-factor CIR model performs the best followed by the two-factor Vasicek model. Regarding the unrestricted model the Gaussian estimates of γ_1 and γ_2 are 1.5732 and 1.3965 for the three-month and one-year rates. There is weak evidence of mean reversion in the three-month rate compared to the one-year rate. The correlation parameters indicates 93% between the two-factors in the CKLS model and 92% in the Vasicek and CIR models. Based on the χ^2 likelihood ratio test under the null hypothesis that the nested models restrictions are valid the results imply that we can reject the two-factor Vasicek and CIR models.

Table 4. Gaussian Estimates of Two Factor Models: 3-Month and 1-Year.

Parameters	CKLS	Vasicek	CIR
α_1	0.0010	0.0025	0.0016
	(0.0005)	(0.0010)	(0.0008)
α_2	0.0017	0.0027	0.0021
	(0.0007)	(0.0011)	(0.0009)
β_1	− 0.0179	− 0.0407	− 0.0281
	(0.0114)	(0.0153)	(0.0134)
β_2	− 0.0285	− 0.0411	− 0.0329
	(0.0127)	(0.0150)	(0.0139)
γ_1	1.5732	0.0	0.5
	(0.0919)		
γ_2	1.3965	0.0	0.5
	(0.1028)		
σ_1	0.3014	0.0050	0.0174
	(0.0791)	(0.0002)	(0.0009)
σ_2	0.1867	0.0053	0.0181
	(0.0529)	(0.0003)	(0.0009)
ρ_{12}	0.9265	0.9189	0.9230
	(0.0098)	(0.0107)	(0.0102)
LogLF	**1194.1000**	**1130.5500**	**1162.9200**
χ^2 ***Test***		127.1000	62.3600

Two-year:
Based on the long rate being the two-year rate. We find based on the maximized Gaussian log likelihood values compared to the unrestricted CKLS model the CIR model performs the best followed by the Vasicek model. Regarding the unrestricted model the Gaussian estimates of γ_1 and γ_2 are 1.4566 and 1.2133 for the three-month and two-year rates. There is evidence of mean reversion in the two-year rate. The correlation parameters indicates 88% between the two-factors in the CKLS model and 87% in the Vasicek and CIR models. Based on the χ^2 likelihood ratio test the results imply that we can reject the Vasicek and CIR models.

Three-year:
Based on the long rate being the three-year rate. We find based on the Gaussian log likelihood values compared to the unrestricted CKLS model the CIR model

Table 5. Gaussian Estimates of Two Factor Models: 3-Month and 2-Year.

Parameters	CKLS	Vasicek	CIR
α_1	0.0010	0.0024	0.0016
	(0.0005)	(0.0009)	(0.0008)
α_2	0.0021	0.0026	0.0022
	(0.0008)	(0.0010)	(0.0010)
β_1	− 0.0172	− 0.0389	− 0.0270
	(0.0107)	(0.0132)	(0.0126)
β_2	− 0.0310	− 0.0371	− 0.0322
	(0.0136)	(0.0129)	(0.0139)
γ_1	1.4566	0.0	0.5
	(0.0969)		
γ_2	1.2133	0.0	0.5
	(0.1330)		
σ_1	0.2177	0.0050	0.0174
	(0.0595)	(0.0002)	(0.0008)
σ_2	0.1159	0.0054	0.0186
	(0.0410)	(0.0003)	(0.0009)
ρ_{12}	0.8801	0.8740	0.8797
	(0.0156)	(0.0162)	(0.0155)
LogLF	**1156.8200**	**1105.1600**	**1133.1800**
χ^2 *Test*		103.3200	47.28

performs the best followed by the Vasicek model. Regarding the unrestricted model the Gaussian estimates of γ_1 and γ_2 are 1.4146 and 1.2107 for the three-month and three-year rates. There is evidence of mean reversion in the three-year rate. The correlation parameters indicates 85% between the two-factors in the models. Based on the χ^2 test the results imply that we can reject the Vasicek and CIR models.

Five-year:
Based on the long rate being the five-year rate. We find based on the Gaussian log likelihood values compared to the unrestricted CKLS model the CIR model performs the best followed by the Vasicek model. Regarding the unrestricted model the Gaussian estimates of γ_1 and γ_2 are 1.3387 and 1.1616 for the three-month and five-year rates. The correlation parameters indicates 82% between the two-factors in the different models. Based on the χ^2 test the results imply that we can reject the Vasicek and CIR models.

Table 6. Gaussian Estimates of Two Factor Models: 3-Month and 3-Year.

Parameters	CKLS	Vasicek	CIR
α_1	0.0009	0.0023	0.0015
	(0.0005)	(0.0009)	(0.0007)
α_2	0.0020	0.0025	0.0021
	(0.0008)	(0.0011)	(0.0010)
β_1	− 0.0155	− 0.0379	− 0.0256
	(0.0102)	(0.0140)	(0.0123)
β_2	− 0.0286	− 0.0353	− 0.0304
	(0.0134)	(0.0142)	(0.0138)
γ_1	1.4146	0.0	0.5
	(0.0942)		
γ_2	1.2107	0.0	0.5
	(0.1436)		
σ_1	0.1936	0.0050	0.0173
	(0.0510)	(0.0002)	(0.0008)
σ_2	0.1130	0.0054	0.0186
	(0.0423)	(0.0003)	(0.0009)
ρ_{12}	0.8505	0.8484	0.8549
	(0.0191)	(0.0192)	(0.0184)
LogLF	**1143.4000**	**1095.7600**	**1122.3400**
χ^2 *Test*		95.2800	42.12

Seven-Year:
Based on the long rate being the seven-year rate. We find based on the Gaussian log likelihood values compared to the unrestricted CKLS model the CIR model performs the best followed by the Vasicek model. Regarding the unrestricted model the Gaussian estimates of γ_1 and γ_2 are 1.3010 and 1.2060 for the three-month and seven-year rates. There is no evidence of mean reversion in both rates. The correlation parameter indicates 80% between the two-factors in the CKLS and Vasicek models and 85% in the CIR model. Based on the χ^2 test the results imply that we can reject the Vasicek and CIR models.

Ten-year:
Lastly, based on the long rate being the ten-year rate. We find based on the Gaussian log likelihood values compared to the unrestricted CKLS model the CIR model performs the best followed by the Vasicek model. Regarding the unrestricted model the Gaussian estimates of γ_1 and γ_2 are 1.2722 and 1.2581

Table 7. Gaussian Estimates of Two Factor Models: 3-Month and 5-Year.

Parameters	CKLS	Vasicek	CIR
α_1	0.0008	0.0022	0.0013
	(0.0005)	(0.0010)	(0.0007)
α_2	0.0016	0.0023	0.0018
	(0.0008)	(0.0013)	(0.0010)
β_1	− 0.0134	− 0.0358	− 0.0230
	(0.0097)	(0.0155)	(0.0114)
β_2	− 0.0223	− 0.0309	− 0.0253
	(0.0127)	(0.0156)	(0.0130)
γ_1	1.3387	0.0	0.5
	(0.0959)		
γ_2	1.1616	0.0	0.5
	(0.1685)		
σ_1	0.1570	0.0050	0.0173
	(0.0419)	(0.0002)	(0.0008)
σ_2	0.0950	0.0053	0.0181
	(0.0410)	(0.0003)	(0.0009)
ρ_{12}	0.8220	0.8206	0.8310
	(0.0226)	(0.0224)	(0.0211)
LogLF	**1133.6400**	**1089.6600**	**1115.4000**
χ^2 ***Test***		87.9600	36.4000

for the three-month and ten-year rates. There is no evidence of mean reversion in both rates. The correlation parameters indicates 79% between the two-factors in the CKLS and Vasicek models and 81% in the CIR model. Based on the χ^2 test the results imply that we can reject the Vasicek and CIR models.

Overall the estimates have plausible values and all indicate that the relationship between the volatility of rates and level of rates is much higher than assumed by the Vasciek and CIR models. Compared to other U.S. results for the single factor CKLS model using monthly one-month U.S. T-bill rates CKLS reported an estimate of $\gamma = 1.5$; Nowman (1998) reports an estimate of $\gamma = 1.0519$ using monthly one-month U.S. Euro-currency rate; Byers and Nowman (1998) report estimates using weekly Euro-currency data for the seven day, one, three, six, and twelve month rates all over one. In the two-factor versions following Nowman's (2001) approach, Byers and Nowman (2001) obtained using monthly Euro-currency rates for the one and twelve-month rates estimates of $\gamma_1 = 1.0625$ and $\gamma_2 = 0.9763$.

Table 8. Gaussian Estimates of Two Factor Models: 3-Month and 7-Year.

Parameters	CKLS	Vasicek	CIR
α_1	0.0008	0.0021	0.0015
	(0.0005)	(0.0009)	(0.0007)
α_2	0.0015	0.0023	0.0021
	(0.0009)	(0.0011)	(0.0010)
β_1	− 0.0136	− 0.0352	− 0.0256
	(0.0103)	(0.0130)	(0.0123)
β_2	− 0.0206	− 0.0295	− 0.0304
	(0.0137)	(0.0133)	(0.0138)
γ_1	1.3010	0.0	0.5
	(0.0979)		
γ_2	1.2060	0.0	0.5
	(0.1905)		
σ_1	0.1416	0.0050	0.0173
	(0.0384)	(0.0002)	(0.0008)
σ_2	0.1022	0.0052	0.0186
	(0.0494)	(0.0002)	(0.0009)
ρ_{12}	0.8003	0.8034	0.8549
	(0.0251)	(0.0242)	(0.0184)
LogLF	**1128.15**	**1086.8300**	**1122.3400**
χ^2 ***Test***		82.6400	11.6200

FORECAST PERFORMANCE OF MODELS

We now discuss how to obtain optimal forecasts of the discrete interest rates from the estimated discrete model. The forecasting procedure was developed by Bergstrom (1989) based on the exact discrete model for the general model of Bergstrom (1986) and it was shown (Bergstrom, 1989, Theorem 2) that the forecasts obtained were optimal. In Byers and Nowman (1998) they compared the forecasting performance of the one-factor CKLS model and its special cases based on weekly Euro-currency rates over a wide range of different maturities for the U.K. and U.S. It was shown that the forecasting performance varied over the models and between markets. In Nowman (2001) a forecasting comparison of the two-factor CKLS, Vasicek and CIR models was also undertaken for Japanese and U.K. Euro-currency rates and for a more extensive range of currencies in Byers and Nowman (2001).

In Tables 10–13 we report a number of summary forecast statistics. In particular we compute the Root Mean Square Error (RMSE), Mean Absolute

Table 9. Gaussian Estimates of Two Factor Models: 3-Month and 10-Year.

Parameters	CKLS	Vasicek	CIR
α_1	0.0007	0.0020	0.0012
	(0.0005)	(0.0008)	(0.0007)
α_2	0.0012	0.0021	0.0015
	(0.0009)	(0.0010)	(0.0010)
β_1	− 0.0128	− 0.0337	− 0.0213
	(0.0098)	(0.0113)	(0.0113)
β_2	− 0.0163	− 0.0269	− 0.0204
	(0.0128)	(0.0114)	(0.0129)
γ_1	1.2722	0.0	0.5
	(0.0992)		
γ_2	1.2581	0.0	0.5
	(0.2017)		
σ_1	0.1309	0.0050	0.0173
	(0.0359)	(0.0002)	(0.0008)
σ_2	0.1120	0.0051	0.0171
	(0.0569)	(0.0002)	(0.0008)
ρ_{12}	0.7881	0.7973	0.8076
	(0.0266)	(0.0249)	(0.0237)
LogLF	**1127.5567**	**1087.9645**	**1112.1305**
χ^2 ***Test***		79.1844	30.8524

Table 10. Summary Forecast Statistics for Two Factor Models: RMSE.

Model	CKLS	Vasicek	CIR
3-Month	0.0050	0.0040	0.0048
1-Year	0.0057	0.0047	0.0052
3-Month	0.0049	0.0040	0.0046
2-Year	0.0056	0.0051	0.0055
3-Month	0.0049	0.0041	0.0047
3-Year	0.0050	0.0047	0.0050
3-Month	0.0049	0.0041	0.0049
5-Year	0.0046	0.0041	0.0045
3-Month	0.0049	0.0043	0.0047
7-Year	0.0035	0.0029	0.0035
3-Month	0.0051	0.0044	0.0049
10-Year	0.0034	0.0030	0.0033

Error (MAE), Mean Error (ME) and Theil's inequality measure (U). If we let the forecast value of $r(t)$ be $r^*(t)$ the four measures arc then given below for the K forecast periods:

$$\text{RMSE} = \sqrt{\left[\frac{1}{K}\sum_{t=T+1}^{T+K}(r^*(t) - r(t))^2\right]}$$

$$MAE = \frac{1}{K}\sum_{t=T+1}^{T+K}|r^*(t) - r(t)|$$

$$ME = \frac{1}{K}\sum_{t=T+1}^{T+K}(r^*(t) - r(t))$$

$$U = \frac{\sqrt{\left[\frac{1}{K}\sum_{t=T+1}^{T+K}(r^*(t) - r(t))^2\right]}}{\sqrt{\left[\frac{1}{K}\sum_{t=T+1}^{T+K}(r^*(t))^2\right]} + \sqrt{\left[\frac{1}{K}\sum_{t=T+1}^{T+K}(r(t))^2\right]}}.$$

If the forecasts are perfect then each of the above measures is zero. If $U = 1$, the predictive performance of the model is as bad as it could possibly be. It should

Table 11. Summary Forecast Statistics for Two Factor Models: ME.

Model	CKLS	Vasicek	CIR
3-Month	− 0.0046	− 0.0036	− 0.0044
1-Year	− 0.0056	− 0.0046	− 0.0051
3-Month	− 0.0045	− 0.0036	− 0.0042
2-Year	− 0.0053	− 0.0048	− 0.0052
3-Month	− 0.0045	− 0.0038	− 0.0043
3-Year	− 0.0047	− 0.0044	− 0.0047
3-Month	− 0.0045	− 0.0037	− 0.0045
5-Year	− 0.0042	− 0.0036	− 0.0042
3-Month	− 0.0045	− 0.0039	− 0.0043
7-Year	− 0.0030	− 0.0022	− 0.0030
3-Month	− 0.0047	− 0.0040	− 0.0045
10-Year	− 0.0025	− 0.0017	− 0.0024

Table 12. Summary Forecast Statistics for Two Factor Models: MAE.

Model	CKLS	Vasicek	CIR
3-Month	0.0046	0.0036	0.0044
1-Year	0.0056	0.0046	0.0051
3-Month	0.0045	0.0036	0.0042
2-Year	0.0053	0.0048	0.0052
3-Month	0.0045	0.0038	0.0043
3-Year	0.0047	0.0044	0.0047
3-Month	0.0045	0.0037	0.0045
5-Year	0.0042	0.0036	0.0042
3-Month	0.0045	0.0039	0.0043
7-Year	0.0030	0.0026	0.0030
3-Month	0.0047	0.0040	0.0045
10-Year	0.0030	0.0026	0.0029

Table 13. Summary Forecast Statistics for Two Factor Models: THEIL U.

Model	CKLS	Vasicek	CIR
3-Month	0.0458	0.0358	0.0436
1-Year	0.0489	0.0401	0.0442
3-Month	0.0445	0.0359	0.0416
2-Year	0.0450	0.0411	0.0442
3-Month	0.0449	0.0375	0.0425
3-Year	0.0400	0.0373	0.0402
3-Month	0.0446	0.0371	0.0447
5-Year	0.0368	0.0323	0.0363
3-Month	0.0449	0.0394	0.0425
7-Year	0.0271	0.0223	0.0273
3-Month	0.0470	0.0401	0.0451
10-Year	0.0274	0.0240	0.0266

be noted that the forecasts are dynamic K step-ahead forecasts. We take the forecast period as $K=6$ starting December 1999. For example, based on the RMSE's for the three-month and one-year rates the Vasicek model performs the best followed by the CIR and CKLS models. Turning to the three-month and two, three, five, seven and ten-year rates respectively the Vasicek model performs the best again followed by the CIR and CKLS models. The other measures confirm the Vasicek model performs the best also (see Tables 10–13

Table 14. Summary Forecast Statistics for VAR Models: RMSE.

Rate	RMSE
3-Month	0.0055
1-Year	0.0059
3-Month	0.0055
2-Year	0.0061
3-Month	0.0055
3-Year	0.0054
3-Month	0.0054
5-Year	0.0047
3-Month	0.0054
7-Year	0.0035
3-Month	0.0055
10-Year	0.0034

for further details). We also estimated a simple VAR(1) model for both rates in each case and the Root Mean Square Errors are reported in Table 14 below. For all maturities the Vasicek model has smaller Root Mean Square Errors than the VAR(1) model.

CONCLUSIONS

In this paper we have provided a review of the Gaussian estimation methods used by Nowman (1997, 2001) for estimating non-linear interest rate diffusion models. These models have important implications for the effective development of risk management tools in banks and are therefore important for practitioners in deciding which model to use. We have estimated two-factor versions of the CKLS, Vasicek and CIR models following on from the study by Nowman (2001). We have found that the relationship between the volatility of rates and the level of rates is much higher than assumed in the Vasicek and CIR models. We have also compared the forecasting performance of the models over a six-month period and found the Vasicek model performs the best and has smaller Root Mean Square Errors than a VAR model. The general Gaussian estimation methods have much wider applications in general areas of financial modelling and further research and applications of these methods are currently underway by a number of econometricians in different countries.

ACKNOWLEDGMENTS

I would like to thank Professor's Tom Fetherston, Rex Bergstrom and Marcus Chambers for their advice.

REFERENCES

Adkins, L. C., & Krehbiel, T. (1999). Mean reversion and volatility of short-term london interbank offer rates. *International Review of Economics and Finance*, *8*, 45–54.

Agbeyegbe, T. D. (1984). The exact discrete analog to a closed linear mixed-order system. *Journal of Economic Dynamics and Control*, *7*, 363–375.

Agbeyegbe, T. D. (1987). The exact discrete analog to a closed linear first-order system with mixed sample. *Econometric Theory*, *3*, 142–149.

Agbeyegbe, T. D. (1988). An exact discrete analog of an open order linear non-stationary first-order continuous time system with mixed sample. *Journal of Econometrics*, *39*, 237–250.

Babbs, S. H., & Nowman, K. B. (1999). Kalman filtering of generalized vasicek term structure models. *Journal of Financial and Quantitative Analysis*, *43*, 115–130.

Bergstrom, A. R. (1966). Non-recursive models as discrete approximations to systems of stochastic differential equations. *Econometrica*, *34*, 173–182.

Bergstrom, A. R. (1983). Gaussian estimation of structural parameters in higher-order continuous time dynamic models. *Econometrica*, *51*, 117–152.

Bergstrom, A. R. (1984). Continuous time stochastic models and issues of aggregation over time. In: Z. Griliches & M. D. Intriligator (Eds), *Handbook of Econometrics* (Vol. II). Amsterdam: Elsevier Science.

Bergstrom, A. R. (1985). The estimation of parameters in nonstationary higher-order continuous time dynamic models. *Econometric Theory*, *1*, 369–385.

Bergstrom, A. R. (1986). The estimation of open higher-order continuous time dynamic models with mixed stock and flow data. *Econometric Theory*, *2*, 350–373.

Bergstrom, A. R. (1988). The history of continuous time econometric models. *Econometric Theory*, *4*, 365–383.

Bergstrom, A. R. (1989). Optimal forecasting of discrete stock and flow data generated by a higher-order continuous time system. *Computers and Mathematics with Applications*, *17*, 1203–1214.

Bergstrom, A. R. (1990). *Continuous Time Econometric Modelling*. Oxford: Oxford University Press.

Bergstrom, A. R. (1996). A survey of continuous time econometrics. In: W. A. Barnett, G. Gandolfo & C. Hillinger (Eds), *Dynamic Disequilibrium Modelling*. Cambridge: Cambridge University Press.

Bergstrom, A. R., & Nowman, K. B. (1999). Gaussian estimation of a two-factor continuous time model of the short-term interest rate. *Economic Notes*, *28*, 25–41.

Brennan, M. J., & Schwartz, E, S. (1979). A continuous time approach to the pricing of bonds. *Journal of Banking and Finance*, *3*, 133–155.

Brennan, M. J., & Schwartz, E. S. (1980). Analyzing convertible bonds. *Journal of Financial and Quantitative Analysis*, *15*, 907–929.

Byers, S. L., & Nowman, K. B. (1998). Forecasting U.K. and U.S. interest rates using continuous time term structure models. *International Review of Financial Analysis*, *7*, 191–206.

Byers, S. L., & Nowman, K. B. (2001). Further evidence on the forecasting performance of two factor continuous time interest rate models in international and Asia Pacific financial markets. *Managerial Finance*, *27*, 40–61.

Chambers, M. J. (1991). Discrete models for estimating general linear continuous time systems. *Econometric Theory*, *7*, 531–542.

Chambers, M. J. (1996). The estimation of continuous parameter long-memory time series models. *Econometric Theory*, *12*, 374–390.

Chambers, M. J. (1998). The estimation of systems of joint differential-difference equations. *Journal of Econometrics*, *85*, 1–31.

Chambers, M. J. (1999). Discrete time representation of stationary and non-stationary continuous time systems. *Journal of Economic Dynamics and Control*, *23*, 619–639.

Chambers, M. J. (2000). Temporal aggregation and the finite sample performance of spectral regression estimators in cointegrated systems: a simulation study. *Econometric Theory*, *17*, 591–607.

Chambers, M. J., & McGarry, J. (2001). Modelling cyclical behaviour with differential-difference equations in an unobserved components framework. *Econometric Theory*, forthcoming.

Chan, K. C., Karolyi, G. A., Longstaff, F. A., & Sanders, A. B. (1992). An empirical comparison of alternative models of the short-term interest rate. *Journal of Finance*, *47*, 1209–1227.

Cox, J. C., Ingersoll, J. E., & Ross, S. (1980). An analysis of variable rate loan contracts. *Journal of Finance*, *35*, 389–403.

Cox, J. C., Ingersoll, J. E., & Ross, S. (1985). A theory of the term structure of interest rates. *Econometrica*, *53*, 385–407.

Dahlquist, M. (1996). On alternative interest rate processes. *Journal of Banking and Finance*, *20*, 1093–1119.

Dothan, U. L. (1978). On the term structure of interest rates. *Journal of Financial Economics*, *6*, 59–69.

Episcopos, A. (2000). Further evidence on alternative continuous time models of the short-term interest rate. *Journal of International Financial Markets*, *10*, 199–212.

Gandolfo, G. (Ed.) (1993). *Continuous Time Econometrics Theory and Applications*. London: Chapman-Hall.

Hiraki, T., & Takezawa, N. (1997). How sensitive is short-term Japanese interest rate volatility to the level of the interest rate? *Economic Letters*, *56*, 325–332.

Langetieg, T. C. (1980). A multivariate model of the term structure. *Journal of Finance*, *35*, 71–97.

Longstaff, F., & Schwartz, E. (1992). Interest rate volatility and the term structure: a two factor general equilibrium model. *Journal of Finance*, *47*, 1259–1282.

McGarry, J. (2000). The exact discrete time representation of a system of fourth-order differential equation. Economic Research Paper No. 15, Loughborough University.

Merton, R C. (1973). Theory of rational option pricing. *Bell Journal of Economics and Management Science*, *4*, 141–183.

Nowman, K. B. (1991). Open higher order continuous time dynamic model with mixed stock and flow data and derivatives of the exogenous variables. *Econometric Theory*, *7*, 404–408.

Nowman, K. B. (1993). Finite-sample properties of the gaussian estimation of an open higher-order continuous time dynamic model with mixed stock and flow data. In: G. Gandolfo (Ed.), *Continuous Time Econometrics Theory and Applications*. London: Chapman-Hall.

Nowman, K. B. (1997). Gaussian estimation of single-factor continuous time models of the term structure of interest rates. *Journal of Finance*, *52*, 1695–1706.

Nowman, K. B. (1998). Continuous time short rate interest rate models. *Applied Financial Economics*, *8*, 401–407.

Nowman, K. B., & Sorwar, G. (1999). An evaluation of contingent claims using the CKLS interest rate model: an analysis of Australia, Japan, and United Kingdom. *Asia Pacific Financial Markets*, *6*, 205–219.

Nowman, K. B. (2001). Gaussian estimation and forecasting of multi-factor term structure models with an application to Japan and the United Kingdom. *Asia Pacific Financial Markets*, *8*, 23–32.

Phillips, P. C. B. (1972). The structural estimation of a stochastic differential equation system. *Econometrica*, *40*, 1021–1041.

Saltoglu, B. (2000). Comparing forecasting ability of parametric and nonparametric methods: application with Canadian monthly interest rates. Unpublished paper.

Tse, Y. K. (1995). Some international evidence on the stochastic behavior of interest rates. *Journal of International Money and Finance*, *14*, 721–738.

Vasicek, O. (1977). An equilibrium characterization of the term structure. *Journal of Financial Economics*, *5*, 177–188.

INCREASING LINKAGES OF STOCK MARKETS AND PRICE VOLATILITY

Nidal Rashid Sabri

ABSTRACT

This study is aimed to discuss forms of linkages that exist between the world stock markets, and to indicate to what extent the present interaction factors are increasing in the last decade. The study analyzed published data, as well as correlation between monthly changes of local price indices for 16 stock markets in 1994 and 1998.

The study indicated that there were significant changes during the nineties arising from introducing liberal regulatory rules, increasing foreign trading, increasing in number of cross listed firms and equity portfolio flows. The study found that there are significant positive increases from 1994 to 1998, in the degree of correlation between the majority of selected stock markets. Increasing linkages suppose to increase data dissemination, thus increase stock market efficiency, but with the existing cross-markets volatility transmission phenomenon, increasing linkages should be scrutinized carefully.

Financial Risk and Financial Risk Management, Volume 16, pages 349–373.

ISBN: 0-7623-0858-3

1. INTRODUCTION

The integration of international stock markets may be considered as the most significant change in the global capital market, which has been introduced to the stock markets in the last two decades. Many stock exchanges removed restrictions and admitted listing of stocks on more than one exchange. The national stock exchanges are moving towards increasing linkages to other international stock exchanges. There are continuous increases in share of the listed foreign firms and in share of the non-residents' stock transactions. The increasing linkages are extended from developed stock markets to other emerging stock markets, as well as from stock markets to other financial and banking systems.

Integration and liberalization of stock markets received and interpreted as a positive signal in the development of global stock markets, which may lead to various advantages, such as: reducing the cost of equity capital as reported by Beakert and Harvey (2000), Stulz, (1999) Doukas and Switzer (2000) and Miller (1999). Increasing liquidity, reducing risk, increasing diversification, and increasing the investor base as reported by Hargis (2000), Claessencs (1995), and Jayaraman et al. (1993), and increasing investments opportunity as concluded by Henry (2000).

On the other side, the increasing of linkages provides some disadvantages such as a mistake in one market or volatility surprises may be transferred to other stock markets (King, 1990) and (Jeong, 1999). The free capital flow and increasing linkages may transfer the volatility of inflation and exchange rate from one market to another as happened to the financial markets in Mexico during 1994 and East Asian region during the years 1997–1998. This may be considered as a risk factor and may lead to stronger co-movements, and reducing the expected gains from international diversification (Shawky et al., 1997). The majority of stock market experts considered the decline in international stock indices as the most risky factor in destabilizing of other national stock markets due to the increasing linkages of stock markets (Sabri, 1995a, b).

Various studies examined the stock market linkages, the majority of these related studies intended to report whether there is positive or negative correlation among stock price volatility, cross-markets in different times and under different conditions, and to discuss the stability of the stock volatility over time. Other studies discussed the issue between stock markets in various times, periods and conditions, before, after and around the 1987 stock market crash. However, there are few studies discussed and explored factors that may create stock markets linkages.

Therefore, this study aims at examining such factors, which is increasing rapidly in the last decade. In more details, this paper intends to accomplish the following purposes: First: to present the forms of linkages which are considered as the main factors in creating interactions between stock markets and may lead to close market integration. Second: to indicate to what extend the present interaction factors are increasing in the last decade. Third: to examine the changes occurred in the international stock market linkages using empirical investigation of the performance indices' movement during two different years (1994–1998).

The rest of paper is organized in the following sections: Section 2 is devoted to present the review of literature, Section 3 presents the methodology. Section 4 explores forms and factors of linkages, between stock markets; Section 5 presents the findings of the empirical investigation, while Section 6 is devoted to summary and conclusion.

2. REVIEW OF THE RELATED LITERATURE

Various studies discussed the issue of international linkages of stock markets in the last decade, especially after the 1987 stock market crises. The majority of those studies used one or more of correlation or regression models to examine the price, returns or indices for different periods. They covered different regions, including developed and emerging markets and examined linkages between both markets. Some studies covered one or more regions, while others covered global samples.

Examples of these studies: Wu and Su (1998) found that there is significant dynamic relation exist among four major stock markets including U.S., Japan, Britain, and Hong Kong, in addition, the correlation among stock markets has been increased considerably after 1987 and it is increasing in the recent years. Arshanapalli and Doukas (1993) results show that the degree of international co-movements among stock price indices increased substantially, with the exception of Nikkei index, and the U.S. stock market had impact on the French, German and U.K. markets in the post crash period. Ramchand and Susmel (1998) found that the correlation between the U.S. market and others are higher in a high volatility market situation, in which foreign markets become highly correlated with U.S. markets.

De Sants and Impohoroglu (1997) found evidence of time-varying volatility, and reported that the level of volatility in emerging stock markets is higher than that of mature markets. Moreover, Koutomos, (1996) and Kanas (1998) discussed the volatility in European stock markets, and found that volatility interactions are extensive and reciprocal between England, Germany, France and Italy. Bracker and Koch (1999) reported that international equity markets move together more when the market is volatile or falling. Janakiramanan and Lamba (1998) found that the U.S. markets influences all other Pacific-Basin Stock markets except the market of Indonesia. Longin and Solnik (2001) found that the correlation among stock markets increases in bear markets, but not in bull markets. The IMF report (2000) concluded that emerging market assets remain heavily dependent upon the mature market developments including the risk perceptions and tolerance of investor. Bekaert and Harvey (1997) reported that capital market liberalization increases the relation between local market returns and the world market.

Finally, the findings of the above studies may be summarized as follows: The linkages among stock markets are existed and began to increase after the 1987 stock market crisis. The correlation of price volatility between stock markets is changing over time. Emerging stock markets become more correlated with developed stock markets. Correlation between stock markets tends to increase during unstable and high volatility periods. The U.S. stock market influences the majority of other European, Asian and Latin American stock markets.

3. METHODOLOGY

This study aimed to investigate the stock market linkages using twofold methods:

First: Analysis of Published Data

This study examined the related published data in regard to various forms of stock market linkages for the last decade (1990–2000), as reported by Emerging Stock Markets Fact books of IFC, International Federation of Stock Exchanges Database, International Capital Markets reports of IMF, and the annual Factbooks of the world international stock exchanges. The forms of stock market linkages may be summarized as follows: stock markets are moving towards globalization. Removing restrictions from foreign ownership and increasing of stock market liberalization. Introducing liberal regulatory rules in stock exchanges to attract foreign equities and investors. Increasing net private portfolio flows across developed and emerging markets. Increasing number of firms issuing equity in multiple international markets. Increasing number of cross listed national corporations in international stock exchanges. Increasing the number of the of cross listed firms in emerging stock exchanges. And increasing linkages between developed stock markets and emerging stock markets.

Second: Empirical investigations
The study examined the linkages of stock markets as presented in the first part of this study. The Pearson Correlation Coefficient between the stock market indices' movement was calculated between each pairs' indices for the selected 16 stock market exchanges. Using the monthly change percentages of the local price indices for the stock exchanges. The monthly changes of stock price index for two years (1994 and 1998) is examined in order to determine to what extend the correlation among stock market exchanges has been increased as a result of the significance changes in increasing linkages. The selected period witnessed significant increasing in stock markets linkages as expressed by introducing more liberal rules in stock exchanges, in increasing number of cross listed companies, increasing of the share of foreign trading and ownership in stock markets, and in trading of stocks outside their home exchanges.

In addition, the output correlation's data between the two periods was tested using T *test*. It used to determine whether the difference between the correlation between each pairs for the selected 16 stock market in 1994 (r_1) is significantly different from the degree of correlation in 1998 (r_2). This covered developed stock markets groups, emerging stock market group and between both developed-emerging stock markets. The value of t test computed and compared for each group at level of 0.05 significant. The stated directional hypotheses for this part was articulated as follows:

- There is a significant increase in positive correlation between developed stock markets based on monthly movement of stock market indices.
- There is a significant increase in positive correlation between emerging stock markets based on monthly movement of stock market indices.
- There is a significant increase in positive correlation between developed and emerging stock markets based on monthly movement of stock market indices.

The used data for the second part were based on International Financial Corporation database for emerging stock markets, and the stock market Factbooks for developed stock markets. The sample of the second part covered 16 national stock market exchanges in both developed and emerging stock markets, covering all geographical regions as presented in Table 1. The trading value of the selected sample of stock markets form about 84% of the total world trade value in 1999 (IFC, 2000).

4. FORMS OF STOCK MARKETS LINKAGES

The stock market linkages have been intensified in the last decade. The evidence of increasing forms and size of stock market linkages may be found

Table 1. The Selected Sample of Stock Exchanges.

Market Groups	Countries	Trade Value IN $ M (1999)	Stock Exchanges and Index
Developed			
	Australia	105.999	Australian (All Ordinaries)
	Singapore	97.985	Straits Time Index
	Japan	1.849.228	Tokyo Nikkei 225 Index
	Hong Kong	244.886	Hong Kong (All Ordinaries)
	Canada	364.625	Toronto Composite Index
	U.K.	1.377.859	London (FTSE 100 Index)
	USA	18.574.100	NYSE (Dow- Jones)
	Germany	1.357.841	Frankfurt (DAX)
Emerging			
	South Africa	72.917	JSE Overall
	Korea	733.591	Korea (KSE)
	Turkey	81.277	ISE Composite
	Greece	188.722	ASE General
	Malaysia	48.512	Kuala Lumbar (KLSE)
	Taiwan	910.016	Taiwan (TSE Average)
	Argentina	7.781	Bolsa Index General
	Mexico	36.042	BMV General

Source: Based on IFC, 2000.

by tracking the stock markets linkages during the last decade between 1990 and 2000. This part of the paper is devoted to explore this issue, covering the most important forms of linkages, which may be summarized as follows:

4.1. Introducing Liberal Rules in Stock Exchanges

The global stock market witnessed a significant change related to the liberalization of its rules, to permit foreign trading and investments. Generally, there are various barriers, which facing the flow of funds between countries. There are direct legal constrains as imposed by governmental laws or individual listed corporations, as well as indirect barriers such as capital gains and income tax regulations, and regulations regarding stock market transactions. In addition, others obstacles, which may hinder the flow of equity portfolio, such as laws of controlling local exchange rates and transferring of funds outside the boarders.

For direct foreign trading restrictions, the restrictions are imposed either by the corporate laws or stock exchanges' laws in the most of middle East countries some of the Latin American countries and south Asia Countries. However, in some countries, the restrictions in foreign investments are imposed by the individual corporation's bylaw, and not by the governmental laws as in Switzerland, Finland and Thailand (Stulz & Wasserfallen, 1995). Other restrictions of ownership may impose only in specific sectors such as financial sector as in Brazil, Russia, and Sir Lanka. In other countries there are special shares issue for local residents, and other shares issue for foreign investors. For example a company in Switzerland may issue bearer shares, registered shares and restricted shares with different vote right (Gardiol et al., 1997). The majority of European companies issue bearer shares, which do not permit control on the ownership of the stock trading.

The world stock market witnessed relaxing in all of the above restrictions in the last decade. The evidence of reducing or eliminating the restrictions in foreign investments may be found in Table 2. It shows that the number of countries introduced changes in their investment regimes from 35 to 60 between 1991 and 1998, and the number of regulatory changes favorable to foreign investments increased from 80 states to 136 states (UNCTAD, 1999). In addition, out of the fifty two emerging stock markets states, thirty five states have removed the ceiling of ownership for listed stocks up to 100% of the total equities by the end of 1998. While the other seventeen states removed the restrictions on foreign ownership partially, such as Brazil: 49%, Trinidad and Tobago: 30%, India 24%, Korea: 49.9%, Philippines: 40%, Taiwan: 30%, Thailand: 49%, Russia: 9%–25%, Ghana: 74%, Jordan: 50%, Saudi Arabia 25%, Tunisia: 49.9%, and Zimbabwe: 40% (IFC, 1999). The liberalization of stock market increases the trading volume of stock markets and liquidity, but may lead to increase the volatility. Levine and Zervos (1998) found that stock markets become more liquid and more volatile as a result of stock markets liberalization.

Table 2. National Regulatory Changes for Foreign Investments Between 1991–1998.

	1991	1998
Number of countries introduced changes in their investments regimes	35	60
Number of regulatory changes favorable to Foreign investments	80	136

Source: UNCTAD, 1999.

4.2. Increasing of Cross Listing Companies

The practice of cross listing is the most significant phenomena that create linkages among stock exchanges. The idea of cross listing is that a listed firm on a domestic exchange is looking for second or more stock exchanges to be listed there at the same time. The number of dual listed firms has been increased significantly in the last decade. Cross listing started in the late seventies, by the large multinational corporations to be listed in two or more of the developed stock exchanges. Today, it is not limited to multinational corporations, but it's extended to many national firms even located in emerging countries. The majority of foreign firms listed in more than one stock exchange have to meet dual requirements of these exchanges. Firms which may not meet the second exchange requirements use the so called depository receipts as alternative for cross listing. Martell (1999) found that 67% of the foreign listed companies in NYSE were using global depositary receipts method.

Table 3 presents a summary of foreign listed firms in the international exchanges which include 12 foreign listed firms or above as in 1999. It indicates that there are 20 stock exchanges in which more than 12 foreign firms are listed and accounted for 98% of the total foreign listed firms in the world stock exchanges in 1999. To compare between 1981, 1994 and 1999, its clear that there are significant increase of cross listing in most of the stock exchanges such as NYSE, NASDAQ, London, Tokyo, Paris, Australian, and Luxembourg.

The top five stock markets based on the number of foreign listed firms is classified as developed stock markets, and is accounted for 62% of the number of foreign listed firms. These are: London, NASDAQ, NYSE, Frankfurt, and Luxembourg. The top five exchanges witnessed significant increase from 1981, to 1994, to 1998. In addition, many stock exchanges started to include foreign firms in the nineties only such as Vienna, Hong Kong and Lima. The cross-listed firms are extended to emerging stock exchanges such as Johannesburg.

In addition, the number of cross listing of Latin American firms in foreign exchanges started by 2 companies in 1989, and increased to 106 listed firms in 1991, mostly in U.S. stock exchanges (Hargis, 2000). The trading value of Mexican, Argentine, and Chilean stocks traded in the U.S. were greater than the total value traded in their respective domestic stock markets during the year 1995 (Hargis, 2000). In addition, the concept of cross listing is expanded to even small stock markets classified as frontier stock exchanges, such as Botswana stock exchange, which includes 9 foreign listed firms (IFSE, 2000).

The number of cross listing is expected to increase, due to the competitions among the international stock exchanges, to attract other foreign stocks for dual

Table 3. Number of Foreign Listed Firms in Stock Market Exchanges Between 1981 and 1999.

Stock Exchanges	1981 a	1994 b	1999 c
London	478	462	499
NASDAQ	0	–	429
NYSE	42	–	406
Frankfurt	177	227	234
Luxembourg	124	217	226
Paris	162	195	176
Zurich	168	242	173
Amsterdam	257	215	154
Brussels	150	141	122
Australian	21	–	70
New Zealand	–	–	58
Toronto	67	–	47
Singapore	167	–	43
Tokyo	15	–	43
Johannesburg	–	–	24
Stockholm	–	8	23
Bermuda	–	–	23
Oslo	–	14	20
Irish	–	–	19
Vienna	0	–	17
Hong Kong	0	–	13
Lima	0	–	12
Total	1828		2831
Total dual listed firms in the world stock exchanges in 1999			2900

Source: Based on, a: Biddle and Saudagaran, 1989, b. FESE, 1994, c: IFSE, 2000 and HKSE Fact Book, 1999.

listing. Mueller (1999), Cheung and Lee (1995) argued that there will be more non-U.S. companies, that would list on the NYSE if it accepts the IASC standards instead of the American accounting standards. The main obstacle of cross listing is the different requirements of accounting standards, which is going to be removed by adapting International Accounting Standards Committee by many developed and emerging countries. This will lead gradually to international accounting harmonization, thus make cross listing process more beneficiary and less costly.

As a consequence of increasing the number and trading of cross listed firms in many of stock exchanges, some leading corporations are traded now in foreign stock exchanges almost the same size as traded in their home exchanges. For example, the trading value of the major Dutch corporations' stocks traded in foreign exchanges from 30% to 46% of the total trading value; the foreign exchanges include NYSE, NASDAQ, London, Germany, and Swiss Exchanges (Amsterdam Stock Exchange, 2000).

4.3. Increasing of the Foreign Trading Value

Beside the increasing number of cross listed firms, there are significant increasing of the traded value of foreign transactions related to foreign listed firms in the last decade. In some of stock exchanges, the ratio of foreign trade value of stock transactions exceeded the value of the domestic transactions such as in the London Stock exchange. In other exchanges the share of foreign trade formed between 1% to 24% of the total trading values of stocks, as presented in Table 4.

In addition, the trade value of foreign transactions in increased significantly in the last few years. For example, the total foreign transactions in German

Table 4. The Value of Foreign Stock Trading in 1994 and in 1999. (Million and percentages)

Exchange	Currency	Foreign % 1994	Foreign % 1999	1999 Total value
London	GBP	54%	58%	2,092,895.20
Stockholm	SEK	1%	24%	2,609,016.60
Johannesburg	ZAR		15%	529,941.00
Frankfurt	EUR	3%	11%	1,472,829.00
New Zealand	NZD		10%	25,621.20
Brussels	EUR		8%	265,403.90
NYSE-USA	USD		8%	8,910,485.30
Lima	PEN		7%	9,308.90
Switzerland	CHF	6%	5%	847,359.80
Oslo	NOK	1%	5%	445,603.40
Luxembourg	EUR	2%	4%	991.80
NASDAQ–USA	USD		3%	10,463,198.60
Paris	EUR	1.8%	2%	3,481,036.00
Amsterdam	EUR	2%	1%	421,724.00

Source: Based on a: IFSE, Database, September 2000, b: FESE, annual Report, 1994.

Stock Markets increased from 10,711 Euro million in 1995 to 193,209 Euro million in 1999, with an increase of 1700% (German Stock Fact book, 1999). This tremendous increase is almost existed in the majority of both developed and emerging stock markets as presented in Table 5. It shows that the foreign trading value of stock transactions increased between 1998 and 1999 of more than 100% in eight stock exchanges. For stock exchanges such as Milan, which started dealing with foreign stock transactions recently, the increasing ratio, was about 553% just between 1998 and 1999.

4.4. Increasing Foreign Ownership in Stock Markets

Up to the nineteen eighties, the majority of ownership of equity portfolio in the major stock markets were mainly owned by domestic residences. Cooper and Kaplanis (1994) found that in 1987, 100% of stock equities in Sweden, 98% in U.S., 91% in Italy, 79% in the U.K., 75%, in Germany, and 94% in Spain were owned by residents. Stulz (1999), Cooper and Kaplanis (1994), and Tesar (1995) argued that this is due to what is know as the home bias and to the cost of transferring investments cross-borders. The home bias concept is related to the fact that equity portfolio are concentrated in local markets and not on

Table 5. Value of Foreign Stock Trading in 1998 and 1999.

Exchange and Currency		1998 (Million, Local Currency)	1999 (Million, Local Currency)	Increase %
EUR	Italy, Milan	513.9	3,355.6	553%
BMD	Bermuda	27,836.5	86,924.0	212%
ZAR	Johannesburg	27,391.1	81,560.3	198%
SEK	Stockholm	211,209.5	616,214.0	192%
CAD	Toronto	459.0	1,248.8	172%
HKD	Hong Kong	1,386.9	3,391.3	145%
EUR	Luxembourg	19.3	43.7	126%
EUR	Paris	36,066.9	73,815.0	105%
TWD	Taiwan	36,398.0	70,707.0	94%
EUR	Germany	88,238.5	167,345.0	90%
EUR	Madrid	1,050.4	1,803.5	72%
USD	NASDAQ	215,848.6	349,144.7	62%
EUR	Amsterdam	1,730.7	2,781.0	61%
USD	NYSE	561,362.4	686,636.8	22%

Source: Based on IFSE, Database, September 2000.

international foreign markets in spite of the benefit which may gained from diversification. Kang and Stulz (1997) reported that foreign investments are strongly biased against small firms, while it biased with large firms and with good accounting performance firms.

However, this situation is changing gradually. For example, the foreign ownership of U.S. stock equities increased from US$11,240 million in 1995 to US$107,522 million in 1999, with an increase of about 957% in five years (IMF, 2000). Many pension funds in developed and emerging markets are spreading their investments to benefit from diversification and reducing risk. For example, the U.K. pension funds owned about 27% of total equity owned by the pension funds in international equity during the period from 1991 to 1997 (Timmermam & Blake, 2000).

For other stock markets, the share of foreign ownership is increasing rapidly as presented in Table 6. It constituted more than 50% of total ownership in London, Amsterdam and Helsinki Exchanges, and more than one third of the total ownership in other five stock exchanges, while the foreign ownership constituted less than 10% only in Japan and U.S. stock markets.

Table 6. Share of Foreign Ownership in Stock Markets Equities. (1995–2000)

Stock Market Exchanges	Sources	Foreign Ownership of Total Equities
Copenhagen Stock Exchange	a	24%
Helsinki Exchanges Groups	a	60%
Amman Stock Market	a	44%
London Stock Exchange	a	66% clients or equities
Amsterdam Stock Exchange	a	50%
Egypt Stock Exchange	a	23%
New Zealand	a	40%
USA	b	7%
Japan	c	6% (Large firms) 1% (Small firms)
Argentina	d	38%
Chile	d	17%
Mexico	d	25%
Peru	d	38%
Venezuela	d	36%

Source: Based on: a: Fact books of the respective stock exchanges (1999–2000); b: For USA: United States, Board of Governors of the Federal Reserve System, 2000; c: For Japan: Kang and Stulz, 1997; d: For Latin American Countries: Campollo-Palmer, 1997.

4.5. Increasing Equity Portfolio Flows

The flows of portfolio equity investments from developed markets to developing countries, increased from 3.7 billion in 1990 to $49.2 billion in 1996 (IFC, 2000). However, the net private portfolio across stock market witnessed high fluctuations during the period from 1995 to 1999 as a consequence of Asia finical crises in 1997–1998 as presented in Table 7. It shows that there are negative flow of equity portfolio from Asia and Russia in the last two years, as well as a decrease of inflow of equity portfolio in other regions. Froot et al. (2001) argued that the sensitivity of local stock prices to foreign fund inflows, is positive and large.

The existed high volatility of equity portfolio flows between stock markets created unstable linkages. Thus, there is some serious criticism against the portfolio capital flow, as a short-term rather than long term investment. Grabel (1996); Singh and Weisse (1998) considered this as not helping developing countries in enhancing long term economic growth, and may lead to various problems such as: economic and financial crises, undermining the existing bank and financial systems, and increase volatility.

The capital flow of equity portfolio is not able to take full advantage of international portfolio diversification, has unstable structure relation between stock markets and less stable aspects compared to the foreign direct investments flow as concluded by the World Bank report (2000), and Shawky et al. (1997). Accordingly, increasing the linkages of stock markets as a consequence of increasing equity portfolio flows to emerging countries may be

Table 7. Net Private Portfolio Investments Flows to Emerging Markets Between 1992–1999.
(in billion $)

Regional Markets	1992	1995	1998	1999
Africa	1.8	1.4	4.3	4.4
Asia	9.0	14.2	− 17.9	− 5.6
Asian Countries: Indonesia, Korea, Malaysia, Thailand	6.4	17.4	− 6.0	6.3
Europe	2.3	14.6	0.7	6.6
Russia	0.0	10.3	3.9	− 1.1
Middle East	12.7	3.8	6.7	7.3
Western Hemisphere	30.3	3.0	17.7	10.6
Brazil	14.5	11.7	14.8	3.2

Source: IMF, International Capital Markets, September 2000.

consider as negative aspect and may lead to destabilizing of emerging stock markets.

5. FINDINGS OF THE EMPIRICAL STUDY

This part of the study aims at testing whether the increasing forms of linkages between stock markets have an impact on the correlation between movements of the stock market indices. Accordingly, this part examined the existed correlation between each pairs for a sample of 16 developed and emerging stock markets from different geographical regions, in two different years (in 1994 and 1998). This done based on the monthly price movements of stock market local indices. The findings of this part are presented in three sections as follows:

5.1. Comparison Between Price Movements

To compare between the emerging and developed markets during the 1994 and 1998 years, Table 8 presents the monthly changes in percentages of the local price indices for the selected stock markets in 1994. Which includes eight developed stock markets (HKSE, 1999, 1994; Germany stock Market, 1999), and eight emerging stock markets (IFC, 1995, 1999). The local price indices' performance shows high volatility during the 1994 between the developed stock markets, such as that at the end of March, June and November. The performance of the related price indices was decreased in the majority of developed stock markets. However, this association movement had limited extend to the other eight emerging stock markets during 1994.

Table 9, shows the price movements of the selected sample during 1998, the association between the performance of prices' indices was closer between the developed and emerging stock markets, especially that in August and in May movements. At the end of August, all of the selected sixteen stock price indices witnessed losses from -8.2% to -39%. A close situation may be found also, during May movements of stock prices. This high association is also applied when the performance of price indices improves. At the end of October and November, the performance for fifteen stock price indices was improved at the same time covering the losses of August. This high association between price movements of the selected sample of stock markets also existed and reported at the end of February.

Table 8. Monthly Changes of the Local Price Index for the Selected Stock Markets during 1994 in %.

Months	1	2	3	4	5	6	7	8	9	10	11	12
Developed												
Australia	6.3	− 5.7	− 5.8	0.6	0.8	− 4.5	3.6	2.9	− 4.4	0.8	− 7.5	1.2
Japan	16.1	− 1.1	− 4.4	3.2	6.3	− 1.6	− 0.9	0.86	− 0.52	2.2	− 4.6	3.4
Hong Kong	− 3.8	− 8.8	− 12.2	− 1.2	5.0	− 7.9	6.7	3.8	− 2.9	− 0.1	− 12	− 3.7
Singapore	− 3.6	0.2	− 11.2	10.3	− 0.2	− 2.9	20.9	4.9	0.9	2.0	25.8	− 0.1
Toronto	5.4	− 2.9	− 2.1	− 1.5	1.4	27.0	3.9	4.1	0.1	− 1.4	− 4.6	3.0
London	2.2	− 5.0	− 7.3	1.3	− 4.9	− 1.8	5.6	5.5	− 6.9	2.4	− 0.5	− 0.5
New York	6.0	− 3.4	− 5.1	1.3	2.1	− 3.5	3.9	3.9	− 1.8	1.7	− 4.3	2.5
Germany	2.0	3.8	− 1.4	− 4.9	7.0	3.0	− 4.8	− 2.7	8.1	− 2.3	1.7	− 2.3
Emerging												
South Africa	− 2.8	1.9	1.9	8.5	0.7	0.2	4.6	3.2	− 2.7	0.9	0.6	1.9
Korea	9.2	− 2.8	− 5.6	4.8	3.4	− 0.7	− 0.6	1.8	11.3	5.3	− 2.8	− 4.4
Turkey	− 2.8	− 25.4	− 6.1	7.2	− 2.3	34.0	10.0	16.2	6.1	− 7.2	13.2	3.3
Greece	10.1	1.1	5.9	− 1.5	− 13.0	− 1.3	− 0.4	0.1	0.6	− 4.3	3.9	2.6
Malaysia	− 13.2	1.7	− 15.4	10.7	− 5.8	1.8	1.6	10	0.0	− 1.9	− 8.6	− 4.1
Taiwan	0.7	− 11.5	− 3.1	9.3	2.7	0.7	13.3	4.3	1.2	− 8.0	− 2.5	12.5
Argentina	12.8	− 5.7	− 12.4	− 0.5	10.2	− 14.5	8.5	8.7	− 3.3	− 5.9	− 7.2	− 11.6
Mexico	6.9	− 7.0	− 6.8	− 4.8	8.3	− 8.9	8.8	9.8	1.6	− 7.1	1.5	− 8.3

Source: IFC, 1995, and HKSE, 1994.

Table 9. Monthly Changes of the Local Price Index for the Selected Stock Markets during 1998 in %.

Months	1	2	3	4	5	6	7	8	9	10	11	12
Developed												
Australia	1.5	1.5	1.7	0.7	− 1.7	− 1.8	1.4	− 8.2	4.3	2.3	4.8	1.4
Japan	9.0	1.2	− 1.8	− 5.4	0.2	1.0	3.5	− 13.9	− 5.0	1.2	9.7	− 7.0
Hong Kong	− 18.4	24.8	− 1.4	− 9.3	− 14.0	− 6.9	− 7.9	− 10.0	9.7	24.3	2.8	− 3.6
Singapore	− 16.7	18.3	− 1.5	− 8.8	− 13.7	− 13.6	0.6	− 15.7	9.8	28.2	17.6	1.7
Toronto	0.1	5.9	6.6	1.4	− 1.0	− 3.0	− 5.9	− 20.2	1.5	10.6	2.2	2.2
London	6.3	5.6	2.9	− 0.1	− 1.0	− 0.7	0.1	− 10.0	− 3.5	7.4	5.6	2.4
New York	0.0	8.1	3.0	3.0	− 1.8	0.6	− 0.8	− 15.1	4.0	9.5	6.1	0.7
Germany	4.5	6.0	8.3	0.1	8.3	5.9	− 0.5	− 17.7	4.4	7.5	− 0.4	
Emerging												
South Africa	5.6	8.3	6.8	8.7	− 7.4	− 11.3	3.7	− 29.9	3.6	14.3	− 3.6	− 3.4
Korea	48.4	− 1.8	− 12.3	− 12.4	− 20.1	− 11.5	15.3	− 9.7	0.1	24.0	17.5	24.5
Turkey	2.8	− 7.8	− 0.4	28.7	− 11.1	10.0	5.4	− 39.0	− 14.0	− 3.1	17.4	0.8
Greece	− 5.7	1.71	41.3	31.0	− 1.2	− 8.7	18.3	− 22.2	− 2.5	2.0	16.1	9.0
Malaysia	− 4.2	30.9	− 3.5	− 13.0	− 14.0	− 13.4	− 11.6	− 24.8	23.3	8.5	23.7	16.9
Taiwan	− 0.7	13.8	− 1.21	− 8.7	− 4.8	− 4.5	1.4	− 14.4	4.3	3.9	1.1	− 10.6
Argentina	− 8.8	8.0	3.0	− 0.7	− 11.6	− 4.8	6.9	− 30.7	12.8	11.8	3.8	− 8.2
Mexico	− 12.6	4.7	4.8	1.6	− 11.2	− 5.5	− 0.9	− 29.5	19.3	14.2	− 7.5	4.3

Source: IFC, 1999, and HKSE, 1998 and Germany Stock Market Fact Book, 1999.

Table 10. The Significant Correlation Between the Selected Stock Markets as Existed in 1994 Based on Monthly Changes of Local Price Indices.

	Japan	HK	Toronto	London	NY	SA	Malaysia	Argentina	Mexico
Australia	0.737	0.758	0.840	0.698	0.985			0.738	
Japan					0.719				
Hong Kong			0.663		0.790			0.726	0.623
Singapore						0.660	0.732		
Toronto					0.866			0.750	0.659
Lodon					0.703				
New York								0.770	
South Africa							0.591		
Argentina									0.894

Note: Correlation is significant at the 0.01 level.

5.2. The Correlation Existed Between Stock Markets Indices

The Pearson Correlation Coefficient between the stock market indices' movement in 1994 was calculated between each pairs' of indices for the selected 16 stock market exchanges. Out of the total possible stock market pairs, only 17% reported significant correlation between stock price movements during 1994 as presented in Table 10. It shows that there is a significant correlation between developed stock markets with the exception of Germany, while only four emerging markets reported significant correlation including South Africa, Argentine, Mexico, and Malaysia, during the year of 1994. The end of month stock price indices shows no associations for Germany, Korea, Turkey, Greece and Taiwan.

However, this situation had been changed significantly during 1998 year, as presented in Table 11. It shows that there is a significant correlation between the stock market indices' movement for more than half of possible relations of the selected 16 stock markets. A significant correlation is also found between the majority of both developed and emerging stock markets. This includes Germany, which had a negative association during the 1994 year, but in 1998, it had a significant correlation of price movements with the majority of the developed countries. In addition, Malaysia, Taiwan, Argentine, Mexico, Greece and Turkey had significant correlation with other emerging and developing stock markets.

Table 12 presents the stock markets which show significant correlation between their price indices and others. It shows that the number of associated

Table 11. The Significant Correlation Between the Selected Stock Markets as Existed in 1998 Based on Monthly Changes of Local Price Indices.

	Japan	Singapore	Toronto	London	NY	Germany	SA	Turkey	Greece	Malaysia	Taiwan	Argentine	Mexico
Australia	0.596	0.639	0.796	0.695	0.860		0.791	0.575		0.736	0.670	0.861	0.752
Japan				0.763	0.548	0.739							
Hong Kong		0.909	0.569		0.668					0.727	0.644	0.662	0.654
Singapore			0.629		0.743					0.791	0.683	0.748	0.667
Toronto				0.832	0.940	0.731	0.864			0.626	0.657	0.773	0.781
London					0.811	0.818	0.744				0.622	0.574	
New York						0.680	0.854	0.570		0.712	0.689	0.890	0.797
Germany								0.600					
South Africa									0.577		0.570	0.834	0.776
Turkey									0.638				
Malaysia											0.859	0.633	0.620
Taiwan												0.635	0.659
Argentine													0.879

Note: Correlation is significant at the 0.01 level.

Table 12. Number of Associated Markets with Other Stock Indices.

Stock Exchanges Indices	Significant Correlation in 1994	Significant Correlation in 1998
Australia	6	11
Japan	2	4
Hong Kong	5	7
Singapore	2	8
Toronto	3	11
London	2	8
New York	6	13
Germany	0	5
South Africa	2	8
Korea	0	0
Turkey	0	4
Greece	0	2
Malaysia	2	8
Taiwan	0	10
Argentina	5	9
Mexico	3	9
Total	38	116

stock markets increased for all selected stock markets between 1994 and 1998, with the exception of Korea. New York, Toronto, Australia, and Taiwan have had the most associated stock markets (more than ten markets) compared to other stock markets during 1998. The number of associated stock markets increased from 40% to 1000% for the selected sample from 1994 to 1998, with the exception of Korea, which had no association with any of the selected markets in both years. In Taiwan, there was no association with any stock market in 1994, while there was a significant correlation with ten stock markets during 1998.

Finally, to indicate to what extend the correlation between each pairs of the selected stock markets has been increased significantly. Table 13 presents a list of stock market pairs which witnessed an increase of more than 100% in the degree of correlation of price index movement between the year 1994 and the year 1998. It shows that there are about 30 pairs of stock markets witnessed an increase of more than 100% in the degree of correlation between 1994 and 1998. Many of the stock market pairs that show negative correlation in 1994 such as Toronto – South Africa, Germany – Toronto, Germany – New York, Turkey – Greece, South Africa – Mexico, and South Africa – Greece had significant correlation of the stock price movements during 1998.

Table 13. List of Stock Market Pairs that Witnessed Increase More Than 100% in the Degree of Correlation Between the Year 1994 and 1998.

Stock Market Pairs	Correlation in 1994	Correlation in 1998
Australia – South Africa	0.135	0.791
Toronto – South Africa	− 0.022	0.864
London – South Africa	0.377	0.744
New York – South Africa	0.102	0.854
Australia – Malaysia	0.154	0.736
Hong Kong – Malaysia	0.378	0.727
New York – Malaysia	0.194	0.712
Singapore – Mexico	0.121	0.667
Singapore – Taiwan	0.227	0.683
Singapore – Argentine	0.321	0.748
Australia – Singapore	0.280	0.639
Hong Kong – Singapore	0.402	0.909
London – Japan	0.263	0.763
Toronto – London	0.457	0.832
Singapore – New York	0.328	0.743
Japan – Germany	0.119	0.739
Germany – Toronto	− 0.224	0.731
Germany – London	− 0.691	0.818
Germany – New York	− 0.330	0.680
Germany – Australia	− 0.393	0.562
South Africa – Turkey	0.063	0.536
South Africa – Greece	− 0.228	0.577
Turkey – Greece	− 0.046	0.638
Malaysia – Taiwan	0.290	0.859
South Africa – Argentine	0.021	0.834
Argentine – Malaysia	0.121	0.633
Taiwan – Argentine	0.293	0.635
South Africa – Mexico	− 0.107	0.776
Malaysia – Mexico	0.032	0.620
Mexico – Taiwan	0.330	0.659

It should be pointed here the impact of regional affiliation on the degree of the correlation between stock price monthly movements. Such as the correlation between Greece and Turkey, the correlation between the Latin American stock markets, the correlation between Australia, Hong Kong, Singapore and Taiwan. Moreover, some of the regional stock markets witnessed closer association to the developed stock markets between 1994 and 1998, such as Asian and Latin American Markets.

Table 14. Average Correlation Between 1994 and 1998 and *t* Test Values for Groups of Stock Markets.

Groups	1994		1998		N	T Test	Significant at
	Mean	SD	Mean	SD			
Developed – Emerging	0.220	0.340	0.512	0.236	64	7.132	0.000
Developed	0.324	0.449	0.604	0.235	28	2.834	0.009
Emerging	0.122	0.298	0.434	0.264	28	4.590	0.000

5.3. Test of the Stated Positive Hypotheses

The study found that the average correlation for the selected sample of both developed and emerging stock markets increased from 0.220 in 1994 to 0.512 in 1998. This means that there was an increase of 133% of the degree of correlation during the period. For the developed stock markets the average correlation increased from 0.324 in 1994 to 0.604 in 1998, with an increase of 86% during the period. For emerging stock markets the average correlation increased from 0.122, in 1994 to 0.434 in 1998, with an increase of 256% during the period.

It is clear that the average correlation between developed stock markets (0.604) is much higher than the association between the emerging stock markets (0.434) in 1998. This may be due to the fact that the positive correlation between many pairs of emerging stock markets was materialized around the 1997 stock market crisis in Asia and thereafter. While the high positive correlation between developed stock markets was initiated since 1987 stock crisis. However, the percent increase for emerging stock market of correlation between emerging stock markets is much higher than that of the developed market during the period.

To indicate whether the increased percentage of correlation between 1994 and 1998 for the selected stock markets was significantly different or not, the t test was calculated and presented in Table 14. It shows that the degree of correlation (r_1) in 1994 is significantly different than the degree of correlation (r_2) in 1998 at less than 0.01, for the three groups of stock markets. Thus, the stated directional hypotheses for the three groups "There is a significant increase in positive correlation between developed, emerging, and both markets based on monthly movement of stock market indices" has been are confirmed.

6. SUMMARY AND CONCLUSIONS

The paper presented forms of linkages between the world stock markets that exist during the period 1990 to 2000. The forms of stock markets linkages include removing restrictions by stock exchanges imposed on foreign ownership fully or partially. Increasing of stock market liberalization dealing with foreign stocks. Introducing liberal regulatory rules in stock exchanges to attract foreign equities and investors. Increasing the flows of net private portfolio between developed and emerging markets. Increasing of the trading volume of firms shares outside home exchanges. Increasing the number of cross-listed corporations in two or more stock exchanges. Increasing number of the cross listed corporations from emerging economies to be listed in other markets, and increasing the volume of foreign transactions of stocks' trading.

The analysis of published data related to the above factors as presented in stock exchange fact books, International Federation of stock Exchanges Database, IFC fact books and other related sources indicated that there was significant increase in the above factors that lead to more linkages among individual and regional stock markets. The study indicated that there were significant changes during the nineties arising from introducing liberal regulatory rules, from increasing foreign trading, increasing number of cross listed firms and transactions' activities and from equity portfolio flows.

Increasing of stock market linkages was reflected in the high correlation of stock price movements between the majorities of the world stock markets. The study found that a significant correlation was found between 38 stock market pairs in 1994, which increased to 117 stock market pairs in 1998. In addition, there was a significant positive increase from 1994 to 1998 in the degree of correlation between the majority of the selected developed and emerging stock markets based on monthly changes of performance' indices.

The increasing linkages of stock market should be considered carefully, due to the fact that many studies reported that stock market linkages are increasing more in high volatile stock prices and during unstable periods, thus may lead to the transmission of stock volatility to other stocks. Example of these studies are: (Login & Solnik, 2001; Lin et al., 1994; De Santis & Imrohoroglu, 1997; Ramchand & Susmel, 1998; Janakiramanan & Lamba, 1998; Jeong, 1999; Solnik et al., 1996; Koutmos, 1999 and Bracker et al., 1999). The increasing of the foreign listed firms may also have negative aspects in this regard than other factors. Due to the fact that the dual listed shares are priced in different market places, with different currencies, different methods of pricing, different methods of settlements and other related conditions, which may increase the movement of stock price volatility as examined by Lin et al. (1994) Kane et al. (2000), Werner and Kleidon (1996), and Chan et al. (2000).

Therefore, the negative aspects of increasing linkages and open borders between stock markets should be considered, which may lead to a stock market crisis as happened in 1987, and 1997. Increasing linkages suppose to increase data dissemination, and thus increase efficiency of the stock market. However, with the existing new situation of stock volatility spillover, this issue should be scrutinized carefully in the coming era. In which linkages and correlation between stock markets in both developed and emerging markets are expected to intensify and be more associated with each other than it is now.

REFERENCES

Amsterdam Stock Exchange (2000). *Amsterdam Stock Exchange: Facts & Figures July.* Amsterdam, Netherlands.

Arshanapalli, B., & Doukas, J. (1993). International stock market linkages: evidence from the pre- and post October 1987 period. *Journal of Banking & Finance, 17*, 193–208.

Bekaert, G., & Harvey, C. R. (1997). Emerging equity market volatility. *Journal of Financial Economics 43*, 29–77.

Biddle, G., & Saudagaran, S. M. (1989). The effects of financial disclosure levels on firms' choices among alternative foreign stock exchange listings. *Journal of International Financial Management and Accounting, 1*, 56–87.

Bracker, K., Docking, D. S., & Koch, P. D. (1999). Economic determinants of evolution in international stock market integration. *Journal of Empirical Finance, 6*, 1–27.

Bracker, K., & Koch, P. D. (1999). Economic determinants of the correlation structure across international equity markets. *Journal of Economic and Business, 15*, 443–472.

Campollo-Palmer C. (1997). Equity investments in emerging markets. NYSE. Conference on the Globalization of Financial Markets, Working paper, Mexico.

Chan, K., Chockalingam, M., & Lai., K. W. L. (2000). Overnight information and intraday trading behavior: Evidence from NYSE cross-listed stocks and their local market information. *Journal of Multinational Financial Management, 10*, 495–509.

Cheung, C. S., & Lee, J. (1995). Disclosure environment and listing on foreign stock exchanges. *Journal of Banking & Finance, 19*, 347–362.

Claessencs, S. (1995). The emergence of equity investment in developing countries: overview. *The World Bank Economic Review, 9*, 1–18.

Cooper, I., & Kaplanis, E. (1994). Home bias in equity portfolios, inflation hedging and international capital markets equilibrium. *Review of Financial Studies, 7*, 45–60.

Copenhagen Stock Exchange (2000). *Factbook 2000.* Copenhagen Stock Exchange, Copenhagen.

De Santis, G., & Imrohorglu, S. (1997). Stock returns and volatility in emerging financial markets. *Journal of International Money and Finance, 16*, 561–579.

FESE (1994–2000). *European Stock Exchanges Statistics Annual Reports.* FESE, Brussels.

FESE (2000). *The Federation of European Stock Exchanges Database.* FESE, Brussels. Available on line: www.fese.be.

Froot, K. A., O'Connell, P. G., & Seasholes, M. S. (2001). The portfolio flows of international investors. *Journal of Financial Economics*, *59*, 189–216.

Gardiol, L., Gibson-Asner, R., & Tuchshmid, N. S. (1997). Are liquidity and corporate control priced by shareholders? Empirical evidence from Swiss dual class shares. *Journal of Corporate Finance*, *3*, 299–323.

Germany Stock Market (1999). *Deutshe Borse Factbook 1999*. Frankfurt, Germany.

Grabel, I. (1996). Marketing the third world: the contradictions of portfolio investment in the global economy. *World Development*, *24*, 1761–1776.

Hargis, K. (2000). International cross-listing and stock market development in emerging economics. *International Review of Economics and Finance*, *9*, 101–122.

Henry, P. B. (2000). Stock market liberalization, economic reform, and emerging market equity prices. *Journal of Finance*, *55*, 529–563.

HKSE (1994). *Hong Kong Stock Exchange Fact Book 1994*. Hong Kong Exchange & Clearing Limited.

HKSE (1998). *Hong Kong Stock Exchange Fact Book 1998*. Hong Kong Exchange & Clearing Limited.

IFC (1995). *Emerging Stock Markets Factbook 1995*, International Financial Corporation, Washington, D.C.

IFC (1999). *Emerging Stock Markets Factbook 1999*, International Financial Corporation, Washington, D.C.

IFC (2000). *Emerging Stock Markets Factbook 2000*. Standard & Poor's, Washington, D.C.

IFSE (2000). *International Federation of Stock Exchanges Data Base*. FIBV, Paris. Available on line www. fibv.com.

IMF (2000). International Capital Markets: Development, Prospects and Key Policy Issues. *World Economic and Financial Surveys*, Washington, September.

Janakiramanan, S., & Lamba, A. S. (1998). An empirical examination of, linkages between Pacific-Basin stock markets. *Journal of International Financial Markets, Institutions & Money*, *8*, 155–173.

Jayaraman N., Shastri, K., & Tandon, K. (1993). The impact of international cross listings on risk and return, the evidence from American depository receipts. *Journal of Banking & Finance*, *17*, 91–103.

Jeong, J. (1999). Cross-border Transmission of stock price volatility: evidence from the overlapping trading hours. *Global Finance Journal*, *10*, 53–70.

Kanas, A. (1999). Volatility spillover across equity markets: European Evidence. *Applied Financial Economics*, *8*, 245–257.

Kane A., Lehmann, B. N., & Trippi, R. R. (2000). Regularities in volatility and the price of risk following large stock market movements in the U.S. and Japan. *Journal of International Money and Finance*, *19*, 1–32.

Kang, J., & Stulz, R. M. (1997). Why is there a home bias? An analysis of foreign portfolio equity ownership in Japan. *Journal of Financial Economics*, *46*, 2–28.

King, M. A. (1990). Transmission of volatility between stock markets. *The Review of Financial Studies*, (Vol. 3, No. 1), 5–33.

Koutmos, G. (1999). Asymmetric price and volatility adjustments in emerging Asian stock markets. *Journal of Business Finance & Accounting*, *26*, 83–102.

Levine, R., & Zervos, S. (1998). Capital control liberalization and stock market development. *World Development*, *26*, 1169–1183.

Lin, W., Engle, R. F., & Ito, T. (1994). Do bulls and bears move across borders? International transmission of stock returns and volatility. *The Review of Financial Studies*, *7*, 507–538.

Longin, F., & Solnik, B. (2001). Extreme correlation of international equity markets. *Journal of Finance*, *56*, Forthcoming.

Martell, T. F., Rodriguez, L. Jr., & Webb, G. P. (1999). The impact of listing Latin American ADRs on the risks and returns of the underlying shares. *Global Finance Journal*, *19*, 147–160.

Miller, D. P. (1999). The market reaction to international cross-listings: Evidence from depositary receipts. *Journal of Financial Economics*, *51*, 103–123.

Mueller, G. (1999). Global financial accounting standards setting at crossroads. *Emerging Issues in International Accounting Proceeding*, 7–11. Niagara University, USA.

Ramchand, L., & Susmel, R. (1998). Volatility and cross correlation across major stock markets. *Journal of Empirical Finance*, *5*, 397–416.

Sabri, N. R. (1995a). Stabilization of stock markets; the case of the Frankfurt exchange. *Journal of Multinational Financial Management*, *5*(3), 23–32.

Sabri, N. R. (1995b). Experts' opinions towards the stock market stability during the stock market crisis. *International Journal of Commerce and Management*, *5*(2–3), 130–146.

Shawky, H. A., Kuenzel R., & Mikhail, A. D. (1997). International portfolio diversification: A synthesis and an update. *Journal of International Financial Markets, Institutions & Money*, *7*, 303–327.

Singh, A., & Weisse, B. (1998). Emerging stock markets, portfolio capital flows and long-term economic growth micro and macroeconomics perspectives. *World Development*, *26*, 607–622.

Solnik, B., Boucrelle, C., & Le Fur, Y. (1996). International market correlation and volatility. *Financial Analysts Journal*, *52*(5), 17–35.

Stulz, R. M. (1999). *Globalization of equity markets and the cost of capital.* BSI Gamma Foundation, Switzerland.

Stulz, R. M., & Wasserfallen, W. (1995). Foreign equity investment restrictions, capital flight, and shareholder wealth maximization: theory and evidence. *The Review of Financial Studies*, *8*, 1019–1057.

Tesar, L. L. (1995). Home bias and high turnover. *Journal of International Money and Finance*, *14*, 467–492.

Timmermam, A., & Blake, D. (2000). *Determinants of international portfolio performance.* BSI Gamma Foundation, Switzerland.

UNCTAD, World Investment Report (1999). *Foreign Direct Investment and the Challenge of Development United Nations*, New York and Geneva.

Werner, I. M., & Kleidon, A. W. (1996). U.K. trading of British cross – listed stocks: An intraday analysis of market integration. *The Review of Financial Studies*, *9*, 619–664.

World Bank (2000). *Global Development Finance 2000.* The World Bank, Washington, D.C.

Wu, C., & Su, Y. (1998). Dynamic relations among international stock markets. *International Review of Economics and Finance*, *7*, 63–84.

TESTING FOR CONTAGION DURING THE ASIAN CRISIS

B. Gerard, K. Thanyalapark and D. Filson

ABSTRACT

This paper uses a stationary multivariate asymmetric GARCH specification of the international capital asset pricing model to investigate contagion effects across five developed and emerging East Asian markets as well as the U.S. and the World markets around the time of the Asian currency crisis of 1997. After controlling for domestic shocks and spillover effects, the results suggest that the region's equity markets volatility processes display interdependence but little contagion. The results indicate contagion effects only from Thailand to Korea.

INTRODUCTION

The region-wide panic struck first in Thailand before spreading to Malaysia, the Philippines, Indonesia, Korea, and eventually to Taiwan and Hong Kong. During the first year following the inception of the Asian crisis, the currencies of the affected countries depreciated by 35% to 80%, reducing wealth substantially. Many analysts argue that the magnitude, severity and geographical reach of the crisis were amplified by contagion effects.[1] However, it is not obvious that the crisis was caused by contagion effects rather than by shared economic weaknesses. Most of the Asian countries that suffered from the crisis shared similar fundamental economic problems. They experienced both external macroeconomic problems (such as fixed exchange rates, high

Financial Risk and Financial Risk Management, Volume 16, pages 375–394.

ISBN: 0-7623-0858-3

interest rates, excessive borrowing from abroad, and domestic political instability) and internal weaknesses (such as inadequate financial supervisory institutions, antiquated banking practices, and poor investment decisions in the private sector).

The goal of this paper is to assess whether contagion took place. This is important for both investors and policy makers. If contagion occurs it undermines much of the benefits of international diversification. Understanding the source and transmission mechanisms of the crisis are important as policy makers contemplate financial market, institutional, and macro-political reforms to foster a recovery while preventing another crisis.

There are several hypotheses that could explain transferred shocks across countries, and each has different policy implications. For example, Glick and Rose (1998) argue that contagion spreads from countries which are closely tied by international trade linkages to the victim countries. However, the evidence suggests that trade linkages are not sufficient for explaining the Asian crisis in 1997–1998. For example, Table 1 reports that Thailand's most important export market among Hong Kong, Korea, and Malaysia was Hong Kong, but even Hong Kong never accounted for more than 6.70% of Thailand's exports during 1997–1998. The numbers in Table 1 are too small to account for the large shocks that occurred in Asia.

The explanation of the Asian crisis that we test is that the spread of the crisis was the consequence of herd behavior by investors.[2] The claim that herd behavior was an important contributing factor to the crisis is widely accepted, but to date it has proved difficult to test this claim.[3] The main approach for testing for herd behavior is to test whether the correlations between the returns in the different countries' stock markets rose after the onset of the crisis. If investors in different markets all respond to a shock in one market then we should observe the correlations between the returns in the different countries' stock markets rise after the onset of the crisis.

Forbes and Rigobon (1998, 1999) use cross-market correlations to test for stock market contagion from Hong Kong to other countries. They measure the correlation coefficient of the returns in Hong Kong and each other country using a linear ordinary least squares model. However, Forbes and Rigobon (1998) show that conventional correlation coefficients are biased upward, especially during the crisis. Therefore, they propose using "adjusted" correlation coefficients to test for contagion. Their analysis has important implications for previous empirical studies because it suggests that high market co-movements during the crisis were simply a continuation of strong cross-market linkages. In other words, there was no contagion – only interdependence.

Table 1. Total Export Shares.
The percentage of Thailand's Exports that go to Selected Countries. Table Entry is Percentage of Total Exports

Share of exports in percentage terms												
1997: Month	**January**	**February**	**March**	**April**	**May**	**June**	**July**	**August**	**September**	**October**	**November**	**December**
USA	17.78	16.52	16.85	17.89	18.79	20.13	21.40	22.07	20.43	20.57	19.96	20.25
Japan	16.20	16.21	16.27	15.32	15.03	15.87	15.80	14.69	14.97	14.32	14.60	12.84
Korea	1.83	2.19	2.10	2.09	2.38	1.98	1.56	1.39	1.74	1.35	1.43	1.25
Hong Kong	4.66	5.78	6.70	6.09	6.31	5.89	5.59	6.31	6.06	5.51	6.13	6.19
Malaysia	4.33	3.64	4.59	4.79	4.33	5.08	4.35	4.46	4.13	3.86	4.24	4.17
Total Exports	100.00	100.00	100.00	100.00	100.00	100.00	100.00	100.00	100.00	100.00	100.00	100.00
1998: Month	**January**	**February**	**March**	**April**	**May**	**June**	**July**	**August**	**September**	**October**	**November**	**December**
USA	21.33	19.85	20.97	20.64	22.70	22.24	24.54	24.81	23.72	23.58	22.18	21.44
Japan	13.28	14.75	14.38	12.86	13.57	13.80	13.36	13.33	13.53	13.55	14.52	13.52
Korea	1.00	1.15	1.39	1.45	1.33	1.04	1.08	0.96	1.06	0.99	1.09	1.25
Hong Kong	4.99	5.71	5.76	5.25	5.67	4.94	4.64	4.75	5.52	4.68	4.60	4.80
Malaysia	3.07	3.11	3.40	3.74	3.36	3.64	3.24	2.85	2.90	3.15	3.38	3.37
Total Exports	100.00	100.00	100.00	100.00	100.00	100.00	100.00	100.00	100.00	100.00	100.00	100.00

We use cross-market correlations to test for stock market contagion during the 1997 Asian crisis, but we propose a different approach to eliminate the bias in the conventional correlation coefficient. We compute the correlation matrix using time-varying estimates. This conditional correlation coefficient is measured at each point in time so it is automatically adjusted for the bias introduced by the change in market volatility. To compute the time-varying conditional variance we use an asymmetric Generalized Autoregressive Conditional Heteroscedasticity (GARCH) process where volatility responds more to negative shocks than to positive ones.[4] The standard GARCH model allows for the variance to change over time as a function of past errors and the past conditional variance but assumes that volatility responds symmetrically to positive and negative shocks. Several papers (for example, Erb, Harvey & Viskanta, 1995; Kroner & Ng, 1999; De Santis & Gerard, 1999) argue that volatility processes increase more following negative shocks than following positive shocks. This is crucial, because during the crisis, when most shocks are negative, the symmetry restriction in GARCH leads to a downward bias in the volatility processes – hence, we use an asymmetric GARCH.

We find little evidence for contagion. The absence of significant increases in correlations between the different countries' stock markets suggests that co-movement across markets are simply due to their historically close relationships. We find evidence for contagion only from Thailand to Korea.

DID CONTAGION OCCUR IN ASIA?

The Data

The sample covers January 1985 to December 1998. For Hong Kong, Japan, the U.S., and the world, we use the monthly dollar-denominated returns on stock indices supplied by Morgan Stanley Capital International (MSCI). For the emerging markets, Korea, Thailand, and Malaysia, we use the dollar-denominated returns on emerging stock indices from International Financial Corporation (IFC). Emerging market country short-term interest rates are from International Financial Statistics (IFS), and developed countries' short-term interest rates come from the Bank of International Settlement.

The Test

There is no exact date for the beginning of the crisis. We follow Manning (1999) and take the commencement of the "crisis" to be January 1, 1997. This date is reasonable. According to Radelet and Sachs (1998), in January 1997

Hanbo Steel, a large Korean chaebol, collapsed with debts of six billion U.S. dollars and was soon followed by Sammi Steel and Kia Motors. In early March, Somprasong Land, one of the biggest Thai real estate companies, defaulted on the payments of its foreign debt. By May 1997, the Thai currency was affected by massive selling, and was finally devalued on July 2. By June 1997, Asian currencies were clearly in "crisis." The volatility of stock market returns (measured by the standard deviation) in Korea, Malaysia, and Thailand increase dramatically during the crisis: 70% in Korea, 100% in Malaysia, and 65% in Thailand.

We investigate contagion effects by examing how correlations among stock markets change during the crisis. Substantial increases in the correlations after the onset of the crisis are consistent with contagion effects. Panel A in Table 2 reports conventional correlations (covariance divided by the product of the standard deviations) and shows that the correlations between Thailand and all other countries rise after the onset of the crisis. Panel B reports conditional correlations from the asymmetric GARCH process and shows that only the correlation between Thailand and Korea rises substantially. Figures 1–3 present

Table 2. Correlation Coefficients.

Unconditional and average conditional correlations between Thailand and selected countries. The stable period is January 1995 to December 1996, and the crisis period is January 1997 to December 1998.

Panel A: correlation coefficients are unadjusted and unconditional

Country	**Stable period**	**Crisis period**
USA	0.51	0.55
Japan	0.21	0.57
Korea	0.29	0.65
Hong Kong	0.56	0.66
Malaysia	0.57	0.73

Panel B: correlation coefficients are adjusted and conditional

Country	**Stable period**	**Crisis period**
USA	0.37	0.30
Japan	0.25	0.26
Korea	0.32	0.54
Hong Kong	0.65	0.52
Malaysia	0.69	0.66

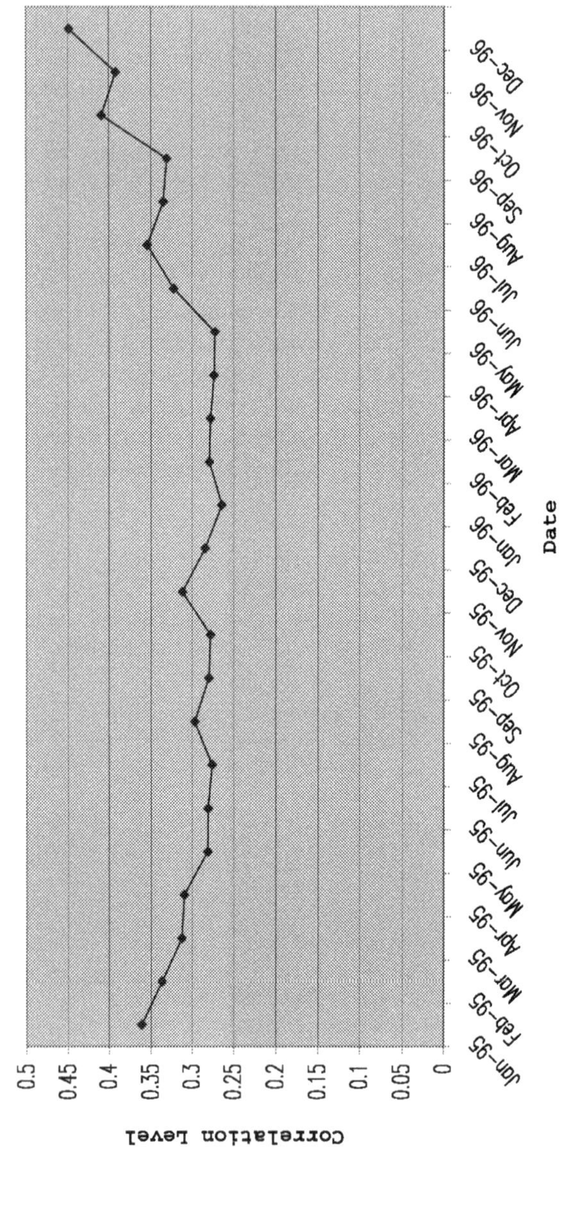

Fig. 1a. Rolling Conditional Correlation Between Thailand and Korea During the Stable Period.

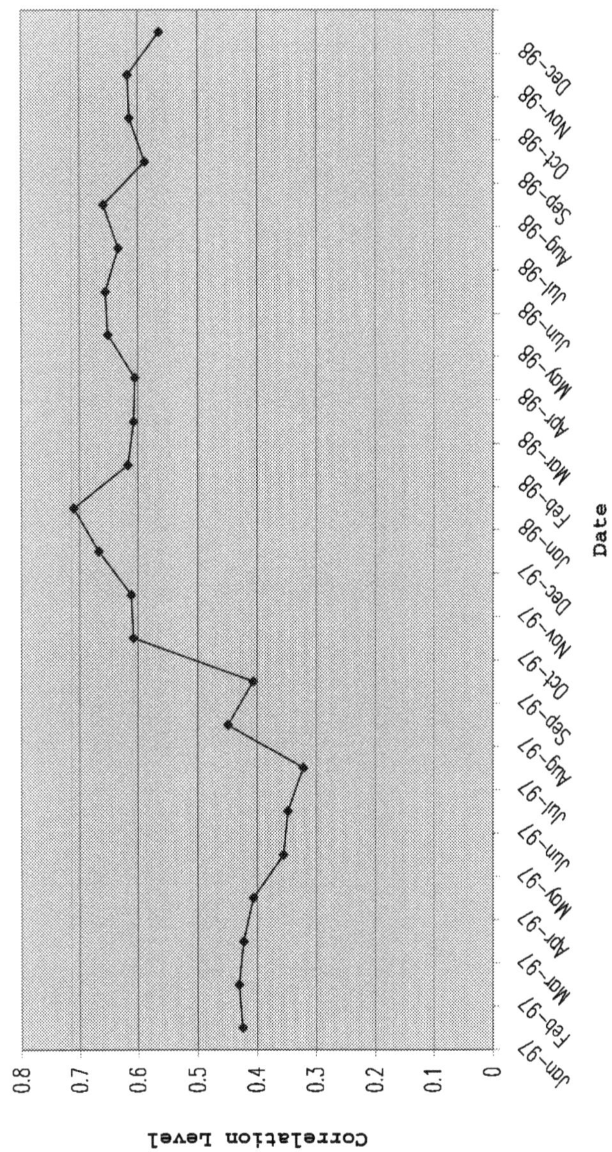

Fig. 1b. Rolling Conditional Correlation Between Thailand and Korea During the Crisis Period.

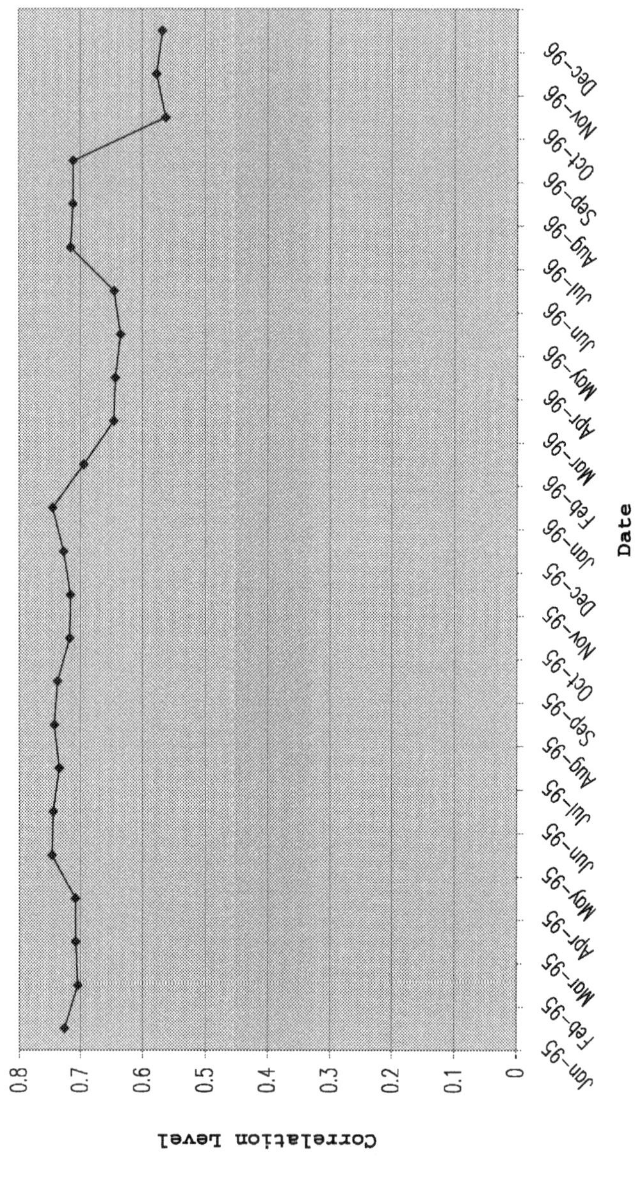

Fig. 2a. Rolling Conditional Correlation Between Thailand and Malaysia During the Stable Period.

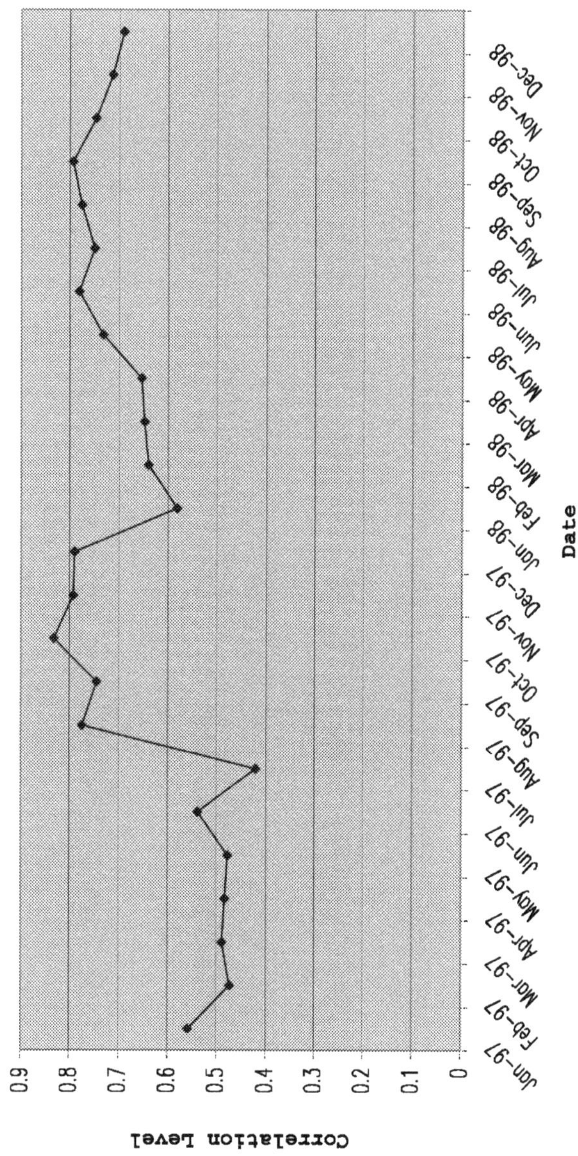

Fig. 2b. Rolling Conditional Correlation Between Thailand and Malaysia During the Crisis Period.

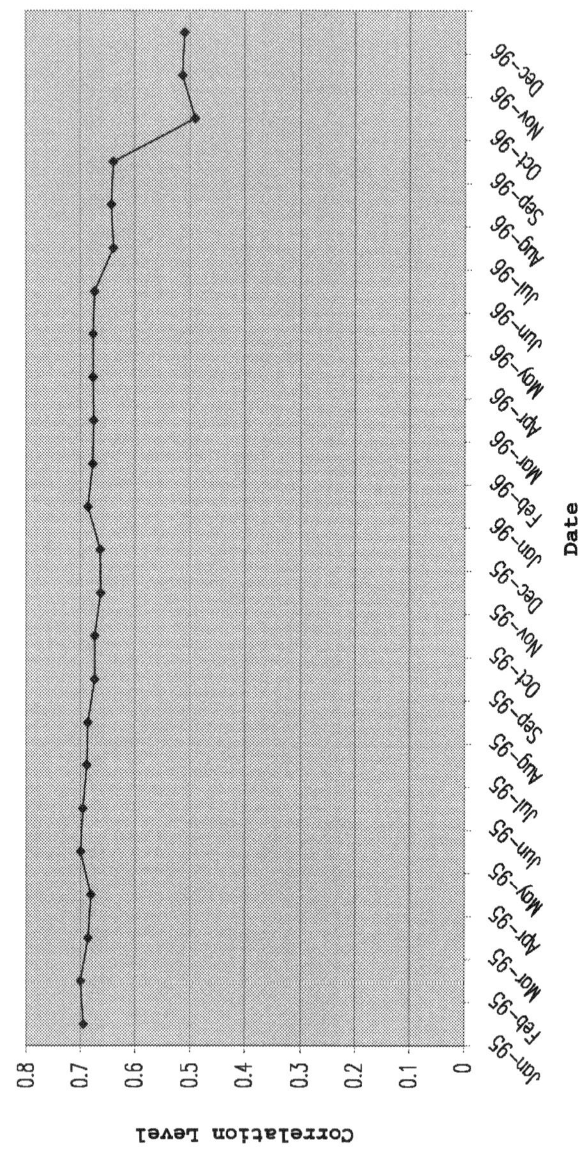

Fig. 3a. Rolling Conditional Correlation Between Thailand and Hong Kong During the Stable Period.

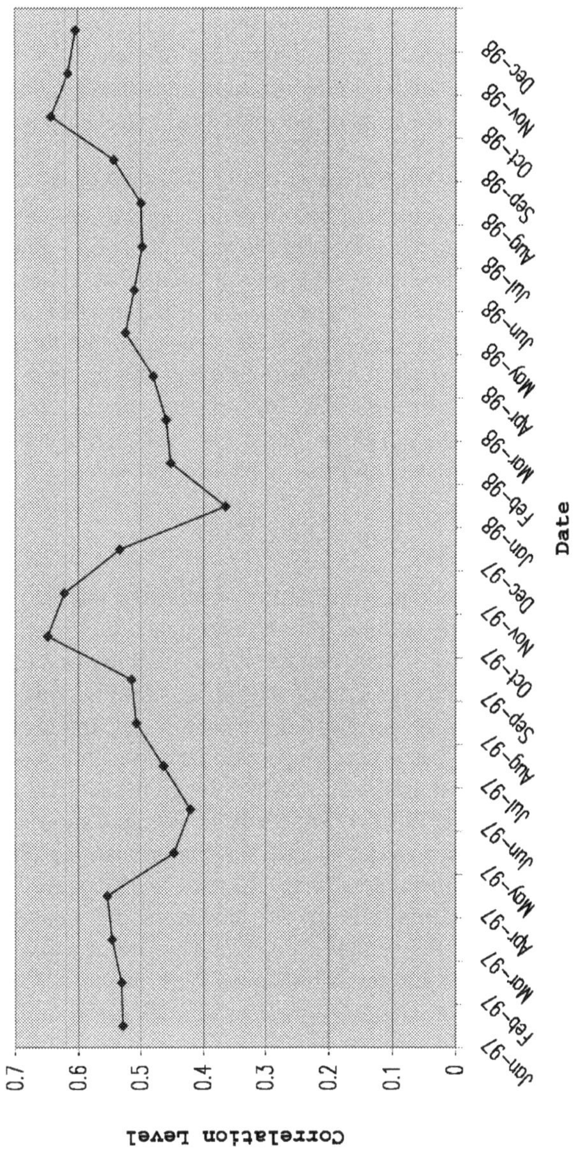

Fig. 3b. Rolling Conditional Correlation Between Thailand and Hong Kong During the Crisis Period.

the rolling conditional correlations during the stable period and the crisis period of Thailand and Korea, Thailand and Malaysia, and Thailand and Hong Kong, and lead to the same conclusion. Evidently, using conditional correlation coefficients has a significant impact on the result of the contagion test. In the stable period, results from both correlations (conditional and unconditional) are very similar, but during the crisis the unconditional correlation is substantially greater.

We follow Erb, Harvey, and Viskanta (1998) and investigate one additional measure of cross-sectional correlation. Table 3 reports the highest fraction of countries who all experienced returns in the same direction (either positive or negative) each month. This measure gives a point-wise estimate of cross-sectional correlations. If the ratio equals to one, it implies that all countries in the region move in the same direction. Table 3 suggests that there is a pattern of high cross-sectional correlation in Asia that has little to do with the crisis. Correlations were high before 1995, too: the regional correlation index is about 0.8 in mid-1987 and rises to 1.00 in mid-1994, well before the onset of the crisis. Therefore, the crisis has minimal impact on this index.

Thailand and Korea

Figure 4 shows that the conditional volatility of shocks in the Thai stock market shock reached about 15% in August 1997 although it had been around 10% throughout the early periods. This number is very striking because it deviated approximately 50% from its pre-crisis conditional volatility. This incident may be seen as an effect of a managed float of the baht in July. Interestingly, the fall in the Thai stock market has a great impact on its correlation with the Korean stock market. Figure 1b shows that after the plunge in the Thai stock market, the correlation rose to over 60% in October 1997. Figure 4 shows that after this rise in correlation, the Korean stock market conditional volatility increased significantly. Conditonal volatility in the Korean market stayed at this high level until December, 1998. These circumstances are consistent with a contagion effect because the negative shock in Thailand led to a sharp rise in the correlation and had an enormous impact on the Korean stock market. Thus, we conclude that there was a contagion effect from Thailand to Korea.

Robustness Tests

In the above estimation we assume that the crisis lasted from January 1, 1997 to December 1998. We repeated the analysis assuming that the crisis started in June 1997 and the main results did not change. There were slight changes

Table 3. Regional Correlation.

Regional Correlation is the highest fraction of countries who all experienced returns in the same direction (either positive or negative).
Countries included are Japan, Korea, Thailand, Hong Kong and Malaysia.
Stable period is from January 1995 to December 1996 and the crisis period is from January 1997 to December 1998.

Date	**Stable Period**		**Crisis Period**
Jan-95	1	Jan-97	0.6
Feb-95	0.6	Feb-97	0.6
Mar-95	0.8	Mar-97	1
Apr-95	0.6	Apr-97	0.6
May-95	0.6	May-97	0.8
Jun-95	0.6	Jun-97	0.6
Jul-95	0.8	Jul-97	0.6
Aug-95	1	Aug-97	1
Sep-95	0.6	Sep-97	0.6
Oct-95	0.6	Oct-97	1
Nov-95	0.6	Nov-97	1
Dec-95	0.8	Dec-97	0.8
Jan-96	0.6	Jan-98	0.6
Feb-96	0.8	Feb-98	0.8
Mar-96	0.8	Mar-98	0.8
Apr-96	1	Apr-98	1
May-96	0.6	May-98	1
Jun-96	0.6	Jun-98	0.8
Jul-96	1	Jul-98	0.6
Aug-96	0.6	Aug-98	1
Sep-96	0.8	Sep-98	0.6
Oct-96	0.6	Oct-98	1
Nov-96	0.8	Nov-98	0.8
Dec-96	0.8	Dec-98	0.6
Average	0.73	**Average**	0.78
SD	0.15	**SD**	0.18

in unadjusted correlations results with the new crisis date; Japan, Korea and Malaysia were all victims of contagion effects. However, results from conditional correlation coefficients still indicate contagion only from Thailand to Korea.

As a second robustness test we consider how an alternative source of contagion affects our results. We follow Forbes and Rigobons (1998, 1999) and use the October crash of the Hong Kong market as the event leading to

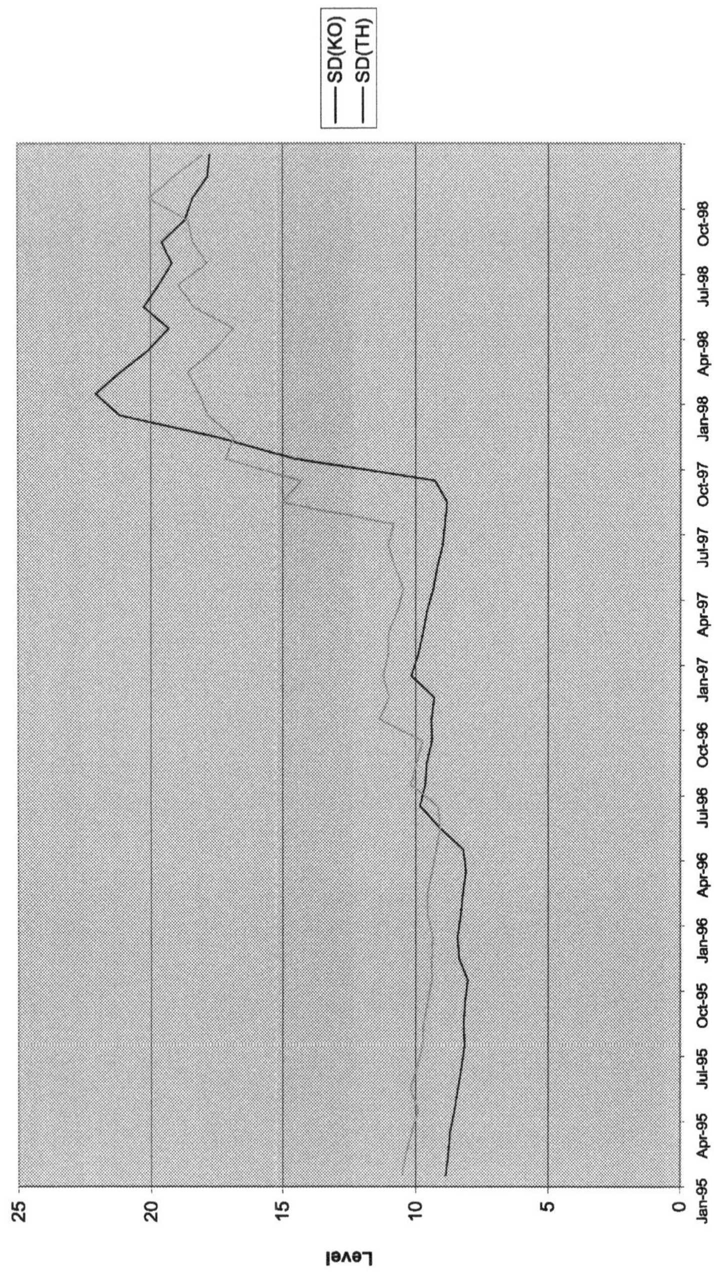

Fig. 4. Conditional Volatility of Korea vs. Thailand.

Table 4. Correlation Coefficients.

Unconditional and average conditional correlations between Hong Kong and selected countries. The stable period is October 1995 to December 1996, and the crisis period is October 1997 to December 1998

Panel A: correlation coefficients are unadjusted and unconditional

Country	**Stable period**	**Crisis period**
USA	0.75	0.54
Japan	0.11	0.49
Korea	0.08	0.23
Thailand	0.57	0.69
Malaysia	0.45	0.67

Panel B: correlations are adjusted and conditional

Country	**Stable period**	**Crisis period**
USA	0.54	0.51
Japan	0.18	0.24
Korea	0.22	0.04
Thailand	0.63	0.53
Malaysia	0.70	0.57

contagion. The period of crisis is October 1997 to December 1998 and the period of relatively stability is October 1995 to December 1996. The conclusions are similar to those of Table 2 – the conditional correlations indicate much less contagion. Table 4 shows that unadjusted correlations indicate that there are contagion effects from Hong Kong to several countries, but conditional correlations indicate only slight contagion from Hong Kong to Japan.

Next, because contagion may occur from any country in the region, Table 5 reports the correlation coefficient matrices for every country in the sample using January 1, 1997 as the onset of the crisis. The unadjusted correlations indicate contagion effects in all countries, whereas the adjusted correlations indicate substantial contagion effects only in Korea and Thailand.

CONCLUSION

To assess whether contagion took place during the Asian crisis, we used an international capital market model to examine the spillover effects among crisis

Table 5.

Average Unconditional Correlation Coefficient for Residuals Shocks in the Stable and Crisis Periods (crisis period in italics). The Stable Period is January 1995 to December 1996, and the Crisis Period is January 1997 to December 1998.

	USA	**JAPAN**	**KOREA**	**THAILAND**	**HONG KONG**	**MALAYSIA**	**WORLD**
USA	1	0.33	0.17	0.51	0.47	0.34	0.45
		0.50	*0.30*	*0.55*	*0.59*	*0.59*	*0.93*
JAPAN		1	0.49	0.21	0.06	0.16	0.18
			0.65	*0.57*	*0.52*	*0.40*	*0.70*
KOREA			1	0.29	0.15	0.20	0.25
				0.65	*0.23*	*0.34*	*0.43*
THAILAND				1	0.56	0.57	0.58
					0.66	*0.73*	*0.63*
HONGKONG					1	0.60	0.63
						0.64	*0.64*
MALAYSIA						1	0.87
							0.61
WORLD							1

Average Conditional Correlation Coefficient for residuals shocks in the stable and crisis periods (crisis period in italics). The stable period is January 1995 to December 1996, and the crisis period is January 1997 to December 1998.

	USA	**JAPAN**	**KOREA**	**THAILAND**	**HONG KONG**	**MALAYSIA**	**WORLD**
USA	1.00	0.23	0.19	0.37	0.52	0.51	0.79
		0.24	*0.16*	*0.30*	*0.52*	*0.37*	*0.78*
JAPAN		1.00	0.47	0.25	0.18	0.24	0.74
			0.31	*0.26*	*0.23*	*0.23*	*0.73*
KOREA			1.00	0.32	0.23	0.29	0.37
				0.54	*0.10*	*0.24*	*0.23*
THAILAND				1.00	0.65	0.69	0.42
					0.52	*0.66*	*0.34*
HONG KONG					1.00	0.70	0.52
						0.58	*0.53*
MALAYSIA						1.00	0.53
							0.39
WORLD							1.00

countries. We interpret contagion in terms of herd behavior – the basic hypothesis is that if herd behavior was a factor in the crisis, then the correlation between the stock markets of the affected countries should rise during the crisis, even after controlling for the important aspects of own-country risk. A sharp increase in correlation during the crisis period implies that the relationships among countries have moved away from their traditional comovements of fundamentals.

Our tests using unconditional correlation coefficients indicates contagion effects in several markets. However, when conditional correlation coefficients are used, contagion effects occur only between Thailand and Korea. The key results from this paper raise several issues for research on stock market co-movements. Although we did not find a significant increase in stock market co-movement after the onset of the crisis, the co-movements are very high in several counties. Similar experiences during the crisis can be accounted for by a continuation in the high level of interdependence between the various markets.

NOTES

1. The term contagion refers to herd behavior that occurs when investors pull out of a market because their expectations have been changed by a shock in another market.
2. Calvo and Mendoza (2000) provide an excellent description of herd mentality in a global portfolio diversification framework. They suggest that it is rational for an investor to acquire less information when there are greater opportunities to diversify globally. As a result, there is a more significant impact of "news" on the allocation of investment funds in any particular country. Investors tend to follow the market instead of making their own assessments of each country's fundamentals, perhaps guessing that market portfolios embodied relevant information, or fearing the consequences of disagreeing with the market (Scharfstein & Stein, 1990).
3. Attempts to assess contagion and investor behavior during the Asian Crisis include Baig and Goldfajn (1998), Forbes and Rigobon (1998, 1999), Glick (1998a, b), Radelet and Sachs (1998), Tan (1998), Manning (1999), Hahm and Mishkin (2000), Ang and Ma (2001), and In et al. (2001).
4. The estimation method is described in the Appendix.

ACKNOWLEDGMENTS

Filson thanks the John M. Olin Foundation and the National Association of Scholars for financial support.

REFERENCES

Ang, J. S., & Ma, Y. (2001). The Behavior of Financial Analysts During the Asian Financial Crisis in Indonesia, Korea, Malaysia, and Thailand. *Pacific Basin Finance Journal*, 9(3, June), 233–263.

Baig, T., & Goldfajn, I. (1998). Financial Market Contagion in the Asian Crisis. IMF Working Paper, No. 115.

Berndt, E. K., Hall, B. H., Hall, R. E., & Hausman, J. A. (1974). Estimation and Inference in Nonlinear Structural Models. *Annuals of Economic and Social Measurement*, *3*, 653–665.

Bollerslev, T., & Woolridge, J. M. (1992). Quasi-maximum likelihood estimation and inference in dynamic models with time-varying covariances. *Econometric Reviews*, *11*, 143–172.

Calvo, G., & Mendoza, E. (2000). Rational Contagion and the Globalization of Securities Markets. *Journal of International Economics*, *51*(1, June), 79–113.

De Santis, G., & Gerard, B. (1997). International Asset Pricing and Portfolio Diversification with Time-Varying Risk. *Journal of Finance*, *52*, 1881–1912.

De Santis, G., Gerard, B., & Hillion, P. (1999). Portfolio Choice and Currency Risk Inside and Outside the EMU. *Swedish Economic Policy Review*, *6*(1), 87–116.

Erb, B. C., Harvey, R. C., & Viskanta, E. T. (1998). Contagion and Risk. Working Paper. Chicago: First Chicago NBD Investment Management Company.

Forbes, K., & Rigobon, R. (1998). No Contagion, Only Interdependence: Measuring Stock Market Co-movements. Working Paper. M.I.T.-Sloan School of Management.

Forbes, K., & Rigobon, R. (1999). Measuring Contagion: Conceptual and Empirical Issues. UNU-WIDER conference on Financial Contagion held in Helsinki, Finland. Working Paper.

Glick, R. (1998a). Thoughts on The Origins of The Asia Crisis: Impulses and Propagation Mechanisms. Federal Reserve Bank of San Francisco. Research Department. Working Paper, No. PB98–07.

Glick, R. (1998b). Contagion and Trade: Why are Currency Crises Regional? Center for Pacific Basin Monetary and Economic Studies, Research Department, Federal Reserve Bank of San Francisco. Working Paper, No. PB98–03.

Glick, R., & Rose, K. A. (1998). Contagion and Trade: Explaining the Incidence and Intensity of Currency Crises. NBER Working Paper, No. 6806.

Hahm, J.-H., & Mishkin, F. S. (2000). The Korean Financial Crisis: An Asymmetric Information Perspective. *Emerging Markets Review*, *1*(1, May), 21–52.

In, F., Kim, S., Yoon, J. H., & Viney, C. (2001). Dynamic Interdependence and Volatility Transmission of Asian Stock Markets: Evidence from the Asian Crisis. *International Review of Financial Analysis*, *10*(1, January), 87–96.

Kroner, K. F., & Ng, V. K. (1998). Modeling Asymmetric Comovements of Asset Returns. *Review of Financial Studies*, *11*, 817–844.

Longin, F., & Solnik, B. (1998). Correlation Structure of International Equity Markets During Extremely Volatile Periods. Working Paper.

Manning, N. (1999). The "Asian Crisis" and Volatility Spillovers: Equities in Indonesia, Malaysia and Singapore. Working paper. Economics Department. University of Wales Swansea.

Radelet, S., & Sachs, J. (1998). The East Asian Financial Crisis: Diagnosis, Remedies, Prospects. *Brookings Papers*, *28*(1), 1–74.

Scharfstein, D. S., & Stein, J. C. (1990). Herd Behavior and Investment. *American Economic Review*, *80*, 465–479.

Tan, J. A. R., III. (1998). Contagion Effects During The Asian Financial Crisis: Some Evidence From Stock Price Data. Center for Pacific Basin Monetary and Economic Studies Economic Research Department Federal Reserve Bank of San Francisco. Working Paper, No PB98–06.

APPENDIX:

The Estimation Procedure

We use an international capital asset pricing model (ICAPM) to describe stock market returns (De Santis & Gerard, 1997), and we use time varying correlation coefficients to determine whether contagion occurred. In the one factor ICAPM, the expected excess return on an asset is proportional to the systematic risk of the asset as measured by its covariance with a market-wide portfolio return:

$$E_{t-1}(r_{it}) = \delta_{m,t-1}\text{cov}_{t-1}(r_{it}, r_{mt} \mid \Im_{t-1}) \tag{1}$$

where r_{it} is the nominal excess returns on asset i, $\delta_{m,t-1}$ is the world aggregate risk aversion coefficient, r_{mt} is the nominal excess return on the world market portfolio between time $t-1$ and t, and $\Im_{t-1}$ is the set of market-wide information variables at the end of time $t-1$.

We assume that Eq. 1 holds for every asset, including the world market portfolio. Let R_t represent the vector of $n-1$ risky assets and the world market portfolio, and let R_{ft} represent the risk free rate of return at time t. Then Eq. (1) can be transformed into a conditional ICAPM as follows:

$$R_t - R_{ft}i = \delta_{m,t-1}h_{mt} + \varepsilon_t \qquad \text{where } \varepsilon_t \mid \Im_{t-1} \sim N(0,H_t), \tag{2}$$

where i is a vector of ones, H_t is the $n \times n$ conditional covariance matrix of asset returns (this is used to compute the conditional correlations discussed in the text), h_{nt} is the nth column of H_t and contains the conditional covariance of each asset with the market, and ε_t is the vector of shocks (ε_{it} is the shock for market index i and is used to compute the conditional volatility numbers discussed in the text).

We use a GARCH model with asymmetry and feedback in the covariance process, as proposed by De Santis and Gerard (1999). We follow the method De Santis and Gerard (1999) propose to reduce the number of unknown parameters. We assume that the ε_t is covariance stationary. Given this assumption, the process H_t follows can be computed as a function of model parameters:

$$H_t = C_0 + A'\varepsilon_{t-1}\varepsilon'_{t-1}A + B'{*}H_{t-1}B + G'\eta_{t-1}\eta'_{t-1}G, \tag{3}$$

where

$$Vec(C_0) = Vec(H_0)[I_m - (A \otimes A)' - (B \otimes B)' - \frac{1}{2}(G \otimes G)' \tag{4}$$

where C_0 is an $n \times \frac{n+1}{2}$ matrix of unknown parameters, A, B, and G are $n \times n$ matrices of unknown parameters, * denotes the Hadamard (element by element) product, and $\eta_{t-1} = \varepsilon_{t-1}$ if $\varepsilon_{t-1} < 0$ and 0 otherwise. Unfortunately, estimating the system with all seven assets is extremely difficult because there are too many unknown parameters to estimate. Therefore, we assume that the off-diagonal elements in B are zeroes, the off-diagonal elements of A are zeroes everywhere except the bottom row, and the elements of G are zeroes except for the bottom row. This implies that the variance and covariance of each asset depends solely on its own residuals, lagged market residuals, and its past conditional covariance.

Under the assumption of conditional normality, the log-likelihood function is

$$\ln L(\theta) = -\frac{Tn}{2}\ln(2\pi) - \frac{1}{2}\sum_{t=1}^{T}\ln|H_t(\theta)| - \frac{1}{2}\sum_{t=1}^{T}\varepsilon_t(\theta)' H_t(\theta)^{-1}\varepsilon_t(\theta), \quad (5)$$

where θ is the vector of unknown parameters in the model. Since the normality assumption is often violated in financial time series, we use the quasi-maximum likelihood (QML) technique proposed by Bollerslev and Woolridge (1992) to estimate the model. The QML procedure yields estimates with properties of maximum likelihood estimators even when the model is mis-specified. Optimization is performed using the BHHH algorithm (Berndt, Hall, Hall & Hausman, 1974).

AN ANALYSIS OF PRIVATE LOAN GUARANTEE PORTFOLIOS

Michel Gendron, Van Son Lai and Issouf Soumaré

ABSTRACT

We use contingent claims analysis to evaluate portfolios of vulnerable private loan guarantees and to investigate their risk diversification properties. We find that for plausible baseline values of the parameters, the diversifiable credit risk can be eliminated in a portfolio of ten insured firms. We also show that further diversification can be achieved by an appropriate choice of insured firms' risk postures and of correlations between them and the guarantor. Our results suggest that, for high leverage cases, guarantors can do better through size portfolio diversification than by seeking cross-sector diversification.

1. INTRODUCTION

A financial guarantee is a promise from a guarantor to make good on payments to the funds providers in case of default of the debt borrowers. Insurance companies, commercial banks, and public agencies will guarantee a number of financial instruments such as a letters of credit, loans, deposits, swaps, mortgages, and municipal bonds (e.g. Merton & Bodie, 1992). Financial guarantees play a major role in the development of international commerce. They improve access to international capital markets at lower costs, longer maturities, and for larger amounts (e.g. *Euromoney*, Dec. 1997/Jan. 1998; The World Bank, 1995). Multilateral development banks, such as the World Bank, endorse several private investment projects in emerging countries (The World

Financial Risk and Financial Risk Management, Volume 16, pages 395–415.

ISBN: 0-7623-0858-3

Bank, 1995; *Wall Street Journal*, 1999). Last but not least, financial guarantees have become a major tool for risk management and financial innovation to facilitate credit enhancement and hedging.

Most of the current literature on loan guarantees focuses on the evaluation of single-loan guarantees.[1] However, in practice, financial guarantors manage portfolios of several guarantees that might be correlated through concentration of credit risk. Insured firms often operate in the same industry or are subject to the same structural factors. Thus, these firms are exposed to common systemic risks that could even threaten the guarantor itself. Hence, our purpose in this paper is to add to the literature on loan guarantees by considering a portfolio of loan guarantees held by a private guarantor, and accounting explicitly for the non-zero correlation among the borrowing firms themselves and between these firms and the guarantor.

We use contingent claims analysis (CCA) to evaluate portfolios of private, hence vulnerable loan guarantees and investigate their risk diversification properties. We show how the value of the guarantee is affected by the covariance structure among the firms and between the firms and the guarantor. Positive correlations among the firms increase the risk of the guarantee portfolio, while negative correlations decrease it. Both positive and negative correlations between the borrowing firms and the guarantor increase the risk of the portfolio of guarantees.

We also show that, depending on correlations, insuring the debts of five to fifteen firms produces a well-diversified portfolio of guarantees. These results parallel those in Evans and Archer (1968) for equity stocks as well as for bonds (McEnally & Boardman, 1979). We demonstrate how the level of diversifiable credit risk (e.g. Babbel, 1989) can be reduced through an appropriate combination of volatilities and correlations of all parties involved. Our results suggest that, for very high leverage cases, guarantors can do better through size diversification, i.e. increasing the number of insured firms in the portfolio, than by seeking cross-sector diversification, i.e. reducing correlations among the insured firms.

The remainder of the paper is organized as follows. Section 2 develops the model based on the CCA framework, Section 3 describes the Monte Carlo simulation procedure and Section 4 presents the simulation results. Section 5 concludes.

2. THE MODEL

To analyse private loan guarantee portfolios, we first consider the value of single guarantees that we aggregate into portfolios. Merton (1977) has established the isomorphism between a single default-free guarantee and a put option. Since we are dealing with private guarantees, this put becomes a complex option on both the value of the guaranteed firm and the guarantor. Under the standard Merton (1974) framework, we first describe the dynamics of the firm and the guarantor, then evaluate the loss per unit of face value, and finally calculate the value of the private loan guarantee.

Under the standard CCA assumptions (e.g. perfect markets, frictionless markets, no taxes, no transaction costs, symmetric information, continuous trading, etc.), we suppose no violation of the absolute priority rule (APR), and we ignore potential agency problems inherent in financial contracting.[2] For each firm, we also assume a simple capital structure consisting of only one zero coupon bond and equity under a constant interest rate regime. The insured portfolio consists of N guaranteed firms ($N \geq 2$). There are no cash outflows from the firms (e.g. dividends) before the bonds mature. All the bonds mature at the same time and we assume no other senior debt.

Firms and Guarantors Dynamics

As in Merton (1974), the firm's asset follows a continuous diffusion process with constant instantaneous mean return and volatility. Since we have N borrowing firms correlated, the dynamics of the firms assets V ($V = [V_1, V_2, \ldots, V_N]'$) are given by the following system of stochastic differential equations:

$$dV/V = \mu_V \, dt + \Sigma \, dz_V + \sigma_{VW} \, dz_{VW} \tag{1}$$

where $\mu_V = [\mu_{V1}, \mu_{V2}, \ldots, \mu_{VN}]'$ is the instantaneous mean vector of the firms' assets returns; $\Sigma^2 = \Sigma\Sigma'$ is the covariance matrix of the firms' assets; $\sigma_{VW} \, dz_{VW}$ is the vector of covariances between the firms and the guarantor times their respective Wiener processes; and dz_V is a vector of Wiener processes.

The guarantor's total assets are also assumed to follow a continuous diffusion process. Let W denote the value of the guarantor's total assets. The dynamics of the guarantor are then described by the following process:

$$dW/W = \mu_W dt + \sigma_W dz_W + [\sigma_{WV}]' dz_{WV} \tag{2}$$

where μ_W is the instantaneous mean of the guarantor's asset returns; σ_W is the volatility of the guarantor's asset returns characterizing its specific risk level; σ_{WV} is the vector of covariances between the firms and the guarantor; and dz_W and dz_{WV} are Wiener processes generating the uncertainties. Equation (2) describes how the dynamics of the guarantor's asset depend on its own characteristics as well as its covariance with the insured firms.

The above equations describe the dynamics and the interaction of each borrowing firm with the other firms and the guarantor. The relation between the firms themselves is captured by the matrix Σ, and the relation between the firms and the guarantor by σ_{VW}. A firm is influenced not only by its own characteristics (i.e. the instantaneous asset returns' mean and volatility), but also by the dynamics of the other firms and the guarantor.

Value of Loss per Unit of Face Value

The value of loss per unit of face value, $L_{i,T}$, to the debtholders of firm i at maturity T is given by Eq. (3):

$$L_{i,T} = \frac{Max(0, F_i - V_{i,T})}{F_i} \tag{3}$$

where $V_{i,T}$ is the firm i's asset value at maturity T and F_i is the face value of the debt issued by firm i. The numerator of Eq. (3) denotes the payoff at maturity of a put on the underlying asset V_i, with exercise price F_i. Rewriting (3) as $Max(0, 1 - V_{iT}/F_i)$, it is clear that the loss is a function of the Merton's (1974) pseudo debt-asset ratio F/V.

At maturity T, the value of loss per unit of face value L_T for the portfolio is the weighted average of $L_{i,T}$:

$$L_T = \sum_{i=1}^{N} \alpha_i L_{i,T} \tag{4}$$

where α_i is the portfolio weight for firm i and is defined as the relative contribution of firm i to the total portfolio debt value.

Using the equivalent martingale argument via the expectation $E^*[\ .\ ]$, the present value of the portfolio loss per unit of face value, L, is the expected value of loss per unit at maturity discounted at the constant interest rate r, or:

$$L = E^*\left[e^{-rT} \sum_{i=1}^{N} \frac{F_i}{F} \frac{Max(0, F_i - V_{i,T})}{F_i} \right] = E^*\left[e^{-rT} \sum_{i=1}^{N} \frac{Max(0, F_i - V_{i,T})}{F} \right]. \tag{5}$$

Analyzing this expression is the same as studying the normalized value for a weighted portfolio of puts, each with exercise price F_i and underlying asset V_i.

Value of Private Loan Guarantee Portfolios per Unit of Face Value to the Debt Lenders

Since a private guarantor can default, the value of the guarantee at maturity is bounded by the value at maturity of the guarantor, W_T. Hence the value of the private guarantee at maturity per unit of face value of the debt, G_T, will be the minimum of the expected loss and the residual value of the guarantor.

$$G_T = Min\left[\sum_{i=1}^{N} \frac{Max(0, F_i - V_{i,T})}{F}, \frac{W_T}{F}\right] = \frac{1}{F} Min\left[\sum_{i=1}^{N} Max(0, F_i - V_{i,T}), W_T\right]. \quad (6)$$

Again, using the equivalent martingale argument, we obtain the following equation for the present value of the guarantee G:

$$G = E^*\left\{e^{-rT} \frac{1}{F} Min\left[\sum_{i=1}^{N} Max(0, F_i - V_{i,T}), W_T\right]\right\}. \quad (7)$$

We interpret Eq. (7) as an option on a portfolio of puts and on the value of the guarantor.

Given the curse of dimensionality due to the large number of underlying assets involved in the problem, we use Monte Carlo simulation to evaluate these guarantees.

3. SIMULATION PROCEDURE

We use the Barraquand and Martineau (1995) procedure to gauge the impact of the parameters that affect the pricing of the portfolio of guarantees, and to estimate the number of guarantees required to obtain a diversified portfolio. This procedure has the efficiency and speed for tackling complex options with multistate variables. The technique combines the Monte Carlo simulation with the stratification of the state spaces (Stratified State Aggregation) to price multivariate securities. Using this technique to price our European options is dictated by the large number of state variables (up to 100 variables) in our simulations.[3]

The Barraquand and Martineau (1995) procedure comprises three major steps: (1) the generation of the trajectory of the underlying assets, (2) the aggregate state stratification along the payoff and the conditional probabilities, and (3) the computation of the guarantee by an iterative backward procedure. Details for these steps are provided in the appendix.

We validate our simulation results for the case of three state variables by using those obtained from the Boyle, Evnine and Gibbs (1989) algorithm, which is based on the Cox, Ross and Rubinstein (1979) binomial tree. Our results are similar in both techniques up to a factor 10^{-2}.

4. SIMULATION RESULTS

Our analysis of private loan guarantee portfolios consists of two types of studies. First, we perform comparative statics on the guarantee portfolio with respect to its value and risk determinants, using the baseline parameters values shown in Table 1. This is done for a basic portfolio comprising three firms and one guarantor. We then investigate the size diversification effect by varying the number of firms in the portfolio from 1 to 100. For this exercise, we draw firms' volatilities (specific risks) randomly in the range of 10% to 35% from a uniform distribution and set the guarantor volatility constant at 15%. The other parameters and variables values are the baseline values shown in Table 2.[4]

Table 1. Baseline Values for a Portfolio of Three Firms and a Guarantor.

Firms and guarantor values	V_1 30	V_2 40	V_3 50	W 80
Firms and guarantor volatilities	σ_1 20%	σ_2 30%	σ_3 50%	σ_W 25%
Correlations between firms	ρ_{12} 0.10	ρ_{13} 0.50	ρ_{23} − 0.30	
Correlations between firms and guarantor	ρ_{1W} 0	ρ_{2W} 0	ρ_{3W} 0	
Face values of firms debts	F_1 20	F_2 30	F_3 30	
Debt-assets ratio	0.67	0.75	0.60	

Note: This table presents the baseline parameters for the simulations. It shows the asset value of the three insured firms and the guarantor, the risk posture of the firms and the guarantor, the correlations among the firms and between the firms and the guarantor, and the face value of the borrowing firms debts. V_i denotes the total asset value of the firm i. W is the total asset value of the guarantor. σ_i is the volatility of the firm i measuring its risk level, and σ_w the volatility of the guarantor measuring its risk level. ρ_{ij} the correlation between the firm i and the firm j, and ρ_{iw} is the correlation between the firm i and the guarantor. F_i is the face value of the debt of the firm i.

Some Comparative Statics for a Portfolio of Three Firms and a Guarantor

Table 1 presents the baseline values for our simulation parameters.

The firms' values are set at 30 for firm 1, 40 for firm 2 and 50 for the firm 3. We assign as the value of the guarantor two thirds of the total value of the insured firms, i.e. 80. Firms' volatilities are 0.20 for the firm 1, 0.30 for the firm 2 and 0.50 for the firm 3 per year. The insurer risk is 0.25 per year. Firm 1 is less risky than the guarantor (0.20 versus 0.25). The correlations between the borrowing firms range from –0.30 to 0.50. Initially, we set the correlations between firms and the guarantor equal to zero. The firms' leverages measured by the debt to firm's asset value ratio are 67% for firm 1, 75% for firm 2 and 60% for firm 3.

We use a constant interest rate of 5% for our simulation experiments, and we vary the maturity from one to ten years. We focus on the effect of key

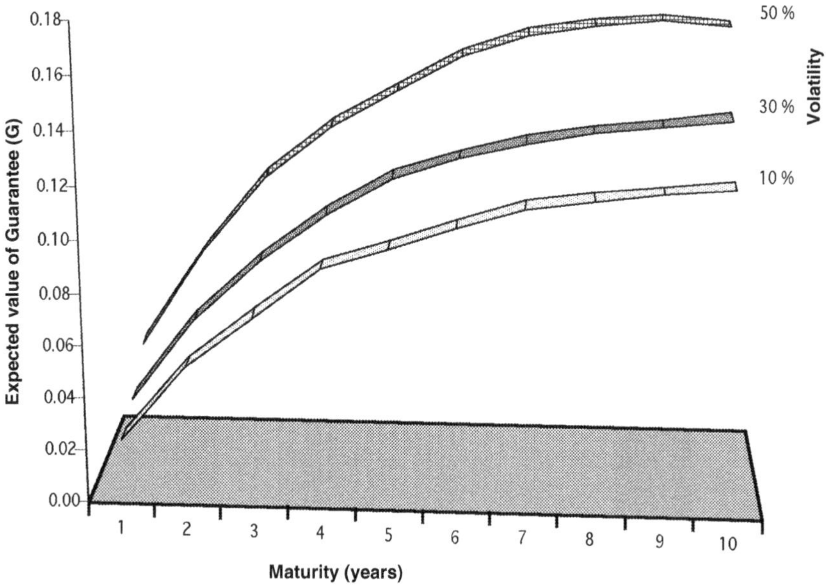

Fig. 1. Expected Value of Guarantee (G) as Function of Insured Firm 1's Asset Volatility.

Note: This figure shows the expected value of guarantee (*G*) for three different volatility values for firm 1 with maturity of the loan varying from 1 year to 10 years. Firm 1's volatility values are respectively 10%, 30% and 50%. Other baseline values are shown in Table 1.

parameters, such as asset volatilities (Figures 1 and 2) and correlations (Figures 3 and 4), on G. Comparative statics with respect to interest rates, debt maturity, asset and nominal debt values of the borrowing firms and firms values and the insuring capacity of the guarantor, not reported here, are in line with the results found in Merton (1974), Lai (1992), Lai and Gendron (1994).

Figure 1 illustrates how the value of the guarantee measured as a percentage of the face value of the debt varies with debt maturity, for firm 1's volatilities of 10, 30 and 50%. This value is an increasing function of the insured firm's risk and of maturity of the debt.

Since a risky guarantor (i.e. not a full faith and full credit guarantor) can default on its obligations, the guarantee depends not only on the firms' dynamics, but also on the guarantor's insuring capacity. Figure 2 plots the value of the guarantee as a function of the debt maturity for guarantor's risk value of 5, 25, and 45%, respectively. This value decreases with the guarantor's risk and increases with the maturity of the debt.

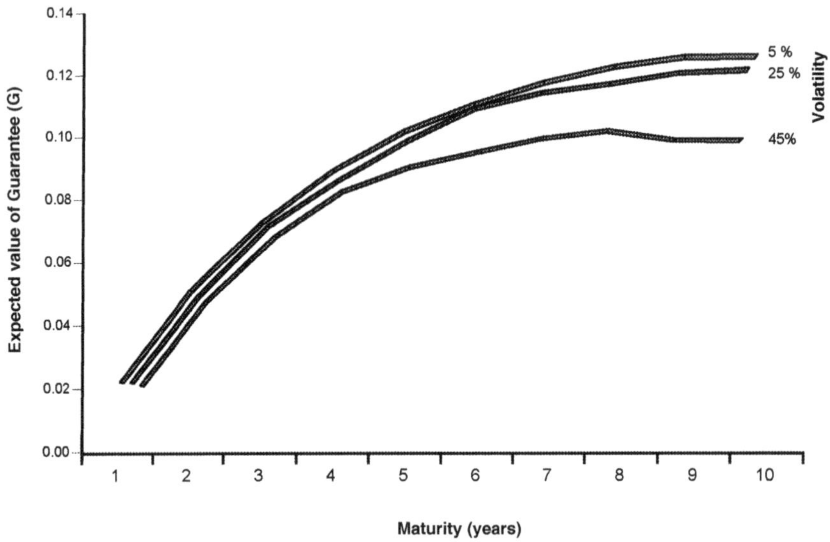

Fig. 2. Expected Value of Guarantee (G) as Function of Guarantor's Asset Volatility.

Note: This figure shows the expected value of guarantee (G) for three different volatility values of the insurer's asset returns as function of the loans maturity. The maturity of the loans is varying from 1 year to 10 years. The insurer's volatility values are respectively 5%, 25% and 45%. Other baseline values are shown in Table 1.

Figure 3 shows that the value of the guarantee G decreases when the insured firms are negatively correlated among themselves. This is consistent with well known diversification arguments. However, in practice, the insured firms will most likely exhibit positive correlations due to sector specialization by the guarantor.

Figure 4 illustrates that the private guarantee is less valuable when the correlations between the firms and the guarantor are zero. The presence of correlation between V and W introduces further variability in those variables, which increases the expected value of the losses. Hence, to reduce variability

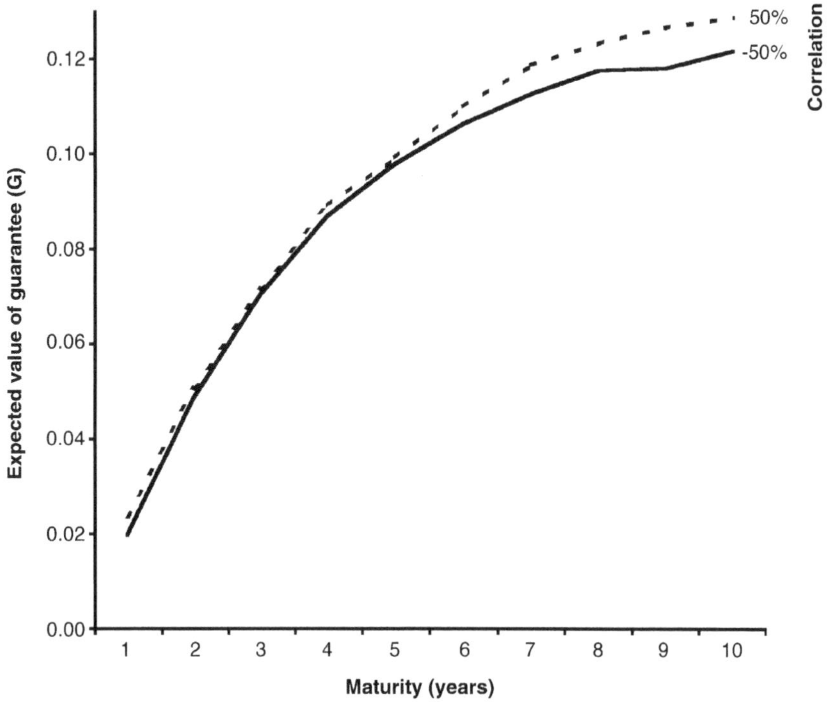

Fig. 3. Expected Value of Guarantee (G) as Function of the Correlation between Insured Firms 1 and 2.

Note: This figure shows the expected value of guarantee (G) for two different correlation values between insured firms 1 and 2 with maturity of the loans varying from 1 year to 10 years. The correlations between firms 1 and 2 are respectively –50% and 50%. Other baseline values are shown in Table 1.

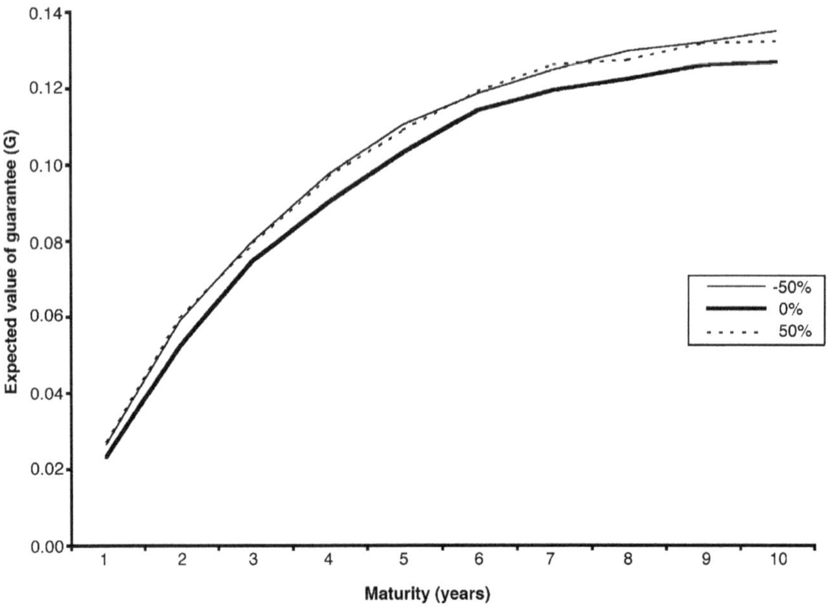

Fig. 4. Expected Value of Guarantee (G) as Function of the Correlations between the Insured Firms and the Guarantor.

Note: This figure shows the expected value of guarantee (G) for three different correlation values between the insured firms and the guarantor with maturity of the loans varying from 1 year to 10 years. The correlation values between firms and guarantor are set respectively to –50%, 0% and 50%. Other baseline values are shown in Table 1.

and expected losses, the guarantor should look for firms with activities uncorrelated with those of the guarantor. We obtain comparable values of G for the same positive and negative correlations of 50%. This result stems from the dynamics of the generating process for V (Eq. (1)) where $\sigma_{VW}\,dz_{VW}$ has a symmetric distribution with mean zero and the returns processes follow a normal distribution.

Portfolio Risk Level as Function of the Number of Firms in the Portfolio

We next address the issue of size diversification of the risk of our portfolio of private loan guarantees. To investigate the extent of the diversification effect suggested by portfolio theory we proceed in the following way. We normalize the standard deviation of the guarantees portfolio by dividing it by the standard deviation of a portfolio of size 1 which then becomes the benchmark (100%). Table 2 presents the baseline parameters used in the simulation. This exercise is done for the base case parameters values and shown in Figure 5. A high leverage and a high correlation scenario are compared to the base case in Figures 6 and 7 in absolute and relative terms respectively.

The simulations proceed as follows. We consider N guarantees from one to hundred. Each firm has a value of 40 but the guarantor has a value of 100. Recall that we draw firms' volatilities randomly in the range of 10% to 35% from a uniform distribution and that we set the guarantor risk at 15%. The baseline correlations are 0.20 among the borrowing firms, and between each firm and the guarantor. We assume the same debt-assets ratio of 0.75 for all the firms.

For each N, we obtain the reported standard deviation of the guarantees portfolio by averaging over 100 batches of 1,000 replications for each batch (as done, for instance, in Barraquand & Martineau, 1995). Since we assume that the firms have the same value and debt-assets ratio, the average losses are the same for all portfolios, and our risks comparison is valid.

Figure 5 shows that increasing the number of insured firms in the portfolio of loan guarantees reduces its overall risk; the higher the number of firms in the portfolio, the lower the risk. The shape of the risk reduction curve is reminiscent of the familiar Evans and Archer (1968) curve, where the

Table 2. Baseline Parameters for the Diversification Analysis of the Guarantee Portfolios.

Firms and guarantor values	V_i 40	W 100
Firms and guarantor volatilities	σ_i Randomly selected between 10% and 35%	σ_W 15%
Firms debt-assets ratio	0.75	
Correlations between the firms and between the firms and the guarantor	0.20	

Note: This table shows the baseline parameters for the diversification effect simulations. It presents the value of the firms and the guarantor, their volatilities, the debt-asset ratio of the firms, and the correlations among the firms and between the firms and the guarantor. V_i represents the value of the firm i and σ_i his volatility with i varying from 1 to N. N is the number of firms in the portfolio, W represents the value of the guarantor and σ_W his volatility.

diversifiable risk (in our case, credit risk) is drastically reduced by increasing the size of the portfolio. The undiversifiable portion of the portfolio risk is the systematic credit risk (e.g. Babbel, 1989; Pedrosa & Roll, 1998). With ten firms, we already reach more than 50% reduction of the total risk level which suggests that size diversification is an efficient way to reduce risk in portfolios of financial guarantees.

To gauge the impact of correlations and leverages on diversification of risk, we compare three scenarios, the base case scenario and two other scenarios with high correlations and high leverage.

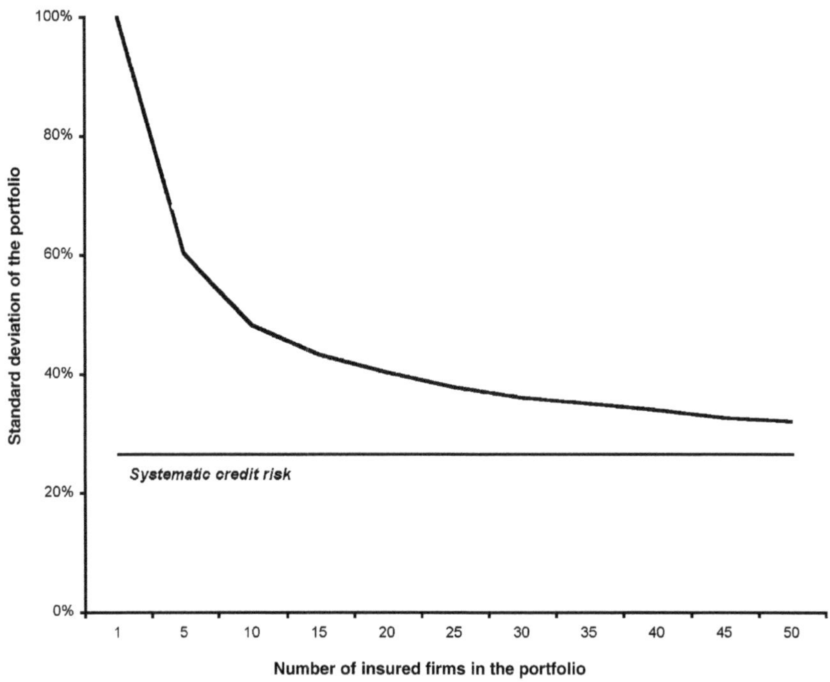

Fig. 5. Portfolio's Standard Deviation as a Function of the Number of Insured Firms in the Portfolio.

Note: This figure shows the risk reduction pattern as the number of insured firms in the portfolio increases. The portfolio risk level is measured by the relative standard deviation, i.e. the standard deviation of the guarantee portfolio divided by the one of the portfolio consisting of only one element. The number of firms in the portfolio varies from 1 to 50. The baseline parameters values are those in Table 2. The dotted line represents the level of systematic credit risk.

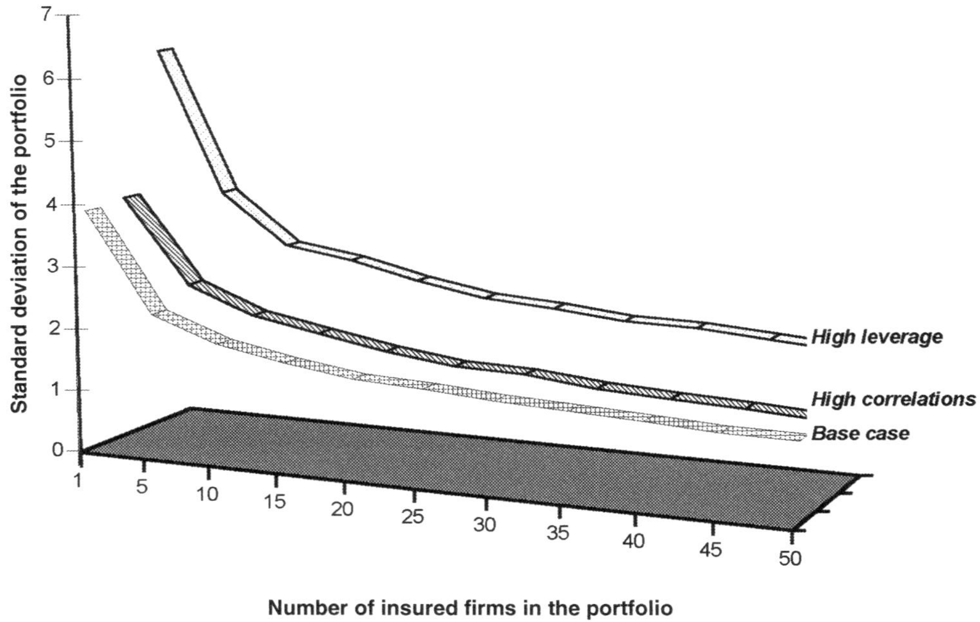

Fig. 6. Risk Reduction Pattern For the Three Scenarios.

Note: This figure shows the risk reduction pattern as the number of firms in the portfolio increases for three scenarios. The scenarios are the base case, high correlations and high leverage. The portfolio total risk level is measured by its standard deviation. The number of firms in the portfolio varies from 1 to 50. The base case scenario corresponds to the one with the parameters shown in Table 2. For the high correlations scenario, the correlations are set to 50% and for the high leverage scenario the debt-assets ratios are set to 95%. All other values are the same as those for the base case scenario.

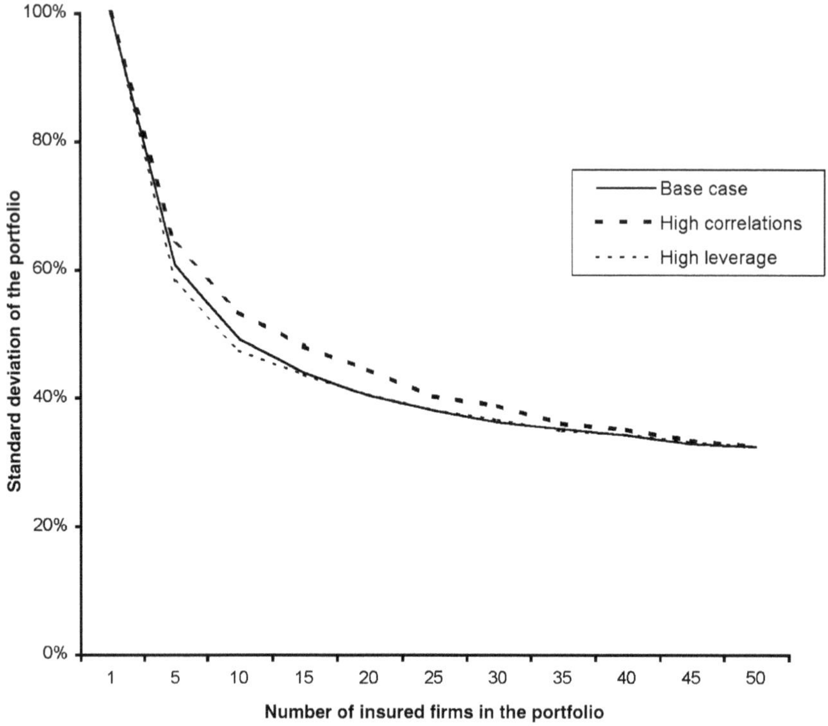

Fig. 7. Relative Risk Reduction Pattern in the Three Scenarios.

Note: This figure shows the relative risk reduction pattern as the number of firms in the portfolio increases for three scenarios. The scenarios are the base case, high correlations and high leverage. The portfolio total risk level is measured by its relative standard deviation (i.e. the standard deviation of the guarantee portfolio divide by the one of the portfolio consisting of only one firm). The number of firms in the portfolio varies from 1 to 50. The base case scenario corresponds to the one with the parameters shown in Table 2. For the high correlations scenario, the correlations are set to 50% and for the high leverage scenario the debt-assets ratios are set to 95%. All other values are the same as those for the base case scenario.

Again, the base case scenario corresponds to the parameters values in Table 2. We set the firms' values at 40, the guarantor's value at 100, the correlations at 0.20, and the debt-assets ratios at 0.75. In the high correlation scenario we increase correlations to 0.50 and in the high leverage scenario the debt assets ratios are set to 0.95.

Table 3. Standard Deviation of the Guarantee Portfolio for Different Levels of Diversification.

Number of insured firms	Base case scenario						High correlations scenario						High leverage scenario					
	2 years maturity		6 years maturity		10 years maturity		2 years maturity		6 years maturity		10 years maturity		2 years maturity		6 years maturity		10 years maturity	
	ABS	REL	ABS	REL	ABS	REL	ABS	REL	ABS	REL	ABS	REL	ABS	REL	ABS	REL	ABS	REL
1	1.88	1.00	3.86	1.00	4.80	1.00	2.12	1.00	3.92	1.00	5.11	1.00	4.71	1.00	6.23	1.00	7.79	1.00
5	1.24	0.66	2.26	0.59	2.72	0.57	1.36	0.64	2.55	0.65	3.18	0.62	2.64	0.56	3.93	0.63	4.30	0.55
10	0.97	0.52	1.88	0.49	2.25	0.47	1.17	0.55	2.13	0.54	2.56	0.50	2.21	0.47	3.10	0.50	3.52	0.45
15	0.87	0.47	1.67	0.43	1.99	0.42	1.04	0.49	1.93	0.49	2.32	0.45	1.99	0.42	2.93	0.47	3.21	0.41
20	0.79	0.42	1.51	0.39	1.90	0.40	1.00	0.47	1.73	0.44	2.12	0.41	1.88	0.40	2.68	0.43	2.96	0.38
25	0.75	0.40	1.46	0.38	1.72	0.36	0.88	0.42	1.59	0.41	1.94	0.38	1.74	0.37	2.48	0.40	2.88	0.37
30	0.70	0.37	1.38	0.36	1.68	0.35	0.83	0.39	1.56	0.40	1.87	0.37	1.69	0.36	2.40	0.39	2.72	0.35
35	0.68	0.36	1.33	0.35	1.64	0.34	0.78	0.37	1.44	0.37	1.73	0.34	1.62	0.34	2.29	0.37	2.57	0.33
40	0.69	0.37	1.28	0.33	1.54	0.32	0.78	0.37	1.38	0.35	1.67	0.33	1.59	0.34	2.27	0.36	2.52	0.32
45	0.64	0.34	1.23	0.32	1.53	0.32	0.73	0.34	1.34	0.34	1.59	0.31	1.54	0.33	2.18	0.35	2.42	0.31
50	0.64	0.34	1.22	0.32	1.49	0.31	0.73	0.34	1.27	0.32	1.54	0.30	1.52	0.32	2.09	0.34	2.41	0.31
100	0.55	0.29	0.99	0.26	1.22	0.26	0.55	0.26	0.98	0.25	1.18	0.23	1.22	0.26	1.76	0.28	1.96	0.25

Note: This table presents the standard deviation of the portfolio loss (ABS) and the ratio of the standard deviation of the portfolio loss over the one from a non-diversified portfolio, i.e. the portfolio consisting of only one element (REL). ABS is the absolute risk level and REL is the relative risk level. The table presents the standard deviation and relative standard deviation of the guarantees portfolio as function of the number of firms, for three scenarios (base case, high correlations, and high leverage), and three maturities (2, 6, and 10 years). The base case scenario corresponds to the parameters values in Table 2. We set the firms' values at 40, the guarantor's value at 100, the correlations at 0.20, and the debt-assets ratios at 0.75. In the high correlation scenario we increase correlations to 0.50 and in the high leverage scenario the debt assets ratios are set to 0.95. The number of insured firms in the portfolio varies from 1 to 100.

Table 3 presents the risk of the portfolios, as measured by their standard deviations for each scenario for maturities of two, six, and ten years. The portfolio size varies from one to fifty firms. In the first column (*ABS*), we show the absolute value of the standard deviation of the portfolio. The second column (*REL*) presents the ratio of the standard deviation of the diversified portfolio on the standard deviation of the unit portfolio, a non-diversified portfolio consisting of only one guarantee.

The results from Table 3 illustrate that risk increases with maturity and decreases with the number of firms in the portfolio. Contrary to Brealey, Hodges and Selby (1983), we obtain the same risk reduction pattern regardless of maturity. This result could be explained by the fact that we consider only zero coupon bonds.

The high correlations and high leverage scenarios show the same risk reduction pattern as that of the base case scenario. However, the risk for the high leverage scenario is substantially higher than the one for high correlations (roughly 100% compared to 10% of the base case results). This feature reflects the fact that financial leverage is a major determinant of firm's creditworthiness. This finding suggests that, for high leverage cases, guarantors can do better through size portfolio diversification than by seeking cross-sector diversification. Of course, we must also account for marginal costs of diversification.

Figures 6 and 7 present the risk reduction pattern for each scenario in absolute and relative terms, respectively. Figure 6 shows that although the diversifiable risk reduction pattern is the same for all three scenarios, the systematic risk level is much higher for the high leverage scenario. Figure 7 confirms that the risk reduction trend is indeed similar. We note that five firms are sufficient to reduce the portfolio risk (measured by its standard deviation) by 40% and only ten firms eliminate 50% of the risk of portfolio of loan guarantees.

5. CONCLUSION

The literature on loan guarantees focuses mainly on the evaluation of single-loan guarantees. However, in practice, financial guarantors manage portfolios of guarantees that can be highly correlated. Insured firms often operate in the same industry or are subject to the same structural factors. Thus the firms are exposed to common systemic risks that could even affect the guarantor itself.

In a portfolio context, we extend the financial guarantees literature by accounting explicitly for the non-zero correlation among the debt-borrowing firms themselves and between these firms and the guarantor. We use contingent claims analysis under the Merton (1974) framework, to evaluate portfolios of private and vulnerable (i.e. the guarantor can default) loan guarantees and to investigate their risk diversification properties. Our results in a portfolio context, which we obtain by using Monte Carlo simulations, support the comparative statics of loan guarantees with respect with the value and the risk posture of the guarantor and a single insured firm.

We show that depending on correlations, insuring the debts of five to fifteen firms produces a well-diversified portfolio of guarantees for a private or vulnerable guarantor. These results parallel those in Evans and Archer (1968) for stocks portfolio, and McEnally and Boardman (1979) for bonds portfolio. We show that the level of undiversifiable credit risk can be reduced by choosing appropriate combinations of firms' volatilities/risk and correlations (e.g. Babbel, 1989; Pedrosa & Roll, 1998). Positive correlations among firms increase the risk of the portfolio and negative correlations decrease it. Positive and negative correlations between the firms and the guarantor increase the risk of the portfolio of guarantees.

The high correlations and high leverage scenarios show the same risk reduction pattern as that of the base case scenario. However, the risk for the high leverage scenario is substantially higher than the one of high correlations (roughly 100% versus 10% of the base case results). For high leverage cases, guarantors can do better through size diversification, by increasing the number of guarantees in the portfolio, than through cross-sector diversification, by decreasing correlation between firms.

ACKNOWLEDGMENTS

This paper benefited from suggestions from participants at the 2001 Canadian Operational Research Society, the 2000 Actuarial Research Conference and workshops organized by the Finance Department of Laval University; the Ministry of Finance of Quebec (Canada); and the Centre de Recherche en Économie et Finance Appliquée, especially Dr. Jean-Pierre Paré. We gratefully acknowledge financial support from the Social Sciences and Humanities Research Council of Canada and the Fonds pour la Formation des Chercheurs et l'Aide à la Recherche. Issouf Soumaré thanks the Chair in Insurance L'Industrielle-Alliance at Laval University for an excellence award.

NOTES

1. Note that Babbel (1996) sketches, at a conceptual level, an outline of a hedging approach to the provision and pricing of multiple insurance/guarantees on sovereign loans.

2. Violation of the APR requires modeling of the bankruptcy trigger point and the distribution of residual assets, which is beyond the scope of this paper.

3. This technique can also handle the non-zero coupon situation and the investigation of time diversification under stochastic interest rates.

4. Note that one has to interpret our simulation results in the context of the Merton (1974) framework, which assumes that firm's total asset value follows a lognormal process with constant instantaneous mean return and volatility.

REFERENCES

Babbel, D. F. (1989). Insuring banks against systematic credit risk. *Journal of Futures Markets, 9*, 487–505.

Babbel, D. F. (1996). Insuring sovereign debt against default. Discussion Paper, Financial Sector Development Department, The World Bank.

Barraquand, J., & Martineau, D. (1995). Numerical valuation of high dimensional multivariate American securities. *Journal of Financial and Quantitative Analysis, 30*, 383–405.

Boyle, P. P., Evnine, J., & Gibbs, S. (1989). Numerical evaluation of multivariate contingent claims. *The Review of Financial Studies, 2*, 241–250.

Brealey, R. A., Hodges, S. D., & Selby, M. J. P. (1983). The risk of bank-loan portfolios In: M. Brenner (Ed.), *Option Pricing: Theory and Applications* (pp. 153–182). Lexington Books.

Cox, J. C., Ross, S. A., & Rubinstein, M. (1979). Option pricing: A simplified approach, *Journal of Financial Economics, 7*, 229–263.

Euromoney (Dec. 1997/Jan. 1998). A special report by Asian Securitization and Infrastructure Assurance (Pte) Ltd. Euromoney Publications, PLC.

Evans, J. L., & Archer, S. H. (1968). Diversification and the reduction of dispersion: An empirical analysis. *The Journal of Finance, 23*, 761–767.

Lai, V. S. (1992). An analysis of private loan guarantees. *Journal of Financial Services Research, 6*, 223–248.

Lai, V. S., & Gendron, M. (1994). On financial guarantee insurance under stochastic interest rates. *The Geneva Papers on Risk and Insurance Theory, 19*, 119–137.

McEnally, R. W., & Boardman, C. M. (1979). Aspects of corporate bonds portfolio diversification. *Journal of Financial Research, 2*, 27–36.

Merton, R. C. (1974). On the pricing of corporate debt: The risk structure of interest rates. *The Journal of Finance, 29*, 449–470.

Merton, R. C. (1977). An analytic derivation of the cost of deposit insurance and loan guarantees: An application of modern option pricing theory. *Journal of Banking and Finance, 1*, 3–11.

Merton, R. C., & Bodie, Z. (1992). On the management of financial guarantees. *Financial Management, 21*, 87–109.

Pedrosa, M., & Roll, R. (1998). Systematic risk in corporate bond credit spreads. *The Journal of Fixed Income, 8*, 7–26.

Wall Street Journal. (1999). Loan guarantees may cost World Bank – Some projects may force agency to make good; Solutions are sought, by M.M. Phillips, October 4.

The World Bank (1995). The World Bank guarantee: Catalyst for private capital flows. *The World Bank Group*, September.

APPENDIX

Barraquand and Martineau (1995) Simulation Procedure

This appendix summarizes the Barraquand and Martineau (1995) simulation procedure for tackling multivariable complex securities. The three steps of the simulation are:

1. Generation of Sample Paths

This step generates a given number, M, of sample paths for the insured firms and for the guarantor assets up to maturity.

We consider a vector $X=(V_1, \ldots, V_N, W)'$, which represent the values of N firms and the guarantor. The values of the firms and the guarantor follow a lognormal process (e.g. Merton, 1974). An explicit Euler scheme on X (X_i, $i=1, \ldots, N+1$) is given by:

$$\forall i \in \{1, \ldots, N+1\},\ X_i(t+\Delta t)=X_i(t)\exp\left(\left(r-\frac{1}{2}k_{ii}\right)\Delta t+\sum_{j=1}^{N+1} v_{ij}\sqrt{\Delta t}z_j^t\right) \quad \text{(A.1)}$$

where

$\Delta t = T/d$ with d the number of time steps in the interval $[0,T]$
z_j^t follows a standard normal distribution $N(0,1)$ for all j and t
$r=$ the short-term riskless interest rate (risk free)
$K=[k_{ij};\ (i,j)\in\{1,2, \ldots N+1\}^2]$ is the covariance matrix of the insured firms and the guarantor (the vector X)
$V=[v_{ij};\ (i,j)\in\{1,2, \ldots N+1\}^2]$ is the volatility matrix, obtained from the Cholesky decomposition of K ($K=VV^T$)

We simulate the sample paths for each element of X over the interval $[0,T]$ by dividing this interval in d subintervals $[t_j,t_{j+1}]$ with a length $\Delta t(t_{j+1}-t_j=\Delta t)$. We repeat this generation procedure M times to obtain M batches. For each batch and at each instant t with $t\in\{t_0, t_1, \ldots, t_d\}$, we calculate the values of the payoff (the value of the losses and the value of the guarantee) $f(X(t))=(f^1(X_1(t), \ldots, X_N(t)), f^2(X_1(t), \ldots, X_{N+1}(t)))$ as follows:

$$f^1(V_{1,t}, \ldots, V_{N,t})=\sum_{i=1}^{N}\frac{Max(0,F_i-V_{i,t})}{F}, \quad \text{(A.2)}$$

$$f^2(V_{1,t}, \ldots, V_{N,t}, W_t) = Min\left[\sum_{i=1}^{N} \frac{Max(0, F_i - V_{i,t})}{F}, \frac{W_t}{F}\right]$$

$$= Min\left[f^1(V_{1,t}, \ldots, V_{N,t}), \frac{W_t}{F}\right]. \quad (A.3)$$

2. Stratified State Aggregation (SSA) and Calculation of Conditional Probabilities and Payoff Expectations

Once we compute the M paths $X^1(t), \ldots, X^M(t)$, we can proceed to the Stratified State Aggregation Along the Payoff (SSAP) of the expected values (For more details, see Barraquand & Martineau, 1995). SSAP consists of dividing the state space in cells on which the payoff values are equal. Next, we calculate the conditional probabilities. The following three equations express the division of the state space in k subcells.

$$p_i(t) = \{X \in \Re^n_+, A(t)\, e^{B(t)(i-2)} < f(X) \leq A(t)e^{B(t)(i-1)}\}, \forall i \in \{2, \ldots, k-1\} \quad (A.4)$$

$$p_1(t) = \{X \in \Re^n_+, f(X) \leq A(t)\} \quad (A.5)$$

$$p_k(t) = \{X \in \Re^n_+, A(t)\, e^{B(t)(k-2)} < f(X)\} \quad (A.6)$$

where

k = the number of desegregated cells

$A(t)$ and $B(t)$ are adjusted automatically to assure

$Prob\{X(t) \in p_1(t)\} \approx Prob\{X(t) \in p_k(t)\} \approx 0.1\%$

The set of $\{P_i, i \in \{1, 2, \ldots, k\}\}$ constitutes a finite partition of the space of the payoff values.

Next, we compute the number $a_i(t)$ of the sample crossing $p_i(t)$ and the number $b_{ij}(t)$ of the samples moving from $p_i(t)$ to $p_j(t + \Delta t)$.

$$a_i(t) = Cardinal\{p \in [1,M], X^p(t) \in p_i(t)\}, \forall i \in [1,k] \quad (A.7)$$

$$b_{ij}(t) = \Sigma_{\{p \in [1,M], Xp(t) \in pi(t), Xp(t+\Delta t) \in pj(t+\Delta t)\}} e^{-r\Delta t}, \forall i,j \in [1,k]^2. \quad (A.8)$$

We compute the sum $c_i(t)$ (payoff expectations) over the samples X^k of the payoff values $f(X^k(t))$ from:

$$c_i(t) = \Sigma_{\{p \in [1,M], Xp(t) \in pi(t)\}} e^{-r\Delta t} f(X^p(t)), \forall i \in [1,k]. \quad (A9)$$

By the law of large numbers, we have the following identities for the value of the conditional probabilities π_{ij} (for the passage from state i to state j, assuming that the process is Markovian):

$$\pi_{ij} = lim_{M \to +\infty} b_{ij}(t)/a_i(t) \text{ and } f_i(t) = lim_{M \to +\infty} c_i(t)/a_i(t). \quad (A.10)$$

3. Backward Integration Algorithm

Using the Monte Carlo estimates of the conditional probabilities and payoff expectations, we can compute the values of losses and guarantee backward in time by using the algorithm described below:

At the maturity date T, the approximate SSAP price is initialized at

$$C(i,T) = c_i(T)/a_i(T). \tag{A.11}$$

At time $T - \Delta t$, we compute for all $i \in [1, k]$,

$$C(i,T-\Delta t) = \max\left(\frac{c_i(T-\Delta t)}{a_i(T-\Delta t)}, \sum_{j=1}^{k} C(j,T)\frac{b_{ij}(T-\Delta t)}{a_i(T-\Delta t)}\right). \tag{A.12}$$

We apply the procedure recursively, backward in time to compute all the prices $C(i,T-2\Delta t)$, $C(i,T-3\Delta t)$, . . . , $C(1,0) = C_{SSAP}$, which represent the values to be computed. These prices are the value of losses to the debtholders (P) and the value of the guarantee (G) that we analyze in the main text.

ASSESSING THE RISK OF HEDGE FUNDS

François-Serge Lhabitant

ABSTRACT

We suggest an empirical model to analyze the investment style of individual hedge funds and funds of funds. Our approach is based on a mixture of the style analysis approach suggested by Sharpe (1988), the factor push approach used in stress testing, and historical simulation. An interesting and straightforward extension of this model is the estimation of value-at-risk (VaR) figures. This extension is tested using a very intuitive implementation over a large sample of 2,934 hedge funds over the 1994–2000 period. Both the in-sample and the out-of-sample results suggest that the proposed approach is useful and may constitute a valuable tool for assessing the investment style and risk of hedge funds.

1. INTRODUCTION

> The review team found that the due diligence and ongoing risk assessments of hedge funds were largely qualitative and lacked quantitative rigor (Federal Reserve Board, March 24, 1999).

Spurred by the increasing complexity of financial instruments and the large losses sustained by some major institutions, market participants have acknowledged the need for a unified method to measure risk that could be useful for both regulatory reporting and internal risk management purposes. As a result of important developments in financial risk modeling, Value at Risk

Financial Risk and Financial Risk Management, Volume 16, pages 417–449.

ISBN: 0-7623-0858-3

(VaR) and scenario analysis have progressively become best practices for assessing the total market risk exposure of institutions. They are now being used within leading financial institutions and corporations, and are supported by the Basle Committee on Banking Supervision, the Group of Thirty, the Bank for International Settlements, and the European Union.

However, trading rooms have adopted VaR more readily than asset management firms. While most asset managers are particularly proficient at measuring returns and constructing benchmarks to evaluate performance, they argue that this expertise does not extend to the measurement of risk. Indeed, asset managers view risk management in general, and VaR in particular, as being inherently at odds with their primary business mandate: taking risks.

Nevertheless, this situation should change rapidly, particularly for asset managers whose portfolio holdings are not transparent to investors at all times. We are particularly focusing on hedge funds, commodities trading advisors (CTAs), and other eclectic investment pools, whose private partnership structure or offshore location frees them from local regulation and disclosure requirements that apply to mutual funds and banks. For all of these, VaR could be used to communicate risk figures in simple terms, answering both regulators and investors' concerns without imposing disclosure of portfolio holdings.

Hereafter, we propose and test a practical framework for the quantification of the market risk and the specific risk of hedge funds and hedge funds portfolios ("funds of hedge funds"). Our model combines the style analysis approach of Sharpe (1988) with the factor push approach applied in stress testing and historical simulation. It is easy to implement, has a high explanatory power, and is not restricted by some of the assumptions that tie down traditional VaR approaches.

The structure of this article is as follows: Section 2 introduces the notions of hedge funds, market risk and VaR. Section 3 reviews the style analysis model introduced by Sharpe (1988) and its economic interpretation. Section 4 extends this model to take into consideration the various particularities of hedge funds. Section 5 suggests some applications, and Section 6 reports the results of the empirical tests. Finally, Section 7 presents some conclusions and opens the path to further discussion.

2. HEDGE FUNDS, MARKET RISK AND VaR

Hedge funds have been embraced by investors worldwide and are now recognized as an asset class in their own right. Originally, hedge funds operated by taking a "hedged" position against a particular event or expectation (whether an increase or decrease in value), effectively reducing risk. Nowadays, some investment funds are categorized as hedge funds, but do not actually hedge anything. Indeed, the term "hedge fund" is applied somewhat indiscriminately and beyond the scope of its original meaning. It refers to any pooled investment vehicle that is not a conventional investment fund – that is, any fund using a strategy or set of strategies other than investing long in bonds, equities, money markets, or a mix of these assets. Consequently, hedge funds are better identified by their common structural characteristics than by their "hedged" nature. These characteristics include, but are not limited to, active management, long-term commitment of investors, use of incentive fees, leverage, and broad discretion over the investment styles, asset classes and investment vehicles.

As with traditional investments, a major source of risk for hedge funds is market risk – that is, the risk that the value of a fund's assets declines because of adverse movements in market variables such as interest rates, exchange rates, or security prices. This risk can be increased by leverage, or reduced by hedging strategies. In addition, each fund has its own investment style and specific risk – that is, a risk that is independent of what the market is doing. For legal reasons, hedge fund managers have traditionally been very reluctant to disclose specifics about their operation or risks even to their own investors[1], resulting in frequent criticisms. In addition, positions are often proprietary – external knowledge of the positions could directly impact anticipated returns. Also, many investors do not have the tools required to gauge the rick of these positions, so that simple discolsure of positions is not necessarily the best option. The solution would be of course to disclose standardized risk information, so that investors could understand precisely what risk reports contain.

In April 1999, in response to the collapse of Long Term Capital Management, the President's Working Group on Financial Markets[2] issued a report calling for a group of hedge funds to draft and publish sound practices for their risk management and internal controls. The answer[3] was the "Sound practices for hedge fund managers" report issued in February 2000, which developed some innovative recommendations for the hedge fund industry. In particular, it suggested that hedge fund managers should employ a VaR (VaR) model for measuring and communicating the risk of loss for their portfolios.

Let us recall that VaR aims to measure the magnitude of the likely maximum loss that a portfolio could experience over a finite time horizon at some specific confidence level. The time horizon typically corresponds to a holding period hypothesis, which should reflect the features of the portfolio on which the risk is being measured. The confidence level indicates the frequency of the maximum loss. The user sets the confidence level according to the purpose at hand (risk management, regulatory reporting, etc.) and within the limits of what is considered as "normal" market conditions[4].

VaR collapses the entire distribution of a portfolio's returns into a single number (see Fig. 1). It aims to do what virtually no other financial tool has ever attempted – provide a unified framework for a meaningful, easy to interpret, aggregate measure of risks for portfolios composed of complex instruments with various market sensitivities, maturity and pricing mechanisms. While the definition of VaR is broad and encompasses – at least in theory – all sources of market risk for a portfolio, actually estimating VaR can be challenging in practice. Once the confidence level and holding period have been decided, the

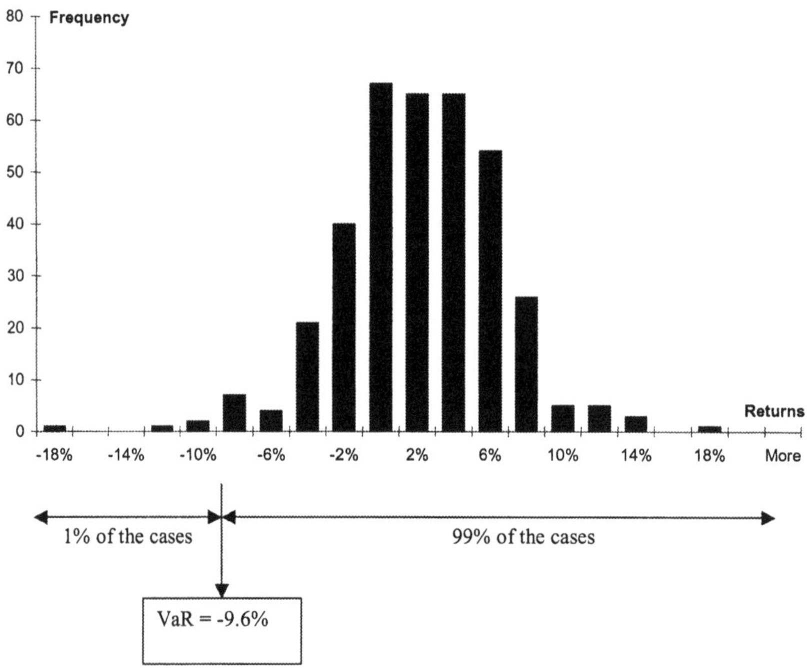

Note: This figure illustrates the historical at risk calculation in the case of the Morgan Stanley Capital Index USA, from December 1969 to October 2000, using monthly non-annualized data. On the histogram, the value at risk at a 99% confidence interval is equal to − 9.6%. This corresponds to the one percent quantile of the return distribution, i.e. one percent of the observed values are lower than the VaR and 99% are higher than the VaR.

Fig. 1. Computing VaR.

next two steps consist of forecasting large future movements of underlying markets and assessing the sensitivity of the portfolio to these movements. Various methods may be used, including parametric methods, extreme value estimates, or historical or Monte Carlo simulations. Each methodology has its own strengths and weaknesses[5].

3. FROM FACTOR MODELS TO STYLE ANALYSIS

Measuring market risk can be summarized as:

(i) finding a good model for assets' returns and;
(ii) deriving assets' risk exposures.

Several descriptive model forms have been, and continue to be, applied in analyzing the sources of projected or realized assets' returns. In the broadest, and most literal sense, most take the form of a linear factor model.

A linear factor model relates the return on an asset (be it a stock, bond, fund or any other asset) to the values of a limited number of factors. The basic equation of a multiple factor model takes the following form:

$$R_t = \alpha_i + \sum_{i=1}^{N} \beta_i \cdot F_{i,t} + \varepsilon_t \tag{1}$$

where:

R_t = the return on the asset at time t;
α_i = the excess return (a constant) of the asset;
$F_{i,t}$ = the value of factor i at time t;
β_i = the change in the return on the asset per unit change in factor j;
N = the number of factors;
ε_t = the portion of the return on the asset not related to the N factors.

An analogy to the familiar relationship that quantity times price equals value provides an easy interpretation of Eq. (1). For a given asset, we can think of β_i as the quantity of type-i risk in the asset and $F_{i,t}$ as the reward of type-i risk at time t. Thus, the product $\beta_i \cdot F_{i,t}$ is the value of the contribution of type-i risk to the expected return of the asset at time t.

The usefulness of a factor model depends crucially on the factor(s) chosen for its implementation. Equation (1) gives no guidance as to which factors should be considered. Selecting the correct factors to explain return dynamics is often more of an art than a science. Several techniques for factor identification have been proposed. They range from principal component analysis (PCA) to arbitrarily specified factors within one of the following categories:

- Factors pertaining to particular observable stock (firm) characteristics, such as a market index, sector index, amount of sales, P/E ratio, market capitalization, leverage, dividend yield, trading volume, etc. Something important to remember is that the corresponding factor should affect all assets under consideration; see for instance Fama and McBeth (1973).
- Macroeconomic factors, such as the shape or level of the term structure of interest rates, foreign exchange rates, industrial production, GDP growth, etc.; see for instance Blake, Elton, and Gruber (1995).
- Returns on relevant portfolios, which themselves capture the broader influences on the assets considered. Examples are decile-portfolios sorted by size or P/E; see for instance Fama and French (1992).

Popular examples of theoretical factor models based on Eq. (1) include the single-factor CAPM and the generic Roll-Ross APT model, as well as fixed income models relying on duration and convexity and all derivative models relying on sensitivities (delta, gamma, etc.). On the practical side, numerous implementations are now available, such as the series of BARRA models, twenty-factor APT model from Advanced Portfolio Technologies Inc., six-factor model developed by Quantec Systems, Ltd, or Salomon Brothers Risk Attribution Measurement (RAM) model, among others.

An interesting application of factor models is the return-based style analysis initially suggested by Sharpe (1988). Return-based style analysis inverses the causality of multi-factor models and asserts that a fund manager's investment style can be determined by comparing its returns with the returns of a number of selected passive indices. For a given fund, the econometric model is as follows:

$$R_t = \alpha + \sum_{i=1}^{N} \beta_i \cdot R_{i,t} + \varepsilon_t \tag{2}$$

where R_t denotes the return on the fund at time t, $R_{i,t}$ is the return on index i at time t, β_i is a factor loading that expresses the sensitivity of the fund's returns to index-i returns, and $\varepsilon_{i,t}$ represents the portion of the fund's return not related to the N factors (idiosyncratic noise). The factor loadings must add-up to one, so that they can be interpreted as portfolio weights within an asset allocation framework.

$$\sum_{i=1}^{N} \beta_i = 1 \tag{3}$$

Each factor loading must also be positive in order to meet the short-selling constraint that most fund managers are subject to.

$$\beta_i \geq 0 \quad i = 1 \ldots N \tag{4}$$

The model in Eq. (2) subject to the constraints of Eqs (3) and (4) can easily be estimated by quadratic programming to provide point estimates for the factor loadings.[6] In practice, the indices represent pre-specified investment styles (e.g. value/growth, small/large caps, high/low dividend, etc.) or particular asset classes (stocks, bonds, real estate, etc.). Following Sharpe's recommendations, they should be mutually exclusive, exhaustive with respect to the investment universe, and have returns that differ. If some indices are too closely correlated or not mutually exclusive, the model will yield unstable or oscillating results from period to period. Likewise, if the set of indices does not span the investment universe, the methodology will fail in identifying a benchmark that consistently explains the fund's behavior.

Application of return-based style analysis has proven to be beneficial, but its results must be carefully interpreted. It is often incorrectly stated that the factor loadings correspond to the effective allocation of the fund's portfolio among the asset classes. In actuality, the most one can say is that the fund behaves "as if" it was invested using these factor loadings.

For an investor or a sponsor, return-based style analysis offers a major advantage: it allows the identification of the effective investment style of a fund even before obtaining end-of-year official figures.[7] This has important consequences for monitoring and judging a fund's investment behavior. For instance, it allows for the monitoring of portfolios' style characteristics at both the individual (i.e. fund) and at the aggregate (i.e. portfolio) levels. It also allows the creation of style benchmarks for performance assessment, providing a detailed breakdown of the various contributions to return from investment styles. The return obtained by a fund in each month (R_t) can be compared with the return on a mix of asset classes with the same estimated style ($\Sigma\beta_i F_{i,t}$). This mix is a viable and identifiable alternative that can be easily replicated, and is an acceptable benchmark. The difference between the fund and its benchmark ($\alpha + \varepsilon_t$) is therefore, the net contribution from the manager, given its style.

A drawback of return-based style analysis is that it assumes style consistency through time, at least over the period of return measurement. A time series of data is used to perform a single constrained regression, providing a single style for the entire period. It is therefore common practice to use moving window regressions to incorporate new information and evaluate a manager's style shifting through time.

Style analysis works remarkably well for investment funds and traditional portfolios; see for instance the results obtained by Sharpe (1992). However, it performs poorly with hedge funds. The reasons are two-fold. First, the factors underlying hedge fund returns have not yet been fully identified. Second, hedge fund managers have different investment styles and market opportunities than traditional stock and bond fund managers. Typically, while the latter are strictly regulated and must hold primarily long positions in the underlying assets, the former have broad mandates, take long and short positions and use varying degrees of leverage in varying market conditions. This results in non-linear returns that can flaw the (linear) return-based style analysis. As an illustration, let us recall the major results from Fung and Hsieh (1998).

Applying principal component analysis to a sample of 2,525 U.S. mutual funds, Fung and Hsieh observe that there are 39 dominant investment styles. Most are sub-sets or mixes of nine broadly defined asset classes.[8] Given that mutual funds do not change their asset allocation frequently, style analysis has a large explanatory power with respect to mutual funds' variations.[9] When applying the same methodology to a sample of 409 hedge funds and CTAs, the results differ dramatically. Fund and Hsieh identify five dominant styles, with two being linked to traditional asset classes (U.S. equity, and high-yield). The remaining three are dynamic trading strategies, i.e. non-linear functions of the traditional asset classes' returns. Even worse, hedge funds often follow aggressive tactical asset allocations between these classes, resulting in the style analysis model having a very low explanatory power, and therefore, a reduced usefulness.

As a consequence, Fung and Hsieh suggest adding regressors to proxy the returns of these dynamic trading strategies. In particular, they use a non-parametric form of regression to find the corresponding dynamic trading strategy to replicate hedge fund returns. They observe that a twelve-factor model – nine asset classes and three trading strategies – provides better results, and could be used to assess the performance of hedge funds. Although we entirely support their proposition, recent academic research[10] has shown evidence that the existence of additional factors such as, convenience yields, market momentum, and other institutional features resulted in potential arbitrage opportunities for hedge fund managers. Accounting for these additional factors, while using monthly hedge funds quotes, would lead to important estimation problems rather than to a solution.

4. OUR MODEL

Fortunately, since Fung and Hsieh's research, new elements have occurred and may provide a solution to the problem. In 1999, Credit Suisse First Boston and Tremont combined their resources to create new benchmarks for hedge fund performance. The CSFB/Tremont Hedge Fund Indices offer several advantages with respect to their competitors:

- They are transparent both in their calculation and composition, and constructed in a disciplined and objective manner. Starting from the TASS + database, which tracks over 2600 U.S. and offshore hedge funds, the indices only retain hedge funds that have at least U.S. $10 million under management and provide audited financial statements. Only about 300 funds pass the screening process.
- They are computed on a monthly basis and asset-weighted. Funds are reselected quarterly to be included in the index, and in order to minimize the survivorship bias, they are not excluded until they liquidate or fail to meet the financial reporting requirements. This makes these indices representative of the various hedge funds investment styles and useful for tracking and comparing hedge fund performance against other major asset classes.
- They do not include the amount of funds of hedge funds and separate accounts. Therefore, each sub-index is mutually exclusive: this should allow the avoidance of most of the multi-collinearity problems in our regression/optimization approach.

Therefore, we suggest adapting the Sharpe (1988) return-based style analysis model by using as asset classes the nine CSFB/Tremont sub-indices, which are described in Table 1. For a given hedge fund, our model can be written as:

$$R_t = \alpha + \sum_{i=1}^{9} \beta_i \cdot I_{i,t} + \varepsilon_t \quad (5)$$

where:

$I_{1,t}$ = return on the CSFB Tremont Convertible Arbitrage index at time t;
$I_{2,t}$ = return on the CSFB Tremont Short Bias index at time t;
$I_{3,t}$ = return on the CSFB Tremont Event Driven index at time t;
$I_{4,t}$ = return on the CSFB Tremont Global Macro index at time t;
$I_{5,t}$ = return on the CSFB Tremont Long Short Equity index at time t;
$I_{6,t}$ = return on the CSFB Tremont Emerging Markets index at time t;
$I_{7,t}$ = return on the CSFB Tremont Fixed Income Arbitrage index at time t;

$I_{8,t}$ = return on the CSFB Tremont Market Neutral index at time t;
$I_{9,t}$ = return on the CSFB Tremont Managed Futures index at time t.

We therefore assume that the return (and risk) on any hedge fund can be split in two components: one explained jointly by the nine systematic factors,[11] and the other that remains unexplained. The latter consists of a constant expected component (α), plus an unexpected one (ε_t) with a zero mean and a variance denoted σ_ε^2.

Our model preserves the analytical tractability and ease of interpretation of Sharpe's model. Rather than referring to traditional asset classes modeled by passive indices, we simply use alternative asset styles represented by indices of active funds. Therefore, for a given hedge fund, the beta coefficients can then be seen as exposures to the different CSFB/Tremont styles. The alpha

Table 1. Definition of Hedge Fund Investment Styles According to CSFB/Tremont.

Category	Strategy
Convertible arbitrage	Invest in the convertible securities of a company. A typical investment is to be long in convertible bond and short in stock of the same company.
Dedicated short-bias	Maintain consistent net short (or pure short) exposures to the underlying market.
Emerging Markets	Equity or fixed income investing in emerging markets around the world.
Market Neutral	Exploit equity market inefficiencies by being simultaneously long and short matched equity portfolios of the same size within a country.
Event-driven	Equity-oriented investing designed to capture price movement generated by an anticipated corporate event (merger, acquisition, distressed securities, etc.).
Fixed-income arbitrage	Profit from price anomalies between related interest rate securities.
Global macro	Leveraged views on overall market direction as influenced by major economic trends and/or events.
Long/short equity	Equity-oriented investing on both the long and short sides of the market, with an objective different from being market neutral.
Managed futures	Systematic or discretionary trading in listed financial and commodity futures markets and currency markets around the world.

Source: CSFB/Tremont.

coefficient is the excess return generated by the hedge fund manager, taking into account its investment style.

Let us now discuss constraints on the sensitivities from Eqs (3) and (4). Should we or shouldn't we impose constraints on the hedge funds' sensitivities? Following Fung and Hsieh's argument, we have decided to set no upward restriction on beta coefficients. The economic justification is the possibility of leverage. However, one should be cautious in interpreting a high beta, since this beta is relative to the average leverage of the CSFB/Tremont style index. In a sense, it is a relative indicator of leverage, but not an absolute one.

However, unlike Fung and Hsieh, we have decided to keep the lower boundary constraint. Although hedge funds may take short positions, we have to remember that our underlying indices are style indices, not standard asset class indices. Therefore, having a negative exposure to a particular style could be hard to justify economically. For instance, what would be the meaning of a negative exposure to the Short Bias style?

5. APPLICATIONS

There are several possible areas of application for our model. The return-based style analysis can be used to monitor a hedge fund manager's investment style, regardless of his claimed exposure or categorization and without necessitating periodic disclosure of the funds' assets. This provides a useful indication as to the economic environment in which a given manager is likely to do well or poorly. It can also provide some evidence of both the probability and extent to which a particular hedge fund performance will diverge from any performance benchmarks it is measured against.

Our multi-factor analysis can also be used for performance evaluation purposes. It helps in identifying what underlying ability, skill or flare has contributed to a fund manager's performance, as opposed to what might reasonably be expected by a fund manager with average abilities adopting the same investment style. It also allows the definition of benchmarks that are based on the characteristics of the strategies applied by the funds that are evaluated, in the spirit of Daniel et al. (1997).

In the following example, we will focus primarily on a new application. Knowing the style exposure of a hedge fund, one can easily apply a two-step procedure to obtain its value at risk, that is, its maximum loss during a specified period of time at a given level of probability. The first step estimates systematic risk. Once we have mapped a hedge fund on the nine indices that constitute our risk factors, the idea is to "push" the price of each individual risk factor in the most disadvantageous direction and estimate the overall impact on the fund, accounting for risk factor correlation. This will give us the VaR due to market moves (i.e. style return moves). We call this first part the "value at market risk". In a second step, we will add up the VaR due to the specific characteristics of the fund, that we will call "value at specific risk".

Let us assume that we want a confidence level of 99% for the one-month VaR. Denoting by F_i* the one percentile extreme move of index i returns over one month, the value at market risk for a fund P over one month is given by

$$\text{Value at Market Risk}_{P,1M} = \sqrt{\sum_{i=1}^{9}\sum_{j=1}^{9} \rho_{i,j}\cdot\beta_i\cdot F_i^*\cdot\beta_j\cdot F_j^*} \tag{6}$$

where $\rho_{i,j}$ is the correlation between monthly returns of hedge fund indices i and j. This formula is inspired by the one used in the variance/covariance method (e.g. Riskmetrics). The procedure to estimate extreme moves is based on extreme value theory and detailed in the appendix.

The second step estimates specific risk. We simply define specific risk (σ_ε^2) as the difference between total risk (observed fund variance σ_P^2) and systematic risk (variance due to the market, i.e. the hedge fund style). We have:

$$\sigma_\varepsilon^2 = \sigma_P^2 - \sum_{i=1}^{9}\sum_{j=1}^{9} \rho_{i,j}\cdot\beta_i\cdot\sigma_i\cdot\beta_j\cdot\sigma_j \tag{7}$$

The error terms $\varepsilon_{i,t}$ are all observable on a monthly basis, so that it is easy to obtain their empirical distribution and calculate its percentiles. In particular, the one percentile will be equal to the 99% value at specific risk of the fund.

Note that if we are willing to accept the assumption of normally distributed errors (which does not imply normally distributed fund returns), we can compute the value at specific risk analytically. For a 99% confidence level, we simply need to apply a factor push of 2.33 times σ_ε (corresponding to a 99% confidence level for a normal variable) to obtain the specific risk of a hedge fund.

$$\text{Value at Specific Risk}_{P,1M} = 2.33 \times \sigma_\varepsilon \tag{8}$$

The total VaR over a one-month interval is obtained by adding up market and specific risk figures, accounting for their zero correlation:[12]

$$\text{VaR}_{P,1M} = \sqrt{(\text{Value at Market Risk}_{P,1M})^2 + (\text{Value at Specific Risk}_{P,1M})^2} \tag{9}$$

How does our VaR model compare to alternatives? VaR is nothing more than a measure of the tail of a distribution, however the key step when assessing the risk of a hedge fund is to model its return distribution. Given the scarcity of data and the low frequency of observations, performing a non-parametric estimation of a hedge fund return distribution is not feasible. Assuming a parametric distribution does not rely on any particular economic intuition, and adhering to the standard default of a normal distribution pattern would be non-realistic, since hedge funds typically have fat tails in comparison to normal distribution (i.e. unusual and extreme events tend to occur more frequently than that implied by the normal distribution).

Therefore, we believe our methodology is superior and provides more information in terms of the fund behavior, its areas of concentration and diversification benefits, its leverage with respect to the market – and all without additional knowledge of the fund's positions. It also allows ease in applying unprecedented volatility levels or breakdowns in historical correlated markets, a critical component of the investment process of multi-manager portfolios.

6. EMPIRICAL TESTS

6.1. Data and Methodology

A major source of difficulty in constructing a hedge fund sample is the lack of performance history. The majority of hedge funds started in the 1990s as private investment partnerships, and as a result, they were not required to publicly disclose their performance and assets under management. Although this may create a selection bias, we are nonetheless restricted to focus solely on hedge funds that voluntarily reported their performance.

Our database is built from a series of historical quarterly snapshots from a number of hedge fund providers (Managed Account Reports, Hedge Fund Research, TASS + and Evaluation Associates Capital Management). In total, it contains 5,228 distinct hedge funds and CTAs, with no restriction whatsoever on their assets under management or duration of existence. It goes so far as to include defunct funds for the time of their existence.

To be selected in the sample used for this article, a hedge fund had to fulfill additional rules: (a) The fund must have been reporting performance figures to one of the above-mentioned agencies for at least three years and one month between January 1994[13] and October 2000. (b) The fund must have been managing at least $5 million or an equivalent amount in another currency. (c) The fund could not have been a managed account, but must have had a legal structure (e.g. a limited partnership). This gave us a final sample of 2,934 investment vehicles, for which we computed monthly holding period returns based on net asset values expressed in U.S. dollars and accounting for eventual distributions.

We distinguish ten different investment styles, namely, Convertible Arbitrage, Short Bias, Event Driven, Global Macro, Long Short Equity, Emerging Markets, Fixed Income Arbitrage, Market Neutral, Managed Futures, and Multi-strategy. Each of these styles corresponds to a CSFB/Tremont Hedge Fund index or sub-index for which monthly holding period returns in U.S. dollar terms are available starting from January 1994. Table 2 provides the standard deviation and correlation for the CSFB/Tremont hedge fund indices.

6.2. Fitting of the Style-analysis Model

The mapping of a particular fund in its corresponding category was performed according to the following rule. We use a 36-month historical window to estimate Eq. (5). This provides us with nine exposure parameters (i.e. betas). If any exposure to an investment style represents more than 50% of the total fund exposure, the fund is mapped into this investment style. Otherwise, the fund is considered to be from the Multi-strategy style.[14] Then, we move one month forward the 36-month window and perform the same analysis using the new dataset. This allows us to capture style movements, if any. Consequently, a hedge fund can change its style on a monthly basis.

Table 3 gives key descriptive statistics of our total sample. Note all figures are expressed in terms of back-testing months rather than in terms of amount of funds in hedge fund, because of the frequent style changes. For a fund, a test period corresponds to the three-year sample period used to estimate style sensitivities. In total, we have 96,549 test periods. We use the resulting sensitivities to classify funds rather than the officially reported style, and we can observe that the largest category corresponds to multi-strategy (29,000 test periods), followed by convertible arbitrage (12,692 test periods) and event-driven (12,251). Surprisingly, very few funds confirmed their so-claimed emerging markets or global macro investment style (with 746 and 807 test periods, respectively). We also observed a large number of strategy changes throughout the life of the funds.

Table 4 provides some statistics about the style regression results. The R-square corresponds to the percentage of cross sectional variation explained by our nine-index style analysis. With an average R-square value of 0.56, there is strong evidence that our style indices capture the long-term behavior of hedge funds well. This was not granted a priority, because our style indices are constructed from a small sample of funds (less than 300), which implies that most of the funds considered in our sample were in fact not included in the

Table 2. Correlation, Extreme Moves and Volatility Figures for Hedge Fund Indices.

	Covertible Arbitrage	Dedicated Short Bias	Event Driven	Global Macro	Long-Short Equity	Emerging Markets	Fixed Income Arbitrage	Market Neutral	Managed Futures
Convertible Arbitrage	1.00	–0.30	0.60	0.36	0.21	0.45	0.75	0.31	–0.61
Dedicated short bias	–0.30	1.00	–0.73	–0.14	–0.77	–0.72	–0.06	–0.56	0.30
Event Driven	0.60	–0.73	1.00	0.40	0.66	0.80	0.41	0.52	–0.53
Global Macro	0.36	–0.14	0.40	1.00	0.52	0.46	0.58	–0.05	–0.04
Long-Short Equity	0.21	–0.77	0.66	0.52	1.00	0.75	0.23	0.30	–0.15
Emerging	0.45	–0.72	0.80	0.46	0.75	1.00	0.35	0.46	–0.38
Fixed Income Arbitrage	0.75	–0.06	0.41	0.58	0.23	0.35	1.00	–0.01	–0.32
Market Neutral	0.31	–0.56	0.52	–0.05	0.30	0.46	–0.01	1.00	–0.17
Managed Futures	–0.61	0.30	–0.53	–0.04	–0.15	–0.38	–0.32	–0.17	1.00
Volatility	1.83	6.41	2.54	4.20	4.76	6.67	1.66	0.76	2.89
Extreme Move (99%)	–4.67	–8.68	–8.69	–9.38	–10.04	–18.39	–5.83	–0.69	–4.54

Note: This table shows the correlation, volatility and extreme move figures for the hedge funds style indices at the end of September 2000. All values are computed from a historical sample of 36 months. Volatility and Extreme moves are expressed on a monthly basis.

Table 3. Summary Statistics on the Hedge Fund Sample.

	1997	1998	1999	2000	Total
Convertible Arbitrage	1’780	3’560	4’093	3’259	12’692
Emerging	102	81	304	259	746
Event Driven	2’546	3’382	3’624	2’699	12’251
Long-Short Equity	2’998	2’803	3’199	2’344	11’344
Managed Futures	238	1’074	2’962	1’953	6’227
Market Neutral	1’362	1’656	3’946	4’033	10’997
Multi-Strategy	6’574	7’835	8’134	6’457	29’000
Fixed Income Arbitrage	3’094	3’278	2’904	2’606	11’882
Global Macro	240	160	219	188	807
Dedicated Short	163	163	188	89	603
All sample	21’094	25’990	31’572	25’887	96’549

Note: This table shows the number of test periods for each investment style. Each test period corresponds to a three-year estimation period for one fund. Note that these numbers include defunct funds, if they were active during the corresponding year.

Table 4. Fitting of the Style Analysis Model (average R-square).

	1997	1998	1999	2000	Total
Convertible Arbitrage	0.46	0.50	0.60	0.59	0.55
Emerging	0.68	0.78	0.75	0.76	0.75
Event Driven	0.50	0.53	0.66	0.64	0.59
Long-Short Equity	0.53	0.61	0.65	0.73	0.63
Managed Futures	0.42	0.65	0.68	0.65	0.66
Market Neutral	0.44	0.49	0.52	0.54	0.51
Multi-Strategy	0.47	0.50	0.55	0.54	0.52
Fixed Income Arbitrage	0.44	0.53	0.57	0.59	0.53
Global Macro	0.55	0.62	0.74	0.75	0.66
Dedicated Short	0.61	0.61	0.72	0.55	0.64
All sample	0.48	0.53	0.60	0.60	0.56

Note: This table shows statistics on the average R-squares obtained when applying the nine-index style model of Eq. (5).

style indices. The best fits are observed for the investment styles that have the least test periods (e.g. emerging markets, global macro and dedicated short). This is essentially due to the presence of outliers in other samples, since the median R-square values are often much higher than the average values.

6.3. VaR and Backtesting

We then compute the VaR according to the methodology described previously. Using the extreme moves of the style indices over the 36-month rolling window and each hedge fund sensitivities to these styles, we compute a one-month VaR figure for each hedge fund at a 99% confidence level, and compared it to the profits/losses realized by the fund over the next month, i.e. out of the estimation window. If the net asset value of a hedge fund experiences a drop larger than its VaR figure, the event is recorded as being an exception. Exceptions will be used later on to determine to what extent our VaR figures are consistent with the future risk of hedge funds.

Table 5 shows the average and volatility of VaR figures for hedge funds by investment styles as well as globally. The VaR is split into its value at market risk (VaMR) and value at specific risk (VaSR) components. All figures are expressed as a percentage of the net asset value to allow comparisons and aggregations across funds.

Overall, hedge funds have a monthly average VaR of 10.97%, which is split (on average) between a monthly VaMR of 8.07% and a monthly VaSR of 6.91%. However, the figures differ widely, both across investment styles and across time. The less risky investment style appears to be Event Driven (average VaR of 8.50%) and the riskier one is Emerging Markets (average VaR of 29.09%). Managed Futures, Global Macro and Dedicated Short styles experienced an overall decrease of their VaR, while all other categories increased their risk figures. The larger increase is observed for Emerging Markets hedge funds, particularly after the Asian crisis of 1997. The major source of risk remains the market risk rather than the specific risk component.

The large VaR volatility figures (at least when compared to the average VaR for each category) give evidence to the wide variety of risks within a style. Therefore, as a rule of thumb, we can say that it is risky to assign a fund to a particular hedge fund index, even if the classification is based on effective returns rather than on a self-declared style. This could somehow be expected: two funds having the same investment strategy but different financial leverage will (and should!) exhibit very different value at risk figures.

Figure 4 details the number of exceptions aggregated on a month-to-month basis. In total, out of 96,549 test periods, 1,026 exceptions were observed,

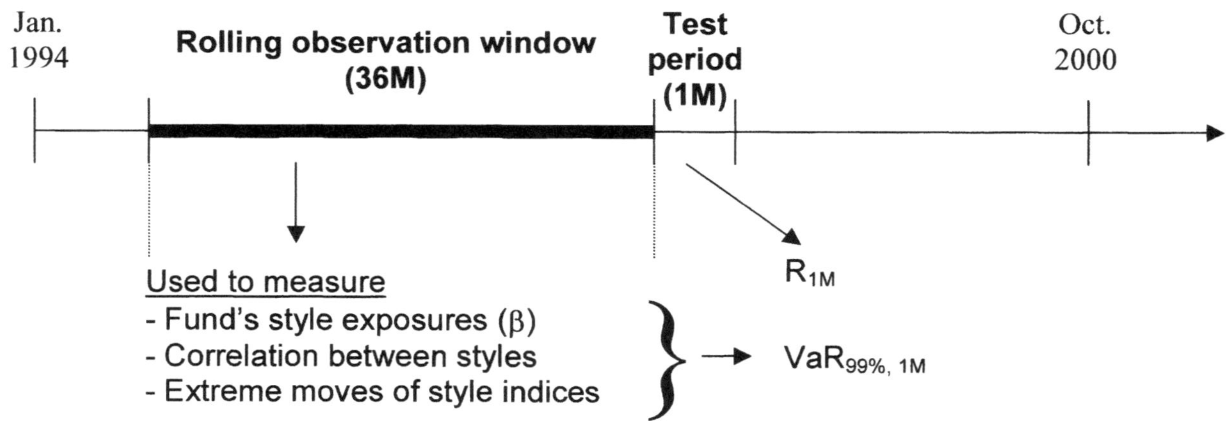

Source: The figure illustrates the methodology used to compute and back-test our VaR figures. All the data available during the observation window is used to "forecast" the VaR at a 99% confidence interval over a one month holding period ($VaR_{99\%,1M}$). This value is compared tot eh realized return of the following month (R_{1M}). Then both the "rolling observation window" and the "test period" are shifted forward by one month, and the whole process starts again.

Fig. 2. Back-testing the VaR Methodology.

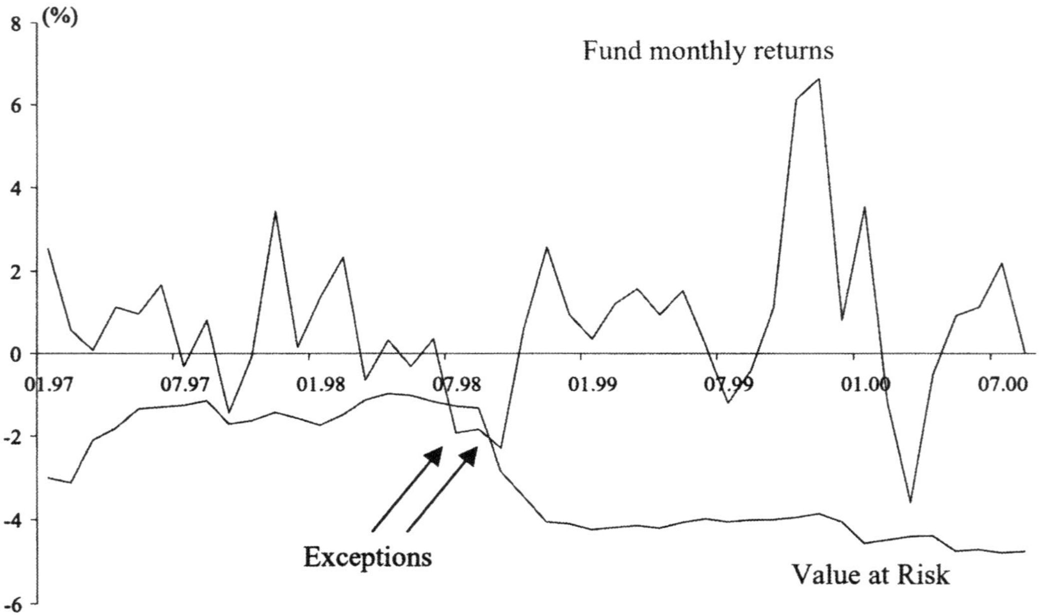

Source: This figure shows the results obtained from back-testing the VaR for a single hedge fund on a monthly (rollover) basis. In this example, the fund experienced two exceptions during the 1998 crisis. An exception is defined as a situation when within a month, the net asset value of a fund drops by more than the forecasted VaR at the end of the previous month.

Fig. 3. Back-testing the VaR.

Table 5. Value at Risk Components (one month, 99% confidence) Over Time.

	Average VaMR					Volatility VaMR				
	1997	1998	1999	2000	Average	1997	1998	1999	2000	Average
Convertible Arbitrage	5.88	5.95	9.04	8.44	7.57	5.16	6.32	8.00	7.40	7.04
Emerging	9.88	29.52	28.71	29.94	26.65	5.06	19.70	13.19	14.42	13.74
Event Driven	5.13	5.27	7.14	7.20	6.22	4.63	4.70	5.21	5.96	5.14
Long-Short Equity	6.77	8.12	10.20	14.10	9.58	3.63	4.75	6.36	8.63	5.99
Managed Futures	4.90	7.02	8.93	7.76	8.08	2.54	4.76	4.97	3.95	4.56
Market Neutral	5.55	6.46	8.50	8.80	7.94	4.38	5.56	6.48	7.03	6.03
Multi-Strategy	6.27	6.76	8.77	8.73	7.65	4.83	5.56	6.48	7.03	6.03
Fixed Income Arbitrage	5.79	7.77	10.72	11.98	8.90	5.30	7.24	7.78	8.00	7.11
Global Macro	8.02	8.34	8.67	8.26	8.31	4.87	4.6	4.62	4.01	4.58
Dedicated Short	11.95	10.62	10.79	7.71	10.60	5.60	4.76	4.94	5.14	5.11
All sample	6.10	6.83	9.15	9.55	8.07	4.70	5.75	6.68	7.18	6.25

	Average VaSR					Volatility VaSR				
	1997	1998	1999	2000	Average	1997	1998	1999	2000	Average
Convertible Arbitrage	6.90	7.02	6.35	6.71	6.71	6.39	6.92	6.02	6.92	6.57
Emerging	5.13	9.76	11.58	12.74	10.90	2.05	6.87	5.14	6.61	5.63
Event Driven	5.93	5.69	4.63	5.17	5.31	5.60	5.11	4.44	5.89	5.21
Long-Short Equity	5.79	5.80	6.77	8.63	6.65	3.67	3.57	4.58	5.64	4.38
Managed Futures	11.22	7.75	7.09	6.98	7.33	8.46	4.21	4.04	4.15	4.35

Table 5. Continued.

	Average VaSR					Volatility VaSR				
	1997	1998	1999	2000	Average	1997	1998	1999	2000	Average
Market Neutral	6.46	6.62	7.60	7.85	7.40	4.88	5.00	5.35	5.14	5.17
Multi-Strategy	7.03	6.84	7.22	7.67	7.17	5.18	5.04	5.75	6.12	5.53
Fixed Income Arbitrage	7.47	6.55	7.47	8.43	7.43	7.14	6.12	5.73	5.89	6.26
Global Macro	7.52	6.29	4.93	5.03	5.99	4.55	4.20	2.90	2.98	3.74
Dedicated Short	7.89	7.64	7.40	8.38	7.74	4.17	3.44	3.18	3.07	3.53
All sample	6.76	6.58	6.82	7.45	6.91	5.53	5.34	5.28	5.83	5.48

	Average VaR					Volatility VaR				
	1997	1998	1999	2000	Average	1997	1998	1999	2000	Average
Convertible Arbitrage	9.29	9.60	11.33	11.04	10.48	7.96	8.97	9.69	9.85	9.31
Emerging	11.55	31.42	31.23	32.75	29.09	4.52	20.37	13.54	15.42	14.32
Event Driven	8.03	8.08	8.74	9.14	8.50	7.05	6.55	6.55	8.08	7.02
Long-Short Equity	9.15	10.23	12.54	16.75	11.94	4.71	5.50	7.34	9.95	7.00
Managed Futures	12.463	10.82	11.56	10.62	11.17	8.57	5.71	6.12	5.39	5.94
Market Neutral	8.74	9.50	11.67	12.08	11.13	6.26	6.53	8.23	8.41	7.84
Multi-Strategy	9.73	9.97	11.68	11.91	10.83	6.65	7.02	8.22	8.95	7.75
Fixed Income Arbitrage	9.75	10.54	13.34	14.93	11.98	8.56	9.06	9.29	9.51	9.09
Global Macro	11.38	10.95	10.23	9.84	10.62	5.97	5.37	4.96	4.65	5.29
Dedicated Short	15.25	13.61	13.65	12.07	13.84	4.58	4.53	4.41	4.44	4.49
All sample	9.42	9.87	11.72	12.42	10.97	6.89	7.41	8.13	8.89	7.93

Note: This table shows the average and the volatility of the value at market risk (VaMR), value at specific risk (VaSR) and value at risk (VaR) over time and split by investment style. All numbers are expressed as percentages of net asset values, and calculated using a one month holding period and a 99% confidence interval.

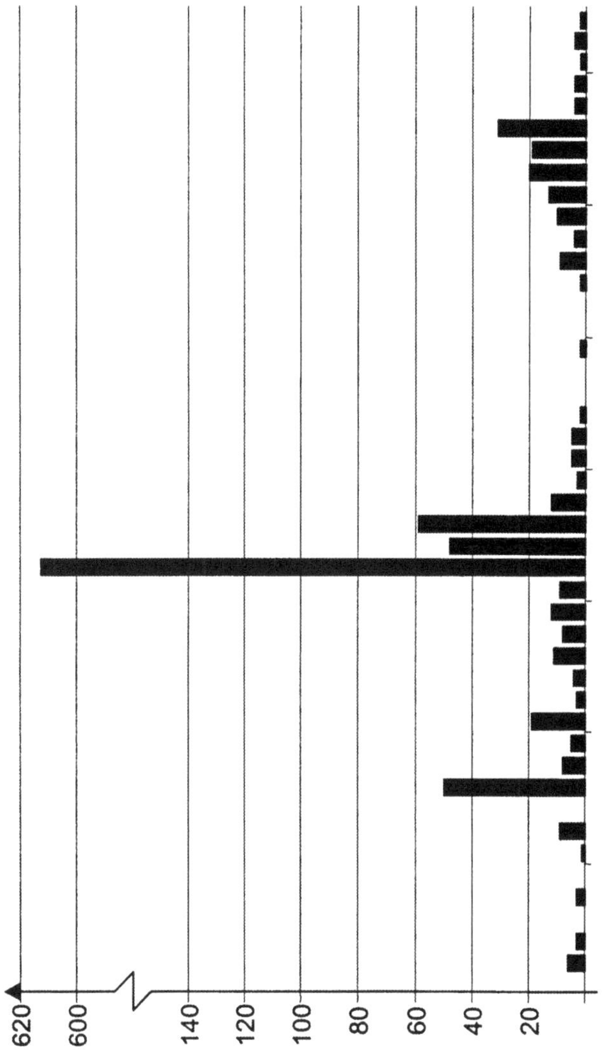

Source: This figure shows the number of exceptions observed during each month from January 1997 to October 2000. An exception is defined as a situation when, within a month, the net asset value of a fund drops by more than the forecasted VaR at the end of the previous month.

Fig. 4. Number of Exceptions Over Time.

including 614 in August 1998 immediately after the LTCM crisis. The other major peaks observed correspond to the 1998 Asian crisis and the 2000 burst of the Internet bubble.

Table 6 regroups interesting statistics about these exceptions. Panel A shows the proportion of exceptions observed year by year for each investment style. The proportion of exceptions corresponds to a binary loss function. If a loss larger than the VaR is observed, it is counted as an "exception". Each loss is equally counted, so that the magnitude of the loss does not matter so far. At time t, for a particular hedge fund, the loss function is therefore:

$$L_t = \begin{cases} 1 & if\, R_t \leq VaR_t \\ 0 & otherwise \end{cases} \qquad (10)$$

where VaR_t is the estimated VaR for month t, and R_t is the realized return figure at time t. If the VaR model is truly providing the level of coverage defined in its confidence level $(1 - \alpha)$, then, one should observe that the average number of exceptions expressed in relative terms to be no more than $(1 - \alpha)$.

The results from Panel A are somewhat mixed. The proportion of exceptions provides a point estimate of the probability of observing a loss greater than the VaR amount over one month and at a 99% confidence interval. Considered globally, the exception rate is 1.06%, slightly higher than the expected 1% level.[15] Fixed Income Arbitrage and Event Driven funds have the highest exception rate (1.84 and 1.47%, respectively). Note that these numbers have to be taken cautiously, given the longevity of the funds in our database. The back testing period being around 29 months on average, an average of one single exception per fund would result in an exception rate of 3.45%!

As a general rule, a large proportion of hedge funds (30.13%) experienced at least one exception during the 1998 LTCM crisis. To illustrate the impact of this single event on VaR figures, we repeat the experiment, but exclude August 1998 from our sample, assuming exceptions within this month were primarily due to the Russian default and/or the collapse of LTCM. As a result, the 1998-year and the overall average, look much better, with exception rates of 0.86% and 0.43% respectively.

Panel B of Table 6 provides some interesting statistics on the magnitude of observed exceptions. In absolute terms, each exception represented an average overstepping of 4.85% over the VaR. At a first glance, this number may appear small. However, expressed in relative terms, this corresponds to an average excess of 63.4% of the VaR. As expected, excluding the month of August 1998 almost always resulted in lower figures.

Table 6. Proportion of Exceptions.

	Exception Rate (%)							
	1997	1998	1999	2000	All	1998*	All*	Aug 98
Convertible Arbitrage	0.11	3.43	0.12	0.31	1.10	1.36	0.49	23.64
Emerging	1.96	3.70	0.00	0.00	0.67	0.00	0.27	60.00
Event Driven	0.63	4.46	0.25	0.15	1.47	0.56	0.39	41.49
Long-Short Equity	0.10	2.75	0.03	0.38	0.79	0.19	0.16	36.73
Managed Futures	0.00	0.28	0.17	0.10	0.16	0.30	0.16	0.00
Market Neutral	0.59	3.20	0.13	0.22	0.68	0.59	0.29	33.33
Multi-Strategy	0.46	2.69	0.11	0.63	1.00	0.58	0.43	26.24
Fixed Income Arbitrage	0.78	5.40	0.03	0.65	1.84	2.19	0.92	36.60
Global Macro	0.00	2.50	0.00	0.53	0.62	1.37	0.38	14.29
Dedicated Short	0.00	0.61	2.13	0.00	0.83	0.68	0.85	0.00
All sample	0.45	3.34	0.13	0.39	1.06	0.86	0.43	30.13

Exception excess loss, as a percentage of NAV

	1997	1998	1999	2000	All	1998*	All*	Aug 98
Convertible Arbitrage	3.10	4.08	6.60	1.22	3.95	2.05	2.32	5.22
Emerging	1.65	6.76			4.72		1.65	6.76
Event Driven	5.06	4.92	3.24	6.68	4.89	3.39	4.23	5.11
Long-Short Equity	3.52	3.40	1.58	8.97	3.94	1.69	5.63	3.52
Managed Futures		0.45	0.40	2.15	0.77	0.45	0.77	

Table 6. Continued.

	Exception excess loss, as a percentage of NAV							
	1997	1998	1999	2000	All	1998*	All*	Aug 98
Market Neutral	10.23	4.60	3.10	3.06	4.92	5.70	5.68	4.38
Multi-Strategy	3.87	4.35	2.61	9.88	5.03	2.65	5.38	4.78
Fixed Income Arbitrage	4.48	6.31	0.73	2.44	5.79	4.36	4.05	7.45
Global Macro		3.25		0.12	2.62	0.82	0.59	5.68
Dedicated Short		5.67	2.04		2.76	5.67	2.76	
All sample	4.78	4.77	2.91	6.43	4.85	3.25	4.27	5.23

	Exception loss, as a percentage of VaR							
	1997	1998	1999	2000	All	1998*	All*	Aug 98
Convertible Arbitrage	23.4	60.6	55.0	7.1	56.0	38.2	34.0	73.3
Emerging	21.9	30.0			26.7		21.9	30.0
Event Driven	41.0	78.6	23.9	54.7	72.0	46.3	40.8	82.7
Long-Short Equity	24.7	37.2	45.2	30.1	36.2	60.5	38.5	35.6
Managed Futures		9.4	2.9	23.0	8.8	9.4	8.8	
Market Neutral	55.3	52.6	49.8	49.5	52.3	58.7	53.7	51.3
Multi-Strategy	37.7	65.3	14.0	56.6	59.6	41.4	43.6	71.2
Fixed Income Arbitrage	35.4	98.0	2.4	40.2	86.2	75.9	60.4	110.9
Global Macro		32.5		0.7	26.1	5.0	3.6	60.0
Dedicated Short		35.3	11.4		16.2	35.3	16.2	
All sample	38.2	70.2	25.0	43.6	63.4	53.4	45.2	75.4

Note: This table shows the proportion of exceptions and their magnitude for each investment style from January 1997 to October 2000. An exception is defined as a situation when, within a month, the net asset value of a fund drops by more than the forecasted VaR at the end of the previous month. The absolute magnitude is expressed as a percentage of the net asset value. The relative magnitude is expressed relative to the forecasted VaR (loss to VaR ratio).

7. CONCLUSION

Since the nineties, there has been growing interest in hedge funds due to their potential for enhancing the overall risk/return profile of traditional portfolios. However, the events of the third quarter of 1998 and the subsequent collapse of LTCM have highlighted the risks associated with hedge funds and prompted strong reactions from virtually all investors. Given the complexity involved with hedge funds strategies, there is a need for adequate tools for measuring and communicating their risk figures. An important challenge is to obtain some form of portfolio transparency from the individual hedge fund managers. Because of specific regulation, lack of liquidity, or other internal reasons, most hedge funds do not disclose their positions or their risk figures.

Our model proposes a simple tool to analyze the investment style of hedge funds, with possible applications for classification, monitoring, performance evaluation and risk management. The risks inherent in a hedge fund portfolio are a function of leverage, market volatility, diversification, and products and markets traded. VaR being a function of all of the above, its use in risk disclosure and monitoring could significantly enhance the decision making at each stage of the investment process of hedge funds, from setting objectives to manager selection, asset allocation, risk monitoring, and performance evaluation.

On the computational side, our VaR model requires the estimation of extreme percentile returns of style indices (which is done once for all), and the calculation of the sensitivity coefficients of a hedge fund to style indices (which needs to be repeated for each fund). The resulting VaR can be split into a specific and a market (style) component. The sources of the latter are also known.

Despite a relatively short observation period, we have tested our model on a large sample of hedge funds. The positive results should provide additional comfort to investment managers by indicating that the realized risks would not be significantly different from the expected ones. The major exception to the previous statement is the month of August 1998, which is considered almost universally to be a "non-representative" event.

However, despite these promising results, one should remember the definition of VaR and its limits. VaR should not create a false sense of security among fund managers, investors and bankers leading to higher leverage and larger exposure positions than would otherwise have occurred. This is definitely not the intended goal. It is important to recognize that VaR is not perfect and has limitations. It should be seen as a quantitative tool used to complement, but not replace, human judgment and market experience. Long

Term Capital Management itself had a fairly sophisticated VaR system, based on historical data, to try to limit potential losses. However, the combination of the exceptional market conditions at the end of 1998 (spreads moving many standard deviations) with excessive leverage, led to a disaster.

There are numerous directions for future research. In particular, the framework presented in this paper does not incorporate all the risk components to which a hedge fund investor is exposed. For instance, we have completely omitted credit and liquidity risks,[16] which are also essential parts of the full risk picture of a hedge fund.

NOTES

1. See Lhabitant (2000) for a review of their major motives.
2. The PWG comprises of the Secretary of the U.S. Department of the Treasury and the respective chairs of the Board of Governors of the Federal Reserve System, the Securities and Exchange Commission and the Commodity Futures Trading Commission.
3. The answering group included representatives of the largest hedge funds in the industry: Caxton Corporation, Kingdon Capital Management, LLC, Moore Capital Management, Inc., Soros Fund Management LLC and Tudor Investment Corporation.
4. A VaR with a confidence level of 99% implies that the loss should not exceed the VaR in 99 cases out of 100. See for instance Jorion (1997) for relevant background material.
5. See Jorion (1997) and Dowd (1998) for a review.
6. Under some conditions, it is also possible to derive the asymptotic distribution for the factor loadings. This allows for inferring confidence intervals and carrying out statistical significance tests. However, because of the constraints imposed by Eqs (3) and (4) on the estimated coefficients, this is not a straightforward exercise. See for instance Gouriéroux et al. (1982).
7. Although a fund's prospectus should obviously provide this information, recent research by DiBartolomeo and Witkowski (1997), Brown and Goetzmann (1997) and Kim, Shukla and Tomas (1999) presents evidence of serious misclassifications when self-reported investment objectives are compared to actual investment styles.
8. These are: MSCI U.S., MSCI non-U.S., and IFC Emerging Market for equities; JP Morgan U.S. Government Bonds, JP Morgan non-U.S. government bonds, and Merrill Lynch High Yield Corporate Bond Index for fixed income; one-month eurodollar rate for cash; gold for commodities; and Federal Reserve's Trade Weighted Dollar Index for currencies.
9. About 73% of the funds considered have a R^2 higher than 0.80, and 56% have R^2 higher than 0.90%.
10. See for instance Chan et al. (1996) or Blake et al. (1999).
11. By systematic, we mean that the corresponding factors influence returns on all hedge funds.
12. Note that if the lower boundary constraint of Eq. (4) is really binding, market risk and specific risk may not be absolutely orthogonal. However, we will neglect that case here.
13. The January 1994 starting date for our sample coincides with the availability of CSFB/Tremont indices.
14. A natural consequence of this particular mapping scheme is that the existence of diversified funds of hedge funds will result in double counting the underlying investment.

15. Note that there are several tests to verify VaR systems; see for instance Kupiec (1995) or Lopez (1998). Unfortunately, the power of these tests is poor in small samples. In our case, we have a large number of funds, and this gives us a large number of test periods. But each fund has a short test history (at most seven years of observations, i.e. four years of test periods), due to the monthly quotes. We are therefore unable to rely on such tests to draw conclusions.

16. Note that the sound practice report also suggested that hedge fund managers should consider incorporating additional measures to capture asset liquidity. That is to say, the change in the value of an asset due to changes in liquidity of the market in which the asset is traded. Suggested measures of asset liquidity that might be captured include the number of days that would be required to liquidate and/or neutralise the position in question, and the value that would be lost if the asset in question were to be liquidated and/or neutralised completely within the holding.

17. This also applies to nonparametric methods such as kernel smoothing.

18. See Smith (1987) for maximum likelihood estimation, Hosking and Wallis (1987) for probability-weighted moments estimation, and Castillo and Hadi (1997) for more specific recommendations.

ACKNOWLEDGMENTS

F. S. Lhabitant is with Union Bancaire Privee (Geneva), HEC University of Lausanne (Switzerland) and Thunderbird, the American Graduate School of International Management (AZ, USA). The opinions expressed in this paper reflect solely the views of the author and do not engage any institution he may belong to. An earlier version of this paper appeared in the Journal of Risk Finance – see Lhabitant (2001).

REFERENCES

Bekaert, G., DeRoon, F., Ferguson, M., & Nijman, T. (2000). Style Estimation. Working Paper. Columbia Business School.

Brown, S., & Goetzmann, W. (1997). Mutual Fund Styles. *Journal of Financial Economics*, *43*, 373–399.

Castillo, E., & Hadi, A. S. (1997), Fitting the generalized Pareto distribution to data. *JASA*, *92*(440), 1609–1620.

Chan, L. K. C., Jegadeesh, N., & Lakonishok, J. (1996). Momentum strategies. *Journal of Finance*, *51*, 1681–1713.

Culp, Ch. L., Mensink, R., & Neves, A. M. P. (1999). VaR for Asset Managers. *Derivatives Quarterly*, *5*(2).

Daniel, K., Grinblatt, M., Titman, S., & Wermers, R. (1997). Measuring mutual fund performance with characteristics-based benchmarks. *The Journal of Finance*, *LII*(3).

DeRoon, F., Nijman, T., & TerHorst, J. (2000). Evaluating Style Analysis. Working Paper Erasmus University Rotterdam (RIFM).

DiBartolomeo, D., & Witkowski, E. (1997). Mutual Fund Misclassification: Evidence based on Style Analysis. *Financial Analysts Journal*, (Sept/Oct), 32–43.

Ditlevsen, O. (1994). Distribution arbitrariness in structural reliability. In: Schuller, Shinozuka and Yao (Eds), *Structural Safety and Reliability* (pp. 1241–1247). Rotterdam.: Balkema.

Dowd, K. (1998). *Beyond VaR: The New Science of Risk Management*. Chichester: John Wiley & Sons.

Blake, E. J., Elton, M. J., & Gruber, C. R. (1995). Fundamental economic variables, expected returns, and bond fund performance. *Journal of Finance*, *50*, 1229–1256.

Blake, E. J., Elton, M. J., & Gruber, C. R. (1999). Common Factors in Active and Passive Portfolios. *European Finance Review*, *3*(1).

Fama, E., & French, K. (1992). The cross section of expected stock returns. *Journal of Finance*, *47*(2), 427–465.

Fama, E., & McBeth, J. D. (1973). Risk return and equilibrium: an empirical test. *Journal of Political Economy*, *81*, 607–636.

Fung, W., & Hsieh, D. A. (1998). Performance attribution and style analysis. From mutual funds to hedge funds, Working paper, Paradigm Financial Product, February.

Gourieroux, Ch., Holly, A., & Montfort, A. (1982). Likelihood Ratio Test, Wald Test and Kuhn-Tucker Test in Linear Models with Inequality Constraints on the Regression Parameters. *Econometrica*, *50*, 63–80.

Hosking, J. R. M., & Wallis, J. L. (1987). Parameter and quantile estimation foe the generalized pareto distribution. *Technometrics*, *29*, 1339–1449.

Jorion, Ph. (1997). *VaR: The New Benchmark for Controlling Derivatives Risk*. Irwin Publishing.

Kim, M., Shukla, R., & Tomas, M. (2000). Mutual Fund Objective Misclassification. *Journal of Economics and Business*, *52*, 309–323.

Kupiec, N. H. (1995). Techniques for verifying the accuracy of risk measurement models. *Journal of Derivatives*, *3*(2), 73–84.

Lhabitant, F. S. (2000). Hedge funds and investment partnerships: a primer, discussion paper. Thunderbird, the American Graduate School of International Management.

Lhabitant, F. S. (2001). Assessing market risk for hedge funds and hedge funds portfolios, *The Journal of Risk Finance*, Spring 2001, 1–17.

Lobosco, A., & DiBartolomeo, D. (1997). Approximating the Confidence Intervals for Sharpe Style Weights. *Financial Analysts Journal*, July/August, 80–85.

Longin, F. (1999). Stress Testing: A Method Based on Extreme Value Theory. Working paper. BSI Gamma Foundation.

Lopez, J. A. (1998). Methods for Evaluating VaR Estimates. Working paper. Federal Reserve Bank of New York.

Mitev, T. (1995). Classification of Commodity Trading Advisors (CTAs) using Maximum Likelihood Factor Analysis. Working Paper. CISDM/SOM, University of Massachusetts.

Pickands (1975). Statistical Inference using extreme order statistics, *Annals of Statistics*, *3*, 119–131.

President's Working Group on Financial Markets (1999). *Hedge Funds, Leverage and the Lessons of Long Term Capital Management*, April.

RiskMetrics. (1996). *RiskMetrics™ - Technical Document* (4th ed.). New York, N.Y.: J. P. Morgan and Reuters.

Schneeweis, T., Savanayana, U., & McCarthy, D. (1996). Informational content in historical CTA performance. *Journal of Futures Markets*.

Sharpe, W. F. (1992). Asset allocation: management style and performance measurement. *Journal of Portfolio Management*, *18*(2), 7–19.

Sharpe, W. F. (1988). Determining a Fund's Effective Asset Mix. *Investment Management Review*, *2*(6), 59–69.

Smith, R. L. (1987). Estimating tails of probability distributions. *Ann. Statist.*, *15*(3), 1174–1207.

Wilson, T. C. (1993). Infinite wisdom. *Risk*, *6* (June), 37–45.

APPENDIX 1

Estimating Extreme Moves

The estimation of extreme moves for hedge funds indices has to be performed very cautiously, since the whole methodology relies on the resulting values. In practice, extreme moves are nothing more than lower or upper extreme quantiles of a hedge fund index return distribution. However, estimating them using traditional statistical and econometric methods is generally not feasible. First, the underlying return distribution is not accurately known, which precludes the use of parametric methods. Second, most estimation procedures are targeted to provide a good fit in regions where most of the data fall, but are ill-suited to the assessment of tail behaviours, where by definition few observations fall.[17] Third, the required estimates are often way in the tails, far beyond the boundaey of the range of observed data.

Fortunately, "Extreme Value Theory" (EVT) has emerged as a powerful approach for estimating extreme quantiles and probabilities. Unlike traditional approaches, EVT focuses on extreme values data rather than all the data, therefore fitting the tail (and only the tail). There are two different, yet related, approaches to modeling extreme values. The first one consists of fitting one of the three extreme value limit laws to the maximum of a time series. Much historical work was devoted to this approach (see Gumbel, 1958). The second one, and the one we will follow hereafter, is to consider values exceeding a given threshold.

Let $r_1, \ldots, r_N$ be the monthly return observations for a particular hedge fund index. These values are considered to be realizations of N independent and identically distributed random variables $R_1, \ldots, R_N$. The order statistics of the sample $\{r_1, \ldots, r_N\}$ will be denoted by $R_{(i)}$, with $R_{(1)} \leq \ldots \leq R_{(N)}$. We denote by F the cumulative return distribution. Let us say that we want to estimate the upper extreme quantile q_α, defined by:

$$1 - F\,(q_\alpha) = Prob(R > q_\alpha) = \alpha$$

with $0 < \alpha < 1/N$.

Traditional estimation methods assume a parametric approximation $F \approx F_\theta$, obtain an estimate $\hat{\theta}$ based on the whole sample $\{R_1, \ldots, R_N\}$ and estimate the quantile $q\alpha$ as $\hat{q}_\alpha = F_{\hat{\theta}}^{-1}\,(1 - \alpha)$. Typical assumptions are the normal distribution (with mean μ and variance σ^2, i.e. $\theta = (\mu, \sigma)$) or any arbitrary fat-tailed distribution. However, cumulative distribution functions from various parametric models may have similar shapes over the sample range, but can differ significantly in their tail behaviors. Since most observations in the sample are central ones, the fit is generally adequate on average values, but ill-suited to the extreme observations. This leads to imprecise estimations, particularly when $\alpha < 1/N$; see for instance Ditlevsen (1994). Fortunately, extreme value methods, and more particularly the extreme value theorem can help us in finding what the distribution of extreme quantiles should be.

Let us say that we choose a (high) threshold value u so that there are m values of r_i above the threshold. We denote y_i the differences $r_i - u$, with $i = 1 \ldots m$. Pickands (1975) shows that the probability distribution of $y_1, \ldots, y_m$ can be approximated by a generalized Pareto distribution, which has the following cumulative distribution functions

$$G(y; \sigma, k) = \begin{cases} 1 - \left(1 - \frac{ky}{\sigma}\right)^{\frac{1}{k}} & if\, k \neq 0 \\ 1 - e^{-\frac{y}{k}} & if\, k = 0 \end{cases}$$

where $\sigma > 0$ is a scale parameter, and $-\infty < k < +\infty$ is a shape parameter. The support is $y \geq 0$ if $k \leq 0$, and $y \in [0, \sigma/k]$ if $k > 0$. The shape parameter k reflects the weight of the tail in the distribution of the parent variable X (low k values correspond to fatter tails). It also gives the number of finite moments of the distribution ($k > 1$ when the mean exists, $k > 2$ when the variance is finite, etc.). Depending on the value of σ and k, the generalized Pareto distribution reduces in special cases. For instance, normal, exponential, log-normal, gamma and Weilbull distributions will result in a Gumbel distribution for extremes values ($k = 0$), while Cauchy, Pareto or student-t, or stable Paretian law returns will result in a Fréchet distribution for extremes values.

To summarize, the algorithm to estimate $q\alpha$ is as follows. Starting from N observations,

(1) Choose a high threshold u so that m observations are greater than u. Keep these m observations, and denote the obtained excess returns $(r_i - u)$ by $y_1, \ldots, y_m$.

(2) For high values of u, the probability distribution of $y_1, \ldots, y_m$ can be approximated by a generalized Pareto distribution, whose parameters σ and k can be estimated using maximum likelihood, method of moments or probability-weighted moments.[18]

(3) The extreme quantile q_α is then estimated by

$$\hat{q}_\alpha = u + \frac{\hat{\sigma}}{\hat{k}}\left[1 - \left(\frac{N \cdot \alpha}{m}\right)^{\hat{k}}\right]$$

In our case, N = 36,and we set arbitrarily m = 9, i.e. one fourth of the data is used to fit the extreme values distribution.

APPENDIX 2

Alternative Parameters

In addition to computing the 99% one-month VaR figure as described previously, we also performed additional tests on our sample.

First, the estimation of the funds' sensitivities to the style indices was performed using an exponentially weighted regression rather than a standard OLS. The goal of this particular weighting scheme was to set more emphasis on recent errors (ε_t) rather than older ones, in order to capture faster any investment style change from the fund manager, if any. The exponentially weighted average approach with a fixed weight parameter has been promoted fairly heavily by JP Morgan in their RiskMetrics (1996) package.

Second, in addition to 99%, we set the VaR confidence level at 97.5% and 95%. Remember that the choice of a particular confidence level depends very much on the application and users: internal risk management, external supervisory agencies, and financial statement users (VaR as a performance measure). A high confidence interval will ensure that alarms are not set off too frequently, while a lower level of VaR may be more appropriate to trigger more frequent discussions.

None of these "improvements" provided significantly different results with respect to the ones we reported in this paper. Using an exponentially weighted regression did not change the funds' style exposures much nor the VaR figures, and changing the VaR confidence level sensibly increased the number of exceptions.

ADR RISK CHARACTERISTICS AND MEASUREMENT

Tom Arnold, Lance Nail and Terry D. Nixon

ABSTRACT

In this study of ADRs, we find several results of interest to the finance community. We find that tests of foreign stock index correlations with the U.S. stock markets are insufficient tests of the diversification impact of ADRs on portfolios of U.S. stocks as the correlations of ADRs with the S&P 500 are significantly lower than the correlations between the S&P 500 and home country indices of the ADRs. We also find differences between risk and return in developed and emerging markets. ADR returns and standard deviations are significantly higher than those of the underlying stocks from developed countries, but the opposite is true for emerging markets. This result is likely caused by greater tax preferences for home country investors and higher transactions costs in emerging markets. The ADRs from emerging markets are also insignificantly correlated with the S&P 500 while those from developed countries are significantly correlated (at a low 0.12). These low correlations result in near zero betas for both developed and emerging market ADRs and lead to reductions in both systematic and unsystematic risk. Finally, on the basis of CAPM-adjusted abnormal returns, we cannot conclude that CAPM is an inaccurate predictor of returns for ADRs of either developed or emerging markets. The same holds true for the underlying stocks in developed countries. However, we can reject CAPM as an appropriate asset pricing model for the home country stocks of emerging markets as it significantly overestimates the expected returns of emerging markets'

Financial Risk and Financial Risk Management, Volume 16, pages 451–472.

ISBN: 0-7623-0858-3

stocks. This result is unresolved and opens an interesting avenue of future study.

1. INTRODUCTION

While a healthy empirical literature exists on international diversification and its benefits, surprisingly few studies have examined the risk characteristics and efficacy of asset pricing models for one avenue of international diversification – investments in American Depository Receipts (ADRs). Originating in approximately 1927, ADRs provide an opportunity for investors to indirectly purchase shares of foreign firms. ADRs represent a claim to a given number of shares of a foreign firm held by a U.S. financial institution (e.g. Bank of New York). With the increasingly significant presence of ADR trading in the American stock markets – increasing six-fold between 1990 and 1999 – an analysis of these securities' diversification impact on a U.S. stock portfolio and tests of the acuity of asset pricing models for predicting their returns should contribute to investors' utility in efficiently diversifying risk.

To date, studies of American Depository Receipts have focused on two main topics: (1) pricing efficiency of ADRs relative to their underlying foreign security, and (2) potential international diversification benefits of ADRs in an individual's stock portfolio.

The studies on the efficiency of ADRs relative to their underlying security find that, on average, exploitable arbitrage opportunities do not exist. ADR prices do reflect changes in the price of the underlying security. Kato, Linn and Schallheim (1991) find no real opportunity for arbitrage profits in a small sample of ADRs between 1981 and 1984. They conclude that the law of one price holds even though the returns of their sample ADRs and underlying securities are not perfectly positively correlated. They attribute some of the difference to tax issues. In a response to Kato et al., Wahab, Lashgari and Cohn (1992) argue that the standard deviations for ADRs will be greater than the standard deviation for their underlying security and again attempt to determine whether arbitrage opportunities can be exploited. Ultimately, they are not able to make a strong case for the existence of arbitrage opportunities. Jayaraman, Shastri and Tandon (1993) find that the listing of an ADR results in positive excess returns as well as increased variance of returns for the underlying security.[1] Sundaram and Logue (1996) provide support for Jayaraman et al.'s finding. Their results indicate that the issuance of ADRs is associated with an increase in the issuing firms equity price. Kim, Szakmary and Mathur (2000) also test whether ADR prices are efficient relative to the price of the underlying shares. They contend (as do others) that ADR prices should reflect the price of the underlying shares in local currency, the relevant exchange rate, and the U.S. market index. They find that the most influential factor on ADR prices is the underlying share price followed by exchange rates.

The other branch of ADR literature finds support for ADRs as a means of increased international diversification in a portfolio. Officer and Hoffmeister (1987) find that ADRs in combination with U.S. stock result in increased diversification possibilities for a given investor's portfolio. Wahab and Khandwala (1993) test whether the ADRs are actually better means of diversification than the underlying stock. Their empirical tests find that the ADRs and underlying stocks have similar returns but that the ADRs do have additional risk reduction benefits. Jiang (1998) finds a portfolio consisting of the U.S. market portfolio and ADRs outperform portfolios containing the U.S. market index and foreign indexes in the short-run, but cannot unequivocally state that these same results hold for the long-run. Choi and Kim (2000) examine ADRs from 1990–1996, and also conclude that ADRs can be beneficial in an individual's portfolio for diversification purposes with emerging market ADRs giving the best chance for diversification.

The sample employed in this study consists of 85 ADRs traded continuously on the U.S. stock exchanges between 1990 and 1999. In particular, we measure the volatility of the ADRs in terms of their volatility in U.S. trading, volatility of trading in their home countries, and the volatility of exchange rates between the U.S. and the home country of the ADR. We then decompose the volatility of the ADR into terms attributable to either home country volatility or exchange rate volatility. Finally, we expand the ADR literature by conducting ex-post tests of the Capital Asset Pricing Model (CAPM) in both the U.S. and the home country of the ADR in order to determine the ability of CAPM to serve as an accurate predictor of returns for ADRs and/or their home country stocks.

Our results show that ADRs can add more diversification to a portfolio of U.S. stocks than the broad indices previously tested. We also find that ADR returns are significantly lower than their underlying stocks in emerging markets but that the opposite is true for developed countries. Our results also indicate that the volatility of ADRs as measured by the standard deviation of return is not significantly different from the volatility of their underlying home country stocks for either developed or emerging markets. However, the volatility in exchange rates causes the correlation between ADRs and the S&P 500 to be much lower than for the average U.S. stock relative to the same index. This result also leads to beta measures near zero for the ADRs in our study and indicates that ADRs can be used to reduce both systematic and unsystematic portfolio risk. We also cannot reject the validity of CAPM in generating expected returns for ADRs or home country stocks in developed countries.

However, CAPM significantly overestimates expected returns in emerging markets.

The remainder of this paper is organized as follows: Section 2 describes our sample and methodology, Section 3 presents our results, and Section 4 concludes.

2. SAMPLE AND METHODOLOGY

We obtained our sample of ADRs from the Center for Research in Security Prices (CRSP) tapes, identifying all ADRs traded on any of the U.S. exchanges between 1990 and 1999. This initial sample resulted in 95 ADRs traded during this time period. We chose our sample period on the basis of three factors – availability of data, size of sample, and span of overall market returns. First, CRSP data were available through year-end 1999 at the time of this study. Second, we had to account for the trade-off between sample size and range of returns for the U.S. stock markets. Longer time periods of analysis lead to more robust results across different market environments, yet longer periods also cause a rapid decrease in the number of observations. For example, reducing our sample period to 1995–1999 would have nearly tripled our sample size, but our entire sample period would have consisted of only positive returns for the U.S. stock markets. Extending our sample period to pre-1990 would have significantly reduced our sample as ADR listings are positively temporally distributed and would introduce the problems associated with small sample properties into our analysis. Thus, 1990–1999 seems to be a logical time period for analysis as it represents an entire decade of stock market returns (both positive and negative) with a sample size that avoids small sample properties. The CRSP listing of ADRs was then checked against *The McGraw-Hill Handbook of American Depository Receipts* to identify the home country of the ADRs. All ADR price and return data were also taken from the CRSP tapes.

For home country stock price and return information and exchange rate data, we retrieved data from either the Bloomberg database or from the *Financial Times*. Our initial sample of 95 ADRs was reduced to a sample size of 89 due to missing data from either Bloomberg or the *Financial Times*. The six excluded ADRs included listings from Bermuda, Finland, Israel, Luxembourg, and four from Mexico. Four additional ADRs from Australia and the United Kingdom were excluded because they traded in a range less than $1.00 and severely positively skewed volatility results in such a small sample. Thus, our final sample size for this study includes 85 observations. Table 1 exhibits a description of our sample distributed by home country.

Table 1. Description of Sample.

This table contains a description of the 85 American Depository Receipts (ADRs) traded on the U.S. stock markets the entire sample period of 1990–1999. The sample is distributed according to ADRs' home country.

Country	*N*	*Index*	*Currency*
Australia	8	All Ordinaries	Australian Dollar
Denmark	1	Copenhagen	Kroner
France	1	CAC-40	French Franc
Ireland	2	Irish Overall	Punt
Italy	3	Milan Index	Lira
Japan	24	Nikkei-225	Yen
Netherlands	4	Amsterdam	Guilder
Norway	1	Oslo	Krone
South Africa	5	Johannesburg	Rand
Spain	5	IBEX	Pesata
Sweden	4	Stockholm	Krona
United Kingdom	27	FTSE-100	British Pound
All countries	85		

Our empirical analysis follows a standard study design – employing t-tests for significance of individual variables and paired t-tests for subsample comparisons. As in prior studies of ADRs, we analyze our full sample of ADRs as well as subsamples according to home country of ADR and classification of the home market as either developed or emerging. Following the convention of Choi and Kim (2000), we classify the markets of Australia, France, Japan, and the United Kingdom as developed and all other countries are classified as emerging markets. This market classification is necessary in order to obtain robust results as ADRs from many countries are sparsely represented in our sample and cannot be analyzed with standard tests of significance.

We selected our market indices according to the primary stock index listed by either Bloomberg or the *Financial Times* for each country. Use of the Standard & Poors 500 Index (S&P 500) for the United States differs somewhat from prior studies, but use of this index is more congruent with the choice of other countries' indices than either of the CRSP indices more commonly used. The indices used in this study are shown in Table 1. The empirical results generated from our sample and design are presented in the following section.

3. EMPIRICAL RESULTS

3.1. Comparisons of Risk Measures Between ADRs and Home Country Stocks

Presented in Table 2 are descriptive statistics for the ADRs in our study. The average annual return for the entire length of the study (1990–1999) in the home market was 9.81% versus a return of 9.13% for the ADRs themselves. Home market returns ranged from a high of 18.83% in South Africa to a low of 2.09% in Japan. Irish ADRs had the highest return at 14.04% while Spanish ADRs had the lowest at 3.52%.

Standard deviations were also very similar between the home markets and ADRs – averaging 45.05% for home stocks and 44.55% for ADRs. The range for home country stocks was a high of 63.19% in France and a low of 23.04% in Norway. ADRs ranged from 55.98% in South Africa to 24.35% in Norway. The standard deviation measures are also highly correlated between home stocks and ADRs at 0.94 (p-value = 0.000).

Differences in betas between markets shows a much different pattern however. The average beta of home country stocks to their home market indices is 1.05 compared to an average beta of 0.06 for ADRs relative to the S&P 500. Home country betas fall into a relatively narrow range of 1.94 for South Africa to 0.61 for Italy. ADR betas are much more dispersed – ranging from 2.14 for Dutch ADRs to –1.40 for South African ADRs. The correlation between home stock betas and ADR betas was an insignificant 0.01.

We also present the volatility of exchange rates over the sample period for each country. The average standard deviation of exchange rates for all countries is 10.32% – ranging from a high of 12.92% for the Italian Lira and a low of 8.42% for the South African Rand.

We next perform paired t-tests to determine if differences exist between measures of risk and return between home country stocks and their ADRs. These tests are presented in Table 3. As can be seen in Panel A, the 0.69% difference in returns between the home country stocks and their ADRs (Home-ADR) is insignificant. A review of individual countries reveals an interesting pattern however. With the exception of Japan, returns are higher in the underlying stocks than in the ADRs. These returns are significantly higher in Australia (1.87%), Italy (5.66%), South Africa (9.39%), Spain (4.62%), Sweden (5.58%), and the United Kingdom (0.55%). Japanese ADRs outperform their underlying stocks by a significant 4.38%.[2] These results support the notion of Kato, Linn and Schallheim (1991) that tax preferences in the home country and transactions costs associated with ADRs may lead to higher home country returns.

***Table 2*.** Descriptive Statistics.

This table contains summary information regarding ADRs, their underlying stocks (home market), and the volatility of exchange rates between the U.S. dollar and home country currency (cross).

			Home market			ADR			Cross
Country	*Mkt*	*n*	*Average annual return %*	*Average annual standard deviation %*	*Average annual beta*	*Average annual return %*	*Average annual standard deviation %*	*Average annual beta*	*Currency standard deviation %*
Australia	D	8	13.74	41.27	1.20	11.87	41.41	0.43	8.82
Denmark	E	1	15.71	42.24	1.10	12.63	38.09	2.14	10.69
France	D	1	10.53	63.19	1.41	6.72	54.39	0.74	10.15
Ireland	E	2	17.25	49.13	1.02	14.04	44.25	1.15	10.32
Italy	E	3	12.03	34.26	0.61	6.38	27.87	–0.27	12.92
Japan	D	24	2.99	41.31	0.62	7.37	46.73	–0.84	9.09
Netherlands	E	4	10.05	41.92	0.85	7.72	38.09	0.09	10.19
Norway	E	1	9.91	23.04	0.55	8.13	24.35	–0.98	9.62
South Africa	E	5	18.83	60.13	1.94	9.44	55.98	–1.40	8.42
Spain	E	5	8.15	35.64	0.66	3.52	32.02	0.60	12.78
Sweden	E	4	13.59	54.60	1.22	8.01	49.78	–0.61	12.62
United Kingdom	D	27	11.72	48.42	1.34	11.16	46.42	0.89	9.72
All countries		85	9.81	45.05	1.05	9.13	44.55	0.06	10.32

***Table 3*.** Univariate Comparisons of Risk Measures.

Presented in this table are mean differences in risk measures between ADRs and their underlying stocks.

Panel A: Differences in beta and standard deviation for each country

			Difference: Home market – ADR					
Country	*Mkt*	*n*	*Average annual return %*	*t-stat*	*Average annual standard deviation %*	*t-stat*	*Average annual beta*	*t-stat*
Australia	D	8	1.87	3.77*	–0.14	–0.11	0.77	2.06
Denmark	E	1	3.07	–	4.15	–	–1.04	–
France	D	1	3.81	–	8.80	–	0.67	–
Ireland	E	2	3.21	4.18	4.70	2.15	–0.13	–0.14
Italy	E	3	5.66	9.63*	6.38	3.00	0.88	3.26
Japan	D	24	–4.38	–13.24*	–5.18	–4.52*	1.46	4.31*
Netherlands	E	4	2.33	5.01	3.83	5.83*	0.76	1.88
Norway	E	1	1.79	–	1.30	–	1.53	–
South Africa	E	5	9.39	22.44*	4.15	13.94*	3.34	6.51*
Spain	E	5	4.62	23.25*	3.62	5.63*	0.06	0.68
Sweden	E	4	5.58	5.85*	4.82	3.49*	1.83	1.85
United Kingdom	D	27	0.55	2.55*	1.99	3.47*	1.75	1.33
All countries		85	0.69	1.54	0.49	0.85	0.99	5.54*

Table 3. Continued.

Panel B: Differences in beta and standard deviation for developed and emerging markets

		Difference: Home market – ADR					
Market	*n*	*Average annual return %*	*t-stat*	*Average annual standard deviation %*	*t-stat*	*Average annual beta*	*t-stat*
Developed	60	–1.19	–3.06*	–1.05	–1.47	0.90	4.18*
Emerging	25	5.20	9.80*	4.19	9.23*	1.21	3.76*

* Significant at the 5% level

Just as with returns, standard deviations between ADRs and their underlying stocks are not significantly different (0.49%, t-stat = 0.85). But as before, individual countries reveal different patterns. Home country standard deviations are higher in every country except Australia and Japan. Standard deviations are significantly higher in the Netherlands (3.83%), South Africa (4.15%), Spain (3.62%), Sweden (4.82%), and the United Kingdom (1.99%). Japan is the only country where ADR standard deviations are greater than in the underlying stocks (5.18%). These results run counter to the conjecture of Wahab, Lashargi and Cohn (1992) that ADR standard deviations will be higher and perhaps more consistent with Kato, Linn and Schallheim (1992) in that ADR markets are informationally efficient. Volatility is virtually the same between the ADRs and the underlying stocks; thus, exchange rate volatility appears to be driving the aforementioned differences in standard deviations.

As might be expected, betas are quite different between ADRs and their underlying stocks. The beta measure contains a limit property that asserts that in the limit the beta of a portfolio of all stocks in a market approaches 1.00 as the correlation between the market index and its stocks also approaches 1.00 in the limit. This property should hold true in any country's market. However, ADRs are different in the sense that they are derivative securities traded on a U.S. exchange with the primary security trading on a foreign exchange. Thus, while the underlying stock would be expected to be correlated with its home country index, the level of correlation of its ADR with the S&P 500 would depend on the degree of correlation between its home country index and the S&P 500 (see Section 3.2 for further analysis of cross-country correlations). This cross-correlation issue leads to large differences in betas between ADRs and their underlying stocks. The average beta is significantly greater in the home country than for that of the ADR. The average difference is a significant 0.99 (1.05–0.06). The largest difference of 3.34 occurs in South Africa and the lowest of –1.04 occurs in Denmark. The only other country in which the ADR beta is higher is Ireland, but the difference is insignificant. Yet, only two countries have significantly higher home country betas – South Africa and Japan (difference of 1.46). On the whole, these results suggest that ADRs possess significantly lower co-movements with the S&P 500 than either co-movements with their own indices or U.S. stocks with the S&P 500. This also implies that systematic risk can be significantly reduced with the inclusion of ADRs in a portfolio of U.S. stocks and also holds important implications for our CAPM tests described in Section 3.3.

We also want to consider the differences in risk and return with regard to developed and emerging markets. As can be seen in Panel B of Table 3, ADR returns are significantly higher for developed countries (1.19%) while underlying returns are 5.20% higher for emerging markets. This result loosely supports Kato, Linn and Schallheim (1991) in their assertion that tax preferences and transactions costs lead to higher returns in the home country relative to ADRs. Both taxes and transactions costs tend to be higher in emerging markets, leading to lower ADR returns vis-à-vis the underlying stocks. However, the reverse situation occurs with developed countries with lower taxes and transactions costs where adverse exchange rate movements cause ADR returns to be significantly higher.

Surprisingly, standard deviations are significantly higher (4.19%) in emerging home country stocks than in their ADRs. This finding lends support to the conclusions of Kim, Szakmary and Mathur (2000) in that ADR returns initially under-react to contemporaneous underlying security and especially exchange rate returns and refutes the contention of Wahab, Lashgari and Cohn (1992) that the standard deviations of ADRs will be higher than those of their underlying stocks. Considering that no significant difference exists between ADR and underlying standard deviations in developed countries, the higher underlying standard deviations in emerging markets might indicate the more liquid and less risky trading environment that exists in developed countries (the U.S. market in particular).

As expected, the ADR betas of both developed and emerging markets are significantly lower than those of the underlying stocks. The differences are 0.90 for developed countries and 1.21 for emerging markets. These large and significant differences imply very different systematic risk measures between domestic and international portfolios for the same stock in both developed and emerging markets.

3.2. Measures of Correlation

As we alluded to earlier in our analysis, levels of correlation play a vital role in determining the level of systematic and unsystematic risk reduction achieved through the inclusion of ADRs in a domestic portfolio. Of course, the sum of weighted covariances formula shows that lower levels of correlation between securities lead to lower levels of total risk in a portfolio. However, the use of beta in the CAPM formula assumes that unsystematic risk has been diversified away and the only relevant remaining risk to consider is systematic risk as measured by beta. Yet, as previously discussed, the limit property of beta no longer holds as ADR correlations with the S&P 500 may or may not approach 1.00 in the limit. Therefore, we must analyze additional correlations between ADR returns and the S&P 500, underlying stocks and their indices, and between the indices themselves. Pearson correlation coefficients for all such pairings are presented in Table 4.

Table 4. Correlations.

This table shows correlations between ADRs and S&P 500, underlying stocks and home index, and home indices and S&P 500.

Panel A: Correlation tests for individual countries

Country	*Mkt*	*n*	*Average correlation of home country stock with home country index*	*p-value* (>0)	*Average correlation of ADR with S&P 500*	*p-value* (>0)	*Average correlation of home country index with S&P 500*	*p-value* (>0)
Australia	D	80	0.44	0.000*	0.19	0.086	0.57	0.000*
Denmark	E	10	0.65	0.043*	0.57	0.084	0.56	0.093
France	D	10	0.75	0.012*	0.47	0.171	0.61	0.062
Ireland	E	20	0.41	0.068	0.13	0.569	0.59	0.006*
Italy	E	30	0.58	0.001*	0.22	0.232	0.47	0.009*
Japan	D	240	0.46	0.000*	0.03	0.646	0.22	0.001*
Netherlands	E	40	0.42	0.007*	0.11	0.499	0.65	0.000*
Norway	E	10	0.79	0.006*	–0.55	0.099	0.11	0.768
South Africa	E	50	0.75	0.000*	–0.22	0.118	–0.06	0.697
Spain	E	50	0.45	0.001*	0.15	0.304	0.63	0.000*
Sweden	E	40	0.70	0.000*	0.17	0.292	0.41	0.009*
United Kingdom	D	270	0.28	0.000*	0.18	0.003*	0.78	0.000*
All countries		850	0.42	0.000*	0.11	0.002*	0.39	0.000*

Table 4. Continued.

Panel B: Correlation tests for developed and emerging markets

Market	*n*	*Average correlation of home country stock with home country index*	*p-value* (>0)	*Average correlation of ADR with S&P 500*	*p-value* (>0)	*Average correlation of home country index with S&P 500*	*p-value* (>0)
Developed	600	0.37	0.000*	0.12	0.002*	0.41	0.000*
Emerging	250	0.57	0.000*	0.05	0.440	0.41	0.000*

* Significant at the 5% level

As can be seen in Panel A, underlying stocks are significantly positively correlated with their home index in all countries with the exception of Ireland (which is significant at the 10% level). The average correlation across all countries is a significant 0.42. ADR returns are generally positively correlated with the S&P 500 (Norway and South Africa being the exceptions), but the only significant correlation is the 0.18 for ADRs from the United Kingdom. For all countries, the average correlation is a significant 0.11. This correlation is significantly lower than the 0.42 for the home country stocks.

Given these results, the fact that home indices are positively correlated with the S&P 500 is not surprising. The only negative correlation with the S&P 500 comes from the South African Johannesburg Index at –0.06 and is insignificant. Indices in Australia (0.57), Ireland (0.59), Italy (0.47), Japan (0.22), Spain (0.63), Sweden (0.41), and the United Kingdom (0.78) are all significantly positively related to the S&P 500. The average correlation for all indices relative to the S&P 500 is a significant 0.39. These results are similar to prior studies.

As shown in Panel B, considering market classification also reveals that correlations are significantly positive – irrespective of whether the home country stocks are from developed or emerging markets. The one exception is in the ADRs in emerging markets which have an insignificant correlation of 0.05 with the S&P 500. Interestingly, correlations between developed and emerging markets' indices with the S&P 500 are an identical 0.41. This compares to ADR correlations to the S&P 500 of 0.12 and 0.05 for developed and emerging markets, respectively. These results lead us to conclude that macro index studies of international diversification such as Harvey's (1991) do not capture the full effect of diversification offered by ADRs as even a diversified portfolio of ADRs (85 for all ADRs, 60 for developed country ADRs, and 25 for emerging market ADRs) offers a lower correlation (0.11, 0.12, and 0.05) than the correlation between indices.

We next consider the impact of these correlations on the validity of CAPM for generating expected returns for both ADRs and their underlying stocks.

3.3. Ex-post CAPM Tests

Our first step in testing the validity of CAPM involves testing for a beta with predictive power (i.e. >0). We do this by estimating beta over a moving five-year period and averaging each of these five-year betas. Thus, we have beta estimates for 1995–1999 for each of our ADRs and underlying stocks and average these five betas for average annual beta estimate. This procedure is conducted for ADRs relative to the S&P 500 and for the underlying stocks relative to their home indices. Results are shown in Panel A of Table 5.

As previously discussed, home country betas are all positive and fall into a fairly tight range of 0.61 to 1.94. The average across all countries is 1.05 and significantly different from zero. For most countries with multiple observations – Australia, Japan, South Africa, Spain, Sweden, and the United Kingdom – betas of underlying stocks are significantly positive. All of the three remaining countries – Ireland, Italy, and the Netherlands – are emerging markets, a point to be addressed later. Thus, beta appears to have significant predictive power for home country stocks – especially those in developed countries. The betas for ADRs behave very differently from their underlying counterparts. The only statistically significant ADR betas belong to Japan (–0.84) and the United Kingdom (0.89). All other ADR betas are insignificant and the average of 0.06 across all countries is not significant. As seen in Panel B, home market betas are similarly significant between developed (1.04) and emerging (1.07) markets. Neither exhibit significant ADR betas. In aggregate, these results suggest that CAPM is most likely to be accurate in developed home markets, followed by emerging home markets and with little predictive ability in the ADR market. We now test to see if this is indeed the case.

Presented in Table 6 are our ex-post tests of CAPM. In conducting these tests for the underlying stocks, we use the five-year beta calculated above and multiply this by the market risk premium as determined by the actual return on the home index for each year minus the one-year U.S. Treasury (risk-free) rate for the same year. This is then added to the risk-free rate to calculate an expected return for the stock. This expected return is then deducted from the actual return of the stock for that year in order to compute an abnormal return for the stock. Just as before, the procedure is repeated rolling forward a year. This results in five abnormal returns and we take the average of these five returns as our measure of abnormal return for the stock. The same procedure is then used to generate ADR abnormal returns by replacing the home country beta with the ADR beta, the home country index return with that of the S&P 500, and the actual underlying stock return with that of the ADR. This procedure is shown in Eqs. 1 and 2 below. If a t-test of mean abnormal returns is significant, then we can reject the validity of CAPM for generating expected returns – at least in an ex-post sense and in realization of the dual hypothesis problem.

$$\textit{Abnormal}\ \text{Return}_i = \textit{Actual}\ \text{Return}_i - \beta_{i-5,i-1} * (\textit{Home Market}\ \text{Return}_i - rf_i) \quad (1)$$

Table 5. Tests of Beta.

This table presents results of the tests for the significance of betas for ADRs and their underlying stocks.

Panel A: Tests of beta for individual countries

Country	*Mkt*	*n*	*Average beta of home country stock relative to home country index*	*t-stat* (>0)	*Average beta of ADR relative to S&P 500*	*t-stat* (>0)
Australia	D	8	1.20	3.13 *	0.43	0.99
Denmark	E	1	1.10	–	2.14	–
France	D	1	1.41	–	0.74	–
Ireland	E	2	1.02	3.99	1.15	1.13
Italy	E	3	0.61	2.35	–0.27	–0.76
Japan	D	24	0.62	4.85*	–0.84	–2.65*
Netherlands	E	4	0.85	1.96	0.09	0.17
Norway	E	1	0.55	–	–0.98	–
South Africa	E	5	1.94	12.72 *	–1.40	–1.93
Spain	E	5	0.66	3.16*	0.60	2.34
Sweden	E	4	1.22	4.23*	–0.61	–0.57
United Kingdom	D	27	1.34	3.46*	0.89	3.55*
All countries		85	1.05	7.59*	0.06	0.41

Table 5. Continued.

Panel B: Tests of beta for developed and emerging markets

Mkt	*n*	*Average beta of home country stock relative to home country index*	*t-stat (>0)*	*Average beta of ADR relative to S&P 500*	*t-stat (>0)*
Developed	60	1.04	5.55*	0.14	0.61
Emerging	25	1.07	8.42*	–0.14	–0.53

* Significant at the 5% level

***Table 6*.** Tests of CAPM.

This table presents results of the tests for the significance of CAPM abnormal returns for ADRs and their underlying stocks.

Panel A: Tests of CAPM for individual countries

Country	*Mkt*	*n*	*Average CAPM-adjusted abnormal return of home country stock relative to home country index %*	*t-stat* (>0)	*Average CAPM-adjusted abnormal return of ADR relative to S&P 500 %*	*t-stat* (>0)
Australia	D	8	5.06	0.72	–5.33	–0.74
Denmark	E	1	10.48	–	–19.07	–
France	D	1	8.71	–	–2.44	–
Ireland	E	2	–10.44	–2.15	–10.99	–0.48
Italy	E	3	4.69	0.57	18.57	2.36
Japan	D	24	10.56	1.68	14.76	2.16*
Netherlands	E	4	–16.65	–3.07	–2.70	–0.27
Norway	E	1	–3.78	–	20.92	–
South Africa	E	5	–13.49	–1.19	21.38	1.63
Spain	E	5	–16.86	–2.50	–11.50	–2.19
Sweden	E	4	–18.03	–1.69	12.07	0.52
United Kingdom	D	27	–3.48	–0.76	–4.62	–1.33
All countries		85	–0.96	–0.36	3.61	1.29

Table 6. Continued.

Panel B: Tests of CAPM for developed and emerging markets

Market	*n*	*Average CAPM-adjusted abnormal return of home country stock relative to home country index %*	*t-stat (>0)*	*Average CAPM-adjusted abnormal return of ADR relative to S&P 500 %*	*t-stat (>0)*
Developed	60	3.48	1.03	3.08	0.90
Emerging	25	–11.62	–3.70*	4.90	0.99

* Significant at the 5% level

$$\textit{Stock or ADR Abnormal } \mathrm{Return} = \sum_{1995}^{1999} \textit{Abnormal } \mathrm{Return}/5 \qquad (2)$$

We present our CAPM tests of individual countries in Panel A of Table 6. The average abnormal return for home country stocks is less than 1% in absolute terms and is not significantly different from zero. This result is not unexpected given that our average beta was significant. What is somewhat unexpected is the insignificant abnormal return of 3.61% for ADRs. While substantially (and significantly) larger than the home country abnormal returns, the insignificant ADR abnormal return cannot lead us to reject CAPM as a valid generator of expected returns. The only individual country to exhibit any significant abnormal return is Japan in its ADRs with a 14.76% abnormal return. No other country's home stocks or ADRs possess abnormal returns; however, this is probably due to small sample sizes for most of the countries. In order to address this issue, we analyze abnormal returns according to market classifications as shown in Panel B of Table 6.

Again, CAPM cannot be rejected for its validity in the ADR market as both developed and emerging markets' ADR abnormal returns are not significantly different from zero. The same holds true for the underlying stocks of developed countries. However, the abnormal returns of the home market stocks in these countries is a significant –11.62% – implying that CAPM significantly overestimates the expected return on these stocks relative to heir actual returns. Although we can only speculate at the cause of this result, the source of the abnormal returns are likely from one of the following – a small sample size leading to erroneous results, higher levels of unsystematic risk in emerging markets, or simply model mis-specification. The result makes for an interesting topic of future study.

4. CONCLUSION

In our study of ADRs traded in the U.S., we find several results of interest to the finance community. First, we find that tests of foreign stock index correlations with a U.S. market index (the S&P 500 in our study) are insufficient tests of the diversification impact of ADRs on portfolios of U.S. stocks as the correlations of ADRs with the S&P 500 are significantly lower than the correlations between the S&P 500 and foreign indices from the home countries of the ADRs. Second, we find differences between risk and return in developed and emerging markets. ADR returns are significantly higher than underlying stock returns for developed countries, but the opposite is true for emerging markets. This result is likely the result of greater tax preferences for home country investors and higher transactions costs in emerging markets vis-à-vis developed markets. The same relationships hold for annual standard deviation measures. The ADRs from emerging markets are also insignificantly correlated with the S&P 500 while those from developed countries are significantly positively correlated with the S&P 500 (albeit a low 0.12). Third, these low correlations result in near zero betas for both developed and emerging market ADRs and lead to reductions in systematic risk as well as unsystematic risk of a portfolio of U.S. stocks.

Another contribution of this study is our tests of the validity of CAPM to serve as an appropriate asset pricing model for ADRs (and their underlying stocks) given that their returns should be determined more by their relationship to their home country index and changes in exchange rates. On the basis of CAPM-adjusted abnormal returns, we cannot conclude that CAPM is an inaccurate predictor of returns for ADRs of either developed or emerging markets. The same holds true for the underlying stocks in developed countries. However, we can reject CAPM for generating expected returns for the home country stocks of emerging markets as it significantly overestimates the expected returns of emerging markets' stocks. This result is unresolved and opens an interesting avenue of future study.

NOTES

1. The day 0 excess return is 0.47%, and the authors note that the Japanese ADRs account for the majority of the excess return.
2. Denmark, France, and Norway each have only one ADR in the sample and cannot be evaluated with t-tests.

ACKNOWLEDGMENTS

The authors wish to thank editor Tom Fetherston for his help and encouragement in the completion of this study.

REFERENCES

Choi, Y., & Kim, D. (2000). Determinants of American depository receipts and their underlying stock returns: implications for international diversification. *International Review of Financial Analysis*, *9*, 351–368.

Coyle, R. (Ed.) (1995). The McGraw-Hill Handbook of American Depository Receipts.

Harvey, C. (1991). The world price of covariance risk. *Journal of Finance*, *46*(1), 111–158.

Jayaraman, N., Shastri, K., & Tandon, K. (1993). The impact of international cross listings on risk and return: the evidence from American depository receipts. *Journal of Banking & Finance*, *17*, 91–103.

Jiang, C. (1998). Diversification with American depository receipts: the dynamics and the pricing factors, *Journal of Business Finance & Accounting*, *25*, 683–699.

Kato, K., Linn, S., & Schallheim, J. (1991). Are there arbitrage opportunities in the market for American depository receipts. *Journal of International Financial Markets, Institutions & Money*, *1*, 73–89.

Kim, M., Szakmary, A., & Mathur, I. (2000). Price transmission dynamics between ADRs and their underlying foreign securities. *Journal of Banking & Finance*, *24*, 1359–1382.

Officer, D., & Hoffmeister, J. (1987). ADRs: a substitute for the real thing? *Journal of Portfolio Management*, *13*, 61–65.

Sundaram, A., & Logue, D. (1996). Valuation effects of foreign company listings on U.S. exchanges. *Journal of International Business Studies*, *27*, 67–88.

Wahab, M., & Khandwala, A. (1993). Why not diversify internationally with ADRs? *The Journal of Portfolio Management*, *19*, 75–82.

Wahab, M., Lashgari, M., & Cohn, R. (1992). Arbitrage opportunities in the American depository receipts market revisited. *Journal of International Financial Markets, Institutions & Money*, *2*, 97–130.

OPERATIONAL RISK AND THE *BIS* CAPITAL CHARGE: FOREIGN VERSUS AUSTRALIAN BANK PRACTICE

Christopher Viney

ABSTRACT

This paper conducts a comparative analysis of the disaster risk management practices of foreign and local banks within the Australian financial system. Results demonstrate that, overall, each group of banks is only in the formative stages of the disaster risk management process. Significant differences are evident between the practices of foreign and Australian banks. The paper concludes that banks are not adequately prepared to respond to a loss of critical business functions. The BIS initiative to develop operational risk management guidelines, encourage nation-state bank supervisors to adopt specific measurement standards and apply an operational risk capital charge are necessary and timely.

INTRODUCTION

Disasters do happen! September 11, 2001 will be forever etched in the memory of the United States of America as terrorist attacks in New York and Washington brought home the reality of disaster. The U.S. financial system was severely tested as financial institutions and markets closed and struggled to recover their critical business operations. The direct and consequential operational and financial losses associated with this disaster will be measured over many years.

Financial Risk and Financial Risk Management, Volume 16, pages 473–496.

ISBN: 0-7623-0858-3

Businesses within the State of Victoria, Australia, faced the reality of disaster in September/October 1998 when an explosion at the Longford plant of Esso Limited, an Exxon subsidiary, resulted in the loss of gas supply throughout the majority of the State. The disruption resulted in significant loss of production, loss of income to both business and employees, and ultimately, bankruptcy for those businesses where the cash-flow burden of the disaster was too great.

Auckland, New Zealand, 1998, and businesses were exposed to an extended loss of reticulated power. Whilst some larger organisations had back-up generators in place as part of their business continuity planning, no business had planned for a situation where, for months, commercial life was sucked out of the whole city. Importantly, Auckland is New Zealand's financial centre and the disaster highlighted the critical exposure of financial institutions, financial systems and economies to operational risk.

Technology advances, coupled with globalisation of the international financial system, has increased the time sensitivity of financial institutions to even limited disruption to critical business operations. This is particularly evident in derivatives transactions, foreign exchange trading and payments system settlements.

The use of the regulatory process to establish boundaries on financial system risks is usually based on a valid perception of these risks, and of their relative importance in the spectrum of system and institutional exposure to all risks. The regulatory process typically focuses on future events, and thus suffers from the limitations of prediction. Ideally, risk regulation should be based on a statistically significant history of similar risk events which are reasonably measurable and which disclose the relevant cause-effect relationships. Unfortunately, such comprehensive quantitative data does not exist, and therefore operational risk management and potential regulation is unavoidably embedded in large uncertainties.

Regulation of banks results, in part, from risk management inefficiencies, or market imperfections, in a competitive market that is reluctant to disclose information on non-regulated risk levels adopted by an institution. Therefore, depositors, shareholders, other associated financial institutions and the financial system are exposed to uncompensated risks. The regulatory process constructs an explicit agreement that minimises overall exposure to uncompensated risk. Nation-states with bank regulatory and supervisory controls attempt to ensure agreement is reached in managing otherwise uncompensated risks of an institution by the application of standards to be observed by all participants. The implementation of capital adequacy standards is an example of such regulatory intervention.

A nation-state's financial system may be described as the life-blood of the real economy. For an economy to grow, and maintain that growth, it must be supported by a highly developed and efficient financial system (Viney, 2000). The modern financial system comprises a range of institutions and markets that are reliant on interrelationships and dependencies; internally, and across a range of other domestic and international institutions and markets. The loss of a bank's critical business operations due to a physical, technical or natural disaster may have a catastrophic effect on the ultimate operational and financial survival of an institution. Operational risk contagion is a further real risk to which financial systems are exposed. The contagion effects may even threaten the overall stability of a financial system. Organisational business continuity, or disaster recovery planning, is the risk management process that develops and maintains specific strategies that will enable an institution to recover and resume disrupted critical business operations.

The then Deputy Governor of the Reserve Bank of Australia, Mr G. J. Thompson stated (1997, p. 15);

> . . . banks are increasingly reliant on computers for information-processing and control. As a result, they are exposed to various kinds of operational risk. For a bank active in derivatives trading, a breakdown in computer systems for even a relatively short time could be disastrous – preventing it from monitoring its changing market positions and disrupting its capacity to trade and to settle outstanding transactions. I recently heard a keen observer predict that the next big banking disaster would come from a (hypothetical) major international bank losing track of its derivatives positions for 24 hours.

Results of a nationwide study in the United States of America by the Center for Research on Information Systems at the University of Texas at Arlington (UTA), and reported in Chantico (1991, p. 4) shows that:

- as the length of an outage increases, loss of functionality and integration worsens;
- reverting to manual backup procedures is totally inadequate;
- horizontal and vertical coordination of business functions decreases markedly;
- computer outages initiate actions that cause the business to incur additional expenses;
- the largest intangible loss is cash-flow interruption; and
- continued loss of customers, competitive edge, and image might prove more damaging than the temporary loss of revenue and additional costs.

Existing research (Hiatt, 2000; Myers, 1999; Wold, 1992; Blair, 1991; Ford, 1990; Arnell, 1990; Toigo, 1989) clearly identifies the high-risk exposure of financial institutions to events of business disruption due to a natural, physical or technical disaster. Major banks operate within a global market and are subject to both international and domestic business continuity demands of government (economic and social objectives); regulators (financial system stability and monetary policy objectives); customers (service and public confidence); other institutions (interrelationships and dependencies); and shareholders (profitability and business survival).

The implications of the above are that banks must manage their exposures to business continuity risk. The Bank for International Settlements (2001) has adopted a position that regulatory intervention is necessary and has moved to develop international guidelines for the measurement of operational risk and the application of minimum capital charges.

BANK FOR INTERNATIONAL SETTLEMENTS OPERATIONAL RISK INITIATIVES

The *Basel Committee on Banking Supervision* operates a secretariat within the Bank for International Settlements (BIS) and comprises senior supervisory representatives from the United States of America, United Kingdom, France, Italy, the Netherlands, Germany, Belgium, Canada, Sweden, Switzerland and Japan. The committee monitors developments in the international financial markets and has instigated a number of operating standards and conventions for participants in the markets; including the capital to risk weighted assets standards. There currently are no international guidelines, or capital charges applied, for the management of operational risk.

The regulation and supervision of operational risk, in particular business continuity risk, varies significantly between nation-state financial systems.

The United States of America provides the most comprehensive example of the regulation and supervision of business continuity risk. The revised version of banking circular BC177, dated 12 July 1989, issued by the Comptroller of the Currency (OCC), and adopted by all financial institution regulators, under the auspices of the Federal Financial Institutions Examination Council (FFIEC), requires institutions to maintain corporate-wide contingency planning. Direct responsibility for business continuity rests with the board of directors and senior management of banks. They must ensure that a comprehensive contingency plan is developed, maintained and tested for the entire organisation. Failure to comply with this policy could result in an enforcement action against the bank. OCC examiners strictly enforce the requirement for an annual board of directors' review of the contingency plan. A further banking circular, BC187, extends bank management responsibility for developing and implementing a contingency plan to service bureau and out-sourced business functions.

The Reserve Bank of Australia (RBA) is the central bank of Australia with specific responsibilities for the soundness of the payments system and overall financial system stability. The Australian Prudential Regulation Authority (APRA) is the bank supervisor. The RBA and APRA acknowledge there are no specific prudential standards, or requirements, for banks to develop and maintain strategies and procedures to manage business continuity for either their computer centre operations, or the total organisation. The RBA notes its past consultative processes, where it stressed to banks the need for appropriate disaster recovery plans, however the data analysed in this paper indicates that not all banks responded to this aspect of the RBA's consultative process. APRA has taken a more direct interest in the appropriateness of banks' organisational disaster risk management processes and has requested that bank external auditors specifically comment on this area of risk in their annual report to APRA.

Two areas of potential operational risk where the RBA and APRA have taken an active approach were the Y2K exposure and the introduction of real time gross settlement (RTGS) within the payments system. Australian banks were required by legislation[1] to report periodically on their level of preparedness to manage Y2K. Australian banks estimate their expenditures in managing the Y2K risk in excess of AUD1.1 billion (APRA, 1999). With the introduction of RTGS, each bank was required to establish backup systems and procedures to ensure their continuous participation in the payments system.

The BIS issued its *Core Principles for Effective Banking Supervision* (1997) which comprise twenty-five basic principles that represent a minimum prerequisite for effective prudential bank supervision. Principle 13 (iii) states that supervisors "should ensure senior management puts in place effective internal control and auditing procedures; also, that they have policies for managing or mitigating operational risk (e.g. through insurance or contingency planning). Supervisors should determine that banks have adequate and well-tested business resumption plans for all major systems, with remote site facilities, to protect against such events."

A survey of operational risk by the BIS (1998) noted that "managing such risk is becoming an important feature of sound risk management practice in modern financial institutions." The committee interviewed thirty major banks from different member countries on the management of operational risk. The report focused primarily on policy and management processes and did not explore the detail of specific risk management practice. In summary, the report found that:

- awareness of operational risk among bank boards and senior management is increasing;
- while all banks surveyed had some operational risk management framework, many indicated that they were only in the early stages of development;
- identification of operational risk as a separate risk category is relatively new;
- few banks currently measure and report this risk on a regular basis; and
- limited institution historical data is available to develop empirical risk management models.

It should be remembered that the banks in this survey are major international banks. If these banks do not adequately manage operational risk, then what lesser standards are practiced by other banks; both within nation-state financial systems, and the global financial system?

The BIS (January 2001) is proposing a regulatory framework for the incorporation of a capital charge for operational risk in its new *Basel Capital Accord*. The BIS is currently gathering data to support the development of three approaches to measuring an operational risk capital charge; that is, the Basic Indicator Approach, the Standardised Approach and the Internal Measurement Approach. Operational risk is categorised as:

(1) internal fraud;
(2) external fraud;
(3) employment practices and workplace safety;
(4) clients, products and business practices;
(5) damage to physical assets;
(6) business disruption and system failures; and
(7) execution, delivery and process management.

Given the proposed BIS operational risk capital charge, and the critical need for banks to maintain continuous operation, this paper analyses the disaster risk management practices of foreign and local banks within the Australian financial system in an endeavour to:

(1) draw conclusions on the level of preparedness of the banks to respond to, and recover from, a significant event of business disruption;
(2) compare the practices of Australian banks versus foreign banks; and
(3) explain the initiative of the *Basel Committee on Banking Supervision* to develop an international standard to address operational risk exposures of banks that should be implemented by nation-state bank regulators and supervisors.

OPERATIONAL RISK MANAGEMENT – MAINTAINING BUSINESS CONTINUITY

An institution with a comprehensive organisational business continuity plan will have a greater chance of survival, and minimise the cost of that survival, in the event of a disastrous business disruption. "Companies that plan for the possibility of a disaster, that formulate strategies for recovering critical business functions, and that train employees to implement those strategies, generally do survive disasters" (Toigo, 1989, p. 3).

Operational disaster risk management facilitates the development of specific disaster recovery planning and disaster response processes. In the event of a disruption to business operations due to a natural, physical or technical disaster, these processes must enable an institution to resume critical business operations in the shortest possible time-frame and facilitate the resumption of normal business operations in an efficient, structured and prioritised manner.

A disaster is an evolving, or immediate, event that may significantly disrupt the critical business functions of an institution. Critical business functions refer to minimum operational requirements necessary to meet an institution's current commitments, maintain customer relationships, ensure market confidence, maintain cash-flows and minimise financial loss. Natural, physical and technical disasters are operational disasters. Natural disasters may include flood, fire, hurricane, earthquake and snow-storm. Physical and technical disasters may include employee error, sabotage, terrorist acts, loss of power, loss of computer systems and applications, and failure of communication systems.

The rapid development and institutional integration of information systems, product delivery systems and communication systems has created an environment in which a disruption to critical business functions of a limited duration potentially could cause severe financial loss, and ultimately may even threaten corporate survival (Christensen, 1992, p. 35). The emphasis of business continuity planning is moving from a myopic focus on a bank's computer centre, to all encompassing organisational disaster risk management processes that incorporate all business units within an institution.

The theory of the organisation contends that the risk management process, in part, derives from an organisation's need to survive. Therefore, organisational disaster risk management should actively reside within a bank's management decision structures; that is, the risk management process will ensure that all critical exposures to business disruption are identified and managed through a structured decision process. However, operational imperatives and constraints may limit the extent of the risk management process. The institution may place constraints on, or even ignore, the pre-emptive management of risk exposures and develop an ethos of reactive risk management.

A CASE FOR AN OPERATIONAL RISK CAPITAL CHARGE

Within the Australian financial system, banks are the dominant financial institutions, representing 43.3% of total assets as at 30 June 2000 (Table 1). Banks' control of funds within the financial system is substantially extended through their life insurance, finance company and funds management subsidiary operations. A broad range of foreign banks operate within the Australian markets. The main categories of institutions, and assets held, are shown in Table 1.

The data in this paper was gathered from a combination of questionnaires forwarded to the bank population within the Australian financial system (N = 35) and scheduled interviews conducted with the disaster risk managers of

Table 1. Total Assets of Financial Institutions.

Financial Institution	30 June 2000 AUD Billions
Reserve Bank	54.1
Banks (% of all assets)	731.0 (43.3%)
Permanent building societies	12.7
Credit cooperatives	21.5
Money market corporations (merchant and investment banks)	63.7
Pastoral finance companies	5.9
Finance companies	44.3
General financiers	20.7
Life insurance offices (% of all assets)	171.5 (10.2%)
Superannuation funds outside life offices (% of all assets)	276.9 (16.4%)
General insurance offices	74.2
Cash management trusts	24.8
Public unit trusts	109.6 (6.5%)
Common funds	7.4
Friendly societies	5.9
Securitisation vehicles	64.7
Total, all financial institutions	1688.9

Source: Reserve Bank of Australia, Bulletin, March 2001, Table B.1, S3.

twenty-one banks. Seventy-one percent of banks responded to the questionnaire. Sixty percent of the bank population was interviewed.

Disaster risk management comprises complex processes that incorporate a multitude of variables, each of which may be at a different stage of development. The data in this paper focuses on a range of specific elements of the disaster recovery planning process and the disaster response process. The data differentiates between foreign bank and Australian bank practices in order to ascertain if significant variances exist between the two types of banks. The 'all banks' data enables conclusions to be draw on the preparedness of banks within the Australian financial system to respond to, and recover from, a disruption to critical business operations. Absolute numerical and percentage results are tabulated and analysed. The chi-square and p-value are calculated to support any evidence of relationships between the different approaches of the foreign banks and Australian banks to elements of disaster risk management. Data addresses selected elements of the disaster risk management processes, and is categorised as:

- disaster recovery plan status;
- policy and resource allocation;
- risk assessment and business impact analysis;
- critical business function identification;
- recovery strategies;
- plan testing;
- disaster response infrastructure, and
- media liaison.

DISASTER RECOVERY PLAN STATUS

Table 2 reports the *organisational* disaster recovery plan status in each bank. Twelve percent of respondent banks (n = 3) indicated they have achieved an organisational disaster recovery planning status where a plan has been fully developed and documented. Eighty percent (n = 20) indicate they are currently developing a plan, comprising 86% (n = 3) of Australian banks and 73% (n = 8) foreign banks. One Australian and one foreign bank have not commenced the planning process. A chi-square of 0.785 and a p-value of 0.385 indicate the population is homogeneous; that is, significant differences in disaster recovery plan status do not exist between Australian banks and foreign banks.

Given the implications of business continuity exposures to the operational and financial performance of a bank, these statistics present a position of some considerable concern. The data indicate that a significant number of banks are

Table 2. Organisational Disaster Recovery Planning Status.

	Australian Banks (n = 14)		Foreign Banks (n = 11)		All Banks (n = 25)	
Organisational DRP Fully Documented	1	7%	2	18%	3	12%
Organisational DRP Being Developed	12	86%	8	73%	20	80%
No Organisational DRP Documented	1	7%	1	9%	2	8%

Note: $\chi^2 = 0.785$; DF = 1; p = 0.385.

only developing an organisational disaster recovery plan. Therefore, it is essential to determine the level of progress of the development process. Analysis of further data provides a clearer understanding.

Having regard to the almost absolute reliance of banks on computer systems it is appropriate to consider banks' computer centre disaster recovery planning status (Table 3). Sixty-four percent (n = 16) of all banks, including ten Australian banks and six foreign banks, maintain fully documented plans for their computer centre operations. Surprisingly, eight banks are only in the development stage and one foreign bank has no plan. The chi-square figure of 0.343 indicates no significant difference between bank groupings.

These statistics reveal that bank management place a higher priority on the management of risk within the computer centre than critical business functions of the overall organisation. Interview responses indicate that senior managers within the computer centre environment are, generally, more aware of the potential impacts of business disruption than are senior managers of other business units in an organisation.

Table 3. Computer Centre Disaster Recovery Planning Status.

	Australian Banks (n = 14)		Foreign Banks (n = 11)		All Banks (n = 25)	
Computer centre DRP Fully Documented	10	71%	6	55%	16	64%
Computer centre DRP Being Developed	4	29%	5	45%	9	36%

Note: $\chi^2 = 0.343$; DF = 1; p = 0.550.

In interviews, bank disaster risk management managers stated that limited board and executive management understanding of operational risk, resultant low priority restrictions, and inadequate budget and resource allocations significantly constrained the progress of the plan development phase. Given these constraints, it is useful to consider the extent of the organisational policy commitment.

POLICY AND RESOURCE ALLOCATION

The formalisation of objectives and policy of a bank is the responsibility of the board of directors. Table 4 data indicate that only 52% (n = 13) of all respondent banks have issued a written disaster recovery planning policy document. Table 2 previously indicated that 92% of banks had implemented, or were currently developing, an organisational disaster recovery plan. There is a significant variance between the results in Table 2 and Table 4. This immediately raises concerns regarding the veracity of that initial response, the extent of the bank policy decision processes, and the functional direction of the decision process within banks. While neither variable is dependent, it suggests that the formal disaster risk management process is not being driven from the top of those organisations. Further analysis by bank grouping reveals that only 43% (n = 6) of Australian banks and 64% (n = 7) of foreign banks have issued policy documentation.

A measure of a bank's commitment to disaster risk management is its allocation of resources. Due to factors of confidentiality and competitive advantage, it was not possible to obtain actual budget expenditures. Banks did provide data indicating whether a formal budget allocation for disaster recovery planning occurred. Fifty-two percent (n = 13) of banks provide a formal budget allocation, however between bank groupings this figure varies, with 64% (n = 9) of Australian banks and a low 36% (n = 4) of foreign banks (Table 5).

This data does not track the dispersion of the budget allocations throughout a bank. A number of interviewees indicated that a formal allocation was

Table 4. Written Policy Document Issued by Board of Directors.

	Australian Banks (n = 14)	Foreign Banks (n = 11)	All Banks (n = 25)
Yes	6 43%	7 64%	13 52%
No	8 57%	4 36%	12 48%

Note: $\chi^2 = 1.066$; DF = 1; p-value = 0.302.

Table 5. Disaster Recovery Planning Formal Budget Allocation.

	Australian Banks (n = 14)	Foreign Banks (n = 11)	All Banks (n = 25)
Yes	9 64%	4 36%	13 52%
No	5 36%	7 64%	12 48%

Note: $\chi^2 = 1.924$; DF = 1; p-value = 0.165.

incorporated in the computer centre budget only, and that budget allocations for bank-wide disaster risk management was significantly lower.

RISK ASSESSMENT AND BUSINESS IMPACT ANALYSIS

Risk assessment and business impact analysis are essential elements of the plan development process. Data in Table 6 sought to determine whether banks had carried out a business impact analysis to identify which business functions are critical to the organisation.

Seventy-two percent (n = 18) of all banks, comprising 86% (n = 12) of Australian banks and 55% (n = 6) of foreign banks have completed a business impact analysis. A chi-square of 2.968 and a p-value of 0.085 indicate a significant difference between the practice of Australian banks and foreign banks. In Table 2, 92% of banks stated they maintained, or were developing, an organisational disaster recovery plan, however this result (72%) indicates that 20% of those banks are in the very early formative stages of development, as they have not completed a business impact analysis.

CRITICAL BUSINESS FUNCTION IDENTIFICATION

Each bank was asked to list in priority order its five most critical business functions. The weighted rank order distribution is presented in Table 7.

Table 6. Business Impact Analysis Completed.

	Australian Banks (n = 14)	Foreign Banks (n = 11)	All Banks (n = 25)
Yes	12 86%	6 55%	18 72%
No	2 14%	5 45%	7 28%

Note: $\chi^2 = 2.968$; DF = 1; p-value = 0.085.

Computer centre operations were identified by 40% (n = 10) of banks as the most critical business function, followed by treasury operations at 32% (n = 8), and retail banking/customer services third at 12% (n = 3). Overall, 96% (n = 24) of banks included treasury operations; 92% (n = 23) included computer centre operations; and 40% (n = 10) included retail banking/customer services in their list of critical business functions.

A comparative analysis of the critical business functions of all banks provides some interesting variations in the weighted rank order results, reflecting to some degree the past development and different market segments in which the banks operate. Treasury operations are ranked number one for the all banks grouping, whereas Australian banks rank computer centre operations as the most critical business function. The bank treasury operation is ranked number two by Australian banks.

The very broad nature of the critical business function identification by respondent banks, raises serious concern regarding the extent of the business impact analysis carried out by the banks. The business impact analysis would normally be expected to provide a much more definitive identification of

Table 7. Percentage Distribution Critical Business Functions All Banks (n = 25) – by Average Rank Order.

Critical Business Functions	5		4		3		2		1		Weighted Rank	
Treasury operations	8	32%	5	20%	8	32%	3	12%			3.60	1
Computer centre	10	40%	5	20%	2	8%	4	16%	2	8%	3.44	2
Retail bank services	3	12%	3	12%	1	4%	2	8%	1	4%	1.40	3
Clearing operations	1	4%	4	16%	2	8%					1.08	4
Telecommunications	1	4%	2	8%	1	4%	1	4%	1	4%	0.76	5
Corporate banking	1	4%	2	8%	1	4%			1	4%	0.68	6
International banking					4	16%	2	8%			0.64	7
Lending services			2	8%	1	4%	1	4%	2	8%	0.60	8
Retail card operation			1	4%	1	4%	2	8%	3	12%	0.56	9
Executive admin.	1	4%			1	4%			6	24%	0.56	9
Custodial services					1	4%	3	12%	2	8%	0.44	10
Other							3	12%	2	8%	0.32	11
General ledgers							1	4%	2	8%	0.16	12
Statutory reporting							1	4%	1	4%	0.12	13
No response			1	4%	2	8%	2	8%	2	8%		

Note: rank order: 5 = most critical business function to 1 = lower ranked critical business function.

specific critical business functions. Further doubt was cast upon the business impact analysis process when, in interview, some banks indicated that a systematic quantitative methodology was not used, but rather the 'experience' method was adopted. Specific critical business functions generally were not identified.

RECOVERY STRATEGIES

Having identified banks' critical business functions, data was gathered on the backup facility capability of the banks, that is, the level of preparedness to recover an identified critical business function in the event of business disruption.[3] In analysing this data it should be borne in mind that each business function has been identified as being *most critical* to the bank, and as such would need to be recovered in a very short time-frame to minimise operational and financial impacts.

Table 8 shows that 24% (n = 6) of all banks maintain hot sites for their most critical business function (treasury operations), and a further 40% (n = 10) maintain warm sites. The percentage of banks with hot site backup facilities falls away as the ranking of criticality reduces, where, at the fifth most critical function (telecommunications), no hot site facilities are available and 36% (n = 9) warm sites are maintained. At the other end of the scale, identified critical business functions with no backup facilities range from 24% (n = 6) to a significant 56% (n = 14).

Within bank groupings there are important variances (Table 8). The chi-square statistics of 7.008, 6.166 and 7.517 indicate significant variances between the approaches of the Australian banks and the foreign banks in relation to critical functions: (1) treasury operations, (2) computer centre, and (4) clearing operations, respectively. The Australian banks maintain a greater level of preparedness. There is no significant difference with critical functions (3) retail bank services, and (5) telecommunications.

The data from this question provides some significant insight into the level of disaster preparedness of the banks. The five business functions listed in the survey responses are the most critical functions identified by the banks, yet the overall capacity to recover those operations, within the very short time-frame necessary, is not high. Again concerns are expressed as to the actual level of organisational disaster recovery plan development, and the preparedness and capacity of banks, as a group, to recover from a major disaster.

Another essential element of a disaster recovery strategy is the off-site storage[4] of critical data; electronic and hardcopy. Table 9 provides data on the form of off-site storage of critical data maintained by the banks. This is

Table 8. Backup Facility Status by Critical Business Function – Ranking 1 to 5.

Critical function 1 Treasury operations	Australian Banks (n = 14)	Foreign banks (n = 11)	All Banks (n = 25)
Hot Site	4 29%	2 18%	6 24%
Warm Site	8 57%	2 18%	10 40%
Cold Site	1 7%	2 18%	3 12%
No	1 7%	5 46%	6 24%

$\chi^2 = 7.008$; DF = 3.

Critical function 2 Computer Centre	Australian Banks (n = 14)	Foreign banks (n = 11)	All Banks (n = 25)
Hot Site	4 29%		4 16%
Warm Site	7 50%	4 36%	11 44%
Cold Site	1 7%	2 18%	3 12%
No	2 14%	5 46%	7 28%

$\chi^2 = 6.166$; DF = 3.

Critical function 3 Retail Bank Services	Australian Banks (n = 14)	Foreign banks (n = 11)	All Banks (n = 25)
Hot Site	3 21%	1 9%	4 16%
Warm Site	6 43%	2 18%	8 32%
Cold Site		1 9%	1 4%
No	5 36%	7 64%	12 48%

$\chi^2 = 4.031$; DF = 3.

Critical function 4 Clearing Operations	Australian Banks (n = 14)	Foreign banks (n = 11)	All Banks (n = 25)
Hot Site	1 7%		1 4%
Warm Site	10 71%	3 27%	13 52%
Cold Site		2 18%	2 8%
No	3 22%	6 55%	9 36%

$\chi^2 = 7.517$; DF = 3.

Critical function 5 Telecommunications	Australian Banks (n = 14)	Foreign banks (n = 11)	All Banks (n = 25)
Hot Site			0 0%
Warm Site	7 50%	2 18%	9 36%
Cold Site	1 7%	1 9%	2 8%
No	6 43%	8 73%	14 56%

Note: $\chi^2 = 2.743$; DF = 2.

Table 9. Critical Data Off-Site Storage Program.

	Australian Banks (n = 12)		Foreign Banks (n = 9)		All Banks (n = 21)	
Total Organisation	4	33%	5	56%	9	43%
Computer Centre Only	1	8%			1	5%
Computer Centre plus Limited Other Data	7	59%	4	44%	11	52%

Note: $\chi^2 = 1.532$; DF = 2; p = 0.900.

categorised by total organisation, computer centre only, or computer centre plus limited other critical data. All banks maintained some level of off-site storage. Fifty-six percent of foreign banks have an organisational program in place, in contrast to 33% of Australian banks. Overall, the chi-square statistic and p-value indicate no significant difference.

The next two questions consider the provision of power, an essential input to two of the identified critical business functions, the computer centre and treasury operations. Banks provided data relating to the maintenance of uninterrupted power supply (UPS)[5] and backup generators for these critical business functions. Seventy-six percent (n = 16) of all banks maintain UPS and backup generators to their computer centre operations, but only 48% (n = 10) maintain the same level of redundancy to their treasury operations (Tables 10 and 11). Disturbingly, 24% (n = 5) and 52% (n = 11) respectively do not maintain backup generators.

The chi-square statistics (2.965 and 0.447 respectively) indicate no significant difference between the practice of Australian banks and foreign banks. This is of particular concern given the previously mentioned treasury operation risk exposures noted by Thompson (1997). This result further

Table 10. Computer Centre – UPS and Backup Generator.

	Australian Banks (n = 12)		Foreign Banks (n = 9)		All Banks (n = 21)	
UPS & backup generator	10	83%	6	67%	16	76%
UPS only	2	17%	1	11%	3	14%
Neither			2	22%	2	10%

Note: $\chi^2 = 2.965$; DF = 2.

Table 11. Treasury – UPS and Backup Generator.

	Australian Banks (n = 12)		Foreign Banks (n = 9)		All Banks (n = 21)	
UPS & backup generator	5	42%	5	56%	10	48%
UPS only	3	25%	2	22%	5	24%
Neither	4	33%	2	22%	6	28%

Note: $\chi^2 = 0.447$; DF = 2; p = 0.800.

highlights concerns regarding the extent of organisational disaster risk management in banks.

DISASTER RECOVERY PLAN TESTING

An advanced form of plan testing, other than actual business interruption or a real disaster, is a full simulation test.[6] Table 12 provides data on the number of banks that had conducted a full simulation test of their currently developed organisational disaster recovery plan. The data indicates only 20% (n = 5) of all banks have conducted full simulation testing; comprising 14% (n = 2) of Australian banks and 27% (n = 3) of foreign banks. The results of this data relate to currently developed plans and are particularly poor. No significant difference exists between Australian and foreign banks.

The bank computer centre was identified as a critical business function. Banks were asked, if a major disaster occurred at the computer centre, how long would it take to recover to an acceptable operational level using backup facilities. As shown in Table 13, there is a wide dispersion in responses. Fourteen percent (n = 3) of all banks, comprising 17% (n = 2) of Australian

Table 12. Full Simulation Testing of Current Disaster Recovery Plan.

	Australian Banks (n = 14)		Foreign Banks (n = 11)		All Banks (n = 25)	
Yes	2	14%	3	27%	5	20%
No	12	86%	8	73%	20	80%

Note: $\chi^2 = 0.649$; DF = 1; p = 0.420.

Table 13. Computer Centre Recovery Time Scale.

	Australian Banks (n = 12)	Foreign Banks (n = 9)	All Banks (n = 21)
Less than 8 hours	2 17%	1 11%	3 14%
8 hours to <24 hours	5 41%	5 56%	10 48%
More than 24 hours	5 42%	3 33%	8 39%

Note: $\chi^2 = 0.853$; DF = 2; p = 0.653.

banks and 11% (n = 1) foreign banks, believe computer operations can be recovered in less than eight hours. A further 48% (n = 10), comprising 41% (n = 5) of Australian banks and 56% (n = 5) of foreign banks, believe computer operations can be recovered between eight hours and less than twenty-four hours.

The data indicates that 39% (n = 8) of all banks are not able to recover computer operations within an acceptable down-time proposed by Arnell (1990); that is, within a period of less than twenty-four hours. Statistical differences between Australian bank and foreign bank response times are not significant.

When asked if a computer centre recovery time had been fully operationally tested, only 57% (n = 12) of all banks, comprising 67% (n = 8) of Australian banks and 44% (n = 4) foreign banks, responded in the affirmative (Table 14). The adequacy of bank management decision processes are brought into question in that all banks identified the time frame in which they could recover computer centre operations, but only 57% had actually fully tested that current recovery response status. Further, care should be exercised in interpreting this data; during interviews a number of banks expressed strong reservations with regard to the estimated recovery times provided by their computer centre personnel.

Table 14. Computer Centre Recovery Plan Operationally Tested.

	Australian Banks (n = 12)	Foreign Banks (n = 9)	All Banks (n = 21)
Yes	8 67%	4 44%	12 57%
No	4 33%	5 56%	9 43%

Note: $\chi^2 = 1.037$; DF = 1; p = 0.309.

Table 15. Treasury Operations Recovery – Intra-day; Overnight.

	Australian Banks (n = 12)	Foreign Banks (n = 9)	All Banks (n = 21)
Both Positions	4 33%	5 56%	9 43%
Overnight/some intra-day	2 17%	1 11%	3 14%
Overnight only	4 33%		4 19%
None	2 17%	3 33%	5 24%

Note: $\chi^2 = 5.000$; DF = 3.

Banks also identified treasury operations as a critical business function. The data provided in Table 15 relate to the recovery of critical treasury data through the application of a disaster scenario. Banks were asked whether they would be able to recover their intra-day positions, and overnight positions, if they lost their treasury operations through fire; that is, immediate evacuation with loss of primary site hardware and data.

Only 43% (n = 9) of all banks, comprising 33% (n = 4) of Australian banks and 56% (n = 5) of foreign banks, believe they are able to recover both positions. A further 14% (n = 3), comprising 17% (n = 2) of Australian banks and 11% (n = 1) of foreign banks, are able to recover their overnight position and some intra-day data. Another 19% (n = 4) of all banks are only able to recover their overnight position. Twenty-four percent (n = 2), including two Australian banks and three foreign banks, would not be able to recover either position. There is no significant difference between the ability of each bank grouping to recover critical treasury positions.

Given the high level of criticality placed upon treasury operations by the banks, and its potential to incur large and immediate financial impacts upon the organisation, the vulnerability of the banks generally to a loss of critical treasury operations data is a further serious concern. This data also implies a very high level of systemic risk that potentially could impact upon financial system stability.

DISASTER RESPONSE INFRASTRUCTURE

The physical structure established for the central control of a disaster response plan, incorporating the then active elements of the organisational disaster recovery plan, may be variously referred to as a recovery control centre or an emergency operations centre. The recovery control centre becomes the

Table 16. Recovery Control Centre Established.

	Australian Banks (n = 14)		Foreign Banks (n = 11)		All Banks (n = 25)	
Yes	12	86%	4	36%	16	64%
No	2	14%	7	64%	9	36%

Note: $\chi^2 = 6.512$; DF = 1; p = 0.011.

management and administrative hub for the coordinated implementation of the disaster response for the total organisation.

Banks provided data on the establishment of predetermined recovery control centres. A high 86% of Australian banks (n = 12) maintain established recovery control centres, but only 36% (n = 4) of foreign banks (Table 16). A number of foreign banks indicated they would revert to a hotel suite, however it was recognised, by some, that critical delays would be experienced in establishing communications systems and providing equipment. A chi-square statistic of 6.512 and a p-value of 0.011 indicate significant differences exist between the approach of Australian banks and that of foreign banks. Foreign banks have not implemented adequate or effective recovery control centre arrangements.

Further data was obtained to ascertain the proximity of the recovery control centre to existing executive management and head office administration (Table 17). The location of the recovery control centre has strategic implications depending on the type of disaster experienced. A disaster that impacts upon a central business district; for example, an earthquake, may result in denial of access to the recovery control centre if it is located in the same geographic area as the organisational operation which it is required to support.

Seventy-five percent (n = 12) of all banks with established recovery control centres, locate the centre within ten kilometres of their existing head office administration, but do not maintain a centre outside that perimeter. Only 26% (n = 4) of all banks have established a recovery control centre outside a ten kilometre radius. In each case the recovery control centre is located interstate.

MEDIA LIAISON

Another important element of the disaster response process is a bank's media liaison or public relations strategy. Media liaison will represent the face of a bank in the event of disaster and will be crucial in maintaining the confidence

Table 17. Recovery Control Centre Strategic Geographic Dispersion.

	Australian Banks (n = 12)	Foreign Banks (n = 4)	All Banks (n = 16)
Within 10 Km	8 66%	4 100%	12 75%
Over 10 Km	4 24%		4 26%

Note: $\chi^2 = 1.778$; DF = 1; p = 0.182.

Table 18. Operational Disaster Media Liaison or Public Relations Strategy.

	Australian Banks (n = 12)	Foreign Banks (n = 9)	All Banks (n = 21)
Yes	11 92%	7 78%	18 86%
No	1 8%	2 22%	3 14%

Note: $\chi^2 = 0.810$; DF = 1; p = 0.368.

of government, the central bank, the prudential supervisor, the media, other financial institutions, the public and shareholders in the bank. The preparedness of banks to respond publicly to a disaster situation through an established media liaison strategy is reflected in Table 18.

Eighty-six percent (n = 18) of all banks, comprising 92% (n = 11) of Australian banks and 78% (n = 7) of foreign banks, indicated that a disaster response media liaison strategy is in place. There is no significant difference ($\chi^2 = 0.810$; p-value = 0.368) between the media liaison practices of the Australian banks and the foreign banks.

CONCLUSION

Modern organisations, and in particular banking institutions, are more than ever exposed to operational risk, incorporating business continuity risk. The elapsed time between when a disaster causes the loss of critical business functions, and when recovery of that function is essential to a bank's survival, is typically accepted as being less than twenty-four hours for a bank's computer centre operations. However, some critical bank functions, such as foreign exchange trading, derivatives dealing and payments system settlements, are time sensitive within minutes. Banks are fundamentally reliant upon technology to support their information systems and deliver their products and services. Coupled with this absolute dependency on technology is an exposure to public confidence and market sentiment.

Banks are exposed to financial and operational risks. The failure of the majority of bank regulators and prudential supervisors to establish organisational disaster risk management standards, or guidelines, indicates that the potential consequences of this form of operational risk to banking institutions and financial systems remains an unresolved issue. It is evident from an analysis of the results of this paper, and further supported by a BIS survey, that there exists a resultant level of institutional and systemic risk within an undefined number of nation-state financial systems that should be of concern to bank regulators and prudential supervisors. Any contention that the majority of Australian banks have fully developed comprehensive organisational disaster risk management practices is not supported by the data. Furthermore, such a contention cannot be supported for foreign banks that operate within the Australian financial system.

The results of this research clearly demonstrate that the majority of banks are in the formative stages of developing disaster recovery planning or disaster response processes throughout their organisations. These conclusions should be qualified in that a very limited number of individual banks may reasonably argue that they have reached a point where they could confidently claim that they are prepared to recover critical business functions in the event of a disaster.

The BIS has recognised that the systemic risk that may eventuate from a major operational disaster in the banking system is significant. The reluctance of most nation-state regulators to implement specific operational risk management guidelines has prompted the *Basel Committee on Banking Supervision* to move to develop international guidelines and encourage nation-state regulators to adopt specific standards to measure operational risk and apply an operational risk capital charge.

Australia is generally regarded within the financial markets as having a modern and efficient financial system that is prudently regulated and supervised, yet there remains an obvious and serious risk exposure. However, when compared with the overall disaster risk management practices of foreign banks, the approach of the Australian banks does not differ significantly. In important areas where significant difference does exist; that is, the completion of a business impact analysis, the establishment of backup facilities, and the maintenance of recovery control centres, the practices of Australian banks outperform those of the foreign banks. Therefore, the international operational risk management initiatives of the BIS and the *Basel Committee on Banking Supervision* appear necessary and timely.

NOTES

1. Year 2000 Information Disclosure Act (Commonwealth).
2. The business impact analysis facilitates an analysis of each identifiable business function, and provides a detailed understanding of the financial and operational impacts of experiencing business disruption, and highlights both internal and external interrelationships and dependencies. The business impact analysis is, to a large degree, the basis upon which the organisational disaster recovery plan is built, in that it provides management with the empirical evidence with which an informed business decision may be made regarding the allocation of resources to the development of a plan.
3. A backup facility refers to an alternate site available to an institution for relocation of business operations in the event of disruption of operations at the primary site (e.g. computer centre, head office administration, treasury dealing room). Backup facilities are described as being a cold site, warm site or hot site. A cold site backup facility is one where no provision of resources or equipment has been made. A computer centre cold site will, for example, incorporate raised flooring and environmentals such as power, telecommunications and air-conditioning). All other equipment and resources required to duplicate existing facilities are only installed if the backup site is activated. A warm site is a facility where resources and equipment are available, but a period of time will elapse while the facility is being made operational; for example, the downloading of current data. A hot site is a backup facility that provides sufficient duplication of the primary site to allow near immediate and continuing operation of critical business operations until the recovery of primary site operations is achieved.
4. Backup copies of all critical data and documentation stored at a site other than its usual operational location. Data or documentation stored off-site may be in various media formats, including computer tape or disc, film or hard copy (paper). Transfer of the data off-site may be electronic (e.g. vaulting or micro wave) or physical (e.g. courier).
5. UPS, supported by a generator system, provides a backup source of clean power (i.e. voltage irregularities are removed) which will allow the continued and uninterrupted operation of equipment and facilities. UPS will generally support the institution's computer centre and other identified critical business operations.
6. A simulation test involves the planned conduct of disaster recovery plan strategies in a manner consistent with actual operating conditions. Initial simulation tests may test individual components of the recovery plan, but will progressively incorporate more business functions until management is confident that the institution can respond effectively in a real disaster situation.

REFERENCES

Arnell, A. (1990). *Handbook of Effective Disaster/Recovery Planning A Seminar/Workshop Approach*. D. G. Davis (Ed.). New York: McGraw-Hill Publishing Company.

Australian Prudential Regulation Authority (1999). *Year 2000 Preparations in the Australian Banking and Financial System*, December, Sydney.

Australian Prudential Regulation Authority (1998). Auckland Power Supply Failure 1998, *The Report of the Ministerial Inquiry into the Auckland Power Failure*, July, Wellington.

Basel Committee on Banking Supervision (2001a). Overview of the New Basel Capital Accord, Consultative Document, Bank for International Settlements, January, Basle.

Basel Committee on Banking Supervision (2001b). Operational Risk, Consultative Document, Bank for International Settlements, January, Basle.

Basel Committee on Banking Supervision (2001c). QIS 2 – Operational Risk Loss Data, Bank for International Settlements, 4 May, Basle.

Basel Committee on Banking Supervision (1998). Operational Risk Management, Bank for International Settlements. (Paper No. 42), September, Basle.

Bank for International Settlements (1997). Core Principles for Effective Banking Supervision, Basle.

Blair, G. (1991). *Corporate Security and Contingency Planning Survey*, Coopers & Lybrand and Price Waterhouse Contingency Planning '91 Conference, 28–29 November, Sydney.

Christensen, S. (1992). Surveying, and Salvaging, the Aftermath of Outage, *Computerworld* (2 October), 35.

Chantico Publishing Company, Inc. (1991). *Disaster Recovery Handbook*. Blue Ridge Summit, PA: TAB Professional and Reference Books.

Ford, M. H. (1990). *Disaster Recovery Planning: How to Develop and Write a Plan*. Florida: American Bankers Association.

Hiatt, C. J. (2000). *A Primer for Disaster Recovery Planning in an IT Environment*. Hershey: Idea Group Publishing.

Myers, K. M. (1999). *Manager's Guide to Contingency Planning for Disasters: Protecting Vital Facilities and Critical Operations* (2nd ed.). New York: John Wiley & Sons, Inc.

Rehesaar, H. (1992). *Secrets of Successful DRP Project Management and Insurance* (4th ed.). New York: Harper Collins Publishers Inc.

Reserve Bank of Australia (1999). *Total Assets of Financial Institutions*. Bulletin, Statistical Table S79, December, Sydney.

Thompson, G. J. (1997). *The Many Faces of Risk in Banking*. Deputy Governor, Reserve Bank of Australia, Bulletin (July), 15, Sydney.

Toigo, J. W. (1989). *Disaster Recovery Planning – Managing Risk and Catastrophe in Information Systems*. New Jersey: Yourdon Press, Prentice-Hall, Inc.

Viney, C. (2000). *McGrath's Financial Institutions, Instruments and Markets* (3rd ed.). Sydney: McGraw-Hill Book Company.

Wold, G. H. (1992). The Disaster Recovery Planning Process – Part I of III, *Disaster Recovery Journal* (Vol. 5, No. 1), 29–34.

Woodcock, D. (1992). *Organisation-Wide Contingency Planning*. Coopers & Lybrand and Price Waterhouse Contingency Planning '92 Conference, 2–3 April, Melbourne.

CREDIT SPREADS BETWEEN GERMAN AND ITALIAN MEDIUM TERM ZERO COUPON GOVERNMENT BONDS – EMPIRICAL ASSESSMENT OF A THREE-FACTOR DEFAULTABLE TERM STRUCTURE MODEL

Bernd Schmid and Anna Kalemanova

ABSTRACT

This article analyzes the model performance of the Schmid and Zagst three-factor defaultable term structure model (Schmid & Zagst, 2000) in the context of credit spread pricing. We estimate the parameters of the model by applying Kalman filter methods to observed daily zero coupon bond data of German and Italian Government bonds from 1999–2000 and discuss the stability of the parameters over a longer time period. The Kalman filter method enables us to filter unobservable rates (such as riskless short rates and short rate credit spreads) from actually observable credit spreads. Hence, we can avoid using proxies for these unobservable rates which would be an additional source of noise. We investigate the developments of the credit spreads between German and Italian bonds through time, examine for the ability of the theoretical model to describe these dynamics realistically and provide various descriptive statistics. Our

Financial Risk and Financial Risk Management, Volume 16, pages 497–533.

ISBN: 0-7623-0858-3

empirical results based on in-sample and out-of-sample tests show that the model is capable of describing various shapes of credit spreads very well.

1. INTRODUCTION

For the valuation of defaultable bonds, defaultable interest rate options and credit derivatives a defaultable term structure model is necessary. One important issue of using such a model in practice is the estimation of its parameter values. This article presents a Kalman filtering method (see, e.g. Oksendal, 1998, pp. 79–106; Harvey, 1989) for estimating the parameter values of the Schmid and Zagst three-factor defaultable term structure model (Schmid & Zagst, 2000). We apply this method to zero coupon bond data of German and Italian Government bonds between September 30, 1999, and October 23, 2000. For that time frame the exchange rates between the German and Italian currencies have already been fixed due to the membership of the two countries to the European Monetary Union. So we don't have to consider any exchange rate risk in our study. We analyze the development of the credit spreads between German and Italian bonds through time and examine for the ability of the Schmid and Zagst model to describe these dynamics realistically.

The Schmid and Zagst model is a hybrid model and as such combines ideas of structural and reduced-form defaultable bond pricing models. The structural approach goes back to the initial proposal of Merton (1974), where he assumes that the dynamics of the value of the assets of a firm across time can be described by a diffusion-type stochastic process and the defaultable security can be regarded as a contingent claim on the value of the assets of the firm. There are a lot of papers dealing with extensions and generalizations of this approach. Some of the most important ones are the following: Black and Cox (1976), who incorporate classes of senior and junior debt; Geske (1977) who considers coupon bonds; Shimko, Tejima and Deventer (1993) and Kim, Ramaswamy and Sundaresan (1993) who allow for stochastic non-defaultable interest rates; Zhou (1997) incorporates a jump process for the underlying asset value. Many papers have recently appeared that follow a quite different approach, for example, those of Jarrow and Turnbull (1995) who present a model where the bankruptcy process is compared to a spot exchange rate process; Lando (1998) who uses Cox processes, which can be thought of as Poisson processes with a random intensity, to model prices of credit risky debt and the papers of Duffie and Singleton, (see, e.g. Duffie & Singleton, 1998) who show that valuation under the risk-adjusted probability measure can be done by discounting the non-defaultable payoff on the debt by a discount rate that is adjusted for the parameters of the default process. Hybrid models like the Schmid and Zagst model combine the strengths of structural and reduced-form models. Their model is a direct credit spread model. One of the factors that determine the credit spread is the so called uncertainty process which can be understood as an aggregation of all information on the quality of the obligor currently available: The greater the value of the uncertainty process the lower the quality of the obligor. The model assumes the underlying short rate to follow either a mean-reverting Hull-White process or a mean-reverting square root process with time-dependent mean reversion level; the uncertainty process is assumed to follow a mean-reverting square root process; finally, in addition to the non-defaultable short rate and the uncertainty index, Schmid and Zagst directly model the short rate spread process: they assume that the spread between a defaultable and a non-defaultable bond is considerably driven by the uncertainty index but that there may be additional factors which influence the level of the spreads: at least the contractual provisions, liquidity and the premium demanded in the market for similar instruments have a great impact on credit spreads; they can easily relate credit spreads to business cycles by replacing the uncertainty index by some index of macroeconomic variables without any change of their theoretical framework. Although structural as well as reduced-form models seem to be interesting we apply the hybrid model of Schmid and Zagst to our data for several reasons:

- Structural models work very well for corporate bonds. Without significant changes of these models or at least of the interpretations of their building blocks they can't be applied to sovereign bonds.
- Intensity based models lose to much structural information.
- The analysis of Düllmann and Windfuhr (2000) shows poor performance of two specific two-factor intensity based models.
- There are closed form solutions for zero coupon bond prices in the Schmid and Zagst model available.

There are large, liquid markets for interest rate derivatives. To price these derivatives, with closed-form solutions or numerical methods, we need estimates of the parameters of the underlying stochastic processes that determine the interest rate dynamics. Hence, parameter estimation is an important step in the application of interest rate option pricing models. The application of Kalman filtering methods in the estimation of term structure models using time-series data has been analyzed, e.g. by Chen and Scott (1995), Geyer and Pichler (1996) and Babbs and Nowman (1999). As far as we are aware, we are the first ones to apply this method to defaultable term structure models, especially to the model of Schmid and Zagst. The great advantage of the application of the Kalman filter to (defaultable) term structure models is that it allows the underlying state variables (in our case the default-free short rate, the short rate credit spread and the uncertainty index) to be completely unobservable. Other approaches usually need to work with proxies for the short rates which induces noise in the parameter estimation process. But which proxy one could use for the values of the uncertainty index is a serious problem. In this paper, we apply Kalman filtering methods to the Schmid and Zagst three-factor defaultable term structure model using data from German and Italian zero coupon Government bonds. We assume German bonds to be riskless and consider Italian bonds to be risky. These two countries are appropriate for our analysis because they are one of the most liquid markets for Government bonds within the European Monetary Union. The daily zero coupon bond prices (from January 1, 1999 until October 23, 2000), are provided by Reuters Information Services.

All yields in our analysis are adjusted to the continuously compounded yields to maturity assuming 365 days a year. Credit spreads are then calculated as the difference between Italian and German zero coupon bond yields. We analyze the development of these credit spreads through time and analyze the performance of the Schmid and Zagst model to explain these dynamics. Empirical investigation of credit spreads – mostly for corporates – has been done by, e.g. Longstaff and Schwartz (1995), Duffee (1996), Wei and Guo (1997), and Düllmann and Windfuhr (2000). Our analysis offers some advantages:

- We use daily data for credit spreads.
- (To our knowledge) we are the first ones to apply Kalman filter techniques to credit spread investigation.
- We don't use proxies for the unobservable state variables but filter their values from observable data.
- We apply different in-sample and – most important – out-of-sample tests.

The paper is organized as follows. Section 2 provides a brief review of the Schmid and Zagst model. The defaultable zero coupon bond pricing formula is presented which is the basic building block of the theoretical pricing and yield calculations. Section 3 describes the data we use for parameter estimation and testing. The complete process from the raw data to the modified data, which is actually used for estimation and testing, is shown. Several important descriptive statistics are presented. Section 4 shows how the Kalman filtering method can be applied to our data and the Schmid and Zagst model. Section 5 discusses the results of the parameter estimation. Sections 6 and 7 analyze the model performance for in-sample and out-of-sample data. Finally, the stability of the parameter estimations is discussed.

2. THE THREE-FACTOR DEFAULTABLE TERM STRUCTURE MODEL

We fix a terminal time horizon T^*. Uncertainty in the financial market is modelled by a complete probability space $(\Omega, \mathcal{F}, \mathbf{Q})$ and a filtration $\mathbf{F} = (\mathcal{F}_t)_{0 \leq t \leq T^*}$ of the three-dimensional standard Brownian motion $\hat{W}(t)' = (\hat{W}_r(t), \hat{W}_s(t), \hat{W}_u(t))$ satisfying the usual conditions (i.e. $\mathcal{F}_0$ is trivial and contains all the $\mathbf{Q}$-null sets of $\mathcal{F}$ and the filtration $\mathbf{F}$ is right continuous). In addition, we assume $\mathcal{F}_{T^*} = \mathcal{F}$. The filtration $\mathbf{F}$ represents the arrival of information over time. We will assume throughout that the price of a security at time t is zero if all dividend payments after time t are zero. All prices are taken to be ex-dividend. The modelling takes already place after measure transformation, i.e. we assume that $\mathbf{Q}$ is a martingale measure and all discounted security price processes are local $\mathbf{Q}$-martingales with respect to a suitable numéraire. As numéraire we choose the money market account $B(t) = e^{\int_0^t r(l)dl}$, where $r(t)$ is the non-defaultable short rate. In the following, all processes are defined on the probability space $(\Omega, \mathcal{F}, \mathbf{Q})$.

Assumption II.1. *The dynamics of the non-defaultable short rate are given by the following stochastic differential equation:*

$$dr(t) = [\theta_r(t) - \hat{a}_r r(t)]\, dt + \sigma_r r(t)^{\beta}\, d\hat{W}_r(t),\ t \geq 0, \tag{1}$$

where $\hat{a}_r$, $\sigma_r > 0$ *are positive constants,* $\beta = 0$ or $\frac{1}{2}$ and θ_r *is a non – negative valued deterministic function.*

This specification implies that the current rate $r(t)$ is pulled towards $\frac{\theta_r(t)}{\hat{a}_r}$ with a speed of adjustment $\hat{a}_r$, and if $\beta = \frac{1}{2}$ the instantaneous variance of the change in the rate is proportional to its level.

Assumption II.2. *The development of the uncertainty index is given by the following stochastic differential equation:*

$$du(t) = [\theta_u - \hat{a}_u u(t)]\, dt + \sigma_u \sqrt{u(t)}\, d\hat{W}_u(t),\ t \geq 0, \tag{2}$$

where $\hat{a}_u$, $\sigma_u > 0$ *are positive constants and* θ_u *is a non-negative constant.*

Assumption II.3. *The dynamics of the short rate spread (the short rate spread is supposed to be the defaultable short rate minus the non-defaultable short rate) is given by the following stochastic differential equation:*

$$ds(t) = [b_s u(t) - \hat{a}_s s(t)]\, dt + \sigma_s \sqrt{s(t)}\, d\hat{W}_s(t),\ t \geq 0, \tag{3}$$

where $\hat{a}_s$, b_s, $\sigma_s > 0$ *are positive constants.*

Given assumption II.1, the price of a non-defaultable zero coupon bond is given by the following proposition.

Proposition II.1. *Under assumption II.1 the time t value of a non-defaultable discount bond with maturity T,* $P(t, T) = P(r, t, T)$*, is given by (compare to Vasicek, 1977; Cox, Ingersoll & Ross, 1980; Hull & White, 1990)*

$$P(r, t, T) = A(t, T)\, e^{-B(t,T)r(t)}, \tag{4}$$

where $A(t, T)$ *and* $B(t, T)$ *are defined by*

$$B(t, T) = \begin{cases} \dfrac{1}{\hat{a}_r}[1 - e^{-\hat{a}_r(T-t)}], & \textit{if } \beta = 0, \\[2ex] \dfrac{1 - e^{-\delta_r(T-t)}}{\kappa_1^{(r)} - \kappa_2^{(r)} e^{-\delta_r(T-t)}}, & \textit{if } \beta = \tfrac{1}{2}, \end{cases} \text{, and,} \tag{5}$$

$$\ln A(t, T) = \begin{cases} \int_t^T (\tfrac{1}{2}\sigma_r^2 B(\tau, T)^2 - \theta_r(\tau) B(\tau, T))\, d\tau & \\ = \ln \dfrac{P(0, T)}{P(0, t)} - B(t, T)\dfrac{\partial \ln P(0, t)}{\partial t} & \textit{if } \beta = 0, \\ -\dfrac{\sigma_r^2}{4\hat{a}_r^3}(e^{-\hat{a}_r T} - e^{-\hat{a}_r t})^2 (e^{2\hat{a}_r t} - 1), & \\ -\int_t^T \theta_r(\tau) B(\tau, T)\, d\tau, & \textit{if } \beta = \tfrac{1}{2}, \end{cases} \tag{6}$$

with $\delta_x = \sqrt{\hat{a}_x^2 + 2\sigma_x^2}$ and $\kappa_{1/2}^{(x)} = \dfrac{\hat{a}_x}{2} \pm \dfrac{1}{2}\delta_x$.

Equations (4), (5) and (6) define the price of a discount bond at a future time t in terms of the short rate at time t and the prices of non-defaultable discount bond prices today. The latter can be calculated from today's term structure. The partial derivative $\dfrac{\partial \ln P(0, t)}{\partial t}$ in Eq. (6) can be approximated by $\dfrac{\ln P(0, t+\varepsilon) - \ln P(0, t-\varepsilon)}{2\varepsilon}$ where ε is a small length of time. In addition, if $\beta = 0$, the deterministic function $\theta_r(t)$ is given by

$$\theta_r(t) = f_t(0, t) + \hat{a}_r f(0, t) + \frac{\sigma_r^2}{2\hat{a}_r}(1 - e^{-2\hat{a}_r t}),$$

where $f(0, t)$ denotes the instantaneous forward rate as seen at time 0 for a contract maturing at time t. If $\beta = \frac{1}{2}$, $\theta_r(t)$ can be obtained iteratively from

$$-\int_0^t \theta_r(\tau)B(\tau, t)\, d\tau = \ln A(0, t)$$

by time discretization.

Under the assumption

$$Cov(d\hat{W}_r(t), d\hat{W}_s(t)) = Cov(d\hat{W}_r(t), d\hat{W}_u(t)) = Cov(d\hat{W}_s(t), d\hat{W}_u(t)) = 0 \quad (7)$$

Schmid and Zagst (2000) generalized the result of corollary II.1 to the pricing of defaultable zero coupon bonds. Let T^d denote the time of default and assume recovery of market value.[1] Then the following proposition holds:

Proposition II.2. *Assuming* $\beta = 0$ *and the dynamics specified by Eqs (1), (2) and (3), the value at time* $t < \tau = \min(T, T^d)$, $P^d(t, T) = P^d(r, s, u, t, T)$, *of a defaultable discount bond is given by*

$$P^d(t, T) = A^d(t, T)e^{-B(t,T)r(t) - C^d(t,T)s(t) - D^d(t,T)u(t)} \quad (8)$$

where

$$C^d(t, T) = \frac{1 - e^{-\delta_s(T-t)}}{\kappa_1^{(s)} - \kappa_2^{(s)}e^{-\delta_s(T-t)}},$$

$$D^d(t, T) = \frac{-2v'(t, T)}{\sigma_u^2 v(t, T)},$$

$$\ln A^d(t, T) = \ln A(t, T) + \frac{2\theta_u}{\sigma_u^2}\ln\left|\frac{v(T, T)}{v(t, T)}\right|.$$

The function $v(t, T)$ *is defined in Appendix A.*

3. THE DATA

In the following analysis we use observed data of credit spreads between German and Italian zero coupon Government bonds. The S&P ratings of the German and Italian bonds are AAA and AA, respectively. Hence, we can assume that the German bonds are default risk free whereas the Italian bonds

Table 1. Summary statistics for the sample of German and Italian zero coupon sovereign bonds.

	Germany	Italy
Number of bonds	33	36
Minimal maturity	0.5 years	0.36 years
Maximal maturity	11.5 years	12.2 years
Average maturity	4.9 years	3.5 years

are defaultable. The credit spreads are calculated as the differences of the yields to maturity of the appropriate bonds. We consider a 22 months time series of daily bond prices from January 1, 1999, until October 23, 2000, provided by Reuters Information Services.[2] All prices are denominated in Euro. As Germany and Italy are both members of the European Monetary Union, we don't have to take care of possible currency risks involved in credit spreads. Note further that our sample only consists of pure zero coupon bonds without any special embedded options such as callability features. From Table 1 it can be seen that we use a universe of 33 German and 36 Italian bonds. The ranges of maturities of the bonds span from 0.5 years to 11.5 years and from 0.36 years to 12.2 years for Germany and Italy, respectively.

To determine the parameter values of the Schmid and Zagst model (Schmid & Zagst, 2000) we need the complete German and Italian zero curves at each time step (i.e. at each observation day), at least up to some maximal time of maturity. But unfortunately only a finite number of points on these zero curves is observable. To infer the entire zero curves for Germany and Italy from the daily prices of the 33 German and 36 Italian bonds on a daily basis, we apply the method of Nelson and Siegel (1987).[3] They fit the yield curve using an exponential decay specification and reduce the problem to a four-parameter model: level, slope, curvature, and a time constant. Besides the construction of the zero curves we expect from the Nelson and Siegel methodology a smoothing effect of our data. Such an interest rate smoothing model avoids the problem inherent in spline-based models of choosing the optimal knot point specification. Nelson and Siegel take the following four parameter approximation model to determine zero curves from bond prices:

$$R(t,T) = \beta_0(t) + (\beta_1(t) + \beta_2(t)) \frac{1 - e^{-\frac{(T-t)}{\beta_3}}}{\frac{(T-t)}{\beta_3}} - \beta_2(t) e^{-\frac{(T-t)}{\beta_3}}, \tag{9}$$

where

$$P(t,T) = 100e^{-R(t,T)(T-t)},\ 0 \leq t \leq T.$$

The components in Eq. (9) determine the appropriate choices of weights that can be used to generate zero curves of a variety of shapes. $\beta_0(t)$ stands for the level or long term factor. $-\beta_1(t)$ stands for the slope or the short term factor. $\beta_2(t)$ stands for the curvature or the medium term component. β_3 is the time constant associated with curve hump positioning. It determines the rate of decay towards the long term rate. We estimate the parameters $\beta_i(t)$, $i = 0, 1, 2$, and β_3, for each day t based on the non-defaultable German zero coupon bond data from a non-linear regression. As Table 1 shows, the German bonds cover a range of maturities from half a year up to 11.5 years with an average maturity of 4.9 years.

Afterwards we apply the same methodology to the defaultable Italian zero coupon bond data. The Italian bonds cover maturities from three months up to 12.2 years with an average of 3.5 years. For each t we fit the parameters $\beta_i^d(t)$, $i = 0, 1, 2$, and β_3^d, of the Nelson and Siegel model

$$R^d(t,T) = \beta_0^d(t) + (\beta_1^d(t) + \beta_2^d(t))\,\frac{1 - e^{-\frac{(T-t)}{\beta_3^d}}}{\frac{(T-t)}{\beta_3^d}} - \beta_2^d(t)e^{-\frac{(T-t)}{\beta_3^d}}, \tag{10}$$

where

$$P^d(t,T) = 100e^{-R^d(t,T)(T-t)},\ 0 \leq t \leq T,$$

to the available Italian defaultable bond data. To make the two models better comparable we assume that $\beta_3 = \beta_3^d$. Finally, based on the estimated parameter values $\beta_i(t)$ and $\beta_i^d(t)$, $i = 0, 1, 2$, for each t, and β_3, we can calculate the estimated yields to maturity for non-defaultable German and defaultable Italian Government zero coupon bonds for each maturity $T \geq t$. It turns out that the best results can be achieved by setting the constant parameter β_3 equal to 3. After having estimated the zero curves we apply a robust outlier test removing all the curves which couldn't be fitted well enough by the Nelson and Siegel methodology.[4] Table 2 presents the quality statistics of our zero curve estimations, i.e. we summarize the analysis of the deviations of the observed German and Italian bond data from the estimated term structures of interest rates. The mean average absolute errors[5] are 18.8 basis points for Germany and 9.0 basis points for Italy, with standard deviations of 11.0 basis points and 10.3 basis points, respectively. Hence, all the curves fit the data fairly well.

Tables 3 and 4 show the parameter summary results of the curve fitting for Germany and Italy, respectively. The results show that the German long term

Table 2. Summary statistics for the deviations of the estimated yields from the observed German and Italian zero coupon bond yields. The deviation results are in basis points. Yields are based on continuous compounding.

	Germany	Italy
Average number of bonds per estimated curve	23.8	15.4
Mean of average absolute deviation	18.8	9.0
Standard deviation of average absolute deviation	11.0	10.3
Maximum of average absolute deviation	49.8	39.2

Table 3. Summary statistics for the Nelson Siegel parameters, results of fitting the German spot (zero coupon) curve. All numbers are given in percent.

	Mean	Standard Deviation	Maximum	Minimum
Level β_0	5.532	0.257	6.414	4.042
Slope $-\beta_1$	2.245	0.994	3.788	−0.556
Curvature β_2	0.102	1.682	4.343	−3.492

Table 4. Summary statistics for the Nelson Siegel parameters, results of fitting the Italian spot (zero coupon) Curve. All numbers are given in percent.

	Mean	Standard Deviation	Maximum	Minimum
Level β_0^d	6.048	0.435	9.967	4.305
Slope $-\beta_1^d$	2.795	0.965	7.478	−0.239
Curvature β_2^d	0.385	2.041	8.391	−4.759

spot rate is, on average, 5.532%, and the spot curve is, on average, upward-sloping, since the mean of the slope is 2.245%. In addition, on average, the German spot curve shows a curvature of 0.102%. The Italian long term spot rate is, on average, 6.048%, and the spot curve is, on average, upward-sloping, since the mean of the slope is 2.795%. In addition, on average, the Italian spot curve shows a curvature of 0.385%. Hence, on average, the level of the Italian yields is higher than the level of the German yields. Some of the German and Italian spot curves are downward-sloping, most of them are upward-sloping. The Italian curves tend to be steeper. Figures 1 and 2 show graphically the results of the German and Italian spot curve fittings on October 3, 1999, and August 24, 2000. On October 3, 1999, both curves are humped and deeply upward-sloping, convex, and fit the data very well: the level, slope, and curvature parameters of the German and Italian spot curves are 5.345%, 2.989%, and 2.942%, and 6.220%, 3.686%, and 1.532%, respectively. Hence, level and slope parameters of the Italian spot curve are higher than the corresponding quantities of the German spot curve. Obviously, this can be explained by the lower rating of the Italian bonds. On August 24, 2000, the situation is quite different. Although the German curve is upward-sloping for short maturities and downward-sloping for long maturities, over all it is very

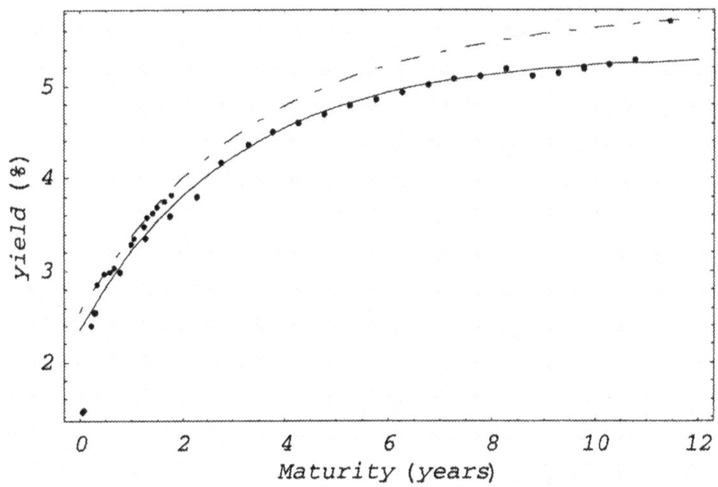

Fig. 1. Nelson-Siegel spot curve fitting on October 3, 1999. The line and the dashed line refer to the fitted spot rates of Germany and Italy, respectively. The dots refer to the estimated spot rates of Germany and Italy.

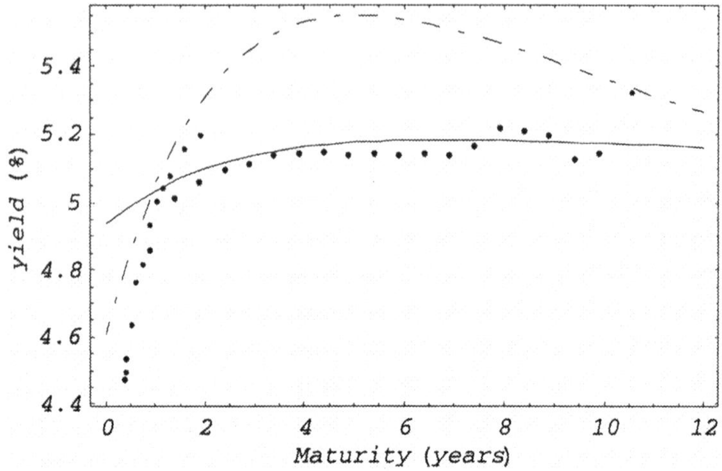

Fig. 2. Nelson-Siegel spot curve fitting on August 24, 2000. The line and the dashed line refer to the fitted spot rates of Germany and Italy, respectively. The dots refer to the estimated spot rates of Germany and Italy.

flat. The Italian curve is steeply upward-sloping for short maturities, humped, and downward-sloping for long maturities. For maturities less than a year, the estimated Italian curve lies below the estimated German curve although all observed Italian yields are higher than the appropriate German yields. Nevertheless, both curves fit the data fairly well. The level, slope, and curvature parameters of the German and Italian spot curves are 5.055%, 0.120%, and 0.602%, and 6.088%, 3.548%, and 2.247%, respectively.

To study the relationship between the German and Italian spot curves, we calculate the correlation matrix of the three-, six-, and nine-year German and Italian spot rates first. The results in Table 5 show that all rates are highly correlated. The correlation of the spot rates of different countries but with the same maturity is almost always higher than the correlation between curves of the same country with different maturities. Overall, we can say, the greater the difference between the maturities the less the correlation of the appropriate curves. Figure 3 shows the comovement of the rates across time. According to the high correlations, the curves mainly differ in their absolute level whereas the shapes are more or less all the same. We then calculate the correlation matrix of the level, slope, and curvature for the German and Italian spot curves.

Table 5. Correlation matrix of 3Y, 6Y, 9Y German and 3Y, 6Y, 9Y Italian spot rates.

	3Y Germany	6Y Germany	9Y Germany	3Y Italy	6Y Italy	9Y Italy
3Y Germany	1.000					
6Y Germany	0.967	1.000				
9Y Germany	0.924	0.990	1.000			
3Y Italy	0.996	0.956	0.911	1.000		
6Y Italy	0.976	0.991	0.973	0.976	1.000	
9Y Italy	0.949	0.990	0.978	0.944	0.992	1.000

To further understand the structural difference between the German and the Italian spot curves we investigate the spread between them. The estimated spread processes for various maturities, calculated as differences between Italian and German yield processes, are presented in Figs 4, 5 and 6.

The spreads are very volatile for all maturities. Because Germany and Italy are one of the most liquid Government bond markets in Europe we can assume that these spreads are real credit spreads and that liquidity risk can be neglected. In the following we want to partition the credit spread by using the

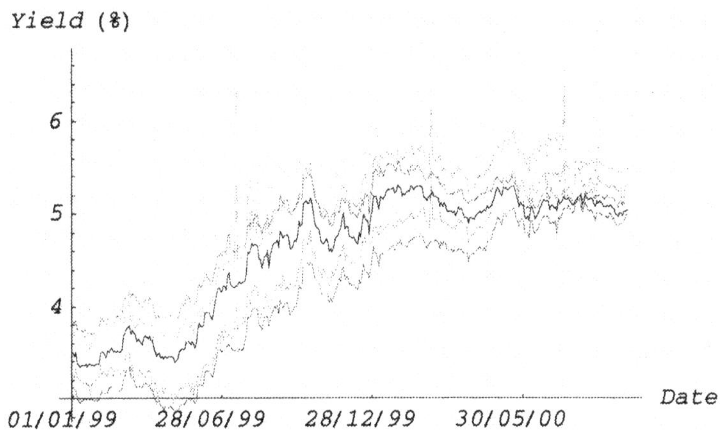

Fig. 3. From below: 3Y German, 3Y Italian, 6Y German, 6Y Italian, 9Y German, 9Y Italian spot rates.

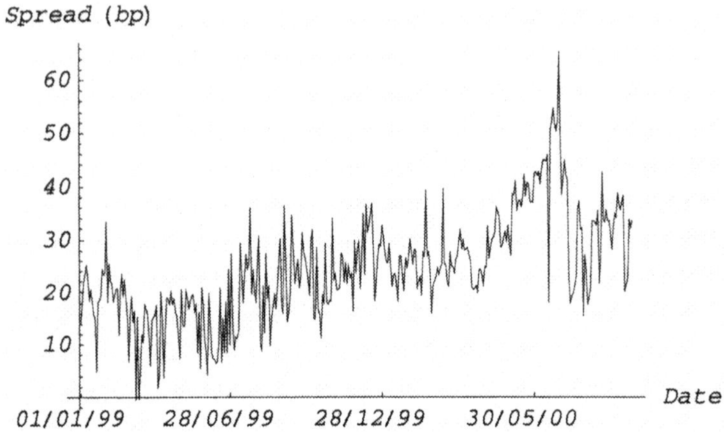

Fig. 4. Estimated credit spreads between Italian and German Government zero coupon bonds with maturity of 3 years. Time period: from January 1, 1999, until October 23, 2000.

Nelson-Siegel formulas (9) and (10). First, we observe that we can rewrite Eq. (9) as:

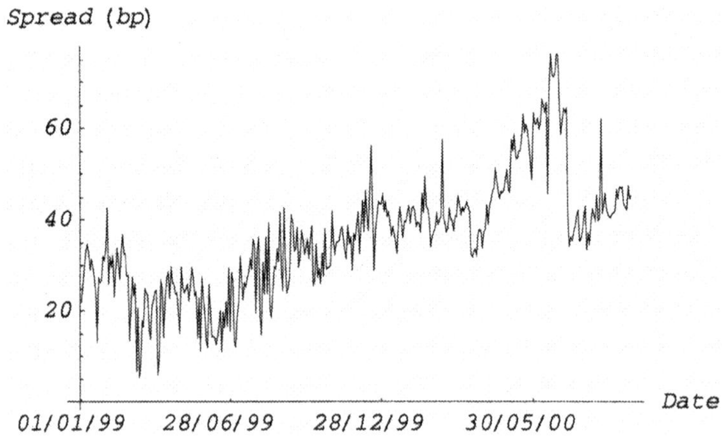

Fig. 5. Estimated credit spreads between Italian and German Government zero coupon bonds with maturity of 6 years. Time period: from January 1, 1999, until October 23, 2000.

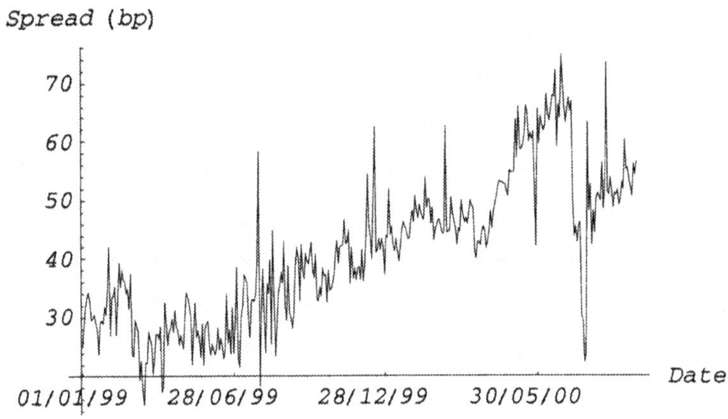

Fig. 6. Estimated credit spreads between Italian and German Government zero coupon bonds with maturity of 9 years. Time period: from January 1, 1999, until October 23, 2000.

$$R(t,T) = \beta_0(t) + \beta_1(t)\frac{\beta_3}{(T-t)}\left(1 - e^{-\frac{(T-t)}{\beta_3}}\right)$$

$$+ \beta_2(t)\frac{\beta_3}{(T-t)}\left(1 - e^{-\frac{(T-t)}{\beta_3}}\left(\frac{(T-t)}{\beta_3} + 1\right)\right).$$

We can obtain a corresponding formula for $R^d(t, T)$. Hence, the credit spread $S(t, T) = R^d(t, T) - R(t, T)$ can be partitioned into three parts:

$$S(t,T) = (\beta_0^d(t) - \beta_0(t)) + (\beta_1^d(t) - \beta_1(t))\frac{\beta_3}{(T-t)}\left(1 - e^{-\frac{(T-t)}{\beta_3}}\right)$$

$$+ (\beta_2^d(t) - \beta_2(t))\frac{\beta_3}{(T-t)}\left(1 - e^{-\frac{(T-t)}{\beta_3}}\left(\frac{(T-t)}{\beta_3} + 1\right)\right). \tag{11}$$

The first term on the right-hand side of Eq. (11) is the level component, the second term is the slope component and the third term is the curvature component for the credit spread at time t with maturity T. In our sample set, $(\beta_0^d(t) - \beta_0(t)) > 0$ for all t. The mean level component contributes to most of the mean credit spread. The mean slope component offsets the mean level

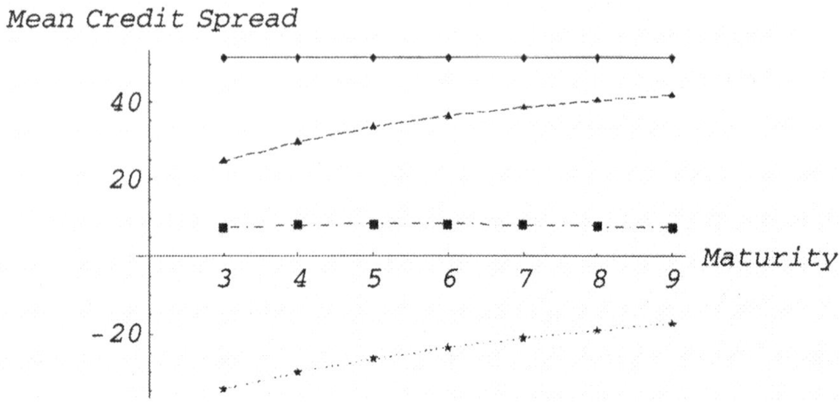

Fig. 7. Components of mean credit spreads for different maturities. From below: mean slope component, mean curvature component, mean credit spread, mean level component. Maturity in years, mean credit spreads and credit spread components in basis points.

component. The mean credit spread increases with maturity. The mean curvature component plays a less important role.

All together we get credit spread curves for 370 days between January 1, 1999, and October 23, 2000. Figure 8 shows the plot of the curves: over the

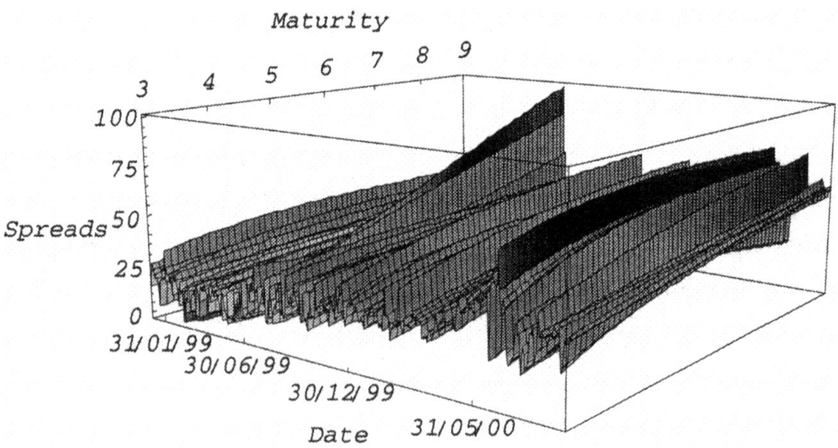

Fig. 8. Evolution of Italian credit spread curves. Credit spreads (bps), Maturity (years).

Table 6. Summary statistics for the credit spreads between Germany and Italy for different maturities. Mean, Standard Deviation and Maximum are given in basis points.

Maturity	Mean	Std. Dev.	Maximum	Skewness	Excess Kurtosis	L
3 years	24.35	10.00	65.33	0.46	0.73	21.02
4 years	29.30	11.97	72.40	0.47	0.89	25.29
5 years	33.05	12.88	75.48	0.47	0.79	22.74
6 years	35.89	13.08	76.24	0.45	0.56	17.33
7 years	38.06	12.91	77.05	0.43	0.23	12.12
8 years	39.75	12.62	76.38	0.40	–0.14	10.01
9 years	41.06	12.39	74.73	0.36	–0.46	11.33

observed time period, we get a range of different shapes: monotonic, humped and S shaped.

In Table 6 we show the summary statistics for the credit spreads between the German and Italian zero coupon bonds for different maturities. Again, the statistics are based on 370 observation days. The range of expected spreads between the two markets spans from 24 to 41 basis points depending on the time to maturity. Spreads are usually higher for longer maturities. The skewness parameters[6] are all positive and suggest that the credit spreads are more likely to be above the mean. The excess kurtosis[7] parameters suggest that the probability density functions are platykurtic for all maturities. For short term debt (maturities of 1 and 2 years) we find very high standard deviations of the spreads. That's why we exclude these maturities from the further analysis. One method that has been suggested for testing whether the distribution underlying a sample of n elements is normal, is to refer the statistic

$$L = n\left(\frac{skewness^2}{6} + \frac{excess\ kurtosis^2}{24}\right) \tag{12}$$

to the chi-squared distribution with two degrees of freedom.[8] The critical values for 5% and 1% are 5.99 and 9.21, respectively. We carry out the test using our credit spread data for the maturities between 3 and 9 years. According to the values of L given in Table 6, we can reject the normality hypothesis for the credit spread samples (for all maturities between 3 and 9 years) on a 1% level.

Table 7. Summary statistics for the credit spread changes between Germany and Italy for different maturities. Mean, Standard Deviation and Maximum are given in basis points.

Maturity	Skewness	Excess
3 years	–0.60	16.17
4 years	–1.05	23.71
5 years	–0.93	11.14
6 years	–0.54	6.31
7 years	–0.35	4.08
8 years	–0.31	4.17
9 years	–0.26	8.18

In addition to the analysis of the credit spread levels we investigate the first-differences in the logs of credit spread levels. The results in Table 7 suggest that credit spread changes are far away from being normally distributed. As, e.g. Duffie and Pan (1997) and Pedrosa and Roll (1998) point out, this implies troubling implications for risk management. The large values of the excess kurtosis are caused by fat tails in the probability distribution. There are much more extreme events than there would have been in the case of a normal distribution.

A prerequisite for producing reliable statistical results is that the credit spread time series is intertemporal stationary, i.e. that there is no unit root. We use the augmented Dickey-Fuller regression (Dickey & Fuller, 1981) to test for unit roots:

$$\begin{aligned}\Delta S_t(\tau) &= S_t(\tau) - S_{t-1}(\tau)\\ &= a_0 + \gamma S_{t-1}(\tau) + a_2 t + \sum_{i=2}^{p} \beta_i \Delta S_{t-i+1} + \varepsilon_t,\end{aligned}$$

where $S_t(\tau)$ denotes the time t credit spread between τ-year Italian and German zero coupon government bonds. The drift term parameter a_0, the linear time trend parameter a_2, γ, and β_i are parameters which have to be estimated by regression. ε_t is the spherical disturbance. We choose p to be the highest significant lag from the autocorrelation function of S. The coefficient of interest is γ. If $\gamma = 0$, the sequence $\{S_t(\tau)\}$ contains a unit root. Table 8 reports the Dickey-Fuller t-test results of $H_0{:}\gamma = 0$. The critical 95% and 99% values are –3.99 and –3.43, respectively. A smaller t-statistic rejects H_0. Hence, according to Table 8 we can reject the existence of unit roots for all maturities at the 99% level.

Table 8. Unit root tests for credit spreads between Italian and German zero coupon government bonds.

Maturity	p	γ	Standard Error	Test Statistic
3 years	5	–0.283617	0.0561638	–5.0498
4 years	5	–0.211004	0.048394	–4.3601
5 years	5	–0.187264	0.0450996	–4.1522
6 years	5	–0.187931	0.0443555	–4.2369
7 years	5	–0.212585	0.0461903	–4.6023
8 years	4	–0.266	0.049571	–5.36603
9 years	4	–0.346507	0.0558706	–6.2019

4. PARAMETER ESTIMATION BY USING KALMAN FILTERING

The application of Kalman filtering methods to the parameter estimation of term structure models has the great advantage that it allows the underlying state variables to be handled as completely unobservable, whereas other methods often must use some short term rates as proxies, which introduces additional noise. In the following we use the Kalman filtering method to estimate the parameters of the three-factor defaultable term structure model described in Section 2 using the German and Italian zero coupon bond data described in Section 3. First we derive the state space model formulation of the defaultable three-factor model and then present the Kalman filter algorithm. This is used in the calculation of the likelihood function of the observed credit spreads and the computation of the unobserved state variables and parameters of the model. Because we use real world credit spread observations in the Kalman filter we must describe the credit spread dynamics under the "real world" measure which we denote by **P.** We follow the assumptions of Schmid and Zagst (2000) and model the dynamics of $s(t)$ and $u(t)$ under **P** the following way:

$$du(t) = [\theta_u - a_u u(t)]\, dt + \sigma_u \sqrt{u(t)}\, dW_u(t), \tag{13}$$

$$ds(t) = [b_s u(t) - a_s s(t)]\, dt + \sigma_s \sqrt{s(t)}\, dW_s(t), \tag{14}$$

where

$$a_i = \hat{a}_i - \lambda_i(\sigma_i)^2 \text{ and } \hat{W}_i(t) = W_i(t) + \int_0^t \gamma_i(l)\, dl,\ i = s, u,$$

with

$$\gamma_s(t) = \lambda_s \sigma_s \sqrt{s(t)} \text{ and } \gamma_u(t) = \lambda_u \sigma_u \sqrt{u(t)},$$

for some constants λ_s and λ_u. Note, that we assume that $dW_s(t)$, $dW_u(t)$, and $dW_r(t)$ are pairwise uncorrelated. We denote the parameter vectors consisting of the unknown parameters by

$$\Phi_{s,u} = (a_s, a_u, \sigma_s, \sigma_u, b_s, \theta_u, \lambda_s, \lambda_u).$$

The theoretical formulas for the observed credit spreads $S(t, t+\tau)$, are given as the differences between the defaultable and non-defaultable continuous zero rates. The zero rate of a defaultable bond P^d at time $t \in [0, T]$ for a maturity time $T \in [t, T^*]$ is given by

$$\begin{aligned} R^d(t, T) &= -\frac{1}{T-t} \ln P^d(t, T) \\ &= -\frac{\ln A^d(t, T)}{T-t} + \frac{B(t, T)}{T-t} r(t) + \frac{C^d(t, T)}{T-t} s(t) + \frac{D^d(t, T)}{T-t} u(t) \\ &= -\frac{\ln A(t, T)}{T-t} - \frac{2\theta_u}{(\sigma_u)^2 (T-t)} \ln \left| \frac{v(T, T)}{v(t, T)} \right| + \frac{B(t, T)}{T-t} r(t) \\ &\quad + \frac{C^d(t, T)}{T-t} s(t) + \frac{D^d(t, T)}{T-t} u(t). \end{aligned}$$

Hence,

$$\begin{aligned} S(t, t+\tau) &= R^d(t, T) - R(t, T) \\ &= a(\tau) + c(\tau) s(t) + d(\tau) u(t), \ \tau \geq 0, \end{aligned}$$

with

$$a(\tau) = -\frac{2\theta_u}{(\sigma_u)^2 \tau} \ln \left| \frac{v(T, T)}{v(\tau)} \right|, \ c(\tau) = \frac{C^d(\tau)}{\tau}, \text{ and } d(\tau) = \frac{D^d(\tau)}{\tau},$$

where $v(\tau) = v(t, t+\tau)$, $C^d(\tau) = C^d(t, t+\tau)$, and $D^d(\tau) = D^d(t, t+\tau)$. Note that a, c, and d don't explicitly depend on t. Rather they depend on the time to maturity of the defaultable bond. We consider N-dimensional vectors of credit spreads with different maturities $\tau_1, \ldots, \tau_N \geq 0$ at times $t_1 < t_2 < \ldots < t_n$:

$$SV(t_k) = SV_k = \begin{pmatrix} S(t_k, t_k + \tau_1) \\ S(t_k, t_k + \tau_2) \\ \vdots \\ S(t_k, t_k + \tau_N) \end{pmatrix}, \ 1 \leq k \leq n.$$

If we denote

$$A = A(\Phi_{s,u}) = \begin{pmatrix} a(\tau_1) \\ a(\tau_2) \\ \vdots \\ a(\tau_N) \end{pmatrix}, \; C = C(\Phi_{s,u}) = \begin{pmatrix} c(\tau_1) & d(\tau_1) \\ c(\tau_2) & d(\tau_2) \\ \vdots & \vdots \\ c(\tau_N) & d(\tau_N \end{pmatrix},$$

and

$$X(t) = X(t, \Phi_{s,u}) = \begin{pmatrix} s(t) \\ u(t) \end{pmatrix},$$

where $\Phi_{s,u}$ is a subset of the parameter set which we want to estimate, we can define the measurement equation as

$$SV(t) = A + CX(t), \; t \geq 0.$$

The system of stochastic differential Eqs (13) and (14) with $X(t) = (s(t), u(t))'$ can be written in matrix form as

$$dX(t) = [HX(t) + J]\, dt + V(X(t))\, dW(t), \tag{15}$$

where

$$H = H(\Phi_{s,u}) = \begin{pmatrix} -a_s & b_s \\ 0 & -a_u \end{pmatrix}, \; J = J(\Phi_{s,u}) = \begin{pmatrix} 0 \\ \theta_u \end{pmatrix},$$

$$V(X(t)) = V(X(t), \Phi_{s,u}) = \begin{pmatrix} \sigma_s \sqrt{s(t)} & 0 \\ 0 & \sigma_u \sqrt{u(t)} \end{pmatrix},$$

and

$$dW = \begin{pmatrix} dW_s \\ dW_u \end{pmatrix}.$$

We allow for noise in the sampling process of the data. Hence, we assume that the spread vectors SV_k are observed with measurement errors ε_k that are jointly normally distributed with zero mean and $(N \times N)$ – dimensional covariance matrix G. Theoretically the matrix G can take various forms. But to simplify the calculations of the Kalman filter we choose the covariance matrix to be diagonal. Because trading activity and therefore bid-ask spreads usually vary across maturities (see, e.g., Geyer & Pichler, 1996) we allow for maturity-specific diagonal elements of G, i.e.

$$G=\begin{pmatrix} g_1^2 & 0 & \cdots & 0 \\ 0 & g_2^2 & \cdots & 0 \\ \vdots & \vdots & \ddots & \vdots \\ 0 & 0 & \cdots & g_N^2 \end{pmatrix}.$$

The diagonal elements g_i, $1 \leq i \leq N$, must be estimated together with $\Phi_{s,u}$, and the vector consisting of these diagonal elements is denoted by $\Psi_{s,u}=(g_1, \ldots, g_N)$. Thus, the measurement equation is given by

$$SV_k = A + CX_k + \varepsilon_k, \tag{16}$$

where

$$X_k = X(t_k) \text{ and } \varepsilon_k \sim N(0, G).$$

ε_k is assumed to be a sequence of i.i.d. random vectors. Now, let $\Delta t_{k+1} = t_{k+1} - t_k$, $k=1, \ldots, n-1$, and approximate the variance vector $V(X(t), \Phi_{s,u})$ over a subinterval $(t_k, t_{k+1}]$ by its value at the beginning of the subinterval, i.e. by $V_k = V(X_k, \Phi_{s,u})$. Then the transition Eq. (15) can be approximated by

$$dX(t) = (HX(t) + J)\, dt + V_k\, dW(t),\ t \in (t_k, t_{k+1}]. \tag{17}$$

For $t \in (t_k, t_{k+1}]$ we rewrite Eq. (17) as

$$e^{-Ht}\, dX(t) - e^{-Ht}HX(t)dt = e^{-Ht}[J\, dt + V_k\, dW(t)]. \tag{18}$$

By applying the two-dimensional version of the Itô formula[9] to $e^{-Ht}X(t)$, we get

$$d(e^{-Ht}X(t)) = e^{-Ht}\, dX(t) - e^{-Ht}HX(t)\, dt. \tag{19}$$

Plugging Eq. (19) into Eq. (18) yields

$$e^{-Ht_k}X_k - e^{-Ht_{k+1}}X_{k+1} = \int_{t_{k+1}}^{t_k} e^{-Hl}J\, dl + \int_{t_{k+1}}^{t_k} e^{-Hl}V_k\, dW(l),$$

which is equivalent to

$$X_{k+1} = e^{H\Delta t_{k+1}}X_k - \int_{t_{k+1}}^{t_k} e^{H(t_{k+1}-l)}J\, dl - \int_{t_{k+1}}^{t_k} e^{H(t_{k+1}-l)}V_k\, dW(l).$$

Easy calculations yield our final transition equation

$$X_{k+1} = e^{H\Delta t_{k+1}} X_k + \int_0^{\Delta t_{k+1}} e^{Hl} J \, dl + \int_0^{\Delta t_{k+1}} e^{H(\Delta t_{k+1} - l)} V_k \, dW(l). \tag{20}$$

The measurement Eq. (16) and transition Eq. (20) represent the state space formulation of our model. Now let $\tilde{X}_{k+1|k}$ and $\tilde{X}_{k+1}$ denote the optimal estimators[10] of the unknown state vector X_{k+1} based on the available information (i.e. the observed credit spreads) up to and including time t_k and t_{k+1}, respectively. The optimal estimators are the conditional means of X_{k+1}which are denoted by $E_k[X_{k+1}]$ and $E_{k+1}[X_{k+1}]$, respectively. Let Cov_k denote the covariance matrix of the estimation error, then

$$Cov_k = E_k[(X_k - \tilde{X}_k)(X_k - \tilde{X}_k)'].$$

Hence, the prediction equations are

$$\tilde{X}_{k+1|k} = e^{H\Delta t_{k+1}} \tilde{X}_k + \int_0^{\Delta t_{k+1}} e^{Hl} J \, dl \tag{21}$$

and

$$\begin{aligned} Cov_{k+1|k} &= E_k[(X_{k+1} - \tilde{X}_{k+1|k})(X_{k+1} - \tilde{X}_{k+1|k})'] \\ &= E_k\left[\left(e^{H\Delta t_{k+1}}(X_k - \tilde{X}_k) + \int_0^{\Delta t_{k+1}} e^{H(\Delta t_{k+1} - l)} V_k \, dW(l)\right) \cdot \right. \\ &\quad \left. \cdot \left(e^{H\Delta t_{k+1}}(X_k - \tilde{X}_k) + \int_0^{\Delta t_{k+1}} e^{H(\Delta t_{k+1} - l)} V_k \, dW(l)\right)'\right] \\ &= e^{H\Delta t_{k+1}} \cdot Cov_k \cdot e^{H'\Delta t_{k+1}} + \int_0^{\Delta t_{k+1}} e^{Hl} \tilde{V}_k \tilde{V}_k' e^{H'l} \, dl, \end{aligned} \tag{22}$$

where

$$\tilde{V}_k = E_k[V_k] = \begin{pmatrix} \sigma_s \sqrt{\tilde{s}_k} & 0 \\ 0 & \sigma_u \sqrt{\tilde{u}_k} \end{pmatrix}.$$

Note, that X_k and the time increments of the standard Brownian motion are independent for $t \geq t_k$. If we rewrite the credit spread vector as

$$SV_{k+1} = A + C(X_{k+1} - \tilde{X}_{k+1|k}) + C\tilde{X}_{k+1|k} + \varepsilon_{k+1},$$

then the optimal estimator of the credit spread vector at time t_{k+1}, given all credit spreads up to time t_k, is given by

$$\widetilde{SV}_{k+1|k} = E_k[SV_{k+1}] = A + C\tilde{X}_{k+1|k}.$$

If we denote the prediction error vector of the credit spreads by υ_{k+1}, then

$$\upsilon_{k+1} = SV_{k+1} - \widetilde{SV}_{k+1|k} = SV_{k+1} - A - C\tilde{X}_{k+1|k}. \tag{23}$$

Obviously, given $SV_1, \ldots, SV_k$ the vector $\begin{pmatrix} X_{k+1} \\ SV_{k+1} \end{pmatrix}$ is conditionally normally distributed with conditional mean

$$E_k\left[\begin{pmatrix} X_{k+1} \\ SV_{k+1} \end{pmatrix}\right] = \begin{pmatrix} \tilde{X}_{k+1|k} \\ \widetilde{SV}_{k+1|k} \end{pmatrix}$$

and conditional covariance matrix

$$Cov_k\left[\begin{pmatrix} X_{k+1} \\ SV_{k+1} \end{pmatrix}, \begin{pmatrix} X_{k+1} \\ SV_{k+1} \end{pmatrix}\right] = \begin{pmatrix} Cov_{k+1|k} & Cov_k[X_{k+1}, A + CX_{k+1}] \\ Cov_k[A + CX_{k+1}, X_{k+1}] & Cov_k[SV_{k+1}, SV_{k+1}] \end{pmatrix}$$

$$= \begin{pmatrix} Cov_{k+1|k} & Cov_{k+1|k}C' \\ CCov_{k+1|k} & F_{k+1} \end{pmatrix},$$

where – according to Eq. (23) –

$$\begin{aligned} F_{k+1} &= E_k[\upsilon_{k+1}(\upsilon_{k+1})'] \\ &= E_k[C(X_{k+1} - \tilde{X}_{k+1|k})(X_{k+1} - \tilde{X}_{k+1|k})'C'] + G \\ &= CCov_{k+1|k}C' + G. \end{aligned}$$

If we apply results from Harvey (1989), chapter 3, we get the updating equations

$$\tilde{X}_{k+1} = \tilde{X}_{k+1|k} + K_{k+1}\upsilon_{k+1} \tag{24}$$

and

$$Cov_{k+1} = Cov_{k+1|k} - K_{k+1}CCov_{k+1|k}, \tag{25}$$

with the so called Kalman gain matrix

$$K_{k+1} = Cov_{k+1|k}C'F^{-1}_{k+1}. \tag{26}$$

In the update step, the additional information given by SV_{k+1} is used to get a better estimate of X_{k+1}, the so called filtered estimate. Hence, the Kalman filter is capable of estimating the unobservable short rates s and u from observable credit spreads. In addition, for parameter estimation, one can define the likelihood function L, evaluated with the Kalman filter (21)–(26), by

$$L(\Phi_{s,u}, \Psi_{s,u} | SV_1, \ldots, SV_n) = \prod_{k=1}^{n} f_{SV_k | SV_1, \ldots, SV_{k-1}}(\Phi_{s,u}, \Psi_{s,u})$$

$$= \prod_{k=1}^{n} \frac{1}{(\sqrt{2\pi})^N} \frac{1}{\sqrt{\det F_k}}$$

$$\cdot \exp\left\{ -\frac{1}{2} (SV_k - \widetilde{SV}_{k|k-1})' F_k^{-1} (SV_k - \widetilde{SV}_{k|k-1}) \right\},$$

where $f_{SV_k | SV_1, \ldots, SV_{k-1}}(\Phi_{s,u}, \Psi_{s,u})$ denotes the conditional probability density function of SV_k given all information up to and including time t_{k-1}. Up to a constant, the log-likelihood function can be expressed as

$$\ln L(\Phi_{s,u}, \Psi_{s,u} | SV_1, \ldots, SV_n) = -\frac{1}{2} \sum_{k=1}^{n} \ln(\det F_k) - \frac{1}{2} \sum_{k=1}^{n} (\upsilon_k)' F_k^{-1} \upsilon_k. \quad (27)$$

The parameter vectors $\Phi_{s,u}$ and $\Psi_{s,u}$ can be estimated by maximizing the log-likelihood function (27) with respect to $\Phi_{s,u}$ and $\Psi_{s,u}$. It can be shown that such estimation yields consistent[11] and asymptotically efficient[12] estimators.

5. ESTIMATION PROCESS AND RESULTS

For the parameter estimation of the two-factor credit spread model, we use seven samples of data, each of length 150 for each country, i.e. in the Kalman filter algorithm we set $N = 7$ and $n = 150$. We use time series with daily data from September 30th, 1999, until May 30th, 2000, excluding several days for which there is no bond data available, the Nelson-Siegel estimates of the credit spreads appear to be negative or the bond data is identified as an outlier. We consider the times to maturity $\tau_i = i + 2$, $i = 1, \ldots, 7$ (expressed in years). Thus, the input data consists of 150 observed spread vectors

$$SV_k = \begin{pmatrix} S(t_k, t_k + \tau_1) \\ S(t_k, t_k + \tau_2) \\ \vdots \\ S(t_k, t_k + \tau_7) \end{pmatrix}, \; 1 \leq k \leq 150.$$

For the iterative calculation of the log-likelihood function (27) we have to initialize the Kalman filter first, i.e. we have to guess some good starting values for $\tilde{X}$ and Cov_0. Often they are set to their unconditional expectation and unconditional covariance matrix, respectively. In our case – as the state vector consisting of the short rate spread and the uncertainty index is not observable – we use starting values that are implied by the observable data. Solving the following system of two equations

$$S(t_0, t_0 + \tau_1) = a(\tau_1) + c(\tau_1)\tilde{s}_0 + d(\tau_1)\tilde{u}_0,$$

$$S(t_0, t_0 + \tau_2) = a(\tau_2) + c(\tau_2)\tilde{s}_0 + d(\tau_2)\tilde{u}_0,$$

yields $\tilde{X}_0 = \begin{pmatrix} \tilde{s}_0 \\ \tilde{u}_0 \end{pmatrix}$. We initialize the matrix Cov_0 simply by setting it equal to $\begin{pmatrix} \frac{1}{2} & \frac{1}{2} \\ \frac{1}{2} & \frac{1}{2} \end{pmatrix}$. After initialization we perform the 150 Kalman filter iterations to

Table 9. Kalman filter maximum likelihood parameter estimates for Italy: Part I. Sample period: 150 days from September 30th, 1999, until May 30th, 2000.

Parameter	g_1	g_2	g_3
Estimation	0.000418245	0.000289569	0.000236120
g_4	g_5	g_6	g_7
0.000225986	0.000057738	0.000143889	0.000241359

Table 10. Kalman filter maximum likelihood parameter estimates for Italy. Part II: Parameters of the short rate credit spread and uncertainty index processes. Sample period: 150 days from September 30th, 1999, until May 30th, 2000.

Parameter	Estimation	Parameter	Estimation
b_s	0.273903738	θ_u	0.000033835
a_s	0.053199919	a_u	0.068884441
σ_s	0.158772058	σ_u	0.030100786
λ_s	−1.868477669	λ_u	−1.190989999

calculate the log-likelihood function (27). Finally, we maximize this function with respect to the two parameter vectors $\Phi_{s,u} = (a_s, a_u, \sigma_s, \sigma_u, b_s, \theta_u, \lambda_s, \lambda_u)$ and $\Psi_{s,u} = (g_1, \ldots, g_7)$. To find the maximum we apply the multi-dimensional Downhill Simplex method of Nelder and Mead (1965). Tables 9 and 10 summarize the parameter estimates of our model derived from the observed credit spreads between Germany and Italy. The average mean reversion level of the Italian short rate credit spread and the mean reversion level of the Italian uncertainty index implied by our parameter estimates equal 25 basis points and 0.049%, respectively, which nicely fit to Figs 9 and 10.

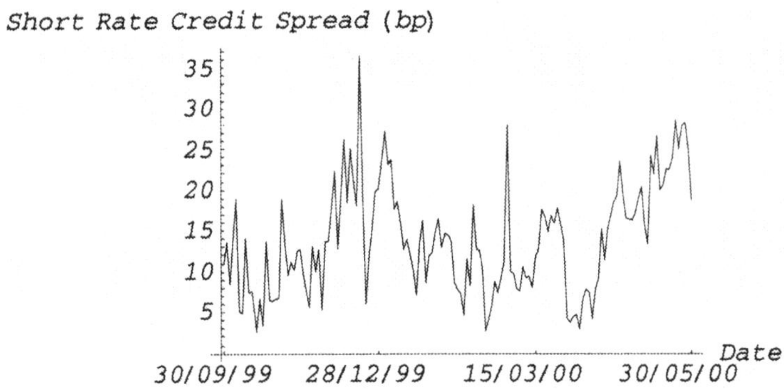

Fig. 9. Kalman filtered Italian short rate credit spread process. Time period: 150 days from September 30th, 1999, until May 30th, 2000.

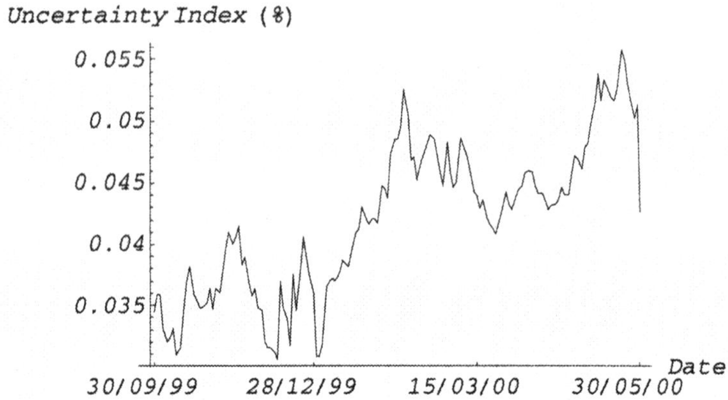

Fig. 10. Kalman filtered Italian uncertainty index process. Time period: 150 days from September 30th, 1999, until May 30th, 2000.

6. TESTING OF THE MODEL PERFORMANCE

First we test the assumption that the standardized Kalman filter residuals are normally distributed. We apply the test statistic (12) to the residuals with the critical values given in Table 11 and find: According to Table 12 we don't reject

Table 11. Critical values of the Box-Ljung test with 150 data points and 10 estimated parameters.

	$\chi^2(2)$
95% quantile	5.99
99% quantile	9.21

Table 12. Test for normal distribution of the Italian standardized Kalman filter residuals. Sample period: 150 days from September 30th, 1999, until May 30th, 2000.

Maturity	3 years	4 years	5 years	6 years	7 years	8 years	9 years
L	1.79604	1.9342	1.0273	0.86506	7.9013	12.113	10.911

the normal distribution hypothesis on the 5%-significance level for maturities of 3, 4, 5, and 6 years. In addition to 3, 4, 5, and 6 years, we don't reject the normal distribution hypothesis on a 1%-significance level for 7 years. We reject the hypothesis on the 1%-significance level for maturities of 8 and 9 years.

To test the standardized residuals for serial correlation we apply the Box-Ljung test on 1% and 5%-significance levels to different maturities. Under the null hypothesis that the standardized Kalman filter residuals for the specific maturities are not correlated, the Box-Ljung Q-statistic $Q(L)$ is asymptotically χ^2-distributed with

$$L\text{-}number\ of\ estimated\ parameters$$

degrees of freedom. As it is necessary, that the lag L grows with the number of observations, we choose $L = 2\sqrt{n} = 2\sqrt{150} \approx 24$. We reject the null hypothesis on the 1% significance level only if the test statistic is greater than the 99%-quantile of 21.67, or on the 5% significance level if the test statistic is greater than the 95%-quantile of 16.92. Table 13 summarizes the results of the Italian Q-statistics for several maturities: for the maturities of 4, 5, 8, and 9 years we find that the correlation is not significantly different from zero on the 5%-significance level, and for the maturities of 3, 6, and 7 years the correlation of the residuals is not significantly different from zero on the 1%-significance level.

Finally, we use the test for homoscedasticity as described in Harvey (1981, p. 157). The 1% and 5% critical values are given in Table 14. According to

Table 13. Box-Ljung tests for Italian standardized Kalman filter residuals. Sample period: 150 days from September 30th, 1999, until May 30th, 2000.

Maturity	3 years	4 years	5 years	6 years	7 years	8 years	9 years
Q-statistic (Box-Ljung)	21.52	14.95	15.96	18.38	21.16	14.24	13.88

Table 14. Critical values of the test for homoscedasticity.

	$F(50,50)$
0.5% quantile	0.476938
2.5% quantile	0.570791
97.5% quantile	1.75195
99.5% quantile	2.09671

Table 15. Test for homoscedasticity of the Italian standardized Kalman filter residuals. Sample period: 150 days from September 30th, 1999, until May 30th, 2000.

Maturity	H-statistic:$H(50)$
3 years	0.81934
4 years	0.459982
5 years	0.526177
6 years	0.611612
7 years	0.700424
8 years	0.791193
9 years	0.846494

Table 15, for Italy we don't reject the hypothesis on the 5%-significance level for the maturities of 3, 6, 7, 8 and 9 years. In addition, we don't reject the hypothesis of homoscedasticity on the 1%-level for the maturity of 5 years.

Overall, based on the various tests we can conclude that the assumptions on the Kalman filter algorithm are sufficiently satisfied by our Italian data set.

In the following we want to test the model performance by applying a test which is similar to that in (Titman & Torous, 1989). We test the power of the model to explain the changes of observed credit spreads. If the results are satisfactory we can conclude that the model can price defaultable bonds and credit spreads accurately. Let $\Delta S_k(\tau) = S(t_k, t_k + \tau) - S(t_{k-1}, t_{k-1} + \tau)$, $2 \leq k \leq 150$, denote the changes of the observed credit spreads with time to maturity τ, and let $\widehat{\Delta S_k}(\tau)$, $2 \leq k \leq 150$, denote the changes of the corresponding fitted credit spreads. The test equation is given by the following linear regression:

$$\Delta S_k(\tau) = a + b\widehat{\Delta S_k}(\tau) + \varepsilon_k^*, \text{ where } \varepsilon_k^* \sim N(0, h^2). \tag{28}$$

We apply the test to the maturities $\tau = 3, \ldots, 9$ (all in years). If $\widehat{\Delta S_k}(\tau)$ is an unbiased estimate for $\Delta S_k(\tau)$, then a and b should be close to 0 and 1, respectively. In addition, the adjusted $\bar{R}^2$ statistics are a measure for the quality of the model. Table 16 shows the results of the regression:

- The test of the hypothesis that $a = 0$ is accepted for all maturities.
- The parameter values for b are always close to 1.
- The test of the joint hypothesis that $a = 0$ and $b = 1$ is accepted on a 5%-significance level for all maturities but 6 years. Hence, the model prices these zero coupon bonds with acceptable accuracy.

Table 16. Test of model explanatory power: linear regression results.

Maturity	a	b	$\bar{R}^2$	P-Value ($a=0$)	P-Value ($a=0, b=1$)
3 years	$6.11333 \cdot 10^{-6}$	0.938757	0.717058	0.814845	0.440907
4 years	$7.63096 \cdot 10^{-6}$	1.03916	0.831121	0.713915	0.452307
5 years	$7.73356 \cdot 10^{-6}$	1.06541	0.907437	0.610017	0.055909
6 years	$6.96232 \cdot 10^{-6}$	1.05084	0.967956	0.414893	0.004006
7 years	$5.64142 \cdot 10^{-6}$	1.01643	0.973381	0.452594	0.355994
8 years	$3.9653 \cdot 10^{-6}$	0.975102	0.882806	0.80251	0.320922
9 years	$2.05174 \cdot 10^{-6}$	0.934458	0.717195	0.937439	0.396085

- The adjusted $\bar{R}^2$ values vary between 71.7% and 97.3%. Based on these values the explanatory power of the model is best for the 7 year credit spreads.

7. OUT-OF-SAMPLE TESTING

In the previous section we did some in-sample testing to examine the performance of the Schmid and Zagst model. To complete the analysis of the model we add an out-of-sample test. We analyze if we can apply the model with the parameters estimated in Section 5 to the pricing of credit spreads after May 30, 2000. Therefore we consider 70 additional time steps $t_k^* = 1, \ldots, 70$, for $k = 1, \ldots, 70$, from May 30, 2000, until October 23, 2000, and apply the Kalman filter to observed credit spreads for this time period. Note, that we keep the parameters from Section 5 fixed, i.e. we filter the values for $s(t)$ and $u(t)$ and determine the credit spread predictors with given values for the vectors Φ and Ψ. To test the out-of-sample model performance we apply the linear regression (28) to the new data. We test the maturities $\tau = 3, \ldots, 9$ (all in years). Table 17 shows the results of the regression:

- The test of the hypothesis that $a = 0$ is accepted for all maturities.
- The test of the joint hypothesis that $a = 0$ and $b = 1$ is accepted on a 1%-significance level for all maturities, on a 5%-significance level for all maturities but 6 and 9 years. Hence, the model prices these zero coupon bonds with acceptable accuracy.
- The adjusted $\bar{R}^2$ values vary between 68.9% and 95.2%. Based on these values the explanatory power of the model is best for the 6 year credit spreads.

Table 17. Test of out-of-sample model explanatory power: linear regression results.

Maturity	a	b	$\bar{R}^2$	P-Value ($a=0$)	P-Value ($a=0, b=1$)
3 years	0.0000150071	0.90796	0.689351	0.828829	0.471914
4 years	0.0000109933	1.03144	0.802159	0.85241	0.134735
5 years	0.0000104826	1.07602	0.888956	0.813476	0.265945
6 years	0.0000122546	1.07674	0.952238	0.667574	0.0374687
7 years	0.0000153419	1.05566	0.951507	0.59085	0.145532
8 years	0.0000190276	1.02615	0.862036	0.701499	0.219308
9 years	0.000022813	0.995921	0.714741	0.766278	0.0440766

Overall the test suggests that the out-of-sample behavior of the Schmid and Zagst model is very encouraging.

8. SUMMARY AND CONCLUSION

In the paper we analyze the model performance of the Schmid and Zagst model. We use credit spread data between German and Italian zero coupon bonds from January 1, 1999, until October 23, 2000. The raw data is smoothed by applying the algorithm of Nelson and Siegel. The quality of the approximation is shown by providing various descriptive statistics. The approximation results for the Italian term structure are very satisfactory. In case of the German term structure the results are not quite as good but not discouraging. The Kalman filter technique enables us to get good estimations for the parameters in the Schmid and Zagst model. In addition, we get filtered time series of the unobservable short rate credit spread and the uncertainty index. Using these parameters and applying in-sample and out-of-sample tests we can show that the model is appropriate in explaining credit spread dynamics very well. Especially, the adjusted $\bar{R}^2$ results of the linear regression (28) are much better than in previous empirical studies on the performance of other theoretical term structure models. To even improve these results, for future research it might be interesting to include liquidity considerations in the theoretical modelling and testing as well.

NOTES

1. We assume that the payoff of a claim upon default is given by

$$Z(\omega, t, F) = w(\omega, t)F(\omega, t-),\ 0 \leq w(\omega, t) \leq 1,$$

where $w(t)$ is a predictable process (such that $E^{Q}[\sup_t |Z_t|^q] < \infty$) describing the recovery rate process and $F(\omega, t-)$ is the value of the claim just before default.

2. Most of the previous empirical studies use weekly or monthly data. Besides Düllmann and Windfuhr (2000) we are the only ones to use daily data – at least to our knowledge.

3. The parsimonious model of Nelson and Siegel is widely used and suggested:

- Litterman and Scheinkman (1991) examine Treasury bonds and find that level, slope, and curvature explain most of the returns on the examined Treasury bonds.
- Jones (1991) shows that the yield curve can be mainly explained by shifts (parallel changes) and twists (changes in the slope).
- Barrett, Gosnell and Heuson (1995) apply it to daily Treasury note and bond data. From the investigation of shifts in the yield curve they draw conclusions for the selection of immunization strategies.
- Willner (1996) uses Nelson and Siegel's approach to extend traditional duration measurement methods to level, slope, and curvature durations.
- The Bundesbank has moved away from its in-house model to the Nelson and Siegel method for estimating the par yield curve (see f.e. *Estimating the Term Structure of Interest Rates* (1997)).
- Brooks and Yan (1999) show that the Nelson-Siegel functional form can be used to fit the forward curve and the spot curve as well.
- Jordan and Mansi (2000) show that the Nelson and Siegel functional form performs better than other yield-smoothing methods.
- Mansi (2000) compares the use of constant-maturity Treasuries as an alternative to on-the-run yields obtained from the Treasury market. He finds that a continuous bootstrapping methodology with the Nelson and Siegel functional form as the interpolation method can reduce pricing errors dramatically.

4. Let SSR_t be the sum of the squared deviations of the observed from the Nelson-Siegel estimated yields at time t. We assume that the curve at time t^* is an outlier if the deviation of SSR_{t^*} from the mean of all SSR_t is more than three times the standard deviation of all SSR_t.

5. By average absolute error of the Nelson-Siegel estimated curve at time t we mean

$$\sqrt{\frac{SSR_t}{\text{Number of bonds used for estimating time } t \text{ curve}}},$$

where SSR_t is the sum of squared deviations of the observed from the Nelson-Siegel estimated yields at time t.

6. Let X be a random variable with mean μ and variance σ^2. The skewness of a probability density function (pdf) can be measured in terms of its third moment about the mean. If a pdf is symmetric, $E[(X-\mu)^3]$ will obviously be 0; for pdf's not symmetric $E[(X-\mu)^3]$ will not be zero. In practice, the symmetry (or lack of symmetry) of a pdf is often measured by the coefficient of skewness, γ_1, where

$$\gamma_1 = \frac{E[(X-\mu)^3]}{\sigma^3}.$$

A variable with a negative skew is more likely to be far below the mean than it is to be far above the mean. (from Larsen & Marx, 2001, p. 233).

7. Let X be a random variable with mean μ and variance σ^2. The excess kurtosis of a probability density function (pdf) can be measured in terms of its fourth moment about the mean. The coefficient of kurtosis, γ_2, is defined by

$$\gamma_2 = \frac{E[(X-\mu)^4]}{\sigma^4} - 3.$$

A pdf whose excess kurtosis is positive has more mass in the tails than a Gaussian pdf with the same variance. Hence, γ_2, is a useful measure of peakedness: relatively "flat" pdf's are said to be platykurtic; more peaked pdf's are called leptokurtic (from Larsen & Marx, 2001, p. 233).

8. See e.g. Greene (2000, p. 161).

9. See, e.g. Oksendal (1998, p. 48).

10. Here we mean optimal in the mean squared error sense.

11. See, e.g. Larsen and Marx (2001, p. 359): An estimator $\hat{\Phi}_n$ is said to be consistent for Φ if it converges in probability to Φ, i.e. if for all $\varepsilon > 0$,

$$\lim_{n \to \infty} (\mathbf{P} \| \hat{\Phi}_n - \Phi \| < \varepsilon) = 1.$$

12. See, e.g. Larsen and Marx (2001, p. 351): Let $\hat{\Phi}$ be a sample estimate of a parameter vector Φ. The estimate is said to be unbiased if $E[\hat{\Phi}] = \Phi$. Now suppose that $\hat{\Phi}$ is an unbiased estimate of Φ. The estimate $\hat{\Phi}$ is said to be efficient if it is the case that for any other unbiased estimate $\hat{\Phi}^*$, the following matrix is positive semidefinite:

$$E[(\hat{\Phi}^* - \Phi)(\hat{\Phi}^* - \Phi)'] - E[(\hat{\Phi} - \Phi)(\hat{\Phi} - \Phi)'].$$

REFERENCES

Babbs, S. H., & Nowman, K. B. (1999). Kalman filtering of generalized Vasicek term structure models. *Journal of Financial and Quantitative Analysis*, *34*(1), 115–130.

Barrett, B., Gosnell, T., & Heuson, A. (1995). Yield curve shifts and the selection of immunization strategies. *The Journal of Fixed Income*, 53–64.

Black, F., & Cox, J. (1976). Valuing corporate securities: Some effects of bond indenture provisions. *Journal of Finance*, *31*, 351–367.

Brooks, R., & Yan, D. Y. (1999). London inter-bank offer rate (LIBOR) versus treasury rate: Evidence from the parsimonious term structure model. *The Journal of Fixed Income*, 71–83.

Chen, L. (1996). *Interest Rate Dynamics, Derivatives Pricing, and Risk Management* (No. 435). In: *Lecture Notes in Economics and Mathematical Systems* (1st ed.). Springer.

Chen, R., & Scott, L. (1995). Multi-factor Cox-Ingersoll-Ross models of the term structure: Estimates and tests from a Kalman filter model. Unpublished Paper. Rutgers University.

Cox, J., Ingersoll, J., & Ross, S. (1980). An analysis of variable rate loan contracts. *Journal of Finance*, *15*, 389–403.

Dickey, R., & Fuller, W. (1981). Likelihood ratio tests for autoregressive time series with a unit root. *Econometrica*, *49*, 1057–1072.

Duffee, G. R. (1996). The relation between treasury yields and corporate bond yield spreads. Working Paper. Washington: Federal Reserve Board.

Duffie, D., & Pan, J. (1997). An overview of value at risk. *Journal of Derivatives*, *4*(3), 749.
Duffie, D., & Singleton, K. J. (1998). Credit risk for financial institutions: Management and pricing.
Düllmann, K., & Windfuhr, M. (2000). Credit spreads between German and Italian Sovereign bonds - do affine models work?
Estimating the Term Structure of Interest Rates (1997). Monthly report. Bundesbank.
Geske, R. (1977). The valuation of corporate liabilities as compound options. *Journal of Financial and Quantitative Analysis*, 541–552.
Geyer, A. L. J., & Pichler, S. (1996). A state-space approach to estimate and test multifactor Cox-Ingersoll-Ross models of the term structure.
Greene, W. H. (2000). *Econometric Analysis* (4th ed.). New Jersey: Prentice Hall International, Inc.
Harvey, A. C. (1981). *The Econometric Analysis of Time Series*. Philip Allan Publishers Limited.
Harvey, A. C. (1989). *Forecasting, Structural Time Series Models and the Kalman Filter*. Cambridge: Cambridge University Press.
Hull, J., & White, A. (1990). Pricing interest-rate-derivative securities. *The Review of Financial Studies*, *3*(4), 573–592.
Jarrow, R., & Turnbull, S. (1995). Pricing options on financial securities subject to default risk. *Journal of Finance*, *50*, 53–86.
Jones, F. (1991). Yield curve strategies. *Journal of Fixed Income*, 43–51.
Jordan, J., & Mansi, S. (2000). Estimation of the term structure from on-the-run treasuries. Working Paper. National Economic Research Associates and George Washington University.
Kim, J., Ramaswamy, K., & Sundaresan, S. (1993). Does default risk in coupons affect the valuation of corporate bonds? A contingent claims model. *Financial Management*, 117–131.
Lando, D. (1998). On Cox processes and credit risky securities. Working Paper. Department of Operations Research, University of Copenhagen.
Larsen, R. J., & Marx, M. L. (2001). *An Introduction to Mathematical Statistics and Its Applications* (3rd ed.). New Jersey: Prentice Hall.
Litterman, R., & Scheinkman, J. (1991). Common factors affecting bond returns. *The Journal of Fixed Income*, 54–61.
Longstaff, F. A., & Schwartz, E. S. (1995). Valuing credit derivatives. *The Journal of Fixed Income*, 6–12.
Mansi, J. V. J. A. S. A. (2000). How well do constant-maturity treasuries approximate the on-the-run term structure. *The Journal of Fixed Income*, *10*(2), 35–62.
Merton, R. (1974). On the pricing of corporate debt: The risk structure of interest rates. *Journal of Finance*, *29*, 449–470.
Nelder, J. A., & Mead, R. (1965). A simplex method for function minimization. *The Computer Journal*, *7*, 308-313.
Nelson, C., & Siegel, A. (1987). Parsimonious modeling of yield curves. *Journal of Business*, *60*, 473–489.
Oksendal, B. (1998). *Stochastic Differential Equations – An Introduction with Applications*. Universitext (5th ed.). Springer.
Pedrosa, M., & Roll, R. (1998). Systematic risk in corporate bond credit spreads. *The Journal of Fixed Income*, *8*(3), 7–26.
Schmid, B., & Zagst, R. (2000). A three-factor defaultable term structure model. *The Journal of Fixed Income*, *10*(2), 63–79.

Shimko, D., Tejima, N., & Deventer, D. V. (1993). The pricing of risky debt when interest rates are stochastic. *The Journal of Fixed Income*, 58–65.

Titman, S., & Torous, W. (1989). Valuing commercial mortgages: An empirical investigation of the contingent-claim approach to pricing risky debt. *Journal of Finance*, *44*, 345–373.

Vasicek, O. (1977). An equilibrium characterization of the term structure. *Journal of Financial Economics*, *7*, 117–161.

Wei, D. G., & Guo, D. (1997). Pricing risky debt: An empirical comparison of the Longstaff and Schwartz and Merton models. *The Journal of Fixed Income*, 8–28.

Willner, R. (1996). A new tool for portfolio managers: Level, slope, and curvature durations. *The Journal of Fixed Income*, 48–59.

Zhou, C. (1997). A jump-diffusion approach to modeling credit risk and valuing defaultable securities. Working Paper. Washington: Federal Reserve Board.

APPENDIX A

The Function v(t, T)

$v(t, T)$ is given by

$$v(t, T) = (\sigma_u^2)^{\frac{\hat{a}_u}{2\delta_s} + \phi(\kappa_1(s))}$$

$$\cdot \left[\frac{\varphi_1}{\varphi_2} (e^{-\delta_s(T-t)})^{\frac{\hat{a}_u}{2\delta_s} - \phi(\kappa_1^{(s)})} F_1(t, T) + (e^{-\delta_s(T-t)})^{\frac{\hat{a}_u}{2\delta_s} + \phi(\kappa_1^{(s)})} F_3(t, T) \right],$$

with

$$F_1(t, T) = F(-\phi(\kappa_1^{(s)}) - \phi(\kappa_2^{(s)}),\ -\phi(\kappa_1^{(s)}) + \phi(\kappa_2^{(s)}),\ 1 - 2\phi(\kappa_1^{(s)}),\ \kappa_2^{(s)}/\kappa_1^{(s)}\, e^{-\delta_s(T-t)}),$$

$$F_3(t, T) = F(\phi(\kappa_1^{(s)}) - \phi(\kappa_2^{(s)}),\ \phi(\kappa_1^{(s)}) + \phi(\kappa_2^{(s)}),\ 1 + 2\phi(\kappa_1^{(s)}),\ \kappa_2^{(s)}/\kappa_1^{(s)}\, e^{-\delta_s(T-t)}),$$

and

$$\phi(g) = \frac{\sqrt{\hat{a}_u^2 g + 2b_s\sigma_u^2}}{2\delta_s\sqrt{g}}.$$

In addition, $\varphi_1 = \varphi_1(T, T)$, and, $\varphi_2 = \varphi_2(T, T)$, where

$$\varphi_1(t, T) = \zeta_2\, e^{-\delta_s(T-t)} F_4(t, T) - \xi_1 F_3(t, T),$$

$$\varphi_2(t, T) = \xi_2 F_1(t, T) - \zeta_1\, e^{-\delta_s(T-t)} F_2(t, T),$$

with

$$\xi_{1/2} = \left(\frac{\hat{a}_u}{2} \pm \delta_s \phi(\kappa_1^{(s)})\right), \zeta_{1/2} = \delta_s \frac{\kappa_2^{(s)}}{\kappa_1^{(s)}} \frac{\phi^2(\kappa_2^{(s)}) - \phi^2(\kappa_1^{(s)})}{1 \mp 2\phi(\kappa_1^{(s)})},$$

and

$$F_2(t, T) = F(1 - \phi(\kappa_1^{(s)}) - \phi(\kappa_2^{(s)}), 1 - \phi(\kappa_1^{(s)}) + \phi(\kappa_2^{(s)}), 2 - 2\phi(\kappa_1^{(s)}), \kappa_2^{(s)}/\kappa_1^{(s)}\, e^{-\delta_s(T-t)}),$$

$$F_4(t, T) = F(1 + \phi(\kappa_1^{(s)}) - \phi(\kappa_2^{(s)}), 1 + \phi(\kappa_1^{(s)}) + \phi(\kappa_2^{(s)}), 2 + 2\phi(\kappa_1^{(s)}), \kappa_2^{(s)}/\kappa_1^{(s)}\, e^{-\delta_s(T-t)}).$$

$F(a, b, c, z)$ is the hypergeometric function.

Remark A.1. *The hypergeometric function is usually denoted by F, has series expansion*

$$F(a, b, c, z) = \sum_{k=0}^{\infty} \frac{(a)_k (b)_k}{(c)_k} \frac{z^k}{k!},$$

where $(a)_0 = 1$, $(a)_n = a(a+1)(a+2) \ldots (a+n-1)$, $n \in \mathcal{N}$, *and is the solution of the hypergeometric differential equation*

$$z(1-z)y'' + [c - (a+b+1)z]y' - aby = 0.$$

The hypergeometric function can be written as an integral

$$F(a, b, c, z) = \frac{\Gamma(c)}{\Gamma(b)\Gamma(c-b)} \int_0^1 t^{b-1}(1-t)^{c-b-1}(1-tz)^{-a}\, dt, \; (c > b > 0),$$

and is also known as the Gauss series or the Kummer series.

ESTIMATION OF MEAN AND VARIANCE EPISODES IN THE PRICE RETURN OF THE STOCK EXCHANGE OF THAILAND

Theodore Bos and Pongsak Hoontrakul

ABSTRACT

This paper extends the novel and useful recent work of Inclán and Tiao (1994). Their invention was a procedure, based on CUSUM statistics, that would estimate the location of change points in the variance of a time series. This paper will show, with a Monte Carlo analysis, that the basic Inclán and Tiao procedure will also estimate changes in the average of a time series. This will invalidate prior work using earlier forms of the procedure. This paper will also introduce a procedure that will statistically identify whether an estimated change point is a change in average, variance, or both. To show the practical value of these new procedures, they will be applied to the daily return on the index of the Stock Exchange of Thailand (SET). This will be augmented with a description of the more important of these turning points in the life of the SET.

1. INTRODUCTION

Recent work of Inclán and Tiao (1994) presented a new procedure that would estimate change points in variance. They called this procedure the iterated

Financial Risk and Financial Risk Management, Volume 16, pages 535–554.

ISBN: 0-7623-0858-3

cumulative sum of squares (ICSS) algorithm. It was immediately obvious to finance researchers that this procedure could help in estimating when risk (variance of return) of an asset changes. The ICSS algorithm has been applied to estimating change points in the volatility of stock returns by Aggarwal, Inclán and Leal (1996). More recently Bos, Ding and Fetherston (BDF, 1998) attempted an improvement in the ICSS procedure and also applied that improved procedure to the volatility of stock returns. That attempt used the critical boundaries of Tanazaki (1995) in the hope that those nonlinear boundaries would improve the estimates of the original ICCS which uses linear boundaries. Bos and Fetherston (1992) showed that the linear boundaries, first used by Brown, Durbin and Evans (1975), lead to higher incidences of breaks in the middle of the data set.

In their empirical work, BDF hypothesized that their estimated change points in the variance of Thai stock returns might be related to changes in the mean of those stock returns. This paper will revisit that concern. Using Monte Carlo analysis, Section 3 of this paper shows that changes in the mean of a process will indeed be picked up by the ICCS as changes in the variance. Thus the original ICCS procedure will pick up both changes in mean and variance. Section 4 introduces a procedure that will estimate whether an estimated change point is either a change in mean, or variance, or both. This new procedure can be grafted to the original ICCS procedure. Section 5 applies this new set of procedures to daily price returns of the Stock Exchange of Thailand (SET).

2. BACKGROUND

In econometrics all the work on cumulative sum (CUSUM) of squares originates with Brown, Durbin and Evans (BDE, 1975). That paper created the CUSUM and CUSUM of squares statistics, and showed how those measures could be used to help determine whether or not the estimated parameters of a regression changes over time. The implicit assumption underlying every regression is that its parameters (the coefficient of the constant, the slopes, and the error variance) are constant over time. The CUSUM statistics are based on what are called *recursive residuals*. These are the standardized one-period ahead prediction errors from estimates of regressions based on data sets which grow one observation at a time.

It is known, but not widely understood, that a regression estimate without any independent variables is simply the mean and variance of the dependent variable. It is in this way that the CUSUM statistics can be used first of all to look for changes in the mean and variance of a series using the methods of

BDE, and now secondly to estimate change points in the variance using Inclán and Tiao's ICSS.

We will now develop the basic CUSUM concepts for a single series. Let

$$y_t = \mu + \varepsilon_t$$

where μ is the constant unknown mean of y_t, and σ^2 is the constant unknown variance of ε_t and y_t. The process of calculating first the recursive residuals, and then the CUSUM statistics starts with the first observation, y_1. With only this one observation, the predicted value of the next observation is equal to the first, as we have no other information. We can standardize the resulting prediction error, add an observation to our information set and estimate of the next observation, and continue to the end of the data set. In this way, the recursive residuals are

$$w_r = \frac{y_r - \left(\sum_{i=1}^{r-1} y_i \Big/ r-1 \right)}{\sqrt{\left(\frac{r}{r-1}\right) s_y^2}} \qquad r = 2, 3, \ldots, n$$

where s_y^2 is the estimated variance of all the y_t. Hence by the definition of the recursive residual, the numerator of w_r is the prediction error, (actual − predicted), while the denominator of w_r is the standard deviation of the one period ahead prediction error.

From these recursive residuals, one can calculate the CUSUM statistics.

The CUSUM statistic is defined as

$$W_r = \sum_{t=1}^{r} w_t \quad r = 2, 3, \ldots, n$$

and the CUSUM of squares statistic is defined by

$$s_r = \frac{\sum_{t=1}^{r} w_t^2}{\sum_{t=1}^{n} w_t^2}, \quad r = 2, 3, \ldots, n$$

Inclán and Tiao (1994) center the CUSUM of squares so that its mean is zero

$$s^*_r = \frac{\sum_{t=1}^{r} w_t^2}{\sum_{t=1}^{n} w_t^2} - \frac{r}{n}, \quad r = 2, 3, \ldots, n$$

Once the CUSUM of squares is centered, the original BDE critical boundaries are then horizontal, instead of diagonal, and hence easier to visualize and work with. In prior work, the time series plot of the CUSUM statistic was popular among users because of the intuition to be gained from it. The simple act of centering the CUSUM of squares statistic did the same thing for the CUSUM of squares.

Inclán and Tiao's ICSS procedure goes as follows:

Starting with the whole time series as the data segment being analyzed:

(1) Calculate the centered CUSUM of squares statistic for the data segment;
(2) Find the largest excursion beyond their version of the centered BDE critical boundaries;
(3) If one is found, mark this as an estimated change point in the variance of the time series segment under study;
(4) Split the particular data segment into two parts at this point.

Then follow the same sequence of steps with each new data segment until no more change points are found.

3. ICCS IN THE PRESENCE OF MEAN CHANGES

In the conclusion of their paper BDF hypothesize that the Inclán and Tiao ICCS procedure is also a predictor of mean changes – as well as a predictor of variance changes. In this section we will test this hypothesis with a Monte Carlo study. This analysis will be somewhat consistent with the simulations of Inclán and Tiao and those of the next section. Thus we analyze the reaction of the ICCS procedure to data segments each of the following characteristics:

(a) 100, 200, and 500 observations;
(b) mean and variance changes of 1 (no change), 2, and 3 standard deviations;
(c) mean or variance changes at 25%, 50%, or 75% of the series length.

This selection will give us information as to the sensitivity of the ICCS algorithm to mean and variance changes of various sizes in data segments of varying lengths.

One hundred thousand replications were carried out for each case. The results are summarized in Table 1 and Figs 1 and 2. From these displays the following can be inferred:

(i) mean changes will be picked up by the ICCS algorithm;
(ii) the longer the data set, the closer the point estimates for both mean and variance changes;
(iii) if the break is near the beginning of the data set, the more unreliable the estimate.

The goal of this section is satisfied by point (i). Although as Inclán and Tiao had intended, the ICCS is able to estimate step changes in variance, it is also able to estimate step changes in the mean. This was not intended by Inclán and Tiao, but yet is to be expected as the formula for the estimated variance contains the estimated mean. Thus when a user of the ICCS algorithm estimates a change point, the user is left with two possibilities – either the change point is a mean change or a variance change. This leaves the ICCS algorithm somewhat weak. The next section will introduce a method to estimate whether an estimated change point is a mean change or a variance change.

4. EXTENSION OF ICCS TO ESTIMATE MEAN CHANGES

The results in the above section clearly show that the ICCS algorithm will signal a change if a series experiences either a mean change or a variance change. Also properties of the point estimate of a break point seem somewhat similar for both mean and variance changes. While at first glance the identification problem between mean and variance changes causes a dilemma in the use of the ICCS, that property is actually beneficial. Research into estimating mean changes can now utilize the ICCS – except for the fact that the identification question exists. In this section we propose a simple solution to this question, and will study the effects of the ensuing extended ICCS using a Monte Carlo analysis. We will call the extended ICCS method ICCS:MV, where MV stands for mean and variance.

We suggest the following addition to the ICCS procedure. After all change points have been estimated using the original ICCS procedure, go through the data again two segments at a time. Let there be k estimated change points – not counting the two end points of the series being investigated. Thus there will be $(k+1)$ statistically stationary segements. Going through the data two segements at a time will help us determine what type of change has occurred at each

Table 1.

Number of Observations	Change Type	Where	Size	Estimated Change Points Probability	Average	Standard Deviation
100	NONE			0.034	50.7	18.7
100	Mean	25	2	0.124	42.2	14.6
100	Mean	50	2	1.000	50.4	6.7
100	Mean	75	2	1.066	73.3	8.0
100	Mean	25	3	0.344	37.7	15.2
100	Mean	50	3	1.168	50.8	6.3
100	Mean	75	3	1.164	74.4	7.1
100	Variance	25	2	0.160	51.7	14.9
100	Variance	50	2	0.523	56.4	10.5
100	Variance	75	2	0.420	71.9	11.5
100	Variance	25	3	0.404	44.7	14.9
100	Variance	50	3	0.947	54.7	8.8
100	Variance	75	3	0.848	73.7	9.7
200	NONE			0.039	99.6	33.6
200	Mean	50	2	0.553	72.6	31.3
200	Mean	100	2	1.133	101.0	14.3
200	Mean	150	2	1.133	147.7	16.1
200	Mean	50	3	1.353	64.7	27.8
200	Mean	100	3	1.159	101.3	13.6
200	Mean	150	3	1.202	149.0	15.0
200	Variance	50	2	0.475	81.8	28.9
200	Variance	100	2	0.898	107.3	18.6
200	Variance	150	2	0.750	143.2	22.0
200	Variance	50	3	1.094	68.6	24.2
200	Variance	100	3	1.065	105.4	15.3
200	Variance	150	3	1.038	147.2	18.1
500	NONE			0.045	250.8	84.5
500	Mean	125	2	1.424	165.2	74.5
500	Mean	250	2	1.138	252.1	37.5
500	Mean	375	2	1.179	371.4	40.5
500	Mean	125	3	1.253	144.9	57.3
500	Mean	250	3	1.145	252.4	36.5
500	Mean	375	3	1.190	371.9	40.0
500	Variance	125	2	1.130	163.0	57.1
500	Variance	250	2	1.071	258.3	39.6
500	Variance	375	2	1.054	361.8	48.7
500	Variance	125	3	1.356	147.7	45.6
500	Variance	250	3	1.091	255.5	36.6
500	Variance	375	3	1.077	368.9	42.9

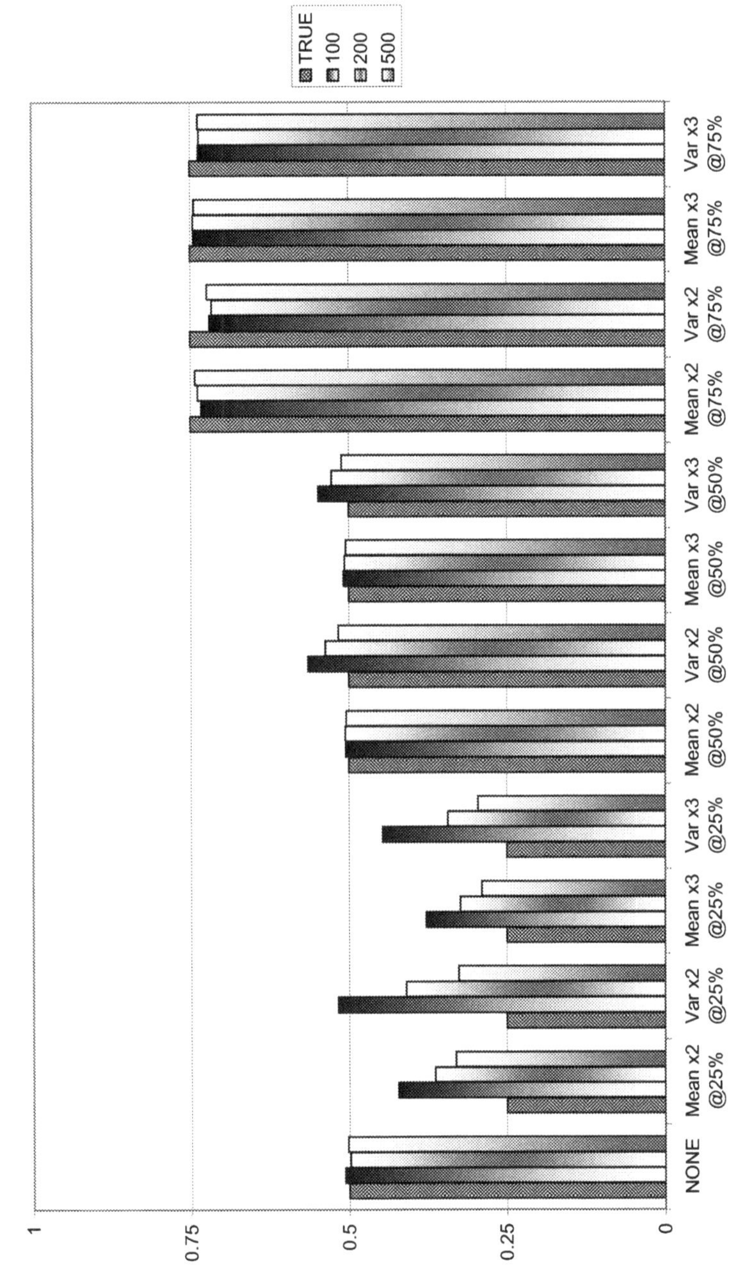

Fig. 1. Average of Estimated Break Points.

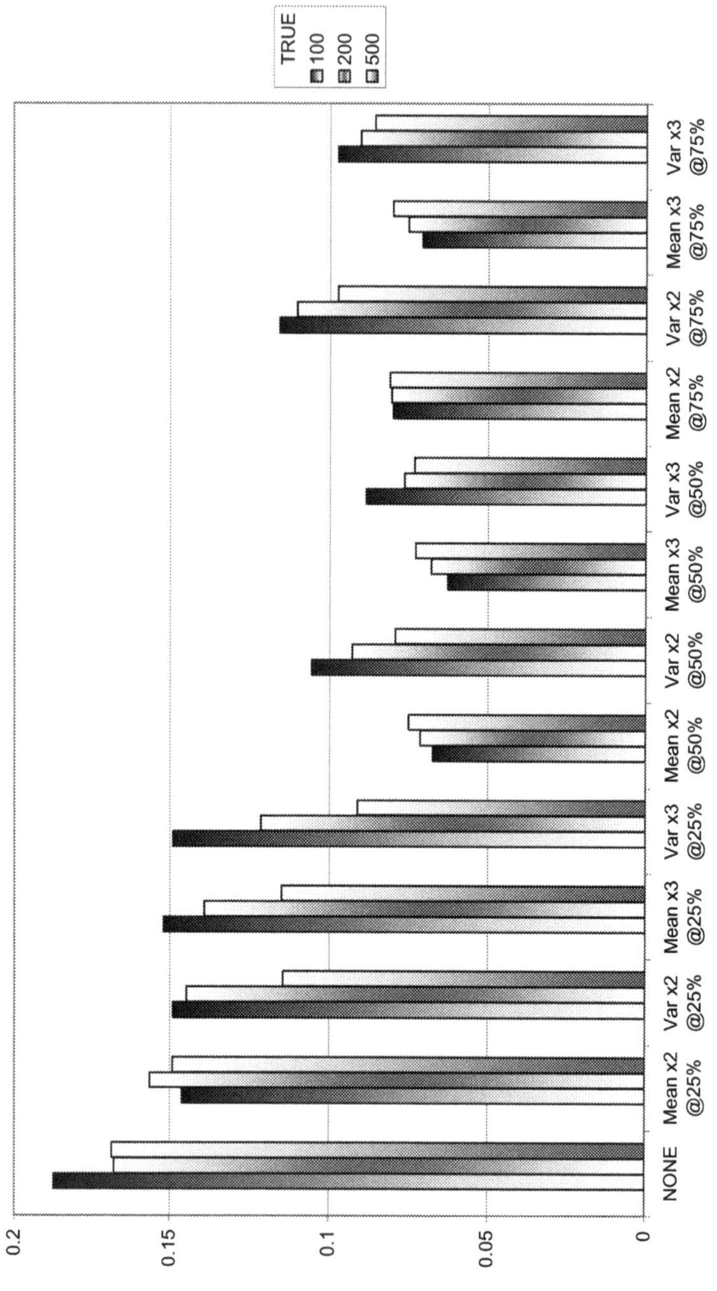

Fig. 2. Standard Deviation of Estimated Break Points.

estimated break point. Let *BPj* denote the *j*th estimated break point. Thus to determine the nature of the break at *BPj* we need the segments on each side of that point. Call these segments 1 and 2 where the elements of segment 1 are x_{1i}, $i = 1, 2, \ldots, n_1$; and the elements of segment 2 are x_{2i}, $i = 1, 2, \ldots, n_2$. We first hypothesize that the break point is a change in the mean. If this is true, then if we mean-standardize both segments then if the combination of the two line segements is passed through the ICCS then the two joined segements are expected to be stationary. By mean-standardize, we mean that each segment is transformed to the deviation from its mean. Thus the two joined segments would become:

$$(x_{11} - \bar{x}_1), (x_{12} - \bar{x}_1), \ldots, (x_{1n_1} - \bar{x}_1); (x_{21} - \bar{x}_2), (x_{22} - \bar{x}_2), \ldots, (x_{2n_2} - \bar{x}_2)$$

Secondly, we hypothesize that the break point is a change in the variance. If this is true, then if we variance-standardize both segments then if the combination of the two line segements is passed through the ICCS then the two joined segements are expected to be stationary. By variance-standardize, we mean that each element is divided by the standard deviation of its segment. Thus the two joined segments would become:

$$\frac{(x_{11} - \bar{x}_{1,2})}{s_1}, \frac{(x_{12} - \bar{x}_{1,2})}{s_1}, \ldots, \frac{(x_{1n_1} - \bar{x}_{1,2})}{s_1}; \frac{(x_{21} - \bar{x}_{1,2})}{s_2}, \frac{(x_{22} - \bar{x}_{1,2})}{s_2}, \ldots, \frac{(x_{2n_2} - \bar{x}_{1,2})}{s_2}$$

We pass the data from the two segments through this process and record the results.

(i) If the mean-standardized segments are *stationary* and the variance-standardized segments are *stationary*, then the break is estimated to be in both mean and variance.
(ii) If the mean-standardized segments are *stationary* and the variance-standardized segments are *nonstationary*, then the break is estimated to be in the mean only.
(iii) If the mean-standardized segments are *nonstationary* and the variance-standardized segments are *stationary*, then the break is estimated to be in the variance only.
(iv) If the mean-standardized segments are *nonstationary* and the variance-standardized segments are *nonstationary*, then the cause of the break is undetermined. The cause for the break could be a change in mean or variance, but most likely it is something else.

The above can be summarized in a table as follows:

Table 2.

		Mean-standardized	
		If stationary	If nonstationary
Variance-standardized	If stationary	Mean and variance change	Variance change
	If nonstationary	Mean change	Undetermined

This additional procedure was put into the Monte Carlo analysis of the previous section. These results are shown in Table 3. This table contains a large amount of interesting information. We direct the reader to the panel with 500 observations per series. From Table 1, we see that if there are no breaks of any kind, then there will be slightly less than the expected frequency of false positives – 4.5% instead of the expected 5%. This is better than the opposite – too many false positves. Referring back to Table 3, if there are no breaks and if the ICCS:MV procedure estimates a break (a false positive), then 92.9% of these will register as variance breaks. One would hope that false positives get evenly distributed among the four choices, but that is not the case.

Now we direct the reader to mean changes in series of 500 observations. Regardless of where the change was, most of the time the change was correctly identified as a mean change (eg. 62.7% for a 2.0 standard deviation change in the mean after observation 125). It is extremely interesting to note that when the ICCS:MV estimates a mean change, then the average point estimate of the location of that change is very close to the true change. Also, and perhaps more important, the standard error of this location is extremely small – meaning that the estimate of the location of the mean change is extremely precise. Although the point and interval estimates of the location of a mean change are very good, it must be noted that if a mean change occurs, the ICCS:MV procedure can still label this as a variance change – an 18.1% chance of being labeled as a variance change for a 2.0 standard deviation change in mean after observation 375.

Now moving to the part of Table 3 with 500 observations and variance changes, we see that the probability of correctly identifying a variance change is very high – much higher than correctly identifying a mean change. Yet, the properties of the point and interval estimates are quite disappointing in comparison to those of the mean changes – the point estimates are clearly biased, and the standard errors are very large.

Table 3.

Number of Observations	Change Type	Where	Size		All Change Points	Estimated Change Type: Both	Mean	Variance	Undetermined
100	NONE			Proportion		17.8%	0.0%	82.1%	0.1%
				Average	50.7	52.3	34.0	50.3	23.5
				Stdev.	18.7	21.5	0.0	18.0	0.5
100	Mean	25	2	Proportion		41.5%	22.6%	33.8%	2.0%
				Average	42.2	43.4	25.4	52.9	25.4
				Stdev.	14.6	12.9	1.7	10.1	3.0
100	Mean	50	2	Proportion		8.3%	78.7%	10.1%	2.9%
				Average	50.4	51.3	50.2	51.9	48.6
				Stdev.	6.7	12.1	2.0	17.0	3.6
100	Mean	75	2	Proportion		75.5%	10.9%	11.8%	1.9%
				Average	73.3	74.5	74.5	65.2	69.8
				Stdev.	8.0	4.8	2.2	17.6	5.9
100	Mean	25	3	Proportion		46.5%	42.4%	7.8%	3.3%
				Average	37.7	48.3	25.2	49.0	25.0
				Stdev.	15.2	12.4	1.0	18.0	1.9
100	Mean	50	3	Proportion		15.9%	72.9%	8.0%	3.2%
				Average	50.8	54.2	50.1	50.9	49.7
				Stdev.	6.3	9.6	0.7	16.6	1.9
100	Mean	75	3	Proportion		20.8%	68.1%	7.2%	3.9%
				Average	74.4	76.0	75.0	65.6	72.9
				Stdev.	7.1	7.4	0.7	20.8	3.1
100	Variance	25	2	Proportion		10.6%	0.0%	89.4%	0.0%
				Average	51.7	57.8	NA	51.0	34.0
				Stdev.	14.9	16.1	NA	14.6	0.0

Table 3. Continued.

Number of Observations	Change Type	Where	Size		All Change Points	Estimated Change Type			
						Both	Mean	Variance	Undetermined
100	Variance	50	2	Proportion		8.0%	0.0%	92.0%	0.0%
				Average	56.4	58.3	NA	56.2	28.0
				Stdev.	10.5	14.6	NA	10.1	23.0
100	Variance	75	2	Proportion		12.1%	0.0%	87.9%	0.0%
				Average	71.9	73.4	81.0	71.7	90.0
				Stdev.	11.5	13.3	0.0	11.2	0.0
100	Variance	25	3	Proportion		14.0%	0.0%	85.9%	0.0%
				Average	44.7	50.1	53.5	43.8	39.2
				Stdev.	14.9	15.6	7.4	14.6	12.6
100	Variance	50	3	Proportion		6.2%	0.0%	93.8%	0.0%
				Average	54.7	55.2	NA	54.7	47.6
				Stdev.	8.8	13.9	NA	8.4	18.2
100	Variance	75	3	Proportion		8.1%	0.0%	91.9%	0.0%
				Average	73.7	73.0	77.0	73.7	NA
				Stdev.	9.7	14.2	0.0	9.2	NA
200	NONE			Proportion		11.4%	0.0%	88.6%	0.0%
				Average	99.6	99.5	NA	99.6	66.0
				Stdev.	33.6	40.7	NA	32.6	0.0
200	Mean	50	2	Proportion		33.0%	51.0%	11.9%	4.1%
				Average	72.6	102.1	50.3	94.9	49.4
				Stdev.	31.3	23.0	2.0	38.6	2.6
200	Mean	100	2	Proportion		5.4%	77.5%	13.1%	4.0%
				Average	101.0	103.6	100.2	105.7	98.4
				Stdev.	14.3	26.3	2.2	34.7	4.8

Table 3. Continued.

Number of Observations	Change Type	Where	Size		All Change Points	Estimated Change Type: Both	Mean	Variance	Undetermined
200	Mean	150	2	Proportion		29.5%	52.1%	13.9%	4.5%
				Average	147.7	149.3	149.6	138.8	142.5
				Stdev.	16.1	12.1	2.4	37.4	8.4
200	Mean	50	3	Proportion		26.0%	62.4%	8.0%	3.7%
				Average	64.7	98.5	50.0	76.3	49.2
				Stdev.	27.8	26.9	0.8	40.9	3.4
200	Mean	100	3	Proportion		10.3%	76.4%	9.3%	4.0%
				Average	101.3	111.3	100.1	100.9	99.7
				Stdev.	13.6	21.9	0.8	36.5	2.2
200	Mean	150	3	Proportion		17.9%	67.2%	11.9%	2.9%
				Average	149.0	152.7	150.0	138.1	149.0
				Stdev.	15.0	14.8	0.7	37.6	2.3
200	Variance	50	2	Proportion		8.5%	0.0%	91.5%	0.0%
				Average	81.8	94.6	70.0	80.6	36.5
				Stdev.	28.9	31.0	0.0	28.4	19.5
200	Variance	100	2	Proportion		5.0%	0.0%	95.0%	0.0%
				Average	107.3	106.9	11.0	107.4	76.0
				Stdev.	18.6	27.3	0.0	18.0	47.0
200	Variance	150	2	Proportion		6.6%	0.0%	93.4%	0.0%
				Average	143.2	142.6	NA	143.3	116.0
				Stdev.	22.0	28.8	NA	21.4	60.8
200	Variance	50	3	Proportion		16.4%	0.0%	83.5%	0.0%
				Average	68.6	86.4	56.7	65.0	76.0
				Stdev.	24.2	26.2	21.4	22.2	39.5

Table 3. Continued.

Number of Observations	Change Type	Where	Size		All Change Points	Estimated Change Type			
						Both	Mean	Variance	Undetermined
200	Variance	100	3	Proportion		4.8%	0.0%	95.2%	0.0%
				Average	105.4	106.1	NA	105.3	96.0
				Stdev.	15.3	25.8	NA	14.5	46.7
200	Variance	150	3	Proportion		4.5%	0.0%	95.5%	0.0%
				Average	147.2	144.1	NA	147.3	164.5
				Stdev.	18.1	30.5	NA	17.2	2.5
500	NONE			Proportion		7.1%	0.0%	92.9%	0.0%
				Average	250.8	247.9	NA	251.1	NA
				Stdev.	84.5	99.6	NA	83.2	NA
500	Mean	125	2	Proportion		22.5%	62.7%	11.1%	3.7%
				Average	165.2	267.0	124.8	202.0	120.9
				Stdev.	74.5	55.4	2.5	107.4	8.3
500	Mean	250	2	Proportion		3.3%	79.3%	12.5%	4.9%
				Average	252.1	271.4	250.1	260.9	248.3
				Stdev.	37.5	72.4	2.0	98.0	6.3
500	Mean	375	2	Proportion		7.8%	70.4%	18.1%	3.7%
				Average	371.4	373.7	374.7	357.5	370.7
				Stdev.	40.5	44.8	2.2	89.0	9.1
500	Mean	125	3	Proportion		12.8%	73.2%	10.0%	4.0%
				Average	144.9	239.6	125.0	177.6	124.0
				Stdev.	57.3	68.3	0.9	106.1	4.2
500	Mean	250	3	Proportion		6.0%	80.0%	9.5%	4.5%
				Average	252.4	291.3	250.1	248.2	249.8
				Stdev.	36.5	59.9	1.0	103.5	1.5

Table 3. Continued.

Number of Observations	Change Type	Where	Size		All Change Points	Estimated Change Type			
						Both	Mean	Variance	Undetermined
500	Mean	375	3	Proportion		12.7%	71.3%	13.0%	3.0%
				Average	371.9	384.1	375.0	342.8	374.7
				Stdev.	40.0	37.5	0.7	99.1	1.9
500	Variance	125	2	Proportion		11.3%	0.0%	88.7%	0.0%
				Average	163.0	207.1	NA	157.4	43.0
				Stdev.	57.1	61.3	NA	54.1	8.0
500	Variance	250	2	Proportion		3.1%	0.0%	96.9%	0.0%
				Average	258.3	255.6	27.0	258.4	313.0
				Stdev.	39.6	61.9	0.0	38.6	15.0
500	Variance	375	2	Proportion		3.2%	0.0%	96.8%	0.0%
				Average	361.8	351.4	NA	362.2	233.0
				Stdev.	48.7	75.5	NA	47.5	164.0
500	Variance	125	3	Proportion		21.2%	0.0%	78.8%	0.0%
				Average	147.7	180.3	154.5	138.9	112.7
				Stdev.	45.6	42.4	5.5	42.3	39.8
500	Variance	250	3	Proportion		3.2%	0.0%	96.8%	0.0%
				Average	255.5	255.6	344.0	255.5	127.4
				Stdev.	36.6	61.7	0.0	35.4	110.2
500	Variance	375	3	Proportion		2.8%	0.0%	97.2%	0.0%
				Average	368.9	360.6	100.0	369.1	241.5
				Stdev.	42.9	74.9	0.0	41.5	170.8

The above properties of the estimates of the ICCS:MV, as expected, get somewhat worse as the series length decreases. We can summarize the properties of the ICCS:MV as follows:

(i) Although not absolutely precise, the ICCS:MV generally does what it is expected to do.
(ii) If the true change is a mean change:
   (a) the probability that the ICCS:MV mis-identifies it is often between 15% and 20%.
   (b) The point estimate is unbiased; and
   (c) The standard error is very small.
(iii) If the true change is a variance change:
   (a) the probability that the ICCS:MV mis-identifies it is very small;
   (b) The point estimate is biased; and
   (c) The standard error is quite large.

Though these properties are not clean as one would like, they are better than the alternative, which prior to this paper was a misunderstanding of the nature of change signals generated by the ICCS.

5. APPLICATION OF ICCS:MV

To gain some practical insight into the ICCS:MV it was applied to 5,514 daily observations of the return in the market index of the Stock Exchange of Thailand (SET). The data used begins on May 2, 1975 and ends on September 22, 1997. Out of those 5,514 observations, 69 changes points were estimated. This level of aggregation corresponds to the application of the ICCS. Of those 69 estimated change points, for only one (November 27, 1978) could the type of change point not be determined – corresponds to the bottom right corner of Table 2. Also of the 69 estimated change points, not one was estimated to be caused by a variance change only. All five estimated variance changes were in conjuction with mean changes. The other 63 estimated change points were mean only changes. The dates of the estimated change points are displayed in Table 4 along with the estimated mean and standard deviations of the intervening episodes. This information is also shown graphically in Fig. 3.

The interesting aspect of this empirical analysis is that the vast majority of the estimated change points were identified as mean changes, and most of the rest were estimated to be both changes in mean and variance. From the Monte Carlo analysis of the previous section of this paper we note that if the true change is a variance change, then it is very likely that the ICCS:MV will identify it as such. Also if the true change if a mean change, then most often

Table 4. Results of ICCS:MV on SET Daily Returns.

#	Episode	Average	Standard deviation	Number of Trading Days
1	May 2, 1975 to May 21, 1975	–0.0117	0.0090	13
2	May 22, 1975 to May 28, 1975	0.0092	0.0090	5
3	May 29, 1975 to July 2, 1975	0.0011	0.0090	24
4	July 3, 1975 to July 28, 1975	0.0048	0.0090	17
5	July 29, 1975 to August 6, 1975	–0.0021	0.0090	7
6	August 7, 1975 to October 6, 1975	–0.0016	0.0090	42
7	October 7, 1975 to October 8, 1975	–0.0017	0.0090	2
8	October 9, 1975 to October 27, 1975	–0.0002	0.0090	12
9	October 28, 1975 to March 8, 1976	–0.0012	0.0081	89
10	March 9, 1976 to June 3, 1976	–0.0008	0.0081	58
11	June 4, 1976 to March 30, 1977	0.0009	0.0081	204
12	March 31, 1977 to April 28, 1977	0.0036	0.0081	19
13	April 29, 1977 to May 3, 1977	0.0128	0.0081	2
14	May 4, 1977 to July 28, 1977	0.0034	0.0081	59
15	July 29, 1977 to August 15, 1977	0.0136	0.0081	10
16	August 16, 1977 to August 23, 1977	0.0072	0.0081	6
17	August 24, 1977 to October 11, 1977	0.0013	0.0081	35
18	October 12, 1977 to December 14, 1977	0.0028	0.0081	43
19	December 15, 1977 to October 13, 1978	0.0010	0.0081	207
20	October 16, 1978 to December 14, 1978	0.0040	0.0081	41
21	December 15, 1978 to March 19, 1979	–0.0017	0.0081	64
22	March 20, 1979 to May 23, 1979	–0.0078	0.0081	42
23	May 24, 1979 to May 30, 1979	0.0314	0.0081	5
24	May 31, 1979 to October 5, 1979	–0.0010	0.0081	90
25	October 8, 1979 to January 18, 1980	–0.0027	0.0081	70
26	January 21, 1980 to November 12, 1980	–0.0007	0.0081	203
27	November 13, 1980 to December 9, 1980	0.0026	0.0081	18
28	December 11, 1980 to August 17, 1982	–0.0004	0.0081	413
29	August 18, 1982 to September 13, 1982	0.0129	0.0081	19
30	September 14, 1982 to September 20, 1982	–0.0212	0.0081	5
31	September 21, 1982 to October 8, 1982	0.0007	0.0081	14
32	October 11, 1982 to December 16, 1982	–0.0003	0.0081	46
33	December 17, 1982 to December 14, 1983	0.0003	0.0081	245
34	December 15, 1983 to October 29, 1984	0.0000	0.0081	218
35	October 30, 1984 to November 6, 1984	0.0000	0.0081	6
36	November 7, 1984 to April 2, 1985	0.0008	0.0081	99
37	April 3, 1985 to July 15, 1985	0.0012	0.0081	67
38	July 16, 1985 to July 3, 1986	–0.0007	0.0081	239
39	July 4, 1986 to June 19, 1987	0.0032	0.0090	238
40	June 22, 1987 to July 22, 1987	0.0106	0.0090	21
41	July 23, 1987 to August 3, 1987	–0.0091	0.0090	8

Table 4a. Continued.

#	Episode	Average	Standard deviation	Number of Trading Days
42	August 4, 1987 to October 16, 1987	0.0071	0.0090	53
43	October 19, 1987 to January 19, 1988	–0.0055	0.0155	62
44	January 20, 1988 to March 25, 1988	0.0047	0.0155	47
45	March 28, 1988 to April 28, 1988	0.0013	0.0155	22
46	April 29, 1988 to September 13, 1989	0.0017	0.0155	339
47	September 14, 1989 to February 5, 1990	0.0014	0.0155	99
48	February 6, 1990 to February 8, 1990	–0.0059	0.0155	3
49	February 12, 1990 to August 2, 1990	0.0030	0.0123	117
50	August 3, 1990 to September 3, 1990	–0.0093	0.0177	21
51	September 4, 1990 to February 26, 1991	–0.0008	0.0177	120
52	February 27, 1991 to July 16, 1991	–0.0014	0.0177	93
53	July 17, 1991 to August 16, 1991	0.0016	0.0177	21
54	August 19, 1991 to August 22, 1991	–0.0032	0.0177	4
55	August 23, 1991 to November 25, 1991	–0.0003	0.0177	64
56	November 26, 1991 to May 4, 1992	0.0013	0.0177	106
57	May 6, 1992 to June 11, 1992	–0.0005	0.0177	26
58	June 12, 1992 to June 23, 1992	0.0025	0.0177	8
59	June 24, 1992 to September 8, 1992	0.0005	0.0177	52
60	September 9, 1992 to November 6, 1992	0.0053	0.0177	42
61	November 9, 1992 to November 25, 1992	–0.0093	0.0177	13
62	November 26, 1992 to October 4, 1993	0.0008	0.0177	208
63	October 5, 1993 to April 19, 1994	0.0021	0.0177	131
64	April 20, 1994 to November 17, 1994	0.0011	0.0177	145
65	November 18, 1994 to May 31, 1995	–0.0003	0.0177	128
66	June 1, 1995 to July 23, 1996	–0.0006	0.0177	278
67	July 24, 1996 to September 27, 1996	–0.0022	0.0177	46
68	September 30, 1996 to June 16, 1997	–0.0040	0.0177	174
69	June 17, 1997 to September 22, 1997	0.0008	0.0177	67

the ICCS:MV will identify it correctly – but also that the ICCS:MV might often identify it as a both in both mean and variance. Thus it is quite certain that the mean changes estimated by the ICCS:MV in this data set are truly changes in the mean, and that the location estimates of these change points are likely to be very accurate. It is also possible that, in this analysis, the points identified as being changes in both mean and variance are truly changes in the mean only.

This outcome seems to be at odds with current thought in financial research. It is common nowadays to posit that the mean return series on an asset is constant over time, while the variance of that series varies perhaps according to some autoregressive scheme.

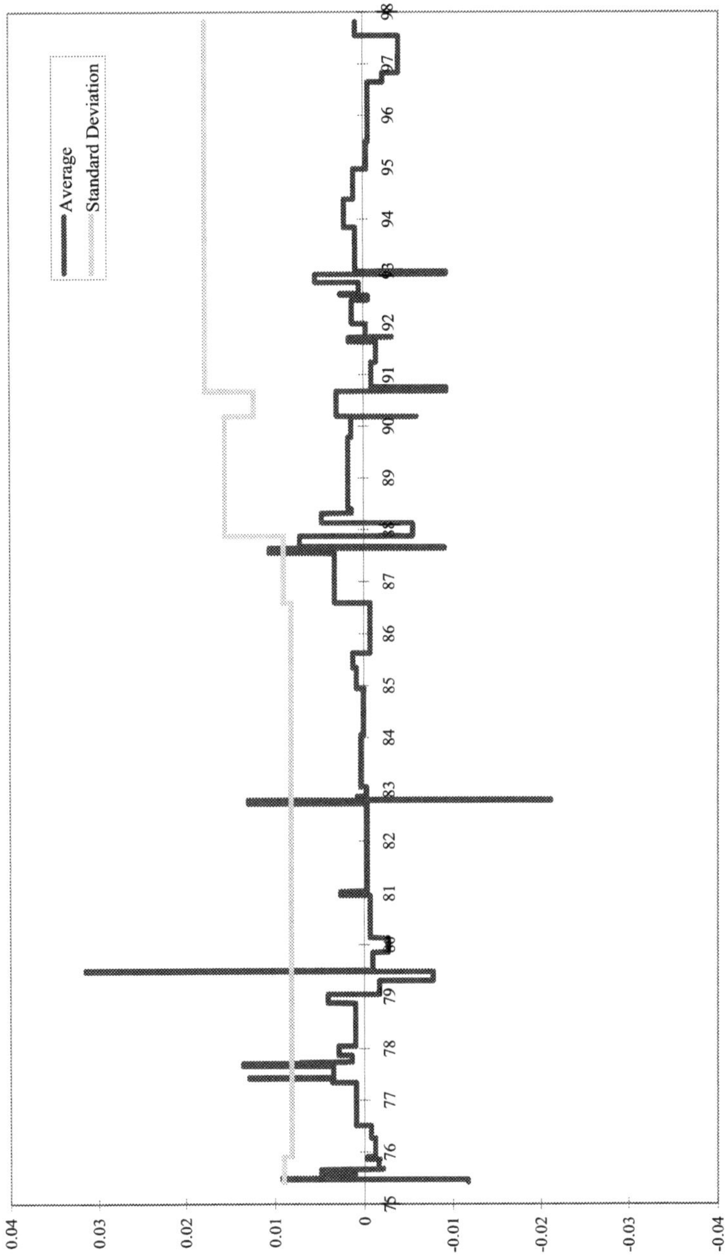

Fig. 3. Results of ICCS:MV on SET Daily Returns.

6. SUMMARY AND CONCLUSION

This paper points out that the IT ICCS procedure erroneously identifies all changes in a series as changes in variance. In particular with a Monte Carlo analysis in Section 3 it is seen that changes in mean will also be picked up as changes in variance by the ICCS. By judicious use of partial mean and variance standardization of segments, this paper introduces ICCS:MV, an extension of ICCS. This extension allows for the statistical identification of the type of change point. While the statistical properties of the new ICCS:MV are not completely desirable, the direction that the new procedure takes has great promise.

As the goal of the ICCS:MV is to estimate when and what mean and variance changes occur in a time series, it is an interesting tool for financial research which, among other things, is interested in the mean and variance – the return and risk – of assets. In the recent annals of financial research, much emphasis has been put on the identification of changes in variance – mostly through ARCH and its derivatives. When the ICCS:MV is applied to daily returns of the index of the Stock Exchange of Thailand, it is discovered that the nearly all, if not all, the estimated changes are attributed to changes in the mean. Some changes are estimated to be changes in both mean and variance, but the ICCS:MV can easily mistake true mean changes as changes in both.

The authors hope that this paper will spark further theoretical and applied work on the ICCS:MV that focuses on its quality control features.

REFERENCES

Aggarwal, R., Inclán, C., & Leal, R. (1996). Volatility in Emerging Stock Markets. Georgetown University working paper.

Bos, T., & Fetherston, T. A. (1992). Market Model Nonstationarity in the Korean Stock Market. In: G. Rhee & R. Chang (Eds), *Pacific-Basin Capital Markets Research, Vol. III*. Amsterdam: North-Holland.

Bos, T., Ding, D., & Fetherston, T. A. (1998). Searching for Periods of Volatility: A Study of the Behavior of Volatility in Thai Stocks. *Pacific-Basin Finance Journal*, *6*, 295–306.

Brown, R. L., Durbin, J., & Evans, J. M. (1975). Techniques for Testing the Constancy of Regression Relationships over Time. *JRSS(B)*, *37*(2), 149–163.

Inclán, C., & Tiao, G. C. (1994). Use of Cumulative Sums of Squares for Retrospective Detection of Changes in Variance. *JASA*, *84*(427, September), 913–923.

Ploberger, W., & Krämer, W. (1992). The CUSUM Test with OLS Residuals. *Econometrica*, *60*(2, March), 271–285.

Tanizaki, H. (1995). Asymptotically Exact Confidence Intervals of CUSUM and CUSUMSQ Tests: A Numerical Derivation Using Simulation Technique. *Communications in Statistics. Simulation and Computation*, *24*(4), 1019–1036.

Lightning Source UK Ltd.
Milton Keynes UK
UKHW021212260420
362142UK00003B/102

9 780762 308583